Handbook of Research on Social Software and Developing Community Ontologies

Stylianos Hatzipanagos
King's College London, UK

Steven Warburton
King's College London, UK

INFORMATION SCIENCE REFERENCE

Hershey · New York

Director of Editorial Content:	Kristin Klinger
Managing Editor:	Jamie Snavely
Assistant Managing Editor:	Carole Coulson
Typesetter:	Amanda Appicello
Cover Design:	Lisa Tosheff
Printed at:	Yurchak Printing Inc.

Published in the United States of America by
Information Science Reference (an imprint of IGI Global)
701 E. Chocolate Avenue, Suite 200
Hershey PA 17033
Tel: 717-533-8845
Fax: 717-533-8661
E-mail: cust@igi-global.com
Web site: http://www.igi-global.com

and in the United Kingdom by
Information Science Reference (an imprint of IGI Global)
3 Henrietta Street
Covent Garden
London WC2E 8LU
Tel: 44 20 7240 0856
Fax: 44 20 7379 0609
Web site: http://www.eurospanbookstore.com

    Library of Congress Cataloging-in-Publication Data

Handbook of research on social software and developing community ontologies / Stylianos Hatzipanagos and Steven Warburton, editors.
    p. cm.
  Includes bibliographical references and index.
  Summary: "This book explores how social software and developing community ontologies are challenging the way we operate in a performative space"--Provided by publisher.
  ISBN 978-1-60566-208-4 (hardcover) -- ISBN 978-1-60566-209-1
  1. Online social networks--Research. 2. Social networks--Research 3. Internet--Social aspects--Research. I. Hatzipanagos, Stylianos, 1963- II. Warburton, Steven.
  HM742.H36 2009
  302.30285'4678--dc22
                    2008035143

British Cataloguing in Publication Data
A Cataloguing in Publication record for this book is available from the British Library.

List of Contributors

Table of Contents

Detailed Table of Contents

Chapter I
> *Jon Dron, Athabasca University, Canada*
> *Terry Anderson, Athabasca University, Canada*

Dron & Anderson provide a framework for understanding the effective use of the Net for learning and teaching by differentiating between three modes of networked social organization. These are defined as the Group, the Network and the Collective. The chapter explores the consequences of this perspective, observing that each has both strengths and weaknesses in different contexts and when used for different applications. They conclude that to gain the greatest benefits from social software it is important to understand the different dynamics of different tools and the different contexts in which they may be used. Taking these into account, they hope that it will now be possible to perform more informed studies that will refine and develop these approaches more fully.

Chapter II
> *Chris Abbott, Reader in e-Inclusion, King's College London, UK*
> *William Alder, Sixth Form Student, Trinity School, UK*

Abbott & Adler contribute to the debate about the apparent dichotomy between the trend for young people to embrace social networking sites enthusiastically while within education we are reluctant to embed social software in our learning and teaching environments. They examine the transition of online practices as a trajectory from personal website use through interactive services to the networking sites today. They conclude that social networking has initiated a series of practices which cannot now be abandoned, and that the challenge for the education system is not control or abolition but the inclusion of social networking within learning and teaching.

Chapter III

Eleni Berki, University of Tampere, Finland
Mikko Jäkälä, University of Jyväskylä, Finland

Berki & *Jäkälä* identify social software as a key technology in communication within cyberspace and recognise they are gradually transforming virtual communities to potentially important meeting places for sharing information and for supporting human actions, feelings and needs. They examine the conceptual definition of virtual community as found in the literature and extend it to accommodate latest trends. Cyber-communities seem to dissolve the boundaries of identity and this questions the trust, privacy and confidentiality of interaction. They present a new way of classifying and viewing self-presentation and identity management in virtual communities, based on the characteristics that participants prefer to attribute to themselves and present to others.

Chapter IV

Werner Beuschel, Brandenburg University of Applied Sciences, Germany

Beuschel uses an exploratory study to examine the value of blogs for learning and teaching, and their potential to support active student participation and collaboration. He shows that cooperative media like blogs cannot just be "prescribed" in an institutional setting, yet the share of informal activities is higher than with other media. Within his target group he found that students needed time and motivation to appropriate the media for their own needs. He concludes that the usage of blogs is generally encouraging, but he also raises some cautionary issues. He recommends that the early processes in a course should devote enough time and effort to explain the specifics of blogs and the activity of blogging in relation to the objectives of a class. He notes finally, that though the importance and prevalence of the social function of blogs was visible, the dimensions of use such as exploration and reflection were sometimes under-employed.

Chapter V

Mark Bilandzic, Technishe Universität München, Germany
Marcus Foth, Queensland University of Technology, Australia

Bilandzic & Foth explore the innovative nature of social software services that enable users to create and share content and develop a collective intelligence. In the context of 'geo-tagging' they examine mobile information systems for collecting and harnessing everyday connections and local knowledge of urban residents in order to support social navigation practices. Network connectivity creates a mediated social environment where mobile phone users turn into in-situ journalists who can upload location based ratings, comments and recommendations to a shared community platform to form a huge social knowledge repository, decentralizing control over information about local services.

Biswas et al introduce the readers to the concept of ontology with particular reference to its philosophical, social and computer science instantiations and tease out the relations between them. They propose a synthesis of these concepts with the term 'social cognitive ontological constructs' (SCOCs) and proceed to explore the role of SCOCs in the generation of human emotions that are postulated to have to do more with cognition than affect. They propose a way forward to address the emotional needs of patients and health care givers through informational feedback that is based on a conceptual framework incorporating SCOCs of key stakeholders. This would come about through recognizing the clinical encounter for what it is: a shared learning experience. The data contained within these records may then be shared between different patients and health professionals who key in their own experiential information to find matching information through text-based tagging on a Web 2.0 platform.

Chapter VII

Code & Zaparyniuk discuss how communities form and develop over time within the context of Internet mediated communication that encourages self-expression and facilitates the formation of relationships based on shared values and beliefs. They consider the psychological challenges unique to understanding the dynamics of social identity formation and strategic interaction in online social networks. They explore how social identity affects the formation and development of online communities, how to analyze the development of these communities, and the implications that social networks have within education. Strategies for social identity experimentation in classrooms allow students to become active interpreters of social interaction and contribute to the student insight into the dynamics of learning and development as a social process.

Chapter VIII

Code & Zaparyniuk explore the emergence of agency in social networks. Agency, defined as the capability of individuals to consciously choose, influence, and structure their actions, emerges from social interactions and influences the development of social networks, and the role of social software's potential as a tool for educational purposes. Practical implications of agency as an emergent property within social networks provide a psychological framework that forms the basis for a pedagogy of social interactivity. They discuss the psychological processes necessary for the development of agency to contribute to an understanding of engagement in online interactions for socialization and learning.

Chapter IX

A. Malizia, Universidad Carlos III de Madrid, Spain
A. De Angeli, University of Manchester, UK
S. Levialdi, Sapienza University of Rome, Italy
I. Aedo Cuevas, Universidad Carlos III de Madrid, Spain

Malizia et al consider the user experience as a crucial factor for designing and enhancing user satisfaction when interacting with a system or computational by exploring collaborative tagging systems that allow users to add labels for categorizing contents. The chapter presents a set of techniques for detecting the user experience through Collaborative Tagging Systems and an example on how to apply the approach for the evaluation of web sites. Their work highlights the potential use of collaborative tagging systems for measuring user experience and user satisfaction and discusses the future implications of this approach as compared to traditional evaluation tools, such as questionnaires or interviews.

Chapter X

Utpal M. Dholakia, Rice University, USA
Richard Baraniuk, Connexions and Rice University, USA

Dholakia & Baraniuk investigate how the learner experience and the effectiveness of Open Education Programs that provide digitized educational resources freely to educators and learners to use and reuse for teaching, learning, and research, can be enhanced by incorporating new social networking technologies along with traditional virtual communities. The implications and impact of how social networking technologies will contribute to the next generation of open education programs is discussed through their experience and engagement with such project.

Chapter XI

Sebastian Fiedler, Zentrum für Sozial Innovation – Centre for Social Innovation, Austria
Kai Pata, Center of Educational Technology, Tallinn University, Estonia

Fiedler & Pata discuss how the construction of a design and intervention framework for distributed learning environments might be approached. They address some current technical and conceptual challenges for the implementation and maintenance of distributed learning environments. They utilise activity theory and the concept of affordance, as perceived possibilities for action, and discuss potential consequences for the design of learning environments. Their contribution is a proposal for a necessary reorientation and a call for debate about design and intervention frameworks for distributed learning environments.

Chapter XII

Yoni Ryan, Australian Catholic University, Australia
Robert Fitzgerald, University of Canberra, Australia

Ryan & Fitzgerald consider the potential of social software to support learning in higher education by outlining a project where social software is used to support peer engagement and group learning. Here they are providing students with opportunities to engage with their peers in a discourse that explores, interrogates and provides a supplementary social ground for their in-class learning. The core of the article describes the results from the survey conducted with students and draws out a number of key issues and emerging trends: that no one-size-fits-all; institutional ICT services are not partners in innovation; open source software and 'free' web services are vital; that cross-institutional innovation is problematic; and a tension exists between decentralised and centralised educational models.

Chapter XIII

Kathryn Gow, Queensland University of Technology, Australia

Gow identifies those competencies that entry level workers, and graduates, will need to acquire to be successful in the 21st Century work environment. In order to succeed in the digital age, augmented ICT skills, including abilities to communicate across the web are prominent in this typology of competencies that includes knowledge and ability in use of social software. Other attributes, such as cross cultural and professional skills, along with an appreciation of web ontologies will facilitate transition of entry-level workers into the world of international liaisons. The chapter addresses the need for teaching institutions to engage in training about digital competencies to ensure a better equipped and competitive workforce.

Chapter XIV

Jerald Hughes, University of Texas – Pan American, USA
Scott Robinson, Global Trading Group, USA

Hughes et al. present a description and functional taxonomy of interaction-oriented virtual communities of spirituality. They identify salient points of similarity and difference between online and offline religious social structures, and show that online spiritual communities as presently constituted, are unlikely to be able to directly replicate the traditional social structures of the offline religious institutions from which they originated. They explore the powers and constraints on action, embodied in social software and the implications for online virtual communities that this finding has. In conclusion they highlight the importance of the issues surrounding identity, authenticity and authority.

Chapter XV

Keegan & Lisewski explore emergent behaviours in the use of social software across multiple online communities of practice, ones where informal learning occurs beyond traditional higher education institutional boundaries. They trace the potentially disruptive nature of social software and social networking practices. They claim that new forms of online learning, with social interaction and metacognition at their core, pose a significant challenge to learners and teachers in terms of: the volume, authority and legitimacy of information; the relatively unbounded nature of communications; traditional assessment practices; and the role of the tutor. They conclude that the tensions between the formal and the informal, the centralised and the decentralised, must be managed effectively, and boundaries need to be negotiated across communities of practice and information networks in order to avoid participants becoming overwhelmed.

Chapter XVI

Kerawalla et al explore the choices that educators have to make when they use social software. They focus on a research programme that investigated the blogging activities of different groups of Higher Education students: (undergraduate, Masters-level distance learners, and Doctoral students). They use their evidence of student experience, perceptions, and expectations of blogging to inform the development of a framework, for course designers and students, that raises awareness of the features of blogging. They present an empirically-grounded framework which can guide course designers and educators on whether and how to include blogging in their course-contexts. It encourages both educators and students to think about the socio-technical context of blogging and how/whether this may generate the potential for community-building.

Chapter XVII

Kervin et al. discuss the activities of an online community of learners developed for beginning teachers in primary and early childhood education and organised around a site with a blogging feature. This provided a space for users to not only reflect critically on their own experiences and developing expertise, but also compare and comment on the experiences of others. Their analysis revealed that it was critical that students set the parameters for blogging and retained ownership of their blogs. They show that the networking opportunities that emerged from the blogging experience provided for focused and meaningful interactions to occur within both the physical and virtual environments.

Chapter XVIII

Jennifer Ann Linder-VanBerschot, University of New Mexico, USA
Deborah K. LaPointe, University of New Mexico Health Sciences Center, USA

Linder-VanBerschot & LaPointe introduce a model that outlines the evolution of knowledge and sustainable innovation of communities through the use of social software and knowledge management. The participatory dimensions of social software increase interaction and introduce a diversity of perspectives into the classroom space. Knowledge management provides the opportunity to capture and store information so that content and learning can be personalized according to learner preferences. Their model describes a circuit of knowledge that includes instructional systems design, individualization of learning, interaction and critical reflection. It also represents a new framework within which communities develop and become more sustainable.

Chapter XIX

Petros Lameras, South East European Research Centre, Research Centre of the University of
Sheffield and CITY College, Greece
Iraklis Paraskakis, South East European Research Centre, Greece & Research Centre
of the University of Sheffield and CITY College, Greece
Philipa Levy, University of Sheffield, Greece

Lameras, Paraskakis & Levy discuss how social constructivist pedagogies that embrace collaborative learning and communities of practice may be supported by the adoption of social software tools. They want to support higher education practitioners in theory-informed design by distilling and outlining those aspects of social constructivism that address the use of social software tools. They claim that the introduction of social software to institutional Virtual Learning Environments, with a strong focus on collaborative learning processes and engagement in online learning communities, will highlight the need for discursive tools, adaptability, interactivity and reflection.

Chapter XX

Dimitris Bibikas, South East European Research Centre, Greece & Research Centre
of the University of Sheffield and CITY College, Greece
Iraklis Paraskakis, South East European Research Centre, Greece & Research Centre
of the University of Sheffield and CITY College, Greece
Alexandros G. Psychogios, CITY College, affiliated Institution of the University of
Sheffield, Greece
Ana C. Vasconcelos, The University of Sheffield Regent Court, UK

Bibikas et al investigate the role of social software in integrating knowledge exploitation and knowledge exploration strategies. They approach these strategies through the lens of dynamic capabilities, organisational learning and knowledge lifecycle models. They argue that while current enterprise Information Technology systems focus more on knowledge lifecycle processes concerning the distribution and application of knowledge, enterprise social software can invoke knowledge exploration strategies and leverage knowledge creation and validation procedures.

Chapter XXI

M. C. Pettenati, University of Florence, Italy
M. E. Cigognini, University of Florence, Italy
E. M. C. Guerin, University of Florence, Italy
G. R. Mangione, University of Florence, Italy

Pettenati et al identify the Personal Knowledge Management (PKM) pre-dispositions, skills and competences of the effective lifelong-learner 2.0 and derive a PKM-skills model centred on a division into basic PKM competences, associated with the social software practices of create-organize-share and Higher-Order skills. These help to identify the enabling conditions and competences that favour the advanced management of one's personal knowledge. Their main purpose is to understand whether such Higher-Order abilities are innate or should be learnt. They claim that they should be taught by educational institutions through the development of specific educational modules or activities.

Chapter XXII

Sharon Markless, King's College, London, UK
David Streatfield, Information Management Associates, UK

Markless & Streatfield question whether the shift from the Web as a vehicle for storing and transmitting information to the new Web as a series of social networking environments requires significant changes in student skills and competencies. They examine the changes in learning being brought about by Web 2.0 and they question whether adjustment of existing information literacy models is a sufficient response to deal with these changes. They conclude that although Web 2.0 developments are not fundamentally undermining the nature of teaching and learning they do provide important possibilities for more effective information literacy development work. A non-sequential framework is offered as a contribution to supporting HE students when seeking to obtain, store and exploit information in the informal social world of Web 2.0 and in their formal academic discipline.

Chapter XXIII

Catherine McLoughlin, Australian Catholic University, Australia
Mark J. W. Lee, Charles Sturt University, Australia

McLoughlin & Lee examine new models of teaching and learning that meet the needs of a generation of learners who seek greater autonomy, connectivity and socio-experiential learning. The advent of

Web 2.0, with its expanded potential for generativity and connectivity impacts on how the dynamics of student learning is conceptualized. Disruptive forces, fuelled by the affordances of social software tools, are challenging and redefining scholarship and pedagogy. In response to these challenges they propose a pedagogical framework which addresses participation in networked communities of learning, personalization of the learning experience, and learner knowledge creation and creativity that offers the potential for transformational shifts in teaching and learning practices.

Chapter XXIV

Alexandra Okada, The Open University, UK
Simon Buckingham Shum, The Open University, UK
Michelle Bachler, The Open University, UK
Eleftheria Tomadaki, The Open University, UK
Peter Scott, The Open University, UK
Alex Little, The Open University, UK
Marc Eisenstadt, The Open University, UK

Okada et al explore how knowledge media technologies create opportunities for social learning in the Open Content movement context. They focus on an Open Educational Resources project which integrates three knowledge media technologies: Compendium (knowledge mapping software); MSG (instant messaging application with geolocation maps); and FM (a web-based videoconferencing application). They show how these tools can be used to foster 'Open sensemaking communities' that are characterised as open and self-sustaining communities that construct knowledge together from an array of environmental inputs by mapping knowledge, location and virtual interactions.

Chapter XXV

Luc Pauwels, University of Antwerp, Belgium
Patricia Hellriegel, Lessius University College, Belgium

Pauwels & Hellriegel use a 'hybrid media analysis' approach to examine YouTube, one of the most popular social software platforms that is challenging the dominant discourse with its focus on community formation and user empowerment. By analysing the steering mechanisms embodied in the infrastructure as well as empirical observations of YouTube's content fluctuations over time, insight is provided into the embedded cultural values and practices and the nature of the ongoing negotiation of power and control between YouTube controllers and 'prosumers'. Their model of analysis is geared towards decoding the multimodal structure of websites and their social and cultural significance. They end by highlighting the subtle struggle for power and control between owners and users as well as pointing at possible effects of cultural mainstreaming or ideological reproduction.

Chapter XXVI

Ismael Peña-López, Universitat Oberta de Catalunya, Spain

Peña-López proposes the concept of the Personal Research Portal (PRP) – a mesh of social software applications to manage knowledge acquisition and diffusion. This is premised on the belief that there is a place for individual initiatives to try and bridge the biases and unbalances in the weight that researchers and research topics have in the international arena. The chapter highlights the main perceived benefits of a PRP that include building a digital identity, information sharing, the creation of an effective e-portfolio, and the sharing of personal and professional networks. He concludes that the main challenges that need to be addressed include access to technology and developing appropriate skills, problems that are recognised as stemming from the digital divide.

Chapter XXVII

Ravenscroft et al. present a new approach to designing learning interactions in the digital age that reconciles learning processes with digital practices in the context of social networking and Web 2.0. They begin by offering some theoretical pointers and methodological perspectives for research and development that play against current educational articulations of Web 2.0; they see a misalignment of social practices that are ostensibly oriented towards and motivated by 'interest' with those that are oriented towards and motivated by 'learning'. They explain how an ongoing initiative in advanced learning design has developed notions of 'ambient learning design' and 'experience design' to address these issues and describe a new methodology for developing digital tools that incorporate these concepts.

Sachdev, Nerur & Teng review the importance of "interactivity" and propose it as an important research construct in the context of social computing. They extend the traditional definition of interactivity by adding three new dimensions to produce what they term Social Computing Interactivity (SCI), a concept that they see as likely to be more useful in understanding issues surrounding social computing. They go on to suggest possible operationalizations of the dimensions of SCI and explore the theoretical bases that could inform a study of the relevance of these dimensions in predicting the continued growth of social computing.

Thomas et al. suggest that transliteracy might provide a unifying perspective on what it means to be literate in the 21st century. They define transliteracy as "the ability to read, write and interact across a range of platforms, tools and media" and open the debate with examples from history, orality, philosophy, literature, ethnography and education. In their approach they record responses to, expansion of, and development of the term. They report that transliteracy is a 'disruptive innovation' which presents challenges that will shape the way we think of teaching and learning in the context of the open economy. In their view, developing transliterate creative production practices and communication across multiple platforms represents a sensory and cultural explosion that will frame new kinds of experience and knowing.

Chapter XXX

Weller & Dalziel have looked at the tension between new forms of social networking, web 2.0 communities and higher education, arguing that there are differences between cultures and values. They claim that both the granularity of formal education and the manner in which we formalise learning are subject to change with the advent of user generated content and distributed and personalised technologies that are informal, and socially oriented. They recommend that the gap between higher education and web 2.0 could be bridged by approaches that meet the diverse needs of learners and utilise the best of social networking.

Chapter XXXI

Wheeler examines the use of wikis, a freely available form of open architecture groupware, and their use as a shared online space to encourage students to generate their own content and foster a supportive and dynamic community of learning. The chapter reports on student perceptions of the limitations and benefits of a wiki as a social writing tool. It focuses on the tension between creative and destructive uses of wikis and offers recommendations on their effective use in mainstream higher education. Interviews with the students revealed a certain amount of disconcertion and readjustment where students share and co-edit the same space on a wiki and some felt that the anonymity of the form denied them appropriate recognition. However, Wheeler argues that when viewed over a period of time, group based generation of content on wikis can be both creative and fulfilling, with long lasting and positive learning outcomes.

Chapter XXXII

Scott Wilson, University of Bolton, UK

Scott Wilson describes some of the key concepts and technologies in presence and puts forward an ontology of presence for social networks and related services. The author shows how presence represents a fundamental component of the online experience, and though it has originated to some extent within the specific demands of instant messaging networks, the concepts and technologies of presence have become embedded within social networks. These include the development of new networks that have presence as a primary purpose, for example Twitter and Jaiku. Wilson argues that these developments reinforce the notion that the next phase of social network technology will have a central role for presence. In the final part of the chapter an ontology is elaborated that can be used to position presence technologies within the existing landscape of social software.

Foreword

"… the way up is the way down and the way forward is the way back"
The Dry Salvages, The Four Quartets (T. S. Elliot, 1941)

Society harnesses technology in astounding and unpredictable ways. Internet and cell phone technology can help us to understand and solve problems related to the environment, sustainability, medicine, education, security, food distribution, and finance, if used well. But for this to happen we need educated citizens, well-designed and accessible technology, and highly skilled specialists. In other words, we need education systems that motivate students to develop the understanding and skills necessary for tackling big societal issues.

Today billions of people use the Internet. No one knows how many computers and cell phones there are in the world. Some people say that half of the world's population will use a cell phone by the end of 2009. Others talk of 3 billion cell phone users by 2010. No one really knows. What we do know is that our world is changing and changing fast. Today's students, many of whom are characterized as "the millennial generation" – those typically born in the 1980s and after - have different social norms and expectations from earlier generations. This generation has grown up with technology: for them surfing the web, sending a quick message to friends on Facebook, or a photo via their cell phone is as much a part of their life as the air they breathe. But this is not so for their parents and educators; even those who have been technology users for many years don't have the "technology smarts" seen in most students, teens and even younger children, who adopt new technology with ease.

Millennials know the way forward, and the way backwards, and they are not afraid of all the different ways of getting from here to there on the Internet. They are surprised that technology is held in awe and handled so clumsily by many educators and parents, because to them it is how you keep in touch with friends, plan events, coordinate activities, do homework, have fun, express yourself, and get noticed. For this generation the problem is not what you can do with technology it is what you do when you don't have it because you lost your cell phone or have been barred from the Internet. Without a cell phone or Internet access to Facebook or Myspace, you are not connected, you're not part of the group, you might as well not exist – at least for now.

This timely, well-written collection of articles addresses the need for educators to understand today's students and to work with them to harness the Internet for education, so that students develop information searching skills and, more importantly, the information literacy skills that will enable them to evaluation the information that they find. This requires students and teachers to work together in mutual respect. Students can help teachers to learn the mechanics of the applications, while teachers can assistant students to evaluate what they do and find. By entering into their students' world, teachers will have greater opportunities to motivate and engage students in meaningful projects that enable them to better understand the complex world in which they live. Well designed projects can engage students in the world's most pressing environmental, political and humanitarian problems. In addition students and teachers can work together in teams locally, nationally and even internationally facilitated by the power of applications such as Skype which enables free voice conversations across the Internet, or texting applications like Twitter and Jaiku, or by sharing photos and videos using Fickr and YouTube. Of course, there will be dangers too that educators must look out for. Pornography, online bullying, and plagiarism are, unfortunately, already well-known to educators. There are even more dangerous threats that include kidnapping, involvement in terrorist activities, drugs and more. Educators need to be aware of these dangers as well as the abundance of good opportunities: their involvement in learners' use of technologies is therefore essential.

Dr Stylianos Hatzipanagos and Dr Steven Warburton have collected an ambitious and broad collection of articles that cover a wide range of topics. The book explores the "disruptive nature of new media" and discusses "learning design and pedagogical frameworks" and "digital literacies and Web 2.0". There are also chapters on "tools, a broad range of "case studies", and a discussion of "social software and knowledge management". Other themes of the book explore "blogs and identity", "communities" and "presence" – prescient topics that will certainly engage readers.

Whether you are an educator, an engaged citizen or a parent and whatever you teach, you will enjoy and learn so much from this book. There is something for everyone. For those who like to read cover-to-cover, you will get good value for your money. If, like me, you like to dip in here and there, you will find many riches to feed your mind, challenge your imagination, and influence how you interact with people. This book should be kept close to hand. It is a gem that should be read by everyone!

Jennifer Preece
University of Maryland, USA

Preface

INTRODUCTION

This book addresses a need for a debate about the future of Web-based technological innovations. We have entered a new phase in the development of the Internet, one that has pushed us to rethink our understanding of the Web as both an active experience and a cultural artefact. The rise of social software and social networking has driven the transition from content-centred to people-centred activity. This shift of focus represents as much a cultural phenomenon as a technological one and has resulted in many commentators assessing the impact on our sense of identity, the meaning of community and the nature of this change.

By examining the impact of new technologies through the particular lens of education, this book says something significant not only about the future of education but also about the future of our relations with new emergent technologies. Importantly, it explores how our interactions with social software are challenging the way we manage ourselves in connected, distributed and increasingly performative spaces.

By engaging the foremost thinkers and researchers in this area to grapple with the critical aspects at the intersection of social software and education—as a shared human activity—the book provides important insights into where new social technologies and emergent behaviours are leading us.

THE 'SOCIAL' IN SOCIAL SOFTWARE: COMMUNITIES AND IDENTITY

Web 2.0 has moved beyond the original meaning given to the term by Tim O' Reilly in 2005 to encompass a set of tendencies exhibited by virtual communities. The terms Web 2.0 and social software are often used together or synonymously, though Web 2.0 describes more the new ways in which the World Wide Web is used, while social software, built on Web 2.0 platforms and services, describes the universe of possible interactions between individuals and communities. The attitudes and behaviours of these communities or social groups have become as significant as the distributed technological platforms that are being exploited by increasing numbers of Internet users.

One of the major characteristics of these new practices has been a shift towards "user-generated content" where:

- Collective and collaborative information is gathered, shared, modified and redistributed in creative acts;
- Personal sites and content increasingly belong to the so called "me media" category;
- The user controls their choice of software, tools and services;
- The "collective intelligence" of users is harnessed through aggregation and large-scale cooperative activities (O' Hear 2005).

Participants in Internet-based social networking are immersed in fragmented digital environments, and engage in acts of computer-mediated communication (Hatzipanagos 2006) through e-mail, e-mail conferencing and mobile texting, podcasting, personal publishing via blogs and Wikis, aggregation[1] and mash-ups[2], voice, chat, instant messaging, and videoconferencing. Social networking is productive of and exercised by virtual communities of people with common interests, and exposes articulations of identity through self-representation, performance and play.

While there is no official agreement on the definition of "social software" it broadly describes the link-up between social entities in a digital network and their interaction (Wellman et al., 2002; Shirky, 2003; Klamma et al. 2006; Prolearn report, 2006).

The term community has been expanded to include the notion of interdependency and encompasses a set of relationships that connect people and groups. Citizens become Netizens, an identity that relates them to the entire world, and moves them outside their local life and work settings.

For example, social network sites, a particular form of social software, have become integrated into the daily practice of millions of users. Boyd and Ellison (2007) describe the key features of these services as allowing individuals to:

1. Construct a public or semi public profile within a bounded system,
2. Articulate a list of other users with whom they share a connection, and
3. View and traverse their list of connections and those made by others within the system.

Blogs, a popular tool across many learning contexts, allow individuals to keep a chronological record of their own thinking over time, facilitate critical feedback by letting readers add comments and as such they become a window on both inner and outer motivations and activities. In this manner, blogs can be interpreted in terms of social action (Miller, 1984) and become loci for identity performance, dialogic interaction, creativity and community formation.

Folksonomy or dynamic ontology production has emerged as a major dimension in the way that users have become embedded in the ordering of content on the Web and one of the cornerstones by which Web 2.0 technologies can be said to afford the harnessing of collective intelligence. This refers to the cooperative manner in which information is categorised on the Web by users. Instead of using a predetermined centralised classification system, content is navigated through context and meaning via an emergent taxonomy of user-generated tags (metadata) and categories. This activity forms the potential realisation of what Tim Berners-Lee first described as the Semantic Web.

Nadin (1997) states that the complexity and abundance of new forms of interconnectivity takes precedence today at many levels, a function for which literacy is ill prepared. Berners-Lee's notion of the Web was based on a "read" and "write" approach. "Reading" and top down content production has dominated the first era of the Internet. Now a participatory bottom up or "read/write" approach is emerging as a dominant future trend. In parallel we can detect a movement from the classical concept of literacy to a more fluid remediation (Bolter, 2001) and diversification towards the development of a range of cognitive, cultural and social skills that need to be acquired.

SOCIAL SOFTWARE AND LEARNING

It has been a turbulent time for educators where new paradigms of user-centred behaviour have contrasted sharply with control-orientated Virtual Learning Environment platforms, placing increasing pressure on institutions and their ICT services to respond to ever widening support demands from learners. The metaphor of the virtual campus has dictated transmissive approaches to teaching and not taken into account those collaborative interactive functions that the Web can support well, instead augmenting rather than disrupting traditional approaches in education. Our systems have remained as firmly transmissive as any other traditional form of teaching, not engaging the learner and frequently putting emphasis on content rather than dialogue and communication.

E-learning has become a devalued concept in higher education (HE) and rethinking the nature and form of technological interventions in the learning and teaching process has been spurred by changes in our relationship with social media. The rise of social software has created a space in which debates concerning fundamental educational values and beliefs are once again being aired. Students have experienced their personal lives as change—moving between communities, charting new territories, benefiting from networking and open computer mediated communication. When these learners come to tertiary education they are often forced to deal with transmissive or "didactic" approaches to education, where significant aspects of leaner community behaviours are not explored or encouraged and creativity is pushed into the margins.

Embedding learning within an educational setting supported by social software does not necessarily mean that learners will become active members of a community of practice of learners. Active membership of communities of practice is a common theme in this book, yet it is still an area that needs to be critically evaluated, as has been done elsewhere for example in sociolinguistics. However the debate and critical approaches to the uses of social software that are inaugurated in this book need to be taken forward, and into other fora. The relationship of communities, social software and digital social networks is a fertile area that needs to be explored further.

What could be termed the emergence of a new "ecology of participation" will continue to blur the boundaries between formal and informal learning spaces (Downes, 2005; Warburton, 2006) and pose serious challenges to the dominant orthodoxy of hierarchical and standards-laden content delivery. One of the answers to overcome this gulf between teacher-centred versus student-centred learning, and a shift towards open content and open learning, may well lie between three related terms "literacy", "multiliteracy" and "transliteracy" (where transliteracy refers to literacy across several media forms). Imbuing our learners with the necessary skills and competencies to manage their own learning effectively is one of the first steps towards embracing the value of openness, dialogue, ownership, and democracy.

CHARTING THE SOCIAL SOFTWARE TERRITORY

These are some of the questions and issues that this book has been drawn towards. Such has been the rapid rise of social software that there have been few complete studies that map the current landscape. We have approached this task with equal measures of enthusiasm and caution. It is the right time to categorise emergent technologies, to extract taxonomies and analyse the outputs from significant adventures in the territory of social software. We also want to explore fully the implications for user communities, and education is a fertile field for this exploration.

We have made a conscious decision to include submissions in the book that were peripheral to the initial vision we had for its structure in targeting only work that related to the "learning in HE" paradigm. However, the comments from reviewers and discussions with the editorial board convinced us we needed to be as inclusive as possible, as the implications for HE in these debates were significant. We believe that the structure and the discourse that this book puts forward emphasises the nature of these implications for the reader and articulates an appreciation of the continuum themes that impact both inside and outside the educational landscape.

The current problems we identify in the educational system are characterised by a call for diversity in response to the changing needs of learners and the transition to more informal and learner-centred spaces. This is compounded by a need for flexibility in the time and place at which learning occurs and determining learner needs depending on background knowledge, expectations and preferred methods of learning. Nowhere is the (digital) divide between social media cultures more evident than inside and out of the school where they appear as stark contradictions. Out of the classroom these social spaces are experienced as diverse, participatory and often commercialised and inside the school they are frequently defined by decontextualised skills and a lack of student motivation (Buckingham, 2003). Postman (1995) argues that the crisis derives from an underpinning failure to supply learners with transcendent, unifying narratives like those that inspired earlier generations.

Past debates on e-learning have highlighted that computer-based technologies would be *disruptive* to traditional models of education. The expectation has been that these models would not be sustainable as technological developments pervade teaching and learning and, as witnessed across many traditional industries, cause disruption to the system. However, despite ongoing developments in e-learning, these predicted changes are not yet evident. It appears that whilst mainstream education, relying traditionally on expository teaching and receptive learning as the main form of instruction, (Bueno, 2005), has been augmented by technology it has been resistant to the potential disruptive effects of technology on both (formal) learning and schooling structures. There is now evidence that this is set to change. The emergence of Web 2.0-based technologies that have seen the enculturation of social software, increasing availability of online collaborative tools and widespread use of social networking spaces such as MySpace, Facebook, and Second Life are gradually shifting established approaches to educational provision.

OVERALL OBJECTIVES AND MISSION

The book follows a critical exploration of current, emerging or imminent, technological and conceptual developments and the effect they have on user communities. It investigates whether developments in social software offer real advantages to learning. It highlights the educational possibilities of technologies and their disruptive effect on learning by elaborating a number of key themes that address the tensions between formal and informal learning, private and public domains, freedom and autonomy, and the implications for new and emerging learning spaces.

In addition, the book:

- Addresses the challenges of new community cultures, new technologies, and networked globalised economies;
- Examines the social shaping of new technologies in education in terms of negotiated meaning, situatedness and interpretative flexibility;
- Examines the theories and technologies of change in education and establishes a possible model that encapsulates current change and future directions;
- Argues that certain advancements in technology are clearly altering traditional pedagogical practices and their associated cultures; and
- Elaborates a typology of literacies in relation to digital media.

We are interested in how new and emerging technologies will impact on formal education and the social implications that surround the reformulation and fluidity of virtual communities.

The book contributes to the debate on what fosters a community, the concept of media literacy and how social networking can impact on learning experiences. These issues are explored from a number of theoretical and grounded perspectives. The book explores computer mediated communication and which approaches promote this, in a variety of contexts. It investigates the challenges posed by the participatory media that forms an important aspect of community engagement around dialogue, shared activity and self-identity. By bringing together key writings in the area of social software, different patterns, developments and examples of good practice, frameworks of effective design and usability will emerge alongside valuable commentary on the future pathways that these new technologies are opening up.

Finally, a note about the organisation of the book itself. It is set around nine complementary and overlapping themes. The submissions include research and evaluation but also position papers reporting developing ideas in social software and social networking:

1. **Disruptive nature of new media:** Chapters II, XXX, XXIII, XIX and XV.
2. **Learning design and pedagogical frameworks:** Chapters I, XXVII and XI.
3. **Digital literacies and Web 2.0:** Chapters XXIX, XIII and XXII.
4. **Tools:** Chapters XXIV, IX, XXXI, XXVI and XXV.
5. **Blogs and identity:** Chapters XVII, XVI and IV.
6. **Social software and knowledge management:** Chapters XXI, XVIII and XX.
7. **Communities:** Chapters VII, XIV, III and VIII.
8. **Presence:** Chapter XXXII.
9. **Case studies:** Chapters XII, XXVIII, V, VI and X.

REFERENCES

Bolter, J. D. (2001). *Writing space: Computers, hypertext, and the remediation of print.* 2nd ed. Mahwah, NJ: Lawrence Erlbaum Associates.

Boyd, D., & Ellison, N. B. (2007). *Social network sites: Definition, history, and scholarship.*

Buckingham, D. (2003). *Media education: Literacy, learning and contemporary culture.* Cambridge. UK: Polity.

Bueno, M. (2005). *Shaping up distance education.* Retrieved December 2, 2006, from http://elgg.net/marcbueno/files/-1/11548/ShapingUpEducation.rtf

Downes, S. (2006). *E-learning 2.0* ACM eLearn Magazine.Retrieved November 21, 2008, from http://www.elearnmag.org/subpage.cfm?section=articles&article=29-1

Hatzipanagos, S. (2006). HOT and flaming spirals: Learning and empathic interfaces in text-based discussion forum dialogues. *European Journal of Open, Distance and e-Learning,* 2006/I.

Klamma, R., Chatti, M. A., Duval, E., Fiedler, S., & Hummel, H. (2006). Social software for professional learning: Examples and issues. In *Proceedings of the 6th International Conference on Advanced Learning Technologies,* Kerrade, Netherlands.

Miller, C. R. (1984). Genre as social action. *Quarterly Journal of Speech, 70,* 151-176.

Nadin, M. (1997). *Civilization of illiteracy.* Dresden: Dresden Univ. Press.

O'Hear, S. (2006, June 20). *Web's second phase puts users in control.* The Guardian Education. Retrieved November 21, 2008, from http://education.guardian.co.uk/elearning/story/0,,1801086,00.html

O'Reilly, T. (2005). *What is Web 2.0? Design patterns and business models for the next generation of software.* Retrieved November 21, 2008, from http://www.oreillynet.com/pub/a/oreilly/tim/news/2005/09/30/what-is-web-20.html

Postman, N. (1995). *The end of education.* New York: Vintage Books.

Prolearn Project Report (2006). *Case study on social software in distributed working environments D15.2.* Retrieved October 25, 2008, from http://my.confolio.org/portfolio/files/Prolearn-CSI/CSI/Participation/WorkPackages/WP_15_-_CSI/Deliverable_15.2/D15.02.pdf

Shirky, C. (2003). Social software: A new generation of tools. *Esther Dyson's Monthly Report, (10).*

Warburton, S. (2006, September 5-6). Everything 2.0? Exploring the potential of disruptive technologies in learning and teaching environments. ALT-C 2006. In *Proceedings 13th International Conference of the Association for Learning Technology.*

Wellman, B., & Hampton, K. (1999). Living networked on and offline. *Contemporary Sociology, 28*(6), 648-654.

ENDNOTES

[1]   Using RSS (Really Simple Syndication) news feeds.
[2]   An application or Web site that combines content from more than one source into an integrated experience (Csharp-online.net)

Acknowledgment

The editors would like to acknowledge the help of all involved in the production and review process of the handbook, without whose support the project could not have been completed. We are grateful to the twelve members of the Editorial Board whose willingness to embrace the project has been very motivational for us and whose recommendations helped us to shape the structure and content of this handbook.

Thanks go to all the reviewers who provided constructive and critical feedback on submissions and engaged in an important dialogue on the themes of the book. Many of the authors of chapters included in this handbook also served as referees for chapters written by other authors. However, some of the reviewers must be mentioned for their willingness to step in and respond to our requests for their opinion and feedback: Philip Barker of Teesside University, Frances Bell of Salford University, Elli Georgiadou of Middlesex University, and Ursula Wingate and Lesley Gourlay of King's College London.

Special thanks also go to the publishing team at IGI Global, whose contributions throughout the whole process from inception of the initial idea to final publication have been more than helpful.

We would like to thank Jennifer Preece of the University of Maryland for embracing the values of the book in her engaging foreword. We would also like to thank Ian Kinchin of King's College who read a draft of the preface and provided helpful suggestions for enhancing its content. And last but not least, our partners and friends for their unfailing support and encouragement during the months it took to produce this book.

In closing, we wish to thank all of the authors for their insights and contribution to knowledge that gave birth to this handbook.

Stylianos Hatzipanagos & Steven Warburton
December 2008

About the Editors

Dr. **Stylianos Hatzipanagos** is an academic working at King's College London. He contributes to the development and delivery of KLI's (King's Learning Institute) graduate and undergraduate programmes. As leader of the e-learning function in the Institute he contributes to the design and development of learning, teaching and research activities that focus on e-learning and the pedagogy of information and communication technologies. He has a first degree in physics and MScs in physics education and in information technology (artificial intelligence); his doctoral research was on the design and evaluation of interactive learning environments. His research portfolio includes: innovation in learning and teaching, formative assessment in higher education, e-assessment, usability and evaluation of e-learning environments and microworlds, computer mediated communication and computer supported collaborative work, social software and social networking in an educational context.

Dr. **Steven Warburton** is an eLearning manager at King's College London and a Fellow of the Centre for Distance Education at the University of London where he chairs the research strategy group. He moved from his initial research background in the area of neuroscience to one that now encompasses a range of research projects in technology enhanced learning. His fields of expertise include: the impact of digital identities on lifelong learning; the use of social software in distance education; pattern languages for Web 2.0; design for learning with multi-user virtual environments; feedback loops in formative e-Assessment; and support for communities of practice in user innovation and emerging technologies. His interests are varied but focus largely on the meaning of identity in online learning, the potential impact of virtual worlds on education, social presence and social networks, and the changing nature of change.

Chapter I
How the Crowd Can Teach

Jon Dron
Athabasca University, Canada

Terry Anderson
Athabasca University, Canada

ABSTRACT

Understanding the affordances, effectiveness and applicability of new media in multiple contexts is usually a slow and evolving process with many failed applications, false starts and blind trails. As result, effective applications are usually much slower to arise than the technology itself. The global network based on ubiquitous Internet connectivity and its uneven application in both formal education and informal learning contexts demonstrates the challenges of effective use of new media. In this chapter the authors attempt to explicate the effective use of the Net for learning and teaching by differentiating three modes of networked social organization. These are defined as the Group, the Network and the Collective. The chapter explores the consequences of this perspective, observing that each has both strengths and weaknesses in different contexts and when used for different applications.

INTRODUCTION

Web 2.0 technologies are becoming increasingly pervasive in e-learning, particularly those that might be characterised as social software. The motivation for using such systems is often pragmatic, the benefits they offer clear and intuitive often relating to increases in access. However, many existing uses of social software in education and informal learning contexts lack distinct theoretical foundations, instead drawing from work in computer mediated communication, science, psychology, sociology and related disciplines. We also note the confusion among communications and psychology theorists (Postmas, 2007) as to the extent to which the Net follows classical media theories such as clues-filtered-out (Short, Williams, & Christie, 1976) and the observations that deep personal relationships and affective interactions can and do develop (Walther, 1996). We suggest that this confusion results from trying to understand and explain the myriad forms of net-based social organization through a single lens. Rather, different forms of social organization have developed on the Net and each affords unique education and learning opportunity.

We also note that our interest in social software in education is grounded on an assumption that distributed education systems offer significantly enhanced forms and degrees of learner freedom in many dimensions. Paulsen (1993) itemized these dimensions in his Law of Cooperative Freedom. In it he postulated that systems that support learners' freedom to negotiate not only the place of learning (as characterizes all forms of distance education) but also freedom to negotiate the time, the pace, the content, the technology and the media will more likely cater for emerging learner needs as the barriers between formal education and lifelong learning disintegrate. To these Anderson (2006) added the freedom for learners to negotiate the type of relationship with other learners and teacher, partially in response to the growing affordance of social software to support a variety of learning relationships. In our own context at Athabasca University we find these freedoms of particular relevance in that, unlike most other distance and open learning organizations, Athabacsa offers all of its undergraduate programming in unpaced, continuous intake model – affording freedom of time, space and pace. Bearing these concepts of learner freedom in mind we devised a definition of educational social software as 'networked tools that support and encourage individuals to learn together while retaining individual control over their time, space, presence, activity, identity and relationship' (Anderson, 2006). This and other broad definitions are perhaps a little over-encompassing, including such applications as email and traditional forums. However, the broadness of definition reminds us that social connectivity predates the Net and

other communications technologies. There is a variety of other definitions of social software (see also Chapter X, this volume) but it is clear that the problems that social software addresses (meeting scheduling and documentation, building community, providing mentoring and personal learning assistance, working collaboratively on projects or problems, reducing communication errors and supporting complex group functions) have application to education use, and especially to those models that maximize individual freedom by allowing self pacing and continuous enrolment.

Social software may have the capacity to effectively leverage the knowledge contained in the minds of others in ways that easily adapt to individual and collective needs. As Bryant (2003) notes *"the value of Social Software is its embedded economies of scope. The ability for an asset to adapt to new uses (its environment) without large transaction costs." With a lower overhead in terms of top-down design, it develops a structure through the interactions and activities of its participants. For example, the use of profiles makes it easy to find like-minded people, link sharing and tagging leverages the collective discoveries of the crowd, blog posts supply a natural structure to discourse surrounding them and wikis can grow into complex documents with relatively little input from a central designer. Because the structure is determined by individuals within the community, it naturally adapts to that community's needs and interests, at least as long as communities are not too large and diverse or where their members have poorly aligned foci."*

Network based education research usually emphasises intentional processes, and often fails to recognise the emergent entity formed by the bottom-up, individual interactions of the many. Dron (2007))has proposed that there is an alternative way of seeing such systems, based on Clay Shirky's (2004) notion that the Group is a first class object within the system, with a part to play that is equal to that of the individuals (teachers and learners) and content in an e-learning environment. Dron defines social software as that in which control arises from the group, not from individuals that form it. While not challenging the notion nor utility of the value of these emergent "Groups" Anderson (2007) adds to this characterisation, extending Downes (2006) usage by suggesting that it is instead the network that is the first class entity that is distinctive about these Web 2.0 trends in social software. In this paper, we will be looking at both points of view, and will suggest that there are actually three distinct entities that are involved in activities supported through the use of social software for education and learning, and that these may be classified under three main headings: the Group, the Network and the Collective. Each entity offers benefits, rewards and challenges to the participants, but comes with potential weaknesses that may undermine the learning experience. We will show how an awareness of the different entities can be exploited by the designers of educational software, the creators of educational programming and the users of existing systems.

We and others have struggled with developing guidelines design patterns (Rohse & Anderson, 2006), and best practices for e-learning activities (Sunal, Sunal C., Odell., & Sunberg, 2003). We have discovered that determining the appropriate kind of application for a variety of formal and informal learning activities is key to successful implementation. For example, there has been keen interest in the use of Weblogs in formal education, but deep differences in opinion as to the levels of security, privacy, evaluation and access that are most appropriate for effective educational use of these tools (Mentor, 2007). We realize that tools can be used in a variety of contexts and they are often socially appropriated for applications that may not be congruent with the developers' original designs (Bijker,1999). Much modern social software is an example of what Patel calls a deferred system: one whose form only emerges after it is designed, through the actions of its users (Patel, 2003). Nonetheless, we are learning that

certain tools and learning activities operate best at different levels of granularity and that each has afford learning opportunities in both formal and lifelong, informal learning.

We suggest that each type of system or level of granularity is specified by a cluster of variables including the number of users, time synchronization, formal leadership, degree of familiarity of users with each other, perceived responsibility to the 'Many' and the privacy afforded to the users. Our classification begins with the often tightly formed and usually temporally bound entity known as the 'group' or, in many corporate settings, as the 'team'. Although some have argued for conceptual differences between groups and teams especially in corporate contexts (Fisher, Hunter & Ketin Macrosson, 1997), we argue that in common use and in educational application the terms are used indistinguishably. From here we move to discussion of the Network, a more fluid form of social entity in which members join, create and remove themselves from numerous informal learning and social connections. Our discussion of groups and networks is similar to Wellman's (Wellman, 2001) discussion of networked individualism, but focuses on the formation and support of these topical entities in formal and informal learning contexts. Finally we discuss the Collective, the most scalable form of social software in which members participate for individual benefit, but their activities are harvested and aggregated to generate the 'wisdom of crowds'. We expand these definitions in the next section.

The classification of diverse activities and the tools to support them, in social contexts rarely produces clean and mutually exclusive categories. Further it is even more challenging to find names for these entities that will be agreed upon by all. We have struggled, and continue to struggle, with these naming issues at some length. To review the major issues, we note that the terms *group* and *team* are used interchangeably by many authors, while some argue that teams are more task orientated and often more time delineated. The use of similar terms such *crew*, *cohort*, and *class* also appear in popular press, in educational circles and in the literature. We find that similarities between the terms far outnumber differences and thus, use the more popular and generic term 'group' to talk about this first level of the many. *Network* can refer to the hardware technology that links electronic devices, but we prefer its more general use in social networking theory to designate the nodes and links between human beings. The term *community* is perhaps the most contentious and confused of the social terms in regular use. As long ago as 1955 Hillery cited 94 definitions of *community* (cited in (Puddifoot, 1995), in the literature of the day. Since then discussion of communities of practice, communities of purpose, communities of inquiry and many other variations have added to the complexity and obfuscation of the term. We thus avoid the term, but note that much of the discussion of dimensions, characteristics, processes associated with the term can be applied to both groups and networks – Thus, we think differentiating groups from networks and generally avoiding the term *community* makes conceptual and parsimonious sense. Finally, we struggled for a term that describes the aggregated activities and opinions that we refer to as the *Collective*. The term has been rather negatively associated with communist economic organization models. Conversely it has been used in metaphysical sense to relate to terms such collective intelligence and collective consciousness and by social activists who refer to collective action. Our own use of the word stems from Star Trek's Borg, a set of cybernetically enhanced beings with an emergent hive mind, which most accurately reflects the combination of independently acting humans and algorithms that is its most distinguishing feature. Our current thinking is that the word, though associated with a large dose of political baggage, is the best term we can think of to describe this most anonymous aggregation of the many.

DEFINING THE GROUP

There are many forms of groups that are identifiable as being (or historically have been) formed intentionally by one or more individuals. Examples are as diverse as countries and clubs, schools and unions, gangs and committees. We are primarily concerned here with those that relate to formal learning, whether in a commercial, an informal or an institutional setting. Groups are cohesive and often have formal lines of authority and roles as for example a designated chairperson, teacher, enrolled student etc. Groups consist of individuals who see themselves as part of that group. It is not uncommon for there to be hierarchies in a group. Groups are often structured around particular tasks or activities that may be term based or ongoing. Groups may institute various levels of access control to restrict participation, or the review of artefacts and transcripts to members so as to provide a less public domain in which to operate- presumably to enhance the security or safety of their members and/or to protect their intellectual property. Group members do not usually expect to see their deliberations appear on a routine search of the Collective space. Given the closeness that a Group engenders and demands, it is perhaps surprising that Groups quite often have an existence that is independent of their membership. For example, a particular class may persist for many years while its students and its teachers may change. The Group itself may be a formal, often task-centred entity which members join and leave without affecting the Group's identity Smith, (2001) overviews many of the models of group development that shows large similarity amongst cyclical, linear and recurring models that attempt to help us understand the ways groups develop over time. Smith has argued that groups develop on three dimensions. The first is the social dimension, and occurs most often at the early stages of group formation when members come to know each other and the roles they are playing in the task. The second dimension relates to task development in which the task that the group sets for itself evolves over times as component parts are completed and new assignments accepted. Finally Smith notes the dimension of group culture that develops as norms, values and standards of behaviour develop.

In a Net centric context these Groups use a variety of tools to support and enhance the efficacy of their Group activities. These may include calendars to synchronize activity, file management systems to distribute and share documents and Group editing systems that support versioning, distribution and review of collaborative work.. Groups are a fundamental kind of human community and, as such, members often feel a need to meet face-to-face or at least in real time using audio or video conferencing. In formal education contexts specialized tool sets have been developed and deployed as Learning Management Systems (LMSs) or, as they are known in some parts of Europe, Managed or Virtual Learning Environments (MLEs or VLEs).

In an educational Group everyone knows your name (or at least has the opportunity to do so). Entry to the Group is usually constrained and controlled sometimes by technology (e.g. only those on a corporate Intranet), or by assignment by organizers (e.g.. the registrar of an institution) or by spoken or unspoken exclusions to entry. Classic examples of Groups with an explicit learning agenda include online education classes, short or long term project work teams, nuclear families and companies or departments.

Active membership in a Group is strongly associated with the development of a social identity defining the individual as a Group member. The social identity is created through individuals associating themselves with the Group and both being categorized and categorizing themselves as members of that Group. When this occurs "then the norms, stereotypes, and other properties that are commonly ascribed to the social Group become internalised; they become subjectively interchangeable with personal norms and stereotypes, influencing thought and guiding action."(Postmes, Haslam, & Swaab, 2005), p. 7).

The sense of knowing other Group members means that Groups rarely use or appreciate anonymity. There are some notable exceptions to this rule, where anonymity can be used effectively for pedagogic purposes, e.g. (Creed, 1996), but it is the very fact that it goes against the grain of the typical group interaction that can make such artificial constructs effective. Group members are responsible for their contributions and have reasonable expectations that these contributions are recognized and appreciated by the Group. Thus, Group members are not likely to seek or to develop a new identity or avatar in immersive environments, but rather to use these and mediated communication tools to further their individual and Group goals.

We have been studying the educational use of networked Groups for some years and their face-to-face instantiation in classrooms for decades. The research and practice of e-learning has to date focussed almost exclusively on Groups. We know that Groups go through stages of introduction, growth, production and eventual demise (Wessner & Pfister, 2001). We also know that high performing and valued e-learning Groups actively create social, cognitive and teaching presence (Garrison & Anderson,2003). Further, much has been written about the need for effective moderating and approaches to nurturing growth (Salmon, 2000), teacher immediacy in online contexts (Christenson & Menzel, 1998), encouraging and rewarding participation in online Groups (Palloff & Pratt,1999) and the need for quality assessment of both individual and Group activity (Mason, 2002).

Finally a sense of group identity is associated with social integration, a significant factor in the reduction of attrition, which remains a key problem in distance education systems (Kember, 1989).

In order for Groups to work effectively, significant levels of trust must be generated among participants. Trust often takes periods of extended time and shared tasks to develop. Educational institutions can play important roles in facilitating and accelerating trust formation in Groups by creating contexts that allow (or induce) members to engage in trusting activities even in the early stages of Group formation when Group members lack detailed knowledge of the trustee (Riegelsberger, Sasse, & McCarthy, 2007). The common cause of successfully completing a course often serves as a motivator for quickly developing effective Group activities and products.

Group activities support development of a growing sense of group membership or as Tinto (1987) describes in educational contexts as identification with the institution. Such integration is associated with higher completion rates and learner satisfaction (Kember, 1989). Educational Groups being relatively closed structures also tend to strengthen bonding forms of social capital in which learners have opportunity to develop trust and deep connections with each other that can utilized by members both within the confines of that group and after the group ceases to operate in a formal fashion. Unfortunately, this closed nature is also associated with development of a "hidden curricula" which has been associated with exclusion, and preserving of economic, class, gender and racial inequalities (Anderson, 2001; Margolis,2001). Thus, the Group is both a powerful tool for building social capital, while containing opportunity for systemic abuse.

Groups in education however are generally not scaleable, meaning that their effectiveness decreases after they reach a certain number of participants. Dillenbourg & Schneider (1995) argue that "most of the mechanisms which explain the effectiveness of collaboration, for example mutual recognition, social grounding, shared cognitive load…can only occur between a few participants" p. 134. Groups in classroom education have been stretched to fill 400 seat theatres, but many of the

Group characteristics and learning benefits associated with collaboration, dialogue and exchange are lost. In online learning to date, groups models seem to be capped at 25-30 students, with very few institutions developing large scale e-learning models that go beyond conventional Group based learning designs

The emergence of educational social software affords new tools and new techniques allowing educators and learners to expand the context of online learning beyond Groups to form the next category of the Many, which we refer to as the Network.

DEFINING THE NETWORK

Networks connect distributed individuals. Individuals are connected to other individuals either directly or indirectly, and may not even be immediately aware of more than a subset of those who form part of the Network. The shape of the Network is emergent, not designed and fluid such that it morphs its intensity, size, and influence in response to internal and external pressures. Notable Networks used in education include the groupings that emerge in syndicated blogs of the blogosphere, the archived mailing list networks focussed on educational or learning content or issues, and the social networking groups that emerge in software systems such as MySpace, LinkedIn, Elgg and Facebook. Network members share a variable sense of commitment to each other, but are typically induced to contribute to the Network as a means to increase their personal reputation, to collaboratively build social capital (Ellison, Steinfield, & Lampe, 2007) and to collectively create a resource that has greater value than individual or Group contribution and perspective. Reward mechanisms for contribution to Networks include peer review/ranking and other forms of both formal and informal contribution recognition (Zarb, 2006).

Networks, unlike Groups, are defined by a mixture of loose and strong ties between members (Granovetter, 1973). Connections amongst Network members are usually of relatively low average density, by which we mean the ratio of personal connections between individual Network members and all possible connections (Granovetter, 2004). However, it is also common for a small number of individuals to be very highly connected, in scale-free and small-world network configurations (Watts, 2003). Thus, members have expectations of using the Network to gain information, viewpoints, contacts and suggestions from those outside of their more familiar Group connections. This capacity to build and sustain new connections allows Networks to exploit emergent connections to the outside world, with potential gains in knowledge, influence, social capital and perspective. However there are often strong ties amongst lead members of the Network, creating inequalities in the influence and prestige of certain network members, though these leaders are rarely officially titled, their leadership is developed through useful contribution to the Network.

Network membership is then usually defined by action, and some author's have argued that passive 'membership' or lurking undermines the network. However choosing if and when to contribute is a complex decision and studies are revealing that lurkers have many reasons for not posting – including the belief that refraining from posting actually enhances the group (Preece, Nonnecke & Andrews, 2004)

Networks are not, of themselves, smart, but the clustering, linking and interaction that occurs within and between Networks creates a structure and form that aids sharing of information and individual and network generation of knowledge. Individuals join learning Networks to associate with others of like interest or vocation or with those who know more. Networks enable users to identify and most importantly to collaborate with the people they want to know, to determine the subjects that fit together, to experience the 'buzz' that is current in a specific subject areas, to personally filter the over abundance of information on the Net and to build new social connections and increase their personal social capital.

Networks are fluid and generative. Most individuals are members of many Networks, some of which are blended with face-to-face contact. The social software built to support Networks normally includes profiles for identifying competencies and mutual interests of current and prospective Network members, blogs to voice individual ideas and commentaries of Network members and heavy syndication such that Network spaces are created from individual contributions. To support Network efficiency and memory organization, document production tools are incorporated to aid the Network in documenting and archiving Network activities. Some of the major social networking systems are proprietary, some of which have reached critical mass such that they attract hundreds of millions of users (Facebook, MySpace, spaces on SecondLife etc)

Our definition of networks implies that they are not (by definition and most not by practice) as restricted in membership as groups, but neither are they designed to meet the needs of everyone. Rather they are parcellated linkings of the Many into manageable clusters that allow for open access and exit and free flow of conversation. They thus provide an environment for loosely organized structures. These organizations often involve forms of self-organizational planning to meet emergent needs. Networks may spawn Groups that are created to meet emergent needs usually associated with more explicit leadership and focused task.

The blog and to a slightly lesser extent the wiki are optimized to support Networks. The blog allows the individual to contribute to a Network, and may allow control of the syndication of that contribution. Similarly Network members use syndication notification to recognize and potentially respond to that post. The linking capacity of blogs (trackbacks, refbacks, pingbacks) by which readers link to blog posting to which they are commenting is yet cumbersome, spammable and not quite functional for Networks that include many new and unsophisticated users. However, the syndication allows information to be exchanged, new contacts to be discovered by blog-specific and general search engines, thus benefiting current and potential Network members while at the same time serving as raw feed stock for later harvesting and aggregation. The wall postings of systems like FaceBook also allow for self disclosure and resulting widening of the Network to not only friends, but to friends of friends, thus allowing Networks to grow and reproduce. Unfortunately, to date, Networks are often subsumed into different proprietary systems with little transfer amongst systems but we await the day for standards based identification, profile and postings systems that allow easy export and import of personal data among many Networks. This is a major source of concern to many in the social software community and some solutions have been proposed and, to an extent, implemented, such as those falling under the umbrella of dataportability. org, including FOAF (Friend Of A Friend), XFN (XHTML Friends Network) , the OpenSocial APIs (http://code.google.com/apis/opensocial/) and OpenID. These standards and technologies go some way towards enabling interoperability between the increasingly large number of systems that employ them.

We next move to the most potentially scalable aspect of the Many, which we refer to as the Collective.

DEFINING THE COLLECTIVE

We define Collectives as aggregations or sets formed of the actions of individuals, bound together by aggregating algorithms that may be as simple as a vote or usage count, or as complex as a multi-layered, pattern-matching collaborative filter. Individuals in a collective do not primarily see themselves as members of a Group nor connected in a Network, yet their aggregated activities and ideas create collective knowledge. Like the Network, the shape of the Collective is emergent, not designed – at least by collective members. It is a kind of cyber-ecology, formed from people linked algorithmically using networked software. It grows through the aggregation of individual, Group and Networked activities. For example, Google's results are aggregated networked links priorized by selection of others, while tag clouds often lead through hyperlinks to others in a Network or even in a Group. The distinctive dynamic is one of aggregation, not networking and the clearest way of distinguishing the two is that Collective systems do not require a commitment to the Many. Rather, through use of collective space and tools, information is continuously gathered and rendered for the benefit of all individuals using the collective tools. They may thus be seen as a combination of individual behaviours and the processing of those behaviours. Examples of collectives exist in which the computer does not play a role – voting in elections is an obvious example – but computers enable more sophisticated processing and more complex algorithms to be brought into play. Perhaps more significantly, computers are at once tools, medium and environment (Dron, 2007) which means that the results of the processing can become part of the fabric of the environment itself, presented back to the participants in an indefinitely large number of ways.

Collectives are, in some ways, smart but may more accurately be described as *clever*. For some kinds of knowledge, the aggregated or averaged behaviour of many intelligent agents can be more accurate, complete or appropriate than that of any one individual (Surowiecki, 2004), but it relies on a number of factors . It is easy to exaggerate the current capacity of the Collective to generate new information and to question at what epistemological point this information becomes knowledge.

Nonetheless, interesting collective applications are emerging. These include the formation of tag clouds from aggregation of interests, postings or other activities, the ordering of results in Google based on backlinks (Brin & Page, 2000) user selection, the collective identification of spam (Han, Ahn, Moon, & Jeong, 2006)], the recommendations of collaborative filters (Rafaeli, Dan-Gur, & Barak, 2005), social navigation in various systems based on prior or current use (e.g. (Brusilovsky, Chavan& Farzan, 2004; Miettinen, Kurhila, Nokelainen& Tirri, 2005), and the selective break down of survey results and other tools querying large numbers of Net users. Each of these examples assumes that explicit or implicit selection or recommendation from the Many is a valuable aide to filtering, decision making and knowledge generation.

One of the problems of collective aggregation is that it is not directly controlled by the users who contribute the data being aggregated. On the public Internet (as opposed to activities within closed educational institutional networks), companies and governments aggregate behaviour and give it back to users (often with commercial advertisements) in ways that they hope users will find useful and, dare we say, compelling. There are efforts being made to empower users by allowing them to sell, aggregate and exchange the data generated by their attention to services of the Net (see for example www.attentiontrust.org). In general, proponents of individual rights versus collective aggregation call for recognition of the owners' rights to data that they generate (open data) and transparency and honesty amongst collective aggregators. The Attention Trust organizers have developed a FireFox plug-in that collects and summarizes Net activities and allows users to decide to which commercial aggregators they will provide explicit access to this data.

It is far too easy for the wisdom of the crowd to transform into the stupidity of mobs, primarily when people become aware of the decisions that others are making (Surowiecki, 2004). The rush to chase popular fads and memes can cause valid knowledge to be filtered out and invalid knowledge to be amplified. This can create mob behaviour that can be arguably smart (Spears, Postmes, Lea, & Wolbert, 2002; Arrington, 2007) or destructive if negative effects of de-individualization emerge (Weinberg & Toder, 2004).

Collectives may fall victims to or benefit from the Matthew Effect (For whoever has, to him more shall be given, and he will have an abundance; but whoever does not have, even what he has shall be taken away from him. Matthew 13: 12) For example, popular sites in Google that appear on the first page of search results, are apt to remain so because of a positive feedback loop: people seldom search much further than that first page, and will only link to pages that they are aware of (Gregorio, 2003) Fortunately, though dominant, Google is far from the only system driving the Web and there are other opportunities for sites to become popular, such as through more explicit recommender sites like Digg and Slashdot. Equally, a significant number of people actively avoid succumbing to the influence of such systems (Dron, 2006)

Collectives often provide collaboration for free – simply using the system may be enough for structures to form. For example, buying books from Amazon, linking one Web page to another (Google's PageRank algorithm), spending time on a particular link or rating a movie or a site for one's personal use may each be used by a system to aggregate behaviours and opinions, thereby creating value. For this reason, Collectives scale very well. Notwithstanding the dangers of the Matthew Principle, the more members a Collective has, the greater its validity and usefulness, at least as long as the focus remains clear and unambiguous.

However, not all of the value of the Collective stems from non-participant actions. In many cases, in order for the Collective to have and add value, some members must add content, whether this is low-threshold (e.g. tagging or rating) or more demanding (e.g. adding content to a wiki or creating a hyperlink on a Web page). Horowitz (2006) estimates that 1% of users are creators or instigators of interaction. A further 10% are synthesizers or commentators who respond to invitation and prompting by creators. The remaining 89% are consumers but who still only add value to the Collective through their tracked consumption. The situation is somewhat less extreme in the case of taggers but there is still a large majority who do not contribute in this way. A recent Pew Internet Study (Rainie, 2007) found that only 28% of online Americans claimed to have tagged content.

While for some the motive may be selfish – for example, tagging in systems like del.icio.us or Flickr serves the useful purpose of organising one's own resources - for others, the motivation may be personal recognition, creative drive and perhaps an altruistic sense of contribution. These elite members of the Collective may add to its value, through interaction, their knowledge and commitment to each other and to their products, ,sometimes creating new Networks or even Groups, as often evolves in large open source software communities. The Collective thus serves as a visible entry point, opening the usually closed and hidden doorway to more intense Networks and Groups. This low stake visibility supports classic social learning (Bandura,1997) in which learners mimic the behaviours of those leaders whom they admire and can lead to cognitive apprenticeship as learners progress and intensify their learning.

Finally we note that Collectives (and to lesser degree Networks) excel at providing access to the unpredictable. Cass Sunstein overviews the essential contribution of this spontaneous and serendipitous affordance of Collectives.

Unplanned, unanticipated encounters are central to democracy itself. Such encounters often involve topics and points of view that people *have not sought out and perhaps find quite irritating. They are important partly to ensure against fragmentation and extremism, which are predictable outcomes of any situation in which like-minded people speak only with themselves (Sunstein,2001, P.8).*

From this general discussion of the functioning of each of the three modes we now focus on their value in educational contexts. We will argue that each mode of Net organization requires different learning strategies, assessment methods and facilitation.

APPLYING THE MODEL

Most individuals make use of all three organizational models and social software tool sets are used to facilitate each: collectives are employed every time we use Google or follow prominent links in a tag cloud; often, when we browse through an aggregated RSS feed or follow links in a blog posting we engage at a network level; and, in formal education, most of us are engaged at one time or another in discussion forums or email correspondence. Membership of any binding of the Many does not preclude membership at any other level. Individual need and use often migrates through all three entities depending upon contextual factors including immediacy, aggregation detail required, and individuals' familiarity, status and past participation in the collaborative entity. Individuals and social groupings may move amongst the three modes as their collective and individual needs are modified over time and context. For example a formal education class may function as Group during a structured semester length session, then many of this Group membership may continue to support and query each other as members of a program or alumni Network when the course completes. Or they may link to, filter or annotate resources listings created by Group and Network members through active or passive tagging and aggregation – thus exploiting and contributing to a Collective.

Similarly identical tools may be appropriated by members of all three levels. For example, wikis may be used by a Group to generate documentation for a collaborative project, or may (like Wikipedia) be a more Collective and/or Networked endeavour. Group blogs may support a Group, be networked through trackbacks and blogrolls, and may be harvested and aggregated to afford a Collective view. We might choose to view any given instance and application of social software, therefore, as moving on a continuum between the three entities.

TEACHING AND LEARNING IMPLICATIONS

Within a formal environment, a range of activities and tools may lend themselves better to one form

of the Many than another. Table 1 provides some examples of how this may occur within a traditional institutional or organisational setting.

We have a growing understanding of the scalability issues and the need to explore ways in which quality e-learning can be designed at lower cost. We argue that the current default position that encompasses e-learning in formal education within a Group paradigm, is not sufficient to gain the advantages presented in a Net-centric learning context. Further, group learning is often associated with excessive teacher control that is not conducive to developing lifelong and self directed learning. Rather, strategies should be devised to use Groups, Networks and Collectives selectively and appropriately such that high levels of learning occur at affordable costs and that learners are equipped with the skills needed for a lifetime of learning..

We end this paper with very brief overview of strategies that e-learning institutions and teachers

Table 1. Uses of social software for learning

	Group	Network	Collective
Metaphor	"Virtual classroom"	"virtual communities of practice"	"wisdom of crowds"
Typical Activities	Collaborative Projects	Discussion & Queries	Data mining, individual submission, search and query
Typical Tools	Threaded discussion, LMS (VLEs), Chats	Mailing Lists Blog syndication	Search Engines Social Network (MySpace, 43 Things etc
Goals	Accreditation, formal learning, task completion	Knowledge generation, expanding social capital	Knowledge extraction
Time Frame	Bounded often by semester, often synchronous	Real time to short term Asynchronous	Long term Asynchronous
Commitment to participate	High, often assessed	Medium - as needed or requested	Low and often passive
Motivation to Contribute	External, required for credit	Altruism & professional reputation	Only as a product of individual use
Expectation for Help	High, often mutual dependence	Med. share and share alike ethos	Low/none, unconscious aggregation
Scalability	Low, usually limited to 25-30 persons	Medium – Can expand as potential membership grows.	High
Operational sizes	Can be effective at low numbers 3-5	Needs 30-50 active members to sustain Network operation	Only provides value when very large numbers of users participate
Social Capital	Bonding	Bridging	Exposing

can use and dangers to avoid when using social software in each of the three modes of organization described above.

Group Strategies

As noted, much of the literature on e-learning is predicated on use of Groups and as such is beyond the remit of this chapter. There are five strategies that we highlight however:

1. Use real time tools (Web, audio and video conferencing) and explore the increased social presence afforded by synchronous and immersive environments
2. Deploy powerful tool sets such as Moodle, through which Groups switch on and off and easily link to various collaborative sharing and production tools, preferably through their own powerful personal learning environments (PLEs)
3. Support standards and tool sets such as Shibboleth, LDAP or Open ID that permit Group control of access to Group conversation and artefacts in a seamless and easy to use fashion
4. Develop and deploy distributed content management tools and expertise such that Group products are easily produced, versioned, tagged and distributed to a variety of audiences
5. Introduce Network tools to continue learning process once the formal group ends

Network Strategies

The literature on support for virtual communities of practice (i.e. Ardichvili, Page, & Wentling, 2003; Dubé, Bourhis, & Jacob, 2005) provides useful insights and lessons for supporting e-learning Networks. In addition, given the varieties of Networks that learners participate in, of crucial importance are tools to manage, filter and control information so as to make learning with and from

Networks efficacious. Specific recommendations include:

1. Use high quality (and, where possible, open) tool sets for finding, joining, forming and supporting new and existing Networks and their archives
2. Develop and deploy tools to support individual control of Network filters
3. Support Network deployment in contexts that are as open as possible,. Generally this means the open Net, however is some larger organizations on closed Intra Networks allow for different types of Networks to evolve.
4. Use tools to support identifying, evaluating and annotating resources by individual and collaborative Network members
5. Create linked profiles and other sophisticated search tools so that Network members can come to know each other and so that contributions to the Network are recognizable and valued
6. Use means of identity management such as OpenID to enable persistence of identity between systems
7. Allow members to morph, parcellate and combine Networks as needs evolve
8. Use tools or processes, such as the soft security of wikis, that promote trust both of Network artefacts and of the people within the Network.

Collective Strategies

Strategies for effective use of Collectives are evolving very rapidly in response to the expanding affordances of the emerging Semantic Web and Web 2.0. Of special importance are strategies to support use and adoption. Many, especially younger net generation learners, are regular and proficient users of the Collective. However a growing digital use divide (Hargittai, 2002) raises questions regarding use among large numbers of

Collective members. There are big differences in skills and preferences among net users, especially between those of different generations and educational backgrounds. To make things worse, the ease with which crowd wisdom can become mob stupidity raises significant issues of trust and reliability. Important strategic initiatives include:

1. Strategies to increase visibility, compatibility and perceived relative advantage by teachers and users

2. Strategies to ensure high levels of Collective literacy and efficacy

3. Strategies to promote contribution to not only increase individual social capital but also increase institutional brand

4. Strategies to support Collective knowledge use in organizational Networks and Groups

5. Support for access to Collective knowledge outside the organization – during work time

6. Support for active harvesting of Collective knowledge to provide insight into threats and opportunities for organization and individuals.

7. The design and deployment of software that uses algorithms that include negative feedback loops as well as interaction design that provides sign posts rather than fence posts, so as to prevent runaway mob behaviour.

Combinatorial Strategies

We have already observed that there are fuzzy borders between each of these modes of the Many, and that there is not always a direct correlation between tools and the kinds of Many that they support. For instance, there is nothng to prevent us from using a system such as Elgg within a Group context, even though it is (arguably) more naturally a network tool. As we begin to use such systems within an institutional context, a number of tensions arise between the traditional group forms and the emergent and/or loosely connected network and collective forms. Based on our experience, we offer the following tentative suggestions:

1. clarify, explicitly or through implicit navigational cues, where the Group ends and the Network and Collective activity begins

2. maintain trusted parcellated areas, whether through access control or (more simply) differently authorised areas within the system

3. allow learners to establish their own comfort zones: ownership is important here. Make sure that they are able to control who sees what and that they are comfortable exercising that control.

4. Provide opportunities within the group to discuss and analyse what goes on outside the gated community of the Group.

CONCLUSION

Collectives and Networks are essentially anarchic: driven primarily from the bottom up, they tend to sit uncomfortably in a top-down hierarchy of the kind found in educational institutions and organisations. The determination of some schools and lawmakers to ban such tools (see for example Doctorow's blog at http://www.boingboing. net/2006/05/11/proposed-law-require.html) bears witness to their perceived disruptiveness. It is true that, even within a relatively walled garden, the attentions of spammers and unintended release of personal data can seriously disrupt each of the three modes of the Many and the lack of control exercised from above can lead to fear and lack of trust, both for the controllers and those they seek to control. But social networking tools, are ubiquitous (Grunwald Associates, 2007) and we ignore them at our peril. We need to find ways to take advantage of such systems, not to censor them. To gain the greatest benefits from social software it is important to understand the different dynamics of different tools and the different contexts in which they may be used. This paper has provided a lens through which the tangled web of disparate social technologies may be viewed and has begun to lay out some approaches to their effective use. It is hoped that it will now be possible to perform more informed studies that will refine and develop these approaches more fully.

REFERENCES

Anderson, T. (2001). The hidden curriculum of distance education. *Change Magazine, 33*(6), 29-35.

Anderson, T. (2006). Higher education evolution: Individual freedom afforded by educational social software. In M. Beaudoin (Ed.), *Perspectives on the Future of Higher Education in the Digital Age.* (pp. 77-90). New York: Nova Science Publishers.

Anderson, T., (2007). Learning with Networks. Retrieved 25th April 2007, from http://terrya. edublogs.org/2007/03/28/46/.

Ardichvili, A., Page, V., & Wentling, T. (2003). Motivation and barriers to participation in virtual knowledge-sharing communities of practice. *Journal of Knowledge Management, 7*(1), 64-77. Retrieved April 2007 from http://www. emeraldinsight.com/Insight/ViewContentServl et?Filename=Published/EmeraldFullTextArticle/ Articles/2300070105.html

Arrington, M. (2007). Diig surrenders to mob. *Tech Cruch,* Retrieved May 2007 from http:// www.techcrunch.com/2007/05/01/digg-surrenders-to-mob/

Bandura, A. (1997). *Self-Efficacy: The Exercise of Control.* New York: Freeman.

Bijker, W. (1999). *Of Bicycles, Bakelites and Bulbs: Towards a Theory of Sociotechnical Change.* Cambridge: MIT Press.

Brin, S., & Page, L. (2000). The Anatomy of a Large-Scale Hypertextual Web Search Engine. from http://www-db.stanford.edu/pub/papers/ google.pdf

Bryant, L. (2003). *Smarter, Simpler Social: An introduction to online social software methodology.* Headshift. Retrieved Nov. 2005 from http://www. headshift.com/moments/archive/sss2.html.

Brusilovsky, P., Chavan, G., & Farzan, R. (2004). Social Adaptive Navigation Support for Open Corpus Electronic Textbooks. Paper presented at the AH 2004, Eindhoven.

Christenson, L., & Menzel, K. (1998). The linear relationship between student reports of teacher immediacy behaviors and perceptions of state motivation, and of cognitive, affective and behavioral learning. *Communication Education, 47*, 82-90.

Creed, T. (1996). Extending the Classroom Walls Electronically. In William Campbell and Karl Smith (Ed.), New Paradigms for College Teaching. Edina, MN: Interaction Book Co.

Dillenbourg, P., & Schneider, D. (1995). Mediating the mechanisms which make collaborative learning sometimes effective. *International Journal of Educational Telecommunications, 1*(2-3), 131-146.

Downes, S. (2006). Networks versus Groups. Talk at Future of Learning in a Networked World event in Auckland, video retrieved Oct 2007 from http://video.google.com/videoplay?docid=- 4126240905912531540

Dron, J. Social software and the emergence of control. In *ICALT 2006:* Retrieved June 2007 from doi.ieeecomputersociety.org/10.1109/ ICALT.2006.293.

Dron, J. (2006). On the stupidity of mobs. Paper presented at the WBC 2006, San Sebastian.

Dron, J. (2007). *Control and Constraint in E-Learning: Choosing When to Choose.* Hershey, PA: Information Science Pub.

Dubé, L., Bourhis, A., & Jacob, R. (2005). The impact of structuring characteristics on the launching of virtual communities of practice. *Journal of Organizational Change Management, 18*(2), 145-166.

Ellison, N., Steinfield, C., & Lampe, C. (2007). The Benefits of Facebook "Friends:" Social Capital and College Students' Use of Online Social Networks. *Journal of Computer Mediated Communication, 12*(4) Retrieved Aug. 2007 from http://jcmc.indiana.edu/vol12/issue4/ellison.html

Fisher, S. G., Hunter, T. A., & Ketin Macrosson, W. D. (1997). Team or Group? Managers' Perception of the Differences," Journal of Managerial Psychology,, 12(4), 232-243.

Garrison, D.R., & Anderson, T. (2003). *E-Learning in the 21st century.* London: Routledge.

Granovetter, M. (1973). The strength of weak ties: A network theory revisited. *American Journal of Sociology, 78*, 1360-1380.

Granovetter, M. (2004). The impact of social structure on economic outcomes. *Journal of Economic Perspectives, 19*(1), 33-50. Retrieved May 2007 from http://www.leader-values.com/Content/detailasp?ContentDetailID=990

Gregorio, J. (2003). Stigmergy and the World-Wide Web. Retrieved 13/12/2003, 2003, from http://bitworking.org/news/Stigmergy/

Grunwald Associates. (2007). Creating *& Connecting: Research and Guidelines on Online Social and Educational Networking.* Washington: National School Boards Association. Retrieved Sept. 2007 from http://files.nsba.org/creatingand-connecting.pdf.

Han, S., Ahn, Y., Moon, S., & Jeong, H. (2006). Collaborative Blog Spam Filtering Using Adaptive Percolation Search. *WWW2006 Workshop on the Weblogging Ecosystem,* Retrieved Oct. 2007 from http://www.blogpulse.com/www2006-workshop/papers/collaborative-blogspam-filtering.pdf

Hargittai, E. (2002). Second-Level Digital Divide: Differences in People's Online Skills. *First Monday, 7*(4). Retrieved April 2007 from http://www.firstmonday.org/issues/issue7_4/hargittai/

Horowitz, B., (2006). Creators, Synthesizers, and Consumers. Retrieved June 2007 from http://www.elatable.com/blog/?p=5.

Kember, D. (1989). A longitudinal process model of drop-out in distance education. *The Journal of Higher Education, 60*(3), 278-301.

Margolis, E. (2001). *The hidden curriculum of higher education.* London: Routledge.

Mason, R. (2002). Rethinking assessment for the online environment. In C. Vrasidas & G. Glass (Eds.), *Distance education and distributed learning.* (pp. 57-74). Greenwich, Co.: Information Age Publishing.

Mentor, K. (2007). Open access learning environments. *Online Journal of Distance Learning Administration.* Retrieved April 2007 from http://www.westga.edu/%7Edistance/ojdla/spring101/mentor101.htm

Miettinen, M., Kurhila, J., Nokelainen, P., & Tirri, H. (2005). OurWeb - Transparent groupware for online communities. Paper presented at the Web Based Communities 2005, Algarve, Portugal.

Palloff, R., & Pratt, K. (1999). *Building learning communities in Cyberspace.* San Francisco: Jossey- Bass.

Patel, N. (2003). Deferred System's Design: Countering the Primacy of Reflective IS Development

With Action-Based Information Systems. In N. Patel (Ed.), Adaptive Evolutionary Information Systems (pp. 1-29). London: Idea Group Publishing.

Paulsen, M. (1993). The hexagon of cooperative freedom. DEOS 3(2), retrieved from www.nettskolen.com/forskning/21/hexagon.html

Postmas, T. (2007). The psychological dimensions of collective action, online. In A. Joinson, K. McKenna, T. Postmes, & U. Reips (Eds.), *Oxford Handbook of Internet Psychology.* (pp. 165-184). Oxford: Oxford University Press.

Postmes, T., Haslam, A., & Swaab, R. (2005). Social influence in small groups: An interactive model of social identity formation. *Europen Review of Social Psychology, 16*, 1-42. Retrieved June 2007 from http://psy.ex.ac.uk/~tpostmes/PDF/PostmesHaslamSwaabERSP05.pdf

Preece, J., Nonnecke, B., & Andrews, D. (2004). The top five reasons for lurking: improving community experiences for everyone. Computers in Human Behavior, 20(2), 210-223.

Puddifoot, J. (1995). Dimensions of Community Identity. Journal of Community & Applied Social Psychology, 5(5), 357-370.

Rafaeli, S., Dan-Gur, Y., & Barak, M. (2005). Social recommender systems: Recommendations in support of e-learning. *Journal of Distance Education Technologies, 3*(2), 30-47.

Rainie, L., (2007). *28% of Online Americans Have Used the Internet to Tag Content.* Pew Internet & American Life Project. Retrieved June 2007 from http://www.pewinternet.org/pdfs/PIP_Tagging.pdf.

Riegelsberger, J., Sasse, M., & McCarthy, J. (2007). Trust in mediated interactions. In A. Joinson, K. McKenna, T. Postmes, & U. Reips (Eds.), *Oxford Handbook of Internet Psychology.* (pp. 53-69). Oxford: Oxford University Press.

Rohse, S., & Anderson, T. (2006). Design patterns for complex learning. *Journal of Learning Design, 1*(3). Retrieved Nov. 2006 from https://olt.qut.edu.au/udf/jld/index.cfm?fa=getFile&rNum=3386817&pNum=3386813

Salmon, G. (2000). *E-moderating: The key to teaching and learning online.* London: Kogan Page.

Shirky, C. (2004). Nomic World: by the players, for the players. Retrieved November 8th 2007, from http://www.shirky.com/writings/nomic.html

Short, J., Williams, E., & Christie, B. (1976). *The social psychology of telecommunications.* Toronto: John Wiley and Sons.

Smith. (2001). Group Development: A Review of the Literature and a Commentary on Future Research Directions. Group Facilitation, 31(3). Spears, R., Postmes, T., Lea, M., & Wolbert, A. (2002). When are net effects gross products? *Journal of Social Issues, 58*(1), 91-107.

Sunal, D., Sunal C., Odell, M., & Sunberg, C. (2003). Research supported best practices for developing online education. *Journal of interactive Online Learning, 2*(1). Retrieved Oct. 5, 2003 from http://www.ncolr.org/jiol/archives/2003/summer/1/index.asp

Sunstein, C. (2001). *Republic.com.* Princeton NJ: Princeton University Press. Retrieved April 2007 from http://press.princeton.edu/chapters/s7014.html.

Surowiecki, J. (2004). *The Wisdom of Crowds.* New York: Random House.

Tinto, V. (1987). *Leaving college: Rethinking the causes and cures of college attrition.* Chicago, IL: University of Chicago Press.

Walther, J.B. (1996). Computer mediated communication: Impersonal, interpersonal, and hyperpersonal interaction. Communication Research, 23(1), 3-43.

Watts, D. J. (2003). *Six degrees: the science of a connected age.* New York: Norton.

Weinberg, H., & Toder, M. (2004). The Hall of Mirrors in Small, Large and Virtual Groups. *Group Analysis,* 492-507. Retrived May 2007 from http://gaq.sagepub.com/cgi/content/abstract/37/4/492

Wellman, B. (2001). The rise (and possible fall) of networked individualism. *Connections, 24*(3), 30–32

Wessner, M.,& Pfister, H.I. (2001). *International ACM SIGGROUP Conference on Supporting Group Work:* IEEE.

Zarb, M. (2006). Modelling Participation in Virtual Communities of Practice. London School of Economics; London. Retrieved April 2007 from http://www.mzarb.com/Modelling_Participation_in_Virtual_Communities-of-Practice.pdf

KEY TERMS

Collective: The loosest aggregation of the Many, an amalgam of algorithm and individual activities, exemplified in tag clouds, collaborative filters and rating systems.

E-Learning: Learning mediated through electronic means, usually over the Internet.

Group: The traditional kind of Many used in education, exemplified in the classroom.

Many: A generic term describing a collection of individuals.

Network: A looser aggregation of the Many, with weaker ties and ever shifting membership, common across the Internet.

Social Software: Software enabling communicaion between people in which the Many plays an active role in structuring the environment.

Web 2.0: A term referring to the trend to more interactive, user-generated Web sites. No different technologically from Web 1.0, it is about the ubiquity of user involvement rather than any particular technological change.

Chapter II
Social Networking and Schools:
Early Responses and Implications for Practice

Chris Abbott
Reader in e-Inclusion, King's College London, UK

William Alder
Sixth Form Student, Trinity School, UK

ABSTRACT

Although social networking has been enthusiastically embraced by large numbers of children and young people, their schools and colleges have been more cautious, and often concerned about the implications for online safety. Social networking used by young people is considered here as part of a trajectory of online practices which began with personal Web sites in the mid 1990s and continued through the use of interactive services to the networking sites familiar today. The response of the education system is examined through interview and anecdotal evidence, and with reference to a growing body of research in this and allied areas. It is concluded that social networking has initiated a series of practices which cannot now be abandoned, and that the challenge for the education system is not control or abolition but the inclusion of social networking appropriately within teaching and learning.

INTRODUCTION

If the placing of a research tender can be seen as indicative of the maturity of a topic for study, then the recent award of a contract by Becta, the UK government agency for ICT in education, to research current in-school and out-of-school Web 2.0 experience is an indication that social networking is a relevant area of study for those seeking to understand educational practices in the UK. The researchers at the three Universities involved (www.lsri.nottingham.ac.uk) will be faced with a range of responses from the education system to the social networking sites that form a key part of current Web 2.0 practice.

Young people of school age frequently use social networking sites in the way that their counterparts of ten years ago used personal Websites: to provide an online representation of themselves and their views and interests, and to communicate with others who may share these preoccupations. Schools and other educational institutions have responded in different ways to this; often by banning such activity but occasionally in a more enlightened way. This chapter will describe how this has happened, outline the positive affordances of social networking for education, and will then suggest a more constructive response from schools and colleges.

SOCIAL NETWORKING AND YOUNG PEOPLE

Social networking has developed rapidly since 2003 and its use by young people has been characterised by successive waves of enthusiasm and ever-changing allegiances. Early alliances with MySpace have given way, for the most part, to institutionally-based networks such as Bebo or culturally-marked sites such as Facebook. At the time of writing, MySpace is seen by many young people in the UK as being more appropriate for younger children, with Bebo having a strong presence within youth in educational institutions and Facebook mostly catering for the late teen and young adult middle class user. This breakdown should be seen as a snapshot in time, however, and, during the period in which this chapter was written, the increasing take-up of Facebook by young professionals has led to a slowing down of its adoption by school-age youth.

It is interesting to note the differing degrees of anonymity in these systems, with the early and largely-anonymised MySpace giving way to Facebook and its supposed use of real names at all times. The youngest children of all have only recently begun to use social networking through systems such as Club Penguin, recently purchased by Disney in a sign of the financial potential of this area of the online market.

Making assumptions about the relative standing of different social networking sites can be a difficult process. Sites which are seen as of great importance and are sought-after one year can then be demoted the next, as is to be expected with a medium which is closely linked with other areas of youth interest such as music and fashion. One of us is an experienced social networking user and explains further, taking issue with some of the assumptions in the popular and academic press.

I'd say MySpace has a particular type of teenage interest, not younger. Also, it focuses on more arty people to a certain extent – ...[there is a] music function, and there are video and other places to display your own work. It also lets you modify your page to make it look how you like, ...but personally I find that extremely annoying. I don't like how you cannot read information about people, because it's in a ridiculous font or too small, or because of the photo behind it all due to someone's bad coding. That's what I like about Facebook, you can easily read what people have written about themselves. The day that Facebook changes that is its downfall!

Also, Facebook is much more institutionalised. It used to be the case that you had to have a school, college or university email in order to have an account on it. They've changed that now. It's based around schools, colleges and Unis and where you come from, different networks.

(Alder, 2008)

In addition to these wide-ranging general social networking sites, users have the opportunity to align themselves to owned social networks such as Friendlink.

Friendlink is a place for young Quakers (members of the Religious Society of Friends) to meet and greet. It is a forum for discussions, with sections for general chat, creative writing, poetry, role play and so on, and an online forum-based games area. Most of the members know each other outside of the forum in real life, but some are from across the world, and are attracted to meeting other young Quakers.

Friendlink differs from Facebook as it is aimed at a specific group, young Quakers, though it does accept others. It is worth examining further not because of any intrinsic importance in itself but as an example of a different style of social networking site, and to which one of us (Alder) belongs. It is also forum based, and although there are places for socialising and putting photos of events and so on (all screened from the public eye), there are many heated discussions about topics that would not be as greatly fought out on places such as Facebook. Although almost all participants come from a Quaker background, there is no common theme in what is believed, and diverse views are represented: Quakerism varies greatly in different countries, having no set beliefs or ways of worshipping. In a sense, where Facebook is more about the individuals and their lives, and is the impression that they wish to give to others (by the use of profiles with photographs, background information, personal profiles and so on), Friendlink is much more about the individual person's beliefs and what they think about particular issues. Although there are spaces to catch up about people (such as *Something that made you smile today* or *Things to love and hate today*), much of Friendlink is about events or current issues that people want to ask about, and apart from groups on Websites such as Facebook, there is no other counterpart to this activity, at least not within a focused community such as Quakers.

In addition to the social networking sites themselves, users have the possibility to add functionality through add-ons. In many cases these are merely intended to amuse, such as the wide variety of virtual gifts possible on Facebook or the aquarium to which friends can contribute

fish bought with virtual currency. In other cases, the add-on may add real information, such as the various maps that show cities visited by the site owner, or new communicative possibilities as in the chat add-ons like Twitter.

Unlike many previous online activities, such as personal Website ownership, there seems to be little evidence of gender or indeed sexuality bias in uptake of these facilities. It is striking to note the rapidity with which change has taken place in this area, as is evident from a reading of a New Scientist article published as recently as September 2006. In this article (Gefter, 2006) the emphasis is still mainly on blogging, an activity which seems increasingly arcane and outdated just a year or two later. The essential stance of the article is that, for young people, blogs have replaced diaries, Flickr has replaced photo albums (but did young people ever have photo albums?) and social networking sites have replaced email. The latter is perhaps the most contentious statement, and others might argue that social networking site conversation is more likely to have replaced instant messaging and that email continues on parallel tracks, but data for this supposition is almost impossible to obtain without large-scale research, and these speculations must therefore remain just that.

Gefter notes in particular the acquisition by News Corporation of MySpace, at the time "ranked number one Website among US internet users, receiving more hits in a one-week period than even Google" (Gefter, 2006: 46). Gefter characterises blogging as essentially a female occupation, although no data is given to justify this apart from the fact that the majority of LiveJournal users are female (or claim to be). As Gefter recognises, the aspect of blogging that comes closest to later social networking sites is the ability to link blogs together into communities of readers and writers. She also makes the key point that, unlike previous communicative online practices such as chatrooms and gaming, the use of social networking sites is not usually anonymous. Gefter's assertion that online and real-life friends are the same is unproven but can be supported anecdotally.

...young people on social networking sites are interacting for the most part not with strangers, but with friends from their real life. Thus their online social life doesn't detract from their real one, as the two are simply different manifestations of the same network of friends.

(Gefter, 2006: 47)

Most young users would agree and would stress that their Facebook interactions build upon and enlarge their face-to-face social activity, and may indeed support these real-life meetings.

Not everyone lives online, but most of my imme- diate friends have Facebook. Certainly it could never replace a real life social life, though in some cases use of the Internet does replace actual go- ing out. However in the majority of cases, it's a great place to arrange events or meeting up with friends. It's very easy to keep track of how many people can come to a particular event, and who you have invited – you can also keep complete tabs on who knows what about the event. Another great use for it I and others have found is that through the networks and also the groups, I've got back in touch with people I was friends with in primary or middle school, and also people that I've met through different things. I find it much easier to find people there than by, [using] say, MySpace or Bebo.

(Alder, 2008)

It is also striking to notice how quickly users can change patterns of uptake and social network- ing practices. Gefter asserted in a conveniently neat turn of phrase that "MySpace connects individuals through friends, Facebook through schools, LinkedIn through professions, and Libr- aryThing through books" (Gefter, 2006: 48). While such a division seems attractively tidy, it is also unconvincing and has not stood the test of time.

In the UK, Facebook, for example, has become the social networking site of choice for young working middle class adults, with LinkedIn more used among formal consultancy partnerships.

Other writers have presented a more nuanced picture of the gendered dimension of social net- working. Research by Danah Boyd at the Uni- versity of California-Berkeley indicated what she termed the "significant cultural resonance" (Boyd, 2007) attached to social networking sites, even though their impact had lessened among the group she studied. Exploring the implications of these sites for youth identity formation, Boyd locates them in what she terms networked publics.

I argue that social network sites are a type of networked public with four properties that are not typically present in face-to-face public life: persistence, searchability, exact copyability, and invisible audiences.

(Boyd, 2007: 2)

This is a useful theoretical framework for an area where theory is largely missing. Persistence and searchability are certainly relevant to the comments of the user quoted earlier, although evidence for what Boyd terms a complication of the ways young people interact and for the abil- ity of social networking to "fundamentally alter social dynamics" (Boyd, 2007: 2) is harder to come by. Boyd reminds us that the persistence of online discourse permits not just asynchronous communication but also the extension of the life of a discourse without limit. Searchability is one of the key drivers of online communities, but replicability is a more hidden aspect which Boyd reminds us about: by use of the ability to copy an original identically, there is no visible differ- ence between the copy and the original. Boyd's concept of invisible audiences inter-relates with her other factors, since persistence, searchability and copyability are all open to these unknown participants.

Boyd's main data came not from Facebook but from the earlier market leader: MySpace. Her two year ethnographical study focussed mainly on urban youth, the majority of them aged from 14 to 18 years. Among her target group, Boyd found users and non-users of MySpace, but almost all had an opinion about it and knew of it, making it, she says, "the civil society of teenage culture" (Boyd, 2007: 3). Her early users were characterised by a high degree of technical knowledge, exploiting their capabilities with CSS or HTML to do more with their MySpace pages than was intended by the site developers. In this way, these early pioneers echo the practices of many of the first young Website owners in the mid 1990s, who have been described by one of us as "technological aesthetes" (Abbott, 2001). The practices of these early MySpace users, and their tendency to help each other and copy and paste code from tips sites, bears remarkable echoes of the Website owners of ten years earlier.

Boyd's main emphasis is on young people's use of the social networking site, the creation of their digital identity – or digital body as she describes it – but she also considers the effect of these practices on home life. Interactions with formal education are less relevant to her research, although she relates a telling story of the reaction of one school to a student applicant whose MySpace profile seemed to present a different picture than that presented by him at interview. Boyd sees school as the structure from which young people seek to escape by creating online spaces and representations, at a time when young people seem to less likely to be outside away from parents than were previous generations. Much of this discussion is US-centric, relating as it does to problems of mobility in a context where public transport may be non-existent or perceived to be unsafe, but a degree of the same concerns exists in UK and European cultures.

Boyd's conclusions include reference to the dilemma facing educational institutions that seek to decide whether to control, support or ignore social networking.

...we need to figure out how to educate teens to navigate social structures that are quite unfamiliar to us because they will be faced with these publics as adults, even if we try to limit their access now. Social network sites have complicated our lives because they have made this rapid shift in public life very visible. ...They are learning how to navigate networked publics; it is in our better interest to figure out how to help them.

(Boyd, 2007: 23)

Beer (2006) has suggested that Boyd's networked publics can also be seen as part of a second media age (Poster, 1996) and sees the demise of artefacts such as Top of the Pops as part of the same process. Beer's central focus of interest is music and the extent to which it is now mediated through social networking, but his discussion of issues such as ownership versus free access or the tension between "various capitalist interests and localised interfaces" (Beer, 2006: 4.3) can be seen as a variant on the education system's concerns about parallel issues.

It is worth considering in passing the extent to which social networking can be accurately seen as youth-oriented any longer, especially as this chapter is being written as Saga Online is launched, in order to offer social networking for the over 50s. It can be a risky business to suggest that social networking is mainly for young people, as BBC Technology Correspondent Rory Cellan-Jones discovered after he described what happened when he suggested in an online article (Cellan-Jones, 2007) that social networking was not for over 30s. He received a great deal of response, including suggestions that the important thing was to have lots of friends – not to know who they were – and someone else set up a *Befriend Rory Cellan-Jones* group. Other more thoughtful responses suggested that Facebook was being used, for example, by lecturers to keep in touch with students overseas. He surmises that "it seems that the virtual worlds... are just a way of managing a thriving real world social life" (Cellan-Jones 2007), a conclusion very much in line with that of Boyd quoted earlier.

Tentative taxonomies of this use put forward in the 1990s included the division of personal Website owners into Technological Aesthetes, Community Builders and Professional Activists (Abbott 1999; 2001). Later work on the use of guestbooks and interactive fora on Websites has highlighted many of the issues that have now come to the fore in the use by young people of social networking sites (Abbott 2005). This developing line of research has highlighted some key methodological and ethical issues associated with this phenomenon, and these have also been explored by one of the current authors (Abbott & Seale 2007).

THE RESPONSE OF THE EDUCATION SYSTEM

Much of the response from the educational system to social networking has related to the real or perceived risks. These risks may relate to current dangers from online predators or be related to concerns for the future of young people who are inadvertently creating a permanent record of youthful indiscretions (Rosenblum 2007), much as the student quoted by Boyd did when his MySpace page came close to causing his rejection by a prestigious school.

Rosenblum titles his article *What anyone can know* and this is in many ways a summary of the concerns of authority figures and institutions. He indicates in some detail the risks associated with posting personal data online in this way, although he recognises that a more guarded approach to sharing information will inevitably result in "some chilling effect on the fluid, no-holds-barred ethos of these sites" (Rosenblum, 2007: 40). In

addition to his recognition of the ways in which Internet-based information is both persistent and accessible, Rosenblum also notes the increasing trend for "prospective employers, government agencies or businesses collecting market data" (Rosenblum, 2007: 41) to have the right to view and make use of this information.

Some social networking sites have responded to these concerns by offering extra privacy options. For example, on Facebook users can choose to let people see only their limited profile, so they are unable to view more personal information such as phone number and address, or even photos. It is possible to control how much anyone sees, even if they are designated friends. These privacy controls, however, are fairly low-profile on the site and do not seem to be widely used, even after the recent announcement that Facebook sites would be searchable with Google (BBC News, 2007).

Schools have been more concerned about online safety than identity theft, probably in reaction to the scale of public and perceived concerns. Discussions with young people who use Facebook, especially those of Sixth Form age, have shown that some have teaching staff in their online friends group and vice versa. However, it seems more common for staff to not accept friend requests and to keep their social life separate from their work. This is no new issue of course; there has always been a difficult line to draw between older students and staff at social events such as graduation celebrations. Identity theft, however, or inadvertent revealing of information that may in future cause problems, is an issue that seems little recognised by schools or by many students.

...an entire MySpace generation could realise, when it is much too late to intervene, that the cyber personae they spawned in adolescent efforts to explore identity have taken on permanent lives in the multiple archives of the digital world.

(Rosenblum, 2007: 49)

Early responses to social networking from schools have been negative for the most part and have revolved around control or prohibition. Many schools have used their filtering systems to block access to sites such as MySpace, Bebo and Facebook. Others have reacted punitively towards pupils found referring to their schools or teachers on these sites. Some educational institutions have ensured that use of social networking sites has led to dismissal or expulsion, but others – although not many - have supported the practice and incorporated it into their pedagogy.

As understanding of the potential of these networks develops, there are signs of a more mature and enabling attitude on the part of a growing number of educational institutions. There is evidence for this in the increasing understanding of the interactive possibilities of institution-based online networks which aim to link together learners, teachers and carers/parents. Although some use of these systems is low-level and mechanical and involves for the most part the maintenance of records, management of homework and registration of attendance, in other cases real interactivity and discursive use is beginning to be recorded. These developments take place against a policy shift in the use of digital technologies by schools, with current Government diktat favouring the "harnessing" of technology (DfES 2005) over its use to free learners to learn, despite the parallel focus on personalised learning.

A number of short anecdotal case studies arising from the personal experiences of both authors of this chapter may go some way to giving examples of the range of responses of educational institutions to social networking.

- Two years ago, a part-time Masters student chose to write a dissertation about the uses of social networking by students at the independent school where he was employed. He began by interviewing his students and discussing the topic with them, but his efforts were overtaken by events when his school featured in a national Sunday newspaper.

It transpired that some students had made comments on Bebo which were highly derogatory about some members of staff at the school. The Masters student himself was relieved to note that he featured in only benign descriptions.

- A student at a prestigious music college set up a Facebook site which included discussion of the college and comments from other students. The next time that the student arrived at the college, he was escorted from the premises by security guards, on the orders of the college administration.

- At least one educational institution in the UK has threatened staff with dismissal after they commented on their place of work in postings on their own and their friends' Facebook sites.

- The social dynamic between teacher and students is changing, as both may appear in the same Facebook group. Whilst some institutions and employers would see this as acceptable, others would be most concerned and would consider it to be an example of unacceptable informality between staff and student. In many ways, this is merely the latest manifestation of a developing pattern, and submission of homework by email has sometimes led to an informalising of teacher-student dialogue as would be expected on that medium. In many schools, the decision for these contacts to occur via school email accounts is seen as keeping the discourse within a professional arena. Text contact via mobile phone between teacher and student is likely to be proscribed, but this may need to be reconsidered as handheld and mobile devices become more accepted in schools and colleges; and e-learning environments have bought online informal discourse practices into the virtual classroom.

- Some school systems have adopted a more open approach. In Denmark, the national schools network also involves parents, and all parents are allocated email usernames by the schools that their children attend. Progress reviews are held twice a year and these can be held online and are always summarised on the network. In this way, social networking has been made part of Danish educational practice.

- Researchers are beginning to explore the potential of avatar-based sites such as Second Life, where social networking can take place either at one remove or through the assumption of an online identity. There is particular interest in the potential of this approach by those working with children who have become disaffected by school. One example of this is the Open University-supported Schome ("not school – not home"). In a depressing example of the difficulties of establishing new practice, Schome was funded firstly by NESTA (National Endowment for Science, technology and the Arts), then by the National Association of Gifted and Talented Youth and then by Becta (UK government agency), but has no current funder (www.schome.ac.uk). Of course, one aspect of the enabling of third-party add-ons for Facebook has been the opening up of dynamic links to other environments, including Second Life.

This mixed picture indicates a range of practices which highlight possibilities as much as constraints, although the unifying factor for the positive uses described is their adherence to a perspective which recognises the socially-constructed nature of most learning. A recent example of Facebook use to facilitate collaborative real-life activity arose during the making of a film during the summer vacation period. Alder explains how Facebook facilitated this activity, and demonstrates the socially collaborative nature of the process.

We used Facebook to initiate the project by creating interest, and are still continuing to do so. A lot of my immediate friends are involved with Drama, Music, and/or technical work, and

I thought that I was in the best place to facilitate such a project. I started by advertising it, and laying down specific dates when we would be filming, and asked people to contact me. This wasn't the sole way of casting, obviously – I had some people in mind for certain characters! We then kept updating the group we had made to try and get extras, crew and musicians to record the soundtrack. One of the co-writers of the initial plot I had only discussed over the internet, and was a friend of a friend – I didn't meet him until after the majority of the filming was over!

I've now created another group to do with the project – the main one is for all the people that may want to be involved in being extras, musicians, or are just interested in the project as a whole, or indeed seeing the final product as their friends are involved. The other for the production crew and cast to discuss when we are going to be filming, analysing the poster campaign I'm making as part of my A2 photography work, and the trailer we have produced. We keep this group closed so that the public, as it were, don't know when/where we're filming or what is going on. All of the cast, and most of the crew of the film are on Facebook, so I can send out mass messages to all of them. Clearly we keep in contact by phone and email, but it's a good way of sorting everyone into one place and sending messages about filming and the suchlike.

(Alder, 2008)

It seems likely that one of the next phases in the development of social networking will be the integration of geographical location information within handheld devices, enabling real-life meetings to take place serendipitously. Early services such as Dodgeball, owned by Google since 2005 but still only available in certain US cities, have made this possible, as has the Bluetooth capability of many mobile phones. This is perhaps what Gefter had in mind when she talked of her belief that the various sites will in the end become conjoined.

"...a meta-network linking together all the various social networking sites will emerge – and an individual's full identity, shown from all sides, will live online. ...We will be more autonomous and mobile than ever, and at the same time discover an unprecedented form of collectivism."

(Gefter, 2006: 48)

CONCLUSION

Social networking offers an unparalleled opportunity to education, although this is not without concomitant risk and concerns. To ignore social networking and what it has to offer to education would not only be short-sighted but would also indicate a basic failure to understand the impossibility of returned to a pre-Internet world. Social networking, like its precursors email, instant messaging and mobile phones, has changed communicative practices permanently. It is now essential that the educational establishment grapples with the implications of that change: the genie is well and truly out of the bottle and no wistful longing will put it back again.

REFERENCES

Abbott, C. (1999). *The Internet, text production and the construction of identity: Changing use by young males during the early to mid 1990s.* Unpublished PhD, King's College, University of London, London.

Abbott, C. (2001). Some young male Website owners: the Technological Aesthete, the Community Builder and the Professional Activist. *Education, Communication and Information, 1*(2), 197-212.

Abbott, C. (2005). Towards Digital Impartiality: learning from young people's online literacy practices. In R. Kupetz & G. Blell (Eds.), *Fremd-sprachenlernen zwischen Medienverwahrlosung und Medienkompetenz* (pp. 31-41). Frankfurt: Peter Lang.

Abbott, C., & Seale, J. (2007). Methodological issues in researching online representations: production, classification and personal Web space. *International Journal of Research & Method in Education, 30.*

BBC News (2007) Google opens up social networking. Retrieved on 13th Nov 2007 from http://news.bbc.co.uk/1/hi/technology/7070815.stm.

Beer, D. (2006). The pop-pickers have picked decentralised media: the fall of Top of the Pops and the rise of the second media age. *Sociological Research Online, 11*(3). Accessed 04/09/2007.

Boyd, D. (in press 2008). Why Youth (Heart) Social Nework Sites: The Role of Networked Publics in Teenage Social Life. In D. Buckingham (Ed.), *Identity*. MIT Press.

Cellan-Jones, R. (2007). How to make friends on Facebook. Retrieved 29th May 2007 from http://news.bbc.co.uk/go/pr/fr/-/1/hi/technology/6699791.stm.

DfES. (2005). *Harnessing Technology: Transforming learning and children's services.* London: DfES.

Gefter, A. (2006). This is your space. *New Scientist, 191*(2569), 46-48.

Godwin-Jones, R. (2006). Emerging Technologies: Tag Clouds in the Blogosphere: Electronic Literacy and Social Neworking. *Language Learning & Technology, 10*(2), 8-15.

Poster, M. (1996). *The second media age.* Cambridge: Polity Press.

Rosenblum, D. (2007). What anyone can know: the privacy risks of social networking sites. *IEEE Security and Privacy, 5*(3), 40-49.

Chapter III
Cyber–Identities and Social Life in Cyberspace

Eleni Berki
University of Tampere, Finland

Mikko Jäkälä
University of Jyväskylä, Finland

ABSTRACT

Information and communication technology gradually transform virtual communities to active meeting places for sharing information and for supporting human actions, feelings and needs. In this chapter the authors examine the conceptual definition of virtual community as found in the traditional cyberliterature and extend it to accommodate latest cybertrends. Similar to the ways that previous social and mass media dissolved social boundaries related to time and space, cyber-communities and social software seem to also dissolve the boundaries of identity. This, in turn, questions the trust, privacy and confidentiality of interaction. The authors present a way of classifying and viewing self-presentation regarding cyber-identity management in virtual communities. It is based on the characteristics that cyber-surfers prefer to attribute to themselves and accordingly present themselves to others. In so doing, the authors coin the terms for five distinct phenomena, namely nonymity, anonymity, eponymity, pseudonymity and polynymity. They subsequently compare and contrast these terms, summarising information from their investigation, and outlining emerging questions and issues for a future research agenda.

INTRODUCTION

Cyberspace and virtual communities are often described by features such as structure, setting or formation. From the view point of the user more important than the features are the social qualities. One of the important social features is the sense of community. Sense of community is often described as a set of subjective experiences of belonging, mutual respect, and commitment that can be gained only through participation (McMillan & Chavis, 1986). It is not just the space but the people with their collective experiences. Furthermore, human empowerment in designing for sociability and usability for socially acceptable information and communication technology has become a research and development issue of increasing importance (Preece, 2000; Earnshaw et al., 2001; Berki et al., 2003). Online communities cannot merely be built, only facilitated in order to provide platforms for people to come and form a community of their choice. This emphasises the human factor within design and research of cyberspaces.

Cyberspace does not have physical borders but social life within cyberspace does have expression boundaries as well as norms and rules for behaviour. These boundaries for social actions and behaviour are either inherited by the structure of a certain e-space or different social software, i.e. discussion forums and work spaces, or imposed by the designers and users of e-spaces. In order to succeed, online communities, e-spaces and other electronic congregations need regular users. Cyberspace does not exist without electronic inhabitants; otherwise it is a deserted cyber place. Recent studies show that the degree of success and functionality of virtual communities is incorporated and built through trustworthy group interaction (Werry & Mowbray, 2001). The rise of social software technologies and online social networks impose new challenges for law, security and trust, identity and interaction (Kollock, 1999; Kimppa, 2007; Berki et al., 2007). The challenges go sometimes so far as to raise questions related to democracy and citizens' degree of participation in private or public virtual communities (Wilhelm, 2000). The existence of cyberplaces also challenges the definition of membership since within digital worlds inclusivity and exclusivity have totally new semantics or terms of definitions

with different applications and tools to facilitate membership management.

Boundless digital spaces also challenge the ways of participation. Entering cyberspace concerns issues of identity and identification. The possibility to participate in online communities anonymously may ease the entrance to digital worlds. Some participants, however, may dislike anonymous people and they, instead, gravitate towards digitally eponymous people welcoming them in an electronically-mediated social environment. To some extent identity, both in real life and cyber life, can be seen as composed of similar qualities. Notwithstanding, questions of security, safety and trustworthiness are often associated with cyberparticipants and their identities. In real life, however, identities are not that often questioned, authenticated or even doubted.

Understanding cyberspace requires exploring the meaning of individual and group (collective) identities, in particular how they are built and how they affect interaction and participation (Renninger & Shumar, 2002; Georgiadou et al., 2004). Arguably, the identity shared by the cyber-societies participants should be empowering to facilitate participation and support communication. An overpowering group identity might block communication and create difficulties in promoting innovative ways of thinking and functioning. A shared, cohesive identity, used by eponymous or anonymous people facilitates the development of mutual trust among the participants and balances communication within a group. On the other hand, a pseudonym or plenty of names may decrease certainty and control in interaction but still increase the willingness to communicate. Technology-mediated-communication is often seen as faceless and task-oriented. However, it seems that communication in cyberspace may speed up initial interaction as well as self-disclosure, which, in turn, may facilitate interpersonal connections and building of relationships (Walther, 1994; Walther and Burgoon, 1992). Without doubt, anonymity, pseudonymity and eponymity affect trustworthiness, credibility and security of e-transactions and e-interactions (Jäkälä & Berki, 2004).

There is a multiplicity of people in e-spaces: e-learners, visitors of different chat rooms, participants of electronic interest groups, and members of support groups and e-communities, all with different needs and different aims (see e.g. Werry & Mowbray, 2001; Jäkälä & Mikkola, 2001; Renninger & Shumar, 2002). In cyberspace, group and community formation as well as identity building, testing and maintenance comprise the social, cultural and psychological aspects of behaviour with communication technologies (Jäkälä & Berki, 2004). Social behaviour online aims at facilitating a trustful communication environment providing acceptable and credible interaction (see Li et al, 2007).

In this chapter, the authors identify and discuss rules that govern interaction in cyberspace. Furthermore, the traditional definition of virtual community (see Rheingold, 1993) is scrutinised and extended. The authors aim at describing and distinguishing different types of identity that are presented or represented in the cyberspace, and associate their research findings to the cyber surfer's identity formation in the context of various virtual communities or e-spaces. Configuring the transformation of individual and collective identity to online identity, the chapter, simultaneously, provides a classification on the pitfalls and certain expectations from five different types of cyber-identity, namely *eponymity, nonymity, anonymity, pseudonymity* and *polynymity*. The authors coin these five terms here for the first time in order to describe five different phenomena in cyber communication that are associated with five different types of cyber-identity. These, though being common phenomena in everyday life on the screen (see e.g. Turkle, 1997, Papadimitriou, 2003), have remained undefined and unclassified while their positive or negative consequences influence online communication

but remain largely unnoticed. There is a need to investigate these phenomena especially since online presence compromises the privacy of the interaction. An improved understanding of the relations between online identity building, online identity types and e-activities could contribute to the design of e-spaces, where people's activation and participation increase. For instance, this new information might lead towards the design of e-learning communities that could increase learners' participation in the e-learning process. Similarly this new knowledge could contribute to open new ways for social inclusion by overcoming biases and digital divides.

Internet is a relatively new means for interaction, where identity and identity formation have recently been paid attention especially from the technical point of view, e. g. authentication, privacy and identity theft. Other scientific domains such as communication and social psychology (see e.g. Bosma et al., 1994; Wallace, 1999; Wood & Smith, 2001) have paid more attention to these concepts. The main investigation approach is examining the recent research findings in the combined domains of cyberspace and identity. In the examination, theories and principles from other scientific domains are combined and utilised for the online identities comprehension. In the discussion and comparison the chapter also draws knowledge from personal experiences in e-learning, e-instruction and cyberspace usage through years of action research in the domain of cyber education, cyber communication and cyber culture.

CONCEPTUALIZING VIRTUALITY AND COMMUNITY

Originating from the Internet and expanding rapidly due to advances of Information and Communication Technology (ICT), virtual communities (VCs) nowadays pervade the public and private life. Within this context, the role of ICT as a facilitator for human interaction becomes gradually a resource of special significance and research study (Wallace, 1999; Earnshaw et al., 2001; Renninger & Shumar, 2002). Recent studies (Earnshaw et al., 2001; Kisielniki, 2002; Werry & Mowbray, 2001) concentrate on the commercial exploitation of leisure and the use of Internet as a means for controlling personal and collective identity (Wallace, 1999; Jäkälä & Berki, 2004). An equally important number of current research scholars concentrate on the growth of and the benefits from online support for a number of needs and every day activities (Jäkälä & Mikkola, 2001; Berki & Cobb-Payton, 2005).

Being part of a community or group fulfils one of the basic human needs, that of belonging (see e.g. Maslow 1987). In our era the use of ICT to build different interest-based and self-identified communities evidently stresses that communities do not necessarily need to interact face-to-face. The development of the Internet resulted in the increase of online communities since ICT enabled geographically dispersed groups to communicate with the aid of different technological solutions. According to Rheinghold (1993, 5), *"virtual communities are social aggregations that emerge from the Net when enough people carry on those public discussions long enough, with sufficient human feeling, to form webs of personal relationships in cyberspace."* Starting from short message exchanges and advancing to more demanding forms of e-discussion and e-interaction, humans express their sympathy, empathy, concern and demonstrate their needs to communicate and ability to support other humans. (Preece, 2000.)

Research-wise, the scientific domain of research in virtual communities includes themes that have recently raised the interest of sociologists, psychologists, anthropologists, computer scientists, communication scholars and information technology professionals. Many opinions have been exchanged in an attempt to coin a successful definition. However, there is not yet a

single accepted definition, except agreement to a few certain elements that should exist in VCs. *"Nearly everybody agrees on certain elements. One of these is inclusivity"* (Werry & Mowbray, 2001), meaning that everybody should be able to participate. Thus, it is challenging to re-define the term online community. One of the very important reasons is that similar or different definitions have been coined and co-exist in an attempt to define e-group, e-environment, e-space, digital space, virtual environment, virtual space, online community, cyberspace, cyberplace, cybercommunity, to name just a few. These terms are often used interchangeably but there might be variations in their use, based on the context.

Internet as such is a large online community. However, quite often the term online community refers to a particular web-based subgroup within the Internet. Furthermore these online communities have labels such as special interest groups, support groups and other. Above all the authors suggest that online communities are technology-supported web-based *contexts* that provide *contact* for individuals and groups, upon specific *content*. Online social aggregations, such as families, groups of friends, distance mode learners, players of online games, and members of political discussion forums are gathered to socialize, discuss, exchange their thoughts, or seek support for their emotional needs. The content of these online communities ranges from entertainment and leisure, e-learning and education or edutainment, to political agenda setting, e-governance, e-democracy and e-health matters.

Inevitably, the Internet has been one way to build communities and promote relationships between individuals and within groups. Wood and Smith (2001) state that the essence of virtual community is more than just a group of people communicating online. Community is based on the feeling of belonging. According to Jones (1997) there are qualities that characterize online communities: i) a minimum level of interactivity among the participants; ii) a variety of communicators for conversation and contribution; iii) a common public space that identifies virtual communities from cyberspace with cyberplace; and iv) a minimum level of sustained membership that maintain and develop the community. These characteristics stress the human factor of online communities and communication.

Inhabitants of virtual worlds and communities might create an alternative identity for themselves that they use exclusively online, or several identities to be used during different online forums or simultaneously within one forum. Some or all of these *identities-on-line* may be complemented with embodiment of the user's image, picture, photo or live video. There are various applications of shared work spaces that equip task-oriented groups such as tele-working teams and virtual organizations. Even when using solely text-based technologies, it is possible to perceive interpretations of personal characteristics and relationships between the communicators. The strength of these interpretations probably varies between individuals. This affects both the notion of telepresence as well as immersion.

Virtual communities are not simply a diminishment or enlargement of personal life. When the real life communities are threatened, virtual communities may provide a shelter needed. In many cases, these communities are based on relationships and feelings. They replicate common and communal features of real life, or, if needed, they may create an environment that is beyond the limits of real life. As observed in real life communities, personal relations whose main objective is sociability, informed by loyalty and authenticity, become as much as part of the social situations of modernity as the encompassing institutions of time-space distanciation (Giddens, 1990). But can they offer commitment or merely a pseudo-community, where commitment could only be virtual? (see e.g. Wilbur, 2001).

Access to cyberspace does not necessarily imply inclusion in any virtual community. Similarly, participation in cyberspace does not automatically imply inclusion in virtual communities. There are different levels of authorisation while permissions are granted after identification and authentication take place. Membership in a certain virtual community does not guarantee access to other exclusive virtual communities; there are always boundaries to cross. However, the feelings of belonging and self-awareness are strongly bound to our group memberships (see e. g. Tajfel, 1982). When privacy is needed the only place to find it might be an exclusive virtual community that identifies and to some degree authenticates its users to guarantee their privacy. This is largely facilitated with the interaction tools that are available and with the cyber-surfers' choice of the cyber-identity that want (or not) others to perceive. Social software may or may not facilitate inclusion and privacy.

TRANSFORMING IDENTITY TO CYBER-IDENTITY

Even though the word 'identity' is often used in diverse scientific domains, it is also considered as an unclear word to be used as a scientific term. It also refers to an increasing number of concepts from personality traits to authenticating computer networks (Camp, 2004). However, the concept of identity has a long history – as long as human beings have been using different types of masks (both material and abstract) to cover their faces and identity (see, Wiszniewski & Coyne, 2002). There are different definitions for identity depending on the context of its use. Identity is often defined as the combination of essential qualities, which characterize and differentiate a person from others. The concept of identity describes the continuum between sameness and differentiation. A person can objectively be identified by physical characteristics: name, date of birth, biographical description; as well as objectively assessed by cognitive and psychological characteristics: Intelligent Quotient, attitudes or personal traits.

Subjective identity, then, refers to the person's mental presentation of these objective identifiers and an awareness of being distinct from the others. (Bosma et al, 1994.). Depending on the time and context, a distinctive identity can be seen as a way to be separated from uniformity; albeit in some cases, it may be seen as social stigma or spoiled identity, as described by Goffman (1986).

People use different sides of their personality and different roles in various situations: e.g. communicating with colleagues, family members, friends, acquaintances or strangers. Identity includes individual's considerations of 'who am I?', 'how do I want to be perceived by others?', and 'how am I actually perceived by others?' Others perceive identity of a certain person as a set of identifiers that distinguish this person from other persons. The meaning of identity in its social context is often viewed in social psychology in relation to the person's or group's inclusion and exclusion from the society, and affects the personal or group considerations about self and groupness, respectively. The transition from the concept of identity in its traditional context to the meaning of identity in a post-modern sense is attempted below, considering the semantics of individual and collective identity as viewed in the post-technological era.

Management of self-presentation takes place when people enter e-spaces. By picking up the username, nickname or alias and selecting or creating personal information that they want to share with others, they simultaneously decide how they wish to be perceived by the other members of the community they are entering. This also emphasizes the relationship between community and identity (Jäkälä & Berki, 2004). The reflection of/on one's identity needs the others, and cyberspace communities help their members to identify and being identified both on the level of personal and collective identities. Real life and virtual communities offer guidelines for becoming 'one of us', distinguishing simultaneously their members from others, outsiders of the commu-

nity. From the viewpoint of social technology, technology does not only provide structures and tools for online communities. In addition to that, technology provides tools for social construction of reality and the outcomes depend on how these tools are being used. Same technology can be used to gain access to community membership and e-space with shared ideas and interaction or space to manifest individuality to all passerby or selected audience. Technology can also be used to block interaction and increase protection. Technology can be the gatekeeper between different users or groups of users. One way of using social technology is to self-manage identity - either personal identity or shared identity of a certain group. In the following paragraphs we will describe and discuss different possibilities for e-identity.

The next five sections refer to, classify and analyse five distinct phenomena that are observed in online communication. We name them: eponymity, nonymity, anonymity, pseudonymity and polynymity. Different context, contact and content of online interaction require different self-presentation rules, and the following types of identity offer opportunities and borders to human participation, inclusion and exclusion from virtual communities.

Eponymity

Eponymity is the state of being identified and recognised by name (eponym) and other distinctive individual features. Being eponymous implies having a set of known, distinctive characteristics, such as name, title and affiliation, used for identification, and to some degree for authentication.

One way of participating in cyber-activities is by being eponymous, when the identity of the communicator is then apparent. Interacting eponymously has often been considered as the way to grant authorization in technology-based communications. Eponymity does not challenge the protection of privacy and declares the responsibility and credibility of the activities. The online group and role formation that is based on *real* identities range from the very traditional roles of educators and learners in virtual learning environments (Putz & Arnold, 2001) to modern research and development collaboration teams for promoting innovation. New cyber-activities that include eponymous interaction are minority groups in society, who seek for re-inventing their roots by creating their own cultural and national identity (Bakker, 1999; Nocera, 1998). For some ethnic minorities or socially suppressed groups, eponymity in cyberspace serves as a step to openness and further recognition (Berki & Cobb-Payton, 2005).

Eponymity may be associated with official communication. For example, in teaching, guidance and customer services real face needs to be seen instead of artificial replica. Being able to transfer the notion of familiarity from virtual world to real world -and vice versa- may also increase trustworthiness. But could artificial and virtual identity be more believable, credible and attractive than the real one?

Nonymity

Nonymity, or rather nonappearance, is the state of not being identified by any name nor any other distinctive individual features. Being at the state of nonymity implies not having a set of known, distinctive characteristics, such as name, title and affiliation, used for identification and/or authentication. Actually, nonymity refers to identity that avoids detection consciously or unconsciously. Nonymity is a stealth mode of identity. Nobody knows whether a person exists when is not apparent while participating. Out of sight, out of mind. No technological means could possibly determine the appearance.

Nonymity is silent, non-observable and no public identity. It is even a non-communicative and non-interactive with other participants, state of identity, where participation and sharing is unidirectional, based on the choice and control

of the nonymous person. No-one is aware of the online presence, sometimes not even of the actions of a person with no identity. For instance, these actions might be malicious in case of stealing others' identities to use them later or gathering useful information for malfunctions. A nonymous person could also benefit in an e-learning virtual community or in an instruction and learning forum, by accessing confidential examination and assessment in online forms of exams. On the other hand, nonymity could also offer protection and safety for the real person behind, in situations where real life communities, persons or identities are threatened.

A nonymous person can hardly ever be distinguished or identified. He or she is a silent participant, whose online silence is different from the silence of the users of other types of identity because no-one else knows or is aware of this silent participation.

Anonymity

Anonymity is the state of not being known by any name. Anonymity is defined as freedom from identification and implies lack of distinctiveness. An unnamed person is someone, who is unacknowledged as the doer of something because of a lack of distinctive features. Sometimes anonymity can be seen as a negative identity. For example within discussion forums the anonymous participant may lurk others - follow their actions without own participation. Online communities have often built-in tools that make other participants visible by adding a feature of awareness of the situation in the online environment. Therefore, other e-participants are aware of the online presence of anonymous persons even without their direct participation, while in the case of nonymous persons are not. Anonymous participants are not necessarily silent, like the nonymous persons. Their participation in a forum, however, can or cannot be identified, while they can be visible or not. Anonymity has been implicated, among other, in research on social facilitation and crowd behaviour. Yet its conceptual status and the processes by which anonymity achieves its effects are still far from clear (Lea et al. 2001).

One way of entering cyberplaces is by strategically choosing anonymity that is the state at which the identity of the communicator is not apparent. Interacting anonymously has often been considered as a questionable identity in technology-mediated communication; it challenges the protection of privacy as well as the responsibility and credibility of the activities (Li et al. 2007). On the other hand, anonymity may facilitate citizens' rights, democratization of processes, consensus participation, and in some cases it may encourage interaction and provide support (Jäkälä & Berki, 2004). While it might be easier to discuss delicate issues anonymously, there might also be doubts about the trustworthiness of other communicators and about security and safety of shared interaction and information. It should also be easier to break up anonymous interaction than interaction with a known other.

Pseudonymity

Pseudonymity is the state of being identified by a pseudonym, that is by a name, which is not somebody's real, correct name. Furthermore, being pseudonymous in virtual communities means bearing a set of false distinctive characteristics, such as name and title that are used for identification and to some degree for interaction of the person concerned. Even though pseudonymity is often addressed with suspicion, it is not always used to mislead others as frequently believed. Sometimes eponymity can be too challenging or the option of anonymity is not available. Sometimes pseudonymity evolves to eponymity, since many cyberspacers are recognised or traced by their nicks or aliases which may lay there to be addressed as their eponyms.

Pseudonymity can offer safety needed when entering virtual communities that otherwise might stay unvisited. For some people, the only option to join a virtual group is by pseudonymity, which provides possibilities to veil under false name or nickname. Pseudonymity offers possibilities to decide on the type of personal information that a person wants to provide, whether real or artificial. While eponymity could be as a desirable property for functioning, and a requirement for inclusivity in reality and in a technological sense (see e.g. Berki & Cobb-Payton, 2005), it is the pseudonymity and its misuse that has raised many questions regarding abuse of language and misbehaviour of humans on the net (see Wallace, 1999).

Pseudonymity could, for instance, enhance self-presentation management for online students and online courses instructors in order to facilitate e-participation, overcome digital divide and increase social inclusion.

Polynymity

Polynymity is the property of having and presenting oneself with many different names. Thus, it is also associated to the state of being identified by several pseudonyms. Having multiple names as identifiers in cyberspace's communities, means possessing and using a mix of real or artificial distinctive names and characteristics, which are presented in interaction with different persons or groups. While communicating with the aid of technology, the management of self-presentation has totally new expression tools. People can have multiple simultaneous roles, each of which is actualised within certain communities (see Papadimitriou, 2003). These roles can totally differ from each other. One person can also participate in the same event with several parallel identities (Turkle, 1997). Nowadays this seems to be the most often used identity in cyberspace. However, that might also be the main reason why some people do not consider virtual communities as a space for *real* interaction.

In case of polynymity, online communication is sometimes seen as loaded with mistrust, since the source of communication cannot always be verified. Sometimes, online participants choose polynymity for fun, but in some cases the user does not have the possibility for choice. At some cases the community guides the community members to polynymity. For example, academic scholars participate in electronic learning environments with their students by using an eponym, while they participate in chat rooms or tutor support groups using a pseudonym; and anonymously evaluate eponymously written but anonymously presented paper proposals for a conference.

THE EMPHASIS FROM CYBERSPACE TO CYBERPLACE

The previous subsections provided a taxonomy of the most frequent types of e-identity formation as phenomena observed in cyberspace and partially described in cyber literature in a limited fashion. Furthermore, the authors provided meaningful names considering the semantics and pragmatics of these cyber-identity types. The five distinct types of identity discussed here, namely eponymity, nonymity, anonymity, pseudonymity and polynymity are subsequently compared and contrasted providing a tabular representation of their features regarding their interaction prerequisites in e-spaces. The following table summarises the information presented above regarding online awareness, visibility, identification, approachability and authentication.

Table 1 itself is a broad summary of the information currently gathered, analysed and classified by the authors. While it depicts significant knowledge on cyber-identities, it is by no means an exhaustive source of what are the advantages and disadvantages of every type of identity or what are the pitfalls and limitations of each one in online communication. It rather comprises issues that set a future research agenda for the technologist, communicator scholar and for the cyber culture scepticism followers. The entries of the table underline the need to get more information about the potential importance of cyberspace to political liberties and established human rights and the ways virtuality is likely to change our experience of the society and e-society in a comparative way. Technological means in the form of social software for achieving this transformation should also be viewed critically since there might be potential pitfalls when mixing technology and human relationships for the sake of communication (or non-communication).

During the last ten years the cyberspace has turned into a populated cyberplace. Before it had merely been an abstract space to present and publish context. Nowadays, it is increasingly becoming a common public place where the virtual communities' users themselves are empowered to produce the content for other users. Cyberspace has been established as an everyday medium for communication, where sociability is increased with the enrichment of personal expression (e.g. applications of social media). It is, thus, important to know which forms of identity might or not facilitate approachability, visibility and authentication (see Table 1).

The number of e-groups in which people participate seems to go on increasing, since pursue of effectiveness is achieved by encouraging people to form different groups, teams and communities. Participation in virtual communities shows a range of diverse interests, different roles and different work tasks. Leisure time and hobbies are more often also net-based which increases the use of different e-spaces also after and during working hours.

One significant aspect of online communication is management of identity. In general, identity formation and self-presentation become significant when there is a desire to regulate the functions and functionality of the virtual community. Apart from regulation, self-expression and self-presentation issues are connected to ease of access to the e-space where all are linked to the content that is provided within a particular

Table 1. Identity types and interaction prerequisites

Identity type / interaction prerequisites	Eponymity	Nonymity	Anonymity	Pseudonymity	Polynymity
Awareness	yes	no	yes	Yes	yes
Visibility	yes	no	limited	Yes	yes
Identification	yes	no	limited	Limited	limited
Approachability	yes	no	limited	Limited	limited
Authentication	limited	no	no	No	limited

context. Table 1 presents a non-definite list of cyber-identity types, which, again, should not be viewed as final and isolated forms of self-expression and presentation. In fact, the entries of table 1, especially those attributed to pseudonymity and polynymity, indicate that identity in cyberspace is not and sometimes cannot be a constant attribute of someone's online presence. It rather is a fluid concept, which evolves during time, enriched or simplified according to the communication needs of the cyber surfer. A significant issue of the future research agenda is the observation of identity changes and the study of the conditions and events that trigger these changes.

SUMMARY AND FUTURE RESEARCH

Online communities can be divided into *permanent* infrastructures, which co-exist with the physical community or can perform as *temporary* virtual environments in order to support the timely functions of real life within a virtual space (Jäkälä & Berki, 2004). For instance, permanent cyber-communities could be perceived as free public networks, public access media and advisory boards, educational collaborations, independent or private media and internet cafes. Cyber-communities of temporary online nature could be the web-based support provided for conferences and symposia, technology centres, governmental

and organisational programs. The latter can be online, supporting by social software, especially when in need to support community activism and research initiatives, or merely for completing a work task. Due to the evolution of technology, the emphasis can not be on the technology as such but on the use of it to support social actions and behaviour online.

The development of the virtual life increased the demands for trust in interpersonal communication. Building, testing and maintaining identity might lead to pretensions and precautions. When referring to nonymity or pseudonymity nontrustable interaction comes to mind, while anonymity and eponymity are associated to domination but also liberation. Liberation and simultaneously deception are terms that are inevitably linked to polynymity, as well as self-expression and creativity. Likewise, the demands for anonymity, eponymity and pseudonymity in different virtual groups have to be approached from the point of view, that best-fitted technological solutions are best-fitted for humans, too. Technology should cater for ethical competition, privacy and transparency in marketing, security in e-sales, individual and intellectual freedom of expression.

The expansion of virtual communities indicated many emerging themes that have not yet been attributed as research objects to a well-formed discipline with a sound scientific and theoretical background. They are, though, promising research areas because onlineness is explored as the possibility for wider participation. Virtuality opens boundaries for new forms of communication and sociability. The concept of identity as a trust-based interaction in online worlds can be realized by considering the power and suitability of technology to create identity assets such as security, integrity and safety for the adequate provision of trust. At the same time, there is a need to combine the principles and capabilities of other disciplines in order to establish cohesive understanding of real people in virtual communities. Real people both in reality and virtuality have different roles and identities. Cyberspace does not demand more out of those, only makes them more visible.

REFERENCES

Bakker, P. (1999, October). Reinventing Roots: New media and national identity. *Second Expert Meeting on Media and Open Societies.* (pp. 21-23). Amsterdam, The Netherlands.

Berki, E., Isomäki, H., & Salminen, A. (2007). Quality and Trust Relationships in Software Development. The Proceedings of E. Berki, J. Nummenmaa, I. Sunley, M., Ross, & G. Staples (Eds.), *Software Quality in the Knowledge Society Software Quality Management XV*, (pp. 47-65). BCS: GB, Swindon.

Berki, E., & Cobb-Payton, F. (2005). Work-Life Balance and Identity in a Virtual World: Facts, Tensions and Intentions for Women in IT. In H. Isomäki, & A. Pohjola, (Eds.), *Lost and Found in Virtual Reality: Women and Information Technology.* University of Lapland Press: Rovaniemi.

Berki, E., Isomäki, H., & Jäkälä, M. (2003, June). Holistic Communication Modelling: Enhancing Human-Centred Design through Empowerment. D. Harris, V. Duffy, M. Smith, & C. Stephanidis (Eds.), *Cognitive, Social and Ergonomic Aspects, Vol 3 of HCI International*, (pp. 22-27). University

of Crete at Heraklion, (pp. 1208-1212). Lawrence Erlbaum Associates Inc.

Bosma, H. A., Graafsma, T. L., Grotevant, H. D., & de Levita, D. J. (1994*). Identity and Development: An Interdisciplinary Approach.* Sage Focus Editions, Vol. 172. Thousand Oaks: SAGE.

Camp, L. J. (2004). Digital Identity. *IEEE Technology and Society Magazine.* (pp. 34-41).

Earnshaw, R., Guedj, R., van Dam, A., & Vince, J. (2001). *Frontiers of Human-Centred Computing, Online Communities and Virtual Environments.* Springer, London.

Georgiadou, E., Hatzipanagos, S., & Berki, E. (2005). Resource-Based Learning and Teaching: Concerns, Conflicts, Consensus, Community. G. A. Dafoulas, W. Bakry-Mohamed, & A. Murphy (Eds.), *e-Learning Communities International Workshop Proceedings.* Jan 3, Cairo. (pp. 89-95). Middlesex University Press: London.

Giddens, A. (1990). *The Consequences of Modernity.* Cambridge, UK: Polity Press.

Goffman, E. (1986) (Repr.) *Stigma: Notes on the Management of Spoiled Identity.* Harmondsworth: Penguin Books.

Jones, Q. (1997). Virtual –communities, virtual settlements & cyber-archaeology: A theoretical outline. *Journal of Computer-Mediated Communication*, 3(3). http://www.ascusc.org/jcmc/vol3/issue3/jones.html

Jäkälä, M., & Mikkola, L. (2001). Technology Makes You Feel Better? Attempts to Mediate Social Support through Technology in Health Care. In M. J. Smith, & G. Salvendy (Eds.), *Systems, Social and Internationalization Design Aspects of Human-Computer Interaction* (pp. 137-141). Lawrence Erlbaum Associates, Mahwah, NJ.

Jäkälä, M., & Berki, E. (2004). Exploring the Principles of Individual and Group Identity in Virtual Communities. In the Proceedings of P.

Commers, P. Isaias, & M. Baptista Nunes (Eds.), *1ˢᵗ IADIS Conference on Web-based Communities* (pp 19-26). Lisbon, Portugal, 24-26 Mar.

Kimppa, K. (2007). *Problems with the Justification of Intellectual Property Rights in Relation to Software and Other Digitally Distributed Media.* Ph.D. Thesis. Turku Centre for Computer Science. University of Turku.

Kisielnicki, J. (2002). *Modern Organisations in Virtual Communities.* IRM Press, Warsaw.

Kollock, P. (1999). The Production of Trust in Online Markets. In E.J. Lawler et al. (Eds.), *Advances in Group Processes* Vol. 16. JAI Press, Greenwich, CT.

Lea, M., Spears, R., & de Groot, D. (2001). Knowing Me, Knowing You: Anonymity Effects on Social Identity Processes Within Groups. *Personality and Social Psychology Bulletin, 27*(5), 526-537.

Li, L., Helenius, M., & Berki, E. (2007). Phishing-Resistant Information Systems-Security Handling with Misuse-Cases. The Proceedings of E. Berki, J. Nummenmaa, I. Sunley, M. Ross, & G. Staples (Eds.), *Software Quality in the Knowledge Society* Software Quality Management XV, (pp. 389-404). BCS: GB, Swindon.

Maslow, A. H. (1987). *Motivation and personality.* New York: HarperCollins.

McMillan, D. W., & Chavis, D. M. (1986). Sense of community: A definition and theory. *Journal of Community Psychology, 14*(1), 6-23.

Nocera, Abdelnour J. L. (1998). Virtual Environments as Spaces of Sympolic Construction and Cultural Identity: Latin-American Virtual Communities. In C. Ess & F. Sudweeks (Eds.), *Proceedings of Cultural Attitudes Towards Communication and Technology '98*, Sydney, Australia, (pp. 193-195).

Papadimitriou, C. (2003). *Turing (A novel about computation).* MIT Press, Cambridge, MA.

Preece, J. (2000). *Online Communities: Designing usability, supporting sociability.* John Wiley and Sons, Chichester.

Putz, P., & Arnold, P. (2001). Communities of Practice: guidelines for the design of online seminars in higher education. *Education, Communication & Information*, 1(2), 181-195.

Renninger, K. A., & Shumar, W. (2002). *Building Virtual Communities Learning and Change in Cyberspace. Learning in Doing: Social, Cognitive & Computational Perspectives.* Cambridge University Press, Cambridge.

Rheingold, H. (1993). *The Virtual Community.* HarperCollins, New York.

Tajfel, H. (1982). *Social identity and intergroup relations.* Cambridge University Press, Cambridge.

Turkle, S. (1997). *Life on the screen: identity in the age of the Internet.* Weidenfeld & Nicolson, London.

Wallace, P. (1999). *The Psychology of the Internet.* Cambridge University Press, Cambridge.

Werry, C., & Mowbray, M. (2001). *Online Communities: Commerce, Community Action, and the Virtual University.* Prentice Hall, Upper Saddle River, NJ.

Wilbur, S. P. (2001). An archaeology of cyberspaces: virtuality, community, identity. In D. Bell & B. M. Kennedy (Eds.), *Cybercultures Reader* (pp 45-53). Routledge, London.

Wilhelm, A. G. (2000). *Democracy in the digital age.* Routledge: New York.

Wiszniewski, D., & Coyne, R. (2002). Mask and Identity: The Hermeneutics of Self-Construction in the Information Age. In K. A. Renninger & W. Shumar (Eds.), *Building Virtual Communities*

Learning and Change in Cyberspace. Learning in Doing: Social, Cognitive & Computational Perspectives (pp. 191-213). Cambridge University Press, Cambridge.

Walther, J. B. (1994). Anticipated ongoing interaction versus channel effects on relational communication in computer-mediated interaction. *Human Communication Research, 20*(4), 473-501.

Walther J. B., & Burgoon, J. K. (1992). Relational communication in computer-mediated interaction. *Human Communication Research, 19*(1), 50-88.

Wood, A. F., & Smith, M. J. (2001). *Online Communication. Linking Technology, Identity & Culture.* Lawrence Erlbaum Associates, Maewah.

KEY TERMS

Anonymity: Anonymity is the state of not being known by any name. Anonymity is defined as freedom from identification and implies lack of distinctiveness. An unnamed person is someone, who is unacknowledged as the doer of something because of a lack of distinctive features.

Eponymity: Eponymity is the state of being identified and recognised by name (eponym) and other distinctive individual features. Being eponymous implies having a set of known, dis-

tinctive characteristics, such as name, title and affiliation, used for identification, and to some degree for authentication.

Nonymity: Nonymity, or rather non-appearance, is the state of not being identified by any name nor any other distinctive individual features. Being at the state of nonymity implies not having a set of known, distinctive characteristics, such as name, title and affiliation, used for identification and/or authentication. Actually, nonymity refers to identity that avoids detection consciously or unconsciously.

Polynymity: Polynymity is the property of having and presenting oneself with many different names. Thus, it is also associated to the state of being identified by several pseudonyms. Having multiple names as identifiers in cyberspace's communities, means possessing and using a mix of real or artificial distinctive names and characteristics, which are presented in interaction with different persons or groups.

Pseudonymity: Pseudonymity is the state of being identified by a pseudonym, that is by a name, which is not somebody's real, correct name. Furthermore, being pseudonymous in virtual communities means bearing a set of false distinctive characteristics, such as name and title that are used for identification and to some degree for interaction of the person concerned.

Chapter IV
Weblogs in Higher Education

Werner Beuschel
Brandenburg University of Applied Sciences, Germany

ABSTRACT

Weblogs are a popular form of Social Software, supporting personal Web authoring as well as innovative forms of social interaction via internet. The potential of Weblogs to emphasize active student participation and collaboration raises great expectations for a new pedagogical quality in higher education. In this chapter, the author explores the value of Social Software, specifically Weblogs, for learning and teaching in institutional education. An exploratory study serves as background for the discussion. Critical issues and areas of research for using Social Software in education are concluding the chapter.

INTRODUCTION

The popular term Social Software combines internet applications like social networking sites, Weblogs, Wikis, Podcasts, and others. Applications under that label have become almost ubiquitous among the younger generation – at least in industrialized countries - but they are also appealing to all other generations (PC Magazine 2006; Time 2007). With the advent of ideas like the "100-Dollar-Laptop", accompanied by the One-Laptop-Per-Child initiative (OLPC 2007), an even bigger and really worldwide audience for Social Software can be expected over the next years, when the technical infrastructure is in place. It seems obvious that a technology that is so widely used cannot and should not be excluded from higher education. Nevertheless, it is necessary to be aware of the frequent hype in technology cycles, so that expectations and limitations of the technology become clearer. On this ground, administrators and educators should to be able to ponder options and strategies for educational use.

Social Software applications in all their variety do have many characteristics in common, but their appearance, user interface and technical functionalities differ to a great degree. The purpose of this chapter is to explore the expectations, options and limitations of a specific form of Social

Software, namely Weblogs. So it seems necessary to discuss their pros and cons in education from both levels, the general view on new qualities of Social Software and the specific view on potentials and limitations of Weblogs.

SOCIAL SOFTWARE, WEB 2.0, AND WEBLOGS

Social Software provides an easy-to-use technical background for computer-mediated communications between individuals or individuals and groups: "Social Software blends tools and modes for richer online social environments and experiences" (Corante 2004). The quote refers to the enabling character of information technology for building new relationships: Social networks and Social Software are seen to be complementing each other. In contrast to the earlier understanding of computer use, where goal-orientation and purposeful uses were in the foreground, now the voluntary, self-organized distribution of information over the internet and the added value for supporting real as well as virtual communities catch the attention of research and business alike. So the appealing effect of the Internet is no longer driven by the technicality of being logged-in, but rather through the personal participation in the co-weaving of the information texture of the World Wide Web. Unlike earlier activities, this is not only done by writing and reading, but also by representing the interests of oneself through pictures, videos or audio streams.

The basic idea behind the term Social Software can be traced back over six decades to Vannevar Bush and others. Vannevar Bush's "memex" was an early blueprint of hypertext, although never manufactured. The device was basically intended to store and associate related knowledge and experiences for personal use (cf. Bush 1945). So the idea to enhance the reach of our personal memory and knowledge by using an external device and providing it with all our individual understanding and experiences as well as that of other people is not so new. Interestingly enough and contained already in the original writing Bush envisioned that other people's knowledge would be equally important and that the exchange of newly associated knowledge would be the crucial asset (for an extensive discussion of the unfolding of Bush's idea cf. Allen 2004). The ease-of-use of the current applications and their widespread adoption, though, creates a new quality with respect to users and innovative interactions.

The term Web 2.0 was coined by Tim O'Reilly, a well-known speaker and writer on issues of the internet (O'Reilly 2005). Rather than trying to define Web 2.0 more precisely some authors distinguish its applications from the presumed world of Web 1.0. While Web 1.0 is supposed to simply present information, Web 2.0 is implying user participation. In popular publications, Web 2.0 is frequently understood as a synonym for Social Software, although it carries a stronger connotation to technical and business aspects. In this chapter, the term Social Software is preferred over Web 2.0, intended to embrace the facets of both terms.

Instant Web-publishing, now embodied through Weblogs, was envisioned since the early days of the internet, e.g. as a "Two-Way-Web" by Berners-Lee (2000). The Web was already perceived of "as a medium for publication, social networking, and collaboration" (Fiedler 2004). With the advent of Weblogs as specific Web-based applications – a term composed of "Web" and "log" file – the vision of an easy way of personal, global publication has come true (Blood 2006, Wikipedia 2007). The easy access via Web-based media obviously hit a real desire. Huge public attention towards media events in 2004 like the tsunami or the US federal election process helped perceiving Weblogs as a way to instantly collect and disseminate the latest news, be it text, picture or video. In journalism, another strong area of applications, Weblogs are credited not only for their capability to quickly spread information but also for swift and critical feedback when an item of doubtful value shows up. Various newspapers and journals make use of Weblogs as kind of a newsgroup for their readers.

Personal Weblog use in the form of openly readable diaries was very attractive to individual users from the beginning and helped to disseminate the idea (Nardi et al. 2005). Several years after the invention, Weblogs are now also making their way into business (cf. Baker et al. 2005).

From an IT-systems view Weblogs are content management systems with a relatively simple user interface. They do not require technical skills like graphics design or HTML programming. Seen as Personal Publishing Systems they put a content item – be it text, photo or video – from a data base on the Web, using a template for layout. The most recent entry is put on top so that a reverse chronological order follows. The entries by an author or a group of authors can be commented and usually the comments make the majority of entries.

Though termed as "Web-diaries", the entries are frequently just a link to something deemed interesting, not a lengthy personal item. Recent developments in Weblog software especially concern the capability of linking Weblogs. Mutual links from one Weblog to other Weblogs - a feature called "Blogrolls" - weave networks of similar topical interest. The standard "RSS" ("Rich Site" or "Real Simple Syndication") allows to subscribe to other Weblogs in order to be kept up-to-date on new entries.

According to the renowned journal Communications of the ACM which devoted an issue to Weblogs in 2004 more than 4.2 million of these applications existed worldwide at the time (CACM 2004). Sometimes the expression "one new blog every second" is quoted in popular magazines, which describes the sharply rising tendency. Currently the number of Weblogs worldwide is estimated to be at 57 million. Nevertheless, all numbers have to be interpreted with caution, as certainly not all Weblogs that are created survive.

To express the cumulative social relevance of Weblogs the journal used the term "Blogosphere" (CACM 2004). The statement in one of the articles: "Blogging's greatest benefit is social, not technological" (Cayzer 2004: 48) points to the relevant dimension which was quoted earlier in this paper: neither technical functionality nor design features of Weblogs seem to be overly innovative or important, but the rapid appropriation by individuals who seek easy means to personally express themselves with relation to a worldwide body of social activities (Nardi et al. 2005).

The quick emergence of a huge number of Weblogs called also for ways to search and systematize this volume. The need created new categories of systems: "Metalogs" are search engines which are constantly indexing Weblogs and thus allow quick topical searches. Surrounding the Blogosphere for professional or non-profit research purposes are also a number of communities who use their own Weblogs (for examples of these systems see Weblog search 2006).

SOCIAL SOFTWARE IN TEACHING AND LEARNING

Social Software leads to high expectations with respect to new forms of computer-supported teaching and learning, sometimes tagged in a popular though imprecise manner as "E-Learning 2.0" or even "Education 3.0" (Alexander 2006).

Though the obvious role of Social Software for the younger generation and their affinity is a good reason to integrating these technologies within educational frameworks it is still necessary to clarify their role with respect to educational environments. Information technology use in education has a long history, which has not always been successful. So the question is justified, why Social Software in general, and especially Weblogs, should play a role in higher education. The following questions need clarification:

- What are new qualities of Social Software for pedagogical scenarios?
- How can these qualities be integrated?
- What are specific requirements with regard to using Weblogs in education?

These questions are taken up in the following subchapters.

New Qualities of Social Software

A vivid observer of the Blogging scenery, Danah Boyd, describes new qualities of Social Software, although as she notes, the technology in itself is not that new. What it distinguishes from earlier forms is mainly the attitude of developers and users. Social Software has to be understood as "a movement, not simply a category of technologies" (Boyd 2007, 17). It is "all about letting people interact with people and data in a fluid way" (ibid.). These qualities are also acknowledged from the side of Web 2.0-protagonists: the much quoted "user provided content" is described as the main characteristic by many publications and conferences (cf. O'Reilly 2005; Tepper 2003). From this starting point, Boyd identifies three important aspects of Social Software, which provide ground for an assessment of chances and limitations for educational use.

The first aspect has to do with the way new applications are designed and put to use on the web. This happens without the long development phases usually employed by traditional system developers. In the case of Web 2.0, the "eternal beta" is a characteristic of system development. It denotes the ongoing addition - or in other cases - the deletion of features and functions. The early start on the market, without being completely defined in all functions, is another outstanding feature. Attributed to this kind of system development is the supposedly lesser need for administrative structures. While traditional system development brings about the ever-growing need of support, this innovative model of system evolution seems

to get along with only minimal bureaucracy (Boyd 2007, O'Reilly 2005).

Secondly, the way participation or membership in Web 2.0 system usage develops over time is much different from traditional systems. "Values are built into the social software and spread through the networks of people who join" (Boyd 2007, 22). As an indication for network membership building there are numerous stories about music groups and their friends gathering on a social networking site, thus attracting new group members with similar taste and interest (cf. TIME 2007).

The third characteristic concerns the question how Social Software creates shifts in user behavior. Since applications are about "connecting people and watching shared interests emerge" (Boyd 2007, 27), the context of interest is important. As Boyd notes, communities with defined interests usually cannot support multiple contexts in the same place. This of course makes growth of systems difficult, thus constraining market value.

These three characteristics – system functions, user participation, and user behavior – interact and unfold in all Social Software applications. It is important to see that members of social networking systems interpret their own role not so much as users of specified system functions, but as members of more or less defined interest groups. While this attitude drives system evolution and community building on one hand, it can also work as restricting factor if the conditions are not perceived as being right. Thus, it is hard to predict which systems are evolving in which direction over time.

The approach by Boyd places much emphasis on the social aspect of the new systems at question, but not many studies of Weblog use have been taken up this perspective. Usually the literature is very optimistic about how far new technologies may change educational environments (e.g. Alexander 2007). Wagner describes an intriguing idea of specialized Weblog use, namely for personal student portfolios (Wagner 2003). Numerous items about Weblog use in education, contributed by various instructors, are collected on the website by Larry Press (Press 2005). Unfortunately, not many in-depth studies exist.

The following case study serves as an explorative background for the discussion of opportunities and limitations of Weblogs in education. Although it was carried out some years ago, it fits into the line of thought, that the "social" is the important feature of Weblog use. So its framework and analysis should still be apt to provide insights.

Integrating Weblogs in the Classroom: An Exploratory Case Study

The project course which was used here to carry the study, "Web-based Information Systems", is usually being offered as an elective course in the 3rd or 4th year of a 4-year-curriculum in Business Informatics. This is regularly offered at a small European university of applied sciences. The course lends itself naturally towards a three-pronged approach of knowledge acquisition by students: a specific system or class of information systems – here Weblogs - is used as subject for technical knowledge, its communicative function is used for reflecting the system itself, and its functionality is used for organizing and coordinating the course itself. In less computer-related curricula the technical aspect would be dismissed, but the latter two approaches could be employed.

Thus, the learning objectives of the course were learning about Weblogs, using Weblogs for communication and organization within the course, and studying Weblog applications. The application aspect for all students was to find out about potential uses and conditions of Weblogs in business and industry. At the time there were few reports on business use of Weblogs, so the course touched right on an up-to-date issue. Still, the importance of Weblog use in businesses seems to hold, so the subject area does not seem dated.

Preceding the course was an empirical study of two students of another curriculum. This study was aimed at the usage of Weblogs for knowledge management in small and medium enterprises. Its results served as an entry point for the start-up discussion about using Weblogs in businesses.

Formal requirements for the students were:

- to implement one Weblog per group
- to contribute as much items as possible to all Weblogs in the course
- to prepare and present a written report on self-selected issues of business or organizational use of Weblogs.

Analysis and findings of the study are based on observation notes during the class and from the interactions with the systems, on document analysis of Weblog entries and seven final home works of the student groups, summing up to some 300 pages.

The study was done in the summer term of 2004. A term amounts to 15 weeks with sessions of six teaching hours duration each week. About 20 students were enrolled, who usually cooperated in groups of two to four, two staying on their own. Eight groups were starting after the group member selection process ended, seven finished the course. All in all eight Weblogs were implemented, adding the instructor's Weblog as the ninth. This Weblog was created ahead and independently of the course and served as an open forum. Another Web-based system, BSCW, developed by the Fraunhofer Institute in Germany and a familiar infrastructure tool to all students in the curriculum, was used for house-keeping of the emerging Weblog-URLs (see BSCW 2008 for the system). A compact overview of the course schedule is shown in the following Table 1.

The second phase after initial task explanations and literature research on the substance topic was to find out about freeware, select it and implement one Weblog per group. With the third phase Weblog usage was encouraged, in all pos-

Table 1. Course overview "Web-based Information Systems/Weblog Project"

Course phase	Approximate duration in weeks	Didactic aspects of Weblog use
Initial phase: Course overview Collaboration infrastructure Student group composition process Selection and definition of one special topic per group (business application aspect)	- three weeks	Weblogs introduced as technical subject, media for course collaboration, and investigative subject of potential business applications.
Task definition phase: Elaboration of special topic Search and select process on Freeware Implementation of one Blog/group	- three weeks	Mainly instructor-group interaction to define project task.
Interaction phase: Blogging activities Special topic elaboration Intermediate presentations of the Weblog-overview and discussion of entries	- eight weeks - throughout the course - throughout the course	Cross-Blogging activities encouraged. Face-to-face meetings reduced. Reflection on cooperation aspects encouraged.
Final phase: Presentation of group results Written homework on the group project	- one week	

sible forms: reading of and commenting on the own group's Weblog, the other's Weblogs, and the instructor's Weblog.

The final assignment consisted of a presentation of the project results and a written report per group. The text elements were the methodological subject of investigation, together with participating observations of Blogging and discussion during the course. Analysis of the study was done by the author after all the written home works were delivered, so that the findings were not available to the students – they were not intended to be – at course time.

Blogging by students was encouraged throughout the course, as soon as Weblogs were made available by the project groups. There was no direction given or limitations set concerning the content. The face-to-face meetings were suspended for about four weeks in order to provide incentives to use the Weblogs.

Analysis and Discussion of Findings

The analysis here emphasizes media-related aspects of Weblog use in education and leaves out technical items, like the freeware systems actually used. All systems deployed were similar in their interface and structure, though.

Analysis of the texts shows that a good share of course time was covered by Weblog selection and implementation. So for about half of the time, circa eight weeks, Blogging was actually possible. The Weblog uses were nevertheless encouraged by the instructor and constantly evolving throughout the second half of the course.

The Canadian researcher Leslie provides a matrix of Weblog usages where the basic opportunities of activity of students and teachers are categorized in four quadrants of Weblog use (Leslie 2003). In the current case, the matrix was applied after the execution of the course. It was perceived as being helpful for analyzing blogging activities in view of the complex structure, as anyone was supposed to write on anyone's Weblog. For future course planning we think the matrix could be used for outlining desired course activities in advance.

If we apply the matrix to sort out the activities during the case study course, it shows that all quadrants were actually employed:

- Writing Weblogs by students: Students posted to their own Weblog as well as to others and to the instructor's Weblog. Though sparely, Weblogs were used as group discussion tools.
- Writing Weblogs by instructor: The instructor gave hints and information in his own Weblog.
- Reading Weblogs by students: Students read Weblogs of others as well as some discussions in external Weblogs.
- Reading Weblogs/Instructor: The instructor read student's Weblogs regularly.

An essential insight from the findings is that the majority of students groups needed some initial time and opportunity to experiment in order to get into active blogging. Although this may seem natural to expect from any new technology, it nevertheless appears to be salient with regard to Weblogs. Weblogs and that is still the current expectation are supposed to support and require every individual to express him- or herself, not just to read entries. This hesitant attitude becomes even more of an obstacle, if students do not enter a course possessing similar experiences in Web-publishing. Thus, several motivational sessions were needed in the beginning to get the process of active blogging started.

With growing familiarity students developed more interest and participated more often in blogging. Some scepticism at the beginning, questioning the relevance of the systems in question for business use, was diluted due to the growing media attention Weblogs got at that time. Nevertheless, for the instructor a constant uphill struggle ensued to motivate students and make them prefer Weblogs for communication over their usual means of Email and informal talk. This was due in part to weekly class meetings, although the meetings were suspended on purpose for some time. So there was no face-to-face forum to discuss the progress of the projects for a while. The traffic took up recognizably during

this time. From the analysis it cannot be claimed, though, that all the issues which would have been discussed in class otherwise went into the Weblogs now. This possible but improbable shift was not investigated. From other courses it is known that students usually do not hesitate to integrate new means like SMS or Instant Messaging into their personal communication architecture, but it seems the open nature of Weblogs made them hesitate to use the tools most of the time.

An important insight following from this discussion is that cooperative media cannot just be "prescribed" in an institutional setting. The share of informal activities, non-planned and spontaneous, is higher than with other media. The target groups need the time to appropriate the systems. As a consequence the early process in the course should devote more time to explain blogging and the specifics of Weblogs. Informal media need much extensive work on motivation and moderation (c.f. Eigner 2004).

The analysis of Weblog entries reveals that explorative and reflective items were not employed to such a high degree compared to the social content. Social content comprises all kind of person-related items like appointments or remarks. Exploring technical prerequisites for the task at hand was in the foreground of group work in the beginning of the course. Later on this effort waned, probably due the limited time of the course and the lack of perspective of continued use of the Weblogs. The same limit in perspective also provides an explanation for the lack of reflective comments in the final phase.

A deeper explanation, which would need verification, goes back to the very media structure of Weblogs. It has been mentioned earlier that their hypertext character mixes regular text and links, which can be just as well be understood as text. Media critics denote Weblogs as "fringeless", being without a clear limitation (e.g. Wrede 2003). This and their "work-in-progress character" make it difficult for casual users to add something. It also hampers the ability to quickly get to the main arguments and logical structure in a lengthy text. The same holds for the requirement to transfer results from Weblogs to other media, especially if a scientific level for the homework has to be satisfied. Weblogs are not in the same format as the usual paper, which is much more formal. As a way out the additional use of a Wiki as a form to store various documents could be considered if the production of regular texts is a requirement in a course. But it shows that the strength of Social Software, the openness towards participation and format-less writing, could turn out to be problematic if several adaptations to other forms are required. Another counter-intuitive aspect of the collective character of Weblog production is the need in most of higher education courses to ascribe a personal achievement and grade to the individual student. Again, a dilemma of counter-acting requirements shows up.

In contrast to the more intricate functions, the social function of blogging was more frequently used: how to go about building the link structures of the implemented Weblogs and informing each other about the other groups' effort. Also hints on the organization of the course were provided so that the media obviously had a positive effect on the self-organization of groups.

Judging from the final results all substantial learning objectives of the course were reached:

- knowledge acquisition about Weblog system ware, system selection and implementation;
- knowledge acquisition about potential and limits of Weblogs in business;
- capability building to describe organizational requirements for using Weblogs individually and in groups, social competence building to analyse experiences with Weblog use in the form of comments across student groups.

Summarizing the discussion, it can be stated that all formal prerequisites for a course should be considered carefully beforehand and on the background of expectations towards students gains of social, exploratory or reflective capabilities. It seems that the use of Weblogs lends itself better to a course framework which is not dependent on rigid milestones or results. Thus, a seminar discussing a subject matter in depth might provide a better environment for Weblog use than a design course for mechanical engineers.

Fields of Tension for Social Software in Education

As with any new technology, the use of Weblogs in teaching and learning scenarios creates its own requirements, and in some aspects even predicaments. In this chapter, we are considering institutionalized education at the level of colleges or universities. In order to judge the merits of Weblog use this framework needs to be acknowledged. Different educational frameworks, e.g. purely informal learning environments, would have to be scrutinized for different outcomes.

While popular expectations toward new qualities of Social Software may be high, the use of Weblogs - and to a certain degree all of Social Software - in education creates two fields of tension. One is between formal and informal requirements: institutional teaching and learning usually requires individual ascription of achievements. But the individual share of collaborative efforts is usually hard to sort out after the collaboration ended. So the question remains open how Blogging achievements can be assessed for the individual grading of students. The other field of tension is the controlled and well-defined world of education compared to the open and peer-to-peer oriented culture of Social Software.

Based on the discussion of literature and the case study results, the following list tries to summarize the experiences and limitations for Weblog use in Higher Education, intended to guide instructors and teachers in planning and setting up a course:

- Weblogs as all Social Software systems are not just technical tools to be used. They need time, motivation and careful preparation if they are to be integrated in the framework of a course.

- Blogging needs extra time and opportunity, thus being a disruptive activity, not part of the usual didactic flow in a classroom (see also Fiedler 2004).

- Requirements in formal education may run the opposite way of activities in Social Software use. The need of grading and ascribing results to single students is in contrast to the motivation of cooperation in groups.

- The hypertext character of Weblogs makes it difficult to denote the body of knowledge, as there are no inherent limits of the text.

- The work-in-progress character of Weblog use makes it difficult to evaluate and archive results.

- Active participation in a class usually differs widely between students, from just reading to frequent posting. Constant attention and motivation seems to be necessary to ease the differences.

- The expectations towards supporting reflexive skills through Weblogs should not be set too high and must be subtly supported.

- Contributions to discussions usually thrive in non-controlled environments; institutions on the other hand usually provide a controlled environment, not necessarily soliciting strong individual expression from students. So it is advisable to talk to students about how and to what degree system entries are supervised.

CONCLUSION AND RESEARCH PERSPECTIVES

The chapter explored the use of Weblogs as an instance of Social Software in learning and teaching. Experiences with Weblogs in education have been discussed according to their special requirements, advantages and disadvantages. One important result is that cooperative media like Weblogs cannot just be "prescribed" in an institutional setting. The share of informal activities, non-planned and spontaneous, is higher than with other media. The target groups of students need time and motivation to appropriate the media from their own needs. The brief discussion of cultural issues in Social Software use in the earlier chapter showed that so far it is unclear to what degree the enthusiasm of private Social Software use can be put to institutional use (cf. Boyd 2007). As a consequence the early process in a course should devote enough time and effort to explain the specifics of Weblogs and the activity of Blogging with relationship to the objectives of a class. This depends of course on the prior familiarity of students in a class with Social Software. Informal media need extensive work on motivation and moderation. The sheer demand to students, "Blog it!" is not enough to initiate and much less to sustain the activity.

The findings of Weblog usage in education are generally encouraging, but they also raise some cautionary issues. In light of students' participation the findings showed the dependency of Weblog uses on articulation and communication skills acquired previously in a curriculum: While the importance and prevalence of the social function of Weblogs was visible, the dimensions of use like exploration and reflection are sometimes underemployed. This is pointing to the necessity to offer Weblogs in an informal and forceless way, while offering contextual support and encouragement for group discussion at the same time.

A great number of investigations into the "Blogosphere" seem to be open for future course experiments, emphasizing the combination of issues of technology, management, and media. As an example for the field of management it should be interesting to see how Web-publishing aspects in relation to the issues of globalization and global knowledge management could be applied within university education. Intercultural aspects of

Weblog use could be another rewarding topic. From a pedagogical view it should be interesting to compare the use of Weblogs in different forms of curricula, either in a predominant face-to-face learning environment or in a more distributed environment, respectively. For an articulate audience of students, a prescription to write "learning diaries" and to evaluate them in a cooperative, social way, could be a rewarding learning experience (for a description see Wagner 2003). In any case, to foster further use and integration of Weblogs into the curriculum is, based on the case study indications so far, a great field for discoveries and therefore strongly advocated.

Harking back to the general view of Social Software it seems that the realm of internet users as a whole could function as sort of a "mass" open source community, where new applications spring up through innovative users who combine publicly available sources to new ones (cf. Markov 2005). Similar effects might be possible through the combination of Weblogs and other applications, especially Wikis. These new forms on the other hand lend themselves for socio-technical investigations where the effects of combinations would build the focus of research.

An important and open question is to what degree non-controlled environments are helpful and contributing to learning and competence building in social networks. Recent events like the shut-down of Weblogs with political topics as well as the fact that newspapers had to close their previously open public access to Wikis or Weblogs for the reason of "vandalism", point to the underestimated aspect of control and socio-technical control mechanisms. We may see that the Blogging phenomenon is not free from all the other dilemmas and disputes surrounding the evolving Web, what is another reason why it makes such an interesting subject of research. While it is obvious that the attitude toward privacy will undergo huge changes in light of the myriads of personal items being put on the Web now, it is unclear however, how the availability of these items will change

the public and private behaviour with regard to personal privacy and identity management in the future. As a consequence it seems necessary to employ much more empirical research towards Social Software.

ACKNOWLEDGMENT

Susanne Draheim, Brandenburg University of Applied Sciences, contributed greatly to various aspects developed in this paper.

REFERENCES

Alexander, B. (2006, March/April). Web 2.0: A New Wave of Innovation for Teaching and Learning? *EDUCAUSE Review,* 41(2), 32–44. www.educause.edu/apps/er/erm06/erm0621. asp?bhcp=1, (11/10/2007).

Allen, C. (2004). *Tracing the Evolution of Social Software.* www.lifewithalacrity.com/2004/10/ tracing_the_evo.html, (04/26/2008).

Baker, S., & Green, H. (2005). Blogs will change your business. *Business Week*, May 2, (pp. 43-51).

Berners-Lee, T. (2000). *Weaving the Web.* San Francisco, Harper.

Beuschel, W. (2003). From Face-to-Face to Virtual Space – The importance of informal aspects of communication in virtual learning environments. In U. Hoppe, B. Wasson, & S. Ludvigsen (Eds.), *Computer Support for Collaborative Learning (CSCL 2003) – Designing for Change in Networked Learning Environments* (pp. 229-238). Bergen/Norway.

Blood, R. (2005). www.rebeccablood.net/essay/ weblog_history.html, (01/30/2006).

Boyd, D. (2007). The Significance of Social Software. In Th. Burg & J. Schmidt (Eds.), *Blog*

Talks Reloaded. Social Software – Research and Cases. Norderstedt: Books on demand.

BSCW (2008). public.bscw.de/de/about.html, (04/26/2008).

Bush, V. (1945). As we may think. *The Atlantic Monthly.* www.theatlantic.com/doc/194507/bush/, (01/27/2006).

Cayzer, S. (2004). Semantic Blogging and Decentralized Knowledge Management, *Communication of the ACM, 47*(12), 47-52.

Corante (2004). www.corante.com/many, (06/20/2004).

de Witt, C. (2006). *Hybride Lernarrangements in der universitären Weiterbildung.* Das Beispiel Educational Media. www.medienpaed.com/03-1/dewitt03-1.pdf, (01/20/2006).

Eigner, C. (2004). Wenn Medien zu oszillieren beginnen. In: Eigner, C. et al. (Eds.): *Online-Communities, Weblogs und die soziale Rückeroberung des Netzes*(pp. 115-125). Graz/Austria.

Fiedler, S. (2004). Introducing disruptive technologies for learning: Personal Webpublishing and Weblogs. In L. Cantoni & C. McLoughlin (Eds.), *Proceedings of Ed-Media 2004* (pp. 2584-2591). Lugano, Switzerland: Association for the Advancement of Computing in Education (AACE).

Leslie, C. (2003). www.edtechpost.ca/gems/matrix2.gif, (01/24/2006).

Markov, J. (2005). Web Content by and for the Masses. www.nytimes.com/2005/06/29/technology/29content.html (06/29/2005).

Mortensen, T., & Walker, J. (2002). Blogging Thoughts: Personal Publication as an online Research Tool. In A. Morrison (Ed.), *Researching ICTs in Context.* Oslo. Intermedia, University of Oslo.

Nardi, B., Schiano, D., & Gumbrecht, M. (2004). Blogging as Social Activity, or, Would You Let 900 Million People Read Your Diary? *Proc. of CSCW'04*, 3(6), 222-231.

OLPC (2007). *One Laptop Per Child.* wiki.laptop.org/go/Home. (11/13/2007).

O'Reilly, T. (2005). *What is Web 2.0?* www.oreilly.de/artikel/web20.html (11/13/2007).

PC Magazine (2006). July 2006.

Press, L. (2005). bpastudio.csudh.edu/fac/lpress/471/blogfeedback.htm (04/30/2008)

Tepper, M. (2003). *The Rise of Social Software. netWorker magazine.* September.

Time (2007). Person of the year. *You, 168*(26).

Weblog search (2006). www.pewinternet.org/PPF/r/144/report_display.asp, www.technorati.com, blogs.feedster.com (04/29/2006).

Wikipedia (2008). en.wikipedia.org/wiki/Weblogs (04/26/2008).

Wagner, C. (2003). Put another (B)Log on the Wire: Publishing Learning Logs as Weblogs. *Journal of Informations Systems Education, 14*(2), 131-132.

Wrede, O. (2003). *Weblog and Discourse.* www.weblogs.design.fh-aachen.de/owrede (10/29/2005/cache).

KEY TERMS

Blog: Short form for >Weblog

Blogging: The individual activity to contribute to a Weblog, either by posts or by comments to posts.

Blogroll: A list of constant links in a Weblog that points to other, somehow related Blogs.

Blogosphere: A thought construct, comprising all existing Weblogs, denoting the social relevance of Blogging.

Informal Learning: Informal learning is neither institutionally planned nor functionally defined, but opportunistic and spontaneous. It can take place within or outside of institutionally planned education.

Posting: Another term for >Blogging

RSS-Feed: Defined as Rich Site Summary (RSS 0.9x); RDF Site Summary (RSS1.0); Really Simple Syndication (RSS2.0). Through RSS, short descriptions of articles or web pages can be represented in machine readable form (XML) and regularly delivered by a news repository. It is also called a newsfeed. This way changes and updates in one site are automatically fed to subscribers,

see http://www.atompub.org/ and http://blogs.law.harvard.edu/tech/rssChangeNotes (06/14/2006)

Social Software: Web-based systems, supporting individual representation, mass interaction, formation and communication of common-interest groups.

Trackback: A technology employed to let users of a Weblog know which other Blogs are linking to them.

Weblog: Artificial word, combining "Web" and "log"file. Web pages with individual entries presented in reverse chronological order, usually maintained by a single author and managed through a specialized software system.

Chapter V
Social Navigation and Local Folksonomies:
Technical and Design Considerations for a Mobile Information System

Mark Bilandzic
Technische Universität München, Germany

Marcus Foth
Queensland University of Technology, Australia

ABSTRACT

Web services such as wikis, blogs, podcasting, file sharing and social networking are frequently referred to by the term Web 2.0. The innovation of these services lies in their ability to enable an increasing number of users to actively participate on the Internet by creating and sharing their own content and help develop a collective intelligence. In this chapter the authors discuss how they use Web 2.0 techniques such as "folksonomy" and "geo-tagging" in a mobile information system to collect and harness the everyday connections and local knowledge of urban residents in order to support their social navigation practices.

INTRODUCTION

Our physical world holds certain characteristics that enable us to interpret what other people have done, how they behaved, and where they have travelled. Sometimes, we can see traces on physical objects that provide hints about people's actions in the past. Footprints on the ground left by previous walkers can show us the right way through a forest or, in a library, for example, dog-eared books with well thumbed pages might be worthwhile reading as they indicate the popularity of the text. The phenomenon of people making decisions about their actions based on what other people have done in the past or what other people have recommended doing, forms part of our everyday social navigation (Dourish & Chalmers, 1994). In contrast to physical objects, digital information has no such 'visible' interaction history *per se*. We do not see how many people have listened to an MP3 file or read a Webpage. In a digital environment people do not leave interaction traces, leaving us, according to Erickson and Kellogg (2000), 'socially blind'. However, the high value placed on social navigation in the physical world has motivated people to start thinking about it as a general design approach for digital information systems as well (A. Dieberger, 1995; A. Dieberger, 1997; Forsberg, Höök, & Svensson, 1998; Svensson, Höök, & Cöster, 2005; Wexelblat & Maes, 1999).

This chapter explores some of the technical and design considerations that underpin the conception and development of a mobile information system called *CityFlocks*. It enables visitors and new residents of a city to tap into the knowledge and experiences of local residents and gather information about their new environment. Its design specifically aims to lower existing barriers

of access and facilitate social navigation in urban places. The technical development phase and the empirical usability research of *CityFlocks* has been reported elsewhere (Bilandzic, Foth, & De Luca, 2008). The purpose and focus of this chapter is to discuss the underlying design concepts that informed this social software. These concepts are positioned at the intersection of three broad areas of research and development that inform human-centred and participatory methods for designing interactive social networking systems on mobile platforms: social navigation, Web 2.0, and mobile spatial interaction (Figure 1).

First, the concept of social navigation and how people make use of it in the physical world are examined. Relevant previous studies and examples are discussed that apply social navigation as a design approach, e.g., for virtual information spaces on the Web. Based on the success and popularity of what has now been coined 'Web 2.0' services, the second part of this chapter analyses a number of Web development trends that foster participatory culture and the creation and exchange of user generated content. Some of these developments that introduced more and more social interaction and navigation methods to the Web, such as user participation, folksonomy and

Figure 1. CityFlocks is placed in an interdisciplinary field, embracing topics in social navigation, mobile spatial interaction and Web 2.0 technology

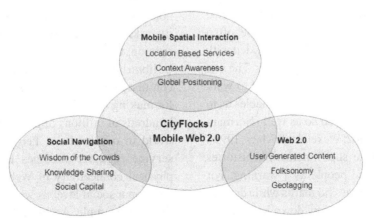

geo-tagging, were reappropriated to inform the design of *CityFlocks*. Given new generation mobile phones that allow global positioning, Web 2.0 technologies that were initially aimed to facilitate social navigation on the Web, can now be used to facilitate social navigation in physical places. The third part of the chapter discusses related projects in the field of mobile spatial interaction, a research area covering mobile applications that deal with information related to the user's surroundings. The review of the aims, strengths and weaknesses of previous research projects in this field refines the research trajectory which guides the development of the *CityFlocks* prototype and potentially similar mobile information systems. The chapter thus reveals further opportunities and issues regarding social navigation in the context of new generation mobile phone services, the 'Mobile Web 2.0' (Jaokar & Fish, 2006).

SOCIAL NAVIGATION

The phenomenon of people asking other people for advice is part of a broader concept called social navigation, at first introduced by Dourish and Chalmers (1994). They describe it as 'moving towards a cluster of other people, or selecting objects because others have been examining them' (Dourish & Chalmers, 1994). It can be seen as a form of navigation, where people make decisions about their actions based on what other people have done or what other people have recommended doing. Tourists in a new town for example, often choose to go to restaurants that are crowded with people rather than picking empty places. The fact that a fair crowd of people has decided to walk down a certain path within a space, enables us to be more comfortable to do so as well (Norman, 1988; Rheingold, 2002; Wexelblat & Maes, 1999). We might also take such interaction histories between objects and people as a warning. For example, if we observe skid marks while driving on a road, we implicitly slow down because the

marks show us that an earlier driver obviously had to brake rapidly.

Mediated and Unmediated Social Navigation

Compared to physical spaces, in the digital world there are no such visible hints that naturally describe an object's interaction history. In contrast to a physical paperback book or a CD, digital documents or music files do not have dog-eared pages or scratches that give us an idea about their amount or time of usage. Similarly, footprints of earlier walkers in the wood might show us the right way, as opposed to virtual information spaces, such as the Web, that do not provide any natural traces and visible paths that could help following navigators. People have recognised that such traces on physical objects provide important information for their navigational behavior in physical spaces and have constantly been trying to transfer the same sort of navigational aid to virtual information spaces, especially to the Web (A. Dieberger, 1997, 2003; Höök, Benyon, & Munro, 2003).

In the recent years people have developed mediated techniques and technologies that provide much more sophisticated social navigation possibilities. In the physical world we are restricted to visual traces on objects (e.g. dog-eared pages on a book) that only give us a vague hint about its quality. Using the second possibility in a non-digital world to find out about a book's quality, asking people directly about their personal opinion, we are restricted to a number of friends or librarians who might have read it before. In contrast to that, the Web has some clear benefits for making use of social navigation. It connects hundreds of millions of people from all over the world in one medium. People have developed services and technologies that leverage this physical connectivity of Web users to connect them on a social level as well. To continue with the book example, Amazon (http://amazon.com)

for instance has created a platform that brings together people from all over the world to comment, review and exchange personal opinions before they purchase a book. The platform keeps track of the books each user has purchased in order to identify and suggest titles that other users with the same shopping history have read as well. As all purchases, reviews and ratings are tracked and saved in a database, collaborative filtering methods can be applied to analyze the taste of many people to automatically predict the book taste of individual users. Providing such a mediated social environment, Amazon has created far more sophisticated social navigation affordances than traditional book stores ever had.

In the last couple of years the social navigation approach for designing Web services has become ubiquitous in the Web due to the appearance of a set of Web 2.0 technologies which facilitate rich user interfaces (e.g. AJAX, CSS), the use of interchangeable data formats (e.g. XML, RSS) and a user based taxonomy (e.g. folksonomy, geo-tagging). The high potential of Web 2.0 technologies combined with the fast development of mobile phone capabilities, such as global positioning technology and high-speed Internet access opens up great capabilities to develop mediated social navigation aids for mobile phone users in physical spaces. Similar to how Amazon leverages the physical connectivity of Web users to provide social aid and recommendations for book shopping, the connectivity of mobile phone users and recent mobile phone technology can be leveraged to enhance social navigational help when searching for places in the physical world.

The Evolution of Social Navigation on the World Wide Web

The problem in the early stages of the Web and its hyperlink based navigation was a lack of navigational and visual structure of space. As Dieberger claims, this very lack of visual structure was the reason that motivated people to start sharing their link references on their personal home pages (A. Dieberger, 1997). Users were ironing out the lack of structure in the Web by providing navigational help to each other. This social sharing of information or hyperlinks with others on the Web is the major enabler of what we call *surfing* or *browsing* the Internet, which turned out to be a popular search strategy for finding Websites on the Internet (Erickson, 1996). People have actually adopted the same strategy they usually apply to find information in the real world: They ask people in their social networks and if they can not help, they would know someone who knows and eventually they would get the information they were looking for. Similarly, people started to search for information on the Web by browsing through personal Websites and following their links to other personal Websites until they found the site with the specific information. Erickson describes this early phenomenon in the World Wide Web as a *"slow transformation from an abstract, chaotic, information Web into what I call a social hypertext"* (Erickson, 1996). With this social hypertext, the Web has become a medium that people can easily browse through the immense pool of social capital and knowledge available in their networks.

Social navigation has become a key principle of how we search for information and navigate the Web today. One example that illustrates its breakthrough on the Web can be seen in the history of search engines. While early search engines until 2001, such as Lycos, Yahoo or Altavista were still based on big Web directories, Google has outpaced all other players with *relevance ranking*, a search concept based on social navigation. Google implemented this concept in its *PageRank* algorithm. For any URL on the Web, it analyses the amount and content of Web pages that refer to it when calculating its position in the search results (Google, 2007). The more people set links to a particular Website, the more important Google considers it to be and the further up it appears on the result page. What Google has achieved with

PageRank is basically an automation of searching for a Website that most other people hyperlink to from their own Webpage. Thus, for any topic or search request it provides a ranking of pages that are obviously considered to be the most popular among other people on the Web.

The CityFlocks prototype is a similar system designed for local places and services in a city. For any type of local service in a city, e.g. 'fish restaurant' or 'tennis court', the system comes up with a ranking of the most popular, relevant places in the city, based on the opinion and ratings of the local community of residents. Harnessing the intelligence of local residents and their participation on a shared knowledge platform can democratise urban information, such as opinions about a local service or place. The next section explains how participatory culture has transformed the Web from something we considered as a pure information space to what it has become today, a thoroughly social medium (O'Reilly, 2005).

WEB 2.0

The term Web 2.0 has been coined to identify – arguably – a second-generation of Web services that aim to facilitate collaboration and sharing between users, such as social networking systems, file sharing sites and wikis. These services provide means for users to engage in participatory culture that are no longer limited to the technically versed or the civically inclined. Scholars such as Jenkins (2006) and Burgess et al. (2006) have identified sociotechnical trends towards a wider ('vernacular') ability of people to participate in digital culture through personal expressions of creativity. Many examples of how participatory culture is enabled by recent technological innovation rely on Web 2.0 applications and services such as blogs, Wikipedia, YouTube, Flickr, and social networking sites such as Facebook, which are arguably more open, collaborative, personalisable, and therefore participatory than the previous

internet experience. According to Kolbitsch & Maurer (2006), the participatory qualities of Web 2.0 encourage ordinary users to make their knowledge explicit and help a collective intelligence to develop. In an urban context, Foth et al. (2007) argue that such capabilities present diverse possibilities for a profound urban epistemology to evolve. New tools and practices, inspired by user-led innovation, are springing up faster than our ability to analyse them individually. It has been claimed that such a social navigation approach can foster a new generation of user experience for mobile applications as well (Höök, 2003; Jaokar & Fish, 2006). Bypassing the terminology debate, whether the term 'Web 2.0' is adequate, this section focuses in particular on three characteristics of Web 2.0 developments, that is, user participation, folksonomy and geo-tagging. It prepares the discussion in the next section about the ways these characteristics can be applied to a mobile spatial interaction service that facilitates social navigation in the physical world.

User Participation: Let the Users Generate Content

Looking back at the history of the Internet, we can see that its real breakthrough as a social mass-medium first came with the introduction of the World Wide Web, the number of users skyrocketing from 600.000 to over 40 million within only five years (Friedman, 2006, p.61). One major reason for this magnificent success of the Internet was that for the first time people were given a medium which allowed them to participate in the content creation process. In contrast to other media such as television or radio which only enables professional information providers to broadcast information, the Web enabled individual users to contribute. Hypertext Markup Language (HTML) offered users means to codify, upload and share their own content with other users on the network. With hyperlinks they were able to refer and set shortcuts to other relevant or interesting pages.

This is in fact how the Internet became a social medium. The combination of user participation and the hyperlink system enabled the Web to be used as a tremendous repository of social knowledge (Erickson & Kellogg, 2000).

However, the majority of Web users were still only information consumers. The lack of technical background knowledge, such as learning a markup language, uploading a site to a Web server or take care of the site administration has prevented many people from creating their own Webpage (Kolbitsch & Maurer, 2006). This is what the introduction of Web 2.0 technologies has dramatically changed. They flattened the technical obstacles and made it easy for anybody, not only geeks and professional information providers to engage in the content creation process. With wikis, Weblogs or file sharing services for example, people do not need to learn HTML anymore in order to publish content on the Web. Such services provide frameworks, templates and tools that abstract from the technical layers and enable ordinary users to easily become authors of Web content. User generated content became a new paradigm for this revolutionary generation of Web 2.0 services (O'Reilly, 2005). Web 2.0 blurs the strict borderline between consumers and information providers which eventually leads to a trend of entirely community-driven Web services (Lindahl & Blount, 2003).

People were given a tool to discuss ideas, exchange information and give advice to each other. With Flickr (http://flickr.com) and YouTube (http://youtube.com) people can easily share their pictures and videos; Blogger (http://blogger.com) and Typepad (http://typepad.com) allow individuals to publish personal stories, and Yahoo Answers (http://answers.yahoo.com) provides a platform for people to answer each other's questions on specific topics. The content of all those services is almost entirely created by the community of its users. This trend towards flattening technical barriers and giving individuals a voice in a mass medium, what Anderson refers to as 'the

Long Tail' (Anderson, 2006), is one of the key success factors of Web 2.0. While conventional Web services have mostly been providing content from a single entity (e.g. a professional content provider), they were outpaced by services leveraging the collaboration of many different entities which would all upload and share their content with others. Following this community driven approach, Wikipedia (http://wikipedia.org), an online encyclopedia, has outpaced Britannica, the most successful encyclopedia till then. The huge amount of Web users, who add or edit Wikipedia articles, renders the content creation process much more flexibly than the relatively small number of Britannica authors. Consequently, the articles in Wikipedia are more current and have a much larger range of topics, covering 3.7 million articles in 200 languages from more than 45,000 registered users who upload about 1,500 new articles every day (Giles, 2006). The benefit of such collaborative information platforms is that their content is based on the collective intelligence of a crowd of people. As Surowiecki (Surowiecki, 2004) puts it, "the many are always smarter than the few", meaning that the information content from a massive user community can not easily be outpaced by a single entity. O'Reilly argues that this paradigm is one of the main drivers of this new generation of Web applications, the Web 2.0 (O'Reilly, 2005).

The community driven design approach of those services transformed the Web in a way that they now take advantage of the dynamic intelligence and content generating power of its community to provide full-blown and highly up-to-date information (Kolbitsch & Maurer, 2006; O'Reilly, 2005). This user participation and uploading of information facilitates social navigation on a much larger scale than we have in the physical world. In fact, the very process of designing proper affordances that allow people to socialise and help each other to navigate digital systems, has been a research topic in various domains (Höök et al., 2003), e.g. online food shopping

(Svensson et al., 2005) or Web browsing (Andreas Dieberger, 1995; A. Dieberger, 1997, 2003; Wexelblat & Maes, 1999), where e.g. Wexelblat and Maes have introduced Footprints, a system that tracks and visualises the navigational behavior of a Website's visitors in order to provide future visitors with navigational aids such as maps and paths (Wexelblat & Maes, 1999).

These studies have shown that social navigation affordances do enhance users' experiences in digital information spaces. They have explored a number of design principles that are significant in different use cases and domains. Additionally, there are suggestions for some key principles, e.g. privacy, trust, personalisation and appropriateness that should be considered in general when designing for social navigation in digital systems (Forsberg et al., 1998).

Folksonomy: Let the Users Organise Content

With the amount of user generated content constantly increasing in Web services, there is a need to structure and organise all the uploaded material. This would ensure that the submitted content could be identified and retrieved at a later point in time. One straightforward way is to set up an indexing system, where all the information would be put in pre-fixed categories. This process usually requires highly trained information professionals and is very inflexible, e.g. for storing information that does not fit in any of the existing categories (Macgregor & McCulloch, 2006; Vander Wal, 2007). In order to provide a more flexible storing and retrieval system, recent Web services that deal with huge amounts of user generated content like Flickr or Del.icio.us, have employed a technique that has come to be known as 'folksonomy' (Golder & Huberman, 2005; Macgregor & McCulloch, 2006; Vander Wal, 2007). Folksonomy is a user created taxonomy for people to generate short keywords about their uploaded content rather that putting them in fixed

categories. By assigning these keywords or so-called tags, the semantics of various information resources can be easily described (Amitay, Har'El, Sivan, & Soffer, 2004; Casey & Savastinuk, 2007; Coleman, 1988; Macgregor & McCulloch, 2006; Torniai, Battle, & Cayzer, 2005). A user submitting a picture of her new car on Flickr could for instance use the tags 'car', 'automobile', 'porsche' and 'cabriolet'. In contrast to an index, the picture will not be saved in any pre-fixed category in the system, but can be retrieved under any of those keywords. As users can assign such decentralised keywords to their content, there are no restrictions to what information one can submit as opposed to the constraints of fixed categories. The organisation of the information resources are completely controlled by the users themselves, which makes the system cheaper and much more flexible. Most recently, the advantages of this user based contextualisation of items have been used to facilitate information retrieval in libraries as well (Casey & Savastinuk, 2007; Courtney, 2007).

This collaborative tagging method, initially developed to organise information on the Web, can be transferred to a mobile information system that people use to describe places in the physical world. Like Delicious (http://del.icio.us) uses collaborative tagging to let Web users identify, describe, recommend and organise Internet-addresses (URLs), CityFlocks was designed in a way that allows the community of local residents to do the same with physical places in a city. Comments on the ice-cream parlor next door could for example be tagged with 'ice-cream', 'dessert' and 'coffee'.

Geo-Tagging: Spatially Contextualised Content

Encouraging ordinary people as content providers for local information can be an effective way to provide a democratic, current and comprehensive pool of local information and news (We Media, 2003). In contrast to citizen journalism platforms, e.g. MyHeimat (http://myheimat.de) or EdgeX (http://edgex.org.au), which enable local citizens to upload extensive stories relevant to their wider city area, there are use scenarios which indicate that spatial contextualisation sometimes requires finer granularity. A story or piece of information might for example only be relevant to a neighbourhood in the city or a specific place, like a shop.

In this cases geo-tagging, a method to attach latitude and longitude identifiers, enables people to put their information resources such as text, pictures or videos into a specific geographic context (Torniai et al., 2005). Such spatially and semantically contextualised information can be applied to overlay the real world with a virtual information space to be used for mobile services (Burrell & Gay, 2002; Jaokar & Fish, 2006), and more specifically, create a mediated social environment that helps people navigate physical spaces by using location aware mobile devices. Qype (http://qype.de) for example provides such a service which uses user-generated, geo-referenced comments in a mobile information service.

Similarly, recent photo cameras can automatically attach the latitude and longitude coordinates of the current geographical position when taking pictures. Later, the pictures can be displayed with special programs or Web services on a map where they were taken. Locr (http://locr.com) for example provides such an online service to organise your picture collection on a geographical map and share them with others. As all pictures are geo-tagged people can compare their own pictures with the photos that other people or friends have taken at the same place or city. Or they can use it to see pictures of a place they plan to visit soon in order to learn about it in advance. Collaborative Tagging has enabled Web users to describe the content and theme of their pictures and make them retrievable for other people. Geo-tagging allows them to additionally share the geographic location of where they have taken each of their pictures. Enriching the metadata of one's pictures with both, folksonomy tags and geographic identifiers enables a very specific and flexible organisation and retrieval of pictures in a shared database. Figure 2 shows a search request on a Flickr-map (http://flickr.com/map) for pictures that were taken in Bangalore, India and Melbourne, Australia and annotated with the tag 'car'.

Dealing with respectively large masses of stored data, Web 2.0 services have developed two very powerful information organisation methods – folksonomy and geo-tagging. With the design of the *CityFlocks* prototype we sought to transfer Web 2.0's participatory culture as well as the

Figure 2. Example from Flickr.com - Folksonomy and geo-tagging enable a flexible organisation and retrieval of pictures

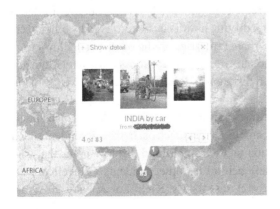

folksonomy and geo-tagging methods to foster a location and context sensitive mobile information system. Applying collaborative tagging and geo-tagging to a community driven, mobile information system enables people to annotate urban places in their neighbourhood with comments and recommendations and describe their entries with tags for later retrieval purposes. Such an urban information system helps collecting local knowledge and experiences in a shared knowledge platform about inner-city places and facilities. The collective intelligence and knowledge of local residents about particular places and local services in a city is much bigger than any single entity like a professional agency could provide. With the geographical identifiers in its metadata, the submitted content is used to support tourists and visitors in finding popular local services in new cities recommended by locals.

MOBILE SPATIAL INTERACTION

The previous sections have covered related projects and literature on social navigation and relevant Web 2.0 technologies. This section is dedicated to related work and research studies undertaken on the mobile platform, specifically mobile spatial interaction, i.e. location and context-aware mobile applications that refer to information relevant to the current surroundings of the user. Such applications can be classified in four different categories: Systems that facilitate navigation and wayfinding in geographic places, mobile augmented reality applications, and applications that create or provide access to information attached to physical places or objects (Fröhlich et al., 2007). In the context of *CityFlocks*, the latter two categories are of special interest.

Lancaster University's GUIDE project for example is an electronic tourist guide that provides users with context-aware information, depending on their profile, interests and location. Its focus is on providing an automated personalised guided city tour with dynamic, interactive services. However it can only read information, but does not provide any content-generating functions to its users (Cheverst, Davies, Mitchell, Friday, & Efstratiou, 2000; Lancaster University). Another example for accessing virtual context-information on mobile devices, are applications that are based on visual codes (Ballagas, Rohs, & Sheridan, 2005; Rohs, 2005; Rohs & Gfeller, 2004; Toye et al., 2004). Using mobile phones with embedded photo cameras, one can select those visual codes and request information related to the object or place where the respective code tag is attached to. A drawback of this method is that the user can request information only in-situ, but not from remote places.

The other type of applications relevant to the context of this work enables users not only to read but also create spatially contextualised content. GeoNotes (Espinoza et al., 2001) and Urban Tapestries (Proboscis, 2003) for example allow mobile users to attach virtual sticky notes to particular latitude / longitude coordinates. Equipped with Wi-Fi enabled Personal Digital Assistants (PDAs), GeoNotes users can see other users' notes that were left behind in their current immediate surroundings. Even though GeoNotes embraces users as information producers rather than just passive consumers, it is not an entirely community driven service. Its major weakness is that the user generated post-it notes are managed in hierarchical, tree-like location structures that have to be set up in advance manually. Thus people can create location based content, but are limited in specifying how it can be retrieved by other users. Urban Tapestries on the other hand allows users to self-organise their comments and relationships to different places with category-like "threads" (e.g. "my favorite pubs and clubs"). E-Graffiti, a context-aware application evaluated on a collage campus, detects each participating student's location on the campus and displays notes that were left behind by other students (Burrell & Gay, 2002). Just-for-Us (Kjeldskov & Paay, 2005) and the George Square project (Brown et al., 2005) represent context-aware real-time applications that provide an enjoyable shared social interaction of remote users that follow a common goal. While Just-for-Us helps a group of friends in a city to identify a good place to meet depending on their individual current locations, the George Square project focuses on location, photography and voice sharing functions to let on-site and off-site users collaboratively explore a city sight.

Much of the previous work in mobile spatial interaction is on enabling users to access or add content to physical places or objects. They focus on techniques that allow people to retrieve locative information or share it with others by attaching stories, thoughts, experiences and knowledge to specific places. Besides the various use scenarios, the applications primarily differ in the interaction design of specific features (Tungare, Burbey, & Perez-Quinones, 2006), e.g. access virtual post-its from remote places (Espinoza et al., 2001; Proboscis, 2003) vs. in-situ access (Burrell & Gay, 2002; Lancaster University, ; Rohs, 2005), push (Espinoza et al., 2001; Kjeldskov & Paay, 2005) vs. pull services, expiration dates of the messages or private vs. public messaging (Burrell & Gay, 2002; Espinoza et al., 2001). While most of the previous projects discuss such different features around indirect and asynchronous interaction methods (i.e. people exchange information by attaching text or multimedia content to specific places), not much work has yet been carried out on studying direct interaction methods (e.g. phone call, text message) in the context of spatial interaction.

CityFlocks focuses on evaluating the performance of people using direct and indirect social navigation methods when gathering information about a specific place. In a similar context, solely the George Square study supported a voice connection and has shown to be the most valuable channel for people when collaboratively exploring a city sight. In contrast to George Square, our participants were not recruited as pairs of friends, but complete strangers. Furthermore, the context

is information and knowledge sharing in urban environments rather than collaborative exploration. *CityFlocks* users can, in addition to leaving relevant text or multimedia content at specific places, also attach their contact information. Other mobile phone users who are interested in more details about the place can then contact the author of the virtual post-it directly via voice-link or a direct text message. In a field study we evaluated which method, direct or indirect communication, users prefer in which situation and context (Bilandzic et al., 2008). The outcomes inform future mobile spatial interaction systems that are targeted in providing information to its users about places and objects in their immediate surroundings.

CONCLUSION

Originally social navigation was restricted to visible interaction histories that were naturally left behind and thus clued on earlier physical interaction between people and the respective object. People interpret these hints as a message, recommendation, warning or just a note telling them something about the type of interaction the previous navigator had with the object. Above, we have seen how online social communities have improved the social navigation experience for special interest groups. With the rapid developments of mobile information and communication technology, the methods which have been developed for such communities on the Web, can also be used to enhance social navigation in physical spaces (Höök, 2003).

There is an emerging trend that sees the network connectivity of mobile phone users leveraged to create a mediated social environment where people who are interested in particular geographic locations can exchange information, personal opinions and experiences with the respective place. This would for example enable visitors of a new city to access the knowledge and experiences from local residents about inner-city facilities. Recent developments in the mobile technology sector indeed have made this scenario become realistic. Multimedia mobile phones with voice recording and photo camera capabilities as well as mobile high speed Internet networks enable users to create and upload location based content anywhere, anytime. Equipped with such a device, people can easily capture and digitise whatever they have experienced at the very point of inspiration, using text, video or audio recordings (Jaokar & Fish, 2006). A mobile Web application would let them upload such location based recommendations and make them available for other mobile users who plan to navigate the same space later on. For example they could create a recommendation for an ice cream parlor, saying *'This place serves the best ice-cream in town. They have a wide range, cheap prices and a very friendly service!'* and attach a rating, e.g. 8 out of 10. Applying collaborative filtering techniques, the service provides a ranking of the most popular places based on all mobile users' entries. This mind-shift in designing mobile services towards a high engagement of individuals has great

potential to enhance peoples' experience when navigating physical spaces (Höök, 2003; Jaokar & Fish, 2006). Turning mobile phone users into in-situ journalist who can upload location based ratings, comments and recommendations to a shared community platform will eventually form a huge social knowledge repository decentralising control over information about local services.

This idea targets a community-driven urban information service. The service is meant to provide an infrastructure to let residents become authors of information regarding their own neighbourhoods and make them available for interested people in the city, e.g. visitors and tourists. User participation, folksonomy and geo-tagging are three design methods that have become popular in Web 2.0 community-platforms and proven to be an effective information management tool for various domains (Casey & Savastinuk, 2007; Courtney, 2007; Macgregor & McCulloch, 2006). Applying such a design approach for a mobile information system (Figure 3) creates a new experience of collaboration between mobile users, a step towards what Jaokar refers to as the 'Mobile Web 2.0' (Jaokar & Fish, 2006), that is, a chance

Figure 3. A resident-driven mobile information system: A mashup of folksonomy tags, location-based user recommendations, and geographic identifiers

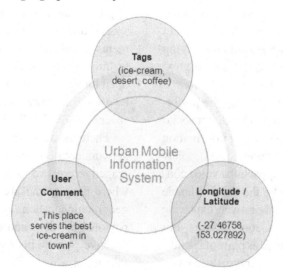

for mediated social navigation in physical spaces on the move.

ACKNOWLEDGMENT

The author would like to thank Helen Klaebe, Greg Hearn, Ronald Schroeter, and all study participants for their support. This study was supported by the Institute for Creative Industries and Innovation at Queensland University of Technology and the Center for Digital Technology and Management at the Technische Universität München. Further support was received through the Australian Research Council's Discovery Projects funding scheme (project number DP0663854), *New Media in the Urban Village: Mapping Communicative Ecologies and Socio-Economic Innovation in Emerging Inner-City Residential Developments*. The author is grateful to be a scholarship recipient of the German National Academic Foundation (*Studienstiftung des deutschen Volkes*). Dr Foth is grateful to be the recipient of an Australian Postdoctoral Fellowship.

REFERENCES

Amitay, E., Har'El, N., Sivan, R., & Soffer, A. (2004). *Web-a-Where: Geotagging Web Content*. Paper presented at the ACM SIGIR conference on Research and development in information retrieval.

Anderson, C. (2006). *The long tail: Why the future of business is selling less of more* (1st ed.). New York: Hyperion.

Ballagas, R., Rohs, M., & Sheridan, J. G. (2005). *Sweep and Point & Shoot: Phonecam-Based Interactions for Large Public Displays*. Paper presented at the CHI 2005.

Bilandzic, M., Foth, M., & De Luca, A. (2008, Feb 25-27). CityFlocks: Designing Social Navigation for Urban Mobile Information Systems. In G. Maden, I. Ladeira, & P. Koze (Eds.), *Proceedings ACM SIGCHI Designing Ineractive Systems* (DIS), (pp. 474-483). Cape Town, South Africa.

Brown, B., Chalmers, M., Bell, M., Hall, M., MacColl, I., & Rudman, P. (2005, 18-22 September 2005). *Sharing the square: Collaborative Leisure in the City Streets*. Paper presented at the Proceedings of the Ninth European Conference on Computer-Supported Cooperative Work, Paris, France.

Burgess, J., Foth, M., & Klaebe, H. (2006, Sep 25-26). *Everyday Creativity as Civic Engagement: A Cultural Citizenship View of New Media*. Paper presented at the Communications Policy & Research Forum, Sydney, NSW.

Burrell, J., & Gay, G. K. (2002). E-graffiti: evaluating real-world use of a context-aware system. *Interacting with Computers, 14*(4), 301-312.

Casey, M. E., & Savastinuk, L. C. (2007). *Library 2.0: The librarian's guide to participatory library service*. Medford, N.J.: Information Today Inc.

Cheverst, K., Davies, N., Mitchell, K., Friday, A., & Efstratiou, C. (2000). *Developing a Context-aware Electronic Tourist Guide: Some Issues and Experiences*. Paper presented at the CHI 2000, Netherlands, April 2000.

Coleman. (1988). Social capital and the creation of human capital. *American Journal of Sociology, 94*, 95-120.

Courtney, N. (2007). *Library 2.0 and beyond: innovative technologies and tomorrow's user*. Westport, Conn.: Libraries Unlimited.

Dieberger, A. (1995). Providing spatial navigation for the World Wide Web. In A. U. Frank & W. Kuhn (Eds.), *Spatial Information Theory, Proceedings of Cosit '95* (pp. 93-106). Semmering, Austria: Springer.

Dieberger, A. (1997). Supporting Social Navigation on the World-Wide Web. *International*

Journal of Human-Computer Studies, special issue on innovative applications of the Web, 46, 805-825.

Dieberger, A. (2003). Social Connotations of Space in the Design for Virtual Communies and Social Navigation. In K. Höök, D. Benyon & A. J. Munro (Eds.), *Designing information spaces: The social navigation approach* (pp. 293-313). London: Springer.

Dourish, P., & Chalmers, M. (1994). *Running Out of Space: Models of Information Navigation.* Paper presented at the HCI'94.

Erickson, T. (1996). *The World Wide Web as Social Hypertext.* Retrieved 03.05.2007, 2007, from http://www.pliant.org/personal/Tom_Erickson/SocialHypertext.html.

Erickson, T., & Kellogg, W. A. (2000). Social Translucence: An Approach to Designing Systems that Support Social Processes. *ACM Transactions on Computer-Human Interaction, 7*(1), 59-83.

Espinoza, F., Persson, P., Sandin, A., Nyström, H., Cacciatore, E., & Bylund, M. (2001). *GeoNotes: Social and Navigational Aspects of Location-Based Information Systems.* Paper presented at the Ubicomp 2001: Ubiquitous Computing, International Conference.

Forsberg, M., Höök, K., & Svensson, M. (1998). *Design Principles for Social Navigation Tools.* Paper presented at the UI4All, Stockholm, Sweden.

Foth, M., Odendaal, N., & Hearn, G. (2007, Oct 15-16). *The View from Everywhere: Towards an Epistemology for Urbanites.* Paper presented at the 4th International Conference on Intellectual Capital, Knowledge Management and Organisational Learning (ICICKM), Cape Town, South Africa.

Friedman, T. L. (2006). *The world is flat: The globalized world in the twenty-first century* (Updated and expanded ed.). Camberwell, Vic.: Penguin.

Fröhlich, P., Simon, R., Baillie, L., Roberts, J. L., Murry-Smith, R., Jones, M., et al. (2007). *Workshop on Mobile Spatial Interaction.* San Jose, CA, USA.

Giles, J. (2006). Internet encyclopaedias go head to head. Retrieved 24.07.2007, 2007, from http://www.nature.com/news/2005/051212/full/438900a.html.

Golder, S. A., & Huberman, B. A. (2005). *The Structure of Collaborative Tagging Systems.*

Google. (2007). Google searches more sites more quickly, delivering the most relevant results. *Our Search: Google Technology* Retrieved 27.04.2007, from http://www.google.com/technology/

Höök, K. (2003). Social Navigation: from the Web to the mobile. In G. Szwillus & J. Ziegler (Eds.), *Mensch & Computer 2003: Interaktion und Bewegung* (pp. 17-20). Stuttgart.

Höök, K., Benyon, D., & Munro, A. J. (2003). *Designing information spaces: The social navigation approach.* London New York: Springer.

Jaokar, A., & Fish, T. (2006). *Mobile Web 2.0: The innovator's guide to developing and marketing next generation wireless mobile applications.* London: Futuretext.

Jenkins, H. (2006). *Fans, Bloggers, and Gamers: Exploring Participatory Culture.* New York: New York University Press.

Kjeldskov, J., & Paay, J. (2005). Just-for-us: a context-aware mobile information system facilitating sociality. *ACM International Conference Proceeding Series; Proceeding of the 7th international conference on Human computer interaction with mobile devices & services table of contents, 111,* 23-30.

Kolbitsch, J., & Maurer, H. (2006). The Transformation of the Web: How Emerging Communities

Shape the Information we Consume. *Journal of Universal Computer Science, 12*(2), 187-213.

Lancaster University. The GUIDE Project. Retrieved 16.06.2007, from http://www.guide.lancs. ac.uk/overview.html

Lindahl, C., & Blount, E. (2003). Weblogs: Simplifying Web Publishing. *Computer, 36*(11), 114-116.

Macgregor, G., & McCulloch, E. (2006). Collaborative Tagging as a Knowledge Organisation and Resource Discovery Tool. *Library Review, 55*(5).

Norman, D. A. (1988). *The psychology of everyday things.* New York: Basic Books.

O'Reilly, T. (2005). What Is Web 2.0 - Design Patterns and Business Models for the Next Generation of Software. Retrieved 20.04.2007, from http://www.oreillynet.com/pub/a/oreilly/tim/ news/2005/09/30/what-is-Web-20.html

Polanyi, M. (1966). *The Tacit Dimension.* Gloucester, MA: Peter Smith.

Proboscis. (2003). *Urban Tapestries.* Retrieved 17.06.2007, from http://research.urbantapestries. net/

Rheingold, H. (2002). *Smart mobs: The next social revolution.* Cambridge, MA: Perseus Publishing.

Rohs, M. (2005). Real-World Interaction with Camera Phones. In *Ubiquitous Computing Systems* (pp. 74-89). Berlin/Heidelberg: Springer.

Rohs, M., & Gfeller, B. (2004). Using Camera-Equipped Mobile Phones for Interacting with Real-World Objects. In A. Ferscha, H. Hoertner & G. Kotsis (Eds.), *Advances in Pervasive Computing* (pp. 265-271). Vienna, Austria: Austrian Computer Society (OCG).

Surowiecki, J. (2004). *The wisdom of crowds: Why the many are smarter than the few and how collective wisdom shapes business, economies,* *societies, and nations.* New York: Doubleday.

Svensson, M., Höök, K., & Cöster, R. (2005). Designing and Evaluating Kalas: A Social Navigation System for Food Recipes. *Computer-Human Interaction, 12*(3), 374-400.

Torniai, C., Battle, S., & Cayzer, S. (2005). Sharing, Discovering and Browsing Geotagged Pictures on the Web.

Toye, E., Madhavapeddy, A., Sharp, R., Scott, D., Blackwell, A., & Upton, E. (2004). *Using Camera-phones to Interact with Context-aware Mobile Services*: University of Cambridge.

Tungare, M., Burbey, I., & Perez-Quinones. (2006). *Evaluation of a location-linked notes system.* Paper presented at the 44th ACM Southeast Regional Conference, Melbourne, Florida.

Vander Wal, T. (2007). *Folksonomy Coinage and Definition.* Retrieved 10.08.2007, 2007, from http://vanderwal.net/folksonomy.html

We Media. (2003). *We Media - How audiences are shaping the future of news and information.* Retrieved 24.10.2007, from http://www.hypergene.net/wemedia/Weblog.php

Wexelblat, A., & Maes, P. (1999). *Footprints: History-Rich Tools for Information Foraging.* Paper presented at the SIGCHI conference on Human factors in computing systems: the CHI is the limit.

KEY TERMS

Folksonomy: In the context of the Web 2.0 discussion, a folksonomy (sometimes also known as a 'tag cloud') is a user-generated taxonomy made up of key terms that describe online content. By assigning these freestyle keywords or so-called 'tags', the semantics of various information resources can be described in a more flexible, decentralised, collaborative and participatory way than fixed categories allow for. The term has been coined by Thomas Vander Wal.

Geo-tagging: An approach which adds latitude and longitude identifiers as metadata to online content. It enables people to embed their information resources such as text, pictures or videos in a specific spatial and semantic context to augment the physical world with virtual information. Such a mediated social environment can help people navigate physical spaces by using location aware mobile devices.

Local Knowledge: Knowledge, or even knowing, is the justified belief that something is true. Knowledge is thus different from opinion. Local knowledge refers to facts and information acquired by a person which are relevant to a specific locale or have been elicited from a place-based context. It can also include specific skills or experiences made in a particular location. In this regard, local knowledge can be tacitly held, that is, knowledge we draw upon to perform and act but we may not be able to easily and explicitly articulate it: "We can know things, and important things, that we cannot tell" (Polanyi, 1966).

Mobile Spatial Interaction: The increasing ubiquity of location and context-aware mobile

devices and applications, geographic information systems (GIS) and sophisticated 3D representations of the physical world accessible by lay users is enabling more people to access information relevant to their current surroundings. The relationship between users and devices as well as the emerging oportunities and affordances are summarised by the term 'mobile spatial interaction'.

Mobile Web 2.0: The suite of systems and mobile devices which either run existing Web 2.0 applications or re-appropriate Web 2.0 characteristics (tagging, user participation, mash-ups, personalisation, recommendations, social networking, collective intelligence, etc.) for the specific context of mobile use and mobile devices.

Social Navigation: The process of guiding activities aimed at determining our position and planning and following a specific route based on what other people have done or what other people have recommended doing. First introduced by Dourish and Chalmers (1994), they describe it as 'moving towards a cluster of other people, or selecting objects because others have been examining them'.

Chapter VI
Social Cognitive Ontology and User Driven Healthcare

Rakesh Biswas
Manipal University, Malaysia

Carmel M. Martin
Northern Ontario School of Medicine, Ottawa, Canada

Joachim Sturmberg
Monash University, Australia

Kamalika Mukherji
Hertfordshire Partnership NHS Foundation Trust, UK

Edwin Wen Huo Lee
Intel Innovation Center, Malaysia

Shashikiran Umakanth
Manipal University, Malaysia

A. S. Kasthuri
AFMC, India

ABSTRACT

The chapter starts from the premise that illness and healthcare are predominantly social phenomena that shape the perspectives of key stakeholders of healthcare. It introduces readers to the concepts associated around the term ontology with particular reference to philosophical, social and computer ontology and teases out the relations between them. It proposes a synthesis of these concepts with the term 'social cognitive ontological constructs' (SCOCs). The chapter proceeds to explore the role of SCOCs in the generation of human emotions that are postulated to have to do more with cognition (knowledge) than affect (feelings). The authors propose a way forward to address emotional needs of patients and healthcare givers through informational feedback that is based on a conceptual framework incorporating SCOCs of key stakeholders. This would come about through recognizing the clinical encounter for what it is: a shared learning experience. The chapter proceeds to identify problems with the traditional development of top down medical knowledge and the need to break out of the well meaning but restrictive sub specialty approach. It uses the term de specialization to describe the process of breaking out of the traditional top down mold which may be achieved by collaborative learning not only across various medical specialties but also directly from the patient and her "other" caregivers. Finally it discusses current efforts in the medical landscape at bringing about this silent revolution in the form of a Web-based user driven healthcare. It also supplies a few details of the attempts made by the authors in a recent project trying to create electronic health records in a user driven manner beginning with the patient's version of their perceived illness with data added on as the patient traverses his/her way through various levels of care beginning from the community to the tertiary care hospital. The data contained within these records may then be effectively and anonymously shared between different patients and health professionals who key in their own experiential information and find matching individual experiential information through text tagging in a Web 2.0 platform.

INTRODUCTION

The human body has a limited range of physiological responses to deal with disease and injury. However, humans have developed social responses to dealing with disease and injury; on the individual level they express their experience as illness (being or feeling unwell), and socially an ill person is allowed to adopt and be accepted in a 'sickness role'(Skoyles 2005, Sturmberg 2007).

Healthcare emerged in hunter and gatherer societies who started to look after their sick and weak group members as this proved to enhance the survival chances of the whole group. Over time the role of caring for a sick or weak group member was ascribed to one person – the birth of the first medical professional – the shaman or medicine man (Sturmberg 2007).

Disease and injury are biological phenomena; illness, sickness and healthcare are social phenomena (Skoyles 2005, Sturmberg 2007). Disease and illness transcend the individual in a socially interconnected world, hence disease and illness and the resulting responses can only be fully appreciated by patients, doctors, policy makers and researchers if viewed as the result of interdependent interactions in broad networks.

Networks function as complex adaptive systems. In brief, complex adaptive systems consist of a large number of components that interact in non-linear ways through many feedback loops. Such systems are open, they interact with their environment. The characteristic of a system is determined by the patterns of its interactions which cannot be reduced to the behavior of its specific components – systems are 'emergent' (Cilliers 1998).

THE DIFFERENT 'NATURES' OF HEALTHCARE

Throughout the ages medicine has always been a collaborative problem solving effort between an individual patient and health professional. However, with time and globalization there have been major changes. The 'localized expert', and thus opinion driven, physician approach to clinical decision-making (as a first step to medical problem solving) has emerged to a 'global expert', collaborative evidence based approach that uses aggregated information as the basis to individual patient care (Biswas 2007 b).

Much of this aggregated information is now available on the Internet allowing patients and health professionals to learn about diseases and their current treatment approaches. (Murray 2003, Larner 2006, Tan 2006, Giustini 2006). Increasingly this mode of information sharing drives the individual consultation, our understanding of acceptable practice and health service planning.

The impact of this information sharing ability can be viewed as 'User driven healthcare'. We previously defined user driven healthcare as a process leading to improved healthcare achieved with concerted collaborative learning between multiple users and stakeholders, primarily patients, health professionals and other actors in the care giving collaborative network across a Web interface." (Biswas 2007a).

Currently the consumer driven healthcare approach is most prevalent. Consumer driven healthcare is essentially a strategy for users (consumers) to decide how they may pay for their own healthcare through multiple stakeholders like employers who provide the money and insurance companies who receive the premiums (Tan 2005).

Patient-centered healthcare, in contrast, is an approach to patient care based on the following ideas: It "(a) explores the patients' main reason for the visit, concerns, and need for information; (b) seeks an integrated understanding of the patients' world - that is, their whole person, emotional needs, and life issues; (c) finds common ground on what the problem is and mutually agrees on management; (d) enhances prevention and health promotion; and (e) enhances the continuing relationship between the patient and the doctor."

And finally there is the concept of the 'expert patient', one who is confident and has the skills to improve quality of life in partnership with health professionals. In many ways this view reflects an understanding of health and illness as 'personal' and healing as 'sense-making exercise' of one's experiences (reflected in the somato-psycho-socio-semiotic notion of health) (Sturmberg 2007).

However research has shown that exploring the patient's understandings about their illness and its management are often ignored having negative consequences in terms of concordance with medications (Horne and Weinman 1999) or appreciating patients' capacity to deal with their multiple conditions (Shaw and Baker 2004, Martin 2003). Patients' expertise is valuable because by understanding the patient's views and situation, the doctor is better equipped to identify a solution that will lead to a successful outcome, however defined.

Health understood as a personal construct described as a balance within a somato-psycho-socio-semiotic framework will necessitate to extend the 'scientific' biomedical worldview with that of the 'naïve' patient's and 'common sense' practitioner's conceptions of this patient's illness (McWhinney 1996). In this chapter we argue that the approach of User Driven Healthcare – seen as a collaborative learning approach among patients, families, health professional caregivers and other actors across a Web interface – might well achieve a common understanding arising from multiple perspectives.

The Spectrum of Ontology

Here we allude to a fundamental philosophical question: "What exists?" or put differently "How do we conceive reality and the nature of being?" The traditional goal of ontological inquiry, in particular, is to divide the world "at its joints," to discover those fundamental categories or kinds that define the objects of the world (IDEF5 methods report 1994). What ontology has in common in both computer science and philosophy is the representation of entities, ideas, and events, along with their properties and relations and the rules that govern them, according to a system of categories ("Ontology-computer science", 2007). An often quoted definition of ontology in computer science is that it is an explicit specification of a conceptualization restricted to different domains

(Gruber 1993). This has been developed further such that for an information system, ontology is a representation of some pre-existing domain of reality which:

1. Reflects the properties of the objects within its domain in such a way that there obtains a systematic correlation between reality and the representation itself
2. Is intelligible to a domain expert
3. Is formalized in a way that allows it to support automatic information processing (Ontology works inc. 2007).

For example if one has to write an ontology of driving a car it would involve representation and retrieval of data specifying certain concepts related to controlling the wheel, clutch, brake as well as concepts of objects such as road on which the car needs to be driven and characters such as trees, other cars and people that need to be avoided. Needless to say the ontology program doesn't actually drive the car (which is more at a spinal level and more to do with robotics) but ontology merely serves to guide with appropriate information delivered in a need based manner (more at a cortical level to use an anatomical analogy).

In philosophy the ontologic domain is existence itself and for an individual sustaining that existence his/her personal ontology is his/her personal conceptualization (although rarely explicitly specified) of the roadmap he would need to drive himself through that existence and the objects s/he would meet on that road that s/he would need to know how to deal with. Social ontology comes close to this as much of an individual human's existence is social.

Health as a personal experience is an individual phenomenon – patients understand and experience their health in the context of their social networks. These networks simultaneously are made up by people and events; structurally they are interconnected and functionally interrelated – and as such interdependent (Bar-Yam 1997).

Over time individual patients therefore build their unique conceptual models of their health and illness in the context of their experiences and everyday social interactions. Equally health professionals develop their main constructs of health and disease from the collective interactions with their colleagues in medical institutions. Frequently these constructs are devoid of the 'white noise' generated by the personal realities of patients, caregivers and other professionals.

These personal individual views form the basis for the socio-cultural construct of health, illness and disease, and the culture of the healthcare system – these understandings are learnt, internalized and enacted. As Berger and Luckmann (1966) point out persons and groups interacting together in a social system, form over time, concepts or mental representations of each other's actions, and these concepts eventually become habituated into reciprocal roles played by the actors in relation to each other. According to Akgün et al. (Akgün et al 2003), the socio-cognitive view of learning can be conceptualized as a higher-order construct (process), construed of cognitive processes and social constructs which are (1) distributed through the social network, (2) unfold overtime, (3) involve people in diverse functions and mind-sets, and (4) are embedded in routines and institutional structures by means of social culture.

Social Cognitive Ontological Constructs and Generation of Emotion

Most humans utilize their individually acquired SCOCs as a result of their learning behavior in relating to the world around them. Our individual social cognitive ontological constructs can make us attract, repel, laugh, cry and go through all the possible human emotions particularly when they overlap acutely with cognitive social ontological constructs of other humans that although may have certain similar attributes, objects and relations in one plane also tend to have very different attributes, objects and relations on another. Commonly emotions of grief or relief are also generated when an individual acutely disconnects or reconnects with whom s/he has been sharing cognitive social ontological constructs. Also in the same individual when there is an acute shift in attributes contained within his/her own social cognitive ontological constructs, it may lead to a sudden outburst of humor, grief depending on the social context. A sudden coming together of two humans of opposite sex or containing SCOCs with different physical attributes generate sexual passion or infatuation depending on which physical attributes share focus, although in such instances the interaction may be tacit as well as cognitive.

All this may have been expressed in a simpler manner by just stating that human emotions are generated in different states of being (philosophically ontology maybe simply expressed as a theory of being). However the above detailing was necessary as it will help us to appreciate how it maybe possible to create human emotions in artificially intelligent computer programs by simply figuring out a way to run two different computer programs containing two different social cognitive ontological constructs (written in code) in a manner that creates an acute friction or overlap between the two, such that the rules contained within them are fractured. This may more likely simulate human-to-human natural social interactions although at present Computer human interaction (CHI) programs currently interpret human emotions mainly by recognizing human emotional states that an individual expresses through its facial musculature or other expressive gestures including physiological variables (Frijda 1986, Juan 2005, Nkambou 2006, Neiji 2007). This may at best be classified as imitation rather than artificial creation of human emotion. Such imitative emotion generation is usually seen in the human system in its infancy although tacit sharing of emotions without cognitive interactions is also a known pleasurable adult activity as outlined previously.

Intuition by definition is a cognitive short cut that cannot be delineated, least in terms of logic. It however doesn't rule out the fact that logical pathways may exist within them. Human to human interaction depends on handling of emotions intuitively such that supposed emotional areas in human brain have been termed the affective domain conveniently separated from its supposed cognitive domain that uses logical thinking. However emotions may just be a product of logically sequenced attributes in an individual cognitive ontology generated due to an acute overlap of divergent ontologies resulting in fractures in rules contained within individual ontologies (at least as far as human-to-human social interaction is concerned).

In effect then our affect may be nothing but cognitive states arising out of acute changes in our social cognitive ontological constructs (SCOCs). Just try thinking of it when you follow/look up any joke etc that makes you laugh (in which case our own SCOCs are tolerant to the challenge in the form of rule breaks the acutely overlapping other divergent SCOC poses) or even angry (wherein our individual SCOCs do not tolerate the rule breakages in the divergent SCOCs).

Affect is a product of social cognition and affection is a behavior of social animals (ranging from humans, dogs, tigers and apes) even shared between different species (for example humans and dogs). An individual without affect (as in a variety of schizophrenia) may appear all alone, in this wide world.

There may be divergent SCOCs in the same human brain and from time to time such humans may generate emotions like joy, sadness etc, states that may be classified as psychotic when observed happening in humans in isolation, without appropriate social stimuli.

All this discussion was necessary to understand that ontology in information science may help to discover ways to logically deal with emotions. Negative emotions may perhaps be curbed by inserting the informational strands that are missing in an individual social cognitive ontological construct acutely compromised by a sudden realization of having run over or banged onto another individual social cognitive ontological construct with different informational attributes.

Only when informational attributes in clashing SCOCs are balanced, emotional information needs may be fulfilled. Also emotional events may signal acute conformational changes in our individual SCOCs essential to learning. The presence of affect is strongest during childhood and gradually diminishes with age which possibly correlates with and is directly proportional to learning activity.

The Emotional Need to Know

To understand one's health is based on having the right information and knowledge. Information and knowledge requirements exceed the biomedical domain and include social and emotional components. The latter "information need" however is particularly poorly explored in the consultation despite it well being the most important need, and the biggest stumbling block when a technical solution needs to be implemented (Smith 1996).

The need to know is emotionally driven, however, in the clinical encounter the role of the emotional need to know is often missed. Emotions are not merely feelings, they are cognitive, and reveal important information about values and beliefs, some of which may well be false or unreasonable, and thus need clarification. Understanding and clarifying the emotions encountered in the consultation is equally important for patients and health professionals (Robichaud 2003).

Uncertainty in Clinical Practice

Many clinical situations occur in the realm of uncertainty (Petros 2003), and both individual patients and health professionals try to seek clarity through more information. However much of the available information is limited and/or difficult to apply to the individual patient (Feinstein and Horwitz 1997).

A gap between the paucity of what is proved to be effective for selected groups of patients versus the infinitely complex clinical decisions required for individual patients has been recently recognized and termed the inferential gap (Stewart et al 2007). The breadth of the inferential gap varies according to available knowledge, its relevance to clinical decisions, access to the knowledge (that is, what the physician actually knows at the time of a clinical decision), the variable ways in which knowledge is interpreted and translated into a decision, the patient's needs and preferences, and a host of other factors. Clinicians are required to fill in where their knowledge (or knowledge itself) falls short (Stewart et al 2007).

An alternative to the currently dominant empirical evidence based approach in medicine has been proposed that has generated considerable discussion (Tonelli 2006). This alternative centers on the case at hand and recognizes the value of considering multiple dimensions, topics and ontologies (SCOCs) in the clinical encounter to aid medical reasoning.

The five dimensions/topics identified by Tonelli (and its representative ontologies) for sense making of a clinical encounter to optimize medical decision-making are in Table 1.

In summary, medical practice is confronted with patients seeking explanations for their suffering in a complex environment consistent in some parts of well proven biomedical but otherwise largely limited knowledge, and multiple understandings of health, illness and disease arising from diverse individual and societal realities. Healing becomes a collaborative effort driven by 'the need to know' – 'to know' being understood in the personal sense (Polanyi 1958) of 'I know'.

THE CLINICAL ENCOUNTER AS A SHARED LEARNING EXPERIENCE

It can be argued that in a collaborative learning environment there are no teachers and learners

Table 1.

The five dimensions/topics identified by Tonelli (and its representative ontologies) for sense making of a clinical encounter to optimize medical decision-making are:
• **Empirical evidence:** derived from clinical research. (biomedical ontology) • **Experiential evidence:** derived from personal clinical experience or the clinical experience of others. (individual ontology) • **Patho-physiologic rationale:** based on underlying theories of physiology, disease and healing. (biomedical ontology) • **Patient values and preferences:** derived from personal interaction with individual patients. (Individual ontology) • **System features:** including resource availability, societal and professional values, legal and cultural concerns. (administrative-bureaucratic and cultural ontologies)

– or in the health context doctors and patients – but rather people with different levels of knowledge and experience (Biswas 2007a).

Such a view overcomes the more traditional structures of learning characterized by a top-down approach where learners are simply expected to learn and memorize the structure of their chosen field and then apply it to patient care. However medical encounters require more than simply recalling memorized medical facts, and at any rate these facts are increasingly superseded by an ever faster growing volume of information.

The Traditional Approach to the Growth of Health Information

The response to the growth of health information has been an ant like division of labor where healthcare workers specialize in certain areas so that they can focus on a smaller volume/area of accumulated information and then offer their 'perceived greater knowledge' as experts in a limited field.

Interestingly there is not much historical evidence to suggest that this approach to information management is doing wonders to present day healthcare (Loeffler 2000). On the contrary today's patient satisfaction with healthcare seems to be at an all time low (Kenagy 2002).

This is especially true for patients with multiple chronic diseases who find it exceedingly difficult to find a health professional able to appropriately manage their particular set of individual problems.

The box offers some of the common narratives around the issues associated with the information explosion.

What we need is a large group of health professionals who are willing to learn more and more about more and more (instead of less and less), i.e. strengthening primary care and the 'all knowing' (though not all powerful) general/family physician. After all primary care physicians are the pillar of the whole healing process. Today the family physician increasingly will share his information and knowledge with a well-informed patient.

The Cycle of Habitualization and Institutionalization of Learning and Its Subsequent Disruption

"All human activity is subject to habitualization. Any action that is repeated frequently becomes cast into a pattern, which can then be reproduced with an economy of effort and which, ipso facto, is apprehended by its performer as that pattern. Habitualization further implies that the action in question may be performed again in the future in the same manner and with the same economical effort. Habitualization provides the direction and the specialization of activity that is lacking in man's biological equipment, thus relieving the accumulation of tensions that result from undirected drives.

Institutionalization occurs whenever there is a reciprocal typification of habitualized actions by types of actors. Put differently, any such typifica-

Table 2.

"Half of what you are taught as medical students will in ten years have been shown to be wrong. And the trouble is, none of your teachers know which half" Sydney Burwell, Dean, Harvard Medical School - 1956 *"Knowing more and more about less and less until one has known everything about nothing"* *"While the quality of the medical care my mother received was extraordinary, I saw firsthand how challenged the healthcare system was in supporting caregivers and communicating between different medical organizations. The system didn't fail completely, but struggled with these phases:* • *What was wrong: it took her doctors nine months to correctly identify an illness, which had classic symptoms* • *Who should treat her: there was no easy way to figure out who were the best local physicians and caregivers, which ones were covered by her* • *Insurance, and how we could get them to agree to treat her* • *Once she was treated, she had a chronic illness, and needed ongoing care and coordinated nursing and monitoring, particularly once her illness recurred.* (Bosworth 2006)

tion is an institution. The institution posits that actors of type X will perform actions of type X.

Institutions further imply historicity and control. Reciprocal typifications of actions are built up in the course of a shared history. They cannot be created instantaneously. Institutions also, by the very fact of their existence, control human conduct by setting up predefined patterns of conduct, which channel it in one direction as against the many other directions that would theoretically be possible." (Quoted from Berger & Luckman 1966).

At a social level, disruptive social forces and innovation challenge established institutional patterns from time to time (Christensen 1997).

De-Specialization as a Disruptive Innovation: Preparing Physicians for People-Centered Healthcare

The context of health professional education in the traditional tertiary hospital setting habituates and institutionalizes the role and the worldview of health professionals. Many health professionals around the world are now exposed to community based experiences providing a greater insight into the realities of people centered healthcare, or haven chosen to implement different approaches

based on the needs of their community. (detailed discussions about this can be found at The Network: Towards Unity for Health and WHO Western Pacific)

The following example describes one potential outcome of the de-specialization approach for a small rural Indian community:

... Physicians here are awe-inspiring. Every one here is in the process of 'de-specializing'. That does not mean that they are losing their skills as specialists. It means, they are learning the other specialties. ENT surgeon here is managing medicine OPD patients for 5 yrs and knows more about approach and management of general OPD issues than I do. A pediatric surgeon has become a general surgeon and has learnt anesthesiology and practices it when no volunteer anesthetist is available. A pediatrician is learning C-sections. Needless to say, they are all able obstetricians.

They all (7 physicians) started without any preconceived notions. Came to a rural setting and started learning how to become rural doctors. Many of my myths were shattered here in the first week itself..."Priyank Jain, Resident Medicine, Wisconsin, Milwaukee on a visit to a rural health set up run by a few committed physicians in Ganiari, Madhya Pradesh, India (personal communication)

Another example is the ECHO (Extension for Community Healthcare Outcomes) model that gives physicians who specialize in the treatment of complex and chronic conditions access to IT-technology, enabling them to share knowledge about best practice to co-manage patients with primary caregivers in rural communities.

The key component of the ECHO model is a disruptive innovation called a Knowledge Network. In a one-to-many knowledge network, the expertise of a single specialist shared with several primary healthcare providers, each of whom sees numerous patients. The flow of information in a Knowledge Network is NOT unidirectional; the specialist and community-based primary care providers gain invaluable feedback and case-based experience through weekly consultations (Arora 2007). Other workers have also created knowledge networks in recent times in rural India utilizing principles of collaborative learning among primary care workers (Ganapathy 2007).

These models sustain themselves through the continued input from all stakeholders, including that of patients (along with those of their relatives) as well as a variety of other health professionals who collaborate to meet the needs of the single patient. This approach transcends the centralized and paternalistic model of healthcare in favor of a truly collaborative one.

Collaborative Learning

In a collaborative learning environment two categories of learners meet. One is the patients, relatives and other primary care givers who have no formal training. The other is physicians, other health professionals and secondary care givers who have received formal training and are the source of care when self-care proves to be insufficient for restoring one's health.

Obviously patients and health professionals gain new information independently, and the collaborative learning effort takes part in the consultation. The learning experience however will transgress the consulting room due to the subsequent exchanges with colleagues, peers and friends.

The medical record on the one level represents a record of the learning in this consultation, yet we would suggest that learning could be progressed over time through a persistent shared electronic health record.

IMPLEMENTING USER DRIVEN HEALTHCARE

Answering multidimensional information needs (AMIN) through persistent clinical encounters (Biswas 2008a-text, tables and figures have been reused with permission)

The Technology

A Web-based solution to integrate healthcare E-learning needs could lie in a simple forum model already in use at present in various Web sites using what is loosely termed as Web 2.0 technology. In Web sites using this technology user-generated tags allow the site to evolve, enabling individual users to conduct more precise searches, make previously unacknowledged associations between facts, and explore a diverse undercurrent of themes to synthesize learning.

It has been recently named Health 2.0 with reference to healthcare and has been described to be all about Patient Empowered Healthcare whereby patients have the information they need to be able to make rational healthcare decisions (transparency of information) based on value.

As more information becomes available as a result of increased transparency, there will be a wave of innovation at all points along the

Figure 1.

full cycle of care (Fig 1), which includes phases where healthcare service providers Educate, Prevent, Diagnose, Prepare, Intervene, Recover, Monitor, and Manage the various disease states (Shreeve 2007).

The present version of Pub-Med, a popular evidence based resource (http://www.ncbi.nlm. nih.gov/sites/entrez) utilizing the Web 2.0 technology displays related publications as soon as a user clicks on to read an article abstract after entering his/her search terms. However this evidence-based resource is chiefly concerned with empirical collective experimental data and even the case reports available on the site do not offer the richness of the individual lived experience. These apart from the fact that most of the articles full text have restricted access.

Introducing and Sustaining an Experiential Network in Routine Clinical Practice

The Shared Learning Space

All humans have the capacity and likelihood of performing both roles of caregiver and care

seeker (patient) in their lifetimes. Each and every individual is an author of his own destiny (as well as his own Web log) that reflects his experiential life processes and decisions that can shape his future. User driven healthcare is an attempt to help make those decisions. It is a proposal to document valuable individual experiences of patients, physicians and medical students in a practicably feasible grassroots manner that has till date regularly gone undocumented and has been lost to the medical literature that may have actually benefited from it.

Regular experiential informational input by any individual in the role of caregiver or care seeker may be posted on to an individual user's password protected Web account that would function as an E-portfolio if s/he were posting as a caregiver and one to his/her private personal health record if s/he is posting as a patient. The individual user could do this through email (or other mechanisms utilizing a unified communication engine: fig 2). Once individual users key in their unique experiential information that could also reflect pathophysiologic rationale, patient values and preferences, system features including resource availability, societal and professional values they would be presented with related individual experiences mashed up with empirical data immediately at the click of a mouse. Later it would be up to the individual to derive meaning from these multiple dimensions of information. To date this experiential information may exist in difficult to search Web logs but most parts of our day-to-day innumerable clinical encounters remain undocumented. As a result the present day user gets far from optimal satisfaction with the information on the net.

Even if one could collate a larger variety of experiential information on the net, it would still be confined to PC literate individuals and to bridge the digital divide there have been recent attempts to develop a unified communication engine for data entry into the Web repository (Biswas 2008b-text, tables and figures have been reused with permission). An individual at his leisure or even while waiting in queue to meet his/her physician may SMS (short messaging service) their thoughts and

queries about their disease onto the forum that could be responded to by anyone on the Web.

Users could choose to use phone, mobile phone, PC/laptop or an embedded system to work with the Web portal (presently in pilot). (Fig 2)

From a community perspective to integrate all these individual experiential data a personal health record for each individual patient in the community needs to be generated again in a user driven manner beginning with the patient's version of their perceived illness with data added on by other actors in the care giving collaborative healthcare network as the patient traverses his/her way through various levels of care beginning from the community to the tertiary care hospital. The data contained within these records may then be effectively and anonymously shared between different patients and health professionals who key in their own experiential information and find matching individual experiential information through text tagging in a Web 2.0 platform.

Figure 2.

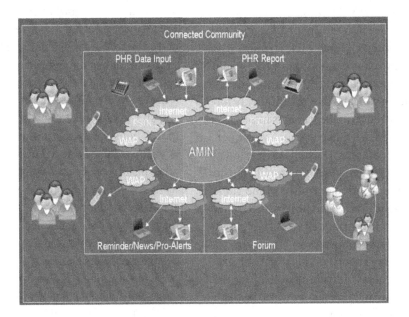

A Dynamic PHR (Personal Health Record) to Answer Multidimensional Information Needs in a Persistent Clinical Encounter (Biswas 2008b)

Analyzing the Personal Health Record (PHR)

The PHR needs to begin with the patient as the vital source of information. Even in present day face to face clinical encounters with the history being recorded by the physician no clinical data entry would have been possible without the patient narrating his/her illness details.

In the sample PHR the individual patient who is the owner of the PHR, is shown to have over a time frame entered her data in her own narrative (Table 3 middle column).

Other than the patient's contribution the data is further processed at multiple levels by different care givers (whoever the patient allows access to his/her data). The physician care giver is by training adept at structuring these narrative data into a compressed front page summary that can be quickly shared between physicians and consequently this comes into the opening page of the PHR as in the sample (Table 3 left column)

Most caregivers accessing this PHR would have a brief structured overview of the patient's problem to begin with and they could quickly follow it up with a glance at the patient's minimally structured thought narrative to gain a wider perspective by simply clicking on the links (generated through text tagging) on this structured page to the minimally structured narrative of the same patient that would be in a separate page or of other patients with related narratives again in separate pages (Table 3 right column).

Relating to different individual patient narratives could generate learning not only for the individual who maintains and browses through his own PHR but also for the other patients who share tagged key words related to their own illnesses in their own PHRs.

In the above example of a dynamic PHR we can further add links to the notes of various other actors in the care giving collaborative network like physicians, nurses, pharmacists and medical administrators all of which would reflect the patient's journey as a persistent clinical encounter through the various processes of healthcare and suffering within an interconnected social framework (Figure 3).

Future Directions: Evolution of Medical Knowledge in Developing Community Ontology

Self-organization is the property of well functioning complex adaptive systems that allows the natural relationships among individuals and groups to shape the nature of an evolving knowledge base (Martin 2007 b).

The organizational complexity of an individual's interactions with his environment defines the level of his functionality. The more the connections an individual is able to develop and more the complexity of his network the more it may reflect his/her vitality (Biswas 2003). This is even witnessed at a micro level inside the human body where there is a demonstrable withering of neuronal connections and complexity with senescense and a resultant loss of neuronal functionality reflected in overall loss of functionality of aging (Lipsitz 1992). Quite a few studies demonstrate the relationship between intimacy and health, and how disease survivors who report positive family relationships or access to support groups consistently live longer than those without them. The challenge for us ahead is coupling our traditional focus on monitoring efficiencies with providing deeper human connections to promote sustainable behavior change (Darsee 2007).

A few physician led companies have already made considerable headway in this direction. SERMO is a Web based US company that uses a forum model to develop experiential knowledge networks among US physicians while 'Patient

Table 3. A sample PHR (personal health record)

First Page: *Structured PHR-individual patient data (centralized SCOCs) with links to further EBM or narrative data*	Linked pages: *Semi structured-individual patient SCOCs)*	Linked pages: *Semi structured-* *Other patient data (other person SCOCs)*
Name: Anonymous **IC Number:** x123 **Contact:** 123 **Diagnosis with duration:** Diabetes 20 years, Hypertension 3 years, Hyperlipidemia 3 years *(Click on: link to patient's own semi structured data)* **Present diabetes status:** Last HbA1C 1month back was 7% *(click on: link to relevant evidence based information on HbA1c)* *Mean BP (measured 1-week back 110/70— a mean of 10 readings in a day (once in a week) measured with an electronic device* (click on: link to relevant evidence based information on Hypertension in diabetes, role of home BP monitoring etc) **Complications:** *Treatment related:* Recurrent hypoglycemias…last episode 6 months back *(click on: link to patient's own semi structured data with relevance to her episodes of hypoglycemias)* *Target organ related:* Microvascular: Kidney (glomerular vessels): Annual test of urine measurement of the albumin-to-creatinine ratio in a random spot collection (preferred method)- normal values *(Click on: link to relevant evidence based information on renal Impairment in diabetes)* Annual test of Serum creatinine for the estimation of glomerular filtration rate (GFR)-normal *(Click on: link to relevant semi structured narratives of other patients with diabetes and chronic renal failure)*	Individual patient's self- profile (Behavioral diabetes institute 2006) *Profile at the time of diagnosis* I was a relatively happy 24-year-old working and eating whatever I wanted, whenever I wanted. My favorite breakfast was sugary cereal, but other than that, I didn't eat a lot of sweets. I typically ate 2 to 3 meals per day, always at different times. *(Link to other patient's semi structured data on dietary changes)* Here is some of what I remember of my first 6 months of having diabetes. **Other people's comments:** My friend D who worked for the local Blue Cross: "Hey good news, Blue Cross now covers kidney transplants for diabetics." (I didn't even know kidney problems were something to worry about.) My friend J - "Be careful of your feet. My uncle just had his leg amputated." *On testing blood sugar* Initially, I found it interesting. But keeping track of results soon became a pain. Plus, my life did not fit the schedule the little logbooks had preprinted. Who eats dinner at the same time every night? What about weekends? **On taking insulin** They showed me how to take injections using an orange as a example. I can't imagine anything less similar to one's leg or stomach than an orange. I don't know if they still do this. *(Link to other patient's semi structured data on taking insulin)* **On my first insulin reaction** I was in the hospital, and the nurse's aide didn't know what was happening. Neither did I, when I ended up starting to pass out, she decided to call in the reinforcements. Over the course of 20 years, I have been taken to the Emergency about 8 times unconscious due to insulin reactions. About 4 of those times were when I was pregnant. The following chronicles my first 20 years with Diabetes.	(http://www.diabetes-stories.co.uk/ research-transcript.asp) **Introductory:** (Greenberg R 2007) In many ways diabetes keeps me far healthier than I would be otherwise. It has improved my diet and weight over the years and some would say my daily walking reflects a woman possessed. Also, getting married for the first time at 48, my motivation to hang around for the long haul – and in good shape – surged…more…(link) http://www.diabetesstories.com/) **Dietary changes:** My diet has changed a lot. The biggest change came to me a few years ago. My next door neighbour's son-in-law had a job where he ended up with a lot of spare fruit and vegetables on a Sunday, and she used to give me this enormous bag and I used to have to try and use it all in the week. And I've really got into fresh fruit and vegetables now, and I really feel a lot better for it…more…(link) http://www.diabetes-stories.co.uk/ research-transcript.asp) **On taking insulin** I think the thought of it was more daunting than the actual injection. The injection, as I've told many people, it doesn't… there's nothing to fear or hurt or anything. It just… well, there is no pain at all, you know. It's in a pen, and you switch up the counts - the amount that you're going to have, the units you're going to have - and then just inject it in, and it's so simple, it's… I mean, I can't see now, so I just... I am lucky that I can hear still and that I can feel the clicks - you can hear the clicks going round on the pen - so each click it counts as a unit. So, you know how many units you're taking, and that's it, you know, it's so simple…more (link)

continued on following page

Table 3. continued

First Page: *Structured PHR-individual patient data (centralized SCOCs) with links to further EBM or narrative data*	Linked pages: *Semi structured-individual patient SCOCs)*	Linked pages: *Semi structured-* *Other patient data (other person SCOCs)*
Retinal vesssels: Annual retinal examination-normal *(Click on: link to relevant semi structured narratives of other patients with diabetes and blindness)* Peripheral nerve function: Annual tests such as pinprick sensation, temperature and vibration perception (using a 128-Hz tuning fork), and 10-g monofilament pressure sensation at the distal plantar aspect of both great toes and ankle reflexes-normal *(Click on: link to relevant semi structured narratives of other patients with diabetes and peripheral neuropathy)* Macrovascular: Coronary vessels: Annual EKG, CXR, Echo—Normal/unchanged Cerebral vessels: No history of TIA or stroke Peripheral limb vesels: No history of claudication pain, peripheral pulses-normal Other organs: Eye: Cataract, glaucoma-annual screening-normal Foot: Assessment of protective sensation, foot structure and biomechanics, vascular status, and skin integrity. Intercurrent illness: Nil **Other risk factor screening for atherosclerosis:** 3 monthly lipid profile: LDL <100 mg/dl (2.6 mmol/l), triglycerides <150 mg/dl (1.7 mmol/l, HDL cholesterol >40 mg/dl (on statins) Smoking-nil Other medications-Aspirin (75mg) and Enalapril (10mg) Present Diet: 50% of each meal plate filled with vegetables and fruits, 25% with cereals and 25% with animal protein *(Link to structured EB data on diabetic diet and semi structured other's experiences in managing their diet)* Exercise: One hour of regular brisk walking Mental health: Psychiatrist notes: *(Links to patient's own semi structured narratives and other patient's psychological reflections)*	**After 1 year - 1986** Somewhere I got the idea that I should have a baby sooner than later, before I had diabetes for too long, so I got pregnant. That didn't give me much chance to get used to the disease, or to learn ahead of time about the impact of pregnancy on Diabetes. What I learned once I found out I was pregnant is that they don't go well together. Then there was the problem I read that babies could die in the last week or two of pregnancy. They also talked about babies being born extremely large. Before I had much chance to worry about that, I started having all sorts of highs and lows and overall the pregnancy was pretty difficult, and included some very bad hypoglycemic reactions that required hospitalization. **After 3 1/2 years - 1989** As time went on, the novelty of the disease wore off and resentment took over. I began to hate the fact that diabetes affected every part of my life and got in the way of doing things I loved. I had to consider it when deciding what to eat, when to eat, what to drink or not drink. I felt guilty every minute of every day, because I felt I was always doing things that were wrong for my diabetes. Eventually, I became so overwhelmed that I kind of barreled into a depression. My marriage broke up. **After 6 years - 1991** I was left with the depression brought on by the diabetes and probably from a life of partying too. Thankfully, I found a therapist who helped me, and introduced me to another patient of hers who is also diabetic. This person was much more accepting and we became good friends for several years. This therapist was the one who helped me put into words how angry I was about being diabetic and how I resented how much it limited me.	**Living with diabetes and blindness** Well, I did lose my sight, of course, other than... that was the only other really downfall with diabetes. I tend to sort of forget about it now, because when you're in your own surroundings, you think you can see... It's just when you go to other places that you haven't been before, you think "oh gosh, where's everything? You tend to sort of live with it, you know... Eventually a social worker came to see me, and she pointed all the different things out that I could have to help me with my blindness. And that was little buttons, proud buttons on the washing machine, that I can still feel free that I can use my washing machine without any help, other than these buttons. She also gave me magnifying glasses, which I could not do without. I have to magnify everything to read, because I can't read any print whatsoever... more...(link)... **Living with Diabetes and renal failure** I was asked by the doctors if I wanted to go on CAPD or - I don't know what they call it - on the machines actually in the hospital, which I'd already had three goes of - four hourly treatments. So, they came along, explained all the CAPD to me, which, at first, I was really very nervous about, because you have to have a tube put into your stomach, which you carry around all the time - you have it taped to your body. And then you have two bags: one which is an outlet, and one which you have to hang up and then drain all that into your stomach, and it's two litre bags. And what I didn't know, to start with, was - I thought it was going to be so easy - "right, we'll just have a bag up, and a bag on the floor, and take it through, and that'll be it". But, as it turned out to be, it's four times a day. Every single day you have to do this, which puts you in, you know - I've got to be there at a certain time; I've got to be there all the time; I'm not going to have time to go out; I'm not going to have time to do anything. But it hasn't proved quite that bad.

continued on following page

Table 3. continued

First Page: *Structured PHR-individual patient data (centralized SCOCs) with links to further EBM or narrative data*	Linked pages: *Semi structured-individual patient SCOCs)*	Linked pages: *Semi structured-* *Other patient data (other person SCOCs)*
Link to scanned paper documents (Investigation results, Digitally converted radiological images and histopathology slides and operative images etc)	**After 7 years - 1993** Technology was helping treatment of diabetes grow by leaps and bounds, testing was so much easier, and each day machines came out that tested in less than a minute and did not require wiping the strip. It was around this time that my doctor put me on Lente Human Insulin once per day and Regular Human insulin for meals. I learned to count carbohydrates and embraced the freedom this gave me. My lunchtime lows all but disappeared, and the biggest problem I had was accurately matching my mealtime doses to the carbohydrates I was eating. Even with those frustrations, my mental health improved. I was thrilled to be able to have an extra cracker or two, or dessert, if I felt like it and not feel guilty, but instead just take a bit more insulin. I loved that I had some choice in my life again. **Years 10, 11 and 12 - 1995 through 1997** I continued to read everything I could about diabetes and various treatments I also got married again in 1996 to a wonderful guy who really took an interest in my diabetes and helped me manage it. He witnessed a couple of bad lows, which was pretty scary for him, and caused him to watch carefully over me, nagging me to test etc. **2003-2006** It was in 2003 my blood pressure started to get dangerously high, and I was put on blood pressure medicine. My cholesterol numbers also went up, and I was prescribed medicine, but convinced my doctor to let me try to control it with diet and exercise. **Where I am now** At my most recent doctor's appointment, my blood pressure was 110/70 with no medication. My bad cholesterol numbers are low, and my good cholesterol numbers are high. My doctor is amazed.	**Living with Diabetes and Depression** My time for depression is when I'm on my own at nighttime. I pretend a lot, because I feel I have to, because sometimes, if I went around feeling, or acting the way I feel sometimes, everybody would disown me; nobody would talk to me. My husband would leave me - I'm surprised he hasn't, really, but! So, you push yourself forward. It's very hard to do sometimes, but then you get in your bedroom at night, and...more...(link)...

opinion' is a UK based setup that aims to access the collective wisdom of patients using Web 2.0 tools where patients can share their stories and rate the care they receive down to ward and department level. This patient opinion aspect of user driven healthcare is about conversations, democracy and improving services by making the individual voice more audible. Curbside.MD is another US based company that goes one step beyond Pub-Med in data mining and presentation by utilizing Semantic fingerprinting to let users key in natural language queries in their search engine, which returns a variety of useful empirical evidence arranged as, all research, systematic

Figure 3. Developing a community medical ontology toward a persistent clinical encounter

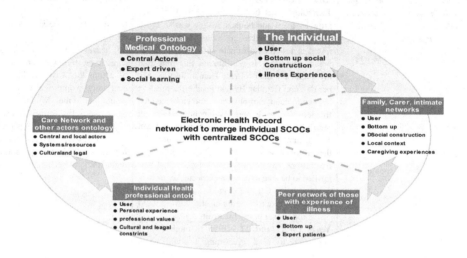

reviews, guidelines, review articles, images etc. It also has begun fingerprinting of individual health profiles and matching similar profiles.

At the present moment user driven healthcare is heavily dependent on human to human interactions augmented by computers but gradually the role of human moderators in this scheme could be taken over by artificial agents that may be able to emote adequately with social cognitive ontological constructs to match their human counterparts. Promising use case studies from W3C computer human interaction researchers are a pointer to this end (W3C Emotion Incubator Group 2007).

CONCLUSION

User driven healthcare is improved healthcare achieved with concerted, collaborative learning between multiple users and stakeholders, primarily patients, health professionals and other actors

in the care giving collaborative network across a Web interface. At an individual level, every human forms his or her own personal cognitive conceptual and operational models as a part of her/his social cognitive interactions labeled social cognitive ontological constructs (SCOCs). Other than this, individuals also form similar conceptual constructs from collective social learning handed down from a collective to individual level in a top down manner. Present learning strategies in healthcare are mostly dependant on top down structured content and non-structured bottom up patient physician experiences are paid less importance.

This chapter discusses the need to merge dominant centralized health professional expert generated medical ontology with decentralized, naïve patient user generated common sense medical ontology in a manner that generates minimum conflict and negative emotions. This may be attained by sharing individual human experiences in healthcare through matching persistent clinical encounters stored in Electronic health records (EHRs). These individual healthcare seeking and care giving experiences may reflect different levels of granularity or leaves budding with time in a larger tree of medical ontology. Regular recording of day to day individual patient physician non-linearly structured experiential data and its meaningful sharing through text tagging by a variety of individuals may be a valuable adjunct to structured average patient data that presently exists in our information bases to promote patient physician E-learning in healthcare. User driven healthcare applying multidimensional approaches of persistent clinical encounters and wisdom of crowds (see glossary) has the potential to be transformational in challenging the complex, high cost, institutional approach that typifies healthcare delivery systems today. Relaxing central control makes local health workers feel more engaged in their projects (Kmietowicz 2007). While dominant players are focused on preserving business models of expensive care and technology arsenals, user driven innovations promise cheaper and simpler access to virtual clinical encounters thus meeting learning needs of the vast majority of patients who may otherwise suffer simply due to lack of information.

REFERENCES

Akgu¨n, A. E., Lynn, G. S., & Byrne, J. (2003). Organizational learning: A socio-cognitive framework. *Human Relations, 56*(7), 839– 868.

Arora, S., Geppert, C. M., Kalishman, S. et al. (2007) Academic health center management of chronic diseases through knowledge networks: Project ECHO. *Acad Med., 82*(2), 154-60

Bar-Yam, Y. (1997). *Dynamics of Complex Systems*. Addison-Wesley.

Behavioral Diabetes Institute (2006). *How medium is a medium apple*. Web page http://www.behavioraldiabetes.org/stories.html. Last accessed September 16th 2007

Biswas, R. (2003). Patient networks and their level of complexity as an outcome measure in clinical intervention. BMJ rapid response to Edwards N, Clinical networks. *British Medical Journal 2002, 324*(63).

Biswas R. (2007a). *User driven healthcare model to answer present day patient physician needs.* Paper presented at the meeting of the IEEEP2407 working group, London, UK.

Biswas, R., Umakanth, S., Strumberg, J., Martin, C. M., Hande, M. & Nagra, J. S. (2007b). The process of evidence-based medicine and the search for meaning. *Journal of Evaluation in Clinical Practice, 13*, 529–532.

Biswas, R., Martin, C., Sturmberg, J., Shankar, R., Umakanth, S., Shanker, S. et al, (2008a). User driven healthcare-Answering multidimensional information needs in individual patients utilizing post EBM approaches: A conceptual model. Journal Eval Clin Pract, *14*, 742-749.

Biswas, R., Maniam, J., Lee, E. W. H., Das, P. G., Umakanth, S., Dahiya, S. et al (2008b press). User driven healthcare- Answering multidimensional information needs in individual patients utilizing post EBM approaches: An operational model. J Eval Clin Pract., *14*, 750-760.

Bosworth, A. (2006). *Healthcare information matters.* (Web page: last downloaded:August 25th) http://googleblog.blogspot.com/2006/11/health-care-information-matters.html

Berger, P. L., & Luckmann, T. (1966). *The Social Construction of Reality: A Treatise in the Sociology of Knowledge*. Garden City, NY: Anchor Books.

Christakis, N. A. (2004). Social networks and collateral health effects. *BMJ, 329*(7459), 184-5.

Christensen, C. M. (1997). *The Innovator's Dilemma*. Harvard Business School Press. ISBN 0-87584-585-1.

Christensen, C. M., Baumann, H., Ruggles, R., & Sadtler, T. M. (2006). Disruptive Innovation for Social Change. *Harvard Business Review*.

Cilliers, P. (1998). *Complexity and Postmodernism. Understanding Complex Systems*. London: Routledge.

Dewey, J. (1938). *Experience and education*. New York: Macmillan.

Feinstein, A., & Horwitz, R. (1997). Problems in the "Evidence" of "Evidence-based Medicine". *American Journal of Medicine 1997, 103*(6), 529-535.

Frijda, N. H. (1986). *The emotions*. Cambridge: Cambridge University Press.

Giustini, D. (2006). How Web 2.0 is changing medicine. *British Medical Journal 2006, 333*, 1283-4

Greenberg, R. (2007). *Diabetes Stories Website* http://www.diabetesstories.com/. Last accessed September 16th 2007

Gruber, T. R. (1993). A Translation Approach to Portable Ontology Specifications. *Knowledge Acquisition, 5*(2), 199-220.

Henderson, J. V. (1998). Comprehensive, Technology-Based Clinical Education: The "Virtual Practicum". *International Journal of Psychiatry in Medicine, 28*(1), 41-79.

Horne, R., & Weinman, J. (1999). Patients' beliefs about prescribed medicines and their role in adherence to treatment in chronic illness. *J Psychosom Res 1999, 47* 555-67.

IDEF5 method report (1994). Retrieved oct 7th 2007 from http://www.idef.com/pdf/Idef5.pdf

Kenagy, J. W., & Christensen, C. M. (2002). *Disruptive Innovation – New Diagnosis and Treatment for the Systemic Maladies of Healthcare, Business briefing: global healthcare*

Larner, A. J. (2006). Searching the internet for medical information: frequency over time and by age and gender in an outpatient population in the UK. *J Telemed Telecare 2006, 12* 186-8.

Loefler, I. J. (2000). Are generalists still needed in a specialized world? The renaissance of general surgery. *BMJ, 320*(7232), 436-40. Review.

Martin, C. (2003). Chronic illness care in General Practice – the practitioner-patient relationship. In C. Walker, C. Peterson, N. Milman, & C. Martin (Eds.), *Chronic Disease: New Perspectives and New Directions*. Melbourne: Tertiary Press.

Martinez-Miranda, J., & Arantza, A. (2005). Emotions in human and artificial intelligence. *In Journal Computers in Human Behaviour, 21*, 323–341.

McWhinney, I. R. (1996). The Importance of being Different. William Pickles Lecture 1996. *British Journal of General Practice, 46*(7), 433-436

Murray, E., Lo, B., Pollack, L., Donelan, K., Catania, J., White, M. et al. (2003). The impact of health information on the internet on the physician-patient relationship: patient perceptions. *Arch Intern Med., 163*, 1727-34.

Neji, M., & Ben Ammar, M. (2007). Agent-based Collaborative Affective e-Learning Framework. *The Electronic Journal of e Learning, 5*(2), 123-134.

Nkambou, R. (2006). Towards Affective Intelligent Tutoring System. Workshop on Motivational and Affective Issues in ITS. 8th International Conference on ITS 2006, (pp 5-12).

Ontology-computer science. (2007, Aug 12) In Wikipedia. Retrieved oct 7th 2007 from http://en.wikipedia.org/wiki/Ontology_%28computer_science%29

Ontology works, inc. What is Ontology? (2008). http://www.ontologyworks.com/what_is_ontology.php

Petros, P. (2003). Non-linearity in clinical practice. *Journal of Evaluation in Clinical Practice, 9*(2),171-178.

Piaget, J. (1977). *The development of thought: Equilibrium of cognitive structures.* New York: Viking.

Polanyi M. (1958). *Personal Knowledge. Towards a Post-Critical Philosophy.* London: Routledge.

Robichaud, A. L. (2003). Healing and Feeling: The Clinical Ontology of Emotion. *Bioethics, 17*(1), 59-68.

Shaw, J., & Baker, M. (2004). Expert patient"--dream or nightmare?' *BMJ, 328*(7442), 723-724.

Skoyles, J. R. (2007). Here's what I believe but cannot prove. "The Edge" Retrieved oct 7th 2007 from http://www.edge.org/q2005/q05_6.html#skoyles

Smith R (1996). What clinical information do doctors' need? BMJ 313:1062-1068

Smith B, Kusnierczyk W, Schober D, Ceusters W. Towards a Reference Terminology for Ontology Research and Development in the Biomedical Domain, Proceedings of KR-MED 2006

Stewart, M. 2001 'Towards a global definition of patient centred care', BMJ 322(7284): 444-5.

Stewart WF, Shah NR, Selna MJ, Paulus RA and Walker JM. Bridging the Inferential Gap: The Electronic Health Record and Clinical Evidence. Health Affairs 2007;26(2):w181-w191

Sturmberg JP. The Foundations of Primary Care. Daring to be Different. Oxford San Francisco: Radcliffe Medical Press 2007

Tan J, Ed. (2005). E-healthcare information systems, Jossey-Bass: Wiley Imprint

Tang H, Ng JHK. (2006) Googling for a diagnosis—use of Google as a diagnostic aid: internet based study *BMJ* 2006;333:1143-5.

The Social Construction of Reality. (2007, July 26) In Wikipedia, Retrieved Oct 16th 2007, from http://en.wikipedia.org/wiki/The_Social_Construction_of_Reality

Uschold M,(2005)An ontology research pipeline. Applied Ontology 1 (2005) 13–16 13. IOS Press

W3C Emotion Incubator Group, (2007) W3C Incubator Group Report 10 July 2007, Internet document retrieved on 7th November, 2007 from http://www.w3.org/2005/Incubator/emotion/XGR-emotion-20070710

Chapter VII
Social Identities, Group Formation, and the Analysis of Online Communities

Jillianne R. Code
Simon Fraser University, Canada

Nicholas E. Zaparyniuk
Simon Fraser University, Canada

ABSTRACT

Central to research in social psychology is the means in which communities form, attract new members, and develop over time. Research has found that the relative anonymity of Internet communication encourages self-expression and facilitates the formation of relationships based on shared values and beliefs. Self-expression in online social networks enables identity experimentation and development. As identities are fluid, situationally contingent, and are the perpetual subject and object of negotiation within the individual, the presented and perceived identity of the individual may not match reality. In this chapter, the authors consider the psychological challenges unique to understanding the dynamics of social identity formation and strategic interaction in online social networks. The psychological development of social identities in online social network interaction is discussed, highlighting how collective identity and self-categorization associates social identity to online group formation. The overall aim of this chapter is to explore how social identity affects the formation and development of online communities, how to analyze the development of these communities, and the implications such social networks have within education.

INTRODUCTION

Central to research in social psychology is the means in which communities form, attract new members, and develop over time. The mechanisms in which communities grow depend on an individual's ability to find and collaborate with others with relevant knowledge, skills, and beliefs that meet a particular need. While these mechanisms of social collaboration are not unlike traditional face-to-face interactions (Tyler, 2002), there are some important differences in the way in which group members interact in online environments. Relative anonymity, selective self-disclosure, physical appearance, and the ease in finding 'familiar others' through search, embedded traits, and predefined groups, are some of the important differences between Internet communication and face-to-face interactions (Bargh & McKenna, 2004; McKenna, Green, & Gleason, 2002; Walther, 2007). Research into Internet social interaction has led to an increased understanding of face-to-face communications and brings into focus the implicit assumptions and biases that exist in traditional communication (Lea & Spears, 1995; Tyler, 2002). Assumptions that mediate face-to-face interactions such as physical proximity and non-verbal cues, assumed necessary to communicate and relate, do not exist in most Internet communications. However, given these limitations, online social communities continue to thrive and grow. The evolution of online communities confronts current views of how social and psychological dynamics contribute to human relationships, communication, and community formation.

Research supports the idea that the relative anonymity of Internet communication encourages self-expression and facilitates the formation of relationships outside of what is considered 'normal' socially mediated communication (Wallace, 1999). The complex origins of shared values and beliefs (Bargh & McKenna, 2004), self-expression through identity experimentation (Ruitenberg,

2003), and relative anonymous interaction (i.e. strangers on the train effect; Derlega & Chaikin, 1977; Rubin, 1975) challenge ideas of an 'individual' identity in relationship formation (Lea & Spears, 1995). As individual identities are malleable, adaptable, and the perpetual subject and object of negotiation within each context (Jenkins, 2004), the notion of identity requires an incessant comparison between the individual, the context in which they are interacting, their intentionality in the context of that interaction, and their 'true' (nominal) identity. The irregular nature in which individuals present arbitrary identities in various contexts, with multiple intentions, and within different social groups, results in a novel dynamic to human community formation and evolution.

In this chapter, we consider the psychological challenges unique to understanding the dynamics of social identity formation and strategic interaction in online social networks. We start with a brief overview of aspects within social psychology that are pertinent to a discussion on social identity formation in online social networks. Specifically, we introduce Social Identity Theory as a perspective in which to frame our current understanding of online social network formation. Next, the psychological development of *social (virtual) identities* (Jenkins, 2004) are explored in online social networks using the conceptualization of *self-presentation* (Goffman, 1959/1997). A discussion of collective identity and self-categorization follows and relates how social identity contributes to online group formation and evolution. Further, to illustrate how to evaluate the effectiveness of online social networks, we review several studies on online social networks using ethnographic methodologies, visualization techniques, and social network analysis (SNA). Finally, we present practical teaching and learning strategies educators can use to facilitate the use of social software for online social network formation within educational environments. The overall aim of this chapter is to explore how social identity affects the formation and development of online communities, to present some methodologies for evaluating the effectiveness of group formation, and to explore the implications of online social networks within education.

SOCIAL IDENTITY AND THE INTERNET

All human identities are social identities (Jenkins, 2004). Social identity concerns how we identify our similarities and differences to other known groups of individuals. Social identify is an ongoing interplay between how we identify ourselves and how others identify us. To identify with any given group of people, whether it is an ethnic group or an online organization, we look for similarities between the group members and ourselves. While similarities initially attract an individual to a group, this initial attraction enables an individual to recognize their individual differences. This comparative process is identified in Social Identity Theory as "*internal* and *external moments of dialectic identification*" (emphasis in original; Jenkins, 2000, p. 7). These internal comparisons are how individuals distinguish themselves from others in both the similarities they share and the differences they recognize. Alternatively, external comparisons involve how others identify individuals, in the similarities and differences they see between that individual, themselves, and a particular group. As internal and external comparisons determine the *active* and *socialized* aspects of a person, they enable the differentiation of the *I* and *me* which make up an integrated *Self* (James, 1891/1950). Given that social identification involves the interplay of internal and external dialectic processes, the Internet further enables individuals to develop and express multiple social identities and experiment with new virtual identities. As individuals' social identities evolve from within social groups, they

also facilitate the alignment or differentiation of an individual from the group. This alignment or differentiation reaffirms an individuals' social identity.

Social identity is a central construct in understanding intergroup relations and is a key element in linking an individual to his or her social group (Tajfel, 1974, 1981). According to Tajfel (Tajfel, 1974, 1981), the foundation of the Social Identity Theory of group membership and behavior recognizes that grouping (social categorization) influences people's perception of others and one's Self. Social identity is "that part of the individual's self-concept [or self-identity] which derives from his or her knowledge of membership to a social group (or groups) together with the value and emotional significance attached to it" (Tajfel, 1981, p. 255). As individuals belong to a variety of social groups, their overall self-concept is composed of multiple social identities (Ashforth & Mael, 1989; Hogg, Terry, & White, 1995; James, 1891/1950; Jenkins, 2004). These multiple social identities enable an individual to adopt various roles and adapt to a variety of social contexts. The contexts in which a social identity exists, supports the pluralistic nature of the Self. As social groups exist at multiple levels, i.e. societal, cultural, industrial, organizational, functional, and professional (Korte, 2007), individual's social identities are facilitated through communication *within* and *amongst* these levels. For example, a professor can identify him or herself as teacher, parent, friend, advocate, and administrator based on social context. The use of Internet-based communication technologies, such as Internet messaging (IM), chat, and social networks, provide an extension of social contexts in which individuals can interact. The various social context and relationships developed using such social technologies, facilitates the development and recognition of an individual's social identification.

Social Identification

Social identification is an emergent product of internal-external dialectic processes (Jenkins, 2004). Emphasizing a distinction between internal and external dialectical processes (Barth, 1969) allows a "wider distinction to be drawn between *nominal identity* and the *virtual identity*: between the *name* and the *experience* of an identity" (emphasis added; Jenkins, 2004, p. 22). A nominal identity is the label an individual identifies his or her Self with, and a virtual identity is the *experience* of that nominal identity. In other words, your nominal identity is who you believe you are (internal dialectic), and your virtual identity is the experience of being that person (external dialectic). In addition, nominal identification varies from context to context and can be associated with numerous virtual identities (Jenkins, 2004). For example, one may identify him or herself as a student (internal identification, nominal identity), but his or her identity and experience as a student is quite different from high school to university (external identification, virtual identity). Similarly, the same student may consider him or herself a quiet, shy person in face-to-face meetings (nominal identity), however, when online they present themself as having an outgoing, animated personality (virtual identity). The experience of an individual's identity, as perceived through thought and action, is influenced through the interplay of the individual and social others. The evolution and development of internal and external dialectic processes occurs through social identity experimentation.

Social Identity Experimentation

Experimenting with social identities is an important part of lifespan development (Wallace, 1999). As individuals develop, particularly through adolescence, they begin to question their place in society; leading them to question their identity and personal values (Erikson, 1963, 1980). Within to-

day's fast paced environment, where lifestyle and career options are abundant and change quickly, many individuals return repeatedly to question their values, beliefs and life goals (Archer, 1989; Wallace, 1999). In particular, the Internet plays an important role in social identity formation and development as it allows individuals to explore their values and beliefs within environments that they perceive to be safe. The anonymity of online interactions facilitates the perception of safety of an individual's nominal identity, allowing users to experiment with multiple virtual identities. As the Internet expands opportunities for social identity experimentation, through online chat, massively multiplayer online games (MMOG), 3D online virtual worlds, and social networks, individuals readily test and experiment with multiple identities. The ambiguity of the Internet in one's life course, is an enabling factor for individuals to explore identities that they could not explore in their 'regular' everyday lives or in their youth (Archer, 1989).

Through adolescence, the uncertainty of identity dominates an individual's development and definition of who they feel they are. As identity is a process of 'becoming', identity experimentation becomes a means of self-exploration. A recent study by Valkenburg, Schouten, & Peter (2005) investigated identity experiments by adolescents and whether pre- and early adolescents engage more often in Internet-based identity experimentation and self-presentational strategies than middle and late adolescents. Of the 600 adolescents surveyed (ages 9-18, $M = 13.37$, $SD = 1.98$), 82% indicated that they used chat or Internet Messaging (IM) on a regular basis. Of those who used these technologies, 50% of them reported that they willingly experimented with their identity. Using such self-presentation strategies as presenting his or herself as older, more 'macho', more 'beautiful', more 'flirtatious', as the opposite gender, as a real-life acquaintance, or as a 'fantasy' person, these adolescents were actively engaged in conscious identity experimentation. The majority of the adolescents surveyed in the study (49.8%) presented themselves as older. Further findings reveal that relative to age differences in the group surveyed, there was a strong influence of age on Internet-based identity experimentation ($b = -.50$, $p < .001$). Meaning, that younger adolescences are significantly more likely than older adolescences to experiment with their social identities, and more frequently use their social identities to facilitate social interaction. Valkenburg et al. also report that introverts engage in identity experiments as social compensation more often than extraverts do. The results indicate that introverts were more likely to experiment with their social identity as a means to explore social communication they lack in the face-to-face world. The study concludes that older teenagers used the Internet most often to communicate with their existing personal network, whereas younger adolescents are more likely to use the Internet more frequently to communicate with strangers. The results of the Valkenburg et al. study validate some existing assumptions about why adolescents use the Internet as a predominate medium of communication, and provides additional evidence of Internet identity experimentation as a means for uninhibited self-exploration

Motives for identity experimentation are varied and diverse. Self-exploration (i.e. to explore how others react), social compensation (i.e. to overcome shyness), and social facilitation (i.e. to facilitate relationship-formation) are a few motives for identity experimentation. Identity experiments such as the one explored in the Valkenburg et al. study, demonstrate the reciprocal nature of Self and social group interaction in the formation of identity. For an individual to develop a social identity, what that individual thinks of him or herself is significant, but no less significant than what others think about him or her. To return to the internal-external dialectic discussed previously, what the Valkenburg study demonstrates is that it is not enough to assert a social identity; others must also validate that social identity through its

reception and recognition. Self-presentation then, is an assertion of a social identity.

Self-Presentation

Self-presentation is an individual's projection of Self and identity in the social world (Valkenburg et al., 2005). In a traditional face-to-face setting, the reality that the individual is concerned with is generally unperceivable. The individual observes the situation and acts according to their perceptions; even if their perceptions are inaccurate. "Paradoxically, the more the individual is concerned with the reality that is not available to perception, the more must he concentrate his attention on appearances" (Goffman, 1959/1997, p. 21). People can change their persona to reflect the social audience and can have as many social 'selves' as there are situations (William James as cited in Abrams & Hogg, 2001). According to Goffman (1959), individuals present an impression by *performing* and observers are the *audience* that judges the effectiveness or the believability of the performance. Goffman describes the performer-audience dialectic as one concerning the maintenance of the impression that the performer is 'living up' to the standards by which their actions are judged. Whether or not these actions are true of the individual's identity, remain the subject of the audience's judgment. Studies reveal that in virtual settings, such as online social networks, inaccuracy of interpretation resulting from individual presentation is a major challenge with Internet communication (Donath, 1999; Lynch, 2005; Valkenburg et al., 2005; Walther, 2007). As previously discussed in the study by Valkenburg et al. (2005) and in the literature on identity experimentation (e.g. Wallace, 1999), the Internet presents many opportunities and motives for identity experimentation. As most participants in online social networks are likely to be actively experimenting with different social identities, 'audience' members need to be aware that people may be presenting an identity that may only be a small part of the 'performers' nominal identity (e.g. Walther, 2007). This awareness brings literal meaning to Shakespeare's assertion that "All the world's a stage, and all men and women players" (As You Like It cited in Haney, Banks, & Zimbardo, 1973).

GROUP FORMATION

Group membership is crucial to the internal-external dialectic negotiation that is identity (Amiot, de la Sablionniere, Terry, & Smith, 2007). Self-categorization theory (Turner, 1985, 1987) suggests that identification with any group is based on the extent to which individuals can enhance their social identity through categorizing themselves as group members (Chattopadhyay, George, & Lawrence, 2004). This theory suggests that individuals must associate themselves and others with particular social categories to derive social identities (Turner, 1985).

Self-Categorization

Social identity involves a process of self-categorization. Categorization as a cognitive function enables individuals to perceive the world as structured and predictable. Categorization is one of the most basic and essential of all cognitive processes that helps one focus on contextually relevant and meaningful aspects of the world; highlighting important distinctions and de-emphasizing unimportant ones (Hogg, 2001). For example, a student may categorize himself or herself as a football player, or other students may categorize that student as a football player. Given this 'football player' categorization, students (and even teachers) make certain assumptions about how that student is likely to behave, with whom he or she associates, and even his or her ability for academic achievement. Categorization of Self, relative to group membership, emphasizes perceived similarities among group members and the characteristics that best define the group in that particular context (Hogg, Cooper-Shaw, & Holzworth, 1993). Self-categorization accentuates attitudinal, emotional, and behavioral similarity to a group *prototype* (Hogg & Hains, 1996). A group prototype involves the salient characteristics that define a typical member of that group. As a prototype is shared amongst group members, it also identifies group norms and stereotypes (Hogg et al., 1993). For example, the *prototypical* football player is an individual who has superior physical abilities, is disruptive in class, and does not obtain high grades in academic subjects. Further to our prototypical football player, if this student deviates from what is stereotypical or 'normal' for this group, such as achieving high grades in their academic subjects, they may be subjected to ridicule from their peers. A group may ostracize a fringe member based on what the group deems as deviant behavior or for ideas that are contradictory to the norms of the group (Marques, Abrams, Paez, & Hogg, 2001). Ultimately, self-categorization depersonalizes perception and conduct such that individual members are not 'processed' as complex multidimensional whole persons, but rather as embodiments of the group prototype (Birchmeier, Joinson, & Dietz-Uhler, 2005; Chattopadhyay et al., 2004; Haney et al., 1973). Research has found that social and group identities are generally more powerful than individual identities, and there is a tendency for individuals to go along with the group in which they identify (Hogg & McGarty, 1990; Korte, 2007; Tyler, 2002). The sense of group identity and the degree of personal identifiability to other group members are conditions known to influence this power relationship (Taylor & MacDonald, 2002). There is also a tendency of the individual to downplay personal attributes in favor of the group prototype or collective identity.

Collective Identification

Collective identification is a representation of how people are similar to each other based on the psychological connection between Self and social group (Abrams & Hogg, 2001; Jenkins, 2004). As discussed previously, social identity is a part of the Self that one identifies with a particular category or group. Put another way, social identity is "the *perception* of self in terms of stereotypical ingroup (*sic)* attributes" (emphasis added; Abrams & Hogg, 2001, p. 433). The in-group is simply the group in which one identifies, conversely, the out-group are those individuals who are not exclusive members. Collective identification, thus, results in a strong association between an individual and the group in which they are member. The individual then assumes the collective identity. Barnum and Markovsky (2007) hypothesized that in-group members would be more influential than out-group members on the collective. For example, using two theoretical approaches based on disagreements with in-group members (self-categorization theory) and the performance expectations (status characteristics theory) of the in-group members, Barnum and Markovsky (2005) observed that group membership affected social influence and that in-group members influenced their subjects more than out-group members. The results of this study support the argument that in the development of a social identity, the new group or collective identity tends to depersonalize the individual in favor of becoming a group member.

Depersonalization

Depersonalization causes people to conform to group prototypes and behave according to group norms. Similar to deindividuation of identity (Festinger, Pepitone, & Newcomb, 1952; Zimbardo, 1969), depersonalization gives an individual a sense of anonymity, in which he or she submits themself to the collective identity. Postmes, Spears and Lea (2002) hypothesized that depersonalization would increase the tendency for intergroup differentiation in attitudes and stereotypes specifically with computer mediated communications (CMC). Based upon previous

research (Postmes, Spears, & Lea, 1998), Postmes et al. state that communication via CMC would potentially increase differentiation between groups on dimensions of bias, stereotyping, and attitude divergence. In addition, they postulate that CMC shifts intergroup interactions from interpersonal ("me" and "you") to intergroup ("us" vs. "them") ultimately depersonalizing interactions and stimulating a tendency for differentiation between social categories (Postmes et al., 2002). Postmes et al. (2002) could not attribute differences in their findings between the groups studied, rather, that CMC likely accentuated differences that already existed. Postmes et al. claim that the results of their study were heightened because of the online context despite the group differences that already existed. The transition from the personal (nominal) to the social (virtual) identity (as originally postulated by Turner, 1987) in which group membership (collective identification) is facilitated, is important for understanding the dynamics of individuals acting as a collective unit or group. The mixed results of the Postmes et al. study reveal that both individuals and groups are in a constant state of social flux. The dynamic nature and negotiation of these groups online makes their structure and evolution fluid and uncertain. Tools, techniques, and technologies for analyzing social networks, will enable further our understanding in social identity development and group formation, and aid in determining the measurable impact of social network tools in education.

ANALYSING ONLINE SOCIAL NETWORKS

Social network formation is a complex process in which individuals simultaneously attempt to satisfy goals under multiple, often conflicting, constraints (Kossinets & Watts, 2006). Social network analysis (SNA) involves theorizing, model building and empirical research focused on uncovering the patterns of links among network members (Freeman, 2000). Social network analysis conceives social structure as a social network. A set of social actors and a set of relational ties connecting pairs of these actors (Wellman, 2000) forms the social network. Social network structures are analyzed using measures such as density, centrality, prestige, mutuality, and role. Demographic data, such as age, gender, and ethnicity, and information about 'user' attitudes and beliefs are collected to gain an understanding of the ethnographic characteristics of group members. Methods used in SNA include graph theoretic, algebraic, and statistical models (Wellman, 2000). Due to the focus and length constraints of this chapter, the specifics of SNA methodologies and analysis are not explored in-depth. Instead, we focus on the analysis of online social networks using examples from the literature that consider linking individuals with community growth, ethnography, social discourse, and data visualization.

Examining Links

Examining links between group members enables researchers to understand how individuals influence, relate, and interact in social networks. Kossinets & Watts (2006), in an analysis of a dynamic social network of more than 45,000 students, faculty, and staff at a large university, found that networks evolve as a result of effects arising between the network topology and the organizational structure the network embodies. Of particular interest is that network characteristics (measures) appear to approach an equilibrium state, whereas individual properties such as linking and bridging are considerably more complex and are more appropriately analyzed using ethnographic techniques (as discussed in a later section). Linking and bridging of individuals-to-individuals and groups-to-groups facilitate connections outside of an individual's circle of acquaintances and promotes a diffusion of information and growth of existing and new communities (Kossinets & Watts, 2006). The rapid and dynamic nature of

linking and bridging in the growth and development of social networks within a relatively stable infrastructure is recognized in the rapid growth of websites such as Facebook (2008), MySpace (2008), Second Life (Linden Research Inc., 2008), and Bebo (2008). Within these web communities, social network connections are far more complex than the technological infrastructure in which they are situated. Understanding how and why bridges occur is central in understanding the circumstances surrounding the formation and growth of online communities.

Research on Community Growth in Online Social Networks

Community growth in online social networks is of great importance to both commercial and social enterprises. As online social networks offer commercial advertising space to a captive audience and is a rapidly evolving environment for social research, understanding how, why, and under what conditions these groups thrive is of paramount importance. For example, a recent study by Backstrom, Huttenlocher, Kleinberg, & Lan (2006) explored three questions in regards to online social network growth and evolution. First, they considered membership and the structural features that influence whether a given individual will join a particular group. Second, they examined how structural features that influence a given group and whether that group will grow significantly over time. Finally, Backstrom et al. explored aspects of group change and how group foci or topics change over time and whether this dynamic affects underlying group membership. Backstrom et al. found that the formation of groups and the determining factors of membership significantly relate to the internal connectedness of an individual's friends. Meaning, individuals whose friends are in a community are significantly more likely to join that community. In a similar way to bridging, as discussed in the last section, information diffusion is similar to membership diffusion in that the more links or bridges one obtains affects the development of the social network and expedites its growth. Backstrom et al. also examined the flow of information within groups; specifically they questioned that "given a set of overlapping communities, do topics tend to follow people, or do people tend to follow topics?" (Backstrom et al., 2006, p. 8). The results to this final query were inconclusive indicating that less technical approaches to understanding community formation and growth, such as the methods used in ethnographic research, would likely provide clearer answers as to the complex dynamics that take place in online social networks.

Ethnography and Social Discourse

Ethnography is a method of research primarily concerned with the description of natural human communities (Munroe, 2000). Ethnography enables the interpretation of the flow of social discourse (Gertz, 1973/2000). In the study of online social networks, ethnography is particularly useful in studying online groups as unique cultural communities. The methodologies and perspectives of ethnography, aids in establishing new questions for research in social networks and complements existing quantitative methodologies. A recent study by boyd & Heer (2006) used ethnographic techniques to study the dynamics of the popular international social networking site Friendster (2008). The ethnographic components consisted of a 9-month participant observation, including interviews, qualitative surveys, and focus groups. Boyd and Heer's particular research questions involved examining how context is created and interpreted in digital environments, how conversations are initiated online, what are the goals of digital conversations, and how are they maintained. Exploring the possibilities and consequences of replicabilitiy, searchability, and persistence, boyd and Heer's ethnographic study revealed several interesting findings. First, in order to derive contextual cues in lieu of the physical

cues present during face-to-face interactions, members of the social network interpreted what boyd and Heer describe as "artifacts of digital performance." The 'artifacts' they describe are traces of interaction history (Wexelblat & Maes, 1999), such as previous discussion postings and images. These artifacts served existing and new network members who use these virtual cues to interpret and build a social profile of the individual who left them. Second, as individuals invited existing friends to their social network, the groups grew and quickly became homogenous. Although boyd and Heer infer that homogeneity is due to the limiting nature of the website itself, the emergence of a homogenous social group exemplifies the homophily principle that similarity breeds connections to "people like us" (McPherson, Smith-Lovin, & Cook, 2001). Homophily, as demonstrated by the boyd and Heer study, serves as a limiter in individuals' social world. As social networks consist of people who know each other offline and who are similar in sociodemographic, behavioral, and intrapersonal characteristics, these networks are less dynamic and are more often a digital representation of most face-to-face social groups. As individuals interact with others similar to themselves (Baym & Zhang, 2004; Jones & Madden, 2002) and attempt to avoid conflicting relationships (Bargh & McKenna, 2004; Gross, 2004), homophily is limiting because it proliferates the divides in our personal environments and limits exposure to people and networks different from our own. Finally, boyd and Heer describe a phenomenon they call "negotiating unknown audiences" (boyd & Heer, 2006, p. 4); meaning as users generate online contexts to serve the needs of a particular group, the individuals in those groups come together already associated the group. Informed by their ethnographic investigation, boyd and Heer used data visualization to provide a macroscopic view of many of the most common behaviors they observed, such as browsing photos, exploring profiles, and searching for common interests.

As qualitative and quantitative analysis of social networks provides insight into the interactions of individuals within the group, data visualization enables a macroscopic view of the social networks in question.

Data Visualization

Visualization aids in the presentation of abstract data. Data visualization enables a visual means to confirm observations made at a local (in this case individual) level, as in the boyd and Heer study (2006), but also provides an alternative perspective on the patterns the data presents, as in a recent study by Golbeck (2007). In the boyd and Heer (2006) study, the visualization served particularly useful in confirming the ethnographic observations concerning the presence and composition of network clusters which allowed the researchers to develop additional narratives. An example of the visualization presented in the boyd and Heer (2006) and Heer and boyd (2008) and represents a single user profile, and demonstrates the interconnectedness between his or her example profile and their 'friends.'

A recent study by Golbeck (2007) used visualization techniques to analyze social network membership and relationship dynamics. The visualization Golbeck uses in the study of social network growth of a sample of social networks show a steady linear growth rate. As awareness of the networks existence grew, mostly through advertising, the membership among the selected networks grew rapidly from 1000 members to more than 10 million. In analyzing the rate of relationship growth relative to membership growth, the 'spacing' of relationships increased significantly over time. 'Spacing' suggests that social networks become more densely connected as they grow larger, which was also observed in the Backstrom et al. (2006) study discussed earlier. Golbeck used visualization to illustrate this spacing effect.

The analysis of online social networks from the macro level provides specific information on community growth, social discourse, and general group dynamics. The addition of this macro-level information to the research on social identity provides further information on the ongoing interplay between the groups in which we identify ourselves and how others respond to this dynamic. The relative strength of collective associations within the group, as evidenced through density, linking, and bridging, associates individual activity with collective (group) level properties. Through this process, further detail of group prototypes and the salient characteristics that define a typical member of that group can be identified, and additional 'narratives' can be developed that further understanding of social identity and group dynamics at the micro (i.e. individual) and macro (i.e. community) levels.

STRATEGIES FOR USING SOCIAL SOFTWARE IN EDUCATION

Social networks already exist in education. Sports teams, social clubs, cheer squads, and social cliques are a few examples that are recognizable in any educational institution. As the context in which social identity supports the pluralistic nature of the Self, the learning environment is a particularly appropriate place for students to explore their nominal identities and experiment with new social (virtual) identities. For educators to capitalize and facilitate identity experimentation within online social networks, such as Facebook, MySpace, Second Life, and Bebo, they need to facilitate social interaction in all learning contexts. We have identified four important areas of research that support identity experimentation and promote the use of online social networks in education. Research important in the use of online social networks in education involves investigating ways in which educators can preserve relative anonymity, enable identity experimentation, manipulate self-categorization, and measuring the effectiveness of online social networks in education.

Preserve Relative Anonymity

To establish an equality of participation, relative anonymity should be preserved (Taylor & MacDonald, 2002). In order for online social networks to be successful in an educational context, anonymity needs to be maintained until social links are established. If anonymity is not maintained, then the social network is likely to fail given that relatively few will participate, and if they do participate, they will 'self-present' in such a way as to make the environment seem false. For example, in traditional or formal learning settings, a student will often demonstrate behaviours expected by the teacher as opposed to behaving as they actually feel. In an online environment, students should feel that they have the freedom to express and interact in ways that are not reflective of outside social influence. The use of anonymity has implications within formal learning structures where anonymity is not often preserved. Further research in this area is necessary to delineate teaching and learning strategies for use within formal learning contexts.

Enable Identity Experimentation

Encouraging identity experimentation facilitates the development of social networks that continually evolve and change with each different educational context. Identity experimentation, keeping a modicum of anonymity, enables a student to present various social identities to his or her peers and the instructor. In other words, identity experimentation through various modes of self-presentation encourages expressions of self that are accepted or rejected by members of the in-group. Identity experimentation is important to education, as it is something that all individuals 'do' and is uniquely possible within online social

networking. Incorporating strategies within the educational context that encourage such experimentation in a safe and equitable way will foster tolerance and understanding of other differing points of view. Identity experimentation promotes social interaction as the individual's identity is in constant negotiation between the individual and social group.

Manipulate Self-Categorization

Building on the first two factors results in a manipulation of self-categorization. Manipulating self-categorization raises individual and collective awareness of the various effects of collective identification. In other words, teaching and learning strategies that enable self-experimentation will also influence how a student develops awareness of their impact on others in their peer group and illustrates how they are accountable for their actions. Through the manipulation of self-categorization, students are able to recognize how their participation within a social group affects the social network and remain accountable for their actions. The use of roles within group interactions enables individuals to understand the difference of their nominal identity and virtual identity in social contexts. This realization can only help students become more cognizant of the influence of social roles in identity formation.

Measuring Social Network Effectiveness

A measurable means for observing changes in the various properties of a social network, such as bridging, linking, and spacing within the network, is important in helping educators determine the level of interactivity in the network overall. For example, a network with low interactivity would have few bridges, few links, and very large spaces between individuals in the network. Alternatively, an active network is one with high interactivity, has bridges, several links, and has less space between individuals in the network. From an educational perspective, an active classroom network, whether face-to-face or online, that has many bridges and many links is a more productive learning environment. It is the ability of the instructor to facilitate these links that will provide an effective social learning environment.

CONCLUSION

Experimenting with social identities is an important part of lifespan development (Wallace, 1999). As individuals develop and change, they question their place in society leading them to question their identity and personal values (Erikson, 1963, 1980). People often change their persona (James, 1891/1950) and have as many social 'selves' as situations (Abrams & Hogg, 2001) and social groups. Categorization of the Self relative to a group accentuates the perceived similarity between individual group members and one's representation of the features that best define the group in a particular context (Hogg et al., 1993). A representation of how people are similar to each other, is based on the psychological connection between the self and social group (Abrams & Hogg, 2001; Jenkins, 2004). Collective identity aids in the development of social identity, but tends to depersonalize the individual in favor of becoming a group member. Although depersonalization facilitates a transition from a personal (nominal) to social (virtual) identity, where group membership (collective identification) becomes increasingly important, social network formation is a complex process in which many individuals simultaneously attempt to satisfy their goals under multiple, conflicting constraints (Kossinets & Watts, 2006).

The use of Internet-based communication technologies facilitates the development of social groups and social identification. Social identity is central in understanding intergroup relations and is a key element linking individuals to their social group (Tajfel, 1974, 1981). As social groups exist at multiple levels, social identity development is facilitated through communication within and amongst these levels. Social identification, as an emergent product of internal-external dialectic processes (Jenkins, 2004), enables an individual to experiment with different virtual identities and explore what it is like to experience those identities in the social world.

Motives for identity experimentation, such as self-exploration (i.e. to explore how others react), social compensation (i.e. to overcome shyness), and social facilitation (i.e. to facilitate relationship-formation) are all important factors in social development. As schools are inherently social institutions, the factors that contribute to healthy social development are of paramount importance for educators to consider for students growth. The strategies for social identity experimentation in classrooms, allows students to become active interpreters of social interaction. Educators that facilitate participation, experimentation, and research of social identity, will ultimately contribute to student's insight into the dynamics of learning and development as a social process.

REFERENCES

Abrams, D., & Hogg, M. A. (2001). Collective identity: Group membership and self-conception. In M. A. Hogg & S. Tinsdale (Eds.), *Blackwell handbook of social psychology: Group processes* (pp. 425-460). Malden, MA: Blackwell.

Amiot, C., de la Sablionniere, R., Terry, D., & Smith, J. (2007). Integration of social identities in the self: Toward a cognitive developmental model. *Personality and Social Psychology Review, 11*, 364-368.

Archer, S. L. (1989). The status of identity: Reflections on the need for intervention. *Journal of Adolescence, 12*, 345-359.

Ashforth, B. R., & Mael, F. (1989). Social identity theory and the organization. *Academy of Management Review, 14*(1), 20-39.

Backstrom, L., Huttenlocher, D., Kleinberg, J., & Lan, X. (2006). *Group formation in large social networks: Membership, growth, and evolution.* Paper presented at the KDD '06, Philadelphia, USA.

Bargh, J. A., & McKenna, K. Y. A. (2004). The Internet and social life. *Annual Review of Psychology, 55,* 573-590.

Barnum, C., & Markovsky, B. (2007). Group membership and social influence [Electronic Version]. *Current Research in Social Psychology, 13,* 1-38, from http://www.uiowa.edu/~grpproc

Barth, F. (1969). *Ethnic groups and boundaries: The social organization of cultural difference.* Oslo, Norway: Universitetsforlaget.

Baym, N. K., & Zhang, Y. B. (2004). Social interactions across media: Interpersonal communication on the Internet, telephone and face-to-face. *New Media & Society, 6*(3), 299-318.

Bebo, Inc. (2008). *About Bebo.* Retrieved April 21, 2008, from http://www.bebo.com/StaticPage.jsp?StaticPageId=2517103831

Birchmeier, Z., Joinson, A. M., & Dietz-Uhler, B. (2005). Storming and forming a normative response to a deception revealed online. *Social Science Computer Review, 23,* 108.

Boyd, d. m., & Heer, J. (2006). *Profiles as conversation: Networked identity performance on Friendster.* Paper presented at the Hawai'i International Conference on System Sciences (HICSS-39), Kauai, HI.

Chattopadhyay, P., George, E., & Lawrence, S. (2004). Why does dissimilarity matter? Exploring self-categorization, self-enhancement, and uncertainty reduction. *Journal of Applied Psychology, 89*(5), 892-900.

Derlega, V. J., & Chaikin, A. L. (1977). Privacy and self-disclosure in social relationships. *Journal of Social Issues, 33*(3), 102-115.

Donath, J. (1999). Identity and deception in the virtual community. In M. A. Smith & P. Kollock (Eds.), *Communities in cyberspace* (pp. 29-59). London, UK: Routledge.

Erikson, E. H. (1963). *Childhood and society (2nd Ed.).* New York, NY: Norton.

Erikson, E. H. (1980). Identity, youth, and crisis. In. New York, NY: Norton.

Facebook, Inc. (2008). *About Facebook.* Retrieved April 21, 2008, from http://www.facebook.com/about.php

Festinger, L., Pepitone, A., & Newcomb, T. (1952). Some consequences of de-individuation in a group. *Journal of Abnormal and Social Psychology, 47,* 382-389.

Freeman, L.C. (2000). Social network analysis: Definition and history. In A. E. Kadzin (Ed.), *Encyclopedia of Psychology,* 7, 350-351. Washington, DC: American Psychological Association.

Friendster, Inc. (2008). *About Friendster.* Retrieved April 21, 2008, from http://www.friendster.com/info/index.php

Gertz, C. (1973/2000). *The interpretation of cultures.* New York, NY: Basic Books.

Goffman, E. (1959/1997). Self-presentation. In C. Lemert & A. Branaman (Eds.), *The Goffman Reader.* Malden, MA: Blackwell.

Golbeck, J. (2007). The dynamics of Web-based social networks: Membership, relationships, and change. *First Monday, 12*(11), 1-15.

Gross, B. M. (2004). *Multiple email addresses: A socio-technical investigation.* Paper presented at the First Conference on E-mail and Anti-Spam (CEAS), Mountain View, CA.

Haney, C., Banks, W. C., & Zimbardo, P. G. (1973). A study of prisoners and guards in a simulated prison. *Naval Research Review, 30,* 4-17.

Heer, J., & boyd, D. (2008). *Visualizing online social networks.* Retrieved July 11, 2008 from http://jheer.org/vizster/

Hogg, M. A. (2001). Social categorization, depersonalization, and group behavior. In M. A. Hogg & S. Tinsdale (Eds.), *Blackwell handbook of social psychology: Group processes* (pp. 57-85). Malden, MA: Blackwell.

Hogg, M. A., Cooper-Shaw, L., & Holzworth, D. W. (1993). Group prototypicality and depersonalized attraction in small interactive groups. *Personality and Social Psychology Bulletin, 19*(4), 452-465.

Hogg, M. A., & Hains, S. C. (1996). Intergroup relations and group solidarity: Effects of group identification and social beliefs on depersonalized attraction. *Journal of Personality and Social Psychology, 70*(2), 295-309.

Hogg, M. A., & McGarty, C. (1990). Self-categorization and social identity. In D. Abrams & M. A. Hogg (Eds.), *Social identity theory: Constructive and critical advances* (pp. 10-27). New York, NY: Harvester Wheatsheath.

Hogg, M. A., Terry, D., & White, K. M. (1995). A tale of two theories: A critical comparison of identity theory with social identity theory. *Social Psychology Quarterly, 58*(4), 255-269.

Linden Research Inc. (2008). *About Second Life.* Retrieved April 21, 2008, from http://secondlife.com/

James, W. (1891/1950). The consciousness of self. In *Principles of Psychology.* New York, NY: Dover Publications.

Jenkins, R. (2000). Categorization: Identity, social process and epistemology. *Current Sociology, 48*(3), 7-25.

Jenkins, R. (2004). *Social Identity.* New York, NY: Routledge.

Jones, S., & Madden, M. (2002). The Internet goes to college: How students are living in the future with today's technology [Electronic Version]. *Pew Internet & American Life Project.* Retrieved October 15, 2007, from http://www.pewinternet.org/pdfs/PIP_College_Report.pdf

Korte, R. (2007). A review of social identity theory with implications for training and development. *Journal of European Industrial Training, 31*(3), 166-180.

Kossinets, G., & Watts, D. (2006). Empirical analysis of an evolving social network. *Science, 311,* 88-90.

Lea, M., & Spears, R. (1995). Love at first byte? Building personal relationships over computer networks. In J. T. Wood & S. Duck (Eds.), *Understudied relationships: Off the beaten track* (pp. 197-233). Thousand Oaks, CA: Sage.

Lynch, D. (2005). *Children's identity development in virtual spaces.* Unpublished Dissertation, McGill University, Montreal, QB.

Marques, J. M., Abrams, D., Paez, D., & Hogg, M. A. (2001). Social categorization, social identification, and rejection of deviant group members. In M. A. Hogg & S. Tinsdale (Eds.), *Blackwell handbook of social psychology: Group processes* (pp. 400-424). Malden, MA: Blackwell.

McKenna, K. Y. A., Green, A. A., & Gleason, M. J. (2002). Relationship formation on the Internet: What's the big attraction? *Journal of Social Issues, 58*(1), 9-31.

McPherson, M., Smith-Lovin, L., & Cook, J. (2001). Birds of a feather: Homophily in social networks. *Annual Review of Sociology, 27,* 415-444.

Munroe, R. L. (2000). Ethnography. In A. E. Kadzin (Ed.), *Encyclopedia of Psychology* (Vol.

3, pp. 267-269). Washington, DC: American Psychological Association.

MySpace, Inc. (2008). About MySpace. Retrieved April 21, 2008, from http://www.myspace.com/index.cfm?fuseaction=misc.aboutus

Postmes, T., Spears, R., & Lea, M. (1998). Breaching or building social boundaries? SIDE-effects of computer-mediated communication. *Communication Research, 25*(6), 689-715.

Postmes, T., Spears, R., & Lea, M. (2002). Intergroup differentiation in computer-mediated communication: Effects of depersonalization. *Group dynamics: Theory, research, and practice, 6*(1), 3-16.

Rubin, A. (1975). Disclosing oneself to a stranger: Reciprocity and its limits. *Journal of Experimental Social Psychology, 11*, 233-260.

Ruitenberg, C. W. (2003). From designer identities to identity by design: Education for identity de/construction [Electronic Version]. *Philosophy of Education 2003*. Retrieved October 12, 2007, from http://www.ed.uiuc.edu/EPS/PES-Yearbook/2003/ruitenberg.pdf

Tajfel, H. (1974). Social identity and intergroup behavior. *Social Science Information, 13*, 65-93.

Tajfel, H. (1981). *Human groups and social categories: Studies in social psychology.* Cambridge, UK: Cambridge University Press.

Taylor, J., & MacDonald, J. (2002). The effects of asynchronous computer-mediated group interaction on group processes. *Social Science Computer Review, 20*(3), 260-274.

Turner, J. C. (1985). Social categorization and the self-concept: A social cognitive theory of group behavior. In E. J. Lawler (Ed.), *Advances in Group Processes (Vol. 2)*. Greenwich, CN: JAI Press.

Turner, J. C. (1987). A self-categorization theory. In J. C. Turner, M. A. Hogg, S. D. Oakes, S. D. Reicher & M. S. Wetherell (Eds.), *Rediscovering the social group: A self-categorization theory* (pp. 42-67). Oxford, UK: Basil Blackwell.

Tyler, T. R. (2002). Is the Internet changing social life? It seems the more things change, the more they stay the same. *Journal of Social Issues, 58*(1), 195-205.

Valkenburg, P. M., Schouten, A. P., & Peter, J. (2005). Adolescents' identity experiments on the Internet. *New Media & Society, 7*(3), 383-402.

Wallace, P. (1999). *The psychology of the Internet.* Cambridge, UK: Cambridge University Press.

Walther, J. B. (2007). Selective self-presentation in computer-mediated communication: Hyperpersonal dimensions of technology, language, and cognition. *Computers in Human Behavior, 23*(5), 2538-2557.

Wellman, B. (2000). Social network analysis: Concepts, applications, and methods. In A. E. Kadzin (Ed.), *Encyclopedia of Psychology, 7*, 351-352. Washington, DC: American Psychological Association.

Wexelblat, A., & Maes, P. (1999). *Footprints: History-rich tools for information foraging.* Paper presented at the Conference on Human Factors in Computing Systems, Pittsburgh, PA.

Zimbardo, P. G. (1969). The human choice: Individuation, reason and order vs. deindividuation, impulse and chaos. In W. J. Arnold & D. Levine (Eds.), *Nebraska Symposium on Motivation* (Vol. 17, pp. 237-307). Lincoln, NE: University of Nebraska Press.

KEY TERMS

Artifacts of Digital Performance: Artifacts of digital performance refer to traces of interaction history (Wexelblat & Maes, 1999), such as previous discussion postings and posted images, that new network members use as virtual cues to interpret and build social context.

Collective Identity: Collective identification is a representation of how people are similar to each other based on the psychological connection between the self and social group (Abrams & Hogg, 2001; Jenkins, 2004).

Depersonalization: Depersonalization causes people to conform to the group prototype and behave according to group norms.

Ethnography: Ethnography is a method of research primarily concerned with the description of natural human communities (Munroe, 2000) and enables the interpretation of the flow of social discourse (Gertz, 1973/2000).

Nominal and Virtual Identity: A nominal identity is the label with which an individual is identified and a virtual identity is an individual's *experience* of the nominal identity. In other words, your nominal identity is what you believe you *are* (internal dialectic), and your virtual identity is the experience of being (external dialectic).

Self-Categorization: Self-categorization theory (Turner, 1985, 1987) suggests that identification with any group is based on the extent to which individuals can enhance their social identity through categorizing themselves as group members (Chattopadhyay et al., 2004).

Social Identity: Social identity is central in understanding intergroup relations and is the key element linking an individual to his or her social group (Tajfel, 1974, 1981).

Social Network Analysis: Social network analysis involves the theorizing, model building and empirical research focused on uncovering the patterning of links among network members (Freeman, 2000). Social network analysis conceives of social structure as a social network: a set of social actors and a set of relations ties connecting pairs of these actors (Wellman, 2000).

Chapter VIII
The Emergence of Agency in Online Social Networks

Jillianne R. Code
Simon Fraser University, Canada

Nicholas E. Zaparyniuk
Simon Fraser University, Canada

ABSTRACT

Social and group interactions in online and virtual communities develop and evolve from expressions of human agency. The exploration of the emergence of agency in social situations is of critical importance to understanding the psychology of agency and group interactions in social networks. This chapter explores how agency emerges from social interactions, how this emergence influences the development of social networks, and the role of social software's potential as a powerful tool for educational purposes. Practical implications of agency as an emergent property within social networks provide a psychological framework that forms the basis for pedagogy of social interactivity. This chapter identifies and discusses the psychological processes necessary for the development of agency and to further understanding of individual's engagement in online interactions for socialization and learning.

INTRODUCTION

Social and group interactions in online and virtual communities develop and evolve from expressions of human agency. Agency is the capability of individuals to consciously choose, influence, and structure their actions (Emirbayer & Mische, 1998; Gecas, 2003) and is an active exercise of ability and will. The ways in which individuals express agency are associated with their motivational orientation, intentionality, and choice (volition), and relates to their ability to engage these characteristics in social contexts to achieve their goals. As agents, individuals formulate intentions, execute decisions, and produce motivation in an effort to communicate. Understanding how agency develops and emerges within social networks is a key factor in identifying *why* online social networks develop and *how* they influence individual processes such as cognition, motivation, behavior, and ultimately learning.

The exploration of the emergence of agency in social situations is of critical importance to understanding the psychology of agency and group interactions in social networks. Research in social psychology provides a context in which to investigate the psychological effects of online social software as it relates to motivation (see Ryan & Deci, 2000), interactions within the social networks (see Thompson & Fine, 1999), and how individuals vary in their ability to express agency (see Martin, 2003, 2004).

Agency emerges out of interactions and goal directed activities within social networks. Similarly, social networks emerge through the interactions and characteristics of agents support their formation, development, and evolution. Socially situated emergent properties of agency and social networks connect them as a dynamic complex system. Social software is software that "supports, extends, or derives added value from human social behavior" (for a review see boyd, 2007; Coates, 2005). Online friendship websites, massively multiplayer online games, and social groupware, such as Facebook (2008), MySpace (2008), Bebo (2008), and Second Life (Linden Research Inc., 2008) provide frameworks in which social dynamics can mediate the development of agency within social networks.

The purpose of this chapter is to introduce the concept of agency as it relates to the formation, development, and evolution of social networks. This chapter explores how agency emerges from social interactions, how this emergence influences the development of social networks, and the potential role of social software as a tool with educational applications. Practical implications of agency as

an ability to engage within social networks provides a psychological framework that forms the basis for a pedagogy of social interactivity. This chapter discusses the psychological processes necessary for the development of agency, how these processes affect an individual's engagement in online interactions for both socialization and learning, and how social software such as Facebook (2008), MySpace (2008), Bebo (2008), and Second Life (Linden Research Inc., 2008) can be used in educational contexts. As agency directly affects how an individual understands their various roles, beliefs, and decisions in social contexts, there are far reaching implications for social software as an educational tool.

AGENCY

Agency is an ability developed through social means and human experience (Mead, 1932, 1934). As an ability to act independently despite the immediate situation, agency engages habit, imagination, and judgment (Emirbayer & Mische, 1998, p. 970). Agency also involves the knowledge, experience, and the ability to achieve one's goals (Little, Hawley, Henrich, & Marsland, 2002). Within the social framework, agency abilities develop through the interaction of social processes, the dynamics of which can be explained using action theory.

For action theorists (e.g. Parsons, 1968), agency is captured in the notion of *effort*. In this view, agency acts as the force that achieves, where conditions for achievement are at one end of a spectrum and the normative rules are at the other (Emirbayer & Mische, 1998). Agency ability is ultimately a *temporal* continuum through which an individual exercises personal influence and in return affects environmental processes that ultimately affect other personal self-processes. Thus, personal influence becomes a reciprocal collective determinant even though it also determines the individual (Martin, 2003). Agency remains a strong dynamic and causal force underlying individual action.

As a dynamic process, agency is a motivating force of action. The ways in which individuals express and develop agency are associated with their motivational orientation, intentionality, and choice, and speaks to their ability to engage these characteristics in social contexts to achieve their particular goals. Internal personal factors, behavioral patterns, and environmental influences require agency ability to facilitate social processes. Agency-related constructs associated with social interaction include self-efficacy, locus of control, and volition.

Self-Efficacy

A belief in one's capability to succeed is an essential condition of human functioning. Whether one believes that they can produce a certain action is as important as having the skills available to succeed (Bandura, 1997). Self-efficacy is a generative property, meaning it is a capacity that originates within the *Self*. It is generative in that it is a belief that an individual holds to be true. Self-efficacy is also an evaluative capacity in which one perceives their ability to perform a particular action. When an individual then deems themselves effective enough to complete a task, they anticipate the result to be positive. Thus, an efficacy belief propagates from the belief in one's own ability and that they have the skill necessary to complete a task successfully. In relation to social networks and social interaction, self-efficacy for socialization is an important part in determining whether an individual feels they can successfully communicate within a social setting. Social software enables the development of self-efficacy for socialization as it removes social barriers that may otherwise inhibit individuals from interacting in certain ways. For example, massive multiplayer online games (MMOG) and social software such as MySpace (2008), Facebook (2008), Bebo (2008), and Second Life (Linden Research Inc., 2008), provide opportunities for interaction where individuals can socialize and develop confidence in their socialization skills without the awkwardness individuals may encounter in a face-to-face setting. Individuals come to believe that they can communicate relatively successfully, and ultimately develop a higher self-efficacy for socialization and feel that they have control over their actions within this particular context. As a result, individuals who have high self-efficacy also have a tendency to believe that they control their actions and the outcomes that result.

Locus of Control

The causal relationship between's one own behavior and that of an outcome affects a range of choices an individual makes (Lefcourt, 1966; Rotter, 1966). Social Learning Theory (Rotter, 1954, 1966), not to be confused with Social Cognitive Theory, posits that control is considered a *generalized expectancy* which operates across a large number of situations and relates to whether or not an individual believes they possess or lack power over what happens to them. How an individual attributes causal beliefs to outcomes is a central argument of Social Learning Theory and the locus of control concept.

Individuals often believe that they have the power to control the outcome of any given situation. If one believes that a cause of an outcome is a result of personal skill, one has an internal control expectancy, or an internal locus of control. Within a MMOG or other online environment, if an individual perceives a threat or is in a situation in which they are required to make a decision, they must first recognize that they have choices available. The individual can then engage the situation or leave it. How an individual reacts to any situation requires self-control and self-regulation in the form of volition.

Volition

Volition incorporates factors of self-control and self-regulation. Contemporary ideas of volition from an information processing perspective were adapted by Kuhl (1985) are based on a theory of motivation and action originally developed by Ach (1910), (as in Corno, 2001). According to Kuhl (1985), self-control and self-regulation are *modes* of volition coordinated through a central executive. *Self-control* is the mode of volition that supports the maintenance of an active goal, whereas *self-regulation* involves the maintenance of one's actions in line with an integrated *Self*. Volition is a "post-decisional, self-regulatory process that energizes the maintenance and enactment of intended actions" (Kuhl, 1985, p. 90). Volition is a self-regulatory process that provides the means for maintaining the commitment and motivation of an individual to their actions. Within social software, volition enables individuals to persist in achieving a desired outcome, such as meeting new friends or getting a date. Volition becomes particularly important in social networks because intentions are fragile and people often waver on commitments especially when they are faced with challenging problems to solve (Corno, 2001). As an agency-related construct, volition ensures that individuals persist in their motivation to achieve their goals.

Volition, self-efficacy, and locus of control are agency-related constructs that demonstrate agency ability. Each of these constructs interacts within the self-system and collectively enables the expression agency. Assumptions within dynamical systems theory assist in interpreting agency as a relationship between several self-processes *emergent* of that relationship.

EMERGENCE OF AGENCY

Agency develops through a socially mediated ability exercised through human interaction (Mead,

1934). As an emergent entity (Martin, 2003; O'Connor & Wong, 2002), agency develops out of the fundamental characteristics of ability (physical, psychological, and behavioral components), will (i.e. volition, locus of control), and action. Emergence, from an ontological perspective is a non-reducible phenomenon, meaning, that if a construct is emergent it has several component parts but is irreducible with respect to them (Martin, 2003; O'Connor & Wong, 2002). For example, water has its own properties that are complex and novel and are not just a collection of the properties of its components, oxygen, and hydrogen. Oxygen and hydrogen are necessary for the creation of water, however, water also has properties that are uniquely its own; in this way the properties of water are *emergent* (Martin, Sugarman, & Thompson, 2003). Martin, Sugarman and Thompson (2003) propose that agency possesses emergence, and that agency itself contains emergent properties generated by a combination of mental and social events. As water has its own properties, when a heat source is applied to water, it boils, as the water molecules act in response to this external force, the property of the water changes from liquid into a gas. Similarly, the properties of agency change when external forces interact with the different *Self*-factors such as self-efficacy, locus of control, and volition. Thus, agency is a systemic construct, a dynamic interaction among a number of associated agency factors. Changes in the properties of agency are a result of mental (internal) and environmental (external) relationships. Similarly, social networks emerge as a construction of the individuals who interact (internal) and the groups they form (external), however, social networks are not simply sum of their parts.

EMERGENCE OF SOCIAL NETWORKS

Individuals are both a product of and producer of their socio-cultural world (Martin, 2003;

Martin et al., 2003). Environmental and social factors through interactions with people are both producers and are a products of social systems (Bandura, 1997) and involve the coordination and interdependence of personal and situational forces (Markus & Nurius, 1984). The dynamics of a social network are a function of both informal and formal factors and affect the emergence of social roles, specifically informally self-generated social roles referred to as virtual identities (see Code & Zaparyniuk, this volume). The emergence of informal social roles have variable effects on the patterns of interaction and connection among individuals in the network and ultimately on the performance, productivity, evolution, and sustainability of the social network (Jeffrey C Johnson, Palinkas, & Boster, 2003). Critical aspects of these emergent properties are the adaptability of the social network to internal and external patterns of change.

The adaptability of a social network is dependent upon the cohesion of individuals within the network. As individuals utilize, model, and emulate behaviors (cognitive and otherwise) projected by their peers and other agents, they effectively co-regulate their development of social competence. Through this process, individuals exploit the abilities of others to enhance their own capabilities, but also to facilitate their achievement of social outcomes. In this context, individuals co-regulate in social networks to achieve personal social goals. This *co-regulation* is a result of an individual resolution to utilize the abilities and efforts of others to achieve personal, social, or other goals. As co-regulation is an on-going collaborative process, the cooperative relationship between individuals within a social network enables adaptation.

During co-regulation, individuals become agents or 'causal contributors' (Bandura, 1997) of their own social experience. Seeking the meditative efforts of others, helps develop the competence to self-regulate. Self-regulatory competence is a skill, an instrument of agency, that is acquired through collaboration (Bruner, 1997). Ultimately, agency is expressed by the capability of individuals to consciously choose, influence, and structure their actions (Emirbayer & Mische, 1998; Gecas, 2003), and in the context of social networks enables them to formulate intentions, execute decisions, and produce motivation in their effort to interact and communicate within the network.

AGENCY AND SOCIAL NETWORKS AS DYNAMIC COMPLEX SYSTEMS

The emergence of agency and social networks involves particular mental and social causations. On the assumption that agency develops as a result of the interaction of these mental causations (Martin, 2003; Martin et al., 2003), and social networks emerge as result of informal social roles and cohesion, agency and social networks can be described as dynamic systems. As agency and social networks are dynamic, they also contribute to their own creation and evolution (see Code & Zaparyniuk, this volume); however, the system is irreducible with respect to them. Just as one individual or group does not embody the dynamics of the social network, the interaction of the group entities brings about group formation. Any one of the agentic factors alone cannot measure agency, but they may be able to indicate it collectively through their interaction. Similarly, each of the individuals within a social network can only create a network (system) through their interactions. Dynamic systems theorists describe general functions of a nonlinear dynamical system (e.g. Carver & Schier, 2002; Neil F Johnson, 2007; Vallacher, Nowak, Froehlich, & Rockloff, 2002), however relative to a discussion of agency and social networks as dynamic systems, four of these factors are briefly outlined.

Factor 1. The system cannot be decomposed into separate additive influences.

As agency is an emergent abstraction of the relationship among factors such as self-efficacy, locus of control, and volition, social networks are similarly an emergent abstraction of the relationships between the individuals within the system. From an ontological perspective, an emergent entity cannot be broken down into its constituent parts. Agency is not merely a sum of self-efficacy, locus of control, and volitional measures. Social networks do not exist without its members; however, each individual member on their own does not characterize it.

Factor 2. The system has memory or includes feedback.

As agentic variables attributed to self-efficacy, locus of control, and volition, are interdependent; they affect and influence each other in both positive and negative ways. From the perspective of agency, self-regulatory competence (e.g. Bouffard, Bouchard, Goulet, Cenoncourt, & Couture, 2005; Wolters, 1999) is affected by a student's self-efficacy for the task (e.g. Loedewyk & Winne, 2005; Schunk & Ertmer, 2001) and motivation to complete the task (e.g. Wolters, 2003; Wolters, Yu, & Pintrich, 1996). Similarly, social networks and the individuals within them are interdependent and influence each other. Within social networks, the presence or absence of factors such as informal social roles has an impact on a network's emergent properties such as stability, adaptability, and robustness (Neil F Johnson, 2007).

Factor 3. The system can adapt itself according to its history, feedback, and environment.

A system's properties and their patterns of change emerge from 'rules' specifying how the system's elements interact. Emergent or 'macro-level' properties can be understood as features (usually in the case of events and processes) that supervene on, and are thus realized in, 'lower-level' features (Henderson, 1994). Related to agency, characteristics of metacognition are identified through personal awareness and cognitive control (Brown, 1987; Flavell, 1979), and provide feedback for such high-order functions as planning, strategy selection, and monitoring (Sternberg, 1999). Alternatively, social networks have 'group' level properties such as cohesion and coherence that supervene on, and are realized in the members of the network.

Factor 4. The system is self-organizing and non-linear.

A system can only exist if it has autonomous organizing capacities (Gergen, 1984). As a system, agency is self-organizing as it is an emergent function of its constituents, as are social networks an emergent function of its membership. Self-organization of cognitive and affective elements into higher order structures have been revealed in experimental work on social judgment and action identification (Vallacher, Nowak, Markus, & Strauss, 1998) and in computer simulations of self-reflection processes (Nowak, Vallacher, Tesser, & Borkowski, 2000).

Agency and social networks as dynamic systems have particular explanatory value on the causes of human action, but also on the formation of particular social groups. Within education, this explanatory value provides new opportunities for teaching and learning.

IMPLICATIONS FOR EDUCATION

Agency and social networks emerge within social contexts. Social software as a tool for facilitating the development of social networks and agency development has far-reaching implications for educational practice. As individuals interact and groups form the purpose of learning, agency and social networks will also emerge within educational contexts. Conceptualizing social software as a cultural tool, using social networks to represents multiple ways of knowing, knowledge-building, promoting communities of practice, and enabling self-regulated learning, enables a clear application of social software as an educational tool.

Social Software as a Cultural Tool

Cultural tools mediate communication within social settings. Social experience involves the interactions between individuals, and involves the tools, symbols, and values that influence the action (Gauvain, 2001). Vygotsky's sociocultural theory of development posits that the transformation and development of cognitive and social skills occurs within social interactions. Vygotsky (1962, 1978) believed that children (and individuals) learn using *cultural tools* which mediate higher-order mental processes such as reasoning and problem solving. Cultural tools include both *technical tools* such as books, media, and computers, and *psychological tools* such as language, signs, writing, and symbols.

"By being included in the process of behavior, the psychological tool alters the entire flow and structure of mental functions" (Vygotsky, 1981, p. 137).

Online social networks and social software changes the way we perceive and act within social settings. As social software is both a social and psychological tool, it provides a computing environment in which actions are mediated through the appropriation of language, writing, signs, and symbols. As a result, online social networks and social software are cultural tools, and are carriers of social, cultural, and historical formations that amplify certain social actions (Jones &

Norris, 2005). The enactment of social software as a cultural tool promotes the development of a unique and particular social language that mediates agentic expression.

Mediated Agency

Mediated agency aids individuals in interpreting the meaning of a situation. As a social construction, agency is mediated within a social setting by psychological tools such as language, and technical tools such as computers. Wertsch, Tulviste, and Hagstrom (1993) refer to agency within a sociocultural situation as *mediated agency* as agency is 'mediated' by the available cultural tools. Psychological and technical tools mediate agency as individuals usually "operat[e] within [these] meditational means" (Wertsch et al., 1993, p. 342). Meditation of thought and action through social software enables the generation of social structures, histories, and ideologies (Jones & Norris, 2005). Individuals and groups use these cultural tools to understand their social world and to draw meaning from their interactions.

Multiple Ways of Knowing in Social Software

Meaning making is entirely situational. Individual construction of meaning is dependent upon the active interpretation of the situation by the participants which is referred to as a *situation definition* (Park & Moro, 2006). Situation definitions are of interest in a discussion of online social networks because how one interprets a situation includes how to use particular mediational means such as cultural tools (social software) and social genres (social language) within a given social context. Understanding how individuals actively interpret situations and construct meaning involves 'multiple ways of knowing' in which individuals use situation definitions to establish contexts for meaning making that are dynamic and only partially shared. Situation definitions enable a shift in authority structure that makes the individual the 'author' of any virtual situation (Rowe, 2005).

Situational definitions within online social software establish *contexts* for meaning making. Contexts describe circumstances that give meaning and form the setting for an event; a focal event set within its cultural setting (Duranti & Goodwin, 1992). Situation definitions activated within the context of online social software have four general attributes as outlined by Duranti and Goodwin (1992) and Gilbert (2006). Relative to online social software, these attributes provide a strong educational context in which learning can take place. First, the situation definition is within a social, spatial, and temporal framework in which individual encounters with events are situated. In other words, social software provides a social, spatial, and temporal framework in which social educational encounters can occur. Second, the situation definition provides a behavioral environment to frame the 'talk' that takes place. Social software provides a collaborative framework to formulate ideas and associate tasks and actions. Third, the use of specific language associated with the focal event enables a situational definition to develop within the socially networked environment. Social software provides a context in which *social languages* or *social genres* (Bakhtin, 1986/1978) are developed. Finally, situation definitions enable individuals to connect relationships between prior knowledge. Social software enables the connection between ideas and tasks situated within the network to be readily associated to background knowledge.

Situation definitions within are only partially shared between individuals and others within the network. Multiple situation definitions can exist simultaneously as individuals change their representation and understanding of events over time (Rowe, 2005). Interaction with others' competing understanding of an event or situation and the process of coming to share situation definitions is

a crucial feature of learning and perspective taking (Wertsch, 1985). Thus, socio-cultural accounts of learning within social software are intersubjective, engaging participants in dynamic and discursive interactions shifting the authority of defining the situation from one individual to another.

Situation definitions within social software are associated with a shift in authority structure. "The authority to define situations is the authority to author one's own life and circumstances rather than simply to respond to what is given" (Rowe, 2005, p. 128). Within the context of social software, this enables individuals to become the authors of their own 'situations' or contexts. As a result, an individual could take on any particular identity by defining the 'rules' in which they choose to engage with others thus enacting on their agency. The *authority* of any given situation resides within the recognition of the power an individual has to create a context (enact a situation definition) rather than simply to engage within one, which by definition is an engagement of agency. The recognition that individuals have authority to enact and define a particular situation contributes to their perceived value in the online social community and for contributions to the community's growing knowledge.

Social Software as a Knowledge Building Environment

Knowledge building is a collective inquiry embedded in cultural practice. "Knowledge advancement is fundamentally a socio-cultural process, enhanced by cultures of innovation" (Scardamalia, 2004). A shift in authority structure encourages agency mediation, which makes online social software conducive to knowledge generation or *knowledge building*.

Knowledge building environments "enhance collaborative efforts to create and continually improve ideas" (Scardamalia, 2004). Embedded in practice, knowledge building characterizes learning as an evolutionary and creative process but also recognizes the importance of 'tools' necessary to facilitate learning as a collective endeavor making learning a complementary process (Bereiter & Scardamalia, 1996).

Social software shares similar characteristics of knowledge building environments. Scardamalia (2004) outlines several characteristics that distinguish knowledge building environments from other similar environments, such as those commonly discussed in the Computer Supported Collaborative Learning (CSCL) literature. Using Scardamalia's outline, each characteristic is adapted to the application of online social software as knowledge building environments for the purposes of education.

1. Online social software provides shared, user-configured spaces that represent the collective contributions of group members. Providing users with shared, user-contributed spaces that represent the collective contributions of group members enables a sense of community 'authorship' in which each member develops a sense of accountability to the group. The value on their individual contributions increases as their motivation to contribute increases. From the perspective of education, collective ownership and accountability enhances collaborative inquiry and cooperation.

2. Online social software supports linking and referencing ideas so that the development of the ideas can be traced. Providing users with the ability to track idea formation and development, social software promotes the recognition of group participation in the idea creation process and acknowledges that ideas have a 'history of thought.' As an educational tool, social software provides a framework for the discovery of the origins of ideas within the collaborative setting, further enhancing a sense of community

authorship, value in individual contribution, and accountability to the collective.

3. Online social software provides ways to represent higher-order organizations of ideas. Social software enables the visualization of idea organization which scaffolds individual schema formation and linkages to prior knowledge. Scaffolding the connection between a learner's prior knowledge is a critical component in aiding in the transformation of conceptual understanding, which is a foundation of learning and development.

4. Online social software provides ways for the same idea to be worked within varied and multiple contexts and to appear in different higher-order organizations of knowledge. As social software enables the visualization of idea organizations, linkages to prior knowledge within multiple contexts promotes cross 'disciplinary' innovation. Further to characteristic 3, social software that enables the connection between multiple contexts promotes cross organizational understanding and individual conceptual change.

5. Online social software has different kinds of systems of feedback to enhance self- and group-monitoring processes. Within the context of social software, users have the ability to provide feedback enabling the group to collectively 'self'-organize and 'self'-monitor ongoing knowledge creation processes. The ability of a learner to be self-reflective is a critical component in self-regulated learning and metacognitive development. As social software enables collective and individual feedback processes, individuals within the social network have frequent opportunities to give and receive feedback on collaborative idea development.

6. Online social software provides opportunistic linking of persons and groups—with the possibility of crossing traditional disciplin-

ary, cultural, and age boundaries. As social software enables temporal relationships among members, opportunity for interactions among individuals is exponential. The possibilities of linking individuals from cross disciplinary fields, cultural, and age groups are more likely, thus encouraging alternative perspective taking; a critical component in higher-order thinking.

7. Online social software supports ways for different user groups to customize the environment and to explore within- and between community trajectories. As social software enables individual and group customization, identity formation at the individual generates a sense of ownership over the 'cultural' space. Further to a sense of community membership, individuals have the ability to construct their own 'situation definitions' and express different aspects of their personalities within the social network.

Characteristics of social software may vary with different kinds; however, if researchers and educators are to understand how to implement social software in education, then identifying the aforementioned characteristics in practice is critical for facilitating learning. Each kind of characteristic *in situ* has its own distinctive knowledge acquired through an individual's complete participation within the 'community of practice' (Bereiter & Scardamalia, 1996).

Social Software Promotes Communities of Practice

Members of an online social community are bound by what they do together and develop around a collective sense of meaning (Wenger, 1998). "Communities of practice are groups of people who share a concern, a set of problems, or a passion about a topic, and who deepen their knowledge and expertise in this area by interact-

ing on an ongoing basis" (Wenger, McDermot, & Snyder, 2002, p. 4). Online social networks form 'communities of practice' as individuals within these environments share concerns, as in advocating for social justice for women (Pierce, 2007), collaborate on a solution to set of problems, as in solving school management issues by principals (Smith, 2007), and deepen their knowledge and expertise, as in contributing to open-source software development projects (Hemetsberger & Reinhardt, 2006). Ultimately, members of a 'community of practice' share a collective sense of purpose supported by the structural elements the social software provides.

Communities of practice arise out of a collective sense of need and intention. To achieve a particular outcome communities of practice develop initially because of a necessity to fulfill a particular purpose, perform a particular function, and produce a particular product or action. Key ideas Wenger (1998) identifies as the primary characteristics of a community of practice involve questions of 1) what is the network about, 2) how the network functions, and 3) what the network produces. Within the context of online social software, particularly in its use in education, these particular questions are essential in determining the context, tasks, and outcomes for learning. Online social software enables the expression of these intentions as it provides particular structural elements that aid in the development of the community.

Online social software establishes a social, spatial, and temporal framework for the development of communities of practice. Structural capabilities of online social software do not inhibit the size of a network (small or large), how long the network exists (long-lived or short-lived), where members of the network are situated (co-located or distributed), whether members are homogenous or heterogeneous, and whether networks develop within (inside) and across boundaries (organizational, corporate, educational, country) (Wenger et al., 2002). Although, traditional social networks and communities of practice also share many of these structural elements, online social software makes each of these capabilities more prevalent and strategically adaptable to the educational and classroom setting. Incorporating social software for the purposes of teaching and learning within and beyond the classroom context engages a student in multiple ways of knowing through knowledge building, which, in turn cultivates a community of practice in the classroom and enables self- and co- regulated learning.

Social Software Enables Self-Regulated Learning

Social and academic competence is a highly improbable occurrence without the ability to self-regulate. The conditions that promote the development of self-regulatory systems are fundamental considerations in understanding the emergence of complex dynamic systems. Agency, social networks, as well as self-regulation are not isolated occurrences. They require the presence of multiple interacting factors that influence their dynamic relationship.

Individuals manipulate and reframe on-going activity to situate meaning construction through self-regulation. Self-regulated learning (SRL) involves an active, effortful process in which learners set goals for their learning and then attempt to monitor, regulate, and control their cognition, motivation, and behaviour (Pintrich, 2000). Guiding and constraining SRL processes are contextual features of the social and learning environments, such as teachers and other students, learning outcomes, and acceptable 'norms and practices' as defined by culture. Thus, SRL is a personal and collective process that is both meta-cognitive and socially mediated by *others*. Social software facilitates SRL as an individual system exercised through socially mediated means, and enables forethought, performance control, and

self-reflection (Bandura, 1986, 1997, 2001, 2006; Zimmerman, 1998, 2004).

Forethought. Influenced by personal motivational factors, the process of forethought involves the ability to anticipate the outcomes of a particular action and then strategically plan for a desired goal. In regards to academic learning, forethought involves goal setting, task analysis, motivational beliefs (goal orientation), and self-efficacy for the specified academic task. For example, a student believes that they are good at organic chemistry and is effacious about their upcoming midterm. The student then sets a goal to achieve an *A* on the midterm and begins to plan on how to study for the exam. In this example, the student believes they will do well, is confident in their abilities in the domain, sets a goal to achieve a particular grade on an assessment task, then makes a plan on how to achieve this academic outcome. Thus, in this manner, the student has "a forethoughtful perspective [that] provides direction, coherence, and meaning" to their achievement (Bandura, 2001, p. 7). Social software provides a supportive environment in which students are scaffolded through the analysis of a task, which in turn affects their motivation and self-efficacy for the task in question. In addition to forethought, learners must also be able to control and monitor the implementation of the plans they consider during forethought.

Performance control. Involving strength of will, self-control, and self-observation, learners engage in strategies to monitor and implement plans developed during forethought. In the development of academic competence, this stage of the SRL process is particularly important as the strategies learners employ, or develop, are of critical import if they are to achieve their desired outcome. For example, research on proactive learners suggests that a large percentage of them control environmental variables. Minimizing distractions in their study space by using earplugs while they study is a type of attention-focusing strategy (Corno, 1993; Corno & Kanfer, 1993), and just one example of the types of self-control strategies competent self-regulated learners use to achieve.

Using self-control strategies, proactive learners exercise self-observation processes to metacognitvely monitor their progress. Self-observation processes include self-monitoring, which refers to mentally tracking one's performance, and self-recording which involves a physical record of how one is doing (Zimmerman, 2004). For example, research on learners who use self-recording strategies demonstrated enhanced self-regulatory processes such as self-efficacy beliefs, which in turn improved goal attainment (Zimmerman & Kitsantas, 1997, 1999). Within social software, students have opportunities to practice regulatory strategies and observe other, potentially more effective strategies through other students in the network and have the control to monitor how they are performing and make adaptations as needed. To develop self-regulatory competence, in conjunction with performance control strategies, learners must also continuously reflect and evaluate on their progress on a task.

Self-reflection. A critical component in the self-regulatory process involves the continuous comparison of present levels of achievement with personal goals and standards. Self-regulatory comparisons or *judgments of success* involve comparisons along three different dimensions (Zimmerman, 2004). First, during self-improvement a learner evaluates their achievement based on progress over prior experience. Second, learners evaluate their achievement relative to the performance of their peers and thus, make comparative judgments along a *social* dimension. Finally, learners also use *mastery judgments* whereby they compare their achievement relative to a mastery source. Through *self* and *other* comparative processes reflective "actions give rise to self-reactive influence through performance comparison with goals and standards" (Bandura, 2001, p. 8). The comparison of goals and standards demonstrates

judgments of success, decision-making, and is an ultimate expression of agency. Social software provides an environment in which self and other comparative processes are possible within the social dimension (network). Agency not only includes the ability to make choices, but also the ability to take appropriate courses of action and evaluate success based on standards set both by the individual learner and by social others.

CONCLUSION

Social and group interactions in online communities develop and evolve from expressions of human agency. Agency is a result of an emergent causal relationship between ability, will, and action. Social networks are a result of mediated expressions of agency that challenge the existing authority structure of classroom discourse. Social software provides students with opportunities to manipulate contexts and strategically interact with other students (agents) to achieve a desired outcome. Thus, agency ability links attributes of motivation to courses of action. Expressions of agency through online social networks, promotes the idea that an individual has authority over their *virtual* cultural space.

Understanding human interaction within online social networks begins with an appreciation of agency. Agency ability is a social construction that develops through mediation, the appropriation of cultural tools, and facilitates a novel means of community formation. Social software in education gives students the power (ability) to do what they want in the absence of internal or external constraints, to understand and reflectively evaluate their intentions, reasons, and motives, and to control their own behavior. The authors suggest that future research explore questions of:

1. The impact of the formal or informal nature of the educational context on agency;

2. The affordances different types of social software tools have relative to the emergence of human agency;

3. The role of the facilitator in orchestrating and encouraging agency emergence; and

4. The potential implications each of these aspects have on learning design.

Education has a responsibility to engage the use of social software to encourage student's development of agency and responsible social action. A shift in authority structure is required to utilize online social networks as a means for knowledge construction, meaning making, and building community within the classroom. Educators can encourage the emergence of agency in social networks through establishing contexts for meaning making, collective inquiry, and knowledge building that develop a community of practice. Recognizing social software's potential as a cultural tool is critical for education as cultural tools not only enhance human thinking, they transform it (Gauvain, 2001).

REFERENCES

Ach, N. (1910). *Uber den willensakt und das temperament. [On the will and temperament]*. Leipzig, Germany: Quelle & Meyer.

Bakhtin, M.M. (1986/1978). Speech genres and other late essays. In C. Emerson & M. Holquist (Eds.). Austin, TX: University of Texas Press.

Bandura, A. (1986). *Social foundations of thought and action*. Englewood Cliffs, NJ: Prentice-Hall.

Bandura, A. (1997). *Self-Efficacy*. New York: W. H. Freeman and Company.

Bandura, A. (2001). Social cognitive theory: An agentic perspective. *Annual Review of Psychology, 52*, 1-26.

Bandura, A. (2006). Towards a psychology of human agency. *Perspectives on Psychological Science, 1*(2).

Bebo, Inc. (2008). About Bebo. Retrieved April 21, 2008, from http://www.bebo.com/StaticPage.jsp?StaticPageId=2517103831

Bereiter, C., & Scardamalia, M. (1996). Rethinking learning. In D. R. Olson & N. Torrance (Eds.), *The Handbook of Education and Human Development* (pp. 485-513). Cambridge, MA: Blackwell Publishers.

Bouffard, T., Bouchard, M., Goulet, G., Cenoncourt, I., & Couture, N. (2005). Influence of achievement goals and self-efficacy on students' self-regulation and performance. *International Journal of Psychology, 40*(6), 373-384.

Boyd, D.M. (2007). The significance of social software. In T. N. Burg & H. Schmidt (Eds.), *BlogTalks reloaded. Social software: Research & cases* (pp. 15-30). Herstellung: Books on Demand GmbH, Norderstedt.

Brown, A. (1987). Metacognition, executive control, self-regulation, and other more mysterious mechanisms. In F. E. Weinert & R. H. Kluwe (Eds.), *Metacognition, motivation, and understanding* (pp. 65-116). Hillsdale, NJ: Lawrence Earlbaum Associates.

Bruner, J. (1997). *The culture of education*. Cambridge, MA: Harvard University Press.

Carver, C., & Schier, M. (2002). Control processes and self-organization as complementary principles underlying behavior. *Personality and Social Psychology Review, 64*(4), 304-315.

Coates, T. (2005). An addendum to a definition of Social Software. *Plasticbag.org (blog)* Retrieved October 12, 2007, from http://www.plasticbag.org/archives/2005/01/an_addendum_to_a_definition_of_social_software/

Code, J., & Zaparyniuk, N. (this volume). Social identities, group formation, and the analysis of online communities. In S. Hatzipanagos & S. Warburton (Eds.), *Handbook of Research on Social Software and Developing Community Ontologies*. New York, NY: IGI Publishing.

Corno, L. (1993). The best laid plans: Modern conceptions of volition and educational research. *Educational Researcher, 22*(2), 17-22.

Corno, L. (2001). Volitional aspects of self-regulated learning. In B. Zimmerman & D. Schunk (Eds.), *Self-regulated learning and academic achievement* (Vol. 191-225). Mahwah, NJ: Lawrence Earlbaum Associates.

Corno, L., & Kanfer, R. (1993). The role of volition in learning and performance. *Review of Research in Education, 19*, 301-341.

Duranti, A., & Goodwin, C. (Eds.). (1992). *Rethinking context: Language as an interactive phenomenon*. Cambridge, UK: Cambridge University Press.

Emirbayer, M., & Mische, A. (1998). What is agency? *American Journal of Sociology, 103*(4), 962-1023.

Facebook, Inc. (2008). About Facebook. Retrieved April 21, 2008, from http://www.facebook.com/about.php

Flavell, J.H. (1979). Metacognition and cognitive monitoring: A new era of cognitive developmental inquiry. *American Psychologist, 34*, 906-911.

Gauvain, M. (2001). Cultural tools, social interaction, and the development of thinking. *Human Development, 44*(2-3), 126-143.

Gecas, V. (2003). Self-agency and the life course. In J. T. Mortimer & M. J. Shanahan (Eds.), *Handbook of the Life Course*. New York, NY: Kluwer Academic Publishing/Plenum Publishers.

Gergen, K.J. (1984). Theory of the self: Impasse and evolution. In L. Berkowitz (Ed.), *Advances in experimental psychology* (Vol. 17, pp. 49-115). New York, NY: Academic.

Gilbert, J.K. (2006). On the nature of "context" in chemical education. *International Journal of Science Education, 28*(9), 957-976.

Hemetsberger, A., & Reinhardt, C. (2006). Learning and knowledge-building in open-source communities: A social-experiential approach. *Management Learning, 37*(2), 187-214.

Henderson, D.K. (1994). Accounting for macro-level causation. *Synthese, 101*(2), 129-156.

Linden Research Inc. (2008). About Second Life. Retrieved April 21, 2008, from http://secondlife.com/

Johnson, J.C., Palinkas, L.A., & Boster, J.S. (2003). Informal social roles and the evolution and stability of social networks. In R. Breiger, K. Carley & P. Pattison (Eds.), *Dynamic social network modeling and analysis: Workshop summary and papers* (pp. 121-132). Washington, D.C.: National Research Council.

Johnson, N.F. (2007). *Two's Company, Three is complexity: A simple guide to the science of all sciences*. Oxford, UK: Oneworld.

Jones, R.H., & Norris, S. (2005). Introducing mediational means / cultural tools. In S. Norris & R. H. Jones (Eds.), *Discourse in Action* (pp. 49-51). New York, NY: Routledge.

Kuhl, J. (1985). Volitional mediators of cognition-behavior consistency: Self-regulatory processes in action versus state orientation. In J. Kuhl & J. Beckmann (Eds.), *Action control: From cognition to behavior* (pp. 101-128). West-Berlin: Springer-Verlag.

Lefcourt, H.M. (1966). Internal versus external control of reinforcement: A review. *Psychological Bulletin, 65*(4), 206-220.

Little, T.D., Hawley, P.H., Henrich, C.C., & Marsland, K.W. (2002). Three views of the agentic self: A developmental synthesis. In E. Deci & R. Ryan (Eds.), *Handbook of self-determination research* (pp. 390-404). Rochester, NY: University of Rochester Press.

Loedewyk, K., & Winne, P. (2005). Relations among the structure of learning tasks, achievement, and changes in self-efficacy in secondary students. *Journal of Educational Psychology, 97*(1), 3-12.

Markus, H.J., & Nurius, P.S. (1984). Self-understanding and self-regulation in middle childhood. In W. A. Collins (Ed.), *Development during middle childhood: The years from six to twelve.* Washington D.C: National Academy Press.

Martin, J. (2003). Emergent persons. *New Ideas in Psychology, 21*, 85-99.

Martin, J. (2004). Self-regulated learning, social cognitive theory, and agency. *Educational Psychologist, 39*(2), 135-145.

Martin, J., Sugarman, J., & Thompson, J. (2003). *Psychology and the question of agency.* New York, NY: State University of New York Press.

Mead, G.H. (1932). *The philosophy of the present.* Chicago, IL: University of Chicago Press.

Mead, G.H. (1934). *Mind, self and society from the standpoint of a social behaviorist.* Chicago, Il: Chicago University Press.

MySpace, Inc. (2008). About MySpace. Retrieved April 21, 2008, from http://www.myspace.com/index.cfm?fuseaction=misc.aboutus

Nowak, A., Vallacher, R.R., Tesser, A., & Borkowski, W. (2000). Society of self: The emergence of collective properties in self-structure. *Psychological Review, 39*, 39-61.

O'Connor, T., & Wong, H.Y. (2002). Emergent properties. In E. N. Zalta (Ed.), *Stanford encyclopedia of philosophy.* Stanford, CA: The Metaphysics Research Lab, Stanford University.

Park, D., & Moro, Y. (2006). Dynamics of Situation Definition. *Mind, Culture, and Activity, 13*(2), 101-129.

Parsons, T. (1968). *The Structure of Social Action.* New York, NY: Free Press.

Pierce, T. (2007). *Women, weblogs, and war: Digital culture and gender performativity. three case studies of online discourse by muslim cyber-conduits of Afghanistan, Iran, and Iraq.* ProQuest Information & Learning, US.

Pintrich, P. (2000). The role of goal orientation in self-regulated learning. In M. Boekaerts, P. Pintrich & M. Zeidner (Eds.), *Handbook of Self-Regulations* (pp. 451-502). San Diego, CA: Academic Press.

Rotter, J.B. (1954). *Social learning and clinical psychology.* Englewood Cliffs, NJ: Prentice-Hall.

Rotter, J.B. (1966). Generalized expectancies for internal versus external control of reinforcement. *Psychological Monographs, 80*(1), 1-28.

Rowe, S. (2005). Using multiple situation definitions to create hybrid activity space. In S. Norris & R. H. Jones (Eds.), *Discourse in action: Introducing mediated discourse analysis* (pp. 123-134). New York, NY: Routledge`.

Ryan, R., & Deci, E. (2000). Intrinsic and extrinsic motivations: Classic definitions and new directions. *Contemporary Educational Psychology, 25*(1), 54-67.

Scardamalia, M. (2004). Knowledge building environments: Extending the limits of the possible in education and knowledge work. In A. Distefano, K. E. Rudestam & R. Silverman (Eds.), *Encyclopedia of distributed learning.* Thousand Oaks, CA: Sage Publications.

Schunk, D., & Ertmer, P. (2001). Self-regulation and academic learning: Self-efficacy enhancing interventions. In M. Boekaerts, P. Pintrich & M. Zeidner (Eds.), *Handbook of Self-Regulation* (pp. 630-649). New York: Academic Press.

Smith, A.A. (2007). Mentoring for experienced school principals: Professional learning in a safe place. *Mentoring & Tutoring: Partnership in Learning, 15*(3), 277-291.

Sternberg, R.J. (1999). *Cognitive psychology.* Fort Worth, TX: Harcourt Brace.

Thompson, L., & Fine, G.A. (1999). Socially shared cognition, affect and behavior: A review and integration. *Personality and Social Psychology Review, 3*(4), 278-302.

Vallacher, R.R., Nowak, A., Froehlich, M., & Rockloff, M. (2002). The dynamics of self-evaluation. *Journal of Personality and Social Psychology Review, 6*, 370-379.

Vallacher, R.R., Nowak, A., Markus, J., & Strauss, J. (1998). Dynamics in the coordination of mind and action. In M. Kofta, G. Weary & G. Seflek (Eds.), *Personal control in action: Cognitive and motivational mechanisms* (pp. 27-59). New York, NY: Plenum.

Vygotsky, L.S. (1962). *Thought and language.* Cambridge, MA: MIT Press.

Vygotsky, L.S. (1978). *Mind in society: The development of higher psychological processes.* Cambridge, MA: Harvard University Press.

Vygotsky, L.S. (1981). The instrumental method in psychology. In J. V. Wertsch (Ed.), *The concept of activity in Soviet psychology* (pp. 134-143). New York, NY: M. E. Sharpe.

Wenger, E. (1998). Communities of practice: Learning as a social system [Electronic Version]. *The Systems Thinker, 9.* Retrieved November 10, 2007, from http://www.ewenger.com/

Wenger, E., McDermot, R.M., & Snyder, W.M. (2002). *Cultivating communities of practice: A guide to managing knowledge.* Boston, MA: Harvard Business School Press.

Wertsch, J.V. (1985). *Culture, communication, and cognition: Vygotskian perspectives.* New York, NY: Cambridge University Press.

Wertsch, J.V., Tulviste, P., & Hagstrom, F. (1993). A sociocultural approach to agency. In E. A. Forman, N. Minick & C. A. Stone (Eds.), *Contexts for learning: Sociocultural dynamics in children's development* (pp. 336-356). New York, NY: Oxford University Press.

Wolters, C. (1999). The relation between high school students' motivational regulation and their use of learning strategies, effort, and classroom performance. *Learning and Individual Differences, 11*(3), 281-299.

Wolters, C. (2003). Regulation of motivation: Evaluating an underemphasized aspect of self-regulated learning. *Educational Psychologist, 38*(4), 189-205.

Wolters, C., Yu, S., & Pintrich, P. (1996). The relation between goal orientation and students' motivational beliefs and self-regulated learning. *Learning and Individual Differences, 8*(3).

Zimmerman, B. (1998). Academic studying and the development of personal skill: A self-regulatory perspective. *Educational Psychologist, 33*(2/3), 73-86.

Zimmerman, B. (2004). Sociocultural influence and students' development of academic self-regulation: A social-cognitive perspective. In D. M. McInerney & S. Van Etten (Eds.), *Big Theories Revisited* (Vol. 4 In: Research on Sociocultural Influences on Motivation and Learning, pp. 139-164). Greenwich, CT: Information Age Publishing.

Zimmerman, B., & Kitsantas, A. (1997). Developmental phases in self-regulation: Shifting from process goals to outcome goals. *Journal of Educational Psychology, 89*(1), 29-36.

Zimmerman, B., & Kitsantas, A. (1999). Acquiring writing revision skill: Shifting from process to outcome self-regulatory goals. *Journal of Educational Psychology, 91*(2), 241-250.

KEY TERMS

Agency: The capability of individuals to consciously choose, influence, and structure their actions (Emirbayer & Mische, 1998; Gecas, 2003) and is an exercise of ability and will through action.

Communities of Practice: Involve groups of people who share concerns, problems, and passions about a topic, and who choose to interact to deepen their knowledge and expertise in this area by interacting on an ongoing basis (Wenger et al., 2002).

Cultural Tools: Mediate higher-order mental processes such as reasoning and problem solving (Vygotsky, 1962, 1978). Cultural tools include both *technical tools* such as books, media, computers, and social software, and *psychological tools* such as language, signs, writing, and symbols.

Emergence: From an ontological perspective is a non-reducible phenomenon. Meaning, that if a construct is emergent it has several component parts but is irreducible with respect to them (Martin, 2003; O'Connor & Wong, 2002).

Knowledge-Building Environments (KBES): Environments that "enhance collaborative efforts to create and continually improve ideas" (Scardamalia, 2004).

Locus of Control: A belief in the causal relationship between's one own behavior and that of an outcome affects a range of choices an individual makes (Lefcourt, 1966; Rotter, 1966).

Self-Efficacy: A belief in one's capability to succeed at a given task (Bandura, 1997).

Self-Regulated Learning

Social Software: Software which "supports, extends, or derives added value from human social behavior" (Coates, 2005).

Volition: A "post-decisional, self-regulatory processes that energize[s] the maintenance and enactment of intended actions" (Kuhl, 1985, p. 90).

Chapter IX
Exploiting Collaborative Tagging Systems to Unveil the User–Experience of Web Contents:
An Operative Proposal

A. Malizia
Universidad Carlos III de Madrid, Spain

A. De Angeli
University of Manchester, UK

S. Levialdi
Sapienza University of Rome, Italy

I. Aedo Cuevas
Universidad Carlos III de Madrid, Spain

ABSTRACT

The User Experience (UX) is a crucial factor for designing and enhancing the user satisfaction when interacting with a computational tool or with a system. Thus, measuring the UX can be very effective when designing or updating a Web site. Currently, there are many Web sites that rely on collaborative tagging: such systems allow users to add labels (tags) for categorizing contents. In this chapter the authors present a set of techniques for detecting the user experience through Collaborative Tagging Systems and we present an example on how to apply the approach for a Web site evaluation. This chapter highlights the potential use of collaborative tagging systems for measuring users' satisfaction and discusses the future implications of this approach as compared to traditional evaluation tools, such as questionnaires, or interviews.

INTRODUCTION

Collaborative tagging is the process by which users add metadata to a community-shared content, in order to organize documents for future navigation, inspection, filtering, or search. The content is organised by descriptive terms (tags), which are chosen informally and personally by the user. The freedom to choose unstructured tags is the main distinctive feature of collaborative tagging systems, as compared to traditional digital libraries or other systems of content organization, where the creation of metadata is the task of dedicated professionals (such as librarians) or derives from additional material supplied by the authors (Bennis et al. 1998, Csikszentmihalyi, 1997). Like all socially-generated structures, tagging is an adaptable process; it takes the form best supported by the content, letting users decide the categorization of such content, rather than imposing a rigid structure on it. Collaborative tagging is most useful in an environment like the World Wide Web, where a single "content classification authority" cannot exist and there is a large amount of data content being continually produced by the users.

The widespread success of collaborative tagging systems over the last few years has generated a large collection of data reflecting opinions on, and evaluation of, web contents. In this chapter, we look into the possibility of exploiting this large database to evaluate the user experience (UX) of web sites. UX is a multi-faceted construct recently introduced into the HCI agenda to describe the quality of an interactive system (Garrett 2003; McCarthy and Wright 2005). This construct is used to indicate how people feel about a product and their pleasure and satisfaction when using it (Hassenzahl and Tracktinsky, 2006). Responses such as aesthetic judgments, satisfaction or frustration, feelings of ownership and identity are the most prominent aspects of user experiences investigated in this new, comprehensive, HCI research area (De Angeli, Sutcliffe and Hart-

man, 2005; Hartman, Sutcliffe and De Angeli, 2007; Norman, 2004). Normally, these responses are collected in formal evaluation settings via questionnaires and/or interviews. Collaborative tagging may offer an interesting alternative, one which is cheaper and less prone to experimental bias. In this chapter, we present a technique to extract semantics from tagging systems, and interpret them to describe the user experience when interacting with on-line content.

This chapter has the following organisation. Paragraph 2 reviews related works on collaborative tagging systems. Paragraph 3 describes three different techniques that can be used to extract semantics from tagging systems. Paragraph 4 reports a method to derive semantics differential attributes from collaborative tagging systems, 3, and its evaluation. Paragraph 5 summarizes the chapter, delineates future trends in the use of collaborative tagging systems for automating evaluation techniques and draws the conclusions.

BACKGROUND

Collaborative Tagging Systems (Golder et al., 2006; Mathes, 2004) offer their users the possibility to index contents for organizing web-related information, sharing knowledge and opinions. There is a growing number of successful web sites which include collaborative tagging, allowing users to index and share different types of contents. Del.icio.us (http://del.icio.us/), for example, specializes on bookmarking, categorizing and sharing URLs, Flickr (http://www.flickr.com/) allows users to tag photographs they own; Technorati (http://technorati.com/) is devoted to tag weblogs; and Youtube (http://www.youtube.com/) allows tagging videos. Other interesting examples are Snipit (http://www.snipit.org/), which offers the functionality of bookmarking sections of web pages, and CiteULike (http://www.citeulike.org/) or Connotea (http://www.connotea.org/) that allow tagging and commenting references to academic publications.

Collaborative tagging systems allow users to become active contributors in the classification of web-content. Because of this characteristic some authors refer to them as "folksonomy" (Mathes, 2004), short for "folk taxonomy", albeit there is still some debate whether this term is accurate (Golder et el., 2006). Users of collaborative tagging systems do not only categorize information for themselves, but they can also share their classification and browse the information categorized by other users. In fact, many collaborative tagging systems have features for sharing contents and their associated tags among users. They also, offer functionalities for keeping contents private, shared only within a pre-set list of users, or public (shared with everyone).Therefore, tagging is both a personal and a social activity. According to the number of people who can tag the same content and/or to the level of privacy of the tag (shared vs. personal).Collaborative tagging systems are distinguished in "broad" and "narrow" systems (Van der Wal, 2005). A broad tagging system is the result of one item being categorized by many people (Del.icio.us is an example). This can generate a very diverse set of tagging, as different users can enter their preferred terms, with obvious semantic and syntactic variations. There will be some terms that are used by many people to describe one item or many items which are described by the same terms. The concentration of terms can take advantage of power laws (like the Zipf distribution (Zipf, 1949; Newman, 2005)) to quickly see the preferred terms for an item or items.). It states that the frequency of the occurrence of a term is inversely proportional to its frequency class. Zipf has discovered experimentally that the more frequently a word is used, the less meaning it carries.

A narrow folksonomy is the result of one person categorizing one item (Flickr is an example). In this case, tags are private, but users could decide to share their own photos allowing others to view their tags and thus their categorization

of contents. When the contents (and tags) are shared with other users a narrow folkosomy can approximate a broad one; nevertheless since the option of sharing contents and tags is leaved to the final user we cannot strictly rely on it.

This paper concentrates on broad collaborative tagging systems, where several users index and share different content. We regard the folksonomy produced by these systems as a result of collective intelligence and social creativity (Fischer 2006): different users contribute to the establishment and dissemination of knowledge. In this vision, collaborative tagging systems are not only important for their primary task (e.g., information retrieval), but they assume a fundamental role in the quest for understanding the user experience. People tag content with words which have both denotative and connotative meaning; these tags are a reflection of their opinion on the content, the service provider and the interface design. We believe that tagging systems act as social dynamics enablers representing the real "vox populi"; in fact, users can take advantage of tagging information shared by others(Nov, 2007). Tagging systems leave the users free to express their own opinion without restricting them in a frame, such as a questionnaire. We believe that this method is more likely to capture the ecological perception of the web site audience. Collaborative tagging systems offer a lot of unstructured metadata (tags) associated to many different contents (web sites, photos, videos, etc.) that can be used for measuring the UX of these contents over the Internet.

Moreover, collaborative tagging systems allow detecting variations over time, by analyzing how tagging evolve. The goal of our research is to develop a methodology to extract meanings from collaborative tagging systems and to use this information in order to understand what people think about on-line contents. This methodology requires a two phased process: (a) detecting semantics from tagging systems; (b) interpreting the meaning of this information.

DETECTING SEMANTICS FROM TAGGING SYSTEMS

Information retrieval (IR[1]) from unstructured contents such as those produced by tagging systems) is a complex task. A major problem relates to the fact that no current tagging systems have synonyms control (e.g. "Mac" and "Macintosh" do not coincide in Del.icio.us). For this reason, in order to use the information contained in a collaborative tagging system, we need to use techniques extracting semantics from users' tags. In the following paragraph, we discuss three information retrieval techniques that can be used to extract semantic features from tagging.

Many information systems use keywords or key phrases to search or browse collection of documents for specific terms and information. Not only are keywords used for searching relevant documents but also to index and categorize the content. Relevant information is indicated by the authors of a document and is placed in appropriate sections for emphasizing them. Typical examples are the title, abstract and author's name written with bold or in appropriate places of the document. This approach is useful if employed within document collection explicitly managing this information, such as newspapers articles. Nevertheless this information is not available in general and providing them manually can be tedious or inapplicable depending on the amount of relevant keywords or terms we want to provide for each document.

IR algorithms were devised to address this problem, trying to automatically extract relevant terms and keywords from unstructured document collection. IR algorithms employ two different phases (Turney, 2002): keywords assignment, and keywords extraction. Usually, there is a training phase where an initial default list of relevant keywords is provided to the system, thus using a controlled dictionary. The wider is the list, the greater should be the number of documents used

to train the system by manually indicating the keywords included in each document (chosen among the given list). These types of algorithms are called training-intensive, i.e. a big training set is required to obtain good performance.; On the contrary, keywords extraction does not need any training since the keywords are directly extracted from the body of each document by using the information learned from the training phase and some similarity measure. In the next section, we present a selection of three IR algorithms that can be used to automatically extracting semantics from collaborative tagging systems.

PMI-IR

The PMI-IR (Point wise Mutual Information – Information Retrieval) algorithm employs the technology of a search engine, such as Google Page Rank, or Yahoo, (Krikos, et al. 2005; Kraft et al. 2006)) to extract the frequency of searched keywords within a collection of documents. In general, the algorithm takes as input a word and a set of alternative terms for that specific word. The output is the selection of the terms whose meaning is the closest to the given word. That is to say, the algorithm finds the synonyms by analyzing the co-occurrences of the terms with the given keyword and among them.

This is exactly the case for tagging systems, where we have a collection of contents labeled with different words representing keywords for that collection and we would like to group words having the same meaning.

There exist different ways of measuring the co-occurrence between two terms, but the one used by PMI-IR algorithm is based on the Point wise Mutual Information (1), where problem represents the given word (tag in a folksonomy), $\{choice_1,..., choice_n\}$ represent the n alternatives for problem and $P(problem, choice_i)$, $i=1,..,n$ the probability of the co-occurrence.

Score (choice$_i$) = log2 (P (problem, choice$_i$) / P (problem) P (choice$_i$))   (1)

If problem and choice$_i$ are statistically independent, then the probability of co-occurrence is described by P (problem) P (choice$_i$). If problem and choice$_i$ are not independent (i.e., they tend to co-occur) the numerator in (1) will be greater than the denominator and the ratio will describe the independence rank between the two terms.

By considering that P (problem) is assuming the same value for each associated choice$_i$ and that the log function is monotonically increasing, equation (1) can be simplified as follows:

Score (choice$_i$) = log2 (P (problem, choice$_i$) / P (choice$_i$)).   (2)

The conditional probability value P (problem| choice$_i$) is assigned as a measure of how close the words are (synonyms). This measure can be computed, for instance, by using a search engine like Google page rank or Altavista advanced search. P (problem| choice$_i$) represents the number of documents returned by the search engine, called hits, when searching for problem and choice$_i$. The term which is the most similar to the problem is the one that maximizes the measure as shown in (3).

To clarify how this algorithm can be used for extracting semantics from tags, let us give an example. In the first instance we consider as co-occurring two words appearing in the same document, for example tags used in del.icio.us for categorizing the same web site; e.g. www.microsoft.com tagged with both the words 'explorer' and 'windows'. In this context, the score assigned to each choice$_i$ is computed as follows:

Score (choice$_i$) = (hits (problem AND choice$_i$) / hits (choice$_i$)).   (3)

The equation reported in (3) assigns as score the value of the ratio between the number of documents containing the two terms (problem and choice$_i$) and the number of documents containing only choice$_i$.

The tag which is most correlated to the problem is the one obtaining the highest score value computed as of (3). This is a reasonable is a reasonable measure of similarity among tags and a given term, yet is has some problems. In fact, a good similarity measure should include the totality of the tags included in a tagging system and not only within a basic set of choice$_i$ terms. Different tags can have different meanings depending on the interpretation of the author of the tags. Thus, this approach is suitable for narrow folksonomies where clusters of tags are created by some users who upload the contents using their own way of categorizing contents which are likely to have a narrow and well defined range of synonyms.

Collaborative Tag Suggestion

A new IR algorithm (Xu et al., 2006) has been recently introduced, which is based on tag suggestions for annotating documents in collaborative tagging systems. This method assigns reputation weights to the authors of tags, on the basis of the accuracy of words entered. The system suggests terms to use as tags for documents based on the words which are most frequently used by users with good reputation (good sense-making).

This algorithm still keeps into account the magnitude of the co-occurrences of terms but using a subset of terms used by certain experienced users. The objective is to evaluate which tags are relevant (keywords) for the documents in the folksonomy. This objective is achieved by a ranking among users indicating which ones participate positively (the most reliable) on the tagging process. The notation used for this algorithm is defined as follows:

- Ps (ti/tj; o): it is the probability that a user labels an object o with the tag ti knowing that the tag tj has already been used for the same object (i.e., document). To measure the correlation between the two tags on the object o, the algorithm considers the ratio between the number of users using both ti and tj, and the number of users using only tj.

- Pa (ti/tj): it is the probability that any object is labeled with the tag ti knowing that the tag tj has already been used for the same object. In this case the observation refers only to the tags and not to the objects. To measure this correlation between the two tags, the algorithm considers the ratio between the number of users using both ti and tj, and the number of users using only tj.
- S (t, o): indicates the score of the tag t on the object o, computed by summing the number of users that labeled o with t.
- C (t): indicates the coverage of a tag, which is the number of objects labeled with t. The greater is the number of objects tagged with t, the less specific is the meaning of the tag t. In other words if t is used very often it is a generic term.

The algorithm works by iterating the selection of the tags ti for which S (t, o) is high and multiplying this by the inverse of C (ti). After selecting the ti with the maximum score, the scores of every other tag t' are changed according to the following statements:

- t' score S (t',o), is decreased removing redundant information, i.e. subtracting the value of the probabilities product of t' and ti used together. In this way the superposition of the suggested tags is reduced, as in $S(t',o) = S(t',o) - Pa(t'/tj) S(/tj,o)$
- t' score S(t',o), is increased if it co-occurs with the selected tag tj over the object o, as in $S(t',o) = S(t',o) + Ps(t'/tj;o) S(/tj,o)$. This procedure allows dealing with basic level variations of tags, normalising the score for tags like BLOG, BLOGGING, and BLOGS.

The drawbacks of this approach are related to the fact that there exist narrow folksonomies, like Flickr, where every object o (i.e. a document) is own by the user that uploaded it, or by users to whom the owner has granted access permissions. In these cases, we do not have access to all the information needed for running the algorithm over a wide number of tags. Thus the clustering process does not necessarily represent the users' opinion on the tagged topic; but a specific feeling about the shared content (e.g. a link to a web site, and thus the web site itself) can be detected by means of finding related words among a community of users sharing the same interests.

The Semantic Halo Algorithm

In our previous work we introduced a Semantic Halo technique in order to deal with word semantics in tagging systems (Dix et al., 2006). The basic idea consisted of using co-occurrences of tags to cluster their relationships and meanings.

The Semantic Halo is defined as a set of search results for a given tag made by a set of four features, labeled as **4A**:

- **Aggregation**. Representing all the tags linked or related to a given tag.
- **Abstraction**. It is similar to aggregation but it relates to a direction (increasing and decreasing), thus it contains two subsets:
  o Generalization, tags increasing abstraction with respect to the given tag,
  o Specialization, tags decreasing abstraction with respect to the given tag.
- **Ambience**. It is the context for a given tag. It includes all the possible tags appearing in the same context, and that will be useful for augmenting or refining the user query. This set is built from a basic context set.
- **Age**. It is a list of the Ambience feature elements over time. It helps in retrieving tags

ordered by meanings given to them over time.

The algorithm was tested within the Del.icio. us community. In this environment, users submit their links to a website, adding some descriptive text and keywords, and Del.icio.us aggregates their posts with everyone else's submissions allowing users to share their contributions. The algorithm was implemented using Del.icio.us programming APIs (Application Programming Interfaces). This procedures allowed to collect results while the users where tagging. Because the Del.icio.us community is very large and active this test resulted in a quite complex but effective test.

For example, given the tag "university", which is quite general, our algorithm searched over Delicious for related tags and retrieved:

Ambience = {'open', {'learning', 'University'}}
Abstraction = {'online', 'education'} U {'colleges', 'high', 'degree', 'distance', 'Commons'}
Age = (('learning', 'University'), ('open'))[2]
Aggregation = {'soccer', 'gradschool', 'corps', 'indoor', 'course', 'masters', 'research institute', 'cites', 'cincinatti', 'peace', 'demographic', 'content', 'courses', 'innovators', 'urban', 'tournament', 'entrepreneurship', 'liverpool', 'york', 'community-college', 'schools', 'Illinois', 'abroad', 'Content', 'latino', 'Course', 'complexity', 'planning', 'Initiative', 'academiclibrary', 'enterprise', 'semantic-web', 'Education', 'grad', 'scholarship', 'teaching', 'college', 'school'}.

We can observe that the Ambience set is composed of two subsets, associated with two different contexts or meanings of the 'university' tag. The algorithm can solve also basic level variations[3] since the tag 'University' with the capital 'U' is strongly associated with the 'university' tag (without using any parser). The first part of the Abstraction set is related to generalization of the

given tag, while the second part is specialization, thus providing a partition of the related tags in increasing and decreasing abstraction. The Age sequence is the ordered set of contexts (meanings) with respect to last updates. The Aggregation set lists all the related tags, and even if there are unwanted tags the majority (as shown in the example above) is clearly related.

The Semantic Halo algorithm is applicable in general to broad and narrow collaborative tagging systems but has the drawback of employing a clustering technique that can be less effective or precise in specific sub-domains originated by users' tags.

Summary

All the different algorithms presented in these paragraphs can be employed for extracting semantics from tags by automatically organising them in classes or synonyms. The designer can choose different algorithms or techniques depending on the characteristics of the considered tagging system.

PMI-IR is quite fast to compute and since it is a standard approach within the IR field, many implementations can be found. The drawbacks of this approach are related to the fact that tags have different meanings depending on the sense-making of the users. As a consequence, for retrieving useful semantics the algorithm should span over the entire collection of tagged contents (considering the different choice$_i$ words). The Collaborative Tag Suggestion approach is very effective but it should be avoided when dealing with narrow tagging systems (Flickr for example) when every tagged content is owned by the user or shared with a specific subset of users granting permissions to them. Finally, the Semantic Halo can be used to extract semantics both from broad and narrow Collaborative Tagging Systems but it is less precise in specific sub-domains of tags (users' annotating contents in on specific domain or topic).

Choosing an IR algorithm is a first step for organizing unstructured content, which is a prerequisite for evaluating the UX over contents shared by tagging systems.

SEMANTIC DIFFERENTIAL IN COLLABORATIVE TAGGING SYSTEMS

This section describes a method to evaluate the information extracted from the tags in order to obtain a measure of the user-experience with web-sites. The evaluation phase in our approach is based on the elaboration of the concept of semantic differential introduced by the psychologist and communication scholar E. Osgood (1975). The original work of Osgood focused on the measurement of meaning, addressing issues of word semantics and psychological differences between words. In his influential research the author proposed a method (the semantic differential) to highlight individual differences in the attribution of meaning to words. The semantic differential measures people's reaction to stimulus words and concepts. Participants are invited to rate the stimulus with a bipolar scale. Each extreme of the scale is labeled by contrasting adjectives, such as bad-good. This technique has been frequently used in psychometrics to measure a number of psychological constructs, and more recently has been employed in HCI to build user satisfaction questionnaires. An example of opposite couples of adjectives used by Osgood methodology is shown in table 1.

Osgood research has demonstrated that ratings on bipolar adjective scales tend to be correlated, and to cluster around three basic dimensions of response, which account for most of the co-variation in ratings. These dimensions, labeled as Evaluation, Potency, and Activity (EPA), have been verified by factor analyses and replicated in an impressive variety of studies.

In our approach, there are no fixed couples

of opposite adjectives but the information is extracted from the adjectives freely introduced by the user. The adjectives are then associated to one of the three dimensions evaluation, potency, and activity

Evaluation

In order to test our methodology of semantic differential through collaborative tagging systems we built a basic collaborative tagging system. Users could add tags for categorizing contents, we explicitly asked users to use adjective as tags for categorizing the contents. Then by employing an IR algorithm we obtained a structured representation of the tags. Successively, we clustered structured tags into groups of adjectives. These groups of adjectives where used for applying the semantic differential technique and obtaining a measure of the UX on the web-site contents.

The objective of our evaluation study was to evaluate the experience of a community of users with respect to the Sapienza University of Rome Italian web portal (www.uniroma1.it). We choose this target because many users of the web portal were complaining about its features and usability. In fact, the Sapienza web portal has now been redesigned.

Table 1. Opposite couples of adjectives used by Osgood

1.	Angular/Rounded,
2.	Weak/Strong,
3.	Rough/Smooth,
4.	Active/Passive,
5.	Small/Large,
6.	Cold/Hot,
7.	Good/Bad,
8.	Tense/Relaxed,
9.	Wet/Dry,
10.	Fresh/Stale.

The community considered in this experiment is composed of 48 people. The majority of users (60%) were students. The remaining sample was split in 20% of administrative staff and 20% of academic staff.

Participants were invited to browse the website and tag it with their preferred set of adjectives. This system provided users with classic collaborative tagging functionalities, such as: presenting the document to be tagged and the text labels where the corresponding tags could be added. Figure 2 shows the tagging systems used for the experiment, even if displayed in Italian the tagging and web site area are clearly visible.

We collected around 162 tags from 48 individuals in a 2 weeks time-frame. As a first step we analyzed the frequency of each tag (adjective) as presented in table 2. Analysing the adjectives, it appears that there is a sort of binary distribution of the general tags among positive and negative

evaluation. Looking at the frequency distribution (for example f= 11), we found that two very different tags (simple and dazed) are the most frequently used. This effect is evident for almost every couple of tags in Table 2. The effect was also evident in the complete dataset, even with less frequent tags. This let us hypothesize that even after the clustering process (assigning tags to the three classes: evaluation, potency and activity) the user perception would be split in two neat categories according to the overall binary perception: positive or negative.

We categorized the tags in the three classes according to the clustering proposed by Osgood in (Osgood et al, 1975), as shown in Table 3. We used the PMI-IR to automatically measure the distance between the selected adjective (Problem) and the couples of adjectives contained in the Osgood scale. This approach has been employed for the positive and the negative meanings of a tag. The three major factors for a tag to belong to a class are:

- **Evaluation:** Representing the overall feelings about the web site (adjectives like good or bad);
- **Potency:** Representing the expressive power and impact on the perception of the web site (adjectives like strong or weak);
- **Activity:** Representing the possibilities and functionalities (at informational level) offered by the web site (adjectives like: active or passive).

By using the clustering results we analyzed the experience of each user, expressed by the tags

Table 2. Table showing the most occurring tags

Tag	Occurrence
Simple	11
Dazed	11
Clear	6
Sad	6
Comprehensive	6
Inconsistent	5
Intuitive	4
Useless	4
Poor	4

Table 3. Classes assigned after the clustering phases and number of tags falling in their relative class; the third rows represent the number of tags per class with positive and negative meanings, (+n) stands for n tags in that category with positive meaning and (-n) for the negatives.

Evaluation	Potency	Activity
82 (+40)(-42)	52 (+11)(-41)	28 (+8)(-20)

Figure 1. The custom collaborative tagging system including tagging labels and interested web site

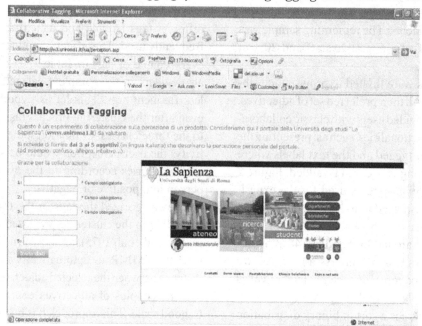

Figure 2. A bar-chart view of the users with respect to the selected classes (evaluation, potency and activity)

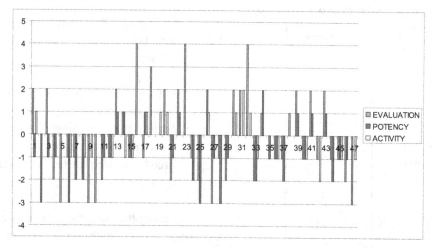

inserted in the system with respect to the selected classes (evaluation, potency and activity) and their positive or negative meaning. Figure 2 shows individual results for each user (1-47[4]).

Figure 3 suggests that, in general, the user evaluation of the web-site has been quite negative as most of the scores fell in the negative half of the scale. Potency is the weakest dimension.

Figure 3. A bar-chart view of the overall evaluation, potency and activity

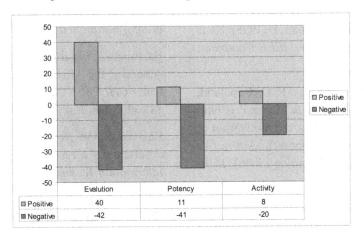

	Evalution	Potency	Activity
▦ Positive	40	11	8
▪ Negative	-42	-41	-20

Furthermore this graph highlights that users with a positive evaluation of the web site focus their attention to that particular class (the Evaluation class), which deals mainly with strong feelings about a web site (adjectives like: good or bad, nice or ugly, etc.).

CONCLUSION

This chapter presented a UX evaluation approach consisting of three steps:: 1) select a collaborative tagging system containing the content for which we would like to evaluate the users' experience (Del.icio.us for web sites, Flickr and YouTube for multimedia content, Technorati for blogs); 2) employ an IR technique to extract semantics for users' tags and group them together by cluster of synonyms or related tags; 3) use the data automatically extracted from the clusters of tags to detect the overall impression of users (UX) over the selected content (web sites, multimedia systems, blogs, etc.) by grouping tags according to the semantic differential technique. We reported an example of how this evaluation approach can

be applied on an ad-hoc collaborative tagging system. Anyway, this procedure can be applied to a wide range of collaborative tagging systems. In our test we asked users to add adjective tags to keep it controlled but generally we will have plenty of available tags already inserted by users of collaborative tagging systems. What do you mean by that? You need to explain further by re-writing this sentence.

Our approach suggests the importance of collaborative tagging systems in the evaluation of the end users experience. It seems to be a promising and cost effective alternative to questionnaires or interviews.

Collaborative tagging systems are becoming increasingly popular on the Internet. There are many reasons why users are motivated in volunteering their time to support these on-line communities (Clary et al., 1998), adding information to collaborative tagging systems over the web; nevertheless such systems keep growing as a social phenomena. We can take advantage of this huge number of users to detect the user experience perceived by them when adding tags for categorizing a content of interest over the web.

REFERENCES

Bennis, W., & Ward Biederman, P. (1998). None of us is as smart as all of us. *IEEE Computer, 31*(3), 116–117.

Clary, E. G., Snyder, M., Ridge, R. D., Copeland, J., Stukas, A. A., Haugen, J., & Miene, P. (1998). Understanding and assessing the motivation of volunteers: A functional approach. *Journal of Personality and Social Psychology, 74*(6), 1516-1530.

Coleman, W. D., & Williges, R. C. (1985). Collecting detailed user evaluations of software interfaces. *Proc. Human Factors Society: Twenty-Ninth Annual Meeting*, Santa Monica, CA, (pp. 204-244).

Csikszentmihalyi, M. (1998). Creativity: Flow and the psychology of discovery and invention. *Perennial*, June 1997.

De Angeli, A., Sutcliffe, A., Hartmann, J. (2006). *Interaction, usability and aesthetics: What influences users' preferences? DIS 2006 Conference Proceedings, ACM*, (pp. 271-280).

Dix A., Levialdi S., & Malizia A. (2006). Semantic halo for collaboration tagging systems. In S. Weibelzahl & A. Cristea (Eds.), *Proceedings of Workshop held at the Fourth International Conference on Adaptive Hypermedia and Adaptive Web-Based Systems (AH2006). Workshop on Social Navigation and Community-Based Adaptation Technologies* (pp. 514-521), Lecture Notes in Learning and Teaching, Dublin: National College of Ireland.

Fischer, G. (2006). *Distributed intelligence: extending the power of the unaided, individual human mind.* In C. Augusto (Ed.), AVI (pp. 7–14). ACM Press.

Garrett, J. J. (2003). *The elements of the user experience: User centred design for the web.* London: Easy Riders..

Golder, S., & Huberman, B. A. (2006). Usage Patterns of Collaborative Tagging Systems. *Journal of Information Science, 32*(2), 198-208.

Hartmann J., Sutcliffe A., & De Angeli, A. (2007*).* Assessing the Attractiveness of Interactive Systems. *CHI 2007 Conference Proceedings* (pp. 387-396), San Jose, CA, USA,.

Hassenzahl, M., & Tractinsky, N. (2006). *U*ser experience - a research agenda. *Behaviour & Information Technology, 25*, 91-97.

Kraft, R., Chang, C. C., Maghoul, F., & Kumar, R. (2006). Searching with context. In *Proceedings of the 15th international Conference on World Wide Web* (pp. 477-486) (Edinburgh, Scotland, May 23 - 26, 2006). WWW '06. ACM, New York, NY.

Krikos, V., Stamou, S., Kokosis, P., Ntoulas, A., & Christodoulakis, D. (2005). DirectoryRank: ordering pages in web directories. In *Proceedings of the 7th Annual ACM international Workshop on Web information and Data Management* (pp. 17-22) (Bremen, Germany, November 04 - 04, 2005). WIDM '05. ACM, New York, NY.

Mathes, A. (2004). *Folksonomies cooperative classification and communication through shared metadata.* Retrieved October 12, 2006, from http://www.adammathes.com/academic/computer-mediated communication/folksonomies.html.

McCarthy, J., & Wright, P. (2005). *Technology as Experience.* Cambridge: MIT Press.

Newman, N. (2005). Power laws, pareto distributions and zipf's law. *Contemporary Physics, 46*, 323-351.

Norman, D. (2004). *Emotional Design: Why we love or hate everyday things.* New York: Basic Books.

Nov, O. (2007). What motivates Wikipedians? *Commun. ACM 50, 11* (Nov. 2007), 60-64.

Osgood, H. M., William, C. E., & Murray, S. M. (1975). *Cross-cultural universals of affective meaning.* University of Illinois Press, Urbana.

Turney, P. (2002). *Mining the Web for Lexical Knoledge to Improve Keyphase extraction: Learning from Labeled and Unlabeled Data*, NRC/ERB-1096, July 19, NRC 44947.

Van der Wal, T. (2005). *Explaining and showing broad and narrow folksonomies*, Personal InfoCloud: February 2005 Archives. Retrieved November 22, 2007, from http://www.personalinfocloud.com/2005/02/.

Xu, Z., Fu, Y., Mao, J., & Su, D. (2006). Towards the semantic web: Collaborative tag suggestions. *In proceedings of the Collaborative Web Tagging Workshop at WWW2006*, Edinburgh, Scotland, May, 2006.

Zipf, G. K. (1949). *Human behaviour and the principle of least effort.* Cambridge MA: Addison-Wesley

KEY TERMS

Collaborative Tagging Systems: Collaborative tagging (also know as folksonomy, social classification, social indexing and other names) is the practice and method of collaboratively creating and managing tags to annotate and categorize content[5].

Distributed Intelligence: In many traditional approaches, human cognition has been seen as existing solely "inside" a person's head, and studies on cognition have often disregarded the physical and social surroundings in which cognition takes place. Distributed intelligence provides an effective theoretical framework for understanding what humans can achieve and how artifacts, tools, and socio-technical environments can be designed and evaluated to empower human beings and to change tasks[6].

Information Retrieval: Information retrieval (IR) is the science of searching for information in documents, searching for documents themselves, searching for metadata which describe documents, or searching within databases, whether relational stand-alone databases or hypertextually-networked databases such as the World Wide Web[7].

Semantic Clustering: Identifying and disambiguating between the senses of a semantically ambiguous word, without being given any prior information about these senses[8].

Semantics Differential: A type of a rating scale designed to measure the connotative meaning of objects, events, and concepts[9].

Usability Evaluation: Usability usually refers to the elegance and clarity with which the interaction with a computer program or a web site is designed[10].

User Experience: User experience, often abbreviated UX, is a term used to describe the overall experience and satisfaction a user has when using a product or system[11].

ENDNOTES

1. Searching a body of information for objects that match a search query, particularly a text or other unstructured forms (http://www.cs.cornell.edu/wya/DigLib/MS1999/glossary.html).

2. Round parenthesis are used in the mathematical sense that we are not enumerating a set here but we consider an ordered sequence in the case of Age feature.

3. Basic level variations are consider to occur when, having two words differing by the case or including or not a dash.

4. One user has been deleted from the sample because inserted tags as spam, due to the anonymous login to the system.

5. Collaborative Tagging Systems. (2007, Nov. 20). In *Wikipedia, The Free Ency-*

clopedia. Retrieved Nov 20, 2007, from http://en.wikipedia.org/wiki/.

6   Fischer, G. (2006). *Distributed intelligence: extending the power of the unaided, individual human mind.*, AVI (Augusto Celentano, ed.), ACM Press, 2006, pp. 7–14.

7   Information Retrieval. (2007, Nov. 20). In *Wikipedia, The Free Encyclopedia*. Retrieved Nov 20, 2007, from http://en.wikipedia.org/wiki/.

8   Semantic Clustering (2007, Nov. 20). In *Wikipedia, The Free Encyclopedia*. Retrieved Nov 20, 2007, from http://en.wikipedia.org/wiki/.

9   Semantics Differential. (2007, Nov. 20). In *Wikipedia, The Free Encyclopedia*. Retrieved Nov 20, 2007, from http://en.wikipedia.org/wiki/.

10   Usability Evaluation. (2007, Nov. 20). In *Wikipedia, The Free Encyclopedia*. Retrieved Nov 20, 2007, from http://en.wikipedia.org/wiki/.

11   User Experience. (2007, Nov. 20). In *Wikipedia, The Free Encyclopedia*. Retrieved Nov 20, 2007, from http://en.wikipedia.org/wiki/.

Chapter X
The Roles of Social Networks and Communities in Open Education Programs

Utpal M. Dholakia
Rice University, USA

Richard Baraniuk
Connexions and Rice University, USA

ABSTRACT

Open Education Programs provide a range of digitized educational resources freely to educators, students, and self-learners to use and reuse for teaching, learning, and research. In the current chapter the authors study how the educational experience for users and the effectiveness of these programs can be enhanced by incorporating new social networking technologies along with traditional virtual communities, such as bulletin boards and chat-rooms. An overview of open education programs is provided, discussing their common characteristics and participants' motivations for joining and contributing to such programs. The authors also consider the roles played by collaboration processes in open education programs, examine how communities evolve on theses sites, their roles in making the programs sustainable, and what site organizers can do to enhance these processes. They conclude the chapter with a discussion of future trends and how social networking technologies will contribute to the next generation of open education programs. Throughout, their discussion is informed by our experiences and engagement with the Connexions project (www.cnx.org).

THE ROLES OF SOCIAL NETWORKS AND COMMUNITIES IN OPEN EDUCATION PROGRAMS

"It isn't about making it cost-free or busting patents. It's about harnessing the latent creativity of a very large number of people who are out of the loop right now" - Dr. Richard Jefferson

Cutting across disciplines, a wide range of academics share a common set of values: that knowledge should be free and open to use and re-use; that collaboration across distances and across disciplines should be easier, not harder; that people should receive credit, accolades, and financial remuneration (if relevant) for contributing to education and research; and that concepts and ideas are linked in unusual and surprising ways and not just in the simple linear forms that textbooks and classroom lectures present (Baraniuk, 2007). Over the last decade or so, aided by technological advances, these values have crystallized into the growing and often grassroots-driven Open Education Movement, which has the potential to fundamentally change the way authors, instructors, and students produce, share, and use educational materials worldwide (e.g., Baraniuk & Cervenka, 2002; Cape Town Declaration 2007; Materu, 2004; see OECD, 2007, for an excellent overview). As an example, over 1,500 individuals representing 153 organizations (as of March 2008) have signed the Cape Town Open Education Declaration (2007) which articulates the principles and strategy surrounding the Open Education Movement, and engenders commitment amongst signatories.

Inspired by developments in open source software such as the Linux operating system and the Apache web server (e.g., Hamm, 2005; Lakhani & von Hippel, 2003), scientific research such as open source bio-technology initiatives (e.g., Hope, 2004), and the open licensing of intellectual property (e.g., St. Laurent, 2004), the open education movement seeks to provide free access to any internet user to high-quality educational materials through an easy to access and easy to use website. Furthermore, the materials can be customized and personalized to match the local contexts of users (language, level, users' educational goals, etc.). Many educational institutions have implemented open education programs (OEPs) over the last few years that make available repositories of teaching and learning materials. These can include text (course notes, curricula, and textbooks), images, audio, video, interactive simulations, problems and answers, and games. These resources are usually digitized and are freely and openly available to educators, students, and self-learners to use and reuse for teaching, learning and research (OECD, 2007). The communication capabilities and connectivity of the internet further enhance the value of these resources by allowing producers and users to collaborate, share materials with each another, and enhance their knowledge and understanding of the materials through these social interactions.

Despite the exploding popularity of OEPs over the last five years (OECD, 2007), most existing analyses of these programs tend to, implicitly or explicitly, view these resources as learning objects that individual users interact with. Relatively little is known about the roles of new technologies that foster online social interactions, social networking, and stimulate interpersonal relationships among users in the functioning of OEPs. Even less is known regarding such questions as what is the best structure of interactions that should be encouraged on OEP sites (synchronous or asynchronous, shallow or deep, etc.), what benefits and detriments partnering with existing or start-up social networking sites will have on OEP success, and the role played by social interaction technologies in making OEP sites financially viable and sustainable(?).

The objective of this chapter is to address this key issue and begin answering these questions. We explicitly study how the educational experience for users and the effectiveness of OEPs themselves can be enhanced by incorporating these new social networking technologies as well as using more traditional virtual communities, such as bulletin boards and chat-rooms on the site.

The rest of the chapter is organized as follows. We begin with an overview of open education programs, discussing their common characteristics and participants' motivations for joining and contributing to such programs. Next, we consider the roles played by collaboration processes in OEPs and then consider how user communities evolve on these sites, their features, and their roles in supporting users' motivations. Then, we discuss the role of social networks and communities in the sustainability of OEPs and specific tools that organizers can provide on their sites to enhance these processes. We conclude the chapter with a discussion of future trends in OEPs and how social networking technologies will contribute to the next generation of OEP sites. Throughout, our discussion is informed by our experiences and engagement with the Connexions project (cnx.org).

AN OVERVIEW OF OPEN EDUCATION PROGRAMS

All open education programs are based on the principle of freely sharing learning resources for use and re-use. However, the structure, i.e., who produces these resources, what type of resources are shared, and how free and open they are, varies by program. Some, like the MIT Open-CourseWare project (mit.edu/ocw) and its OCW consortium (ocwconsortium.org), are top-down organized institutional repositories that provide open access to educational content such as courses developed solely by their faculty, scholars, and instructors.

Others such as the *SEP* (*Stanford Encyclopedia of Philosophy*) provide open access to content that is contributed by faculty from many universities but restricted to a single discipline. Some programs like the *Open Learning Initiative* at Carnegie Mellon University emphasize innovative online instructional tools such as cognitive tutors, virtual laboratories, group experiments, and simulations. Finally, OEPs such as *Connexions* are grassroots organized and provide a broad-based repository of free, interconnected materials in a modular format along with an open software platform so that the materials can be used, reused, and re-contextualized by anyone globally.

Regardless of their structure, OEPs as a whole have the potential to change traditional educational content creation and delivery models significantly in a number of ways. First, they accelerate the blurring of formal and informal learning processes by melding entertainment and collaboration (games, online chat, etc.) with learning, and of educational and broader cultural activities of participants (Downes, 2007; Hylén, 2005). Anyone can go to one of these sites and learn about any subject that interests them at any time. With knowledge and confidence acquired from the learning, they can then contribute to, re-contextualize, or expand the base of existing knowledge.

Second, at a time when the effective use of knowledge is viewed as the key to economic success (e.g., OECD, 2007), OEPs empower many groups that have been "shut out" of traditional publishing domains. These under-served groups include talented K-12 teachers and community college instructors, scientists and engineers that work in corporations, and the world majority who do not speak and write English.

Third, these programs can be an effective way of promoting specific educational opportunities that are currently at the margin of emphases for mainstream educational institutions such as lifelong and continuing education for individuals, the delivery of high-quality technical education (e.g., mathematics, engineering) in languages of the developing countries, on-the-job and refresher training for technology workers, and the collaborative creation of new intellectual content within a discipline or across disciplines (e.g., Tapscott & Williams, 2007).

The institutions that launch, support, and sponsor OEPs, typically universities, do so for a number of reasons. One reason is altruism, that is, that it is a good thing to do. However, there are also many substantial economic reasons for organizing OEPs. One, it reduces the cost of content development for the educational institution through sharing and reuse when compared to traditional linear methods. Second, it can mitigate the time lag between producing course materials and textbooks and getting them into the hands of their students. Third, by showcasing its values, OEPs affiliated or launched by educational institutions can boost their image among key constituents such as the student body, alumni, foundations, and the local and global communities that they serve. In some cases, it may even help build the brand worldwide as a progressive and conscientious institution.

Authors participate in OEPs to gain exposure to a larger audience and to be able to disseminate and update their teaching and research materials in a timely fashion (Downes, 2007). They may even be able to increase the demand for their commercial products like books (Oberholzer & Strumpf, 2004), or earn royalties through on-demand publication of their materials (Baraniuk, 2007). Finally, students participate because they are able to access a body of educational content for free or at a significantly lower cost if purchasing an on-demand book rather than paying exorbitant sums for conventional textbooks (Horwitz, 1965). At the same time, they are able to obtain the most current information as authors can update materials in real time on the OEP site.

COLLABORATION, NETWORKING AND SOCIAL VALUE IN OEPS

Contemporary theories of education posit that a key set of benefits from learning accrue from an increase in the person's *social capital* (Schuller, 2007), defined as creating and maintaining a network of friends, business and personal acquaintances. Likewise, individual learning, defined in terms of both quality and degree, is enhanced by judicious collaboration with others (Bowen, 1996; Tinto, 1998). Based on the logic that collaboration is good, by and large, rather than uploading and/or consuming educational materials on an individualistic basis, OEPs encourage interactions between the producers and consumers of educational materials. Take the example of Connexions. Instead of the traditional content development model of one author to one textbook or course used in education, Connexions invites and links worldwide communities of authors to collaboratively create, expand, revise, and maintain its educational resources. In colloquial terms, borrowing from an Apple Computer slogan and a book by Lawrence Lessig (2001), Connexions (cnx.org) welcomes authors, teachers, and learners everywhere to "Create, Rip, Mix, and Burn" educational resources.

Specifically, Connexions users are free to create educational materials and contribute them to a globally accessible educational resource repository in the form of either small modules or larger collections of modules (Create); they can customize and personalize the materials according to their needs (Rip); they are able to mix the materials together into new collections and courses (Mix); and they can create finished products like web courses, CD Roms, and even on-demand printed books (Burn). Such affordances are available in other OEPs as well (OECD, 2007). In performing each one of these activities effectively, social interactions with other users are important.

Like many other OEPs, Connexions has three distinct user groups that derive more-or-less distinct types of value from using the site: (1) *authors*, who create original educational content and make it available in the open commons of the repository, (2) *instructors*, who select available content from different authors and compile or otherwise manipulate it to create instructional materials for use in their classes and teaching activities, and (3) *students*, who consume the educational materials to learn. It is worth noting here that "students" includes both traditional students enrolled in high-schools, colleges, graduate and professional schools, etc. as well as informal learners who may teach themselves, or belong to study groups. Our own research with all three Connexions user groups (e.g., Baraniuk 2007; Dholakia, Roll, and McKeever 2005), as well as other studies (e.g., Downes, 2007), have suggested that a significant component of value to users from participating in OEPs is *social* in nature.

One important benefit derived by authors is from gaining exposure to the community of individuals interested in their subject matter. Accolades, a book contract, promotion and tenure may all follow as a result. Providing social networking technologies may enable them to initiate new contacts with other authors, publishers, and subject area experts to further their goals. To enable the initial linkage to develop, Connexions offers its users the ability to create a profile page, much like those created on social networking sites like MySpace and facebook, to break the ice with strangers.

Instructors rely on access to a broad set of quality materials to choose from, insights into how to choose and combine the chosen modules into a quality course, and feedback on the content, delivery and grading of their course, all of which involve social interactions. To facilitate the selection process, users contribute to a reputation and rating system called "Lenses" within Connexions that we describe in more details later on in the chapter. Finally, students learn better

in an environment where they can brainstorm, receive clarifications and guidance from others well-versed in the subject domain, and can return the favor to others who begin participating after them. For instructors, synchronicity of communication is less important, and the interactivity offered by bulletin boards may be sufficient; students are likely to find the synchronous communication afforded by char-rooms to be more useful. Connexions offers bulletin boards on the site linked to subject areas, courses, and modules. Additionally, users may be able to chat in real time by using other internet chat services like Skype or Google chat.

PROGRESSION OF COMMUNITY DEVELOPMENT IN OEPS

As the three user groups – authors, instructors, and students – begin participating on the OEP site, our research shows that their view of the user community and their support of it evolves (Dholakia et al. 2005). To begin with, users tend to view the OEP site mostly as a *resource* or a *repository* (depending on whether they are primarily students or authors). Usually, students discover the site through a keyword search on a search engine when they are searching for a specific subject keyword. Others may discover the site because their instructor uses Connexions to support his or her course, and requires them to visit. Authors discover the site either through word-of-mouth or because they are looking for a means to self-publish their manuscript or store the educational materials they have compiled in an online venue.

In this initial stage, virtually none of the users think of themselves as "community members" of the site, nor do they really think of themselves as a social group or "us". Their primary motivation is to achieve their own individual goals efficiently. Authors might participate to put their content online and to gain exposure to the marketplace;

instructors might participate to obtain access to free and high-quality content; and students might participate because they have to, or because they find the materials to be useful. Such an initial emphasis on individualistic functional motivations has been observed in other types of online social interaction venues as well (Dholakia, Bagozzi, & Klein Pearo, 2004). For many OEP users, the evolution to the next stage of user community perceptions may never occur; in this case, they will continue to use the site for seeking knowledge about subjects they are interested in (students) or placing their content or course online (authors/ instructors). Such users are less likely or not at all likely to engage in social interactions with others.

As they participate more in the OEP site and begin interacting with others on it, however, users' view of the site changes to one of a *user network*, where participants feel some affinity to the social network as a whole and are willing to help other members, but only if it is not too inconvenient or effortful. A sense of "we-ness" begins to form, and the individual begins to care about the well-being and goal achievement of others on the site. Instructors may answer some questions of students from a different country that they are not directly responsible for, authors may be willing to receive feedback from instructors or students and make some changes to their content, but none of the participants are willing to spend too much time or effort interacting with other community members. At this stage, users are still like a vast majority of "friends" or "connections" in an individual's network on social networking sites, where the links between members are "mutual, public, unnuanced, and decontextualized" (Donath & Boyd, 2004) and of a weak nature.

In the final stage of the evolution towards a real community, OEP site users' interest and involvement with the site increases, participants have a genuine interest in the well being of other members, and are willing to invest significant amounts of their time and effort in helping oth-

ers. They begin to demonstrate the three markers that sociologists have identified as being necessary for a social grouping to be characterized as a community (see Muniz & O'Guinn, 2001, for a detailed discussion). First, participants feel a "consciousness of kind" or an intrinsic connection toward one another, and a collective sense of difference from others that do not belong to the community (Gusfield, 1978). For example, Connexions users may begin to see the site as markedly superior to its competitors, appreciate and publicly extol its openness and accessibility, and disparage alternative OEP sites. Second, the community comes to be marked by the presence of shared rituals and traditions that help to perpetuate the community's shared history, culture and consciousness. Students may see themselves as unique, because of their preference for open content rather than traditional text-books, for example. The third marker is a sense of moral responsibility, that is, a sense of duty or obligation to the community as a whole, and to its individual members, among users. As these markers begin to become evident among OEP user groups, the site can be viewed as an *engaged community*. To evolve to this stage, a core set of users must be given the opportunities and the incentives to spend significant amounts of time on the site, form relationships with each other, and form a small friendship group (Bagozzi & Dholakia, 2006). Rather than just linking to other users, participants must be provided with occasions and reasons to form a multi-faceted relationship, or in the words of sociologists, a "strong tie" (Granovetter, 1973; Montgomery, 1992)

THE ROLE OF SOCIAL NETWORKS AND COMMUNITIES IN THE SUSTAINABILITY OF OEPS

A common and critical challenge facing all OEPs is planning for and ensuring their sustainability (long-term viability and stability). The complication is that the traditional revenue models employed as a matter of course in other educational settings (earning revenue from knowledge creation and dissemination such as enrolment fees, tuition, book sales, subscriptions, and so on) do not directly apply to OEPs, since their materials, and often times their software platforms, are freely available on the web (Downes, 2007; see Dholakia, King, & Baraniuk, 2006, for a detailed discussion of these issues).

Consequently, it is important to understand not only the social value that users derive from using the OEP site, but also how this value can be harnessed to a financial business model. One important way in which social value translates into sustainability is by increasing the OEP's *brand equity*. In marketing terms, brand equity is "the added, usually intangible value endowed to products or services by the brand which results in tangible positive outcomes" (Keller, 1993). Brand equity arises from creating a differentiated, consistent, and meaningful brand image in users' minds, where they associate the OEP site with key elements or attributes that are important to them personally, and unique to the site so that they cannot find the attribute(s) elsewhere.

The OEP site users' social networks and/or communities offer the opportunity to produce an important brand association. Perhaps the prototypical example of a corporation that has used the customers' social capital to create a successful brand is Harley Davidson Motorcycles. Harley buyers purchase the motorcycle primarily for the ability to enjoy a certain lifestyle associated with freedom, rebellion, and the open road, as well as interactions with Harley Owners' Group members and participation in group-related activities such as rides, rallies, and concerts. In a similar fashion, OEPs may be able to leverage the existing social networks and communities of their users and the value from collaboration arising from their participation therein to attract new users. Collaboration with quality partners is another way to increase users' and potential members' social

value. Connexions collaborates with groups such as Teachers Without Borders, the University of California, and firms such as Texas Instruments, AMD, and National Instruments to accomplish this purpose. Such collaborations also allow the OEP to seek on-going funding from foundations, philanthropic institutions, professional societies, trade or industry groups, individual firms, and governmental and/or non-governmental agencies that are focused on the particular niches.

Given subject matter diversity, focusing on a few subjects (instead of many) may facilitate the formation of social networks on an OEP site. For example, at Connexions, there has been a systematic and deliberate effort to build a community of authors, instructors, students, and practicing engineers to develop a critical mass of inter-connected Digital Signal Processing (DSP) materials. The DSP community is supported by a "community page" built on the Connexions site that contains information about the community, a discussion forum, a "to do" list of modules and courses that are needed, and a statistics section detailing how much traffic the community is generating. In OEPs, strong and densely connected networks help to move beyond open-access publishing toward truly "collaborative publishing", where not only is the access free for users, but collaboration and innovation of the materials is encouraged.

Finally, strong user networks provide the framework on which to place other mechanisms such as co-production of content and reputation creation (discussed in-depth in the next section). These processes require volitional effortful actions (such as rating content, enforcing community norms, etc.) for the community-oriented features of the site to be successful.

SOCIAL NETWORK ENHANCING TOOLS IN OEP SITES

As discussed earlier, there are many challenges facing OEP projects that directly impact the engagement and involvement of the user community. One important issue is the sheer volume of content on the site. Additionally, within the OEP universe, educational materials exist in various stages of development and, hence, at various quality levels. Ability to re-use content may further create numerous versions of the same basic concepts. Finally, the same concepts may be discussed by different authors who bring different levels of expertise, involvement, and personal competence to the task. Within this ample content, variable quality environment, the ability to access high-quality materials easily is crucial to bringing users back to the OEP site, to their being able to network with other users, and to fostering a sense of community in them.

How do we ensure that users are able to easily find and access high-quality OEPs? This requires both a means for individual users to be able to evaluate and rate educational materials and a means to direct new users to those materials that are deemed by others to be of high quality. Tradi-

tional publishers, as well as some institution-based OEP projects like MIT's OpenCourseWare project (OCW), employ a careful review process before the content is made publicly available.

Connexions recognized early on that a pre-publication review process would not scale to the eventual large size and activity level of the repository nor would it foster social networking or community. So, rather than acting as a gate keeper and making a single centralized accept/reject decision regarding each module or collection, Connexions admits all contributions and then opens up the editorial process to third-party reviewers and editorial bodies for *post-publication review*. While Connexions users have access to all modules and courses in the content repository (whatever their quality), users also have the ability to preferentially locate and view modules and collections rated high quality by choosing from a range of different *lenses* provided by the third parties (see Figure 1 and cnx.org/lenses).

Each lens has a different focus; examples include lenses controlled by traditional editorial

Figure 1. Connexions lenses for peer review and quality control

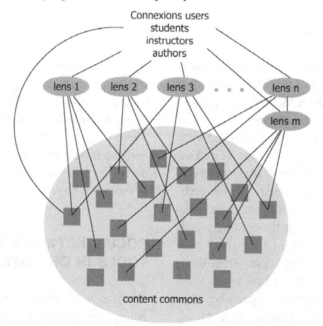

boards, professional societies, or informal groups of colleagues as well as automated lenses based on popularity, the amount of (re)use, the number of incoming links, or other metrics. As one example, the National Council of Professors of Educational Leadership (NCPEA) has launched a Connexions lens based on a rigorous peer review process involving both faculty from educational leadership programs and practicing principals and superintendents. The IEEE Signal Processing Society is launching a reviewing and certification process for Connexions materials in the DSP area. Index-based educational resources such as Merlot (merlot.org) could also naturally serve as Connexions lenses as could interest, geography, or profession-based societies, user groups or special interest groups. While lenses were hypothesized from the inception of Connexions, the emergence of Web 2.0 "social software" has greatly simplified their implementation. Indeed, the first incarnation of the NCPEA Lens was based on the site/software del.icio.us. Generally speaking, reputation mechanisms such as Lenses are intertwined with and supported by the OEP social networks and communities.

A VIEW TO THE FUTURE

In this last section of the chapter, we consider the future role of social networks and communities in OEPs as they evolve (see Baraniuk, 2007,

for a detailed discussion of these issues). To do so, it is instructive to draw a parallel with the evolution of the World Wide Web that enables it. Following the taxonomy of Spivack (2007), Web 1.0 emphasized building and deploying the basic infrastructure for broadcasting simple HTML content from "big content" websites. The emphasis was on the individual's interaction with content. Web 2.0 added XML, social networking, user-generated content, and mash-ups to create exponentially growing sites like Craigslist.com, MySpace.com, and Wikipedia.org. The emphasis is on social interactions and collaboration. Web 3.0, also known as the "semantic web", promises to add intelligence via natural language processing, data-mining, machine learning, and other artificial intelligence technologies. The parallel developments for OEP are illustrated in Table 1 and expanded upon below.

OEP 1.0 – Open educational broadcast. These programs broadcast their institutionally generated educational resources freely to the world over the internet. The prototypical examples of such programs are MIT OpenCourseWare and the members of its OCW Consortium; these are top-down organized institutional repositories that expose HTML and PDF versions of the course web pages and other curricular materials prepared by their faculty. Outside-of-institution contributions are not accepted, and quality control is performed pre-publication by a dedicated staff. Social networking and interaction opportunities are minimal or non-existent in such programs.

Table 1. The first three phases of open education

	Example	Tools	Contributors	Product	Pedagogy
OEP 1.0 (broadcast)	MIT OCW	HTML, PDF	institutions authors	course, textbook	in author's mind
OEP 2.0 (remix)	Connexions today	XML	author, instructor communities	modules collections	in community's mind
OEP 3.0 (interactive)	Connexions tomorrow	XML + smarts	authors, instructors, learners	improved learning	in community's mind and in the machine

Figure 2. An architecture for OEP 3.0 – the production and delivery mechanisms of OEP 1.0 and 2.0 are supplemented by strong feedback loops that link the learning communities and drive evolutionary improvement

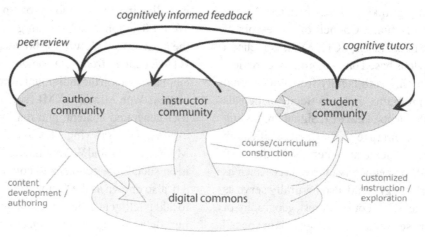

OEP 2.0 – Open educational remix. These programs enable community participation and user-generated content that is continually remixed into new educational materials. In one sense, they are really "open" educational materials because they rely on the contributions of participants for the value of the knowledge to be unlocked. The prototypical example of this type of OEP is the XML-based Connexions, as discussed throughout the chapter.

What's missing? OEP 1.0 and 2.0 programs have both focused on re-inventing the textbook and learning materials dissemination (OEP 1.0) and development (OEP 2.0) processes. They have only indirectly targeted the end goal of *better learning*. Indeed, it is not the information students are given that determines learning, but what they do with it, how they process it, how they construct knowledge, and how they use knowledge in collaboration with others. To summarize in the language of control theory, OEP 1.0 and 2.0 run in a substantially "open loop" mode. Missing from both these types of OEPs is *feedback* that "closes the loop" and makes educational materials' design, delivery, and redesign more *interactive*.

OEP 3.0: Interactive open education. OEP 3.0 will not just deliver content to the student, but

also monitor their interactions with it, analyze those interactions, and then send feedback to the student, the instructor, and the author, all of whom can act in response (see Figure 2). These feedback and adaptation processes will occur continuously on a time scale commensurate with the activity: for the learning process for individual students in minutes or hours, not the current weeks or months; for the iterative authoring process in weeks or months, not the current years.

Over the last several decades, researchers in cognitive science have demonstrated significantly improved learning outcomes using interactive education systems such as intelligent tutors. Unfortunately, such systems are not scalable; they take PhD-level cognitive scientists, working with domain experts, years and millions of dollars to create. Thus, these systems have generally been closed and proprietary, greatly limiting their impact. An excellent example of cognitively informed OEP that combines elements of OEP 1.0 and 3.0 is Carnegie Mellon University's Open Learning Initiative (cmu.edu/oli); This program has demonstrated significantly improved learning outcomes, but only in eleven courses that have taken five years and several million dollars to develop.

OEP 3.0 will achieve scalability to a large number of courses and students by integrating cognitive science, learning theory, and machine learning into the community authoring and remix culture of OEP 2.0. Many of the mechanisms required for students, instructors, and authors to accept feedback are already built into OEP 2.0 projects like Connexions and are fueled by the strong social networks that domicile within the OEP. Moreover, OEP 2.0 projects can harness the efforts of a large community of authors to generate the many problems, correct and incorrect answers, and feedback hints required by intelligent tutors. The pressing need is for an extensible, open-source platform for probing, measuring, analyzing, and tracking student learning. While this Semantic Web infrastructure will be time-consuming and costly to develop, it enable us to move from the current OEP culture of authoring and sharing to a culture of learning within a supportive community of learners.

REFERENCES

Bagozzi, R. P., & Dholakia, U. M. (2006). Antecedents and purchase consequences of customer participation in small group brand communities. *International Journal of Research in Marketing*, *23*(1), 45-61.

Baraniuk, R. G. (2007). *Challenges and opportunities for the Open Education Movement: A Connexions case study*. White paper, Rice University. http://mitpress.mit.edu/catalog/item/default. asp?ttype=2&tid=11309

Baraniuk, R. G., & Cervenka, K. (2002). *Connexions white paper: Building communities and sharing knowledge*.

Bowen, H. R. (1996). *Investment in Learning: The Individual and Social Value of Higher American Education*. New Jersey: Transaction Publishers.

The Cape Town Open Education Declaration (2007). Available online at: http://www.capetown-declaration.org/read-the-declaration

Dholakia, U. M., Bagozzi, R. P., & Pearo, L. K. (2004). A social influence model of consumer participation in network- and small-group-based virtual communities. *International Journal of Research in Marketing*, *21*(3), 241-263.

Dholakia, U. M., King W. J., & Baraniuk, R. (2006). What makes an open educational program sustainable? The Case of Connexions. *OECD-CERI papers*.

Dholakia, U. M., Roll, S., & McKeever, J. (2005). Building community in Connexions. *Market Research Report for Connexions Project*, Rice University, January.

Donath, J., & Boyd, D. (2004). Public displays of connection. *BT Technology Journal*, *22*(4), 71-82.

Downes, S. (2007). Models for sustainable open educational resources. *Interdisciplinary Journal of Knowledge and Learning Objects*, *3*, 29-4.

Granovetter, M. S. (1973). The strength of weak ties. *American Journal of Sociology*, *78*(6), 1360-1380.

Gusfield, J. (1978). *Community: A Critical Response*. New York: Harper & Row

Hamm, S. (2005). Linux, Inc. BusinessWeek, January 31, (p. 60).

Hanley, G. (2005). MERLOT: Enabling open education. *Presentation at the COSL Conference*, Utah State University, Logan, UT.

Hope, J. E. (2004). *Open Source Biotechnology*. Unpublished doctoral dissertation, Australian National University.

Horvitz, P. M. (1965). A note on textbook pricing. *The American Economic Review*, *55* (4), 844-848.

Hylén, J. (2005). *Open Educational Resources: Opportunities and Challenges.* OECD-CERI.

Keller, K. L. (1993). Conceptualizing, measuring, and managing customer-based brand equity. *Journal of Marketing, 57*(1), 1-22.

Lakhani, K. R., & Eric von Hippel (2003). How open source software works: Free user to user assistance. Research Policy, 32(6), 923-943.

Lessig, L. (2001). *The Future of Ideas: The Fate of the Commons in a Connected World.* Random House.

Materu, P. (2004). *Open source courseware: A baseline study.* The World Bank, Washington DC.

Montgomery, J. D. (1992). Job search and network composition: Implications of the strength-of-weak ties hypothesis. *American Sociological Review, 57*(5), 586-596.

Muniz, A. M., & O'Guinn, T. C. (2001). Brand community. *Journal of Consumer Research, 27*(1), 412-432.

Oberholzer, F., & Koleman, S. (2004). *The Effect of File Sharing on Record Sales An Empirical Analysis.* http://www.unc.edu/~cigar/papers/FileSharing_March2004.pdf

Organisation for Economic Co-operation and Development (2007). *Giving knowledge for free: The emergence of open educational resources.* Available online at: http://213.253.134.43/oecd/pdfs/browseit/9607041E.PDF

Raymond, E. S. (2001). *The Cathedral and the Bazaar: Musings on Linux and the Open Source by an Accidental Revolutionary.* O'Reilly.

Schuller, T. (2007). Reflections on the use of social capital. *Review of Social Economy, 65*(1), 11-28.

Spivack, N. (2006). The third generation web is coming. *KurzweilAI.net.*

Stephenson, R. (2005). *How to Make Open Education Succeed Conference,* Utah State University, Logan, UT

St. Laurent, A. M. (2004). *Understanding open source and free software licensing.* Sebastopol, CA: O'Reilley Media.

Tapscott, D., & Williams, A. D. (2007). *Wikinomics: How mass collaboration changes everything.* New York: Portfolio.

Tinto, V. (1998). Colleges as communities: Taking research on student persistence seriously," *The Review of Higher Education, 21*(2), 167-177.

KEY TERMS

Community Development: Progression of users' view of community from being a resource or repository (stage 1), to a user network (stage 2), to an engaged community (stage 3).

Connexions: Connexions is a non-profit start-up launched at Rice University in 1999 that offers a rapidly growing collection of free, open-access educational materials and an open-source software toolkit to help authors publish and collaborate, instructors rapidly build and share custom courses, and students explore the links among concepts, courses, and disciplines. It is internationally focused, interdisciplinary, and grassroots organized.

OEP Sites: Websites hosting Open Education Programs

Open Education Programs: Education programs offering teaching and learning materials such as text (course notes, curricula, textbooks), images, audio, video, interactive simulations, etc. for free use and reuse online.

Social Capital: Creating and maintaining a network of friends, business, and personal acquaintances.

Chapter XI
Distributed Learning Environments and Social Software:
In Search for a Framework of Design

Sebastian Fiedler
Zentrum für Sozial Innovation – Centre for Social Innovation, Austria

Kai Pata
Center of Educational Technology, Tallinn University, Estonia

ABSTRACT

This chapter discusses how the construction of an adequate design and intervention framework for distributed learning environments might be approached. It proposes that activity theory has some interesting concepts and perspectives to offer in this regard. In addition, it discusses the concept of affordance, understood as perceived possibilities for action, and its potential consequences for learning environment design. Furthermore, some current technical and conceptual challenges for the implementation and maintenance of distributed learning environments are addressed. The authors consider their text as a proposal for a necessary reorientation and a call for contributions to the search for an adequate design and intervention framework for distributed learning environments.

INTRODUCTION

In recent years higher-education systems are undergoing a considerable transformation process on various levels. The implementation of leadership-, evaluation- and accreditation schemes that are mainly modelled after entrepreneurial solutions, are fundamentally re-shaping our higher educational institutions. This new regime also influences how communicative and productive practices like teaching, facilitating, and collaborating are technologically mediated. Many educational institutions apply now strategies and policies that aim for the implementation of large-scale, homogeneous, and centrally administered technological landscapes of tools and services to support and manage teaching and studying activities. Thereby they largely ignore that disciplines or areas of study still differ to a considerable degree on how they relate to certain occupations and professions, the labour market in general, and on what educational traditions they have developed over time Bleiklie (2004). From an observer's point of view, all actors appear primarily as "residents" of such an institutional landscape of pre-selected and decreed sets of tools and services. Everyone is expected to perform all necessary mediated activities within its boundaries.

Apart from general communication systems, content repositories and digital library systems, institutional landscapes of universities are still dominated by Course Management Systems, that are often somewhat misleadingly named Learning Management Systems (LMS). These Course Management Systems are the prototypical technological expression or "flag ships" of the mainstream institutional strive for centralisation and control. Thus, it comes as no surprise that the ongoing development of these all-comprising platforms is driven by a continuous desire for expansion and assimilation of additional features and functionalities. At the same time very few of the Course Management Systems currently in use, provide interfaces for interaction and data exchange with a wider ecology of networked tools and services. The majority of these platforms rather operate as "closed clubs" and try to restrain all activities within their particular boundaries.

All these systems feature an unequal distribution of power and ownership with a clear distinction of roles (such as educational authority vs. participants) producing asymmetric relationships (Wilson *et al.*, 2006). Furthermore, they foster a general educational intervention approach that

seems largely based on the rather illusionary expectation that human change processes can, and indeed should be, modelled on the basis of simple cause-and-effect relationships. We would like to argue that the socio-technological practices that are encouraged by the majority of today's Course Management Systems in higher education demonstrate clearly that the majority of instructional design and educational intervention models are still conceptualising humans, or the social systems they form, as "trivial machines" (Foerster, 1999). It seems like decades of multi-disciplinary work on system theory (see e.g. Willke, 2005) constructivist theories of knowing (see e.g. Glasersfeld, 1995), second-order cybernetics (see e.g. Maturana & Varela, 1980), and aspects of self-direction (see e.g. Candy, 1991; Fischer & Scharff, 1998) and self-organisation (see e.g. Harri-Augstein & Thomas, 1991; Jünger, 2004) in education have simply been brushed aside or entirely ignored.

Instead of treating humans as systems of (self) organising complexity that develop particular qualities like operational closure (and thus self-referentiality and highly selective interaction patterns with their environments), technological mediation in higher education and its underlying (instructional) design is mainly based on the idea that human change processes, and the intentional interventions that are supposed to "cause" such changes, can be reduced to simple cause-and-effect relations, simple purpose and goal attribution, and simple sequential temporal patterns (Willke, 2005). Thus, many technologically mediated environments that follow a traditional instructional design approach are fostering almost exclusively the teaching of codified knowledge and skills. Emphasising a clear distinction between educational authorities and students and their respective responsibilities, expert instructional designers and course facilitators are responsible for guiding the participants through a sequence of pre-structured events and interactions with pre-selected materials, towards a set of pre-defined instructional goals (Kerres, 2007). In general this creates rather sheltered and non-challenging environments that offer only a limited amount of prescribed interaction patterns and forms of expression. This predominant institutional approach to technological mediation of teaching and studying appears to be rather incompatible with a variety of contemporary conceptualisations of how human- and social systems evolve and function and what this implies for intervention and intentional change. Apart from this conceptual incompatibility the status quo in many educational institutions contrasts sharply with two major ongoing developments.

SOCIO-POLITICAL AND SOCIO-TECHNOLOGICAL CHANGE

From a socio-political perspective we have to attest that all post-industrial societies have seen a dramatic shift towards more symbolically mediated and information driven work processes. We can observe a general increase of "constructive" or "design"-practices that focus on the production of artefacts in the ongoing work process. Architects produce technical drawings and sketches, psychologists create diagnostic reports or treatment plans, programmers develop new prototypes, and so forth. What all these activities have in common is an evolutionary design- and development process that inevitably produces challenges and demands for change and "learning" on a regular basis. The progression of such design- and development processes is generally hard to predict, since goals and strategies often have to be changed and expectations have to be adjusted. Authentic challenges and tasks often require collaboration, communication, acting under (at least partial) uncertainty, and an overall working style that has been described as bricolage (J. S. Brown, 1999). Bricolage refers to the localisation, selection and combination of artefacts and objects (things, tools, documents, programme-code, etc) in a novel con-

text. Beyond accessible artefacts, the systematic integration of other people and what they know and are able to do (see e.g. the work on distributed cognition by Hutchins, 1991, 1995), becomes a core component for successful problem solutions in information-intensive work settings.

Thus, in numerous work and life settings new important "areas of challenge" emerge. Many people, for example, find themselves increasingly operating in distributed and technologically mediated environments. They need to build up viable dispositions for collaborating, self-directing (intentional change projects), and social-networking successfully within these environments, while making use of new potentials for mediated action on one hand, and compensating the limitations and constraints of such a mediated form of (inter-)action on the other. Some scholars, particularly in the area of vocational education, have acknowledged this trend. Their conceptualisation of competence, for example, explicitly emphasises the role of dispositions such as orientations, values, and volitional aspects for (self-organising) action that can be successful in situations that carry a high level of uncertainty and complexity (Erpenbeck & Heyse, 1999; Heyse *et al.*, 2002). Thus, these scholars try to shift our focus away from dispositions such as factual knowledge and procedural skills that made up the core of the old concept of "qualification". Of course, factual knowledge and procedural skills are necessary dispositions in all contexts, but they are not sufficient to act successfully in many authentic problem situations. They might offer a starting point and some guidance but certainly not a straight solution in many areas of life and work.

In parallel to the changing nature of work and life challenges, we can observe from a more socio-technological perspective the emergence of a myriad of decentralized, only loosely-coupled, networked tools and services. These tools and services increasingly provide individuals and collectives powerful means to augment a myriad of activities and practices that transcend all kinds of institutional and organisational boundaries. The emergence of these small, simple, and networked tools and services, often labelled as social software or social media, is generally considered to be an important expression of the ongoing evolution of the Web towards a general computing platform and a renaissance of some core ideas of the Two-Way-Web (Berners-Lee, 2000). This looming evolutionary step is frequently labelled with the rather fuzzy marketing term Web 2.0. However, we believe that this development could potentially fuel a counter-movement to the mainstream, application-centred, institutional approach to technology provision in higher education outlined above. Many interesting lightweight, cost-efficient systems and tools have emerged in the personal Web publishing realm, including varied content management systems, content syndication and aggregation services, and a range of tracking and mapping tools of hyperlink economies and social networks (Paquet, 2003). These tools offer powerful means for the support of collaborative and individual work and study activities as they occur within contemporary information-intensive design- and development work outside of formal educational settings (Mejias, 2005).

In recent years we saw the emergence of a growing "avant-garde" of people who indeed support and improve their own personal work- and "learning" environments with a patch-work of preferred, networked tools and services. Empirical data on the size of this group is hard to obtain, but there are many indicators that the way people are using the Web for (self-)educational matters and collaborative actions has begun to change (Downes, 2005). In this realm, personal and collaborative Web publishing activities like Weblog or Wiki authoring, Webfeed publication and aggregation, social book-marking and so forth, are currently the iconic practices. Some individuals and collectives already apply these emerging means in creative ways to support projects of all kinds, including their intentional advancement of competencies (in the sense of dispositions for self-organising

actions) in formal and informal contexts. These individuals have acquired the means and capabilities to construct and maintain their personal landscapes of technological instruments. They make use of such networked tools and services to establish new relationships and to construct extended social networks to support their own educational projects. They take responsibility for all necessary instructional functions such as selecting and acquiring material resources, pacing and monitoring themselves, establishing criteria of evaluation, generating feedback, and so forth. From a technical point of view establishing such patterns of actions is entirely feasible and the palette of mediating tools and services is constantly expanding and evolving.

We have argued elsewhere (Efimova & Fiedler, 2004; Fiedler, 2003; Fiedler & Sharma, 2004) that these emerging and evolving personal landscapes of tools and services are well suited to support a more open, conversational approach to learning and change, inside and outside of formal educational settings. The authoring of Weblogs, for example, in combination with the surrounding practices of Webfeed monitoring, reading and aggregation, social book-marking, and so forth, can be meaningfully conceptualized from such a perspective (Fiedler & Sharma, 2005; Sharma & Fiedler, 2007). If used properly these practices can support ongoing "conversations" with self, others, and artefacts. However, bringing these practices into formal educational settings creates considerable difficulties and tensions. Since these practices originated in the context of technological landscapes that can be described as open, distributed, networked, and publicly accessible, they often tend to be perceived as disruptive to existing approaches to technologically mediated teaching and learning in educational institutions. Therefore, some institutions try to control, suppress, and even ban them entirely (Attwell, 2007).

We would like to argue that the continuously expanding array of social media and social software solutions offers an interesting and somewhat promising technological tool set for particular design and intervention purposes in higher education. However, we believe that the application of such a tool set needs to be set in an adequate conceptual framework. Making systematic use of social media and social software looks particularly promising, if the overall goal of one's design and intervention efforts is the establishment of learning environments that attempt to foster the advancement of dispositions (for self-organising action) that are required to cope with high levels of situational uncertainty and complexity. Furthermore, we think that the ongoing socio-political and socio-technological developments that we sketched above, merit such considerations. In the remaining chapter we want to outline what conceptual and theoretical aspects could be worked into a framework for the design and support of distributed learning environments that try to make systematic use of social media and social software following a particular set of educational intervention goals.

BUILDING A CONCEPTUAL FRAMEWORK FOR THE DESIGN OF DISTRIBUTED LEARNING ENVIRONMENTS WITH SOCIAL MEDIA AND SOCIAL SOFTWARE

We suggest that a framework for the design of distributed learning environments could make use of some core ideas of activity theory (Yrjö Engeström, 1987). According to this line of theorising, activity systems arise when an actors want to realize certain objectives. Since we are mainly concerned with formal educational settings in higher education, these objectives are predominantly educational. For fulfilling their personal or group objectives in technologically mediated settings, actors need to construct, adopt and adjust their landscapes of tools and services to meet these purposes, adapt their activities to the co-actors' preferences, and jointly plan and coordinate their activities with studying-partners and facilitators. Different artefacts mediate the processes in such an activity system. Artefacts, as the materialised outcomes or by-products of goal-driven actions, may also serve as new inputs for other activity systems.

To analyze how actors in a given activity system perceive themselves, the artefacts and tools in use, and other participants, we find it useful to integrate the concept of affordances into our considerations for a learning environment design model. Gibson (1986) originally defined affordances as opportunities for action for an observer, provided by an (physical) environment. Gaver (1996) emphasized that affordances emerge in human action and interaction and, thus, go beyond mere perception. This contrasts with the common interpretation that affordances simply refer to situations in which one can see what to do (Gibson, 1986). Neisser (1994) elaborated Gibson's concept of affordance and distinguished three perceptual modes: 1) Direct perception/action, which enables us to perceive and act effectively on the local environment; 2) Interpersonal perception/reactivity, which underlies our immediate social interactions with other human beings, and; 3) Representation/recognition, by which we identify and respond appropriately to familiar objects and situations. Besides the affordances related to the environment, Neisser's interpretation introduces the interpersonal perception of subjects in action as an additional source of affordances in the social and regulative domain.

The mainstream view on affordances in educational technology seems to consider them as objective properties of the tools, which are perceptible in the context of certain activities. Thus, it is commonly suggested that tools have concrete technological affordances for certain performances that can be brought into an actor's perception through specific instructions (Gaver, 1996; Norman, 1988). This use of the concept tends to ignore its self-referential and subjective nature and observer-dependence. It seems to imply that affordances should be located in the environment or specific artefacts or tools. Kirschner (2002), for example, defines pedagogical affordances as those characteristics of an artefact that determine if and how a particular <u>learning behavio</u>r could possibly be enacted within a given context. Kreijns et al. (2002) have defined social affordances as the "properties" of a collaborative learning environment that act as contextual facilitators for social interactions. However, we do not want to follow this common (mis-)understanding of affordances being the "property" of a particular learning environment. From an interaction-centred view (Vyas & van der Veer, 2005) affordances are <u>perceived possibilities</u> for action. They refer to what people perceive and signify during their actual interaction with an artefact or tool. While interacting with an artefact or tool actors continuously interpret the situation, and construct or re-construct meanings. Thus, we propose that instead of relating affordances "objectively" with certain features of software applications or other complex tools and artefacts, they should rather be related to the activity system. Actors must realize how they perform joint actions with artefacts and tools in order to accomplish their shared objectives. Affordances then emerge and potentially become observable in actions that people undertake to realize shared objectives.

A conversational grounding of objectives and tools for particular actions inevitably brings along the development of certain implicit or explicit rules for effective action in particular settings. In return these rules constrain how tools can be used in specific actions. In educational settings constraints for using tools in a particular way also arise from the perception of predetermined tasks, objectives and artefacts that are meant to guide and contextualise the activities. Furthermore, activities within an activity system are also constrained by the technical functionalities of tools and services, and the artefacts conveying meanings in a specific domain context. Actors must develop a (at least partially) compatible understanding of the affordances (for action) within a given setting, to make effective, coordinated performances possible within an activity system. This holds true both for facilitators and participants who need to collaborate. In our framework for the <u>design of distributed learning environments</u> we acknowledge that facilitators cannot pre-define, but only somewhat anticipate affordances that might be perceived in a particular learning environment. A distributed learning environment, however, has to evolve and cannot be "ready" when the participants start to (inter-)act. Cook and Brown (1999) and Vyas and van der Veer (2005), for example, assume that affordances should be conceptualized as a somewhat dynamic concept. In an ongoing interaction with tools, artefacts, and other people, actors are not only affected by the dynamic situational changes but also by their personal dispositions. Our personal dispositions strongly influence what affordances we actually perceive in a given situation at a certain point in time. This dynamic understanding of the affordance concept appears to be entirely compatible with the ideas of Engeström et al. (1999), who describe the dynamic nature of interactions between the various components within activity systems.

We suggest that a framework for the design of distributed learning environments needs to take into consideration that the perceptions of all actors within a distributed learning environment dynamically change over time. From such a perspective iterative cycles of grounding and regulating through conversational actions become increasingly important for all actors. Though facilitators cannot fully pre-determine an "objective" range of affordances for all participants, the production and communication processes still need some structuring and guidance. We propose that these processes can be structured around activity descriptions. Such activity descriptions involve participants and facilitators, their objectives, mediators of their activity (tools and artefacts) and anticipated affordances that are likely to be perceived in relation to suggested actions.

Instead of entering into a pre-defined landscape of tools and services where all objectives, actions and evaluation means are defined and selected by an instructor, actors in our distributed learning environments design framework would be offered activity descriptions that allow them to set up and carry out certain educational challenges or interventions. The realization of each activity description in a particular institutional setting requires a conversational grounding process for establishing and maintaining a distributed learning environment on the basis of loosely-coupled components that can interoperate and interrelate on various levels. To start this process an initial set of tools and services needs to be selected that can support the productive and conversational actions of participants and facilitators. In more traditional instructional design models the instructors are expected to plan appropriate support strategies and tools before the actual activity. These models suggest instructors (or designers) need to (and in fact can) predict the outcomes of learning, define the ways, how to reach these outcomes, and determine which tools are appropriate for mediating these processes. This approach mostly reduces learning environment design in technologically mediated education to the selection of a set of tools, which offer objective functionalities for doing something. The instructor's task is to make use of these tool functionalities in pedagogically sound ways, creating instructional intervention strategies for using these tools in the activities. In addition, instructors are supposed to make learners aware of these tool functionalities in order to guarantee their success.

In our framework for the design of distributed learning environments, however, we understand environments for intentional learning and change as a broad and subjectivist concept. A "personal learning environment" entails all the instruments, materials and human resources that an individual is aware of and has access to in the context of an educational project at a given point in time. We think that our psychological and somewhat

ecological perspective on that matter sets us apart from the majority of the current contributions on "personal learning environments". Though some authors continuously point out that they consider "personal learning environments" as a conceptual approach rather than a piece of software or technological toolset, a review of the existing literature on the topic reveals an overall tendency to use figures of speech and expressions that suggest the contrary (see e.g. Chan *et al.*, 2005; Harmelen, 2008; Johnson *et al.*, 2006a; Johnson *et al.*, 2006b; Milligan *et al.*, 2006; see e.g. Wilson, 2008; Wilson *et al.*, 2006). While we certainly share the general analysis of the shortcomings of the mainstream approach to technologically mediated teaching and studying on one hand, and the proposed transformation of the technological landscape towards loosely-coupled services, interfaces, and tools on the other hand (Attwell, 2007; Wilson, 2008), we find it useful to start from a more comprehensive and radically individualistic perspective that treats the mediation of actions with the means of networked, digital technologies, as one particular realisation of what a person tries to achieve in her "personal learning environment" and what potentials for action (affordances) she perceives. A recent contribution from Johnson and Liber (2008) offers an interesting explication of a cybernetic and more comprehensive perspective on that matter that seems to be compatible with our thinking. It is quite clear, that networked communication and information technologies play an increasingly important role in this regard, but it is misleading to assume that all relevant actions in the context of human learning and change are inevitably technologically mediated all the time One author of this chapter explores this in more detail elsewhere (Fiedler, 2008).

Another important aspect that does not seem to get enough attention in the ongoing discourse on "personal learning environments", is the qualitative differences that emerge if the intended outcomes of work and study are to be produced through collaborative action among a group of actors. While many personal projects of learning and change greatly benefit from the engagement of peers, experts, and facilitators of all kinds, we would argue that the amount of regulation and co-ordination that is required for collaboration poses challenges and requirements that are qualitatively different from what an individual actor experiences if she is only following her individual trajectory of actions and goals. If, however, an individual takes part in some collaborative work- and study activities with other actors, some common goals and objectives for action need to be established and maintained. In this case parts of a personal learning environment inevitably start to show qualities of a human activity system. Again, if this takes place in a, at least partially, distributed setting, the conversational and productive actions will need to be technologically mediated. From an observer's perspective the actors involved have to form a distributed learning environment as long as the collaboration among these actors is still going on. One the productive goals of the collaboration have been reached such a distributed learning environment might dissolve entirely. On the other hand some weak-ties between the former collaborators might be maintained and become a more constant element of the personal learning environment of particular actors. Needless to say that successful collaboration might pre-dispose certain collaborative learning environments to be re-enacted again for other purposes.

From our perspective such distributed learning environments generally have the following characteristics:

- They cannot be set up and defined comprehensively before any activity is carried out together.
- Their components need to be grounded conversationally by participants and facilitators.
- They integrate diverse elements of distributed social software and social media tools and services that support social networking,

collaborative artefact production, sharing hyperlinks and resources, self-reflecting, aggregating and monitoring of all kinds of information and activity flows, and so forth.

- They are constructed and run upon the conversationally grounded and continuously monitored objectives, activities and evaluation means of the collaborating actors
- They mediate activity descriptions, which are constrained by the affordances that are perceived in respect to tool functionalities and their interoperability, characteristics of the artefacts and objects, and the participating actors' dispositions, such as preferences for certain objectives, working-styles, tools, co-workers and so forth.

The systemic nature of such environments suggests that scaffolding issues and tool are highly interwoven. Our framework presupposes that the participants' perception of affordances in concrete activities need to be taken into account. For example, in the context of an educational challenge that focuses on mediated collaborative work, all actors and facilitators have to observe the participants' actions and infer the affordances they perceive (or not) in relation to the tools and services present in a given distributed environment. Furthermore, facilitators need to provide feedback and guidance if it appears that the affordances perceived by the various actors differ considerably and don't allow for an effective realisation of the overall activity goals.

Thus actors and facilitators who want to help to establish and support distributed learning environments need to consider the following issues:

- How can one _infer_ the affordances perceived by various actors within different activities?
- How can actors judge the effectiveness of the inferred affordances for the realisation

of the overall objectives of an ongoing collaborative project?

• What type of feedback has the potential to broaden or advance the actors' perception of affordances within a given distributed learning environment?

• What mental models guide the judgements of actors on the effectiveness of the observed actions within a distributed learning environment?

• How can one support actors in establishing consensus on the affordances within distributed learning environments during various activities?

REMAINING TECHNICAL AND CONCEPTUAL CHALLENGES

One of the major challenges for growing a particular distributed learning environment is the selection of appropriate and interoperable tools according to the actors' perceived affordances in a specific activity context. There is a need to reach a common understanding and to find a consensus among collaborators in respect to the perception of affordances. This raises the question of how to locate and make choices regarding the selection of tools and systems for intended activities. The application of a framework for the design of distributed learning environments requires practices that support setting up and shaping technological landscapes made of loosely-coupled, networked tools and services of various kinds. A new emerging generation of aggregation- and mash-up tools and services look very promising in this regard (Severance *et al.*, 2008). The mash-up tools that we envision would not only allow all participants full control over the selection of information flows and feeds but also over the combination of production tools and workflows for realising their shared objectives for action. Collaborating actors could simply combine tools and services according to their needs for conversational and productive

actions. In turn, their collaborative actions and their tool selections could be recorded and used as the informational basis for the development of additional decision-support tools that help to select tools and services in relation to particular activities. Here we speculate that activity-based, decision-support tools could be beneficial. They could facilitate choosing tools from heterogeneous technological landscapes. The iCampFolio is an example of an early prototype of a decision support tool that attempts to facilitate the selection of tools and services (Väljataga *et al.*, 2007). The main purpose of iCampFolio is to provide people with an opportunity to find tools according to their planned activities. Among other views, the tool provides a community perspective that enables users to position themselves within the tool landscape in comparison to the affordances perceived by other actors. Hence, it enables one to find people with a similar perception of affordances and a similar use of tools for supporting their activities. The main design principle behind that tool is the intentional attempt to couple certain activity descriptions with the affordances typically perceived in its context in relation to particular tools and services (instead of their mere functionalities). However, the usefulness of such tools still needs to be evaluated in the field.

We have indicated before that a critical factor for an effective use of diverse technological landscapes of networked tools and services for the design of distributed learning environments, is the possibility to monitor the selection and use of particular tools and services and the information flows between them in the cause of action. The same holds true for successful scaffolding and coaching in these kinds of setting. Thus, we think that the use of distributed and networked social software and social media components for collaborative projects of intentional learning and change could greatly benefit form the selective aggregation of visible traces of different activities, like Weblog authoring, commentaries with certain tags, artefacts created and stored in different repositories, Wiki-nodes, discourse logs, and so forth. In places where distributed content flows and artefacts meet again, actors can even propagate themselves as connectors between various activity systems or networks of interest. If they intentionally mix their distributed activity traces with the traces of other actors (like in the aggregated feeds of the micro-content publishing service Jaiku - http://jaiku.com/) the aggregated information flow might work as a trigger for perturbation and dissonance and thus for change and learning in the long run (Glasersfeld, 1995; Harri-Augstein & Thomas, 1991; Thomas & Harri-Augstein, 1985). As far as these content flows are openly accessible, this potential effect is not only limited to the group of actors that inhabit a particular distributed learning environment. As long as a distributed learning environment makes use of open publishing and open access principles it always carries a potential for transcending the immediate circle of actors that make up the actual activity system. In general, social-networking and cross-pollination with other individual actors or activity systems is entirely possible and a lot more likely if distributed learning environments are mediated by social software and social media applications. We think that a framework for the design of distributed learning environments should try to conceptually integrate such a perspective and explicate some of the principles that are required to ensure an appropriate level of "openness" and connectivity of these environments (Downes, 2007).

Some social software applications already enable the visualisation of the distribution of simple meaning making activities like tagging within larger groups of actors (see Klerkx & Duval, 2007). What is still needed, however, is the visualisation of activities and the anticipated or perceived potentials for action (affordances) in relation to various components of a given technological landscape. Certainly, such a mapping or visualisation would not indicate which of the available potentialities are actually put into action. If we wanted to gain some insight on that matter, we would need to study the actual interactions that are carried out via specific social media and software tools and the content flows between those tools. This would also pertain the use of asynchronous or synchronous interaction tools when working collaboratively with artefacts. A growing number of these tools can increasingly be integrated with different Web pages, social software applications and mash-up tools. However, the development of tools and services that can keep and display interrelations between recorded conversational exchanges (like a text chat) and productive actions that created a particular artefact should greatly enhance reflective and communicative actions within distributed landscapes.

CONCLUDING REMARKS AND OUTLOOK

Most technologically mediated learning environments in higher education still reflect a design- and intervention approach that either ignores or even contradicts significant social and technological changes. The rise of symbolically mediated and information driven processes in work and life increasingly produces challenges that call for a particular set of dispositions and coping styles. We increasingly rely on collaborating and communicating with others, and our general capacity to act under partial uncertainty. For more and more people all this takes place in distributed and technologically mediated environments. It seems quite obvious that traditional ideas of qualification that overly emphasised the acquisition of factual knowledge and procedural skills are falling short in the light of these developments. While factual knowledge and procedural skills are certainly not becoming obsolete, they need to be embedded in a broader set of dispositions including internalised orientations, values, and volitional aspects necessary for (self-organising) action (Erpenbeck & Rosenstiel, 2007; Heyse *et al.*, 2002; Jünger, 2004).

Furthermore, in many work and life contexts, action becomes progressively more symbolically and technologically mediated.

In recent years, one outstanding driving force for this development has been the gradual evolution of the Web into a general computational platform. Step by step the Web embraces a growing number of decentralized, and only loosely-coupled, networked tools and services. Needless to say that these tools and services can be, and in fact will be, instrumentalised for an ever-expanding range of human purposes. We have outlined above that we see the design of distributed learning environments in higher education as one potential and somewhat promising field of application. However, traditional instructional design approaches and their underlying set of assumptions do not appear to be overly compatible with the qualities and characteristics of the practices that are emerging around social media and social software applications. We suggest that the same incompatibility holds true for an educational intervention perspective that emphasises the advancement of dispositions for self-organising action beyond factual knowledge and procedural skills. Thus, we need to carefully reflect and analyse the theoretically assumptions that are still driving most design and intervention efforts in formal education and formulate new frameworks that allow us to respond to the significant changes that we have outlined above. We are fully aware that this is not an easy undertaking, since it requires the rethinking of some core ideas within pedagogy and instructional design, such as agency, predictability, control, direction, and so forth.

We consider our text to be a preliminary and rather modest proposal for such a reorientation and a call for contributions to the search for an adequate design and intervention framework for distributed learning environments. In this regard we think activity theory has some interesting concepts and perspectives to offer. In addition, we discussed the concept of affordance, under-

stood as perceived possibilities for action, and its consequences if used in the context of learning environment design. We have briefly outlined our overlap and difficulties with current contributions on "personal learning environments" and proposed a more psychological use of the term that takes all aspects of an individuals environment into account that are relevant within the context of a given project of intentional learning and change. Technologically mediated actions are seen as a realisation or expression of the potentials for actions perceived by a human actor in her particular environment. We argued for the emergence of qualitatively different challenges and requirements if human actors place their learning and change in the context of collaboration (in the sense of shared production) with others. Furthermore, we addressed some current technical and conceptual challenges for the implementation and maintenance of distributed learning environments, such as the selection of tools and services in a particular activity context, a lack of robust and versatile mash-up tools for combining and integrating selected tools and services, the aggregation of distributed content flows and activity traces, the explication of design principles that can ensure an appropriate level of "openness" and connectivity of an environment, and the visualisation of activities within a given technological landscape.

Currently, our conceptual framework for the design of distributed learning environments is nothing more than an outline of core components and related concepts. However, within iCamp, an ICT design and development project funded under the 6th framework programme of the European Union, we are following a design-based research approach (A. L. Brown, 1992; Cobb *et al.*, 2003; Collings *et al.*, 2004; Edelson, 2002) that allows us to explore some of our core ideas in a series of field studies. In this context we design and implement some prototypical educational challenges on the basis of our current understanding of how distributed learning environments can be initiated and supported within formal education. The empirical insights that we gain through our field research are then fed back into the next round of improvement and refinement of the overall design framework. The revised framework in turn will guide and inform further field trials. We expect this iterative process to support a gradual abstraction of principles and concepts and the overall development of a robust framework. In the meantime we hope that our preliminary contribution can spur some interest and debate on the potentials and limitations of distributed learning environments in higher education.

REFERENCES

Attwell, G. (2007). *Personal learning environments - future of elearning?* Retrieved June 16, 2007, from http://www.elearningpapers.eu/index. php?page=doc&doc_id=8553&doclng=6

Berners-Lee, T. (2000). *Waeving the web: The original design and ultimate destiny of the world wide web.* New York, USA: Harper Collins.

Bleiklie, I. (2004). Diversification of higher education and the changing role of knowledge and research. *UNESCO Forum Occasional Paper Series.* Paper No 6. Retrieved June 15, 2006, from http://unesdoc.unesco.org/images/0014/001467/146736e.pdf

Brown, A. L. (1992). Design experiments: Theoretical and methodological challenges in creating complex interventions in classroom setting. *The Journal of the Learning Sciences, 2*(2), 141-178.

Brown, J. S. (1999). Learnig, working and playing in the digital age. Retrieved May 25, 2004, from http://serendip.brynmawr.edu/sci_edu/seelybrown/

Candy, P. (1991). *Self-direction for lifelong learning.* San Francisco: Josey-Bass Inc.

Chan, T., Corlett, D., Sharples, M., Ting, J., & Westmancott, O. (2005). Developing interactive logbook: A personal learning environment. In *Proceedings of the ieee international workshop on wireless and mobile technologies in education.* Washington, DC, USA: IEEE Computer Society Press.

Cobb, P., Confrey, J., diSessa, A., Lehrer, R., & Schauble, L. (2003). Design experiments in educational research. *Educational Researcher, 32*(1), 9-13.

Collings, A., Joseph, D., & Bielaczyc, K. (2004). Design research: Theoretical and methodological issues. *Journal of the Learning Sciences, 13*(1), 15-42.

Cook, S. D. N., & Brown, J. S. (1999). Bridging epistemologies: The generative dance between organisational knowledge and knowing. *Organization Science, 10*(4), 381-400.

Downes, S. (2005). *E-learning 2.0.* Retrieved February 3, 2006, from http://www.elearnmag. org/subpage.cfm?section=articles&article=29-1

Downes, S. (2007). *Learning networks in practice.* Retrieved April 5, 2008, from http://partners. becta.org.uk/page_documents/research/emerging_technologies07_chapter2.pdf

Edelson, D. C. (2002). Design research: What we learn when we engage in design. *Journal of the Learning Sciences, 11*(1), 105-121.

Efimova, L., & Fiedler, S. (2004). Learning webs: Learning in weblog networks. In P. Kommers, P. Isaias & M. B. Nunes (Eds.), *Proceedings of the IADIS International Conference Web Based Communities 2004* (pp. 490-494). Lisbon, Portugal: IADIS Press.

Engeström, Y. (1987). *Learning by expanding.* Helsinki: Orienta-konsultit.

Engeström, Y., Engeström, R., & Vähäaho, T. (1999). When the center does not hold: The importance of knotworking. In S. Chaiklin, M. Hedegaard & U. J. Jensen (Eds.), *Activity theory and social practice: Cultural-historical approaches* (pp. 345-374). Aarhus, DK: Aarhus University Press.

Erpenbeck, J., & Heyse, V. (1999). *Kompetenzbiographie - Kompetenzmilieu - Kompetenztransfer* (No. 62). Berlin: Arbeitsgemeinschaft Betriebliche Weiterbildungsforschung, e.V.

Erpenbeck, J., & Rosenstiel, L. v. (Eds.). (2007). *Handbuch Kompetenzmessung*. Stuttgart, Germany: Schäffer-Poeschel.

Fiedler, S. (2003). Personal webpublishing as a refective conversational tool for self-organized learning. In T. Burg (Ed.), *BlogTalks* (pp. 190-216). Norderstedt, Germany: Books on Demand.

Fiedler, S. (2008). The notion of personal learning environments reconsidered (in press).

Fiedler, S., & Sharma, P. (2004). Seeding conversational learning environments: Running a course on personal webpublishing and weblogs. In T. Burg (Ed.), *BlogTalks 2.0* (pp. 271-294). Norderstedt, Germany: Books on Demand.

Fiedler, S., & Sharma, P. (2005). Navigating personal information repositories with weblog authoring and concept mapping. In S.-O. Tergan & T. Keller (Eds.), *Knowledge and information visualization* (pp. 302-325). Berlin: Springer.

Fischer, G., & Scharff, E. (1998). Learning technologies in support of self-directed learning. *Journal of Interactive Media in Education, 98*(4). Retrieved June 16, 2004, from http://www-jime.open.ac.uk/98/4/

Foerster, H. v. (1999). Triviale und nicht-triviale maschinen. In A. P. Schmidt (Ed.), *Der wissensnavigator. Das lexikon der zukunft* (pp. 102). Stuttgart: Deutsche Verlagsanstalt.

Gaver, W. W. (1996). Affordances for interaction: The social is material for design. *Ecological Psychology, 8*(2), 111-129.

Gibson, J. J. (1986). *The ecological approach to visual perception*. Boston: Houghton Mifflin.

Glasersfeld, v. E. (1995). *Radical constructivism: A way of knowing and learning*. London: Falmer Press.

Harmelen, M. v. (2008). Design trajectories: Four experiments in ple implementation. *Interactive Learning Environments, 16*(1), 35-46.

Harri-Augstein, S., & Thomas, L. (1991). *Learning conversations: The self-organised way to personal and organisational growth*. London: Routledge.

Heyse, V., Erpenbeck, J., & Michel, L. (2002). *Lernkulturen der zukunft. Kompetenzbedarf und kompetenzentwicklung in zukunftsbranchen* (No. 74). Berlin: Arbeitsgemeinschaft Betriebliche Weiterbildungsforschung, e.V.

Hutchins, E. (1991). Organizing work by adaptation. *Organization Science, 2*(1), 14-39.

Hutchins, E. (1995). *Cognition in the wild*. Cambridge, MA: MIT Press.

Johnson, M., Beauvoir, P., MIlligan, C., Sharples, P., Wilson, S., & Liber, O. (2006a). Mapping the future: The personal learning environment reference model and emerging technology. In D. Whitelock & S. Wheeler (Eds.), *Alt-c 2006: The next generation - research proceedings* (pp. 182-191). Totton: Association for Learning Technology.

Johnson, M., & Liber, O. (2008). The personal learning environment and the human condition: From theory to teaching practice. *Interactive Learning Environments, 16*(1), 3-15.

Johnson, M., Liber, O., Wilson, S., & MIlligan, C. (2006b). The personal learning environment: A report on the cetis ple project. Retrieved April 5, 2008, from http://wiki.cetis.ac.uk/image:plereport.doc

Jünger, S. (2004). *Selbstorganisation, lernkultur und kompetenzentwicklung*. Wiesbaden: Deutscher Universitätsverlag.

Kerres, M. (2007). Microlearning as a challenge to instructional design. Retrieved April 5, 2008, from http://mediendidaktik.uni-duisburg-essen.de/system/files/Microlearning-kerres.pdf

Kirschner, P. A. (2002). Can we support cscl? Educational, social and technological affordances for learning. Retrieved November 12, 2007, from http://www.ou.nl/Docs/Expertise/OTEC/Publicaties/paulkirschner/oratieboek_PKI_DEF_Klein_ZO.pdf

Klerkx, J., & Duval, E. (2007, September 17-20, 2007). *Visualizing social bookmarks.* Paper presented at the SIRTEL 2007 Workshop on Social Information Retrieval for Technology-Enhanced Learning, Crete, Greece.

Kreijns, K., Kirschner, P. A., & Jochems, W. (2002). The sociability of computer-supported collaborative learning environments. *Educational Technology & Society, 5*(1), 822.

Maturana, H. R., & Varela, F. J. (1980). *Autopoiesis and cognition. The realization of the living.* Dordrecht: Reidel.

Mejias, U. (2005, November 23, 2005). A nomad's guide to learning and social software. *Knowledge Tree Journal, 7,* from http://flexiblelearning.net.au/knowledgetree/edition07/download/la_mejias.pdf

Milligan, C., Johnson, M., Sharples, P., Wilson, S., & Liber, O. (2006). Developing a reference model to describe the personal learning environment. In W. Nejdl & K. Tochtermann (Eds.), *Innovative approaches for learning and knowledge sharing - first european conference on technology enhanced learning, ec-tel 2006* (pp. 506-511). Berlin/Heidelberg: Springer.

Neisser, U. (1994). Multiple systems: A new approach to cognitive theory. *The European Journal of Cognitive Psychology, 6*(3), 225-241.

Norman, D. (1988). *The design of everyday things.* New York: Basic Books.

Paquet, S. (2003). *A socio-technological approach to sharing knowledge across disciplines.* Universite de Montreal.

Severance, C., Hardin, J., & Whyte, A. (2008). The coming functionality mash-up in personal learning environments. *Interactive Learning Environments, 16*(1), 47-62.

Sharma, P., & Fiedler, S. (2007). Supporting self-organized learning with personal webpublishing technologies and practices. *Journal of Computing in Higher Education, 18*(2), 3-24.

Thomas, L., & Harri-Augstein, S. (1985). *Self-organised learning. Foundations of a conversational science for psychology.* London: Routledge.

Vyas, D. M., & van der Veer, G. C. (2005). Experience as meaning: Creating, communicating and maintaining in real-spaces. In M. F. Costabile & F. Paternò (Eds.), *Human-Computer Interaction – INTERACT 2005* (pp. 1-4). Berlin, Heidelberg: Springer

Willke, H. (2005). *Systemtheorie II: Interventionstheorie.* Stuttgart: Lucius & Lucius.

Wilson, S. (2008). Patterns of personal learning environments. *Interactive Learning Environments, 16*(1), 17-34.

Wilson, S., Liber, O., Beauvoir, P., MIlligan, C., Johnson, M., & Sharples, P. (2006). Personal learning environments: Challenging the dominant design of educational systems. Retrieved November 20, 2007, from http://hdl.handle.net/1820/727

Chapter XII
Exploring the Role of Social Software in Higher Education

Yoni Ryan
Australian Catholic University, Australia

Robert Fitzgerald
University of Canberra, Australia

ABSTRACT

This chapter considers the potential of social software to support learning in higher education. It outlines a current project funded by the then Australian Carrick Institute for Learning and Teaching in Higher Education, now the Australian Learning and Teaching COuncil (ALTC) (http://www.altc.edu. au/carrick/go) to explore the role of social software in supporting peer engagement and group learning. The project has established a series of pilot projects that examine ways in which social software can provide students with opportunities to engage with their peers in a discourse that explores, interrogates and provides a supplementary social ground for their in-class learning. Finding creative ways of using technology to expand and enrich the social base of learning in higher education will become increasingly important to lecturers and instructional designers alike. This project represents one small step in testing the applicability of social software to these contexts. While many of our students are already using various technologies to maintain and develop their personal networks, it remains to be seen if these offer viable uses in more scholarly settings.

INTRODUCTION

The evolution of the Web in the 1990s saw a parallel development of commercial Learning Management Systems (LMS) and, by 2001, the widespread adoption of the latter in Australian universities, in response to growing demands for flexibility or convenience for students. Yet much of the research indicates that in the main, LMS have been used more for administrative purposes

(Dalsgaard, 2006; Hedberg, 2006; OECD, 2005; Reeves, Herrington & Oliver, 2004) and educators themselves most frequently use LMS as a content management system rather than exploiting the interactive potential of digital media (Boezerooy, 2003; Fiedler et al., 2007). With the official emergence of Web 2.0 in 2004 (O'Reilly, 2005), and the explosion of activity in social networking applications afforded by the technology, it is timely to consider whether the LMS, and the static learning environments they have typically modelled, should at least be complemented by (and perhaps even give way to) more interactive applications.

The original intention of Berners-Lee 'was all about connecting people' (Anderson, 2007). However, the Web was quickly colonised by vendors intent on using it for education purposes as a tradeable global commodity (Cunningham et al., 1998). LMS vendors promised a universal 'Economics 101' subject developed by the best professors in the world, and accessible - at a price - to all (Cunningham et al., 1998). Educators and the instructional designers who developed online materials were paradoxically complicit in this static model, recreating in their online materials the transmission model of pedagogy they inherited as 'the university teaching model' (Laurillard, 2002). Berners-Lee was not alone in his vision for a different technological future. In his book *Mindstorms*, Seymour Papert (1980) developed a compelling case for the potential of technology to mediate thinking in ways that reveal, enrich and expand learning. The prominent educator Paulo Freire (1985) argued that transformative education can only be achieved through a pedagogy that values learning as a process of *asking* questions not just *receiving* answers. The dominance of the administrative functions of e-learning has already been noted, with its preference for *content* over *process* most frequently achieved through one-way (vs. two-way) models of interaction. In these applications the *answer* seems much more important than the *question*. Papert

(2000) argued that transformative shifts in the way we use technology will only be possible when educators have time to rethink both the *why* and *how* of its use. Given the widening gap between formal education and Internet culture, and the rise of the millennial learner, it is clear that we can no longer afford not to take time to reconceptualise technology-mediated learning. This will involve the design of a pedagogy that connects and engages learners in activities that value the question as much as the answer. Finding creative ways of using technology to expand and enrich the social base of learning in higher education will become increasingly important to academics and instructional designers alike. However, it is not clear that even the experts in higher education and e-learning can envisage such a pedagogy, with Guess (2007) assessing discussion at the Seattle Educause conference as producing 'more questions than answers' about capitalising on the contemporary enthusiasm for social networking in educational settings.

The project reported in this chapter represents one small step towards testing the applicability of different technologies to higher education contexts. While many of our students are already using various technologies to maintain and develop their social networks, it remains to be seen if these offer viable uses in more scholarly settings.

BACKGROUND

There are a multitude of Web 2.0 services that are readily available to students and educators such as blogs (e.g. Edublogs), wikis (e.g. Wikispaces), collaborative word processors (e.g. Google Docs), syndication and aggregation using RSS (e.g. Bloglines, PageFlakes and iGoogle), social bookmaking (e.g. del.icio.us), shared calendars (e.g. Google Calendar and 30 Boxes) and creative content exchange (e.g. Flickr for images, ccMixter for audio, and YouTube for video). The project reported here arose as a result of intense interest in the use of Web 2.0 technologies in higher education by a group of teacher-scholars. Although some of the group were using several applications successfully in their own teaching, predominantly in the area of media studies, they had little in the way of comprehensive research studies to support their belief that Gen Y students would be more engaged in their learning if formal study programmes incorporated Web 2.0 modalities, with their potential for more interactive construction of knowledge, skills and values.

Since 2002, conventional media and IT consultancy firms have reported exponential uptake of social technologies such as Facebook, YouTube and MySpace, and the near universal use of converged technologies like mobile telephones, at least in the West. Social commentators such as Prensky (2001), and educational technologists and managers such as Diana Oblinger (2004) have argued strongly that 'digital natives', in Prensky's term, demand a new pedagogical approach given their routine use of social technologies in their daily lives. Arguably, this is supported by the growing influence of constructivism as an underpinning tertiary learning theory (Biggs, 1999; Marton & Saljo, 1976), and social constructivism (Renner, 2006), since these theories propose that students mentally 'construct' their own learning, based on a variety of resources, including teachers and peers. Increasingly however, these resources are web-enabled.

Over the past five years in Australian universities, traditional face-to-face delivery has declined as the major mode of university teaching, for several reasons. The first is economic, as funding for teaching activities has decreased (Go8, 2007), and programme hours have been cut in consequence. The second is also economically related: as students' personal costs for tuition have increased, their paid-work commitments have risen to an average of over fifteen hours per week (Universities Australia (UA), 2007). The result has been declining attendances at sched-uled lectures (UA, 2007), and demands for more 'flexible' access to learning materials.

As will be discussed further below, the literature presented the research team with contradictory findings. Krause (2006) for example, in her analysis of the decade long studies of the 'First Year Experience' in Australian Universities, argues from her data that students are less comfortable and familiar with new media in their learning environment than has been supposed. Ramsay's early data analysis (2007), supports that view. Berg, Berquam & Christoph (2007) also report some students at the University of Wisconsin-Madison warning off administrators considering muscling in on 'their spaces': 'Don't bother with IM or Facebook – that's **our** way to network. Leave us alone. This is my way to procrastinate. I don't want to feel guilty about it.' Yet Kvavik & Caruso (2005) argued that in their US survey, students were overwhelmingly positive about the attraction of IT in education: it was about 'convenience', easy off-campus access.

The issues underpinning the present project cross the usual boundaries of disciplinary study, making analysis and a standard literature review problematic. Indeed, Cobcroft et al. (2006, p.11) in their 138 page literature review on e-learning, assert that a literature review in this area 'cannot be exhaustive'. This chapter has sought to canvass the more recent and 'typical' of the research, and locate it within industry approaches. A thorough review would take into account not only the more 'academic' studies of technology usage that have methodological rigour, but the 'grey literature' of self-promotional industry reports, mass media reports, and the thousands of opinions available through the affordance of Web 2.0 technology itself, in the form of blogs, wikis etc. It would also situate this literature in the broader context of social and higher education systemic change, such that 'the university experience' no longer encompasses the 'withdrawal' from the world of work of an elite group of the young, to focus on preparation for life and work via study. Clearly such a thorough review is problematic.

Any summary of the literature is also complicated by the nature of inquiry into the phenomenon of social networking: some approaches focus on the technical aspects of social software, others on the sociological implications (the 'generational' or 'digital native/immigrant' line), others still on the philosophical implications of pervasive social technologies, while only a few consider the pedagogical and cognitive dimensions of social networks. Yet another approach is to speculate on the nature of institutional 'disruption' as a result of social and technological networking. This is an immense range of fields to canvass.

There is no doubting the uptake of social applications of technology. The explosion of subscribers to social networking sites is truly astonishing. YouTube, invented only in 2005, reports 70 million viewings per day. It was *Time*'s 'Invention of the Year' in 2006, according to *Time* writer, Lev Grossman, because it promotes 'authenticity'. Australia MySpace claimed on 27 June 2007 that over 48,000 videos had been uploaded in the past three days. It is the most popular social networking site in the country, according to HitWise, an Internet research company based in the UK. 27 % of all Internet users regularly use MySpace, and it claims over 160 million subscribers. On that same day in June, Flickr claimed nearly 3000 photos had been uploaded in the last minute — at 9.20 am. HitWise reported that Bebo 'surpassed MySpace in weekly market share of UK Internet visits to become the most visited social networking site in the UK for the week ending 5th August 2006', and is the 11th most popular site on the Internet with 22 million users. SecondLife, opened in 2003, claims 7.4 million accounts have been opened, although many are never really 'peopled'. It seems to have over one million active users. The Australian-based Prospect Research (2006) claims that in 2006, 34% of Gen Ys had their own blog, and 13% their own website. Facebook claims 200,000 people sign up each day, and boasted 42 million members in October 2007.

The literature around Gen Y students and social technologies presents a conundrum with much of it falling into five categories:

- **Category 1.** A plethora of 'pop pieces' or 'op ed' pieces in conventional media, typically by amazed later age adults 'discovering' the worlds of Second Life and Facebook, and issuing alarmist warnings about identity theft and potential career damage.
- **Category 2.** The large number of industry reports, typically by IT consultants, and based on limited surveys of Gen Y usage.
- **Category 3.** More considered investigations of the youth demographic and their propensities in regard to technologies and learning approaches.
- **Category 4.** A number of studies, which investigate the pioneering use of new applications in selected universities, although many do not evaluate the efficacy of these applications in learning.
- **Category 5.** A small category canvasses new media usage as the object of academic interest in its own right.

Typical of the Category 1 literature is a piece in the *Weekend Australian Magazine* March 2007, which reflects the amazement of the 'newbie' to the world of social sites. Nussbaum, the writer, reprises the intimate details of one of her featured MySpace users, Kitty, including her sexual experiences and her reaction to the death of her parents at 22. Nussbaum characterises the reaction of the older generation to Gen Y's tendencies to 'self-exposure' in these terms: 'They have no sense of shame. They have no sense of privacy. They are show-offs, fame whores, pornographic little loons who post their diaries, their phone numbers, their stupid poetry — for God's sake their dirty photos! — online. They have virtual friends instead of real ones. They talk in illiterate instant messages. They are interested only in attention — yet they have zero attention span...' (Nussbaum, 2007, p.24).

Alarmist stories about the potential for identity fraud in social networks (www.abc.net.au/news/stories/2007/10/24/2068766.htm?section=justin) deepen concern among many in the general population and older academics regarding Web 2.0.

A common attribute of Category 2 type studies into Web 2.0, which examine its educational implications, is the predominance of IT consultants rather than traditional disciplinary academics among authors. This might be explained by a general lack of knowledge of new technologies among traditional academics, given the aging profile of Australian academics (Hugo, 2005), and their status as 'digital immigrants'. It might also be related to self-interest in promoting new technologies on the part of IT consultants, who also predominated in commentary during the 1990s 'tech boom' in e-learning systems. As then, commentary is usually accompanied by brave predictions on media futures and mobile devices (Franklin & van Harmelen, 2007; Livingstone & Bober, 2005; The Horizon Report, 2007).

Typical of such Category 2 publications is the late 2007 Franklin and van Harmelen study, both authors being IT consultants scanning the practices of five European universities in relation to the impact of Web 2.0 on institutional policy and strategy, and changes in pedagogical practices. The significance of this study is its environmental scan of European institutional approaches and policies around Web 2.0. Like the boosters of the 1990s, Franklin & van Harmelen parlay the 'profound potential' of Web 2.0, including its 'pedagogical efficiency' as well as its promise of 'greater student independence and autonomy' (2007, p.3).

Nevertheless, the Franklin and van Harmelen (2007) study offers cautions:

Because Web 2.0 is a relatively young technology, there are many unresolved issues relating to its use in universities. These include intellectual property rights for material created and modified by university members and external contributors;

appropriate pedagogies for use with Web 2.0 (and equally which pedagogic approaches are enhanced by the use of Web 2.0); how to assess material that may be collectively created and that is often open to ongoing change; the choice of types of systems for institutional use; how to roll out Web 2.0 services across a university; whether it is best to host the services within the university or make use of externally hosted services elsewhere; integration with institutional systems; accessibility, visibility and privacy; data ownership; control over content; longevity of data; data preservation; information literacy; and staff and student training. At this stage all that we have to go on are the results of experiments with Web 2.0, rather than a set of solutions that are ready for widespread adoption (p.1).

These are all important issues and need appropriate technical and legal investigation, although the present concern is with pedagogical implications. As one would expect, the report concludes with a recommendation that institutions not 'impose' unnecessary regulations 'in order to avoid constraining experimentation with Web 2.0 technologies and allied pedagogies' (Franklin & van Harmelen, 2007, p.4). As will be seen in our conclusions, we endorse this view.

Franklin & van Harmelen (2007) explore several areas that have bearing on the present study. The first is a finding relayed (Franklin & van Harmelen 2007, p.7) from Arthur (2006) that in Web 2.0, 1% of users create content, 10% comment on that content and therefore add to it, and 89% simply 'consume' it. This, if verified in an educational context, poses difficulties if the learning objective is to *create* content. It is less problematic if the objective is to *disseminate* knowledge.

Franklin & van Harmelen consider that 'much (of the use of Web 2.0 technologies) is still experimental work carried out by enthusiastic lecturers who are willing to devote the time to *make the technologies work for their teaching*' (2007, p.

14; our emphasis). The evidence of this project in terms of the challenges faced at institutional and technical levels would support this observation: enthusiasts 'make' the technologies 'work'; institutional systems are not geared for the systemic incorporation of Web 2.0 in routine teaching practices. Given the case studies presented in the Franklin and van Harmelen report, it would seem that in the European universities surveyed at least, the technologies' most pervasive use has been in social support and building a community ethos, rather than in 'direct' academic work.

This project team supports the notion of using a variety of web applications as providing the most appropriate philosophy and pedagogy for academic users of Web 2.0, consistent with our Manifesto (http://wiki.openacademic.org/index. php/CookBookManifesto), but recognises that this position will be in conflict with many IT systems professionals who try ever harder to manage the unmanageable (Wilson, 2007).

Notwithstanding the many examples of IT consultants as authors of institution-oriented reports, there are a growing number of Media Studies academics conducting small scale research on student use of and attitudes to new technologies in their teaching. Such studies generally focus on particular aspects of technological applications. For example, in the brief report on students' use of Google as a research tool, Head (2007) suggests that the supposed and much deplored reliance on search sites and sources like Google, Yahoo! or Wikipedia has a limited basis in fact, once students have realised the limitations of these tools in providing depth in content. Most students turned first to their subject references as provided by the academic; only 10% used these general sites first in a research assignment. (Head's publication in itself is an indication of the transformation of scholarly publication as a result of the Internet: *First Monday*, its place of publication, is a peer-reviewed online-only journal).

Category 3 studies include those by the highly respected Demos Group: one study reported by the group found that 'one-third of the children surveyed, including one in five 11 year olds, regularly use the Internet for blogging, yet two-thirds of parents do not know what a blog is, and only 1% thought that their child used them' (Demos, 2006, p. 73). Such studies provide valuable background information on the aspirations of Gen Y, and their attitudes to new technologies.

In Category 4 is Anderson's (2007) JISC report from the UK, 'What is Web 2.0? Ideas, Technologies and Implications for Education' - an excellent introduction to various applications and their possibilities and implications. It is particularly useful in that it situates the applications within the wider literature on social, cultural and pedagogical change. EdNA (2007) also lists a number of resources relevant to Web 2.0 in higher education.

Finally, Category 5 is an emerging area where media researchers are closely examining the role of social software in education. Examples include the Rochester Institute of Technology's laboratory for Social Computing (http://social.it.rit.edu), and Seton Hall's virtual worlds projects (http://tltc. shar.edu/virtualworlds).

MAIN FOCUS

The main focus of this chapter is a discussion of the Digital Learning Communities (DLC) project that was funded by the then Carrick Institute for Learning and Teaching in Higher Education. The primary aim of this project was to apply an evidenced-based approach to increasing undergraduate and postgraduate student engagement, especially peer-to-peer interaction and communal learning, through innovative applications of social software in university teaching (http://mashedlc. edu.au/). The context of the three universities involved (University of Canberra, Queensland University of Technology, and RMIT University) was an important consideration: none could be considered 'bleeding edge' in relation to systemic use of sophisticated technologies, although each has a small group of innovative researchers in new media. Two of the universities are large (30,000+ students), with strongly centralised management. The third is small (12,000 students), and its IT services were in flux during the project. An important element of the study for the team as new media researchers was to 'test' the responsiveness of institutional systems to innovative pedagogies.

The general intentions of the DLC project were to:

- enhance student community and peer engagement through socially mediated content creation, classification, aggregation and sharing.
- apply existing free services and applications to maximise accessibility.
- document and disseminate the results in a way that allows immediate and sustainable take-up of these techniques by Australian university teachers.

From the outset of the project it was clear that to gain a better insight into this rapidly changing area we would need to build a multi-faceted evidence and resource base that would help universities understand their student body and offer ways of using social software. To this end we:

- developed a project manifesto that outlined the project team's shared understanding of what constitutes good learning and teaching in higher education.
- conducted a survey to characterise university students' present and emerging use of technology for study, work, and play. In particular we wanted to examine the quantity and quality of the data channels used by students and provide some baseline measures of the uptake of these technologies.
- developed a series of pilot projects to help focus attention on the identification, development and evaluation of how social software

can be used to engage learners with emerging social technologies.

- developed a wiki-based resource (called a cookbook) that would help lecturers explore how to use social software in their teaching.

For the purposes of this chapter we will only report some of our preliminary survey results and briefly detail the pilot projects that are currently still in progress.

Table 1. Age distribution

18-25	58%
26-35	18%
36-45	11%
46-55	9%
56-65	4%

Table 2. Respondents by discipline

Economics	6	1%
Business	78	9%
Law	34	4%
Commerce	23	3%
Information Technology	146	16%
Engineering	14	2%
Science	50	6%
Medicine	5	1%
Education	68	8%
Nursing	7	1%
Languages	13	1%
Communications/Media	124	14%
Creative Industries	112	13%
Design	45	5%
Arts	22	2%
Creative Writing	23	3%
Other	112	13%
International Studies	10	1%
	N=892	100%

Table 3. Choose the three main ways you usually communicate with your colleagues or fellow students

Face to face meetings	30%
Phone calls	16%
Email	27%
Text messaging	15%
Instant messaging	6%
Listserv or group emails	2%
A group website or blog	4%

Social Software Survey

In August 2007 we conducted an anonymous web-based survey of students and staff across three Australian universities. In total we had 853 respondents (41% male and 59% female), 63% undergraduates, 16% postgraduates and 21% university staff. Our preliminary analysis of the data seems to indicate that as a whole, this is a fairly 'connected' group and as such may represent the leading edge of users. Of this group 56% indicated they had their own website, while 39% said they maintained a blog. Further analysis and comparison by discipline grouping will explore this more fully in subsequent reports. Nearly 92% had broadband access with the most common point of access being home (63%), fol-

lowed by university (22%) and workplace (14%) and 93% had two or more email addresses. The age distribution is shown below.

To get a sense of the ways respondents connected with their peers we asked them to identify the three main ways they choose to communicate (Table 3). Face-to-face meetings and email were most popular, followed by phone and text messaging. The importance of text messaging relative to phone calls perhaps points to potential of texting to deliver a cost effective, reliable messaging platform with minimal disruption for both sender and receiver. Instant messaging (IM), blogs and discussion lists did not figure much at all. One should not read too much into this result, as on many university campuses, blogs and IM are not well supported.

Examining the use of popular social networking applications we asked respondents to characterise their use as either an Internet 'Browser', 'Participator' or 'Contributor'. We suggested that each of these characterisations could be defined in the following way:

- **Browsers:** Tend to mainly read, surf or watch Internet content
- **Participators:** Browse but also make comments, suggestions and critiques of Internet content
- **Contributors:** Browse, participate but also create and upload Internet content

Table 4. Which of the following sites do you: Browse, participate or contribute to?

	Browse	Participate	Contribute
Social Networking (e.g. MySpace, Facebook)	36%	30%	34%
Social Bookmarking (e.g. Del.icio.us, Digg)	58%	23%	19%
Blog Sites (e.g. LiveJournal, Blogger)	48%	25%	27%
Wikis (e.g. Wikipedia, Citizendium)	77%	24%	9%
Photo Sharing (e.g. Flickr, Photobucket)	50%	29%	21%
Video Sharing (e.g. Youtube, Blip.tv)	70%	17%	13%
Music Networking (e.g. Last.fm, CCMixster)	67%	20%	13%
Average	**58%**	**23%**	**19%**

In the three universities we surveyed, most students used social software to browse information (58%). Interestingly for most students, wikis, often held up as the archetypal content creator application, were mainly used as an information resource. Given the success of wiki projects such as Wikipedia (http://wikipedia.org/) it is our view that this result may be more a reflection of users' limited understanding of how wikis work rather than a specific flaw of the application. However, specifically designed social networking applications such as Facebook (http://www.facebook.com/) suggest more sophisticated patterns of use with the highest levels of contributors being reported (34%) followed by blogging (27%), photo sharing (21%) and social bookmarking (19%). The questions that arise here are what content is being created and has that content got any educational significance? It is fair to say that at this point we do not know enough about the nature of the content to respond with confidence. Having said that, it is our view that much of the content on, for example Facebook, appears to be directed towards more recreational than educational applications.

In another question, we asked respondents to rate the usefulness of various features of social software on a five-point scale (1-not useful through to 5 -extremely useful). Table 5 shows that the top four features of social software were their search capabilities, opportunities for self publishing,

Table 5. Rate the following features of social software

Self publishing	3.3
Tagging	2.9
Ratings	2.7
Buddylist/Friends	3.2
Search	3.7
Recommendations	3.0
RSS feeds	2.8
Commenting	3.3

commenting and maintaining friend/buddy lists. All of which suggests students value a role as an author (i.e. able to publish and comment) who can be easily connected with people (i.e. friends) and information (i.e. search) – what O'Reilly (2005) and others have referred to as the 'architecture of participation' in which software systems are designed to help users connect with other users.

Pilot Projects

The pilot projects we have established include the use of wikis, blogs and related social networking applications. The underlying pedagogical rationale for the pilot studies was a recognition by each lecturer that the current form of e-learning was too restrictive and that they wanted to explore a different model that might increase student interaction. In one pilot a lecturer explored the use of MyToons (http://www.mytoons.com/), to support the teaching of animation in a New Media course. In a first year Information Systems course, another lecturer is supplementing her WebCT site by using a corporate implementation of the wiki application, Confluence (http://www.atlassian.com/software/confluence/), to build an information systems jobs registry. In a first year Applied Ecology course, another lecturer has given her students a blog through a Drupal-based application (http://community.mashedlc.edu.au) to encourage students to record and share their field notes and laboratory reports. In two similar projects based in two different universities, lecturers are testing a whole-of-programme approach to the use of blogs in New Media courses. Recently, one of these lecturers began using a staff retreat as an opportunity to use a wiki to engage in a curriculum re-design process by getting his teaching staff to work face-to-face undertaking joint curriculum writing activities. The reports from these pilots are still being developed however we can provide some reflection on the Mytoons pilot project.

MyToons (http://www.mytoons.com/) is animation site "...where people who really love animation - from seasoned industry pros to rabid animation fans - can upload and share their creations and animated favorites with the entire world for free". It offers students a wide range of functionality including an online gallery for their work, a personal online portfolio, off-campus access, documentation of personal and group processes, an authentic community of practice, global networks through groups and friend-lists, experience with social protocols and online culture, peer benchmarking, peer critique and technical support.

From the outset of the pilot there were a number of technical problems that prevented students uploading their animations files to the site. While that problem was eventually solved, it did create an initial level of concern amongst the students that they were relying on prototype software to complete their university studies. However by the end of the course students rated themselves as competent users of MyToons and generally believed the site supported their work. While the pilot group identified themselves as experienced users of social software, their participation in this online community helped further raise their awareness of the risks of internet fraud and spamming and presented the lecturer with an opportunity to talk about ways they could manage their identity through the use of online screen names.

A key recommendation arising from the pilot was that the syllabus should be reoriented from technical mastery of animation tools to also consider the skills students require to effectively engage in an online community. Another outcome of posting their work in such a public space was the heightened awareness of copyright issues. In the lecturer's explanation as their work was now under wider public scrutiny, plagiarism became increasingly socially risky (Barrass & Fitzgerald, 2008). The technical problems early in the unit served to highlight that innovation and experimentation can be risky and that adopting longer implementation time frames would help mitigate some of this risk.

EMERGING ISSUES AND FUTURE TRENDS

While this project continues into 2008 with a second social software survey being conducted in May, we are beginning to see a number of issues emerging that we will briefly detail here.

No One-Size-Fits-All

The rich variety of alternatives and complementary tools available online to support learning and teaching can make the selection of the best tools for a particular purpose difficult. In our experience there is no single application or tool that meets all these needs. What is becoming clear is the potential value of networked repositories and aggregation services that university teachers can subscribe to or track easily. Our project remains founded on the belief that there are a multitude of web services that are readily available to students and educators, and we continue to seek the underlying principles that make these services valuable in learning and teaching rather than building or significantly modifying large information systems. The ALCT is developing an online resource to facilitate sharing and exchange. Referred to as the ALCT Exchange (http://www.alctexchange.edu.au), this project seeks to create an online social networking hub for the exchange of ideas about teaching practice in the Australian and international higher education sector. While this work will be a significant development for higher education, the reality is that it will not be the only space for social networking. We will require a multiplicity of social networks that are designed in interconnecting ways that facilitate communication and exchange across different university networks. Interestingly, students themselves are not seeking ICT solutions as alternatives to traditional teaching. Some recent surveys (Berger, 2007; Ipsos MORI, 2007; Salaway & Caruso, 2007) note that students are wary of too much ICT in teaching and prefer a balance between online and face-to-face instruction. They are also concerned that instructors may not have sufficient expertise to use ICT effectively in teaching: some students feel that they have more expertise than their teachers (Ipsos MORI, 2007).

Institutional ICT Services are not Partners in Innovation

Centralised ICT services departments with their focus on management and standardisation have proved a barrier to the exploration of innovative emerging online technologies and services. There is a pervasive view that external services should not be used for teaching as they represent unacceptable risk. It is not just high profile applications such as Facebook that are frowned upon but often decisions are taken in the interests of simplification and standardisation that effectively limit the choices available to lecturers. In one of our universities, a request to have the Firefox web browser included on the standard computer image was denied by ICT Services because they argued Internet Explorer provided equivalent functionality. Despite concerted efforts both within and outside the university to document the pedagogical strengths of Firefox over Internet Explorer 6 (see http://talo.wikispaces.com/Browsers), only Internet Explorer was retained on student labs. Staff were given the opportunity to use Firefox but only if they were able to develop a business case for their application.

In another example, our need to alert students to our survey highlighted difficulties and gaps in the ways universities communicate electronically with students. Many students do not regularly use their university email accounts due to limited mailbox storage limits and the fact that many university portals cannot be easily configured by students to meet their particular communication needs. The result is that it can be difficult to contact students. There are arguments for standardisation and common approaches for institutional services, but as Franklin and van Harmelen (2007)

argue, there is also a need to support innovative and creative activity that explores additional or alternative learning and teaching techniques and environments

Open Source Software and 'Free' Web Services are Vital

Much of what others and we have been able to achieve in the DLC project is the result of the availability of open source software like Drupal and 'free' online services like Google Groups, MediaWiki and MyToons. In institutions where ICT departments can be unresponsive or hostile to requests from academics to use this new software or an online service for research or teaching, access to the Internet's growing range of accessible services provides a more than viable alternative to in-house supplied services. ICT departments are actively discouraging such approaches where they can, for example by denying the easy availability of appropriate browsers on university computers or closing ports on routers used for video collaboration. While there are risks to privacy, questions of accountability, and no guarantees of reliable or continuing services associated with external services, equally there are questions of quality of service, responsiveness and availability of expertise when using institutional services.

Cross-Institutional Innovation is Problematic

Cross-institutional collaboration can be richly rewarding for students and staff. The benefits include raising awareness of best practices, re-use of resources, peer review and economies of scale generally, but there are barriers, not just of time and place. There is a not-invented-here attitude that may have some credibility: individual institutions have their own cultures and timetables that don't necessarily align with others but this should not be a reason to reject outright an approach or resources developed elsewhere. Part of the challenge of working across the sector is that while each institution continues to run its own ICT services, there will be barriers such as authentication issues to impede seamless cross-institutional collaboration. It is time to investigate opportunities to provide ICT systems (like student email, financial management, student management, human resources, student portfolios, alumni services, even a common learning management system) across the higher education sector, not just to facilitate collaboration but also to provide a more efficient and effective service to the community. This is not unprecedented: while the ALCT Exchange may not provide a total solution for collaborative services across the sector, it does provide resources that individual institutions will no longer need to provide for themselves.

Decentralised and Centralised

Our original project was inspired by the loosely connected nature of Web 2.0 services. We have also seen the need to experiment with approaches that offer more stable and managed systems that could integrate with core university systems. In this regard we have been using OpenAcademic (http://openacademic.org/) and their work, to build the Content Management System (CMS) Drupal (http://drupal.org/) as a functional social networking environment. Some of our work and feedback has contributed to the GPL (General Public Licence) release of the Drupaled code base (http://www.drupaled.org/). Drupal has a strong reputation in the field because of its capacity to support both individuals and communities with their web needs from personal web sites or blogs, to community web portals, e-commerce applications or social networking applications. As detailed on the Drupal website (http://drupal.org), the current release of Drupal (Version 6.2) supports a wide variety of uses including:

- Content Management Systems
- Blogs
- Collaborative authoring environments
- Forums
- Peer-to-peer networking
- Newsletters
- Podcasting
- Picture galleries
- File uploads and downloads.

Perhaps the key point in the debate around the use of centralized or decentralized technologies is not really about whether the technology sits inside or outside the institution's firewall but rather how can universities better manage the interconnectivity in a way that is truly student-focussed? As Wilson et al. (2007) explain:

The devolution of technology management from higher education institutions to students is an important step in promoting the transfer of responsibilities, as higher education offers an environment with substantial resources for support, guidance, and community forming. If universities do not make a strategic change to their policy on IT provision, there is considerable risk that education becomes a 'technology ghetto' that offers an increasingly restrictive and un-engaging technology environment that requires constant and expensive care, and feeding by harassed IT staff. (p. 1395)

CONCLUSION

It is clear from the mass popularity of social technologies that a generational shift to working with peers has already occurred in contrast to the individualism that characterised earlier generations, and that we should be capitalising on that social trend in more technologically-mediated ways than we are currently doing. Our approach over the past decade in higher education has been to add a measure of 'group work' to our assessment tasks, but rarely have we deliberately taught the skills of productive groupwork and collaboration to our students: we have simply assumed that groups will 'form, storm and norm' intuitively. However, consider the way MySpace friendship groups develop: the 'intent' is to create the group, not to produce an outcome in the form of an assessment task. We have assumed that students can use their mobile technologies to undertake group work, even if they do not always come to campus to work as a group. But we have not built into our programmes even the simplest of ways to engender a learning group ethos. Nor can we expect our students to make their own connections between formal education and their leisure use of social media. Mass use of such media will always be for diversion, leisure, for 'grazing' and informal interest-driven learning, as Franklin & van Harmelen (2007) have noted. That does not mean we should not make the effort to locate and use the potential of social media for our educational purposes.

Finding creative ways of using technology to expand and enrich the social base of learning in higher education will become increasingly important to lecturers and instructional designers alike. This project represents one small step in testing the applicability of social software to these contexts. While many of our students are already using various technologies to maintain and develop their social networks, it remains to be seen if these offer viable uses in more scholarly settings. Projects such as this, and the Ramsay project mentioned above, provide some baseline data on current students' familiarity with various social technologies, and the efficacy of learning applications of these technologies. Clearly, we are not yet in a position to measure with any validity how Web 2.0 technologies will affect the experience of higher education for our students, but this project, and others, flag ways we might further consider the role of peer learning in universities.

ACKNOWLEDGMENT

The authors thank Dr. Peter Donnan, University of Canberra, for contributing some appropriate references.

REFERENCES

Anderson, P. (2007). *What is Web 2.0? Ideas, technologies and implications for education.* JISC Technology and Standards Watch, Feb. 2007. Bristol: JISC. Retrieved October 25, 2007 from http://www.jisc.ac.uk/media/documents/techwatch/tsw0701b.pdf

Barrass, S. & Fitzgerald, R.N. (2008). Social software: Piloting MyToons as a digital learning community for teaching new media. Paper to be presented at ED-MEDIA 2008 - World Conference on Educational Multimedia, Hypermedia & Telecommunications, June 30-July 4, 2008, Vienna, Austria.

Berg, J., Berquam, L., & Christoph, K. (2007). Social networking technologies: A 'poke' for campus services. *Educause Review,* March/April, 32-44.

Biggs, J. (1999). *Teaching for quality learning at university.* Buckingham, UK: SRHE and Open University Press.

Boezerooy, P. (2003). *Keeping up with our neighbours: ICT developments in Australian higher education.* Retrieved November 11, 2007 from http://www.surf.nl/en/download/Australian_book.pdf.

Caruso, J. B., & Salaway, G. (2007). *The ECAR Study of Undergraduate Students and Information Technology, 2007* (September 2007). EDUCAUSE Center for Applied Research Key Findings. Retrieved November 21, 2007 from http://connect.educause.edu/library/abstract/TheECARStudyofUnderg/45076.

Cobcroft, R., Towers, S., Smith, J., & Bruns, A. (2006). *Literature review into mobile learning in the university context.* Brisbane: QUT.

Cunningham, S., Tapsall, S., Ryan, Y., Stedman, L., Flew, T., & Bagdon, K. (1998). *New Media and Borderless Education.* Canberra: AGPS.

Demos (2006). *Digital curriculum: Their Space.* Retrieved June 2, 2007 http://www.demos.co.uk/ projects/digitalcurriculumproject/overview.

EdNA (2007). *EdNA.* Available online at http://www.edna.edu.au/edna/go/highered/hot_topics/pid/2019 Web 2.0 resources.

EDUCAUSE *Learning Initiative & The New Media Consortium.* (2007). *The Horizon Report.* Retrieved February 15, 2008 from http:// http://www.nmc.org/pdf/2008-Horizon-Report.pdf.

Fiedler, S., Fitzgerald, R.N., Lamb, B., Pata, K., Siemens, G., & Wilson, S. (April 2007). *Proceedings from World Conference on Educational Multimedia, Hypermedia and Telecommunications* 2007. Chesapeake, VA: AACE.

Franklin, T., & Van Harmelen, M. (2007). *Web 2.0 for content for earning and eaching in igher ducation.* Bristol: JISC. Retrieved December 15, 2007 from http://www.jisc.ac.uk/media/ documents/programmes/digitalrepositories/ web2-content-learning-and-teaching.pdf.

Freire, P. (1985). Towards a pedagogy of the question: Conversations with Paulo Freire. *Journal of Education, 167*(2), 7-21.

Grossman, L. (2006). *Best invention YouTube.* Retrieved June 27, 2007 from http://www.time. com/time/2006/techguide/bestinventions/inventions/youtube.html.

Guess, A. (2007). Well, if they're already using it… *Inside Higher Ed.* Retrieved October 29, 2007 from http://insidehighered.com/layout/set/print/ news/2007/10/25/educause.

Hedberg, J. (2006). E-learning futures? Speculations for a time yet to come. *Studies in Continuing Education, 28*(2),171-183.

HitWise (2006). *Is Bebo next?* Retrieved June 29, 2007 from http://weblogs.hitwise.com/heather-hopkins/2006/11/bebo_and_myspace_network_ maps.html.

Hugo, G. (2005). Academica's own demographic time bomb. *Australian Universities Review, 48*(1), 16-23.

Ipsos MORI (2007). *Student expectations study.* Retrieved November 5, 2007 from http://www. jisc.ac.uk/media/documents/publications/studentexpectations.pdf.

Krause, K-L. (2006). *Student voices in borderless higher education: The Australian experience.* June Report for The Observatory on borderless higher education. Retrieved July 25, 2007 from http://www.obhe.ac.uk. Subscription required.

Kvavik, R., & Caruso, J. (2005). *ECAR study of students and information technology: Convenience, connection, control and learning.* Boulder: EDUCAUSE Center for Applied Research.

Laurillard, D. (2002). *Rethinking university teaching in a digital age.* Retrieved November 1, 2007 from http://www2.open.ac.uk/ltto/lttoteam/Diana/Digital/rut-digitalage.doc.

Livingstone, S., & Bober, M. (2005). *UK children go online: Final Report.* Swindon: ESRC.

Marton, F., & Saljo, R. (1976). On qualitative differences in learning-1: Outcome and process. *British Journal of Educational Psychology,* 46, 4-11.

Nussbaum, E. (2007). Kids, the Internet and the end of privacy. *The Weekend Australian Magazine* March 23-24, (pp. 23-27).

O'Reilly, T. (2005). *What is Web 2.0? Design patterns and business models for the next generation of software.* Retrieved November 1, 2007 from http://www.oreilly.com/lpt/a/6228.

Oblinger, D. (2004). Boomers, gen-exers and millenials: Understanding the new students. *EDUCAUSE Review, 38*(4), 37-47.

OECD (2005). *E-learning in tertiary education: Where do we stand?* Paris:OECD

Papert, S. (1980). *Mindstorms: Children, computers and powerful ideas.* Brighton, Sussex: Harvester Press.

Papert, S. (2000). What's the big idea? Steps toward a pedagogy of idea power. *IBM Systems Journal, 39*(3-4), 720-729.

Prensky, M. (2001). Digital natives, digital immigrants. *On the Horizon, 9,* 5.

Reeves, T. C., Herrington, J., & Oliver, R. (2004). A development research agenda for online collaborative learning. *Educational Technology Research & Development, 52*(4), 53-65.

Renner, W. (2006). Proceedings from EDU-COM 2006. Nong Khai:Thailand:Publisher?

Universities Australia (2007). *Australian student finances survey 2006 final report.* Retrieved November 1, 2007 from http://www.universities-australia.edu.au/documents/publications/policy/survey/AUSF-Final-Report-2006.pdf.

Wilson, S., Liber, O., Griffiths, D., & Johnson, M. (2007). *Proceedings from World Conference on Educational Multimedia, Hypermedia and Telecommunications 2007.* Chesapeake, VA: AACE.

KEY TERMS

CMS: Content management system. A general description for a database-driven Web site that allows web-publishing.

Drupal: A popular opensource content management system that allows both individual and community web publishing whose functionality can be extended with an extensive range of add-on modules.

Facebook: A popular social networking site launched in 2004 and originally designed for university and college students.

Firefox: A Web browser developed by the Mozilla Foundation that features numerous add-ons and extensions.

Google Groups: A free groups and mailing list service from Google that includes access a searchable archive of Usenet.

GPL: General public licence. A popular license for free software.

MediaWiki: The opensource software that runs Wikipedia and its related projects.

MySpace: A popular social networking site launched in 2003 and owned by Rupert Murdoch's News Corp.

MyToons: A social networking site designed for animators.

Web 2.0: A term coined by Tim O'Reilly to refer to the shift from static web pages to more interactive web applications controlled by the user.

YouTube: A popular video sharing Website.

Chapter XIII
Identifying New Virtual Competencies for the Digital Age:
Essential Tools for Entry Level Workers

Kathryn Gow
Queensland University of Technology, Australia

ABSTRACT

This chapter focuses on the identification of a range of competencies that entry level workers, and thus graduating students, will need to acquire to be successful in the 21st Century of work. While core or basic competencies will still form the prerequisite generic skills that all entry level workers must demonstrate, as the first year progresses, depending on the field in which they are employed, they will be asked to utilise self management, entrepreneurial, and virtual competencies in order to maintain their employment status. Even if they have ICT skills, they will need to have the knowledge and ability in social software, as well as the ability to communicate across the Web, in order to succeed in the digital age. Other attributes, such as cross cultural and professional skills, along with an appreciation of Web ontologies will facilitate entry-level workers as they move into the world of international liaisons.

OVERVIEW

This chapter deals with the interface between education and the workplace by focusing on entry level worker requirements. It emphasizes the imperative for life long learning, in that digital attributes need be garnered through academic learning and throughout life by individuals mastering a range of tools, languages and processes. The chapter will address the need for teaching institutions to engage in training about digital competencies for the global workplace to ensure a better equipped and competitive workforce.

A review will be undertaken of the field of research and practice in the domains of what has been known as basic, key and core competencies, along with virtual and enterprise and cross cultural competencies. These competencies will be elaborated and assumptions about their underlying structure examined. This platform will then provide the springboard for the elaboration of the domain of digital competencies that are required across the world to enable more satisfactory communication via social software. Samples of policies from different countries (such as Norway and Singapore), programs and projects promoting a range of digital competencies, will be included.

BACKGROUND

Social software facilitates a number of actions within Virtual learning environments: creating, sharing and collaborating. According to Time Magazine (2006/2007), social software empowers people to: (i) make it; (ii) name it; (iii) work on it; and (iv) find it. The net generation swims through social software and becomes frustrated in school and university systems without appropriate resources and adequately trained teachers who can speak their language and engage with them in learning by breaking through the new digital divide. Teachers need sufficient knowledge to pick the right software for different activities and occasions. Later in the chapter, we return to the move to upgrade teacher education.

Social software can be "defined as a range of Web-based software programs ……. that allow users to interact and share data with other users." (Wikipedia: http://en.wikipedia.org/wiki/Social_software). According to McLoughlin and Lee (2007, p. 666) "Social software tools such as blogs, wikis, social networking sites, media sharing applications and social bookmarking

utilities are also pedagogical tools that stem from their affordances of sharing, communication and information discovery. An affordance is an action that an individual can potentially perform in their environment by using a particular tool (Affordance, 2007)." Social software tools include: virtual conferencing; blogs; wikis; podcasting; moblogging; photo publishing; digital stories; and social bookmarking (Australian Flexible Learning Systems, 2007).

The type of virtual and digital competencies that are needed in the engagement with the social software environments include additional specialist competencies that are framed around human interaction and technology. However, an individual cannot engage in digital communities without a wide array of competency domains that might not be readily identifiable to those who have not been involved in discerning and enumerating, and then ascertaining the importance of such knowledge, skills and abilities (KSAs) with Web technicians, employers, teachers, students, guidance officers, and entry level workers. In other words, there are KSAs that underpin success in the digital world of work, and without careful delineation of such underlying KSAs (known in educational fields in the UK and Australia as competencies), it is not appropriate to speak of digital competencies as if they were stand alone "attributes".

Individuals will not be of wider value to the organisation which employs them, without being able to display a range of other key, core, generic, virtual and professional competencies. In the 1990's, Gow (Gow, 1992; 1994; 1995a, b; Gow & Chant, 1998) tracked grade 12 students into the workforce, and found that as they progressed from being new recruits to more experienced recruits, the "high flier" recruits were distinguished from the "middle of the road" recruits, in that the former were more highly achievement orientated and had better networking skills than the latter. In the oft-predicted virtual work scenario, networking skills will be critical for survival. This is generally not a skill taught in formal education, except where there are extra curricula activities incorporated into the school system, or where students engage in team Internet communication projects at school or at home. Ten years later, it became evident that a technology revolution had arrived with digitally skilled children avidly exploring the virtual world not just through computer games, but chat rooms, LANS and WANS. Equipped with mobile technology, such as mobile phones and personal digital devices, they became bored with the slow and linear world of secondary education, as they teleported themselves to other worlds about which adults knew very little. In a few instances, educators moved quickly to adapt to this new phenomenon. Wood (see Wood & Gow, 1996, 1997) highlighted the incredible effect of cascading students' and teachers' learning across distance and within virtual teams.

While it looked like fun and seemed like play, serious learning was occurring, not just for the students, but for the teachers as well. All that remains is for the drive underlying their highly motivated search behaviours to be translated into legitimate income generation activities with the assistance of work and community coaches (Gow, 1995c; 1996). Such achievement motivation is important in the world of work.

Competencies Research

A considerable amount of research has been undertaken on the type of generic/key/core competencies (all captured in this chapter by the overarching organisational term of KSAs) that both school leavers and college and university graduates will need on entry to the workforce. The next section of the chapter will outline the general KSAs needed by all entering new and older recruits, as viewed by themselves, guidance officers, and employers.

From 1997 onwards more intensive research was conducted around the whole perimeter of generic, virtual, entrepreneurial, and cross cultural competencies that new workers would have

to demonstrate on entry to a much changed and evolving workplace (Gow, 1999-2000).

Gow and McDonald (2000) devised a survey that was conducted with 127 employers and 84 educators at secondary and tertiary levels. The survey investigated which competencies would be required of secondary and tertiary graduates in the workplace in the year 2010. Utilising factor analysis, they determined that, of the 57 virtual competencies presented in the survey, four factors (which are referred to here as competency domains) had emerged as necessary for graduates to have on entry to the world of work; Accountability, Adaptability to Changing Work Environments, Business Management Skills and Cross-Cultural Competence. Appendix A contains the source of the 57 competencies which were gleaned from a wide array of sources and in most cases re-engineered into competency language.

Gow and Birch (2006) built on these findings and those of Gow's earlier studies on workforce entry level competencies required of school and university students. Taking a wider perspective in terms of income generation, Birch and Gow surveyed 70 employers, 50 guidance officers and 122 students about the attributes they considered important for secondary school graduates to be able to generate an income in the 21st Century. From the analysis of this survey data, four factors once again emerged, but were different in nature and content from the previous factor analysis. The four factors (presented in order of rated importance by employers and guidance officers) were labelled as: Core Administration Attributes, The Self as a Learning System, Achievement Capability and Global Data Gathering Skills.

Delors and others (1996) in "Learning: The Treasure Within" had exhorted us to educate people to learn to live together, by understanding others and their histories, traditions and spiritual values. In 1999, Gow incorporated the Delors competencies with generic KSAs (Gow, 1999a, Gow, 1999b) and in 1999/2000, surveyed the literature on global and multi/cross cultural competencies in order to ascertain the global skills that successful graduates would need in the new work place. What was finally distilled were basic awareness competencies, more advanced cross cultural skills for those persons working in foreign countries and sets of inter- and multi- cultural competencies. In the next five years, further extensive research was conducted on the generic and professional competencies that sociologists, psychologists, counsellors, and human service workers would need on entry to the workplace (see Gow, Litchfield, Sheehan, & Fox, 1998; Gow, Litchfield & Sheehan, 2002).

It is now time to enumerate some of the competencies that were consolidated from the various research projects.

VIRTUAL AND ENTREPRENEURIAL ATTRIBUTES FOR THE FUTURE WORKPLACE

In a wide survey of the literature, Gow and colleagues produced a range of articles and reports which mentioned or articulated basic, key core and generic competencies, varying in application and scope. From these reviews, competencies were gleaned or composed for research purposes. There was no indication then of the domains that would later become known as digital competencies. Moreover, there was little indication of information and communication technology being a generic competency per se. It may well be that educators believed that ICT was a field in which these generic competencies could be modified and applied, rather than a separate domain.

In the first study, both employers and academics were asked to rate the importance of a large list of competencies that graduates would have to demonstrate on entrance to the workplace. In the second study, which asked the respondents to think about their responses within the scenario of graduates being able to generate income, the views of guidance officers were sought.

The four domains that emerged from the Virtual Competencies subset of items (Gow & McDonald, 2000) were similar to those described in the literature on the future of work: (1) Accountability; (2) Adaptability to Changing Work Environments; (3) Business Management Skills; and (4) Cross-Cultural Competence. The first, "adaptability to changing work environments" had been identified by several authors (e.g., Gow, 1996a; Hollenbeck, 1994) as being essential for participation in a continually changing work environment. It became obvious that graduates would no longer be able to structure their careers using systematic, planned approaches, but would instead need to acquire new skills quickly while continually looking for alternative employment opportunities (Association of Graduate Recruiters, 1995). The new psychological contract between employer and employee created through increased corporate restructuring, outsourcing (McLagan, 1996) and contracting (Defillippi & Arthur, 1994) would also require "adaptability to changing work environments", including a positive approach to change per se. Examples of the competencies within this domain include being able to: Network to create new business; Demonstrate tolerance for ever-changing environments; Respond quickly to change; and Self-direct behaviour and operate independently.

The second highest rated competency domain in this subset was "business management skills". Again, although in the past it would have been a very rare occurrence for individuals leaving school, vocational colleges or university to start out as self-employed, market opportunities have become more suited to the application of business management skills. The Industry Task Force on Leadership and Management Skills (1995) had already promulgated that more graduates would have to demonstrate these skills. Gow (1995) also had realised that new graduates, who were employed by an organisation, would need to manage their careers as though they were self-employed, although, then and now, given the increasingly high rates of youth unemployment in some countries, commencing a small business might be the only opportunity that many graduates would have of securing an income. Some of the items that loaded on this domain included: Recognise the value of the customer; Demonstrate leadership; and Strategically plan for the future of the organization.

The third domain of new skills (also rated third in importance) that emerged from this data was "Accountability", which can be generally described as self-management abilities. It appears that while in the past, union employees were expected to do what they were told, in the future, graduates would require a great deal of maturity in taking responsibility for their personal conduct. This would include skills such as meeting deadlines (Hollenbeck, 1994), monitoring and correcting personal performance (Association of Graduate Recruiters, 1995) and valuing own skills and services (Lam, 1990). This scenario has proven to be correct. Examples of the related competencies in this domain comprised: Exercise a sense of responsibility and accountability; Meet deadlines; and Monitor and correct personal performance.

"Cross-cultural competence" (the fourth domain that emerged from the Virtual Competencies subset) which was rated the lowest overall by employers, but still as moderately important, also needs to be developed by graduates to participate in an increasingly global business context. Over the past 10 years and continuing into the future, substantial deregulation of the economy in many countries means that each country will be operating in an international, rather than in a local, context as envisaged by the Industry Task Force on Leadership and Management Skills (1995). The world's current labour force mobility means that knowledge and appreciation of other cultures and global events and the ability to apply that knowledge to intercultural communication and international business issues, is and will continue to be an important competency for

participation in almost all industries and occupations. Two of these items in this domain were: Demonstrate knowledge of political systems of other nations; and Display knowledge of current global events.

The vision of the boundary-less company, flatter hierarchies, contracting and outsourcing of services means that graduates need to be more able to generate their own business contacts, and in an increasing number of instances in many western countries, to be able to generate their own income. Additionally within organisations, corporate entrepreneurs will be highly valued and actually headhunted in today's competitive global business world. Obviously a graduate displaying such entrepreneurial talent would exhibit high achievement motivation. In Gow and Birch's (2006) study on income generation KSAs, Achievement Capability was highlighted as being a very important competency domain. It included attributes such as: Valuing success highly; Being achievement orientated; and Possessing a low tolerance for failure.

While there are a number of instruments that prospective employers can utilise to assess achievement motivation, the type of task that motivates the graduate may vary greatly between school and work employment environments. Hence the high achiever at school, who works hard to "toe the line" to achieve high grades, may not be the type of person who is able to handle the change and uncertainty in the workplace of the future. However, one would imagine that they would be rated highly on the "Self as a Learning System" domain competencies.

Handy (1996) had predicted that many people would have to be self contractors and service into organisations, rather than be employed within organisations. Thus it is interesting that the second most highly rated competency domain in the Gow and Birch study on final year secondary school students was "The Self as a Learning System"; and indeed if Handy's scenario continues to unfold as rapidly as is occuring now, being prepared to keep on learning and improving one's performance and knowledge will be essential for survival. Moreover, if one is to generate one's own income, then the ability to generate new ideas about service and products, and to learn from one's mistakes, is vital. This second domain is rather critical as it relates to the recruit being able to manage themselves and covers such items as: Exercising an active, inquisitive and open mind; Giving and receiving feedback; Showing self confidence and personal drive; and Monitoring and correcting personal performance.

Certainly this domain indicates that the graduating senior student should be open to change, be creative, be adaptable and to be able to learn from experience in a wide range of environments.

Global Competencies

Both these studies identified that there are global competencies, such as global data gathering skills and cross-cultural attributes. However, while these attributes were considered to be important for entry-level workers, they were not rated as highly as other domains. In both studies, while the global data gathering/cross cultural competency domains were considered to be important, they were rated as only "moderately important", whereas all other domains were rated as "quite" or "very important" for graduates to demonstrate. In some ways they are both similar to but different from the findings of the first study, as these samples will show: Compiling lists/statistics; Displaying knowledge of current global events; and Speaking a language other than English.

Earlier Gow and McDonald's (2000) research had highlighted similar competencies for graduates, although the factor analysis included further items such as: knowledge of political, legal and economic systems of other countries; assessing domestic and foreign markets; appreciating the cultures of other nations; and communicating interculturally. It is interesting that the data gather-

ing skills in the second study were linked to this global arena, whereas in the first study there were no data gathering skills incorporated within the global/crosscultural competency factor. We can see in the competencies listed above the beginning of the iteration of basic competencies that underpin digital literacy: compiling lists/statistics; displaying knowledge of current global events; interpreting the meaning of picture/illustrations; selecting, using, evaluating, adapting and using mathematical ideas/techniques in completing tasks.

The most highly rated competency domain in the second study, which focused exclusively on the competencies required of secondary school graduates, were Core Administration Attributes. There is no doubt that there are some basic skills that all graduates are required to have. Newcomers in the Education and training fields may not be aware that in the early 1990s, Finn (1991) and Mayer (1992) had established the need for the seven key competencies to be addressed in the secondary education curricula within Australia. These key competencies had been nominated by employers for over 50 years in the western world, as lacking in entry level workers, who came to work straight from school, without any prior work experience.

This emphasis on the necessity of basic skills in entry level workers was evidenced in the results of the Birch study with the Core Administration Attributes Domain being considered as "very necessary" by both employers and guidance officers alike. Examples included: Using correct spelling, punctuation, grammar; Having good time management skills; Having ability to seek wisdom and skills to avoid repeating mistakes; and Setting out/presenting/arranging/displaying – in all forms. Readers will recognise these as being repeatedly demanded by employers. Indeed many of them are also required for successful university study. It is as if these attributes are essential building blocks, without which the other competency domains would have no foundation.

BASIC CULTURAL AWARENESS EXPERTISE

Whether students live in Australia, New Zealand, Sweden, South Africa, India, or Thailand, they will be living in a more multi-cultural society in the next century. In 1999-2000, Gow gleaned or extracted from the literature a list of more than 350 competencies in the cross/multi/intercultural arena. According to "Dillard, Andonian, Flores, Lai, MacRae, & Shakir (1992, p. 721), cultural competence is an "awareness of, sensitivity to, and knowledge of the meaning of culture". Gow (see Gow, 1999c; 2001, for multiple sources of items in the list) elaborates on this fundamental requirement by adding other basic communication competencies that all professionals, regardless of their discipline or business, need to demonstrate in order to operate successfully with peoples of other cultures.

Just six of these basic **cultural awareness attributes** are listed here: Possessing an awareness of one's own negative and positive emotional reactions and stereotypes and preconceived notions towards other racial and ethnic groups; Demonstrating cultural sensitivity; Having a capability to empathise and genuinely connect with individuals who are culturally different from themselves; Displaying respect (conveyed through eye contact, body posture, voice tone and pitch); and Possessing an awareness of similarities and differences of cultures, backgrounds/lifestyles and attitudes/values.

Gow (1999c) attempted to distinguish between basic and global competencies and inter-cultural, multi- cultural competencies. However most secondary and technical College graduates would be well equipped for their beginning work life, if they could simply demonstrate these basic cultural awareness competencies. Hopefully they will already have been utilising such skills at school, home and in the community.

TAPPING THE FULL POTENTIAL OF STUDENTS

The lists of competencies, outlined in this chapter have merely "scratched the surface" of the wealth of development and capability that we want our young people to have. Neither do they begin to address the issue of capability, of which competencies are one type of measure (see Gow, 1996b; Gow & Gordon, 1998). Snoke, Underwood and Bruce (2002) emphasized the need for universities to specify the generic competencies that information systems graduate would need on entry to the workplace, and research has been conducted by Coll and Zegwaard (2006) on 24 graduate competencies that undergraduate and recent graduates, employers and faculty considered desirable in science and technology graduates, with the outcome being that while all 24 competencies were desirable, the single most desirable competency was the ability and willingness to learn. Additionally Male, Chapman and Bush (2007) explored gender differences on certain competencies in engineers, but unfortunately the list of competencies they drew on was not included in the publication; similarly with the article by Coll and Zegwaard.

Digital competencies will become part of the generic competencies required of graduates who will have to work in an environment, in which the need to be involved with social software excludes those who have not adopted a life long learning approach to remaining "skilled up"; one of the basic skills is to be open to learning and this means that one is constantly learning in the world of ICT and global communications. Attwell and Elferink (2006) researched how social software could bring together different forms of learning for lifelong competence development.

The great energy behind the competency movement started to falter around 2003, and it was not really until the explosion of social software on the Web that teachers, employers and students alike began to consider the critical nature, not only of ICT competencies and digital capability, but the KSAs that were needed to interface with the social software that had become available to share, learn and create on the Web.

Engendering Transferable Skills in a Digital Era

It became clear that it was not just sufficient to be ICT competent in order to gain and retain successful employment, an entry level worker also must have the general skills outlined in this chapter. An individual can have certain skills, yet not have the "knack" to know how to apply them in a different setting, or in a different way; or to know when to use them and when not to use them (capability by any other name). Opportunity finding is one competency that is rarely addressed, and yet is crucial to surviving in the business world. Even an ICT graduate who may be working in Web design needs to know where and with whom information and resources can be sourced. Competencies for opportunity finding could be listed as follow: knowing about community ontologies; being able to solve problems; possessing knowledge of IT; demonstrating a wide range of computer skills demonstrating opportunity finding skills; having the capacity to network; having creative ability in design and being able to plan effectively

Information literacy, according to Hughes (2006), comprises "understandings, capabilities and critical approaches that collectively underpin effective online information use and foster learning." Tuckett (1989, in Shankar et al., 2005, p. 356) breaks down this multi-faceted dimension of information literacy into a hierarchy of three levels of skills in the following ascending order of complexity: (1) Simple information skills - Using a single information tool; (2) Compound information skills - Combining simple information skills/tools; and (3) Complex/integrated information skills - Making use of a variety of information networks, evaluating and repackaging information.

NCREL (2003) details eight functions of digital literacy: **basic, scientific, economic, technological, visual, information literacy, multicultural and global.** *They define all the functions, but it is the following three functions which are of direct interest to this chapter:*

1. Knowledge about what technology is, how it works, what purposes it can serve, and how it can be used efficiently and effectively to achieve specific goals.
2. The ability to interpret, use, appreciate, and create images and video using both conventional and 21st century media in ways that advance thinking, decision making, communication, and learning.
3. The ability to evaluate information across a range of media; recognize when information is needed; locate, synthesize, and use information effectively; and accomplish these functions using technology, communication networks, and electronic resources.

As Erstad (2005) points out, in many countries around the world digital literacy is now defined as a key area of competence in curricula for schools.

DIGITAL COMPETENCIES IN THE VIRTUAL ERA

The world has rapidly changed in the new technological era, perhaps faster than in the industrial era and the whole workforce has had to upskill continually to be globally competitive.

More than two decades ago, professionals were calling for an acknowledgement of the role that ICT was to play in the future: Cetron (1988) estimated that by 2000, approximately 44% of the labour force would be involved in collecting, analysing, synthesising, structuring, storing, or retrieving information as a basis of knowledge. Kerka (1993) noted the important role that IT would play in employment opportunities, because in order to find and perform a job, locating information is essential. Spender (1997) forecast that trade professions would have to utilise information technology in order to participate in workplace training and to upgrade their qualifications, and Levin and Rumberger (1989), along with many others, postulated that new ways of incorporating IT would free up workers to operate outside the office space.

It is, perhaps, not surprising that it is the librarians who have driven the digital literacy agenda with their wealth of knowledge and abilities in information sourcing, collecting, sorting, storing and retrieving. Librarians have become one of the most digitally competent professionals of any field outside the ICT sector and, in addition to the IT experts, are adept at searching and communicating in ways that are not taught to ICT students. They seem to know a great deal about Information Communications Technology, software tools, search engines, and Web ontologies generally, and have become capable trainers of other professionals, particularly university students. The British Library promulgated its vision that all of its staff would have digital competencies and would collaborate locally and nationally. Significantly, one of their concerns was that that global digital literacy needed cooperation on standards, protocol, and services (Mahoney, 1996).

As our workforce and society in general becomes more digitally and ICT literate, more will be expected of the worker in all fields of work and at all levels of the organisational hierarchy. It will not be uncommon for a professional person or even a volunteer in, for instance, emergency services to be expected to read an electronic GIS (geographical information systems) map about the latest storm weather pattern, flood or bushfire potential and to choose what program to utilize from the available software to obtain up-to-date information on current critical regions.

Togsverd (2002) points out that Denmark, like most western countries, is experiencing a constantly increasing need for engineers in the Information and Communications Technology (ICT) field. He describes some of the challenges for industry and universities in order to secure a high knowledge base and a competitive industry. He argues that the new network society requires that the curricula for ICT engineers have to be redefined in order to ensure that candidates have broader skills, such as those needed to match industry needs. So apart from having generic and specialist skills in engineering and ICT, the entry level workers need to know how to transfer those KSAs to a different work context to assist their employers to stay competitive in a global marketplace.

It has become evident that as the digital universe has evolved, digital literacy is not the same as ICT literacy; digital literacy can be seen as skills, knowledge, creativity and attitudes which are necessary in order to cope with learning and teaching with digital media in a knowledge society (Almas & Nilsen, 2006). It has also been promoted by Johannessen (2006) that "digital literacy comprises the ability to develop the potential embedded in ICT and to exploit it innovatively in learning and work". Its link to information literacy is clarified by Shankar et al. (2005) who define information literacy as "the ability to access, evaluate, and apply information from a variety of sources in appropriate contexts to construct knowledge." (p. 355). They refer to the importance of the competencies of starting, browsing chaining, differentiating and extracting.

Moreover, it is pertinent to mention here that ICT and digital competencies are two domains that are clearly transferable to other work and community contexts, and yet outside of the ICT and Library contexts in which they have burgeoned, they are treated as "add-ons" to learning in education and the workplace. Indeed, it would appear that many entry level workers learn more ICT and digital competencies on the job than prior to commencement. On the other hand, it can be argued that just as many new entry level workers bring with them a collage of knowledge and skills that enrich the workplace with "virtual class teams, connected classrooms archived lectures and advancements in broadband and wireless access" (Dean, 2007, p. 1).

Training for the Workforce

It is difficult for individuals who have completed almost two decades of education to accept that education and training is to be an ongoing part of the rest of their lives in a fast changing work and social environment. It is no wonder that universities consider that the responsibility for life long learning falls into the realm of on-the-job learning, vocational education and training institutes.

Indeed, at tertiary level in some universities, generic skills still seem to be the main discussion in teaching and learning arenas. However, Hager, Holland and Beckett (2002) simply make a mention of ICT literacy in a review of what is required of graduates in terms of competencies. It may well be that it is taken for granted that university students have to have ICT and digital literacy, in order to be able to operate and survive in the tertiary education sector in the first place (indeed if an applicant does not know how to search and navigate the Web, they are unlikely even to manage to enrol in their desired courses); however, it may also indicate that it requires the passage of time for such generic skill bases to be determined and then updated. Nevertheless, as Cretchley notes "employer expectations have changed: university students are expected to graduate with computer competencies appropriate for their field" (2007, p. 29). However, some universities, such as the RMIT (Royal Melbourne Institute of Technology), have enumerated exactly what ICT competencies they want their staff to have, if not their exiting graduate students (Kenny, Quealy & Young, 2002). For a full elucidation of their 25 or so competencies, see Kenny et al. (2002).

Initiatives in Education and Training Involving Digital Literacy

There are two strategies for upskilling the global workforce in digital literacy; one is to re-educate the teachers who are already delivering the training and the existing workforce, and the other is to directly train students at all levels of education and training within the educational environment, and within the workplace.

Two of the countries that have governments which have placed digital literacy on the national education and training agenda are Norway and Singapore. Norway has introduced digital competencies as one of the five basic competencies in schools and has revamped its teacher training; 80% of their school computers have broadband technology linked to the internet (Almas & Nilsen, 2006).

With respect to education policy agendas, UNESCO (2008) has developed ICT Competency Standards for Teachers which aim to improve teacher practice so that a higher quality student will play their part as more equipped citizens and members of the workforce, which in turn should assist in promoting the economic and social development of the countries in which they live and work. In Norway, more than 20,000 teachers have undertaken Teacher ICT training. The feedback from the training varies according to the individual's prior KSAs and experience, as well as its relevance and application in the classroom (Almas & Nilsen, 2006).

The vision of Singapore has consistently been to enable every graduate to be ICT literate by providing the resources in education and training institutes to achieve that goal. They are part of the e-Generation and, as Jones-Kavalier and Flannigan (2006, online) point out, the e-Generation possess "digital competencies to effectively navigate the multidimensional and fast paced digital environment".

At the higher end of the educational tree, Jacques du Plessis (2007) lists digital competencies for information professionals that could be applicable to any professional:

- Use computer text processing software for simple Web page design
- Prepare a budget report using a spreadsheet program
- Construct a simple database for data manipulation
- Use graphics to supplement data reports and presentations
- Specify computer hardware and software requirements for diverse situations
- Understand the role of application software as a decision support system
- Evaluate application software for information management purposes
- Construct a basic Web page with hyper text links.

Gow (2001a) had invited education providers, to face up to the challenges that the new digital work world would require in adjusting our attitudes, skills and ways of thinking about new technologies, and highlighted the nexus that had then been reached by the highly technologically adept students attempting to navigate through old educational systems. Later, Jones-Kavalier and Flannigan (2006) pinpointed the dilemma of children who are "high tech" being led by technologically stymied teachers. While Wood and Gow (1997) had proposed that the way around that problem was to simply employ an Internet cascade model across connecting schools, where students became the teachers for those occasions, they pointed out that to change the current system in schools throughout the world might take a major revolution of problem solving with teachers and students alike. Students do amazing things and, according to Harbutt (2007), school students have been using a multi-user virtual environment (MUVE) program developed by Harvard University to solve health problems in a virtual scenario set in the 19th Century. Thus many pockets of innovative teaching and learning are occurring all around the world.

What of the Disenfranchised?

Interestingly, a topical article in Business Week (4th Oct., 2007) focuses attention on "the digital Divide"; it was not speaking about the gap in skills in a workforce that lives and operates in an ICT- aware society, but rather pointed to the fact that many people across the world, and that includes children, do not have access to such technology; reasons for this include low income, lack of local information, literacy barriers, language barriers (as most Webpages are in English), lack of cultural diversity, and lack of Web content that is ADA compliant; also they cannot access text readers and other necessary technology tools, let alone the prescriptive social software to engage in international trade and education. According to the United States Justice Department, the ADA also applies to the cyberspace "world." The U.S. Department of Justice (see Waddell & Thomason, 2008) has stated that: "Covered entities under the ADA are required to provide effective communication, regardless of whether they generally communicate through print media, audio media, or computerized media such as the Internet. Covered entities that use the Internet for communications regarding their programs, goods, or services must be prepared to offer those communications through accessible means as well."

Another key factor is that most business, including banking business, is now conducted electronically. Without access to ICT and therefore digital upskilling in digital competencies, in many schools in emerging countries and in some rural and isolated areas in first world countries, children may not just be deprived of learning IT and digital skills, but they will also have to surmount the barriers to learning all other subjects taught in the Education curriculum, because learning in the 21st Century already requires new and advanced levels of ICT literacy and access to the latest communication technology and social software.

Passman (2007) notes that Microsoft has a vision that by 2010, every person seeking work or who has lost a job will have access to the necessary training and education that they need to achieve this goal. Earlier Gow (1999d) had made an innovative suggestion that could solve access to university education through use of the internet and every available new piece of technology, by opening a University for the Rural Poor in third world countries (Gow, 2001b, 2005). Not surprisingly, however, in the past couple of years, something akin to this idea has commenced, without being labelled as such, by the opening of Websites onto which units of training courses are placed that are freely available to anyone who can access the internet. Their accreditation at this stage, however, has not yet been accomplished.

Thus access to the Internet, plus the availability of social software programs and experience in cooperative information sharing systems, are the critical resources necessary before young people can participate in the digital workplace, locally and globally.

CONCLUSION

Research consistently shows that there are certain foundation skills that employers want, along with a range of KSAs that have become known as transferable skills. A key domain is that of information computer technology and in order to survive in the 21st century of work, all current and entering workforce members will not only have to be ICT literate, but must have flexibility and versatility in the selection and utilization of social software. Government policies will need to ensure that young children in their countries are given adequate education in the ICT and digital fields, as well as in what has come to be known

as the basic competencies of speaking, reading, writing and arithmetic. Tertiary graduates will need to study additional courses in ICT, computer mediated communication, including the use of social software in order to make a successful transition to the world of work. Those workers who are more adventurous, especially managers and professional graduates, will have little choice but to adapt their portfolio of KSAs (knowledge, skills and abilities) to suit the culture in which they find themselves, whether that be in Asia, America, Europe, Africa or Australia, or wherever it is that the firm, company or government directs them to work. This preparedness, mobility, flexibility, and adaptability, are critical attributes that graduates must have on entry to the workforce.

REFERENCES

Affordance. (2007). In *Wikipedia*. http://en.wikipedia.org/wiki/Affordance Accessed 17.08.07.

Almas, A. G., & Nilsen, A.G. (2006). *ICT competencies for the next generation of teachers.* Formatex. Online. Accessed 20.04.08.

Association of Graduate Recruiters. (1995). *Skills for graduates in the 21st century.* Cambridge: The Association of Graduate Recruiters.

Attwell, G., & Elferink, R. (2006). *Next Generation Learning and Personal Learning Environments.* Paper presented at Alt C conference, Edinburgh, September, Symposium #733 - "E-learning, Social Software and Competence Development.

Australian Flexible Learning Systems (2007). Social software and its contribution to teaching and learning - a report by Australian Flexible Learning Framework (part ii). Online. Accessed 19.04.08 http://www.masternewmedia.org/news/2007/05/24/social_software_and_its_contribution.htm

Bailey, T., & Noyelle, T. (1988). *New technology and skill formation: Issues and hypotheses.* New York: Conservation of Human Resources.

Bikson, T. K., & Law, S. A. (1994). *Global preparedness and human resources: College and corporate perspective's.* Santa Monica, California: Rand Corporation, Institute on Education and Training.

Center for Remediation Design (1992). Survey *of Basic Skills Remediation Practices in JTPA Youth.*

The Center for Remediation Design and Brandeis University. (ERIC Document Reproduction Service No. ED328786)

Cetron, M. (1988). *Seventy-one trends that may affect entrepreneurial education for future world markets.* Arlington, Virginia: Forecasting International Ltd. (ERIC Document Reproduction Service No. ED 294 041)

Coll, R. K., & Zegwaard, K. E. (2006). Perceptions of desirable graduate competencies for science and technology new graduates. *Research in Science & Technological education, 24*(1), 29-58.

Conger, J. A. (1993). The brave new world of leadership training. *Organizational Dynamics, 21*(3), 46-58.

Cordery, J., Sevastos, P., Mueller, W., & Parker, S. (1993). Correlates of employee attitudes toward functional flexibility. *Human Relations, 46*(6), 705-707.

Cretchley, P. (2007). Does computer confidence relate to levels of achievement in ICT-enriched learning models? *Education and Information Technologies archive, 12*(1), 29-39.

Dean, B. (2007). *The challenge of creating a continuous learning culture: Linking the value chain between higher education and corporate learning.*

DeFillippi, R. J., & Arthur, M. B. (1994). The boundaryless career: A competency-based perspective. *Journal of Organizational Behaviour, 15*(4), 307-324.

Delors, J. (1996). *Learning: the Treasure Within.* Report to UNESCO of the International Commission on Education for the Twenty-first Century. Paris: UNESCO.

Dillard, M., Andonian, L., Flores, O., Lai, L., MacRae, A., & Shakir, M. (1992). Culturally competent occupational therapy in a diversely populated mental health setting. *American Journal of Occupational Therapy, 46*(8), 721-726.

du Plessis, J. (2007). Syllabu*s for 632 Digital Competencies for Information Professionals.* Online. Accessed 01.10.07. http://Web.sois. uwm.edu/632%20duPlessis/Document/index. asp?Parent=163.

Erstad, O. (2005). *Conceiving digital literacies in schools - Norwegian experiences.* Proceedings of the 3rd International workshop on Digital Literacy, 1-10. Online. Accessed 30.04.08. ftp. informatik.rwth-aachen.de/Publications/CEUR-WS/Vol-310/paper01.pdf

Filerman, G. L. (1994). Health Care and Education Reform: The Time to Manage for Change Is Yesterday. *Educational Record, 75*(1), 47-51.

Finn, B. (Chair) (1991). *Young People's Participation in Postcompulsory Education and Training: Report of the Australian Education Council Review Committee.* Australian Publishing Service, Canberra.

Goos, M., & Cretchley, P. (2004). Teaching and learning mathematics with computers, the internet, and multimedia. In B. Perry, G. Anthony, & C. Diezmann (Eds.), *Research in mathematics education in Australasia 2000-2003* (pp. 151-174). Flaxton, Queensland: Post Pressed.

Gow, K. M. (1992). *Reconciling school leavers' expectation about work with those of their employ-*

ers. Unpublished doctoral dissertation, University of Queensland, Brisbane.

Gow, K. M. (1994). Recruithood: Smoothing the Transition. *Journal of Applied Social Behaviour, 1*(1), 29-44.

Gow. K. M. (1995). The Transition from school leaver to effective worker. *Social Sciences Monographs (2).* (ERIC Document Reproduction Service No. ED397259)

Gow, K. (1995a). Are school leavers themselves the best resource in the transition from school to work? *Journal of Applied Social Behaviour, 1*(2), 40-49.

Gow, K. (1995b). In and out. Entry-level competencies for school leavers and university graduates. *Australian Training Review,* Sept/Oct/Nov. 15-16.

Gow, K. M. (1995c). *Unless you become as effective coaches, they will not enter into the realm of committed workers.* Paper presented at the "Learning to Earning" International Conference. Port Douglas, 30 September - 6 October, 1995. (ERIC Document Reproduction Service No. ED 389835).

Gow, K. (1996a). Coaching: the link between school, community and the workplace. *Australian Journal of Career Development, 5*(3), 22-26.

Gow, K.M. (1996b). *Is capability a function of competencies required of the more experienced worker?* Applying capability to the workforce. Paper presented at the Second Conference of the Australian Capability Network, Brisbane, 5-6 December.

Gow, K. (1999a). *Competencies required of graduates in the 21ˢᵗ Century.* Paper presented at the UNESCO Conference, December, Bangkok.

Gow, K. (1999b). *The Delors Report and graduate competencies.* Keynote Address at the Post Compulsory Educators Conference, August, Adelaide.

Gow, K. (1999c). *Cross-cultural competencies for counsellors in Australasia.* Culture, Race and Community. International Conference, Melbourne, 19-21 August.

Gow, K. M. (1999d). *A University for the Rural Poor in the Third World.* Paper presented at the World Education Fellowship Conference, Launceston, Tasmania. 30th Dec- 4ᵗʰ Jan. (ERIC Document Reproduction Service No. ED 426232)

Gow, K. (1999-2000). Entrepreneurial and virtual competencies. *VOCAL: Australian Journal of Vocational Education and Training in Schools, 2* (1), 32-34.

Gow, K. (2001a). *Impact of Globalisation and Technology on Teaching and Learning: The Good, The Bad, And The Challenging.* Paper presented at the International Conference on Education. Manila, Philippines, July 1-5.

Gow, K., & Birch, A. (2006). Do Employers and Secondary School Stakeholders View the Core Skills as Important? *Canadian Journal of Career Development, 5*(1), 28-33.

Gow, K. & Chant, D. (1998). Australian Supervisors and Recruits: Closing the gap in understanding each others' viewpoints. *Journal of Constructivist Psychology, 11*(4), 309-332.

Gow, K. & Gordon, R. (1998). What constitutes a capable manager? *Capability Network Newsletter.*

Gow, K., Litchfield, K. & Sheehan, M. (2002). Delineating Professional Competencies for Sociologists and other Health Social Scientists. *Journal of Applied Health Behaviour, 4* (1&2), 21-30.

Gow, K., Litchfield, K., Sheehan, M. & Fox, T. (1998). *How Academic Sociologists rate the importance of generic and specialist competencies.* (ERIC Document Reproduction Service No. *ED 426685)*

Gow, K. & McDonald, P. (2000). Attributes required of graduates for the future workplace.

Journal of Vocational Education and Training, 52(3), 373-394. (ERIC Document Reproduction Service No EJ617391)

Hager, P., Holland, S., & Beckett, D. (2002). *Enhancing the learning and employability of graduates: The role of generic skills. Round Table Business Higher education.* B-Hert Position Paper No.9, July, 16 pp. Melbourne, Australia.

Handy, C. (1996). *Beyond certainty: The changing worlds of organizations.* Boston, MA: Harvard Business School Press.

Harbutt, K. (2007). Students strive to avert virtual epidemic. *Education Times, 15*(11), 15.

Hines, A. (1993). Transferable skills will land you a job in the future. *HRMagazine, 38*(4), 55-56.

Hollenbeck, K. (1994). *The workplace know-how skills needed to be productive.* (Technical Report). Michigan: Upjohn Institute for Employment Research. (ERIC Document Reproduction Service No. ED 413 712)

Howard, J. (1995). The future of work in Australia. In Department of Employment, Education and Training (Ed.), *The future of work* (pp. 119-126). Sydney: Australian Council of Social Service.

Hughes, H. (2006). Responses and influences: A model of online information use for learning. *Information Research, 12*(1). Online: Accessed 14.06.07. http://eprints.qut.edu.au/view/person/Hughes,_Hilary.html

Industry Task Force on Leadership and Management Skills. (1995). *Enterprising nation: Renewing Australia's managers to meet the challenges of the Asia-Pacific century.* Canberra: Australian Government Publishing Office.

Johannessen, O. (2006). *Digital competencies in the national education policy.* Ministry of Education and Research, Norway. EU eLearning Conference 2006. 4th-5th July 2006. Espoo 04072006. Online. Accessed 09.09.07. http://www.google.com.au/search?hl=en&q=norwegian+ministry+digital+competencies&meta=

Jones-Kavalier, B.R. & Flannigan, S.L. (2006). Connecting the digital dots: Literacy of the 21st Century. EDUCAUSE Quarterly, 29, 2, 8-10. Online. Accessed 11.11.07. http://www.educause.edu/ir/library/pdf/EQM0621.pdf.

Kenny, J., Quealy, J., & Young, J. (2002). *RMIT ICT DLS Competency Framework - A basis for effective staff development.* UltiBase Online Journal, November. Accessed 29.04.08. http://ultibase.rmit.edu.au/Articles/nov02/kenny1.pdf

Kerka, S. (1993). *Career education for a global economy.* (Digest No. 135). Ohio: Clearinghouse on Adult, Career and Vocational Education. (ERIC Document Reproduction Service No. ED 355 457)

Lam, M. (1990). *Use your initiative. Enterprise skills for the future.* Canberra: Australian Government Printing Service.

Levin, H., & Rumberger, R. (1989). Education, work and employment in developed countries: Situation and future challenges. *Prospects, 19*(2), 205-224.

Mahoney, J. (1996). *Building the digital library. Networked information in an international context.* Paper presented at a Conference organized by Ukoln in conjunction with the British Library, CNI, CAUSE & JISC, Ramada Hotel, Heathrow, UK. 9th-10th February.

Male, S. A., Chapman, E. S, & Bush, M. B. (2007). Do female and male engineers rate different competencies as important? *Proceedings of the 2007 AaeE Conference*, Melbourne. The University of Melbourne, 2007. http://www.cs.mu.oz.au/aaee2007/papers/paper_61.pdf

Mayer Committee. (1992, September). *Key competencies.* (Report of the Committee to advise the Australian Education Council and Ministers of Vocational Education, Employment and Training on employment-related key competencies for post-compulsory education and training). Melbourne: Mayer Committee.

McLagan, P. A. (1996). Great ideas revisited. *Training and Development, 50*(1), 60-65.

McLoughlin, C. & Lee, M. J. W. (2007). Social software and participatory learning: Pedagogical choices with technology affordances in the Web 2.0 era. *Proceedings Ascilite Conference, Singapore,* (pp. 664-675). www.ascilite.org.au/conferences/singapore07/procs/mcloughlin.pdf -

Miles, R. E., & Snow, C. C. (1995). The new network firm: A spherical structure built on a human investment philosophy. *Personnel Journal, 67*, 5-18.

National Board of Employment, Education and Training. (1994). *Converging Communications and Computer Technologies: Implications for Australia's Future Employment and Skills.* Victoria: Australian Government Publishing Service.

NCREL. (2003). 21ˢᵗ Century Skills enGauge ® 21ˢᵗ Century Skills: Literacy in the Digital Age. Online. Accessed 11.11.07 (http://www.ncrel.org/engauge/skills/agelit.htm)

Passman, P. (2007). *Microsoft unlimited potential: Enabling sustained social and economic opportunity in the Unites States and around the world.* Online. Accessed 04.11.07. http://www.microsoft.com/about/adulteducation.mspx

Shankar, S., Kumar, M., Natarajan, U. & Hedberg, J.G. (2005). A profile of digital information literacy competencies of high school students. *Issues in Informing Science and Information Technology,* (pp. 355-368).

UNESCO (2008). *ICT Competency Standards for teachers.* Paris: UNESCO. http://unesdoc.unesco.org/images/0015/001562/156207e.pdf

Snoke, R., Underwood, A., & Bruce, C. (2002). *An Australian view of generic attributes coverage in undergraduate programs of study: An information systems case study.* Proceedings of HERDSA Conference, Perth: Edith Cowan University, (pp. 590-598). Online: accessed 29.04.08. http://www.ecu.edu.au/conferences/herdsa/main/papers/ref/pdf/Snoke.pdf

Sonnesyn Brooks, S. (1995). Managing a horizontal. *HR Magazine, June,* (pp. 52-58).

Spender, D. (1997). Online upskilling in the digital renaissance. *Australian Training Review, 21,* 4-5.

Time (Canadian Edition) December 25, 2006/January 1, 2007.

Togsverd, T. (2002). Denmark at the Forefront of Information and Communications Technology (ICT) Competencies. *Global J. of Engng. Educ., 6*(2), 175-178.

Vukovic, A. (1997). Information literacy. *Management,* April, 10-11.

Waddell, C. D., & Thomason, K. L. (2008). Is Your Site ADA-Compliant or a Lawsuit-in-Waiting? *International Center for Resources on the Internet.* Accessed 24.07.08. http://www.icdri.org/CynthiaW/is_%20yoursite_ada_compliant.htm

Webber, I. (1991). The changing nature of work and careers. *Business Council Bulletin, 75,* 24-26.

Wood, D., & Gow, K. (1996). Virtually a reality. *Australian Training Review, 20,* 26-27.

Wood, D., & Gow, K. (1997). Educating students for the virtual business era. *New Horizons in Education, 96,* 36-45.

KEY TERMS

Competency: A primary skill or ability that a person has which is required for a particular work task.

Digital: The representation of information in binary form (ones and zeros), discontinuous in time. www.thesaudi.net/vsat/vsat-glossary.htm

Entry Level Worker: Young person (or re-entering adult) joining the workforce.

Generic: Basic skills or aptitudes needed in the workplace.

KSAs: Knowledge, skills and abilities that a person possesses.

Transferable Skills: Knowledge, skills and abilities that are learned in one environment and then transferred to another context; e.g., from university to work.

Virtual: A situation in which communication can be exchanged without being face to face, generally involving advanced technology.

APPENDIX A: SOURCE OF VIRTUAL COMPETENCIES USED IN THE FUTURE WORKER COMPETENCIES QUESTIONNAIRE

ITEM	LABEL	SOURCE
1	Value education as a continuous, routine part of career	Filerman, 1994; Wood & Gow, 1996
2	Speak a language other than English	Hollenbeck, 1994
3	Network to create new business	Association of Graduate Recruiters, 1995; Defillippi & Arthur, 1994; Wood & Gow, 1997
4	Take personal responsibility for career development	Association of Graduate Recruiters, 1995; Hollenbeck, 1994; Kerka, 1993; Miles & Snow, 1994
5	Learn and perform multiple tasks	Bikson & Law, 1994; Cordery et al, 1993; Hollenbeck, 1994
6	Demonstrate tolerance for ever-changing environment	Hollenbeck, 1994; Industry Task Force On Leadership and Management Skills, 1995; Webber, 1991; Wood & Gow, 1997
7	Respond quickly to change	Hines, 1993; Hollenbeck, 1994
8	Trust processes rather than structure	Kerka, 1993
9	Demonstrate motivation	Kerka, 1993; Wood & Gow, 1996
10	Identify the best personal learning strategy and style	Miles & Snow, 1994; Vukovic, 1997
11	Learn in a range of environments	Bikson & Law, 1994; Hines, 1993
12	Display knowledge of current global events	Bikson & Law, 1994; Conger, 1993; Hollenbeck, 1994; Webber, 1991
13	Strive for continuous self-development	Filerman, 1994; Kerka, 1993; Lam, 1990; Vukovic, 1997
14	Demonstrate understanding of international business issues	Bikson & Law, 1994; Conger, 1993
15	View change as opportunity	Industry Task Force On Leadership And Management Skills, 1995; Kerka, 1993
16	Assess domestic and foreign markets	Association of Graduate Recruiters, 1995; Conger, 1993
17	Work with people from diverse backgrounds	Conger, 1993; Industry Task Force On Leadership And Management Skills, 1995; Levin & Rumberger, 1989; Wood & Gow, 1996
18	Strategically plan for the future of the organisation	Lam, 1990; Sonnesyn Brooks, 1995
19	Demonstrate knowledge of economic systems of other nations	Bikson & Law, 1994; Conger, 1993; Kerka, 1993
20	Work in highly decentralised organisations	Filerman, 1994; Hollenbeck, 1994
21	Tolerate diverse viewpoints	Conger, 1993; Hollenbeck, 1994; Howard, 1995
22	Acquire specialist knowledge and skills as needed	Bikson & Law, 1994; Levin & Rumberger, 1989; Wood & Gow, 1996
23	Possess awareness of the need to develop networks of contacts	National Board of Employment, Education & Training, 1994; Wood & Gow, 1996
24	Show willingness to take risks	Bikson & Law, 1994; Hollenbeck, 1994; Industry Task Force on Leadership and Management Skills, 1995
25	Recognise the value of the customer	Hollenbeck, 1994
26	Financially manage business	Wood & Gow, 1996
27	Demonstrate leadership	Hollenbeck, 1994
28	Represent organisation in a positive way	Hollenbeck, 1994
29	Exercise a sense of responsibility and accountability	Cherry, 1993
30	Meet deadlines	Hollenbeck, 1994

continued on following page

APPENDIX A: CONTINUED

ITEM	LABEL	SOURCE
31	Self-directed behaviour and operate independently	Hollenbeck, 1994; Lam, 1990; Webber, 1991
32	Explore new ideas and resources	Association of graduate recruiters, 1995; Conger, 1993; Industry task force on leadership and management skills, 1995
33	Show knowledge of legal systems of other nations	Kerka, 1990; Bikson & Law, 1994
34	Cope with stress and tension	Hollenbeck, 1994; Lam, 1990
35	Maintain a satisfying personal life	Hollenbeck, 1994
36	Follow performance indicators rigorously	Cherry, 1993
37	Create and envision new ways	Bikson & Law, 1994; Hollenbeck, 1994; Kerka, 1993; Lam, 1990; Levin & Rumberger, 1989; Wood & Gow, 1996
38	Demonstrate willingness to diversify	Cordery et al, 1993; Industry Task Force on Leadership and Management Skills, 1995
39	Demonstrate knowledge and appreciation of culture of other nations	Bikson & Law, 1994; Conger, 1993; Kerka, 1993
40	Demonstrate knowledge of political systems of other nations:	Bikson & Law, 1994; Conger, 1993; Kerka, 1993
41	Demonstrate flexibility	Cordery et al, 1993; Hollenback, 1994; Industry Task Force On Leadership And Management Skills, 1995; Kerka, 1993; Wood & Gow, 1997
42	Appraise, assess, and certify and quality of a product or service	Levin & Rumberger, 1989
43	Possess business awareness	Bikson & Law, 1994; Hollenbeck, 1994; Industry Task Force On Leadership And Management Skills, 1995
44	Display knowledge of history of other nations	Bikson & Law, 1994; Kerka, 1993
45	Display product knowledge	Webber, 1991
46	Recognise and report hazards in the workplace	National Board of Emp, Ed'n & Training, 1994
47	Monitor and correct personal performance	Association of Graduate Recruiters, 1995; Center for Remediation Design, 1992; Kerka, 1993; Lam, 1990
48	Responsibly challenge existing procedures and policies	Center for Remediation Design, 1992; Gow, 1996; Hollenbeck, 1994
49	Maintain and fix problems associated with complex equipment	Center for Remediation Design, 1992; Filerman, 1994; Kerka, 1993
50	Handle complaints	Howard, 1995; Lam, 1990
51	Give and receive feedback	Center for Remediation Design, 1992
52	Behave ethically in the workplace	Hollenbeck, 1994
53	Value own skills and services	Hollenbeck, 1994; Lam, 1990
54	Comprehend own or organisation's services and capabilities and link them with customer needs	Bailey & Noyelle, 1988; Filerman, 1994; Industry Task Force On Leadership And Management Skills, 1995; Sonnesyn Brooks, 1995; Webber, 1991
55	Communicate interculturally	Hollenbeck, 1994; Kerka, 1993; Bikson & Law, 1994; Levin & Rumberger, 1989
56	Understand the hidden tensions and power struggles within organisations	National Board of Employment, Ed'n & Training, 1994
57	Market oneself and one's ideas	Association of Graduate Recruiters, 1995; Hollenbeck, 1994; Wood & Gow, 1996

Chapter XIV
Social Structures of Online Religious Communities

Jerald Hughes
University of Texas – Pan American, USA

Scott Robinson
Global Trading Group, USA

ABSTRACT

This chapter examines interaction-oriented virtual religious communities online in the light of socio-logical theory of religious communities. The authors find that the particular importance of identity, authenticity and authority in religious communities populating online discussion forums may give rise to special problems online, which are demonstrated here to be direct outcomes of the necessary reliance on information technology to carry out functions of online religious social groups which are intended to correspond to offline religious categories. The authors draw upon both sociological theory of religious communities and information systems theory of computer-mediated communications to identify salient points of similarity and difference between online and offline religious social structures, and conclude that online religious forum communities as presently constituted are unlikely to be able to directly replicate the traditional social structures of the offline religious institutions from which they originated, due to the particular powers and constraints on action embodied in social software.

INTRODUCTION: RELIGION IN CYBERSPACE

The history of the Internet has repeatedly seen the transference, sometimes successful, sometimes less so, of categories and activities familiar from the pre-Internet world, into cyberspace. Personal mail, for example, been widely adopted as an activity appropriate to the electronic realm; so has gaming, including not just cutting-edge 3D games like World of Warcraft, but also traditional board games such as chess or Scrabble. Online personal auctions have transferred a market model familiar from the offline world of art houses and farm sales to cyberspace, with brilliant success. On the other hand, some models appear to transfer less transparently to the Internet realm. For example, while hard-copy magazines and newspapers in pre-Internet times successfully acquired subscribers willing to pay for content, subscription-based delivery for news content on the Internet has been marked by considerable difficulties in transferring the offline model to the online world—the technological channel through which information was delivered changed the user perception of the transaction taking place. Research has also determined that the technological conditions of computer-mediated communications, the potential for anonymity in particular, can affect human behavior online in ways which affect the usability of online social domains (Davis, 2002). In these latter cases, in which the offline paradigm does not necessarily translate in a straightforward manner to the online world, the potential is present for significantly increased understanding of the specific impacts and import of the information technologies themselves. This paper aims to examine such a case, contemporary attempts to employ offline formal religious categories of personal identity in online social contexts of computer-mediated communications conducted through forum software platforms. In order to understand this particular manifestation of religious activity online, we believe it is useful to examine the intersection of theories from two different disciplines: the sociology of religion, for an understanding of the foundations of religious community, and the information systems discipline, for an understanding of the constraints and powers of the technological components which provide for the possibility of computer-mediated communications. This paper will explore that intersection.

Modern religious life is increasingly taking place online (Pew Internet Research, 2004). More specifically, since the introduction of easy-to-use social software for online text-based user interactions, commonly referred to as bulletin boards or forums, websites hosting persistent conversations specifically aimed at religious topics have appeared, in which adherents of various faiths can affirm their religious identity and participate in religious communities online. In the sections which follow, we will provide information and analysis of some of the issues associated with the virtual communities of users whose loci in cyberspace are the URL's of the websites hosting threaded discussions on religious topics through the use of forum software. Thus we are addressing the notion of user-to-user interactive "online religion" as opposed to "religion online", per the distinction proposed by Helland[2] (2000). Some of these fora are associated exclusively with specific formal religious institutions, while others are more or less open to the public on a broader range of beliefs associated generally with religious practice.

These online religious communities share characteristics with virtual communities generally:

- Shared interests – in this case, religious topics;
- Technology-mediated interactions – micro-computer-based, Internet/browser-based forum software;
- Guided by protocols and norms – emergent from the interaction of users with the technology (Porter, 2004)

Some important dimensions of difference between different religious forums include:

- Degree of association with specific religions/sects
- Formal/Informal nature of protocols and social norms
- Conditions for access to site or specific site areas
- Methods of administration

Internet searches using a phrase "*x* forum", in which *x* may stand for the name of any religion, will return long lists of active forums, so it is clear *a priori* that the spiritually-minded are finding activities of value to them personally in religious communities in cyberspace (see also Pew Internet Research, 2004). However, what they find online may differ considerably from their face-to-face[3] experiences of religious community (e.g., Scott's (2002) discussion of Mormons online). We propose that among such differences are those which stem from fundamental constraints on the notions of identity, authenticity and authority that are specific to the information technologies presently employed by Internet virtual communities; we further propose that these constraints are sufficiently pervasive and long-lived to warrant the prediction that online virtual religious communities as currently implemented on forum-based software platforms cannot replicate the familiar social structures of local face-to-face spiritual communities, and thus will necessarily instead develop into new and hitherto unanticipated structures of social relations. Our arguments in support of these propositions constitute the main body of the paper which follows.

The remainder of the paper is organized as follows. In part II, we employ an analysis based on Emile Durkheim's sociology of religion in order to create a basic picture of the social structures of offline (face-to-face) religious communities. In part III we apply the same style of analysis of virtual religious communities on the Internet, in order to produce a side-by-side comparison, highlighting both similarities and differences between the two (online vs. offline) types of religious communities. The analysis in part IV discusses the impacts of the technologies used in virtual communities upon the fundamental notions of identity, authenticity and authority in religious contexts, as a means of explaining the observed differences. Finally, part V will discuss the implications of these technological capabilities (and impediments) for online virtual

religious communities now and in the future, and summarize our overall conclusions.

SOCIAL STRUCTURES OF RELIGIOUS COMMUNITIES

Emile Durkheim in his seminal volume *The Elementary Forms of Religious Life* (1912) carries out a meticulous analysis in order to arrive at the end of his first chapter with the following definition:

"a religion is a unified system of beliefs and practices relative to sacred things, that is to say, things set apart and surrounded by prohibitions—beliefs and practices that unite its adherents in a single moral community called a church."[4]

A particular religious community thus may define itself in terms of particular beliefs and practices which the participating members assent to, typically as a pre-condition of inclusion in the group. For this analysis we intend to make use of this idea in a perfectly straightforward way, referring to the actual statements and activities of the face-to-face religious community. Thus, for example, many religious organizations, including Christian (e.g., the Apostolic Creed), Islamic (e.g., the Shahada), and Jewish (e.g., the Sheloshah-Asar Ikkarim), may make use of a creed which sets forth the beliefs of the group. When members of a particular religious community assent to a common creed, they provide an observable signal of their commitment to the shared revelation which functions as an important basis for the social cohesion of that group. Having a shared revelation codified in a creed creates a critical basis for shared religious community, in other words, while the authenticity of individual members' commitment to that community can be supported by their actual performance, in the physical presence of other members, of the tradition's rituals associated with that creed (Vinscak, 2000).

Among the practices of religions we may extend this notion to find not only the rituals of the religious service, but also the practices which create and sustain the institution itself as an agent in its social context. Our concern here is primarily those practices which may be employed by religious communities to establish and confirm the sources of identity, authenticity and authority in the face-to-face religious context. As such, the analysis we undertake per Durkheim's theory is of limited application: to only those religious communities in which the forms of religious practice do in fact appear to rely significantly upon personal identity, authenticity, and authority. While we recognize that the range of human spiritual activity is extraordinarily broad, an analysis which could encompass all such forms is beyond the scope of this paper. The following table summarizes some of the familiar characteristics typical of many face-to-face religious communities.

From this list, the questions of Administration and Credentials are particularly important, as they affect how decisions are made and how authority is enforced in the religious community. Priests, for example, may have a particular authority which is conferred upon them by their academic credentials and/or by their official employment by the group, what Weber (1947) termed 'legal' authority, the authority which derives from the office one holds. It is worth noting that the functionality, criteria and limits of authority within any particular group

need conform to no particular standard with respect to religion in general; historically, individual groups may, and have often been, free to define these features arbitrarily, with the consequence that the implementation of Administration and Credentials can vary considerably between various real-world religious groups.

Rituals are also central to the face-to-face religious community[5]. Lorenz (1977) points out the role of rituals in "ensuring the cohesion of the group and distinguishing it from others." The regular, repeated physical activities of attending weekly worship services, performing ablutions, reciting a creed, tithing, praying, and reading sacred texts together thus serve to establish the identity of the local religious community as a group of members committed to each other for the purposes of embodying the religious institution. Because these activities *are* carried out in a face-to-face social context, the authenticity of identity is, in general, a given. The authenticity of a face-to-face participant's commitment to the official belief statements of a particular group is not necessarily quite as secure, but the risk of being challenged in person, were one to visibly dissent, may play a role in supporting the relative homogeneity of specific local, traditional religious social groups. One's visible willingness to actively participate in the group's rituals, such as baptism, prayer, and recitation of a creed serves as a proxy for the in principle unknowable inner mental state of the participant.

Table 1. Face-to-face religious communities: Practices

Feature	Style	Examples
Administration	hierarchical[1]	board, pastor, elder deacon, imam, rabbi, priest
Credentials	ordainment, degrees	seminaries – Catholic, Protestant, Muslim, Buddhist, Hindu, Jewish
Legal Status	non-profit	-chartered, incorporated
	theocracy	-national "official" status (e.g. Church of England)
Location	local - physical buildings and land	cathedral, church, temple, mosque
Meeting	sacred service/worship service	rituals: prayer, communion, liturgy, readings, meditation, offerings

SOCIAL STRUCTURES OF VIRTUAL RELIGIOUS COMMUNITIES

The picture which emerges in virtual religious communities is quite different. Virtual communities are generically described as "social aggregations that emerge from the Net when enough people carry on those public discussions long enough, with sufficient human feeling, to form webs of personal relationships in cyberspace" (Rheingold, 1993). This definition was derived from phenomena of 'persistent conversations' in newsgroups, a form of asynchronous text-based communications still carried on today, on a considerably greater scale, by Web forums powered by message-posting software such as vBulletin. Already at this coarse level of analysis it is possible to discern major differences between the online and offline groups. Face-to-face religious communities are born of history and traditions, the establishment and growth of churches, temples or mosques in specific places, as intentional acts of their founders, and providing a wide variety of activities and rituals for their members. The virtual religious communities we are examining here, on the other hand, as participants of online forums, are generally emergent, and provide just one primary activity, what Hummel and Lechner (2002) refer to as "community multi-lateral" communication, in cyberspace.

Participants in virtual communities of online forums are typically individuals in one of at least three basic categories: administrators, who own and/or run the site; posters, who register with a user name and a password, and contribute to the available online content by submitting text messages (posts); and so-called 'lurkers', who frequent such sites in order to read the content, but do not register and thus may not post content of their own. The content of a site may extend to anything associated with religious topics, and often beyond into merely casual posts about hobbies and entertainments, or just daily life in general, reflecting, from a content standpoint, the social reality of the online community's real-world analog. The administrators of such sites use the controls made available in the software platform to create and label various topic areas they believe will prove to be of interest, and threaded discussions on those topics are gradually built up by the users themselves. As thread content drifts, and new areas of concern are developed, maintenance of threads and topic areas becomes a significant task for administrators.

As long as a forum is very small, this work can be done by the creator(s) of the site alone. However, as membership grows, site owners may need to recruit helpers, known as 'moderators', to carry out the chores of the site. These may include:

- Spotting and deleting spam (advertisements, usually for drugs or pornography)
- Spotting and editing or deleting inappropriate content posted by members
- Enforcing site policies
- Informing users about technical or policy changes
- Handling conflicts between members

Additional layers of site administrative roles are developed as the size and complexity of a forum grows, with varying powers of access and control on the site[6].

An analysis of the same type as that in Table 1 above can be performed for online religious communities. The contents of Table 1 are included below in a contrasting font, in order to facilitate direct comparisons. Features which are the same for both types are marked as such.

ANALYSIS

Although a great many of the activities available to users of the Internet are directly analogous to pre-Internet activities such as shopping or attending a class, the same is not necessarily true of participation in online virtual religious communities. Upon their arrival at a particular URL, a user will typically find not a presiding pastor or priest, but instead a technologically-mediated host in charge. The person who actually owns the website, or person(s) designated by that owner, can at will withhold or reveal any or all information about themselves. Unless there is a pre-existing offline relationship between a user and the site owner, it may be difficult or impossible to obtain any confirmable information about the bona fides (or lack thereof) of the host's religious ideas and commitments. Instead of a pre-determined set of rehearsed, timed activities which constitute an offline religious community's rituals, the religious forum user typically finds a community of discourse (e.g., Scott, 2002). The terms of that discourse are under the control of the site's administrators and staff, since they possess the means to access the purely technological software-based controls on what gets posted, by whom, and under what conditions. It is true that some websites attempt to provide virtual rituals online, which substitute mouse clicks and typed text for the face-to-face components of the ritual (e.g., Casey, 2006). However, it is not clear in what sense these CMC-oriented activities could be said to be actual substitutes for the traditional rituals of the community, especially given that they necessarily lack "co-presence" (Casey, 2006) and therefore cannot constitute shared activities in the physical sense that real-world rituals do.

According to Hummel and Lechner (2002), "From the view of computer-mediated communication, the most important elements of a virtual community are shared resources, common values, and reciprocal behavior." While to a minimal extent it is the case that virtual religious communities share resources of the digital medium (data and IT resources), the nature of CMC-supported interactions—remote location, text-based interaction, and potential anonymity—make "common values" and "reciprocal behavior" necessarily more problematic. An Internet-based religious forum is typically an open door, through which practically any Internet user may pass, even one whose only intention is to post advertisements. Likely of greater interest is the open door's contribution to the phenomenon of multiple users with differing religious beliefs collectively participating in the creation and maintenance of a virtual online community. In the face-to-face context, the chances of a particular, say, Southern Baptist coming into regular and repeated contact with a practicing Zen Buddhist—specifically in order to discuss questions of religious belief—might be quite small, while online encounters with those of significantly differing beliefs are quite common. The notion of "common values" thus may under the right conditions shift from the traditional offline form of a creed, to a set of meta-values about the importance of carrying on dialogues on spiritual topics, maintaining a resilient and courteous response to personal differences, or just the value of communicating freely online. Reciprocal behaviors among the members of a virtual religious community may revolve around such meta-values in the case of more doctrinally open websites, or may be reserved only to those who profess the creed designated as appropriate to the site—a notion which significantly differs from the creed required by a religious institution, since it is being enforced by an agent whose actual identity offline is often completely unknown. Such professions may be generally considered tentative at best, as the forum provides none of the explicit supporting observable cues of authenticity found in face-to-face environments. It is primarily the impact of CMC technology on identity which forces this difference; we will now look individually at the impacts of technology on identity, authenticity and authority—three factors of particular importance to many religious communities.

Identity

In the face-to-face context, of course, identity is functionally established by physical presence

Table 2. Virtual religious communities

Feature		Style	Examples
Administration	*F2F*	*hierarchical*	*board, pastor, elder deacon, imam, rabbi, priest*
	Virtual	*hierarchical*	site owner, administrator, moderator,…
Credentials	*F2F*	*ordainment, degrees*	*seminaries – Catholic, Protestant, Muslim, Buddhist, Hindu*
	Virtual	?	reputation, # of posts, chronological seniority
Legal Status	*F2F*	* *non-profit* *	-chartered, incorporated
		theocracy	-national "official" status (e.g. Church of England)
	Virtual	*non-profit*	Virtual communities hosted by religious institutions which provide both actual physical buildings, and websites online. (e.g. http://www.baptist.org/index.php?name=PNphpBB2)
		private ownership	Ad hoc virtual communities created by self-motivated individuals (e.g. http://foru.ms/)
Location	*F2F*	*local - physical buildings*	*cathedral, church, temple, mosque*
	Virtual	Cyberspace - URL	'Forums' feature of a comprehensive website which includes other features such as an events calendar, links to resources, etc. Stand-alone forums website
Meeting	*F2F*	*sacred service/worship service*	*rituals: prayer, communion, liturgy, readings, meditation, offerings*
	Virtual	Asynchronous CMC (Computer-Mediated Communication)	Public bulletin board posts, member-to-member private messages, restricted-access posts
		Synchronous CMC	Chat

– the community recognizes the body that goes with the name. Online, one typically registers with a nickname—in fact, Internet users are cautioned *not* to use actual personal identifiers in public websites, in order to reduce the risk of identity theft. Any nickname not already in use on the website might be used, regardless of what it signifies (such as the reverse of actual gender), since there is no practical means of confirming the meaning of the nickname used. Thus, the publicly visible 'identity' of the member, the nickname, can function only as a placeholder behind which other members can at best only indefinitely suspend judgment about the reality of the claimed personal characteristics. This anonymity poses a

potentially severe problem in terms of trust at the very front end: how does one establish trust in a religious online environment which as a software feature universally employed deliberately masks the identities of the participants? Someone with administrator privileges on the website may have somewhat improved but still insufficient means of establishing the actual identity of the user. Registration typically requires an e-mail address, and administrative software may include the means to identify the IP address associated with a user; however, both of these point at most to a particular network location, not a person, leaving the administrator ultimately as powerless as any other member to authenticate a user's identity in any reliable way. Furthermore, there is nothing to prevent a participant from developing multiple additional identities (nicknames) on the same website (Krüger, 2005), sometimes referred to pejoratively among users as 'sock puppets'[7]. Users may have recourse to such strategies if they become 'banned' from a particular website they enjoy, in order to bypass the punitive measure. Further, a user employing a 'sock puppet' may obscure identity to an even greater degree by deliberately exhibiting opinions and behaviors contrary to those publicly established under the user's primary identity, taking up 'devil's advocate' positions and so on, and raising the philosophical question of which identity, if any, reflects the "real" person behind the online identity. Even with IP address checks, a user may succeed in rejoining simply by taking care to log on from a machine with a different address, and tracking down such practices requires an investment of time and energy which may be impractical on sites which register thousands of users. The problem here lies in a fundamental, heretofore unavoidable feature of Internet-based virtual communities: the technology identifies (not altogether reliably) only machines, not persons[8]. In this respect, virtual religious communities have pushed to the extreme a feature of online religion noted by Campbell (2004), "the movement toward dynamic and fluctuating relationships". Because of the anonymity conferred (in some cases, required) by the technological platforms employed, the relationships of the members of the virtual religious community can be tenuous indeed, severable by as little as a change of one's nickname. Issues of trust and identity which might be settled easily in personal encounters at traditional physical religious institutions must be suspended indefinitely in online virtual communities (Prusak, 2000).

Authenticity

Websites which intend to serve particular religious traditions may ask as a condition of registration that participants confirm a particular religious doctrine as their personal belief, or as a promise to conform their online actions to the requirements of that specific religious doctrine[9]. Once the registrant has done so, the website has no practical means of establishing the authenticity of the profession of faith. In face-to-face communities, as we noted earlier, that authenticity is established by the ongoing participation in the rituals of the faith such as communion or the recitation of the creed. A virtual online community has no such face-to-face rituals, nor can it. The primary activity in cyberspace on such sites is text-based discourse. Regular users and administrators alike may (and do) resort to parsing the text content of posts for signals which indicate fidelity or lack thereof to particular doctrines, and unhappy 'flame wars' have been fought over such problems.

Technological responses to the problem of authenticity include the provision of additional signifiers which serve to provide direct cues to the community about one's personal beliefs: essentially, putting one's religious affiliations visibly up front. These may include the choice of avatar, icons, tag lines, signature lines, and many more, producing a sometimes dizzying array of signals to other users of the member's place in the online social structure (see Fig. 1). These labels and indicators are "shortcuts to communication" which not only provide information, but also serve as community-specific jargon that separates insiders from outsiders, based in part on their ability to interpret the signs and participate in their use (Goodfellow, 2005). It is clear that this solution is double-edged, increasing not only the potential for bolstering one's authentic presentation of affiliation, but also the potential for more effectively misrepresenting it.

Is the person represented by the images in Figure 1 actually old? A Catholic? A priest? Short of an extensive investigation offline, who is to say? While these signifiers provide guideposts to what is being claimed by the specific user, they do not at all address the fundamental

Figure 1. Online signifiers of social roles

problem of answering the question of the actual internal (and in principle unknowable) mental state of the claimant. In a face-to-face spiritual community, such as a Catholic diocese, resolution of such questions could begin to be addressed by visual inspection (age?), by viewing diplomas or certifications provided by seminaries or other applicable ordaining institutions, by talking to those who might authoritatively vouch for a claimant's bona fides such as the long-term members of the community or superiors in a religious hierarchy, or by simply observing their day-to-day activities in support of a local religious fellowship. While a determined impostor in a face-to-face context might defeat such methods, doing so would require considerable investment of time and effort; yet, in online contexts, the more tenuous nature of the means of social connection—basically, text and images viewed remotely—makes it much easier to make personal religious claims, without providing immediate means for others to check their authenticity.

The same kind of problem arises in connection with claims of religious authority within a particular tradition, even if the basic religious affiliation is not in question. An online participant may mark themselves as 'Pastor', 'Priest', 'Rabbi', etc., simply by putting that text on the screen next to the nickname. What real significance can this possibly hold for other users? It is an in-practice unconfirmable claim when used in cyberspace, whereas in face-to-face context one might reasonably demand and receive the visible

proofs of clerical office, such as the credentials of a particular seminary. While in theory one could imagine an online religious virtual community in which such reliable credentials were demanded by administrators before the use of a marker such as "Reverend" was allowed, in practice the very high burden of time and effort required to actually carry out such a rigorous vetting procedure makes it impractical for most.

Again, these problems are fundamental to the use of computer-mediated communication as a platform for the religious virtual community[10]. The time-honored rituals of religious communities which are the fundamental means of establishing the cohesion of the face-to-face social group simply do not admit of execution by means of text and images on a screen.

Authority

The problems of identity and authenticity become particularly fraught when the exercise of authority in virtual communities is involved. Cases such as the deletion of spam are unproblematic, since the miscreant registrants involved are in clear violation of site rules, and not attempting to seriously disguise their intent. However, moderators of online religious forums may also police posts for their religious doctrinal content[11], and in this respect severe impediments can arise. The fundamental difficulty is the technological means by which authority is exercised online. The ability to edit or remove posts, to restrict users, or ban them altogether, is a technological ability conferred by the CMC software being used. Typically a tiered set of administrative powers is made available to the site's software license holder—whoever founded the site has essentially god-like powers with respect to that website. They can create and destroy entire areas of use with mouse clicks, and even shut down the entire site altogether in a moment, if they choose. Physical religious sites such as cathedrals or mosques can indeed be created or dismantled, but only with far greater expenditure of time and resources than is required to alter digital representations online. Furthermore, the social checks and balances of the real world, which limit the ultimate authority and influence of any single individual and give incorporated non-profit religious groups avenues for addressing catastrophic behavior on the part of their most powerful member(s), have no necessary direct analogs in this online context.

The site founder has, and keeps, administrative control via technological means, typically a particular ID-password pair which is the software's check of the legitimacy of the power being exercised. Furthermore, delegation of certain administrative powers, such as the ability to edit or delete posts, can only be accomplished by the assignment of those powers by the site owner to the secondary-tier participants, such as moderators. In practice, then, the development of authority in the context of a virtual religious community rests upon one's connection, whatever that may consist of, to the site owner and her/his designated agents (such as moderators). It is immediately obvious that this social structure has nothing to do with the traditional face-to-face social structures of boards, pastors, priests, and so on. Yet the actions of online 'authorities' such as administrators and moderators may strike users as intensely personal and important, when one's doctrinal correctness according to the dictates of the site is questioned[12]. There is a potentially severe cognitive dissonance at work between the unreliability of religious credentials and therefore

authority online, and the consequences of religious moderation online, such as having one's contributions summarily removed by a moderator (whose actual religious authority may be under serious question by the user) who is offended on religious doctrinal grounds by its content. Being told that one is not a 'true' believer, or that one's statements lie beyond the pale, is an intensely personal blow to a religious participant. The fact that such a blow is delivered by the notoriously blunt and often harsh instrument of mere online text makes it all the more difficult.

It is a serious problem for virtual religious communities, as attested by the many painful disputes over moderator actions visible in forum threads on such websites. Yet there is no current alternative to the online social structure of site owners, administrators and moderators. This is how the software of Internet CMC works—it is necessary, of course, to have the ability to remove, say, posts from 'drive-by' attacks which put up pornography or vulgarities. The conditions of the technology itself can give rise to the temptation to use such necessary powers in the (perceived) defense of the faith.

CONCLUSIONS AND FUTURE IMPLICATIONS

The social structures which emerge in virtual religious communities are heavily conditioned by the imposition of the restrictions of social software as the channel of communication between members. Online, users discover that the problems of establishing identity, authenticity and trust can interfere significantly with even the most basic notions of commonalities among members. Furthermore, the power of the administrators over the community is greatly magnified, since they have the ability to utterly exclude members[13] temporarily or permanently, and even to destroy the site altogether if they wish. The result is that the social structures associated with traditional face-to-face religious group cannot be realistically mapped to the online community, even such basic notions as whether a particular person is a practicing member of the religion. There is a fundamental and irrevocable mismatch between the nature of religion itself, and the constraints of the technologies which enable the emergence of virtual communities, per the state of the technology in its current form.

Virtual religious communities therefore cannot analogize point-for-point to the face-to-face social structures of formal religious traditions which preceded them. Instead, something entirely different is emerging in cyberspace: a social milieu in which the burden of establishing one's place is carried only by one's productions within the constraints of the software employed. The play of pure ideas, floating free of any necessary connection to a particular physical presence, establishes who one is in the online religious community. So completely divergent is this identification paradigm from its face-to-face counterpart that it can conceivably render an online community fundamentally different-in-kind, rendering established patterns of identity-mitigated discourse obsolete and enabling new possibilities in community self-expression and dialog, wherein member contributions to the discourse are abstracted and freed of limitations imposed upon who-may-say-what by traditional hierarchies – less personal, by necessity, but ultimately availed of potentially greater range of response and, paradoxically, the possibility of greater intimacy through unfettered discourse.

The differences-in-kind in administrative machinery between real-world and virtual communities, can give rise to shortfalls with respect to member expectations, and may alter the nature and potential satisfaction of participation to such a degree that long-term commitment of the sort observed in face-to-face communities may prove immensely difficult or even impossible. The limitations in range of activity and depth of interaction between members make it unlikely that online-forum religious communities can ever compete with face-to-face religious communities in a meaningful way, or provide analogous service to their members.

New Possibilities

It is important to note that the features of online community which can weaken it in the context of traditional religious community may conversely serve to empower members in ways that are seldom if available in traditional, face-to-face communities. Given that identity in online community is ultimately an abstraction, a community member might ultimately gain more than is lost, in terms of potential contribution. Thus, an individual participating in online religious community (and in online communities in general) is potentially an abstracted identity, free of hierarchical constraint. How liberating for the member of an online community, to have equal voice with all others, without respect to religious rank or standing! This liberation opens up new possibilities for communication and the expression of ideas by an individual in an Internet context, and in a religious context in particular, where authoritarian constraint upon self-expression is so arbitrary.

We may envision, then, a new kind of online community that does not replace, but rather augments, the spiritual experience of the individual, offering features seldom if ever found in traditional religious community: egalitarian evaluation of religious concepts, freedom to depart from dogma in favor of more open discourse, freedom to examine and criticize traditional interpretations, and acceptance of others purely on the basis of their contribution, without social prejudice. Moreover, the online environment enables many individuals at the most basic level: all things being equal, they are free to speak their minds without social consequence, a condition seldom realized in the face-to-face world. This alone is a liberating feature of online spiritual community with the potential to enhance the spiritual experience of vast numbers of participants. Online religious communities, then, may in the long run begin to fulfill a different social function, offering spiritual parity to those who cannot achieve it in a traditional setting, and enabling progress in discourse on religious matters that is slowed or obstructed by authoritarian institutional restraints (Campbell, 2005).

It should also be pointed out that the limitations that presently exist in online community are not necessarily static. New forms of virtual community are beginning to introduce components into the online community participant's experience which may alter the dynamics enumerated above. These include the real-time, synchronous interaction provided by emerging new communities like Second Life, and the Internet facility that binds together video game enthusiasts into effective real-time groups, as teammates or opponents. The implications of a move from asynchronous online community to a synchronous experience are profound: the emergence of online communities of this type could enable shared virtual rituals in real time, thereby mitigating a current constraint against member authenticity of belief explicated above. But the innovations and potential offered by real-time virtual environments have even deeper implications for online community, permitting the user to abstract identity to a far greater degree, and in ways that have far greater impact on those with whom one interacts: one may create a façade that is far more compelling (and potentially attractive or deceptive) than mere labels or icons, fashioning a physical appearance and presence that is empowering on many levels that might be unachievable in a face-to-face environment.

Looking ahead farther still, we might envision virtual environments hosting communities of users interacting in real time to collectively undertake community activities unachievable in the face-to-face world, simulating everything from feeding all the hungry of the world to visualizing the Armageddon of Revelation. Real-time virtual environments could also yield interesting ques-tions for study in enabling not only traditional but new shifts in online community authority patterns, as both the visual and real-time interactive facility will still be under arbitrary control of a behind-the-curtain administrator, but could enable new means of acquiring and displaying local power and influence within the online community. It is possible that the recreation of reality within cyberspace might take the currently constrained online community experience and stretch it to the opposite extreme, empowering participants far beyond what is possible in reality, enabling both cooperation and confrontation on scales exceeding current face-to-face experience. As the ability of Internet technologies to support multimedia-intensive communications continues to grow, we should continue to expect the fundamental issues of personal identity, authenticity and authority to be both shaped and constrained by, the powers of the technologies employed.

REFERENCES

Campbell, H. (2004). Challenges created by online religious networks. *Journal of Media and Religion, 3*(2), 81-99.

Campbell, H. (2005). Who's got the power? Religious authority and the Internet. *Journal of Computer-Mediated Communication, 12*(3).

Casey, C. (2006). Virtual ritual, real faith: The re-virtualization of religious ritual in cyberspace. *Online-Heidelberg Journal of Religions on the Internet, 2*(1).

Davis, J. (2002). *The experience of bad behavior in online social spaces: A survey of online users*, internal paper of Microsoft Social Computing Group, available at http://research.microsoft.com/scg/papers/Bad%20Behavior%20Survey.pdf, last accessed 4/29/2008.

Durkheim, E. (1912). *The elementary forms of the religious life*. English translation by Carol Cosman: 2001, Oxford: Oxford University Press.

Erikson, E. (1977). *Toys and reasons: Stages in the ritualization of experience.* New York: Norton.

Goodfellow, R. (2005). Virtuality and the shaping of educational communities. *Education, Communication & Information, 5*(2).

Grimes, R. (1994). *The beginnings of ritual studies.* Columbia, SC: University of South Carolina Press.

Heinze, R. (2000) *The nature and function of rituals.* London: Bergin & Garvey.

Helland, C. (2000). Religion online / online religion and virtual communitas. In J. K. Hadden & D. E. Cowan (Eds.), *Religion on the Internet: Research prospects and promises.* JAI Press: New York.

Hummel, J., & Lechner, U. (2002). Social profiles of virtual communities, In *Proceedings of the 35th Hawaii International Conference on System Sciences..*

Krüger, O. (2005). Discovering the invisible Internet: Methodological aspects of researching religion on the Internet. *Online-Heidelberg Journal of Religions on the Internet, 1*(1).

Lorenz, K. (1977) *Behind the mirror: A search for the natural history of human knowledge.* New York: Harcourt Brace Jovanovich.

Pew Internet and American Life Project (2004). *Faith online.* Available at http://www.pewinternet.org/pdfs/PIP_Faith_Online_2004.pdf , last accessed 4/29/2008.

Porter, C. E. (2004). A typology of virtual communities: A multi-disciplinary foundation for future research. *Journal of Computer-Mediated Communication, 10*(1).

Prusak, L. (2000). Interviewed in "How Virtual Communities Enhance Knowledge", *Knowledge@Wharton*, March 21, 2000, available at http://knowledge.wharton.upenn.edu/article.cfm?articleid=152, last accessed 4/29/2008.

Rheingold, H. (1993). *The virtual community: homesteading on the electronic frontier.* Cambridge: Addison-Wesley.

Scott, R. (2002). Matchmaker, matchmaker, find me a mate: Examination of a virtual community of single Mormons. *Journal of Media and Religion, 1*(4), 201-216.

Turner, V. (1969). *The Ritual process: Structure and anti-structure.* Chicago: Aldine.

Vinscak, T. (2000). The function of rituals among the Buddhists in Mustang District, Nepal. In R-I. Heinze (Ed.), *The Nature and Function of Rituals.* London: Bergin & Garvey.

Weber, M. (1947). *Theory of social and economic organization.* New York: Oxford University Press.

KEY TERMS

Administrator: In the context of computer systems, including those which support online virtual communities, the 'administrator' is one with complete control over all aspects of the system; typically the administrator is the name under which a website is registered, and who bears legal and financial responsibility for it

Asynchronous: In communication, this term refers to channels which can operate with only one member of an interaction present at any time; one leaves a message, and later someone else reads it and perhaps responds; email is asynchronous

Avatar: On Internet forums, an image which represents a particular user; these could be photos of the actual person, altered images, images of celebrities, or of practically any object; in virtual worlds which operate interactively in real time, avatars are animated characters designed in part by the members, using the controls made available by the system host software

Computer-Mediated Communication (CMC): Communication channels provided by means of computer systems, such as email, instant messaging, Internet chat rooms, etc; a key feature of many CMC channels is the possibility of anonymous messaging

Face-to-Face: This term refers to interpersonal communication which takes place in the physical presence of the other person; in other words, NOT via Internet or other electronic channels

Forum: In this context, refers specifically to software which provides an Internet-based public bulletin board, in which mostly text messages are available for anyone to read, organized by topic and tagged with the poster's online nickname

Synchronous: In communication, this term refers to channels which require both (or all) participants to be present simultaneously, communicating in real time; face-to-face, telephone and Instant Messaging communications are synchronous

ENDNOTES

[1] The authors recognize that not all religious institutions are administered in a hierarchical manner, that some might be better described as egalitarian or democratic; the table entry above is intended only to indicate a typical (and in our experience the most prevalent) organization.

[2] In Helland's formulation, "religion online" refers to the provision by institutions of religious information on the Internet, with little or no interactivity provided.

[3] The term "face-to-face" throughout this paper is intended to denote the distinction between communications which are conducted in the physical presence of another person, and those which are mediated by a

technological communications channel such as telephone or the Internet.

[4] Durkheim here was obviously referring to the forms of religion of his time and place, thus his use of a term not necessarily employed by religions generally, "church". The authors' intention is to address online religious communities generally in which identity, authenticity and authority play important roles,, not only those which are described by the Christian-specific term "church"; however, by way of providing particular examples of the phenomena in question, we will also from time to time use terms and concepts specific to particular religions.

[5] The sociological literature on rituals is extensive. Widely cited authors include Victor Turner (1969), Erik Erikson (1977) and Grimes (1994). Those with an interest in the topic may wish to inspect the references available in Heinze (2000).

[6] There may be many more categories: moderators, super-moderators, mediators, supervisors, and team leaders are just a few of the many possible echelons of administrative duty and/or power which may be observed in online religious forums.

[7] See for example the troubles caused by multiple online identities at this Mormon forum: http://www.lds.net/forums/general-discussion/3345-final-thread-recent-member-bans.html

[8] Were open-standards biometric technology such as fingerprint readers to become ubiquitous among Internet users, or nearly so, then confirmation of personal identity as a condition of online participation might actually become technologically practical. However, that day has not yet arrived, and in light of privacy concerns already pervasive with respect to Internet use, it is probably not wise to rely upon any near-term future realization of this possibility.

9   See for example the extensive guidelines at http://www.islamicboard.com/faq/forum-rules/#faq_liforum_rules, the doctrinal requirements for joining at http://www.mannacabana.com/cabanaboards/showflat.php?Cat=&Number=137&page=0&view=collapsed&sb=5&o=&fpart=1, the notice concerning content posted at http://www.chabadtalk.com/forum/showthread.php3?t=5908, or the Profile rules at http://www.catholicforum.com/forums/showthread.php?t=10553-- notice the plea for honesty here.

10   See for example the disclaimer in point #6 at http://islam.about.com/mpboards.htm.

11   See for example, the Code of Conduct here: http://xsorbit29.com/users5/fundamental-baptistforum/index.php?topic=1089.0

12   See for example the post and subsequent linked discussion at http://christianforums.com/t6798314-discussion-of-announcement-amendment-to-non-nicene-annoucement.html

13   Bear in mind, however, that in the online arena, a "member" is a particular single-factor authentication nickname/password pair which confers privileges to participate, NOT an actual person, as would be the case in a face-to-face religious community. Because of the intervening CMC technology, that nickname/password might actually be just one of many online identities used by a person, or conversely a single identity used by more than one live person.

Chapter XV
Living, Working, Teaching and Learning by Social Software

Helen Keegan
University of Salford, UK

Bernard Lisewski
University of Salford, UK

ABSTRACT

This chapter explores emergent behaviours in the use of social software across multiple online communities of practice where informal learning occurs beyond traditional higher education (HE) institutional boundaries. Employing a combination of research literature, personal experience and direct observation, the authors investigate the blurring of boundaries between work/home/play as a result of increased connectivity and hyper availability in the "information age". Exploring the potentially disruptive nature of new media, social software and social networking practices, the authors ask what coping strategies are employed by the individual as their online social networks and learning communities increase in number and density? What are the implications for the identity and role of the tutor in online HE learning environments characterised by multiple platforms and fora? The authors conclude by posing a series of challenges for the HE sector and its participants in engaging with social software and social networking technologies.

Wholly new forms of encyclopaedias will appear, ready-made with a mesh of associative trails running through them... there is a new profession of trailblazers, those who find delight in the task of establishing useful trails through the enormous mass of the common record. The inheritance from the master becomes, not only his additions to the world record, but for his disciples the entire scaffolding by which they were erected....

—Vannevar Bush (1945)

INTRODUCTION

Online social networking is to some extent a cultural phenomenon. As emerging social web-based technologies are being explored and adopted by educators and learners, we are beginning to witness the emergence of new forms of cooperation and collaboration across boundaries of time and space. Much learning takes place beyond institutional boundaries, instead through social interaction across multiple online 'communities of practice' which Wenger, McDermott and Snyder (2002: 4) define as 'groups of people who share a concern, a set of problems, a passion about a topic, and who deepen their knowledge and expertise in this area by interacting on an ongoing basis'. The speed with which information is produced and accessed in an increasingly networked society, and the ease with which communications can take place across multiple platforms and fora, give rise to what Barnett (2000) refers to as 'supercomplexity' where the professional judgement of HE teachers involves using multiple data sources, and often conflictual decision-making choices. The vast amount of information available online, and the ease and speed with which learners and tutors can communicate in the co-construction of knowledge, both require productive boundary making processes in order to lessen the risk of information and communication overload. Alongside the inherent tensions of informal learning taking place across online social platforms which stand apart from the formalised structures of traditional institutions, questions are often raised regarding the authority of knowledge and the legitimacy of participants. These challenges require learners and tutors to demonstrate ongoing reflexivity in terms of the practice of educational interaction in dynamically changing environments and constantly changing information sources.

The use of social software in higher education, such as blogs, wikis and social networking services, has seen a surge in the number of active online learning communities and networks for both staff and students, where members are easily connected and engaging in the social construction of knowledge. Much learning is decentralised (the individual being the locus of control as opposed to the HE institution) and often informal in the sense that it is not prescribed or assessed. There is a resulting tension between the informal or 'feral' nature of social software-enabled learning webs, and the formal teaching accountability of HE institutions in terms of 'what is learned' and the respective assessment practices.

Within the context of his 'communities of practice' analytical tool, Wenger (1998: 267) describes such a tension as the 'interaction of the planned and the emergent - that is, the ability of teaching and learning to interact so as to become structuring resources for each other'. The authors have adopted Wenger's concept of a community of practice to characterise social networking processes as informal and organic 'constellations of inter-related communities of practice' (Wenger, 2000: 229) whereby communities of practice emerge across multiple online social platforms via the ways their participants use the virtual spaces on offer. Within such environments 'members have different interests, make diverse contributions to activity, and hold varied viewpoints... participation at multiple levels is entailed in membership in a community of practice. Nor does the term community imply necessarily co-presence, a well-defined, identifiable group, or socially visible boundaries. It does imply participation in an activity system about which participants share understandings concerning what they are doing and what that means in their lives and for their communities' Lave and Wenger, (1991: 98). Community membership is a matter of mutual engagement which does not necessarily entail homogeneity but diversity. Furthermore, 'since the life of a community of practice as it unfolds is, in essence, produced by its members through mutual engagement, it evolves in organic ways that tend to escape formal descriptions and control' (Wenger, 1998: 118).

These communities of practice can have different levels of expertise that can be simultaneously present, fluid peripheral to centre movement that symbolises the progression from being a novice to an expert and authentic tasks and communication (Johnson, 2001: 45). In effect, these online communities of practice can be conceptualised as 'shared histories of learning' (Wenger, 1998: 86) where both staff and students can participate in multiple communities at once and in doing so may portray different identities. Within these communities learning is a 'social phenomenon, reflecting our own deeply social nature as human beings capable of knowing' (Wenger,1998: 3) and is underpinned by the idea of 'situated cognition' where 'situations...co-produce knowledge through activity' given that 'learning and cognition... are fundamentally situated' (Brown, Collins and Duguid, 1989: 1). Therefore, knowledge is situated and results from the activity, context and culture in which it is developed and employed. Learning arises through 'legitimate peripheral participation' which Lave and Wenger (op cit: 29) characterize as an enculturation 'process by which new learners become part of a community of practice' and thereby 'acquire that particular community's subjective viewpoint and learn to speak its language' (Brown and Duguid, 1991: 48). Furthermore, joining a social networking community of practice involves entering, not only its internal configurations and interactions but also, by hyperlinking its relations with the rest of the digital world.

The ability of the learner to actively engage in dialogue with others in socially interactive online learning communities is seen to be democratising and empowering, echoing the ideas and implementations of radical pedagogical thinkers such as Ivan Illich (1971) and Paulo Freire (1993). Illich (op cit) put forward the idea of self-directed education, supported by intentional social relations, in fluid, informal arrangements - ideas which are found in today's cultures of lifelong and informal learning and the increasing emphasis which is now being placed on learner autonomy; in calling for the use of advanced technology to support 'learning webs', Illich demonstrated a pedagogical vision which is becoming a reality of our learning landscape. In contrast to institutional VLEs, the content of which is most often characterised by standalone modules and learning objects, students can roam freely across the web, accessing vast amounts of information, engaging in social interaction and metacognition through dialogue with others in online communities and participating in blog-based discussions which are characterised by commentary and hyperlinks; learning both formally and informally, and playing a dualistic role of both consumer and producer on the read/write web.

Traditional conceptions of learning, teaching and the role of educational institutions themselves are being challenged by new web-based pedagogies which are by their nature distributed and decentralised. As the use of online social networking services and other forms of social software have reached critical mass in mainstream society, an increasing number of learners and educators are using blogs, wikis and virtual worlds as spaces for communication and collaboration, complemented by faster forms of asynchronous discussion via instant messaging or chat (e.g. Skype, MSN) and now 'microblogging' (e.g. Twitter, Jaiku). Many of these technologies are applications which run outside of the virtual boundaries of the institution. Educators and learners will need to renegotiate shifting paradigms and boundaries such as formal vs. informal; VLE vs. PLE; and centralised vs. distributed interactions across multiple communities of practice. These boundaries may also be constantly shifting according to the level of participation within each community, while communication itself necessitates a degree of reflexivity due to expectations when using multiple and increasingly convergent technologies which are characteristic of a high-speed, always-on culture.

In an educational culture where online learning across multiple, hyper-connected communities may be energising as a result of seemingly never-ending opportunities for dialogue-based learning, there may also be a risk of communication and information overload. New boundaries need to be negotiated in order to allow for quality thinking time – time away from communication and information in order to reflect. If such boundaries are not set, the negative socio-emotional effects of information and communication overload may adversely affect the individual's ability to function and participate effectively within their multiple online communities and networks. Information and communication overload, coping strategies and boundary-setting within multiple online communities of practice (based on the authors' experiences of online social networking, social software and mobile technologies) are the focus of this chapter.

BACKGROUND

Information Overload: Myth or Reality?

Information overload is generally accepted to be "that moment when the amount of available information exceeds the user's ability to process it" (Klapp 1982, 63) and is commonly viewed as being a symptom of living in a high-tech age. Despite this, it is far from being a modern-day phenomenon; the concept of information overload has been traced back to ancient times (Bawden et. al. (1999) Nevertheless, as the means of communicating and disseminating information have increased through the ages, from the arrival of the printing press, through to the advent of telecommunications and now the internet, so too has the risk of feeling overwhelmed due to the ability to process information being limited as a result of cognitive and temporal constraints. The effects are further exacerbated in networked electronic

environments by the speed and ease with which information may be accessed through multiple electronic devices in an increasingly networked culture (Castells, 1996), and complaints of information and communication overload have increased in line with the growth in information and communication devices and fora. Bawden et. al. (*op cit*) describe large scale reports from the 1990s which appear to confirm that information overload is becoming a very real problem, leading to feelings of being overwhelmed and resulting in damage to health.

Much recent literature on information overload has focused on the use of email in workplace and the effects of instant electronic communications on worker productivity (Levy, 2006; Zeldes, 2007). Mobile technologies and web-based communications have resulted in the boundaries between work, home and play being broken down due to the ease with which people can communicate; as web-based communication becomes the norm, work-related discussions via email may be entered into during leisure time, while users are able to use web-based technologies to engage socially online in the workplace. The accelerated nature of electronic communication is not without its consequences as people are both easily reached and immediately available. A pattern of behaviour emerges whereby rapid response times (to emails) breed rapid response times; meetings are arranged easily and rapidly, the irony of which is that through partaking in such rapid communications in order to arrange and negotiate tasks, actual output in terms of productivity may be reduced (Levy, *op cit*). Zeldes et al (*op cit*) state that "field research demonstrates that restoring daily segments of contiguous "Quiet Time" can have a major effect of increasing productivity in development teams (Perlow, 1999). Additional research shows a correlation between a fragmented work mode and reduced creativity (Amabile, 2002)." In relation to organisational networks, Watts (2004, p.274-275) discusses limitations in production and information processing, noting that "from a production perspective, efficiency requires that an organisation constrain the non-productive activities of its workers... network ties are costly, in terms of time and energy... individuals have finite amounts of both, it follows that the more relationships one actively maintains at work, the less actual production-related work one can do..."

MAIN THEMES

Considering Information Overload in the Context of HE

As the emerging social web-based technologies are explored and adopted by educators and learners, new forms of cooperation and collaboration are emerging across boundaries of time and space. Taking the 'blogosphere' as an example, growing numbers of groups, networks and communities are able to share and scaffold knowledge with increasing velocity as a result of the lack of physical and temporal barriers when communicating across cyberspace. Connections of thoughts and concepts, of individuals and networks, are formed at a seemingly exponential rate; a societal shift which is both energising and exciting, and yet can rapidly become exhausting as increased connectivity and hyper availability results in a culture which is information rich, yet time poor[i]. One of the concerns of living in a high-speed, always-on culture which is defined by immediacy and seemingly infinite amounts of information is the risk of spending so much time communicating and actively seeking information that little time remains to reflect (Levy, 2006; Eagleton, 2006). One of the paradoxes of the blogosphere is that blogs are commonly seen as a reflective medium, yet without setting boundaries it is quite possible to follow links ad infinitum from blog to blog, accessing seemingly unlimited amounts of information without taking time out to engage in reflection. A further consideration is that of much

of the learning within blog-based communities coming from not only the posts themselves, but the comments that are left by others. Through following the ensuing dialogue within the commentary, participants are exposed to multiple viewpoints which, when viewed as a whole, serve as diverse and rich sources of new knowledge. This does however have implications for blog-based community participation, as members may be faced with considerably more information than is contained in the original post.

Many educators are exploring ways to harness the potential of social-software enabled 'feral learning' (Nunan 1996) and decentralised learning networks within formalised educational structures. The ability of tutors and students to roam freely among multiple online learning communities and seemingly never ending and constantly updated web-based information requires new skills in time and information management. Multiple fora and tools with which to communicate mean added complexity; when faced with more information that can be processed in the time available; the resulting overload may be a significant cause of stress (Bawden et. al. *op cit*; Klapp *op cit*; Savolainen *op cit*). This is not a phenomenon which is seen as being a result of the use of social software per se; more as a result of technological advancement as a whole, (McLuhan 1967; Poster 1995; Virilio 1995; Erikssen 2001).

The challenge for learners and educators is to harness the power of the network without becoming overwhelmed by the sheer volume of communication and information within the network itself. Just as businesses are beginning to designate 'quiet time' for their employees, away from email in order to focus on productivity (Wakefield, 2007); networked learning requires participants to agree on boundaries and employ methods to manage information and communication expectations in order to avoid both information and communication overload.

Multiple choices within multiple fora create supercomplexity; learners often use a variety of social networking sites (Facebook, MySpace), instant messaging clients (Skype, MSN) and have multiple email addresses independently of education. The introduction of online social tools into the learning process means that learners have additional networked information and communication technologies to negotiate which increases the likelihood of information overload. Learners and educators in a networked society adopt strategies for avoiding or coping with information overload, and commonly employed methods involve either filtering or withdrawal (Savolainen, 2007). Filtering is a characteristic of sound information and digital literacy, while withdrawal is more affectively oriented and may involve actions such as avoiding checking emails and logging into social networking sites, disguising online status and switching off mobile phones in an attempt to remove oneself from the perceived onslaught of communication. While filtering and withdrawal are common strategies for coping when bombarded with information and communications, it is important for learners and educators to ensure that the right sort of 'noise'[2] is filtered out, or that essential communications are not missed as a result of withdrawal.

One common paradox which has been noted by the author(s) is that whereby useful technologies are so heavily used that their usefulness is lessened in some way. Zeldes et. al. (*op cit*: 2007), describe a state where:

"Rapid communications (first order effect) mean more distractions and overload (second order effect) which reduces people's ability to react. This paradox causes people to adopt various strategies to communicate less (third order effect). The outcome is that people are less responsive to many messages than they were a decade ago, when communications were much slower."

This pattern, whereby a useful technology is used so heavily that it's usefulness is diminished, occurs frequently and rapidly with many web-based technologies; for example coping with email overload by 'chunking' and checking less frequently in order to focus on the task in hand reduces the validity of email as a rapid communications tool. The practice of 'chunking' is so widespread that email is now seen by many as a 'slow' technology in comparison to live chat applications such as Skype and MSN. In turn, as increasing numbers of people adopt these 'faster' communication technologies so the likelihood of noise is increased. Coping strategies are again adopted which often take the form of disguising one's online status or turning off messaging alerts in order to filter out noise.

A further example of this paradox in terms of useful technologies is that of RSS (Really Simple Syndication or Rich Site Summary). RSS feeds are used to bring relevant web content to the user, with the intention of creating more personalised information streams with reduced noise, thereby increasing efficiency and filtering out less-relevant information. One of the key uses of RSS is its role in blog aggregation; users can subscribe and follow multiple blogs easily. However, this tool which is designed to filter out noise is then used so much that it becomes a source of noise in itself, with an increasing number of bloggers complaining of RSS and blog overload (Richardson, 2007; Dawson, 2007; Hughes, 2004).

Information and communication overload may be more of an issue for those whom these technologies have appeared in later life, while the 'net generation' may be more at ease living in a culture which is characterized by multitasking, the use of multiple media simultaneously and constant digitally-enabled communication (Barnes et. al, 2007; Oblinger & Oblinger, 2005). Nevertheless, there may well be implications for the introduction of new and emerging technologies into education, due to the exponential nature of the viral-like growth of the network.

Essentially any individual is limited in the amount of networks within which they can actively participate at any one time, and as educators striving to bring communities of learners together through social software, tutors may be competing with online communities within which learners are already engaged informally such as MySpace and Facebook. While the 'net-generation' are generally perceived as being comfortable communicating across multiple platforms simultaneously, the ease with which users can participate within, and move between, online communities and the potential blurring of the boundaries between work and play as institutions try to engage learners through moving in to the realms of popular social networking sites has implications in terms of both student/tutor identity and the risk of information 'grazing', where learning becomes surface as a result of 'too many networks, too little time'.

How this translates in terms of pedagogy remains to be seen, but as an increasing number of educators introduce social software into the classroom it is not difficult to envisage a point at which some learners may feel 'blogged down and blogged out' (Richardson, *op cit*; Dawson, *op cit*.), drowning in a sea of communication and collaboration and reacting by withdrawing from the very learning communities to which they belong. The challenge for learners and educators using social software is the need to negotiate new pedagogies and educational boundaries (time, space, cultural differences) in a global web which is characterised by exponential growth and constantly changing information sources, in contrast to the relatively static nature of the local institution and the requirements of a HE system which requires transparency, accountability and easily measurable outcomes. Learner empowerment must involve a more equal relationship between the tutor and student, with the acknowledgement that, in the more open and global contexts, the tutor is not the sole provider of subject knowledge. That said, there is likely to remain a responsibility on the tutor to provide an enabling structure within which learners, especially those new to subject domains, are likely to develop learning independence.

Tutor as Educational Broker and 'Bridge': Searching for a New Identity within Dynamic Multiple Systems

Communication and social interaction lie at the core of web-based social constructivist pedagogies and communities of learners can be well-supported by new forms of social software; however, the majority of educators in everyday practice are subject to institutional constraints and accountability mechanisms which pose a real challenge to new forms of social and online learning. The role of the tutor in supporting learners through new forms of online learning may be one of guidance; helping learners to explore their own needs and navigate their personal learning pathways. However, many tutors are working in an educational climate characterised by reduced funding and the corresponding pressure to recruit in order to increase student numbers. The tension between what participants in online learning communities believe to be democratic and empowering, and the requirements of a HE system which emphasises easily measurable outcomes, is tangible. Accountability is key: institutional audits, benchmarking, league tables – such frameworks do not lend themselves easily to decentralised models of education and new conceptions of learning which are student-centred as opposed to autocratic, where the role of the tutor is that of a mentor or guide, as opposed to the authoritarian voice.

The exponential rise of social networking sites as informal environments for HE raises issues of teachers' identities and roles given their growing participation within multiple virtual communities of complex interactions. For example, Rheingold (1993: 61) foresaw enormous cultural changes of Internet usage on the individual: 'are relationships and commitments as we know them even possible in a place where identities are fluid?...We reduce and encode our identities as words on a screen, decode and unpack the identities of others'. On a grander scale, Anthony Giddens (1991) describes the over arching features of a dynamic modern society as being the separation of time and space, the disembedding of social systems and the reflexivity of institutions and individuals. Applied within the context of social networking processes we can see that the concept of space has undergone a transformation in that we can be in the same virtual space but not necessarily in the same locale. Furthermore, social relations within HE learning contexts can no longer be limited to the local face to face interaction whereby we are faced with the 'lifting out of social relations from local contexts and their re-articulation across indefinite tracts of time-space' (Giddens, *op cit*: 18). Both these conditions require in particular not only the 'reflexive monitoring of action' (Giddens, *ibid*: 20) but the need for say teachers and learners in online environments to constantly collect, store and interpret ever larger amounts of information within the dialectic of the local and the global interaction of knowledge. This reflexivity of modernity involves a 'fundamental uncertainty about the truth of the new knowledge, because we cannot be sure that this knowledge will not be revised' (Kasperson, 2000: 89). Not only does this undermine the certainty of knowledge but Giddens also argues that it may also be 'existentially troubling' for individuals and thereby threaten their 'ontological security' which he defines as 'a sense of continuity and order in events, including those not directly within the perceptual environment of the individual' (*ibid*: 243).

In an environment of multiple virtual communities of practice; time-space distanciation and faceless commitments may undermine one's sense of self-identity and trust in both the authority of the knowledge and the legitimacy of the participants. Within these dynamic, changeable, and volatile conditions there will be a constant need to undertake a form of recurrent 'mental housekeeping' or 'sense-making' as new information and contributions come to light. Giddens (1990: 139) likens the dynamic features of modernity to 'riding a juggernaut' which 'sometimes seems to

have a steady path', [but] 'there are times when it veers away erratically in directions we cannot foresee'. Such a scenario can be imagined within the context of different social networking tools where one has the ability to operate in multiple environments and make use of unfettered hyperlinking possibilities in the pursuit of authoritative knowledge construction.

Within multi-scenario and collaborative virtual communities of practice, there is a need for teachers to engage in ongoing reflexivity in how to practice educational interaction in dynamically changing environments and constantly changing information sources. This may involve developing productive 'boundary making' processes and negotiating with each other new cultural forms of managing online interaction. The very concept of a community of practice implies the existence of a boundary (Wenger, 2000: 232). That said, participation in an online community of practice involves engaging not only in its internal configurations but also with its external relationships, particularly given the many hyperlinking possibilities. Wenger (2000: 233) argues, that boundaries are important within learning systems because they connect communities and provide opportunities for learning. Practice boundaries are often informal and fuzzy and do not have to be disciplinary specific. Boundaries are the 'edges of communities of practice, to their point of contact with the rest of the world...no matter how negotiable or unspoken -refer to discontinuities, to lines of distinction between inside and outside, membership and non-membership, inclusion and exclusion (Wenger, 1998: 119).

Wenger, McDermott and Snyder (2002: 153) state that interacting across different practices and their respective boundaries initiate a 'deep source of learning' given that boundaries are 'learning assets in their own right'. However as Hayward (2000) points out, in her study of power, social boundaries (such as laws, rules, norms, routinised procedures, institutional arrangements) can constrain as well as enable participants within different social practices. In the context of social networking communities and their respective educational practices, agreed boundaries may on the one hand; provide a structure for neophyte learners, define what constitutes knowledge, create a space for action, establish the nature and urgency of problems and generate a collection of identities, whilst on the other hand, they can exclude participation, limit the further co-construction of knowledge and hamper innovation.

The key here is to connect boundary crossing and knowledge interaction between different virtual communities of practice some of which may be formal like institutional VLE's such as Blackboard and some of which may be informal such as social networking tools like Facebook. Wenger (2000: 235) offers three kinds of connections with regard to knowledge transfer: brokering, boundary objects and a variety of forms of interactions among people from different communities of practice (multi-membership). The focus here is on brokers who according to Wenger (1998:109) are people who are: 'able to make new connections across communities of practice, enable co-ordination…and open new possibilities for meaning'. Brokering can take various forms: such as 'roamers' who are able to create connections and move knowledge from one community to another and 'outposts' where community members can bring back news from the 'forefront' and explore new 'territories'.

Within the context of HE, this will involve - to different degrees - individuals such as tutors belonging to, and participating in, multiple virtual communities of practice simultaneously. Fox (2007) has drawn attention to students' use of social networking tools such as Facebook and compared it to their lack of participation within formalised institutional VLE's. Social networking sites like Facebook display informal, unmoderated and emergent participation with relatively open and fluid boundaries with virtual spaces used by students for socialising and learning - not controlled by the university whereas VLE's, such as

Blackboard tend to have formal, tutor moderated and designed participation with relatively fixed and closed boundaries and hierarchical virtual spaces for structured learning - publicly owned, controlled and surveilled (Land and Bayne, 2001) by the University under licence.

Fox (*op cit*) notes that the popularity of the former was leading to her increasing lack of success in getting student interactions going in the latter. When she browsed Facebook, she found it a useful way of getting to know her students through their profiles. She reports that she was eventually invited to join the social networking group they had formed, associated with her module, and used it to integrate discussions for her seminars. She continues by saying: 'it is a tricky relationship to negotiate, you have to be sensitive because it is a personal space for students, so they don't want it to be too interactive' In effect, tutors must have 'legitimacy' with students whereby the tutor is not seen to be invading their virtual space. This example shows how 'tutors as brokers' are able to make new connections across virtual communities of practice, enable cross participation and open up new possibilities for knowledge co-construction within a more egalitarian HE learning context.

It may be that the tutors of the future will have to develop the skills of translation, co-ordination, and alignment between different perspectives and establish their participatory 'legitimacy' whilst undertaking simultaneous multi-membership of many virtual online social networking learning spaces. As Wenger (1998: 110) argues: 'Brokering therefore requires an ability to manage carefully the existence of membership and non-membership, yielding enough distance to bring a different perspective, but also enough legitimacy to be listened to'. Thus, the HE 'tutor as broker' will have to display the negotiating skills - and feel comfortable enough - to operate between informal and formal virtual communities and within, in particular, multiple informal ones. The challenge is thus to negotiate information and communication boundaries and expectations across the tensions between traditional HE institutions and formalised educational structures, and informal decentralised social learning platforms.

Saunders (2006: 17) in considering relationships between education, learning and work offers additional perspectives on boundary crossing processes. He emphasises the importance of two-dimensions: firstly, moving across boundaries 'yields the potential for learning as sense making processes' and secondly, 'informal learning is given impetus to produce 'ontological security' in the new environment'. He highlights the need for a wide range of 'bridging tools' to help learners, and those supporting them to navigate these transitions from one environment to another. The term 'bridging' is used as the relevant metaphor, because 'it implies a journey and a connection between places in two senses: just as a bridge takes an individual or group from one point to another, it also joins one place to another. This narrative has a strong vision of the world learners inhabit overwhelmingly characterised by rapid change' (Saunders, op cit: 18).

CONCLUSION: FUTURE TRENDS AND CHALLENGES

New forms of online learning, with social interaction and metacognition at their core, pose a significant challenge in terms of the volume, authority and legitimacy of information, relatively unbounded communications, traditional assessment practices and the role of the tutor. Within many online communities of practice learning is fluid and informal, while through participating in such communities tutors can observe learning 'as it happens', guiding students along the way. However, when faced with large student cohorts (which are increasingly commonplace as a result of reduced funding and widening participation in HE) tutors may need to explore alternative methods of monitoring and measuring learning within such communities, such as peer assessment,

Summative self-reporting and more intentional uses of technology in ways designed to capture students' knowledge and what is learnt. Tensions between the formal and the informal, and centralised versus decentralised models of education, must be managed effectively, while boundaries need to be negotiated across communities of practice and information networks in order to avoid participants becoming overwhelmed by information and communication.

More pressingly, our conclusion offers a series of challenges for the HE sector in networking with these new forms of learning and social interaction:

1. How are HE institutions going to participate in these informal settings without 'disrupting' students' informal and voluntary engagements in them?

2. HE institutions are going to have to address issues around 'curricular control', assessment strategies, quality assurance, accountability and ownership of process and product within informal social networking groupings.

3. HE tutors, in particular, are going to have to develop as 'educational brokers' and 'information guides and nurture their own professional reflexivity and increased empathy with students operating within their own organically developing informal social networking communities. This may involve a more equalised teacher-learner relationship where teachers may have to concede some 'designing curricula' power within these contexts. That said, tutors may have to provide the 'bridging' function between the formal learning environments of HE practice and the informal learning environments within social networking contexts and their infinite hyperlinking possibilities.

4. Individuals are going to have to construct coping strategies in addressing 'information overload within the work/life, teaching/

217

learning balance and engage in productive boundary making and negotiating across multiple and dynamic social networking communities.

5. Within the context of these informal and organic 'constellations of interconnected practices' and their relationships with the rest of the digital world, we are going to have to develop what Gee (2000: 522) calls 'reflective communities of practice' and acquire 'reflection literacy' (Hasan, 1998) where both teachers and learners 'engage in both subject-centred design knowledge and the world-building design knowledge through which they imagine and enact new more moral worlds and futures'. This according to Gee (op cit: 517) is 'knowledge about how to design and transform environments, relationships…and identities'.

REFERENCES

Amabile, T., Hadley, C. N., & Kramer, S. J. (2002, August). "Creativity Under the Gun," Special Issue on The Innovative Enterprise: Turning Ideas into Profits. *Harvard Business Review*, 80(8), 52–61.

Barnes, K., Marateo, R. C., & Ferris, S. P. (2007). Teaching and Learning with the Net Generation. *Innovate, 3*(4). Retrieved November 5th 2007, from: http://innovateonline.info/index.php?view=article&id=382&action=article

Barnett, R. (2000). *Realising the University in an Age of Super Complexity*. Buckingham: Society for Research into Higher Education and Open University Press.

Bawden, D., Holtham, C., & Courtney, N. (1999). Perspective on information overload. *Aslib Proceedings, 51*(8), 249-255.

Brown, J. S., Collins, A., & Duguid, P. (1989). Situated cognition and the culture of learning. *Educational Researcher, 18*(1) 32-42.

Brown, J. S., & Duguid, P. (1991). Organizational learning and communities of practice: towards a unified view of working, learning and innovation. *Organization Science, 2*(1) 40-57.

Vannevar Bush, V. (1945). As We May Think. *Atlantic Monthly*.

Carlson, C. N. (2003). Information overload, retrieval strategies and Internet user empowerment. In L. Haddon (Eds.), *Proceedings The Good, the Bad and the Irrelevant (COST 269), 1*(1), 169-173. Helsinki (Finland).

Castells, M. (1996). *The Rise of the Networked Society*. Oxford: Blackwell Publishers Ltd.

Dawson, K. M. (2007) Blog Overload. *The Chronicle of Higher Education*. Retrieved November 6th 2007, from: http://chronicle.com/jobs/news/2007/01/2007013001c/careers.html.

Duguid, P. (1989). Situated cognition and the culture of learning. *Educational Researcher, 18*(1) 32-42.

Eagleton, T. (2006) Your thoughts are no longer worth a penny. *Times Higher Education Supplement. 10th March 2006*.

Eriksen, T. E. (2001). *Tyranny of the Moment: Fast and Slow Time in the Information Age*. Pluto Press, London, UK.

Fox, J. (2007). Quoted in 'Networking Sites: Professors - keep out'. *The Independent*, 18th October 2007, Retrieved November 15th 2007, from: http://student.independent.co.uk/university_life/article3068385.ece

Freire, P. (1993). *Pedagogy of the Oppressed*. New York: Continuum.

Gee, J. P. (2000). Communities of Practice and the New Capitalism. *The Journal of the Learning Sciences, 9*(4), 515-523.

Giddens, A. (1990). *The Consequences of Modernity*. Cambridge: Polity Press.

Giddens, A. (1991). *Modernity and Self-Identity: Self and Society in the Late Modern Age.* Cambridge: Polity Press.

Hayward, C. R. (2000). *De-facing Power.* Cambridge: Cambridge University Press.

Hasan, R. (1998). The Disempowerment Game: Bourdieu and language in literacy. *Linguistics and Education, 10*, 25-87.

Hughes, G. (2004) *RSS/Blog Overload - How do you deal with the glut of information?* Retrieved 6th November 2007, from: http://www.greghughes. net/rant/BloggerConRSSBlogOverloadHowDoY-ouDealWithTheGlutOfInformation.aspx

Illich, I. (1971). *Deschooling Society.* New York: Harper & Row.

Johnson, C. M. (2001). A Survey of Current Research on Online Communities of Practice. *Internet and Higher Education, 4*, 45-60.

Kasperson, L. B. (2000). *Anthony Giddens: An Introduction to a Social Theorist.* Oxford: Blackwell Publishers Ltd.

Klapp, O. (1982). Meaning lag in the Information society. *Journal of Communication, 32*(2), 56–66.

Land, R., & Bayne, S. (2001). 'Screen or monitor? Issues of surveillance and disciplinary power in online learning environments. In C. Rust (Ed.), *Proceedings of the "001 Ninth improving Student Learning Symposium* (pp. 125-138), Oxford: Oxford Centre for Staff and Learning Development.

Lave, J., & Wenger, E. (1991). *Situated Learning: legitimate peripheral participation.* Cambridge: Cambridge University Press.

Levy, D. M. (2006). More, Faster, Better: Governance in an Age of Overload, Busyness, and Speed. *First Monday, special issue number 7* (September 2006). Retrieved November 8th 2007, from: http://firstmonday.org/issues/special11_9/levy/index.html.

McLuhan, M. (1989). *The Global Village: Transformations in World Life and Media in the 21st Century.* Oxford University Press, UK.

Nunan, T. (1996) *Flexible Delivery - What is it and Why a part of current educational debate?* Paper presented at the Higher Education Research and Development Society of Australasia Annual Conference Different Approaches: Theory and Practice in Higher Education Perth, Western Australia, 8-12 July, 1996.

Oblinger, D., & Oblinger, J. (2005). Is It Age or IT: First Steps Toward Understanding the Net Generation. In D. G. Oblinger & J. L. Oblinger (Eds.), *Educating the Net Generation,*(p.21). EDUCAUSE, Washington, D.C.

Perlow, L. (1999). The time famine: Toward a sociology of work time. *Administrative Science Quarterly, 44*(1), \ 57–81, and at http://interruptions.net/literature/Perlow-ASQ99.pdf

Poster, M. (1995). *The Second Media Age.* Cambridge: Polity Press.

Richardson, W. (2007) *Random thoughts and admissions.* Retrieved 10th October 2007, from: http://weblogg-ed.com/2007/random-thoughts-and-admissions/

Rheingold, H. (1993). A Slice of Life in my Virtual Community. In L. Harasim (Ed.), *Global Networks: Computers and International Communication.* Cambridge, MA: MIT Press.

Savolainen, R. (2007). Filtering and withdrawing: strategies for coping with information overload in everyday contexts. *Journal of Information Science, 33*(5) (Oct. 2007), 611-621.

Saunders, M. (2006). From 'organisms' to 'boundaries': the uneven development of theory narratives in education, learning and work connections. *Journal of Education and Work, 19*(1), 1-27.

Virilio, P. (1986). *Speed and Politics: An Essay on Dromology* (trans. M. Polizotti). New York: Semiotext(e).

Virilio, P. (1995). *Speed and information: Cyberspace alarm!* In A. Kroker & M. Kroker (Eds.), *CTHEORY, 18*(3), 1-5.

Wakefield, J. (2007). Turn off e-mail and do some work. *BBC News Online 19 October 2007.* Retrieved 5th November 2007, from: http://news.bbc.co.uk/1/hi/technology/7049275.stm.

Watts, D. J. (2004). *Six Degrees (The Science of a Connected Age).* Vintage U.K.: Random House.

Wenger, E. (2000). Communities of practice and social learning systems. *Organization, 7*(2) 225-246.

Wenger, E. (1998). *Communities of Practice: learning, meaning and identity.* Cambridge: Cambridge University Press.

Wenger, E., McDermott, R., & Snyder, W. M. (2002). *Cultivating Communities of Practice.* Boston: Massachusetts Harvard Business School.

Zeldes, N., Sward, D., & Louchheim, S. (2007). Infomania: Why we can't afford to ignore it any longer. *First Monday,* 12(8) (August 2007). Retrieved 5th November 2007, from: http://firstmonday.org/issues/issue12_8/zeldes/index.html

KEY TERMS

Blogs: Shortened term (weblogs) describing online journals displayed in reverse chronological order.

Boundaries: Practice boundaries are the 'edges' of communities of practice which can be fluid and fuzzy but offer the point of contact with other practice communities and provide lines of distinction between membership and non-membership.

Boundary Crossing: Different forms of interaction among people from different communities of practice.

Brokering: Those who are able to make connections and move knowledge across different practice communities by for example, introducing elements of one practice into another.

Communities of Practice: Organic developments composed of social and informal learning processes which revolve around joint enterprise, mutual engagement and produce a shared understanding and repertoire of communal meaning and resources.

Information Overload: When an individual is faced with more information than can be processed with available time and resources.

Ontological Security: An individual's sense of order, security and continuity within a rapidly changing perceived environment.

Reflexivity: The recurring examination and formation of self identity and social practices within a social environment of ever changing information.

Social Networking: Joining and participating in interconnected Internet communities (sometimes known as personal networks).

Social Software: Web-based applications which are characterised by personal publishing and the sharing and remixing of user-generated content (commonly referred to as 'Web 2.0').

ENDNOTES

[1] There are fundamental concerns about the effects on the individual as a result of the increase of 'fast' time at the expense of 'slow' time (Eriksen, 2001). Paul Virilio (1986, 1995) is known for his explorations of the cultural implications of instantaneous

digital communications, suggesting that the notion of real-time technology management shows an instrumental disregard for lived time and human experience, although it may be argued that Virilio misses the democratizing aspects of new computer and media technologies.

[2] The signal-to-noise ratio is an often-used metaphor for describing information overload... In the context of the Information Age, the term is used to describe the proportion of useful information found to all information found' (Carslon, 2003)

Chapter XVI
Supporting Student Blogging in Higher Education

Lucinda Kerawalla
The Open University, UK

Shailey Minocha
The Open University, UK

Gill Kirkup
The Open University, UK

Gráinne Conole
The Open University, UK

ABSTRACT

With a variety of asynchronous communication and collaboration tools and environments such as Wikis, blogs, and forums, it can be increasingly difficult for educators to make appropriate choices about when and how to use these technologies. In this chapter, the authors report on the findings from a research programme on educational blogging which investigated the blogging activities of different groups of Higher Education students: undergraduate and Masters-level distance learners, and PhD students. The authors discuss empirical evidence of students' experiences, perceptions, and expectations of blogging. We provide an empirically-grounded framework which can guide course designers and educators in their decision-making about whether and how to include blogging in their course-contexts so as to create value and to generate a positive student experience. Also, this framework can help guide students who are either thinking about blogging for themselves, or who are undertaking course-directed blogging activities.

INTRODUCTION

Blogging started in the form of Web pages or Websites through which people informed one another about other Websites or Web pages through links and comments. Tim Berners-Lee in 1992 created the first 'What's new' page; later Marc Andreessen set up a similar page with links to new Web pages that were coming up on the Internet. Justin Hall started a filter log in 1994 which was effectively pages with recommended links for others surfing on the internet. In December 1997, the term 'Weblog' for 'logging the Web' was coined by Jorn Barger. From these link-driven sites, a community arose, and in 1999 the Websites Blogger and Pitas offered a simpler way to creating a Weblog without having to know HTML. Soon Web-log or we-blog was shortened to 'blog' by the programmer Peter Merholz and blogs evolved into personal journals or diaries. For a history of blogging from its origins and until 2000, please see Blood (2006).

With free blog-creation services, it was now possible for anyone to publish both events and opinions without the mediation (or cost) of professional media. Blogging moved into wider public consciousness when independent eyewitness reports in the form of a Web diary on the invasion of Iraq by the 'Baghdad Blogger' (Salam, 2003) were read and republished in print newspapers (e.g. the Guardian in the UK). Blogging activity has expanded and journalists now engage in blogging alongside the more traditional forms of journalism. It is now possible to set up a commercial blogging-organisation. For example 'BlogHer' (retrieved on 19th March 2008 from http://www.blogher.org/about-blogher-0) exists as a network for US homemakers, which is funded by venture capital and it accepts advertising, thereby providing employment for its originators.

Blogging has become another genre of text, and bloggers range from the amateur diary keeper, with no audience except for family, to commercial business blogs (Bruns and Jacobs, 2006, Nardi *et*

al. 2004). In 2006, a US telephone survey reported that 8% of US adult internet users kept a blog and nearly 40% reported reading one. More than half saw the activity as a form of self-expression and were not concerned about whether others read their blog, while about one third felt that they were engaged in some form of 'journalism' and wrote for others to read (Lenhart and Fox, 2006). Businesses are seeing the huge potential of the conversational nature of blogging and have begun to adapt it for marketing, advertising, and even as a recruiting tool (Scobel & Israel, 2006). It is within this context that educational use of blogging is developing, and it's not clear how educational blogging is being perceived by students who would have been exposed to different genres of blogging. It is against this backdrop that we have carried out a research programme in educational blogging which we report in this chapter.

Previous researchers have attempted to define different types of blogs, such as a 'personal journal' or a 'filter blog' (Herring *et al.*, 2004) both of which may, at first glance, support learning. However, these descriptions seem to focus on the end product (i.e., the blog), rather than on the activity of blogging. In this way, the virtues of blogging are reduced to what ends up on the blog, to the detriment of considering the activities involved in creating and posting material to the blog. This approach also fails to recognise whether, how, and why blogging in a public online space is of benefit to the blogger.

Boyd (2006) defines blogging as "a diverse set of practices that result in the production of diverse content on top of what we call blogs" (p1), which suggests that 'blogs' and 'blogging' can mean different things to different people. This suggests that blogging software can be used for an infinite number of activities, and raises the question of how educators a) can exploit the potential of blogging and the available software for blogging; and b) encourage their students to participate in blogging.

Research into blogging in Higher Education has reported mixed success, with some studies suggesting that blogging can support learning (e.g. Du and Wagner 2007), and other authors offering words of caution about issues such as low levels of student engagement with the educator-suggested blogging activities (e.g. Williams and Jacobs, 2004). Problems are, perhaps, unsurprising given that, although the technology itself is relatively simple to use, its potential role to support learning is not fully understood. We discuss this and other challenges in the following section.

BACKGROUND

The Challenges of Student Blogging in Higher Education

Research suggests that blogging can support learning in a number of ways in higher education. Educators viewing blogging from a constructivist learning framework perceive blogs as having the potential to offer students a place to keep a learning log (Homik and Melis, 2006) which they, as teachers, have access to and where the student can engage in authentic presentation of self (Joinson, 2001) and articulate their opinions. Williams and Jacobs (2004), in their study of course-directed blogging by MBA students, report that the majority of students either agreed or strongly agreed that blogging facilitated their learning and increased the level of intellectual exchange of thoughts and ideas between the students on the course. Oravec (2003) discusses the potential for blogs within a blended learning environment and proposes that blogging can promote critical reflection, facilitate the exchange of hyperlinks and the generation of knowledge communities. From a more social perspective, Dickey (2004) suggests that blogging can alleviate the feelings of isolation associated with distance-learning. Farmer (2006) argues that blogs offer students an opportunity to develop an online social presence and to project themselves as 'real' people. Others have been exploring blogs as a new genre which allows for different kinds of literacy practices (Penrod, 2007).

However, previous research illustrates also that course-related blogging can be problematic. For example, Krause (2004) designed collaborative blogging activities for a post-graduate writing class and reports that the students made haphazard contributions to their blogs. Krause found that there was minimal communication between students through their blogs and that the quality of reflection upon the course materials, as indicated in blog content, was poor. Krause acknowledges that this was due to three shortcomings: the blogging software did not offer adequate support for the collaborative activity; students felt that instructions on how to use their blogs were "vague" in terms of the amount and type of posts that were expected from them; and the specific role of the blogs, in conjunction with the use of email, was not clear. Homik and Melis (2006) report that students in their study engaged in blogging only to the extent of meeting assessment requirements. Clearly, the expectations of educators with regards to blogging can be difficult to implement in practice.

The studies discussed here suggest that matching blogs to specific learning activities can be a challenge for course designers. Conole *et al.*'s (2004) Learning Activity Taxonomy identifies seventy-two possible learning tasks including: analysing, creating, explaining, listing, refining, summarising and testing. This wide range of tasks is an illustration of the complexity of learning design. For example, when would it be appropriate to suggest blogging as a means of achieving some of these learning tasks? Learning design is made more complex on courses where more than one medium of communication is used (e.g. materials on the Web, seminars, lectures, laboratory work) and more than one mode of communication and collaboration is used (e.g. e-mail, forums, face-to-face); how are the roles of different media and technologies differentiated? It is important that blogs are matched to appropriate learning activities that enable students to achieve the learning outcomes of the course (e.g. Weller *et al.*, 2005).

It could be argued that subtle differences between the functionalities of some of the new e-learning technologies used on courses (e.g. blogs, wikis or discussion forums) mean that it can be difficult to decide which technologies to use to support particular learning activities. For example, a blog as well as an online discussion forum can facilitate communication between students, so how can course designers and educators decide when and how to use each tool? It is important for course designers to not only 'appropriately' integrate blogging into the learning activities of their courses but to also determine how blogs are used instead of, or in conjunction with other tools. In addition to learning tasks, blogging can also be used for a variety of other activities, many of which are not educational, such as posting pictures of holidays, or posting personal videos, and these activities or posts may conflict with the educational aims, values, or social norms envisaged by the course. At present educators should approach blogging circumspectly. Until we understand more about its affordances as a student-controlled educational activity, we should be careful about how much we promote blogging in education.

This chapter discusses the empirical investigations of the blogging experiences of four different groups of students at the UK's Open University (OU). We focus our student-centred enquiry on the student experience of blogging because it is the students themselves that can best provide first-hand reports of how blogging can support their study. The range of student groups provided us with an insight into the different ways in which blogging can support learning. We have used empirical evidence from our research programme to develop a framework which may be used to raise awareness of some of the features of blogging.

Our Research Context

The overall aim of our research programme was to investigate the ways in which students, at various stages in their post-school education, use blogs to support their learning, with a view to generate: guidance for educators for their design of learning activities using blogs; and guidance for students which would help inform their blogging activities.

Some of our participants were mature undergraduates and Masters-level distance learners who studied part-time alongside managing their jobs, family responsibilities, and life events. Other participants were PhD students located at various UK universities, and one European university, who were either part-time or full-time. Hence, our findings are not from young, full-time students at a campus university, which has enabled us to bring a new perspective to the existing literature on blogging in higher education. The research questions and the different sets of participants in our study are listed in Table 1 and will be discussed later in this section.

Prior to carrying out the research described in this chapter, and in order to understand students' existing experience of, and attitudes towards blogging, we evaluated the findings from a survey of 1,893 OU students. We found that 53.3% of them had read a blog and that only 8% had their own blog. Surprisingly, only 22% of blog owners could see a great use of blogs in their studies (Kerawalla, *et al.* 2007). These findings suggest that course designers will need to consider this lack of student experience of blogs and blogging.

Following this background survey work, we set out to answer three research questions. The research involved carrying out studies with four different groups of students who blogged in different contexts, and whose actual and potential blogging communities were varied. The research questions and the corresponding participants for each of the research questions are listed in Table 1.

The details of the four groups of students and their learning contexts are as follows:

1. Fifteen students (mean age 47.7 years, range 29-55 years) (36.4% male and 63.6% female) studying an international, online OU Masters course (course A in Table 1) – *The eLearning Professional* – which is designed for e-learning professionals and addresses their professional practice and professional development. Reflective learning and being reflective practitioners were central themes of this course: the students reflected on their learning and also reflected on their own practice in the light of what they had read on the course (in our paper, Kerawalla *et al.*, 2008, we have provided a comprehensive discussion of the blogging behaviours of students on this course).

    Blogging was not mandatory; the course materials suggested that blogs may be a suitable environment in which to reflect. Beyond this, students could use their blogs as they wished. As well as assignments, the students iteratively developed an e-portfolio for their final assessment. Reflections carried out in a blog could be submitted as part of the e-portfolio. Students used an asynchronous text-based discussion forum and email as well as blogs. The students were provided with a freely-available Moveable Type blog that was hosted on the OU server and visible only to their tutor and other students on the course, and to any one else to whom the student had given their URL (or Web link). Students were able to link to online resources within their blogs but their blogs were not openly visible to the world.

2. Ten students (mean age 43.5 years, range 29-54 years) (60% female and 40% male) enrolled on an online OU Masters course (course B in Table 1)–*Innovations in eLearning* – which was part of the same MA programme as course A (above). This particular course focused on exploring the application of new technologies to educational settings. The students were given only *one* standalone blogging activity in which they summarised four case studies (out of a total of ten) and shared their summaries with fellow students in their blogs. The students could gain extra marks in their first assignment by including quotes from other students' case-study posts to support their own arguments. Beyond this, they could use their blogs as they wished. Students used an asynchronous text-based discussion forum and email as well as blogs. Eight of these ten students had studied the 'The eLearning Professional' course, and three had been interviewed previously by us. The students were provided with a blog with the same socio-technical configuration as described above in 1 (for the first set of participants) (in our paper, Kerawalla *et. al.*, 2009, we have reported our research on blogging by students on this course).

3. Ten distance education students (mean age 45.2 years, range 30- 56 years) (50% female and 50% male) who blogged autonomously about a wide variety of OU Masters or undergraduate courses (e.g. Geology, Ecology, Ancient Greek, Philosophy and Photography). These students started blogging of their own volition, using various off-the-shelf, freely available, blogging software. All but one of the students made the content of their blog visible to the world. They had been studying between one and three years and had blogged about one to fourteen courses, all of which contained no course-directed blogging activities. Some students maintained a single blog whilst others started a new blog with every new course; the number of blogs per student ranged from one to four. There was variation in whether or not the OU study-related content represented all of the total content of their blog/s (2 students), most of the total content of their blog/s (3

students), or part of the total content of their blog/s (5 students).

4. Ten PhD students (mean age 31.5 years, range 23-48 years) (50% female and 50% male) who blogged autonomously about their research and/or experiences of carrying out a PhD. They used a variety of freely-available blogging software and their blogs were open to the world. They were registered with the OU (4 students), other UK universities (5 students), and one student was studying in the Netherlands. Their research was in Computer Science, Mathematics, Health and Social Care, Art, and Psychology. They had been involved with research-related blogging between six months to five years. Four were full-time students and six were part-time students. There was variation between whether PhD-related posts constituted all of their total blog posts (5 students), most of their total blog posts (3 students), or part of their total blog posts (2 students).

We adopted a common methodology in our research with the four sets of participants listed in Table 1. First, we developed a generic semi-structured interview schedule for students. Following this, we created additional questions for each separate study (with each different set of participants) reflecting the nature of the differ-ent learning contexts. Interview questions in the generic interview schedules were derived from the literature and also from our research questions described in Table 1.

Secondly, we analysed the blogs prior to interviewing students. Our aim was to identify broad types of blog content (e.g. reflection, sharing photos, catharsis, or evaluating a paper) and any additional questions to be addressed in individual interviews. Finally, analysis of the blogs was fol-lowed-up by an audio-recorded, semi-structured, telephone interview with each student.

Using the research questions to guide us through the collated data, we performed a dual-coder qualitative inductive analysis (by the first two authors of this chapter) of the various accounts of students' experiences and their perceptions to identify the emerging themes, sub-themes and the inter-relationships between them. This involved: collecting the data into a Microsoft Word© docu-ment; reading the different sociological accounts in detail to identify the top-level common themes; the lower-level themes were found from multiple readings of the data; and the cataloguing scheme was validated through dual-coding in order to ensure that the sorting criteria were operation-alised effectively and that the sorting process was consistent.

The process was iterative and the two research-ers met weekly to examine any discrepancies.

Table 1. Research questions and four groups of students (participants)

	Research questions	MA students on course A	MA students on course B	Autonomous course-related bloggers	Autonomous PhD bloggers
1	How do students use their blogs: what does blogging achieve, and how?	✓	✓	✓	✓
2	What are students' experiences of blogging and what are their perceptions of its role in their learning?	✓	✓	✓	✓
3	What are the challenges of writing in a public space?	✓	✓	✓	✓

Table 2. *An overview of the authors' research into blogging in higher education*

Phase	Empirical research and consolidation	Research outputs
1. Elicitation	Interviews with students on a Masters level course (course A), and analysis of their blogs	-An understanding of blogging behaviours within the context of this course -- Identification of four emergent themes that represent the main factors students attend to when blogging
2. Elicitation	Interviews with students on a second Masters level course (course B), and analysis of their blogs	-An understanding of blogging behaviours within the context of this course and how they differed to students in phase 1 - Application of the four themes identified in phase 1, to analysis of phase 2 interviews
3. Consolidation		-Development of a framework to guide students' course-related blogging based upon the four emergent themes from phases 2 and 3.
4.Elicitation	Interviews with students studying a variety of OU courses, who blogged about them of their own volition, and analysis of their blogs	- An understanding of the blogging behaviours of these students
5. Elicitation	Interviews with PhD students from the OU and other institutions, who blogged about their research of their own volition, and analysis of their blogs	- Application of the four themes identified in phase 1 to the analysis of phase 4 and 5 interviews
6. Consolidation		- Reconfigured framework to take account of the fifth emergent theme identified in phases 4 and 5

These were resolved through discussion, and the sort criteria (the themes) were merged and documented each time. The process was repeated through different subsets of data until discrepancies were minimized. Each time, the categories of themes and sub-themes became more concrete and more fully articulated.

The research programme is summarised in Table 2.

During phase 1, (see Table 2) our qualitative analysis of interviews with the students revealed four emergent themes:

1. perceptions of, and utility of, the *audience* (defined as whoever reads the student's blog)
2. perceptions of, and utility of, the blogging *community* (defined as the group/s of people to whom a student may feel attached to through blogging)
3. perceptions of, and utility of, *comments* (defined as the communication between students through use of the commenting facility in their blogs)

4. *presentation* of the students' work in their blog in terms of grammar, spelling and academic rigour etc

In phases 2, 4 and 5 as listed in Table 2, our aim was to validate the four themes found in phase 1, so we looked for evidence of these themes in our interview data. However, we kept an open mind for the emergence of additional themes. These four themes occurred in the interview data of phases 2, 4 and 5. The analysis of the interview-data in phases 4 and 5 revealed a fifth theme: 'use of the blog content as a product'. This refers to how students used the *content of their blog* once it has been posted (e.g., as a revision aid).

In phase 3, which involved consolidation from the research in phases 1 and 2, we developed a framework encapsulating the four themes we had identified so far. Once we had identified the fifth emergent theme 'use of the blog content' in phases 4 and 5, we reconfigured the framework in phase 6 to include the fifth theme. Figure 1 shows the consolidated framework. The framework illustrates the process, or activity, of blogging, as well as the outcome of the blogging activity which is the content of the student's blog. The four themes that represent the activity of blogging are mutually constitutive and the dashed lines in Figure 1 visually represent this relationship. For example, a community is constituted by the audience; comments come from the audience and/or community; and blog content is presented to the audience and/or community. The double-headed arrow linking the process of blogging to the product (blog content) represents two things:

- the way in which the content of an active blog is not a static artefact but instead is evolving with each new post; and
- that the content of previous posts may affect what is being actively written in a new post. For example, a post about a particular psychological theory may build upon an earlier post on a similar topic.

In the following sections of this chapter we will:

- describe the contexts in which each of the student groups (Table 1) were blogging;
- present the opinions of students engaged in course-directed blogging regarding the suitability of the suggested activities to blogging;
- discuss these students' views on how blogging was used in conjunction with an online text-based discussion forum that was also available on their courses;
- provide an overview of how the students in each of the four phases addressed working in a public space, in terms of their audience, community, comments and the presentation of their blogs; and
- discuss how the students made use of the content of their blog once it had been posted.

COURSE-DIRECTED BLOGGING ACTIVITIES IN PHASES 1 AND 2

Most of the students on courses A and B undertook the blogging activities that were suggested by their respective courses. In this section, we describe these activities and present students' perceptions about the extent to which they thought that the activities were suited to blogging. Also, we discuss students' views about the way in which blogs and blogging were integrated alongside the asynchronous text-based discussion forum.

Figure 1. Framework representing the activity of blogging and the blog as the end-product

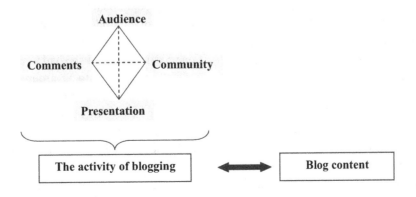

Reflective Writing

Five students studying course A in phase 1 of our research, said that they thought blogging was a good way of carrying out their reflective activities. The following reasons were cited by them:

- their reflections were open for others to comment on;
- they could learn about the reflective process by reading the blogs of others; and
- they could 'think aloud' in their personal space (blog); ask others for help; make links between concepts; and ask themselves questions.

However, some students found that reflecting in their blog was problematic because:

- it was difficult to sit down at a computer and engage in *"directed"* or *"artificial"* reflection on demand;
- the unstructured blogging space offered no opportunity for scaffolding reflection compared to their previous experience of using a template with structured questions; and
- some students felt self-conscious and inhibited about revealing their 'personal' thoughts and reflections to others.

Two of the ten participants avoided the blogging activities on this course. They said they could not find a use for blogging and that they were happy with their pre-existing learning approaches.

Ten of the fifteen students on course A said that they had developed a clearly defined role for their blog in relation to other tools such as the asynchronous text-based discussion tool and email. They cited two reasons for this:

Firstly: a blog is owned by the **individual** student and is **personalised**. It is a space for personal learning, thinking, planning, note-taking, reflections and opinions. It is a space where a student can socialise and *"let my hair down".* Family photographs and humour can accompany academic work. Blog posts may or may not receive a response (through on-line comments to individual posts). On the other hand, a forum is an impersonal shared discussion space that is usually more formal and where responses are expected. Also, writing in a forum is short, impersonal and more concise and reveals less about the student as an individual.

Secondly: the individual nature of a blog means that students are in **control** of the content. They can control, for example, the degree of formality of posted material, the amount written, colour-schemes, and they can decide whether or not to receive, accept and publish comments. In a forum a student has control over their own contributions only.

Summaries of Case Studies

Seven of the students studying course B in phase 2 of our research, expressed reservations about the suitability of the suggested activity of summarising some case-studies for blogging. First, they felt that the limited selection of 10 case studies for the total number of 102 students on this course meant that posts were repetitive. Secondly, the course materials stated that the students could write as little or as much as they liked and did not suggest that students critique what they had read. This meant that many summaries did not offer engaging opinions or raise questions. This resulted in some of the students reading each other's blog-posts solely to meet the course requirements and one participant said she had to change the focus of her assignment to fit around the blog posts that she could find. Another student did not post anything in his blog but used others' posts in his assignment to gain the extra marks. However, one student preferred this activity of summarising with follow-on discussions to the reflective learning activities that she had been encouraged to carry out previously as part of course A because issues of confidentiality in her workplace made reflection on her work-practices difficult.

Five students on the course B said that they had been confused about whether to post their case-study summaries in their blogs or in the asynchronous text-based discussion forum. Sometimes, the students used the forum to discuss the case studies, in which case they found it necessary to post their summaries in both locations. Consequently, there was often confusion about whether to write a comment on a post in the recipient's blog or in the forum. One student found this particularly problematic and eventually stopped using his blog because he felt *"there were too many places to have to go to".*

ADDITIONAL BLOGGING ACTIVITIES BY STUDENTS IN PHASES 1 AND 2

Many students on the two courses developed their own ways to use their blogs to support their own learning needs and some of the activities were beyond those suggested by their courses. Some of these activities were:

Resource-Network Building

Two students on course A blogged in order to build-up a resource network. They conceptualised their blogs as being a collection of resources, ideas, and contacts. They worked hard to make their posts appealing to their audience because they wanted to create a community with whom they could share resources. They sought and welcomed comments from others. These blogs contained little personal information apart from an introductory photograph of the student themselves, as the students saw their blogs as strictly study-related. They wanted to make their blogs places where fellow students would want to visit, and so they ensured that the blogs were well-written, clear and engaging.

Social-Network Building

Three students on course A built up a support network through blogging. They developed into a small community of students who used their blogs to reach out to each other for both academic and social support. Their posts were written in an informal, friendly style, and often addressed the reader directly. They contained high quality academic work that was peppered with details of the students' personal life, such as photographs of their children and also humour.

Blogging to Fulfil Course Requirements

Four students on course A said that would have preferred not to blog but did so because they thought it was required of them. They felt anxious and self-conscious about blogging in a public space because they felt that they might reveal their own perceived incompetence. These students did not seek comments from their fellow students, and did not involve themselves in the course blogging community. Their blogs tended to be rather formal and carefully crafted.

Self-Sufficient Blogging

Several students on both courses engaged in self-sufficient blogging where they blogged mainly for themselves. They did this for a variety of reasons: one student was travelling frequently and, therefore, had no time to communicate with others but yet felt the need for a central online repository. Other students preferred to work on their own, and some students on course B said they had no choice other than to blog for themselves as the case-study activity had failed to stimulate any course blogging community. These students used their blogs as a learning journal or as a place to collect their thoughts to maintain, or raise, their motivation to study on the course. The themes of audience and community did not feature highly for these students, although they were aware that their posts were public and were conscious of spell-checking and grammar, etc.

BLOGGING ACTIVITIES BY AUTONOMOUS BLOGGERS (PHASES 4 AND 5)

In this section we discuss the blogging activities of the autonomous bloggers studied in stages 4 and 5 of our research. These students were either enrolled on OU courses where blogging was not included, or they were undertaking a PhD. They decided to blog of their own volition.

Explaining or Describing to an Audience

Some students explained their learning materials to their audience and, in doing so, they were able to recognise salient points, clarify their understanding, reinforce their understanding and retain knowledge for assignments and exams. Describing learning experiences in a public space was also a useful form of catharsis for some students. Others said that writing helped them to develop their academic argumentation skills.

Sharing with an Audience

Some autonomous bloggers blogged to enlighten the audience about things they had done (e.g. to report on a conference). Also, they wrote about their research domain (e.g. details of a theory), or shared general life events with their family and friends. Two students conducted blogging to promote their on-line profile.

Asking for Feedback or Help

Many students used the commenting facility of their blogs to get feedback from others. For example, students criticised the content of

course-related reading materials, shared their own opinions and arguments with others, and asked for feedback. One undergraduate was confused about some details of a fieldtrip so asked for advice from her fellow students.

Being Motivated by Committing to an Audience

Several students made commitments to their known or unknown audience and doing this motivated them to meet their goals. This included posting work plans and assignment marks to be improved upon next time.

Becoming Part of a Community

Some of the autonomous bloggers said that they felt part of a community through blogging even though they were geographically distant. This enabled the development of friendships, the exchange of information, and recognition at conferences. However, some students discussed how they had become frustrated because the creation of a community had been difficult to achieve. This occurred if, for example, the student's interests lay within a niche area such as an ancient language that is no longer spoken.

The constitution of communities varied between the students, with some interested in maintaining contact with their friends only, whilst others worked hard to build up contacts within their field of interest. Others took the initiative of asking for feedback and comments: for example, one student contacted professional photographers to ask for their comments on photographs that she had taken as part of her photography course which she had posted on her blog.

Working on a Shared Project

One PhD student had used his blog to keep fellow students up-to-date with developments on a shared project. Commenting on blog posts, as well as face-to-face meetings, helped them all to exchange ideas and opinions.

Utilising Blog Content Once It Has Been Posted

Several of the autonomous bloggers used their blog as a resource, for example as a memento, or a revision aid, or a resource for assignments and publications. Some of the PhD students found that reading their previous posts was useful for making sense of their ideas and thoughts and for synthesising ideas and for identifying a research focus. Other students found their blog was a useful memory aid, such as a place marker or as a reminder for exam and assignment dates. Some students included photographs of field-trips and revision activities to help them to make sense of and remember what they had done.

To summarise what we have discussed so far: in the previous three sections we have addressed our research questions by illustrating how the students in our studies have used their blogs and what they have achieved through blogging. Their activities ranged from carrying out course-directed blogging activities to activities that they have engaged in, of their own volition, to meet their individual learning needs. We have demonstrated how these students have negotiated writing in a public space in terms of: their perceptions of, and use of their audience; the ways in which they have utilised the potential of a blogging community; the utility of receiving and giving comments; and the ways in which they have presented their work and/or thoughts in the blog. Also, we have illustrated some of the issues surrounding the integration of blogging into courses that utilise additional communication and collaboration tools, such as a discussion forum or e-mail.

In the next section we discuss how the research programme has led to the development of an empirically-grounded framework to raise awareness amongst educators or course designers and students of some of the characteristics of blogging.

TOWARDS AN UNDERSTANDING OF THE NATURE OF BLOGGING

The studies reported in this chapter have illustrated the variety of ways in which blogging can be conducted. This range of possibilities highlights how difficult it can be for course designers to decide how to utilise blogs to their full potential in their courses, and this can be even more challenging if blogs are to be used alongside other means of remote and/or face-to-face communication and collaboration.

The wide variety of pedagogical contexts, learning outcomes, e-learning technologies and background experiences of students suggests that, rather than prescribing rigid guidelines, it would be most appropriate for us to propose an empirically-grounded framework from our data and research. This framework may be used by both educators and students for raising their awareness of some of the features of the activity of blogging. Based on our research, we have developed and elaborated the framework presented in Figure 1 to include some questions in the framework presented in Figure 2. This framework in Figure 2 may be useful either for course designers when deciding whether blogging would be an appropriate activity for their students, or for students who are either thinking about blogging for themselves, or who are undertaking course-directed blogging activities (e.g. as in course B, above) or course-suggested blogging activities (e.g. as in course A, discussed above).

Figure 2 guides the 'user' of the framework about *blogging as an activity* and the ways in which the students' *blog content* could be used once it has been posted. The framework poses three main questions for course designers to consider. Question 1 and its associated sub-questions were derived from our interviews with students in phase 1 (see Table 2) of our research programme, when the students discussed how they differentiated blogging from their use of an asynchronous, text-based discussion forum. The sub-questions are designed to support initial decisions about the appropriateness of blogs.

Question 2 of the framework is based on the findings from our interviews with students in this research programme. We have suggested that answers to question 2 can be developed with reference to the four themes (audience, community, comments and presentation) that students in our research have identified as factors that mediate their blogging behaviour in a variety of learning contexts. Each of these themes is accompanied by a further set of sub-questions, drawn from our empirical research, which may help in decision-making about how to address each of the themes. Also, the data we have presented in this chapter could be considered as providing examples of successful blogging activities (such as reflective writing and learning, describing learning materials to an audience, or socialisation with other students) and examples of activities which have proved to be relatively uninspiring and unsuccess-

ful (such as asking students to write summaries of case studies in their blogs).

Question 3 of the framework refers to how the students could be encouraged to use the content of their blog once it has been posted. Our findings may also be used to as a trigger for thinking about and discussing the role of blog content, as, for example, a resource for assignments or course-work, materials for an e-portfolio, or as a revision aid.

We hope that the framework in Figure 2 begins to differentiate some of the features of blogging and blogs which are distinct from other asynchronous modes of online communication and collaboration such as the use of wikis and discussion forums, and synchronous modes such as face-to-face meetings, instant messaging, or Web and video conferencing tools. The framework highlights the features of blogging which may help both educators and students to think about the potential and appropriateness of

Figure 2. An empirically-grounded framework to guide blogging activities

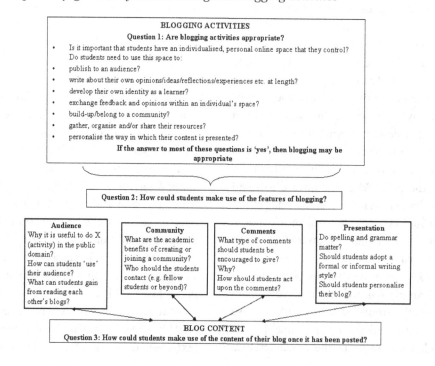

blogging in their own particular teaching and learning contexts.

FUTURE TRENDS

In this chapter, we have seen that the participants engaged in a variety of blogging activities such as socialisation, diary-keeping, sharing, conducting research, support-seeking or giving support, and carrying out activities suggested by courses. This rich mix shows that blogging can support both social and academic life. It may be that, in the future, course designers will need to acknowledge social blogging and support this alongside academic blogging. However, the extent to which students find blogging to be an important element of their study will vary depending on whether or not they are studying online or face to face and also on their preferred blogging behaviours. There will also be the issue of how to curb excessive social use whilst maintaining the institution's code of conduct, giving the opportunity for students to express themselves, and for them to network and build-up communities, if they choose to do so.

Despite the fact that blogging is perceived generally to be a social activity, several students in our research, whether they were blogging on a course or were autonomous, blogged for themselves (e.g., as a research or learning journal). This was in contrast to another set of students who found it beneficial to blog with their audience and community in mind. Thus, course designers may need to reconsider the commonly-held assumption that blogging is a social endeavour aimed at the sharing of experiences and thoughts with others.

CONCLUSION

We hope that the research that we have presented here has provided some insights into students' blogging behaviours and the ways in which blog-ging can support learning. Our studies into the self-initiated blogging activities of undergraduates, Masters and PhD students have highlighted some of the ways in which students may engage with blogging to support their courses or research initiatives, outside the confines of institutional platforms, or course-provided tools. Self-initiated blogging by students has not received much attention by researchers in the past and may well become more important as this relatively new technology is increasingly adopted. What seems to be clear from our research is that self-expression through blogging is important, and that, against the backdrop of other social networking and sharing tools such as Facebook and YouTube, blogging that is strictly and only academic may be resisted by students if it does not sit comfortably with their exposure to blogs elsewhere.

We have used our findings to inform the development of a framework, for course designers and students, to raise their awareness of some of the features of blogging that differentiate it from other communication and collaboration tools, such as discussion forums, wikis and email. The open-ended nature of the questions in the framework makes it possible to think about blogging in terms of both academic and social purposes. We suggest that this framework could overcome some of problems reported in previous research, such as the hesitation of students to blog. This framework will guide course designers to adopt a student-centred approach to blogging and to think about how the *activity* of blogging (as opposed to the use of blogs as a technology) could support learning on their courses. Also, the framework encourages both educators and students to think about the socio-technical context of blogging and how/whether this may generate the potential for community-building.

We recognise that there are other types of blogging activities in higher education that need closer investigation, such as educators' blogs and students' group blogs. As higher education institutions develop virtual and personal learning environments and make blogs available to students throughout the period of their studies, further research will be needed to investigate, for example, the comparative utility of a student having a single blog across all courses and over a programme as opposed to a separate blog for each course. This will raise questions of how blogging behaviours evolve over time and whether and how they are continued when a programme of study comes to a close.

REFERENCES

Blood, R. (2006). Weblogs: A History and Perspective. *Rebecca's Pocket.* 07 September 2000. 25 October 2006. Retrieved 21st May 2008 from http://www.rebeccablood.net/essays/Weblog_history.html.

Boyd, D. (2006). A blogger's blog: exploring the definition of a medium. *Reconstruction* 6.4. Retrieved 21st May 2008 from http://reconstruction.eserver.org/064/boyd/shtml

Bruns, A., & Jacobs, J. (2006). *Uses of blogs.* New York: Peter Lang Publishing.

Conole, G., Dyke, M., Oliver, M., & Seale, J. (2004). Mapping pedagogy and tools for effective learning design. *Computers and Education, 43*(1), 17-33.

Dickey, M. (2004). The impact of Web-logs (blogs) on student perceptions of isolation and alienation in a Web-based distance-learning environment. *Open Learning, 19*(3), 279-291.

Du, H. S., & Wagner, C. (2007). Learning with Weblogs: enhancing cognitive and social knowledge construction. *IEEE Transactions of Professional Communication, 50*(1), 1-16.

Farmer, J. (2006). Blogging to basics: how blogs are bringing online learning back from the brink. In A. Bruns & J. Jacobs (Eds.), *Uses of Blogs* (pp. 91-103). New York: Peter Lang.

Herring, S., Scheidt, L., Bonus, S., & Wright, E. (2004). Bridging the Gap: A Genre Analysis of Weblogs. In *Proceedings of 37th Hawaii International Conference on System Sciences*, Hawaii. (*HICSS*-37). Los Alamitos: IEEE Computer Society Press. Retrieved 21st May 2008 from: http://csdl2.computer.org/comp/proceedings/hicss/2004/2056/04/205640101b.pdf

Homik, M., & Melis, E. (2006). Using Blogs for Learning Logs. *In Proceedings of ePortfolio*, Oxford UK.

Joinson, A. N. (2001). Self-disclosure in computer-mediated communication: The role of self-awareness and visual anonymity. *European Journal of Social Psychology, 31*, 177-192.

Kerawalla, L. J., Minocha, S., Conole, G., Kirkup, G., Schencks, M., & Sclater, N. (2007). Exploring students' understanding of how blogs and blogging can support distance learning in higher education. In S. Wheeler & N Whitton (Eds.), *Beyond control: learning technology for the social network generation.* Research Proceedings of the 14th Association for Learning Technology Conference (ALT-C 2007), Nottingham University, England UK; (pp. 169-178).

Kerawalla L. J., Minocha S., Kirkup G., & Conole G. (2008). Characterising the different blogging behaviours of students on an online distance learning course. *Learning Media and Technology, 33*(1), 21-33.

Kerawalla L. J., Minocha S., Kirkup G., & Conole G. (2009). A framework for blogging in Higher Education. *Journal of Computer Assisted Learning.* [electronic version]. Retrieved December 2008.

Krause, S. D. (2004). When blogging goes bad: a cautionary tale about blogs, email lists, discussion, and interaction. *Kairos*, *9*(1). Retrieved 21st May 2008 from http://english.ttu.edu/kairos/9.1/binder.html?praxis/krause/index.html

Lenhart, A., & Fox, S. (2006). *Bloggers. A portrait of the internet's new storytellers.* Report for Pew Internet and American Life Project. Washington DC.

Nardi, B. A., Schiano, D. J., & Gumbrecht, M. (2004). Blogging as social activity, or, would you let 900 million people read your diary? In *Proceedings of the 2004 ACM conference on Computer supported cooperative work,* New York, (pp. 222-228).

Oravec, J. A. (2003). Blending by blogging: Weblogs in blended learning initiatives. *Journal of Educational Media, 28*(2-3), 225-233.

Penrod, D. (2007). *Using blogs to enhance literacy: The next powerful step in 21st century learning.* London: Rowman & Littlefield Education.

Salam, P. (2003). *Salam Pax: The Baghdad Blog.* London: Guardian Books.

Scoble, R., & Israel, S. (2006). *Naked Conversations: How blogs are changing the way businesses talk with customers.* New Jersey, US: John Wiley & Sons.

Weller, M. J. (2007). *Virtual Learning Environments - using, choosing and developing your VLE.* Oxford: Routledge.

Weller, M., Pegler, C., & Mason, R. (2005). Use of innovative technologies on an e-learning course. *Internet and Higher Education, 8,* 61-71.

Williams, J., & Jacobs, J. (2004). Exploring the use of blogs as learning spaces in the higher education sector. *Australasian Journal of Educational Technology, 20*(2), 232-247.

KEY TERMS

Blog: Weblog or blog is a Web publishing tool. Functionality of different blogging software varies but, generally, blog entries or posts may include a variety of materials including text, video files, sound files, photographs or screen shots, and URLs/hyperlinks to other Web pages or blogs. Readers can leave comments for the blogger(s) (i.e. the person(s) who own the blog). Access to blogs can be controlled by the blogger(s) so that, for example, it may be accessible to the world, or to a small group of friends, or it may be private and visible to the blogger(s) only.

Blog Post: The term 'post' can be a verb or a noun. Noun: entries to a blog are called 'posts'. Posts are usually in reverse chronological (date) order, with the most recent appearing first. Verb: a blogger 'posts' material to their blog.

Blogging: To write entries in, add material to, or to maintain a Weblog.

Distance Education: The delivery of education to students who are not physically on site. Students do not attend courses in person, but teachers and students may communicate through the exchange of printed media (e.g. books or course materials) or electronic media (e.g. email, blogs, wikis, asynchronous or synchronous discussion forums).

Higher Education: In the UK, this refers to degree level, Masters level, or PhD level education (usually) for people aged over 18 years.

Reflection: It is the re-examination and re-interpretation of one's experiences. It is introspective contemplation of the contents or qualities of one's own thoughts or experiences. Experience on its own does not guarantee learning. It is the product of reflecting on that experience that helps to acquire deeper insights.

Socialisation: Socialisation is one of the outcomes of blogging where the Web is being used as a medium to interact with people and 'socially' network with them. Socialisation is about people being able to interact with one another and establish connections on one or more levels by sharing ideas, views and information.

Chapter XVII
Blogs as a Social Networking Tool to Build Community

Lisa Kervin
University of Wollongong, Australia

Jessica Mantei
University of Wollongong, Australia

Anthony Herrington
University of Wollongong, Australia

ABSTRACT

This chapter examines blogging as a social networking tool to engage final year preservice teachers in reflective processes. Using a developed Web site, the students post their own blogs and comment upon those of others. The authors argue that opportunity to engage with this networking experience provides avenue for the students to consider their emerging professional identity as teachers. The blogging mechanism brought together the physical university context and virtual online environment as students identified, examined and reflected upon the intricacies of what it means to be a teacher. The authors hope that examining the findings that emerged from this research will inform other educators as to the affordances of blogging as a social networking tool.

INTRODUCTION

A recent US survey conducted by Pew Internet and American Life Project found that eight percent of internet users, or about 12 million American adults, keep a blog while thirty-nine percent of internet users, or about 57 million American adults, read blogs (Lenhart & Fox, 2006). This social networking phenomenon is not confined to the pursuit of leisure but is also seen as a strategy for professional learning through shared reflection on theory and practice. The professional identities of teachers and preservice teachers can potentially benefit from this experience.

This chapter explores the use of blogging within the context of a final year university subject for teachers in the Faculty of Education at the University of Wollongong, Australia. Using authentic learning (Herrington & Oliver, 2000) as a theoretical framework, the 'Beginning and Establishing Successful Teachers' (BEST) Website was created. Blogging opportunities were incorporated within the Website design to foster and support social networking amongst site users.

The chapter describes how providing students with opportunities to interact within both the physical university and the virtual Website communities led to reflection, networking and identification of professional goals, all of which contributed to their identity as teachers. In particular we examine how blogging as a tool facilitated reflection for shared understandings as individuals moved between two spaces. The virtual community afforded students opportunities for articulation of their own understandings and engagement with the experiences of others. Supporting and enriching this was the physical context, where 'theory' and professional relation-ships were explored through the more structured environment of tutorial workshops. The inter-action between the virtual and real contexts, captured through blogging activity, contributed to each individual's professional identity. This is represented in Figure 1.

TEACHER AS REFLECTIVE PRACTITIONER

In describing teaching as a 'profession of con-science', where teachers are accountable to themselves, the students and their parents, Maarof (2007) identifies the practice of reflecting on one's teaching as important in allowing teachers to better understand their philosophy of learning and to identify strengths and limitations of the decisions they make. Teachers who are reflective in their approach to teaching can make meaning-ful change within their classrooms, schools and broader communities because they use a critical approach to questioning what it is they do in their classrooms, why they have made such decisions and how their practice might be improved (Bintz & Dillard, 2007).

Rather than a simple tool for thinking about teaching, reflection is defined as a complex and rigorous process that takes the practitioner in a 'forward moving spiral' linking theory with prac-tice and practice with theory (Rodgers, 2002, p. 863). For teachers to be able to engage with such a cycle, they require sustained opportunities to explore both theory and practice within socially supported communities that deepen not only their professional identity, but also their understanding of the skills required for reflection (McCormack, Gore & Thomas, 2004).

For preservice and early career teachers in particular, opportunities for reflection on their own learning and the ways that they achieve new understanding are valuable in fostering ac-tive learners whose interest resides in pursuing ongoing professional growth (Bransford, Derry,

Figure 1. Blogging for professional identity

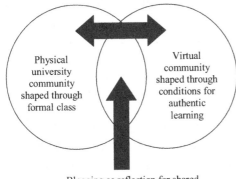

Blogging as reflection for shared
understandings to develop
professional identity

Berliner & Hammerness, 2005; McCormack et.al., 2004). The period of transition from preservice to inservice teacher is identified in the literature as a time where support in developing the skills of reflection is crucial for the construction of professional knowledge (Griffin, 2003; Peters & LeCornu, 2006). It is through opportunities to 'practice and reflect on teaching while enrolled in their preparation programs' that teachers can develop the necessary reflective tools for interpreting their observations and experiences in the early years of teaching (Hammerness, Darling-Hammond & Bransford, 2005, p. 375) and to build their professional identities.

TEACHER PROFESSIONAL IDENTITY

The notion of professional stages within a career is acknowledged in the literature (for example, Guskey, 2002). Our experiences concur that a critical stage for teachers is when they move from being a preservice teacher in the university context to an early-career teacher in a school. Such change requires significant adjustments be made to one's professional identity; adjustments that can be achieved through the development of reflective practices.

Identity is a concept used in the field of social sciences to investigate human behaviour (Jepperson, Wendt & Katzenstein, 1996; Nicolosi, 1991; Turner, 1975) arguing a clear relationship between the way people behave and how this defines their identities (Burke & Reitzes, 1981; Sparks & Shepherd, 1992; Stets & Burke, 2000). As people interact with each other within their environments, they learn about the norms, values and beliefs of the communities within which they operate. This knowledge forms identities as individuals come to know who they are, what they are, how they should behave and what they still need to know.

Learning a profession means learning about the culture of the occupation (Lacey, 1995). Blackledge (2002) argues that each profession has its own disposition and learnt behaviour. Thus, a teacher as a professional needs specific knowledge and skills related to curriculum, pedagogical understandings and awareness of how children learn and their impact upon each of these. Sachs (1999) observes that professional identities include retrospective and prospective identities; retrospective identities use the past to explain the present within the profession, while prospective identities examine the future nature of the profession. Allen (2005) details that aspects of teacher professional identities are not taught; rather teachers' past critical incidents including the workplace and an individual's professional and social networks shape them. These perspectives need to be explored through reflection to consider how individual experiences can come together to create shared meanings and understandings.

Connelly and Clandinin (1988) observe that teachers are not necessarily interested in what they know and what they can do when they reflect upon their role in the profession. Rather, they question their own identity within a situation. They argue teachers appear more interested in understanding their immediate professional situation in connection with their previous personal and professional experiences. Thus, instead of the question what do I know, or what can I do, for many teachers their interest is in the question who am I, what relationship do I have with the learner, what is my relationship with school leaders, and how have my personal experiences contributed to my development as a teacher. These questions demonstrate the role played by both the physical workplace and the individual's networks in the development of a teacher's professional identity.

Professional identity theory indicates that teachers continually develop their own understandings of the teaching profession as they reshape and modify their understandings of their role. Their experiences in the classroom as teachers, the culture of the school of employment, and interactions with other teachers and key stakeholders all contribute to ongoing development of professional identity. Lockyer, Patterson, Rowland and Hearne (2007) describe:

as teachers move from their preservice and induction stages through competency building and into enthusiastic and growing, they are eager to develop skills, support their peers, and investigate and implement new practices and innovations (p. 332).

Given these understandings, it is necessary to consider how social software can be used to provide a forum through which teachers can reflect upon their own experiences, and engage in professional dialogue with others to develop shared community ontologies.

THE NEED FOR SOCIAL SUPPORT

Dewey (1937) has long argued the importance of social activity to support learning. Social activism theory promotes learning that emerges from students' interests, an integrated approach and learning as a way of understanding the complexity of culture and individual roles within that culture (Krause, Bochner & Duchesne, 2003). Lankshear and Snyder (2000) concur in their definition of learning as "...becoming proficient in social practices" (p. 42). This is further reinforced by Gee (2004) who argues, "...people learn best when their learning is part of a highly motivated engagement with social practices they value" (p. 77). Teaching is a complex profession where much learning can occur through social engagement with others.

Whilst the social nature of learning is acknowledged, so too is the notion of belonging to social groups while retaining individuality. This is seen as paramount to active engagement with learning. Gee (2003) names three key require-

ments for active learning: 'experiencing the world in new ways, forming new affiliations, and preparation for future learning' (p. 23). Burnett (2002) describes 'learning comes about when we understand what motivates us or attracts us to a particular set of ideas or practices' (p. 142). Such perspectives can help to explain what happens when people interact within virtual communities as formal and informal educational spaces. For early career teachers, the opportunity to engage with others helps to establish networks to identify and achieve learning goals. The possibilities for social software to facilitate and support such networks are enormous.

For some time, a wide body of research has focused on the value of 'Communities of Practice' (for example, Gee, 2004; Lave & Wenger, 1991). The notion of apprentices working and learning within a group who share the same vision, practices and goals characterises this research. Lave and Wenger's (1991) caution about the relationship between definitions of Communities of Practice and how these may actually transpire in individual settings has characterised the research presented within the chapter. While we acknowledge the fundamentals within theories surrounding the social nature of learning, and consider how these might look as individuals participate in both physical and virtual communities of practice, using these to create shared community ontologies remains our focus.

SOCIAL NETWORKING TO 'UNLEASH' PROFESSIONAL IDENTITY THROUGH REFLECTION

Computer Supported Social Networks (CSSN) have been examined for some time. Wellman, Salaff, Dimitrova, Garton, Gulia and Haythornthwaite (1996) identify that such networks began in the 1960s with the US Government's use of an *Electronic Information Exchange System* to connect users with large university computers. Since this time, there has been exponential growth in the number and range of social networks. Sites such as Facebook, Classmates.com, Flickr, Fotolog and MySpace have re-shaped our understandings of what it means to belong to a "group" and interact with others within those spaces. Gee (2003) describes that interaction within the 'contemporary high-tech global world' poses a range of challenges to one's identity (p. 3-4). To meet such challenges it is necessary to consider contexts, issues and dilemmas associated with the complexity of the profession.

The membership of social networks contributes significantly to the interaction that occurs within them. For there to be a sense of affiliation and support within the group participants need to be aware of and support the founding philosophies of the group to establish a sense of common goals to shape interactions (Donath, 1999). Blanchard and Horan (1998) observe that virtual communities are most powerful when they develop around physically-based communities and expand upon needs and interests.

Notions of identity appear integral within virtual communities. Gee (2003) notes that 'We are fluid creatures in the making, since we make ourselves socially through participation with others in various groups' (p. 4). As such, awareness of oneself and other members within the community become paramount as interactions are assessed according to judgements about reliability, accuracy and trustworthiness of the source. Donath (1999) suggests that the experiences offered within virtual communities and their 'claims of real-world expertise or history' are closely connected with how individual participants are received and valued within the community. It is important to carefully consider the rationale for social software and its goals in bringing together community around issues and problems that are relevant to the real or authentic world of that community.

AUTHENTIC LEARNING AS A THEORETICAL FRAMEWORK

Research has identified the traditional learning environment of educational institutions as insufficient in meeting the needs of the modern student (Harste, 2003; Jonassen, 2003; Oblinger, 2005; Anstey & Bull, 2006; Herrington & Herrington, 2006; Leu, Mallette, Karchmer & Kara-Soteriou, 2005). A principal criticism of traditional teaching approaches is the reliance on delivery of knowledge by 'discipline experts' and passive reception and retention of content by learners in an environment that separates theory from practice (Herrington & Herrington, 2006). Compounding the issue, Lombardi (2007) argues that many university students operate within a dualistic learning model – the notion that there is a single 'right' answer and it is the obligation of the teacher to reveal it and therefore such learners prefer traditional teaching methods. Although 'ambiguity and conflicting perspectives' are identified as important in the development of critical thinkers and problem solvers, such a state is uncomfortable for many learners interested in discovering a single truth (Lombardi, 2007, p. 10). The challenge then, is for educators to maintain the supportive learning environment, while modifying the way they operate in order to facilitate connected learning experiences that more accurately reflect the expectations placed on learners in the community today – authentic learning experiences.

Authentic learning tasks are defined as the ordinary practices of a culture (Brown, Collins & Duguid, 1989) simulated in real world contexts to support learners' development of 'survival skills they...need in the 21st century' (Jonassen, 1995, p. 60). Authentic learning tasks are identified as a teaching approach better suited to the needs of the modern learner because of the potential for incorporating the typical problems and challenges present in the real community in the learning experiences of the student (Herrington & Herrington, 2006; Jonassen, 2003).

Herrington and Oliver (2000) argue that authentic learning experiences:

- reflect the way knowledge will be used in real life
- offer opportunities for exploration of problems
- provide access to expert modelling of real life processes
- allow for engagement with multiple roles and perspectives throughout the process
- provide opportunities for the collaborative construction of knowledge
- encourage reflection on learning and articulation of growing understandings
- offer coaching and scaffolding, from teachers and other learners
- employ authentic assessment of the learning

Authentic learning experiences encourage learners to reflect on their learning in relation to the effect this new understanding will have on their personal outlooks and actions (Bonnet, 1997) and the ways they can move toward expert practice (Teal, Leu, Labbo & Kinzer, 2002). For students in the late stages of their tertiary study and the early stages of their teaching careers, this move toward expert practice is crucial. A learning community intersected by both physical and virtual interactions provides authenticity for these students' learning experiences as they reflect on the theory learned throughout their study in light of their initial teaching experiences.

Description of the BEST Website

An online community of learners called the "BEST site: Beginning and Establishing Successful Teachers" was developed specifically for primary and early childhood students in the Faculty of Education at the University of Wol-

longong. A theoretical framework of authentic learning underpins the content and structure of the site by drawing on the principles of authentic learning experiences identified by Herrington and Oliver (2000) in its design. A Weblog feature within the site provides space where students can post blogs about their teaching experiences. Here, the users can not only reflect critically on their own experiences and developing expertise, but also compare and comment on the experiences of others (Herrington, Herrington, Kervin & Ferry, 2006). Figure 2 depicts the home page for the BEST site.

Blogging is identified as a valuable social practice as opportunities are afforded to reflect on the teaching profession, to learn about oneself and to engage with others for professional learning (Cleine & Darcy, 2006). In this research, blogging was identified as an appropriate medium for facilitating and documenting the development of reflective practice for these early career teachers for a number of reasons. The blogs create a chronological record of the postings of the blog entries and subsequent postings from others within the community. These not only serve as a record of engagement and interaction, but also a text for further reflection. The opportunity to revisit blogs and to build on the posting in response to new understandings gathered from within the virtual or physical community of the classroom allows the blogger to reflect and think critically about their professional identity in response to the stories they have shared.

The genre of blogs was also considered to add unique qualities other virtual mediums (such as forums) may not have enabled. The flexiblility of blogs – they can mimic print based journals in content and layout or they can adopt multiple modes such as sound, movement and links to other sites (Lankshear & Knobel, 2005) - allow the blogger to engage with the reflective process at a level commensurate with their computer skills. Further, bloggers retain control over their learning because they choose the content for discussion,

Figure 2. The BEST site

the layout of the text and they can accept or delete comments posted by others. Finally, bloggers can access their own and others' blogs at anytime, providing the type of 'on the go' learning identified as important for learners today (Beldarrain, 2006; Lombardi, 2007; Anstey & Bull, 2006).

Links between the principles of authentic learning environments and the affordances offered by the BEST site for blogging are identified in Table 1.

The Faculty of Education at the University of Wollongong has an approximate enrolment of fourteen hundred undergraduate and postgraduate students. The areas of preservice teacher education include Early Childhood, Primary, Secondary and Physical & Health Education. A Bachelor of Teaching degree can be completed over a three-year period (full time). Each year two semesters are offered (Autumn and Spring); a full time student can study up to four subjects per semester. Successful completion of the three-year degree qualifies the participant to teach in primary schools within the state of New South Wales. Upon completion of a Bachelor of Teach-

ing degree, participants are eligible to apply for a fourth year of study to complete the Bachelor of Education (Primary) or apply for Bachelor of Education (Honours) degree. This qualification enables the participant to teach in most other Australian states and overseas. These students are engaged with the field as they are already qualified teachers. Their part-time mode of study and demands on time are catered for with a mixture of on campus and virtual networking practices.

Unlike many similar sites, the BEST site does not attempt to create communities from scratch. Instead, it builds on existing communities—those established at university among students. Study in the Faculty of Education is cohort-based, where students enrol full time and progress with their peers through the structured years of training. Generally students who enrol in the fourth year of study for the Bachelor of Education do so at a part-time level while working as either part-time or full-time teachers. During this fourth year of study there are compulsory subjects for students, one of which is entitled *Reflective Practice* and is the focus of this research.

Table 1. Connections between principles for authentic learning and the blogging component of BEST

Principles of authentic learning environments (Herrington & Oliver, 2000)	Affordances of the BEST site for blogging
Authentic learning environments: - reflect the way knowledge will be used in real life	**Structure and blogging affordances of the BEST site:** - problems explored through blogs are identified by undergraduate students and early career teachers from their experiences in classrooms - problems are shared through story and dialogue
- offer opportunities for exploration of problems	- others within the community can respond to stories shared through blogs - 'anytime' access to the site for exploration of the problems shared by others affords community members the time necessary for exploration of the problems shared
- provide access to expert modelling of real life processes - offer coaching and scaffolding, from teachers and other learners	- access to blogs is given to mentors and subject tutors who are experienced classroom practitioners, available to respond to complex problems with deeper understandings - links are provided on the site to authoritative sources such as policy documents, trusted Websites and experienced teachers who act as mentors to inform the blogger's reflections
- allow for engagement with multiple roles and perspectives throughout the process	- sharing of knowledge within the community allows members to adopt different roles as they respond to problems according to their level of experience and expertise
- provide opportunities for the collaborative construction of knowledge	- sharing experiences through publicly posted blogs allows for negotiation of understandings through collaboration
- encourage reflection on learning and articulation of growing understandings	- communication tools enable and support reflection on both personal blogs and the blogs of others
- employ authentic assessment of the learning	- learners within the community identify themes emerging from analysis of their blog postings, identifying areas of growth and learning over time

RESEARCH METHODOLOGY

In 2007, 60 students completed the *Reflective Practice* subject, posted blogs and provided a written report. The written report required students to consider different professional decisions, issues and challenges that they then describe in their blogs. Each student was required to consider:

- The underlying issues that contribute to their complexity;
- The moral, practical and other dilemmas that underlie the decisions, issues and challenges;
- The social and educational consequences of these;
- The social, institutional and political contexts these are located within and the impact of these upon the work of a teacher;

- Professional support that can be connected with to further explore the decisions, issues and challenges.

Each student provided significant text-based data for analysis through both their blog reflections, and their own analysis of these in the prepared report. This provided a foundation upon which we could examine their emerging professional identity. Through the analysis of collected data, the researchers were searching for answers to the following three questions:

- What happened when the students were encouraged to create blogs?
- How did the students engage with the blogging tool as authors and readers?
- How did the blogging experience intersect with the affordances of the tool for social networking?

Blog entries and synthesis tasks were examined in connection with the researchers' own observations of students in the virtual and actual contexts using the following criteria:

- Frequency of student use of the BEST site through user log-in data, blog postings, comments made on other blogs and discussions of the blogging tool in university workshops
- Analysis of blog text
  - o Themes and issues explored within the blogs
  - o Language choices (such as modality of writing)
  - o Connections made between the theory of their university studies and the practical examples discussed
  - o Interaction between students through the blogs
- Analysis of synthesis task
  - o Themes and issues identified within the blogs
  - o Reflections as to why these themes and issues were prevalent
- Analysis of interaction during tutorials
  - o Students identifying 'like' minds and selecting them as study partners
  - o Contribution to class discussion on issues that were 'blogged'

Initial analysis was focused on content where categories were developed and instances recorded (Denzin & Lincoln, 1994). These categories were connected to the previously mentioned criteria. Once the content within the text was investigated, the researchers then focused on coding it into categories based on the emerging themes (Miles & Huberman, 1984). The analysis was comparative and interpretive. Conclusions were checked and discussed between the researchers.

RESEARCH FINDINGS FROM ANALYSIS OF BLOGS

Three key emerging themes were identified.

- ➤ Exploring the genre of a blog
- ➤ Student interactions with blogs and environment
- ➤ Examining the affordances of blogs

Each is explored in connection with data.

Exploring the Genre of a Blog

The blog differed from other genre that the students traditionally use in the university setting. The journal aspect of the blog provided the students with a space to vent their feelings, ideas, anxieties and understandings without the pressure associated with academic writing. One student's blog is representative of many of the students' reports about the nature of blogging,

'I liked that we could write using informal language. Because of this I did not have to worry about perfect grammar. Professional language is something I struggle with and something that I think loses marks for me in assignments... because we were only reflecting, I found it much easier to share my thoughts'.

Another described blogging as *'great being able to write freely without having to quote someone you agree with'*. It would appear that the opportunity to blog provided students the forum for exploration of their profession and professional identity while reducing the burden associated with traditional academic writing.

Although a blog is 'published' or 'saved' onto the site, the opportunity to edit the text remains available to the author. Analysis of the data indicated that some of the students revisited their blogs in response to new understandings emerging from discussions in tutorial workshops (both the *Reflective Practice* subject and others within the course), academic reading, casual teaching experiences or through the postings and comments of others. One student reported, *'Blogging is a good way of reflecting – good way of recording your thoughts and going back to them...',* while another indicated the value of blogs in developing reflective practice, *'... it was interesting to read what I had written over the course of the semester...what worked and didn't etc. I can look back on it to improve my teaching practice'.* The physical interactions occurring through the tutorial workshops were observed to provide students with new perspectives, deeper understandings or increased empathy with their colleagues. Blog entries included such comments as *'I agree with...', 'In light of the readings this week...', 'I found myself taking a lot of what* [tutor] *had suggested onboard', 'As many people in the class today may have felt...'.* The flexibility provided by the blog genre supported students as they made changes to existing entries or created new ones. No blog need be considered finished, its incomplete state allows the author to make tentative constructions of meaning in the face of ambiguous and complex perspectives. Further, their familiarity and comfort with the blog genre emphasised its connection to regular life activities.

Student Interactions with Blogs and Environment

The students and tutors met in both the physical environment of the University and the virtual community through the blogs on the BEST site. These connected interactions between community members were observed to foster genuine relationships and a trusting rapport. Analysis of the blogs revealed empathy between fellow teachers as they struggled with common issues such as classroom management and teacher expectations. For example, one student blogged about her 'worst teaching experience'; *'I found that it's not until you're on your own in the classroom as a casual teacher, with little knowledge of the students that you face the worst possible scenarios'.* The student went on to describe a confrontation with a Year 6 child resulting in the child running away. Another student empathised, *'I think you did all you could in that worst situation. I am yet to have an experience like that, but I'm sure I would find it rather confronting'.* The physical environment further strengthened the connection these two students made through the virtual community as they later collaborated on a group assessment task for this subject. Comments posted in response to other blog entries provide further evidence of the growing rapport and sense of community felt by these members; *'I have had exactly the same bad experience!', 'I can definitely relate to what you say...', 'Nice point, I hadn't thought about* [that] *before'.* Such comments provide example of the social nature of their learning as they moved between physical and virtual communities.

The blogs allowed for spontaneous social networking within the community. Some students found the convenience of reflecting through blogs at times suitable to them was supportive of their developing reflections; one student, on returning from her first day of casual teaching, gushed, *'I had to come home and blog straight away!',* while others reported being able to access the postings at any time was both convenient and helpful. Most students reported reading the postings of others for a variety of purposes. Some described the benefit as providing ideas for personal reflections and alternative perspectives from their own. Others reported that reading others blogs demonstrated that their peers were experiencing similar issues and feelings as their own, resulting in a developing empathetic rapport between students. The final reflection of one student summarises the reports of many,

'A few times I read them before I wrote my own as sometimes I wasn't sure where to go with my writing. A few times I read their blogs and just thought, I know exactly what you're talking about, or, I've had that same experience which was good to know I wasn't the only one out there with those same experiences'.

Not all students found reading the blogs to be affirming, however, a small number reported that reading the blogs was *'intimidating'*, leaving them feeling inexperienced with much still to learn. This was a point of growth for one student, who said, *'It was intimidating reading the blogs of others',* but I also learnt from their blogs'.

Examining the Affordances of Blogs

The blogs provided a 'safe' environment for the students to record their reflections. Analysis of the content of the blog reflections revealed that the students felt comfortable and secure within the virtual community, as though the barriers existing in physical interactions were removed providing some anonymity in sharing. Insights into these beginning teachers' professional identity illustrated both insecurity and growing confidence. Reflections posted suggested a desire to share with the community that, although teaching was a challenge and many mistakes had been made, this teacher was coping and improving. For example, one teacher began a reflection about his final practicum experience; *'I made every mistake possible to even think about writing in blogs'.* However, he finished the posting with the observation, *'By the end of the practicum, I had begun to crawl out of the deep hole I had dug for myself... with lessons being taught that I will never forget and mistakes I will endeavour never to make again!!!!'.* Another student described having to *'get over fear and apprehension and take charge'* of a class which included students

with special needs. Although the student described a difficult beginning, she finished her blog reflection, *'Throughout the day we had our ups and downs but I found that I managed quite well... If I was to have this day over, I would go in with more control and not as scared and not worry about how the students would react to my being there'.*

The safe environment of the blogs also afforded the students the opportunity to explore relationships between themselves and the more experienced teachers they met through casual teaching. Still, the reflections revealed the attitude that although the early years of teaching are difficult, they can cope. A student observed that many of the teachers at her regular casual teaching school *'pretend I am not there because I am a casual teacher'.* She described the ways she had tried to build a relationship with these teachers (so far unsuccessfully), but concluded, *'I guess it takes a while to "fit in" to a school, especially as a casual teacher'.* Responding to observations such as these, a student within this community who was somewhat older with more teaching experience offered support through a blog entitled *'Casual teaching tips'* encouraging others to *'have a quick glance and see if you can get anything from it'.* Although the blog was posted on the BEST site, there was no compulsion for any student to follow the advice; the power to accept or reject remained with each person.

The opportunity to read the reflections of others within the virtual community allowed for exploration of a range of solutions to problems around professional identity. Data analysis revealed that reading alone (without posting a comment) was sufficient in building the social network within the community, as it allowed for identification of likeminded students who could be sought out in person for further professional networking. *'It was good to read other people's blogs and gain ideas or see that others were encountering similar issues and problems as well as successes'.* Most students described feeling initially anxious or vulnerable when authoring their own reflections because of their peer audience, but that this feeling subsided over time and with the understanding that there were many similarities between all members. *'I found this* [writing to an audience] *intimidating at first, but didn't give it much thought as the subject progressed'.*

Blogs as a social networking tool afforded the students opportunities to make personal explorations into the complex nature of professional identity and the way it grows and changes over time. The students reported feeling less isolated and better supported as they identified their experiences within the blogs, responded to the reflections of others and reflected on their shaping identities. Although reflecting through blogs was challenging and initially uncomfortable for many students, most identified it as beneficial. Blogging was initially described as *'intimidating', 'challenging', 'forced', 'daunting'* and *'difficult'*, but also as *'worthwhile', 'useful'* and *'providing a new outlook after deeper thinking'*. One student who at first described blogging as *'scary knowing that others were going to read it'* concluded her reflection saying *'the blogging really helped me to reflect on the choices and decisions I had made during my teaching'.* This finding would suggest that the nature of blogging is akin to many things in life, such as eating muesli or going to the dentist; no one likes it, but they do it because they know it's good for them!

Evidence of the value of blogging as a social networking tool lies in the identification of reflection as a worthwhile professional activity for teachers and also in the increased confidence of these students as beginning teachers. The power of networking and reflection are evident in the final blog made by one student who had struggled with the theoretical and academic nature of university study,

'I really enjoyed reflecting, but had it not been for the blogs, I probably wouldn't have done it. From writing and reading my blogs over again, I realise that I have skills that I didn't know. I would dismiss myself as a teacher that wasn't that fantastic – but after reading my blogs I actually do have some desirable skills'.

CONCLUDING COMMENTS

Participating in the process of creating and posting blogs appeared to provide avenue for these students to reflect on their emerging professional identity as teachers. Opportunity to share both similar and unique issues that arose provided scope to reflect individually and collaboratively as they examined the culture of their profession (Lacey, 1995). Our research revealed that these students were continually developing their understandings of their role as a teacher as they examined and reflected upon their role through their blogs.

The blogging mechanism enabled the physical and virtual contexts to come together in two key ways. As teachers of the *Reflective Practice* subject it gave us avenue to explore the reflections of the students, which then fed into subsequent teaching experiences. This enabled the 'forward moving spiral' described by Rodgers (2002) to come into play. For the students, it provided a virtual space where they could share the decisions, issues and challenges they faced as early career teachers, while also presenting opportunities to engage with the experiences of others as immediate professional situations were examined (Connelly & Clandinin, 1988). This supports the affordances of blogs described by Cleine and Darcy (2006).

What became critical throughout the entire experience was that the students set the parameters for blogging. While there was a requirement within the subject that they post blog entries, it was the students who determined what to share in each entry, the frequency of their postings and responses to others. The ability to edit their own text, and any text encapsulated as comment to their posting, meant that they retained ownership of the blogs. Further, the ability for the students to read other entries and/or respond to these, gave them more power as they made decisions about what to do with that information. For some students, this information fed into and stimulated their authorship of new blog entries; others made selections in the physical tutorial environment about who to sit next to, who to collaborate with on group tasks and the topics for conversation based on what they had read. We believe it is telling that from the sixty participants, only two selected not to read entries composed by others! These findings present example of 'on the go' learning essential for contemporary learners (Beldarrain, 2006; Lombardi, 2007; Anstey & Bull, 2006).

The networking opportunities that emerged from the blogging experience provided for focused and meaningful interactions to occur within both the physical and virtual environments. Students were able to explicate and articulate the different facets of their professional identity as they identified, examined and reflected upon the intricacies of what it means to be a teacher.

REFERENCES

Allen, S. (2005). *The missing link in alternative certification: Teacher identity formation*. Available [Online]: www.umbc.edu/llc/llcreview/2005/The_Missing_Link.pdf, Retrieved on 25 August 2006

Anstey, M., & Bull, G. (2006). *Teaching and learning multiliteracies: Changing times, changing literacies*. Kensington Gardens: International Reading Association and Australian Literacy Educators' Association.

Beldarrain, Y. (2006). Distance education trends: Integrating new technologies to foster student interaction and collaboration. *Distance Education, 27*(2), 139-153.

Bintz, W. P., & Dillard, J. (2007). Teachers as reflective practitioners: Examining teacher stories of curricular change in a 4th grade classroom. *Reading Horizons, 47*(3), 203-228.

Blackledge, A. (2002). The discursive construction of national identity in multilingual Britain. *Journal of Language, Identity, and Education, 1*(1), 67-87.

Blanchard, A., & Horan, T. (1998). Virtual Communities and Social Capital. *Social Science Computer Review, 16*(3), 293-307.

Bonnet, M. (1997). Computers in the classroom: Some values issues. In A. McFarlane (Ed.), *Information technology and authentic learning* (pp. 145-159). London: Routledge.

Bransford, J., Derry, S., Berliner, D., & Hammerness, K. (2005). Theories of learning and their roles in teaching. In L. Darling-Hammond & J. Bransford (Eds.), *Preparing teachers for a changing world: What teachers should learn and be able to do* (pp. 40-87). San Francisco CA: Jossey-Bass.

Brown, J. S., Collins, A., & Duguid, P. (1989). Situated cognition and the culture of learning. *Educational Researcher, 18*(1), 32-42.

Burke, J. & Reitzes, C. (1981). The Link between Identity and Role Performance. *Social Psychology Quarterly, 44*(2), 83-92.

Burnett, R. (2002). Technology, learning and visual culture. In I. Snyder (Ed.), *Silicon LIteracies: Communication, Innovation and Education in the Electronic Age* (pp.141-153) London: Routledge / Taylor & Francis Group.

Cleine, M., & Darcy, C. (2006). Blogging and professional learning. In B. Doecke, M. Howie & W. Sawyer (Eds.), *Only connect: English teaching, schooling and community* (pp. 166-178). Kent Town SA: Wakefield Press.

Connelly, M., & Clandinin, J. (1988). *Teachers as curriculum planners: Narrative experience.* New York: Teachers College Press.

Denzin, N., & Lincoln, Y. (eds). (1994). *Handbook of Qualitative Research.* Thousand Oaks, CA: Sage

Dewey, J. (1937) *Experience and education.* New York: MacMillan.

Donath, J. S. (1999). Identity and deception in virtual community. In P. Kollock & M. Smith (eds.). *Communities in Cyberspace* (pp. 29 – 59). London: Routledge.

Gee, J. P. (2003). *What video games have to teach us about learning and literacy.* New York: Palgrave MacMillan.

Griffin, A. (2003). 'I am a teacher - Oimigod!' The construction of professional knowledge for the beginning English teacher. In B. Doecke, D. Homer & H. Nixon (Eds.), *English teachers at work: Narratives, counter narratives and arguments* (pp. 312-325). Kent Town, SA: Wakefield Press in association with AATE.

Guskey, T. R. (2002). Professional development and teacher change. *Teachers and Teaching: Theory and Practice, 8*(3/4), 381-390.

Hammerness, K., Darling-Hammond, L., & Bransford, J. (2005). How teachers learn and develop. In D.-H. Linda & J. Bransford (Eds.), *Preparing teachers for a changing world: What teachers should learn and be able to do* (pp. 358-389). San Francisco CA: Jossey-Bass.

Harste, J. (2003). What do we mean by literacy now? *Voices from the middle, 10*(3), 8-12.

Herrington, A., & Herrington, J. (2006). What is an authentic learning environment? In A. Herrington & J. Herrington (Eds.), *Authentic learning environments in higher education* (pp. 1-13). Hershey, PA: Information Science Publishing.

Herrington, A., Herrington, J., Kervin, L. & Ferry, B. (2006). The design of an online community of practice for beginning teachers. *Contemporary Issues in Technology and Teacher Education, 6*(1), 120-132.

Herrington, J., & Oliver, R. (2000). An instructional design framework for authentic learning environments. *Educational Technology Research and Development, 48*(3), 23-48.

Jepperson, R., Wendt, A. & Katzenstein. P. (1996). Norms, identity, and culture in national security. In Katzenstein, P. *Culture and Security,* (pp. 33–78). New York: Columbia University Press.

Jonassen, D. (1995). Supporting communities of learners with technology: A vision for integrating technology with learning in schools. *Educational Technology, 35*(4), 60-63.

Jonassen, D. (2003). Designing research-based instruction for story problems. *Educational Psychology Review, 15*(3), 267-297.

Krause, K., Bochner, S., & Duchesne, S. (2003). *Educational psychology for learning and teaching.* Southbank, Australia: Thomson.

Lacey, C. (1985). Professional socialisation of teachers. In T. Husen and T. N. Postlethwaite (Eds.) *The International Encyclopedia of Education,* (pp. 4073-4084). Oxford: Pergamon.

Lankshear, C., & Knobel, M. (2005). Digital literacies: Policy, pedagogy and research considerations for education In *Opening plenary address presented at the ITU Conference.* Oslo, Norway.

Lankshear, C., & Snyder, I. (2000). *Teachers and techno-literacy: Managing literacy, technology and learning in schools.* Crows Nest, Australia: Allen & Unwin.

Lave, J., & Wenger, E. (1991). *Situated learning: Legitimate peripheral participation.* New York: Cambridge University Press.

Lenhart, A., & Fox, S. (2006). Bloggers: A portrait of the internet's new storytellers. Retrieved 12 November 2007 from: http://www.pewinternet. org/PPF/r/186/report_display.asp

Leu, D., Mallette, M., Karcher, R., & Kara-Soteriou, J. (2005). Contextualising new literacies of information and communication technologies in theory, research and practice. In R. A. Karchmer, D. J. Leu, M. M. Mallette & J. Kara-Soteriou (Eds.), *Innovative approaches to literacy education: Using the Internet to support new literacies.* (pp. 1-12). Newark: International Reading Association.

Lockyer, L., Patterson, J. W., Rowland, G. S., & Hearne, D. B. (2007). ActiveHealth - Enhancing the Community of Physical and Health Educators through Online Technologies. In M. Keppell (Eds.), *Instructional Design: Case Studies in Communities of Practice* (pp. 331-348). Hershey, New York: Information Science Publishing.

Lombardi, M. M. (2007). Authentic learning for the 21st century: An overview. In D. G. Oblinger (Ed.), *Educause Learning Initiative. Advancing learning through IT innovation* (pp. 1-12): EDUCAUSE.

Maarof, N. (2007). Telling his or her story through reflective journals *International Education Journal, 8*(1), 205-220.

McCormack, A., Gore, J., & Thomas, K. (2004). *Learning to teach: Narratives from early career teachers.* Paper presented at the Australian Association for Research in Education, University of Melbourne, Melbourne.

Miles, M., & Huberman, A. (1984). *Qualitative Data Analysis.* London: Sage.

Nicolosi, J. (1991). Constructing ethnicity: Creating and recreating ethnic identity and culture. *Reparative therapy of male homosexuality.* Northvale: Jason Aronson.

Oblinger, D. G. (2005). Learners, learning and technology. *EDUCAUSE review, September/October*, 66-75.

Peters, J., & Cornu, R. L. (2006). *Successful early career teaching: More than engaging pedagogy.* Paper presented at the AARE 2006 International education research conference, Adelaide.

Rodgers, C. (2002). Defining reflection: Another look at John Dewey and reflective thinking. *Teachers College Record, 104*(4), 842-866.

Sachs, J. (1999). Teacher Professional Identity: Competing Discourses, and Competing Outcomes. Paper Presented at the AARE Annual Conference Melbourne November. Available [Online]: http://www.aare.edu.au/99pap/sac99611. htm. Retrieved on 11 September 06.

Sparks, P., & Shepherd, R. (1992). Self-identity and the theory of planned behavior: Assesing the role of identification with "Green Consumerism" *Social Psychology Quarterly*, Vol. 55, (4) 388-399.

Stets, E., & Burke, J. (2000) Identity theory and social identity theory. *Social Psychology Quarterly, 63*(3), 224-237.

Teal, W., Leu, D. J., Labbo, L., & Kinzer, C. (2002). The CTELL project: New ways technology can help educate tomorrow's reading teachers. *Reading Online.* Retrieved March 12, 2007.

Turner, J.C. (1975). Social comparison and social identity: Some prospects for intergroup behaviour. *European Journal of Social Psychology.* 5, 5-34.

Wellman, B., Salaff, J., Dimitrova, D., Garton, L., Gulia, M., & Haythornthwaite, C. (1996). Computer networks as social networks: Collaborative work, telework, and virtual community. *Annual Review of Sociology, 22*, 213-238.

KEY TERMS

Authentic Learning: Learning that is connected to knowledge that is required within a particular cultural setting.

Blog: An online text that captures reflections. It may also contain pictures, hyperlinks and sound.

Networking: The interaction of participants for shared knowledge and understandings.

Physical Community: Actual interactions between participants, in this research this occurred through workshop sessions on the University campus.

Professional Identity: One's conception and perception of themselves as a member of their selected profession.

Reflection: Reflection is complex and rigorous, taking the practitioner through the process of linking theory with practice and practice with theory.

Virtual Community: Online interactions between participants, in this research this occurred through engagement with the BEST site.

Chapter XVIII
A Model for Knowledge and Innovation in Online Education

Jennifer Ann Linder-VanBerschot
University of New Mexico, USA

Deborah K. LaPointe
University of New Mexico Health Sciences Center, USA

ABSTRACT

The objective of this chapter is to introduce a model that outlines the evolution of knowledge and sustainable innovation of community through the use of social software and knowledge management in an online environment. Social software presents easy-to-use, participatory technologies, thus bringing increased interaction with others and a diversity of perspectives into the classroom. Knowledge management provides the opportunity to capture and store information so that content and learning can be personalized according to learner preferences. This model describes a circuit of knowledge that includes instructional systems design, individualization of learning, interaction and critical reflection. It also represents a new framework within which communities develop and become more sustainable.

INTRODUCTION

In this chapter, we suggest that the field of online education adopts effective practices from knowledge management, and the best social software tools to create a knowledge community. As social software tools become more available for formal online learning environments, current conceptualizations of online communities must be modified. Where are these social technologies leading us and what are the impacts?

This model proposes a more dynamic online classroom where learners use cutting-edge social software tools to capture and disseminate collective knowledge from the participants in the course, as well as the virtual and local community.

This model facilitates the evolution of knowledge within the classroom, and encourages a sustainable knowledge community, wherein innovation may be enhanced. Our vision of this dynamic partnership of knowledge management, online education, and social software is described in the following scenario (Table 1).

Although the case scenario may seem like a list of items for online instructors to buy, the reality is that these tools are currently available for learners and instructors alike to manipulate to create meaningful and long-lasting online interaction. Granted, adaptation is a constant challenge, but it is our hope that through describing this model,

Table 1.

Futures of Technology and Knowledge in an Online Classroom

Fiona, Tim, and Vita are enrolled in Organizational Learning and Instructional Technologies (OLIT) 565, a graduate course designed to function as an interactive online course using multimedia content, information literacy tools, tests, assignments, and small group projects. The course requires intensive study of the content available in numerous formats for many devices, including desktop computers, iPods, and smart phones. The content can be read online or offline. Interactions with classmates, instructor, mentors, and experts are a critical component of the course and occur through discussion forums, chats, and Web conferencing in the learning management system (LMS), as well as wikis, blogs, and virtual content outside the LMS.

Through a pre-assessment the students completed when registering for the course, the LMS captured their profiles, past performance, and interests. With this information, the LMS organizes several approaches to present course content according to learner preferences. An interactive concept map presents multiple ways of exploring and integrating the content with prior knowledge and outlines the suggested path for each learner. Clicking on the nodes in the concept map brings up the content, supplemental materials, assessments, and group discussions. The concept map also lists the times and places that experts who produced the examples will be available for discussion. The learners explore the content, applying their own structure to it. Additionally, the social networking software inside the LMS connects the three learners based on their shared interests.

During the orientation, the instructor provides an introduction to the synchronous and asynchronous communication technologies, LMS and social software. The instructor, mentors, and learners negotiate ground rules, expectations, roles and responsibilities when using asynchronous and synchronous communication and social software technologies. The ground rules and expectations support active participation in achieving the development of a future sustainable community. The students come to realize that careful attention to one's online presence, reputation, and contributions to discussions is crucial, as they influence trust, cognitive presence and social interaction for learning purposes.

On her way home from a movie, Fiona posts an audio message and a journal article she scanned using her mobile phone. She tags the document with metadata enabling future searching and sharing for reuse and repurposing. The wiki notifies Tim's iPhone and Vita's e-mail account. Tim responds to the message, agreeing with her ideas but providing minimal additional information. The LMS and Fiona both note Tim's brief response and prompt him to think more critically and elaborate on his message.

Essential components of the online environment are evaluation and reflection. For this reason, users provide feedback on the user-created content, the contributions to the discussions, wikis, blogs, and podcasting, and the system. Learners are encouraged to rate each posting using rating systems similar to e-Bay or Slashdot. The ratings are used to continuously improve the posted content and to identify gaps in the material. With the abundant amount of choice in the ways information and knowledge are created and shared, Fiona looks for the tagging, certification of fact-checkers and group rating systems before making a content selection.

Course designers specify multiple routes through a collection of learning objects. Just-in-time information is organized into small units and presented to learners precisely when they need it. The LMS identifies Fiona's preferences for learning, as well as recognizes that she needs to develop other ways of learning in case she encounters online courses without such individualized features. The LMS monitors and logs the student's individual learning processes and creates a collaborative memory to offer aid when needed. The instructor and group mentor review the logs before communicating with the individuals and group, and responding to the group's requests for guidance.

The enrolled learners are not the only participants in the course. In previous courses in the OLIT program, instructors have encouraged emergent leadership from the group—meaning that learners with great interest in the content and technologies take a leadership role in the course. Some of these learners were so stimulated by the content and interaction that they have organized a community in which members meander in and out of courses, as they see fit. Additionally, the social software outside the course LMS is hosted, and the content created, reviewed, and shared by community members. Previous course enrollees and program graduates bring their work experiences to the community. The lessons they have learned through interacting in the world, reflecting on the experiences, and making sense of them through collaboration with others in the community become powerful stories that create part of the community's resources and memory.

This community of learners and experts may choose to participate in the online OLIT courses; however, they may also decide to focus on spreading the collective knowledge co-constructed in the community to local schools and organizations. This knowledge community expands and contracts throughout its existence, but the common feature is that a passionate group of contributors collaborate to solve problems within the community and share their learning and expertise with others outside of the community. The interaction within and between the course and the community creates a space for reflection where learners, leaders and instructors constantly consider necessary changes that need to be made so that the course continues to evolve, as does the learning. Belonging to such an innovative community that provides valuable learning opportunities gives identity to the members and further motivates their participation. This evolutionary process facilitates the innovation and sustainability of the learning community.

more practitioners will realize the potential for incorporating social software tools and knowledge management in online learning. This model breaks the previous boundaries presented by virtual communities and suggests possibilities for increased collaboration and participation.

DEFINITION AND HISTORY OF KEY TERMS

Knowledge Management

Knowledge Management (KM) was a concept initially established by Peter Drucker in the 1970s. However, it was not until the 1990s with Nonaka and Takeuchi's introduction of a knowledge organization, that it became a more integrated concept in business practices. At that point, publications and university courses expanded peoples' understanding of the benefits of KM (Wiig, 1997). Within the past few years, a larger number of educational institutions have begun implementing KM systems to enhance the community knowledge and encourage innovation (Hirschbuhl, Zachariah, & Bishop, 2002; Kidwell, VanderLinde, & Johnson, 2000; Na Ubon & Kimble, 2002).

Traditional KM initiatives are often divided into three processes: (a) design, (b) development and (c) technology (Conway & Sligar, 2002). Not all KM plans follow a rigid process flow; some are flexible enough to incorporate, "how people learn, how they implement what they learn, and how they share their knowledge" (Bassi, 1997, p. 426). By connecting the KM system to the users, the advantages become more apparent. The terminal goal of a KM plan is to create a sustainable system that enhances the growth of the organization's knowledge (Salisbury, 2003) with the ultimate purpose being to enhance organizational creativity and innovation.

Online Education

Distance education supports the learning process when learners and instructor are physically separated and hence rely upon technology to interact (Moore and Kearsley, 2005). Distance education has made great advances since its inception in the 1800s, with the most recent innovation being online education (OE), defined as distance education delivered through the Internet. Current trends in OE include the incorporation of social software, which is a central feature in this chapter.

One of the major benefits of OE is that instructors are forced to be as technologically savvy as the students that they are teaching. Another advantage is that learners have access to the professor and to a community of peers all hours of the day so that they can debate, problem-solve and discuss the concepts associated with their course. OE has been especially helpful in connecting remote students to each other to form an online learning community. Most important to the progress of education, the online platform encourages learner-centered activities, where the instructor guides learners to co-create knowledge, and share that knowledge with other members of the learning community.

Social Software

Social software (SS) is not a single type of software, but instead a combination of two or more modes of computer-mediated communication, resulting in the formation of a community. A social network built from SS allows members to create and participate in a self-made community. With the rise of Web 2.0, SS applications seem to be introduced at such a rate that not even the most technologically savvy can keep up. Yet these communication and interaction tools influence how virtual communities form, and how they sustain themselves even after the online course has ended. The affordances of SS include ubiquity, searchable content and referral to people with common interests. These benefits then support multi-scale social spaces and conversation discovery.

Some of the latest applications include 30 Boxes, a social calendar; Lazybase, a site where individuals are given the tools to create and share a database; Zoho Show, a tool that helps create and publish presentations; and voo2do, a task management tool (Brown, 2007). In fact, this paper was developed using *PBwiki*, a secure, open-source wiki that allowed us to co-create this chapter at a time and place that was convenient for each of us. When one person edited the chapter, the other person received an email update, so she could see the progress being made. When we needed to communicate synchronously, we used *Yahoo! messenger*.

Although SS tools have not been typically applied to educational settings, we side with Dalsgaard (2006) in that we believe SS tools can and should be used to support learning. These tools encourage the creation and contribution of user-created content and facilitation of learning instead of management of learning—a paradigm shift that calls for a new model for OE.

This model acts as a plea for the target audience including researchers, teaching practitioners, and educational technologists to embrace a paradigm shift that applies social systems in OE. SS can increase the diversity of perspectives in the content, virtual presence of a community and establish and enhance peer-to-peer social networks, as suggested by the case illustration. The incorporation of this emerging trend in this proposed model will facilitate the dynamic evolution of knowledge beyond the classroom and contribute to the innovative and sustainable community outside of the formal learning environment.

EXISTING LITERATURE

The first collaboration of OE and KM was envisioned by Albert and Thomas (2000) who taught at the Business School at Britain's Open Univer-

sity. They focused on the tools and technologies used to teach an online course on KM. Similarly, Townley, Geng and Zhang (2002) collaborated between New Mexico State and Beijing University to teach a class on KM. They explained that global education was becoming a rapidly growing field that addresses the need for the development of international relationships. Both collaborations were primarily interested in the course management tools used, not on learning or community development.

Fry (2001) explained how many organizations turn to OE as a strategy for transition and corporate development. The Ernst and Young Center for Business Knowledge, for example, has applied components of OE to assist in the organization's strategic development by using asynchronous discussion groups and online communities of practice, as well as personalization and profiling techniques. Different from the studies mentioned above, Fry (2001) uses OE to enhance current KM practices.

Universities are working to close the gap between the change in technology and the learning needs in an online environment. Hirschbuhl, Zacariah and Bishop (2002) suggest that this gap can be minimized by using KM tools to deliver OE. By fitting the instruction to the individual learning needs of the student, KM can provide increased success for all learners, regardless of their ability or familiarity with technology. Hirschbuhl, Zacariah and Bishop (2002) encourage students and instructors to shift their mental model of teaching methodologies and collaborative strategies in order to develop successful online courses that can be customized to meet individual learner needs. KM is the suggested remedy to smooth and prepare all participants in the paradigm shift from traditional face-to-face classrooms to OE. Almost opposite from the study above, in this case, KM tools are supporting OE.

Saxena (2007) proposes that the integration of KM tools within OE will provide online distance education administrators and instructors with data that could result in improved decision making, reduced course development time, improved academic and administrative services, and reduced costs. He believes the integration of the two will reveal patterns and relationships that provide the knowledge necessary for improving OE. Lytras, Naeve and Pouloudi (2005) also believe in the promise of KM in contributing to the evolution of online learning, and believe that, "The convergence of e-learning and knowledge management will be evident in worldwide initiatives that will foster a constructive, open, dynamic, interconnected, distributed, adaptive, user-friendly, socially concerned, and accessible wealth of knowledge" (p. 68). Only one article was located that connected the fields of OE, KM and SS. Pettenati, Cigognini, Mangione, and Guerin (2007) built a model in which SS was used to track personal knowledge in an online learning environment. However, they do not consider the potential for knowledge development and innovation in a dynamic community environment.

Gaps in the Literature

KM and OE share several common elements, including community, collaboration, trust, knowledge sharing and SS tools (Na Ubon & Kimble, 2002; Saxena, 2007). Despite the availability of tools and technologies and increase in familiarity with these tools, universities seem reluctant to integrate OE and KM. This is demonstrated by the minimal capturing and sharing of knowledge assets in the university environment. An additional gap in the KM literature is the lack of information related to the affective domain which is frequently described as underlying cognition. Emotions and attitudes are critically important in order to interpret experiences positively and to learn effectively, as well as support and trust others.

Although there is literature on the combination of KM and OE, there is not a true collaboration where they are working together towards an im-

proved system as envisioned in the case scenario. Since SS tools are such a recent introduction to the field, there is even less literature on their role in this relationship. Saxena (2007) recommended that KM be used to gather data on students so that universities can then use that data to better understand distance learners and their learning environments. He concludes his article by encouraging researchers to more deeply explore the opportunities for KM in an online setting. This chapter provides a model and an outline for a system where KM, OE and SS combine to create a more dynamic formal online learning environment, as described in the case illustration.

DESCRIPTION OF MODEL

The model shown below represents a cyclical process with five major components: (a) critical reflection with leadership, (b) instructional design, (c) individualization, (d) collaboration and interaction among course participants, and (e) an innovative and sustainable community. This community development of graduates and interested others is ongoing, and feeds experiences and resources back into the model.

The interplay among the components that contribute to the evolution of knowledge occurs throughout the online course. There is not a particular order in which it happens—the boundaries are blurred. For example, instructional design may be the first step for the instructor, followed by implementation in which individualization of the learning experience is considered. Critical reflection may be a structured process at the end. And it may not be until the course ends that learners diverge from the cycle and engage in the community development process. On the other hand, the community development may be a carry-over from a former online course or provide authentic learning opportunities during the course, thus allowing the interaction to be a central component of the online course, with learners who already know each other well. We will describe each component of the model in the section below.

Instructional Design

We will explain the innovative relationship among KM, OE, and SS beginning with instructional design. Instructional design provides the template for determining learner needs, collecting appropriate content and designing interaction to enhance the growth and development of future professionals. A significant amount of the work of instructional designers and instructors is not accomplished through declarative and procedural knowledge alone. Working with instructors and students involves affective aspects, such as responding to emotional or evaluative responses. We remind designers that affective and social content must be a part of the implementation process.

Content

The goal of a majority of KM systems is to capture the most essential knowledge assets for the users (Conway & Sligar, 2002). This may include course projects, archived dialogue or recorded voice conversations. Content will not magically appear in the learning environment—learners and instructors must collaborate to select, contribute, and rate the knowledge that is pertinent to the learning environment. Often times in KM systems, a Subject Matter Expert (SME) is selected to maintain cohesion in the community and distinguish the most essential content to be shared with the group. In the corporate setting, the SME is typically the most knowledgeable member of the community, yet in an online course, it might be more effective to have a rotating SME so that a variety of perspectives can be a part of the knowledge capturing process. An outside member of the community, such as an expert in

Figure 1. Evolution of knowledge and community development model

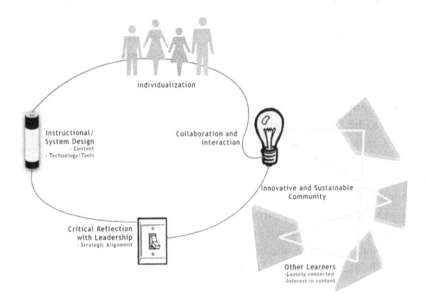

the field or a former class member, may also act as the SME, providing relevant content that is applicable to the course objectives. All members of the learning community must work with the SME to continually reflect upon and refine the content that is captured and stored. New information should be frequently reviewed and assessed, and older information should be regularly revisited to determine if it is still valuable to the learning community.

In order for these captured knowledge assets to be accessed frequently, the content must be prepared in standardized formats that can be later customized in ways that are meaningful for individual users and support carrying the content forward. As LMS programs become more sophisticated, they allow online courses to offer more individualized content that is adaptable to needs of each learner, as indicated through describing the process of tagging in the case illustration above. Until that becomes common practice, passionate content creators and fanatical reviewers are needed to maintain a dynamic system so that learners look forward to accessing and applying content to different contexts (Conrad & LaPointe, 2007).

Technology and Tools

It does limited good to have extensive knowledge sharing without the technological means to enhance the information. Fortunately, advancements in technology afford users from around the world the ability to participate in the knowledge sharing process in real-time (Kilby, 2001; Lan, Xian, & Fu, 2000; Na Ubon & Kimble, 2002). All technology and tools chosen to support the learning process must facilitate the multiple phases of learning, including exploration, reflection, collaboration, testing out new ideas, knowledge construction and feedback. These technologies do not necessarily need to be complex. Instead, the critical characteristic is that the technologies allow easier

communication in the online course to facilitate in the process of interaction.

RSS feeds notify learners whenever a new entry, podcast, email message or wiki posting has been added. Instead of checking in frequently with the constantly updated LMS, an RSS feed allows learners to create and distribute a list of Web links to quickly review at a time and location that is convenient for them. This provides organization for the online participants to know what they have already accessed in contrast to what they still need to review. Online participants depend on ease of use to get started and build confidence in using the tools. Thereafter, accessible support is essential. The technology helps learners organize and find their way through the LMS, as well as make sense of the content presented in many formats and through multiple perspectives.

The type of technology used should depend on the participants. If learners do not understand the functionality of the interface where content is displayed, then the significance of the content may be lost. Content should also be available in the platform preferred by learners, such as computer, cell phone, mp3 player, instant messenger, wiki posting, etc. Na Ubon and Kimble (2002) encourage the use of advanced technologies because they have the potential to increase the sense of trust, identity and commitment of the community. Pre-established standards help guarantee a useful and progressive product. Despite the recommendation to use cutting-edge software and tools, we suggest that the instructor establish a balance between user-friendly and innovative technologies.

Individualization

Although content, technology and tools are essential components of the instructional design process, as illustrated in the model, they are not the only factors to consider. Throughout the design and development process, instructors and course designers must think of the learners for whom they are developing the course because KM and OE are more complex than technology and multimedia tools (Liebowitz, 2001; Na Ubon & Kimble, 2002). The focus cannot simply be on the use of technology, but also on the human issues behind the success or failure of the technology (Davenport, 2005).

All participants enter a course with different levels of familiarity and confidence in terms of technology and content. Whereas some learners are willing to immediately engage in online communication and capturing knowledge, others are more hesitant to participate in this type of online interaction. Other still may apply signaling to present themselves as different people to the online class. It does not come as a surprise that a small percentage of individuals usually create a majority of online content (Kamel Boulos & Wheeler 2007). Instructional designers and instructors must determine how to develop an individualized system that encourages equal participation from all learners. Fisher and Baird (2005) encourage the use of peer mentoring to build students' levels of confidence in using online tools. Similarly, Gunawardena, Linder-VanBerschot, LaPointe, Barrett, Mummert, Cardiff, et al. (2007) reported that e-mentoring facilitated in cross-cultural learning transformation. Community members may volunteer to be mentors for students, establishing their confidence in the learning platform at a pace that is appropriate for each individual. Once students become more familiar with tools and determine how to best apply them for their personal needs, a stronger sense of community begins to emerge. Due to these benefits, instructors are increasingly utilizing community programs like Living Treasures to bring community members and community culture into the classroom to localize course content.

Additionally, there must be space for users to provide feedback on the system (Wiig, 1997) so that the effectiveness can continuously be improved. When communication between knowledge creators and SMEs is limited, the knowledge

often becomes outdated and users stop accessing the system after losing interest (Ravitz & Hoadley, 2005). LMSs such as WebCT Vista have a rating option on discussion messages, so learners can rate messages that they find useful, as described in the scenario. When a particular message has a high rating, learners are more likely to visit it because they want to be accessing the most pertinent information in the course, as described in the case illustration. This rating system allows all users to become SMEs in capturing data that is most important to the collective whole.

Interaction

Interaction is a central component to OE. Moore (1989) outlines three types of interaction: learner-content, learner-instructor and learner-learner. A fourth type of interaction is especially important in OE—learner-interface (Hillman, Willis & Gunawardena, 1994). Similarly, interaction is a foundational component of KM and is facilitated by SS tools. It has even been found that groups of individuals who regularly share knowledge tend to perform better than those who do not (Davenport, 2005). Through interaction, individuals learn to analyze, question, interpret, and make sense of phenomena. Members of the community facilitate their thinking and innovation through the questions, problems, issues, solutions, resources, and tools that members bring to the community.

Collaboration is not always a natural process for learners in an online environment. In fact, Annand (2007) expresses concern that online services coupled with KM software may reduce the need for human interaction. Therefore, instructors must minimize transactional distance and establish a strong sense of social presence so that learners *want* to interact with each other. SS tools can be used to develop and enhance interaction and social presence in the course. Online learners often have different personal goals, and, thus, there is not one tool that will fit the interaction needs of all learners. An additional concern to consider in an international online course is Internet accessibility of all learners (Beldarrain, 2006). McLoughlin and Oliver (2000) provide several suggestions for online instructional designers, one of which is to include communication tools that encourage social interaction so that all learners have the opportunity to co-construct knowledge.

Conrad and LaPointe (2007) remind us that just because these tools are included, it is not guaranteed that they will necessarily facilitate enhanced interaction, or even be used. Their research revealed that collaboration depends on the design, nature, purpose and structure of the SS tool. In their course wiki learners were willing to post content, but did not want to edit other classmates' content. Instead, the learners wanted additional opportunities to discuss the content on the wiki. This adds to our growing awareness that merely capturing and sharing information does not necessarily lead to deeper understanding. New information can only lead to shared knowledge when it is integrated with prior data and tested through dialogue with other learners. In the end, it is the learners who will decide whether or not they will accept and apply the tools to their thinking and learning processes through interaction within the course.

Critical Reflection

In order to make sense of an experience, learners must interpret it. This interpretation then guides learning actions. Mezirow (1990) suggests that this process of reflection "enables us to correct distortions in our beliefs and errors in problem solving" (p. 1). It is a necessary strategy for all online users, as it directs future professional practice and improved performance through the discovery of personal meaning. *Critical* reflection takes the learning process a step further to include "challenging our established and habitual patterns of expectation" (Mezirow, 1990, p. 12). This process provides a potential transformative learning or teaching experience.

Although reflection is embedded in every step of the process, we believe it is important enough to explicitly detail through the description of strategic alignment and leadership. Instructors and instructional designers must reflect on every step of process. For example, instructors must reassess the applicability of the content in the online class. As course objectives change, the content must also be adapted to support learners' needs. Additionally, the instructional designer must reflect on the applicability of the tools chosen to meet course objectives. Both the instructor and instructional designer should review the sense of individualization of content that then encourages collaboration both within and outside of the online course. Finally, we recommend that the instructor and instructional designers ensure critical reflection holds a central position within the learning activities so that learners can also participate in the process.

Strategic Alignment

The goals and objectives of the online course must drive the selection of SS and KM tools. What works for a problems-based biology course cannot be plugged into a lecture-based math course and expect comparable results. Similarly, cultural differences hinder the effectiveness of the drag and drop method. For example, an instructional technology course taught at a university in southwestern United States must be culturally adapted before implementing it at a Chinese university. This has become more apparent as open content and open educational resources are shared between academic institutions, as described in Caswell, Henson, Jensen and Wiley's (2008) recent article on universal education.

All SS tools and KM processes must be connected to the institutional culture and overall course goals so that users feel like it is a valuable use of their time. In fact, Liebowitz (2001) mentioned that one of the three reasons for a failed KM strategy is that it was not connected to the central goals of the institution. If that is the case, users will not see the functionality of the initiative and will most likely not engage. The model proposed in this chapter provides a broad structure within which instructors can adapt to fit their course objectives.

Alignment of the proposed initiative with the organizational strategic plan should be closely related to leadership characteristics, internal organizational structure and external characteristics of the institution (Rogers, 1995). The degree of centralization of power and control in an organization, the formalization of rules and policies, and the degree to which new ideas can flow among organizational units all impact organizational innovativeness and its implementation. Additionally, strategic alignment supports the future sustainability of the initiative.

Leadership

As mentioned above, leadership has the ability to minimize or maximize the impact of this innovative model. Leadership's purposes, expectations, and goals for the model will vary, depending upon the lens through which it views the system. In a formal educational setting, most people define the leader as the instructor or instructional designer who may perceive the model as a way to encourage learners to become involved in a community to create, share, and use content to solve problems and instigate change. Yet, if the leader is unwilling to recognize, encourage and share the collective knowledge, s/he is putting the entire online course community at risk of losing vital information.

Openness to a variety of perspectives enables new understandings and encourages innovation. Sustainable improvement depends on successful and sustainable leadership (Hargreaves & Fink, 2006). This may mean that the leadership is equally distributed across the course—members of the online course take turns in holding the leadership role. This not only provides different perspectives,

but also encourages emergent leadership within and beyond the course.

Community Development

When learners take responsibility for their learning goals and take on a leadership role in their online class, they develop confidence not only in their knowledge of the content and technology, but also in their ability to lead others. They further value the interdependence and the responsibility of all members of the community to teach and to learn.

Knowledge management uses the term Community of Practice (CoP) to describe a place where people unite for a common purpose so that they can work together to achieve a particular goal (Conway & Sligar, 2002; Wenger, McDermott & Snyder, 2002). A CoP may emerge from the community development process. However, we feel that a knowledge community does not have to be as structured as a CoP in order to be successful. Learners may come in and out of the community, as they feel necessary. Some learners may share their knowledge from the online course with the community, while others may distribute information from the community with the online course. The community development moves beyond the classroom to peer networks before, during and after the online course. It is this flexible interplay of expertise that creates an environment of knowledge sharing and innovation.

People choose to belong to social organizations where value is gained through the exchange of information and life experiences from highly credible sources. The value received reinforces the connections between course members and the community. The partnership of community with online course participants allows flexible groupings of students and practitioners to work on projects. Students have increased opportunities for authentic experiences and research that they can bring back to the online classroom.

Innovation

Organizations cite innovation as one of the primary benefits of implementing KM practices into organizational practices (Conway & Sligar, 2002; Davenport, 2005). It is an educational institution's responsibility to determine how to encourage innovation at all levels (Kidwell, VanderLinde & Johnson, 2000; Rogers, 1995). Brown (1998) suggests that "innovation is everywhere; the problem is how to learn from it" (p. 156). Through having the capability to search and navigate a diverse, extensive knowledge base, learners may build new connections, and in turn, enhance the likelihood of developing further innovative products (Merlyn & Välikangas, 1998). Innovation contributes to a greater institutional knowledge base, providing information of value that the community members want to continually access and contribute to; thereby, creating a sense of community rather than a collection of content.

Even the best innovations will get lost in the shuffle if leadership does not know how to communicate them with other members of the community (Brown, 1998; Rogers, 1995). Leaders cannot pass a memo and expect the innovation to be diffused in to everyday practice. Brown (1998) suggests that users need to have the opportunity to experience it in a way that "evokes power and possibility" (p. 168). Sustainability of the innovation is more likely to occur if learners participate and give input throughout the generation and diffusion process (Rogers, 1995).

Sustainability

Organizations that use KM and SS to enhance OE must plan for a dynamic system. Barron (2000) mentions that online content can be considered outdated in less than eight months. Additionally, learner experiences are consistently transforming and are always open to reinterpretation. For these reasons, the dynamism of economic and social change requires a flexible system that is created to adapt to future changes. Thus, the role of KM is to keep the knowledge base "alive and vibrant" (Wiig, 1997, p. 2) with knowledge gained through everyday practice in the community as well as with current research in order to secure the online course's buy-in and later sustainability of the learning community.

The learning and performance supported by this model are based on the recognition and philosophy that learning is a way of being. It is an ongoing set of attitudes and actions by a community of learners who try to keep abreast the myriad of events that are occurring in their field. The leader must embrace the vibrant nature of the online community and work to sustain it. All participants can participate and contribute to knowledge building. Trust and confidence must also be nurtured to support the sustainability. Again, it is recommended to apply shared leadership so that the leader does not burn out and cause the captured knowledge to be outdated and minimally applied.

FUTURE TRENDS

With the rapid expansion of the fields of OE, KM and especially SS, leaders in the field must step back and review broad trends in the field, as well as reflect what those trends mean for the field. Social software presents easy-to-use, participatory technologies, thus bringing increased interaction with others and a diversity of perspectives into the classroom. Knowledge management provides the opportunity to capture and store information so that content and learning can be personalized according to learner preferences. Online education offers instructional design and facilitation of presence and learning. The relationship of KM, OE, and SS supports participation that encourages innovation. This will bring opportunities and challenges.

Security of content and provision of a safe learning experience while inviting the community into the online course will require a solution. Copyright and digital rights management will impact the viability of the model and our case illustration. Websites such as Creative Commons has found a way to provide a space for users to share content with one another with the goal of creating something greater than what one person could develop working independently. Content and interaction, as described in the current model, will blend with virtual world technology. Extensive future evaluative and research opportunities exist to determine the pragmatic value of the model and to build a body of knowledge related to the convergence of technologies and communities to support continued innovation of the organization through the dynamic development of faculty, students, and interested others. Additionally, international interpretations of this model are welcomed.

CONCLUSION

This model describes the evolution of knowledge and sustainable innovation of community through the use of SS and KM in an online environment. Two major limitations to this model exist. First, it was developed using western pedagogy. However, an international literature base was used to build the model. The second major limitation is the lack of a discussion of the model's security concerns—given the extensiveness of this topic, it could not be covered in this chapter.

The model describes a new method of learning—one in which the tools from KM and SS facilitate the learning cycle of an online course. Feeding into this model is innovation that comes from our relationships with the community outside the classroom. We are long past the time of believing that instructors are the only people who can create and maintain the course. Emergent leadership is needed to sustain the evolution of knowledge, thus leading to increased innovation. As online education, knowledge management and

social software become better known, research must be done to combine these fields in order to effectively integrate more formal and informal learning communities.

ACKNOWLEDGMENT

The authors would like to thank Nate Schneider for his contribution in developing the graphics for the model.

REFERENCES

Albert, S., & Thomas, C. (2000). A new approach to computer-aided distance learning: the 'Automated Tutor'. *Open Learning, 15*(2), 141-150.

Annand, D. (2007). Re-organizing universities for the information age. *International Review of Research in Open and Distance Learning, 8*(3). Retrieved April 11, 2008, from http://www.irrodl.org/index.php/irrodl/article/view/372/956

Barron, T. (2000). *A Smarter Frankenstein: The Merging of E-Learning and Knowledge Management.* Retrieved April 11, 2007, from http://www.learningcircuits.org/aug2000/barron.html

Bassi, L. J. (1997). Harnessing the power of intellectual capital. *Training and Development, 21*(12), 422-431.

Beldarrain, Y. (2006). Distance education trends: Integrating new technologies to foster   student interaction and collaboration. *Distance Education, 27*(2), 139-153.

Brown, J. (2007). *Web 2.0.* Retrieved September 28, 2007, from http://www.judybrown.com/tools.html

Brown, J. S. (1998). Research that reinvents the corporation. In *Harvard Business Review on Knowledge Management.* (pp. 153-180). Boston, MA: Harvard Business School Press.

Bruening, T. H., Scanlon, D. C., & Hodes, C. (2001). *The status of career and technical education teacher preparation programs.* National Research Center for Career and Technical Education. Retrieved April 7, 2006, from http://www.nccte.org/publications/infosynthesis/r&dreport/Status_of_CTE/Status%20of%20CTE.html

Caswell, T., Henson, S., Jensen, M., & Wiley, D. (2008). Open content and open educational resources: Enabling universal education. *International Review of Research in Open and Distance Learning, 9*(1). Retrieved April 11, 2008, from http://www.irrodl.org/index.php/irrodl/article/view/469/1009

Conrad, C., & LaPointe, D. (October 2007). Wikis: Collaborative by Nature or Design? *Poster session at the South Central Chapter of the Medical Library Association Annual Conference.* Albuquerque, NM.

Conway, S., & Sligar, C. (2002). *Unlocking knowledge assets.* Redmond, WA: Microsoft Press.

Creative Commons, San Francisco, CA. Retrieved April 12, 2008, from http://creativecommons.org/

Dalsgaard, C. (2006). Social software: E-learning beyond learning management systems. *European Journal of Open, Distance and E-learning, 2.* Retrieved October 17, 2007, from http://www.eurodl.org/materials/contrib/2006/Christian_Dalsgaard.htm

Davenport, T. H. (2005). *Thinking for a living.* Boston, MA: Harvard Business School Publishing.

Fisher, M., & Baird, D. E. (2005). Online learning design that fosters student support, self-regulation, and retention. *Campus-Wide Information Systems, 22*(2), 88-107.

Fry, K. (2001). E-learning markets and providers: Some issues and prospects. *Education and Training, 43*(4/5), 233-239.

Gunawardena, C. N., Linder-VanBerschot, J. A., LaPointe, D., Barrett, K., Mummert, J., Cardiff, M. S., et al. (2007). *Learning Transformations through Cross-Cultural E-Mentoring:Perspectives from an Online Faculty Development Forum.* Paper presented at the Seventh International Transformative Learning Conference, October 23-26, 2007, Albuquerque, New Mexico.

Hargreaves, A. & Fink, D. (2006). *Sustainable leadership.* San Francisco: Jossey-Bass.

Hillman, D. C., Willis, D., &, & Gunawardena, C. N. (1994). Learner-interface interaction in distance education: An extension of contemporary models and strategies for practitioners. *The American Journal of Distance Education, 8*(2), 30-42.

Hirschbuhl, J., Zachariah, S., & Bishop, D. (2002). Using knowledge management to deliver distance learning. *British Journal of Educational Technology, 33*(1), 89-93.

Kamel Boulos, M. N., & Wheeler, S. (2007). The emerging Web 2.0 social software: An enabling suite of sociable technologies in health and health care education. *Health Information and Libraries Journal, 24*(1), 2-23.

Kidwell, J. J., Vander Linde, K. M., & Johnson, S. L. (2000). *Educause Quarterly, 4,* 26-33.

Kilby, T. (2001). The direction of Web-based training: A practitioner's view. *The Learning Organization, 8*(5), 194-199.

Lan, K. G., Xian, Y. Y., & Fu, Z. Y. (2000). Putting knowledge management technologies into distance education. *Proceedings of 2000 IRMA International Conference,* Anchorage, Alaska, USA, 1129-1130.

Liebowitz, J. (2001). Knowledge management and its link to artificial intelligence. *Expert Systems with Applications, 20,* 1-6.

Living Treasures of Los Alamos. Retrieved April 11, 2008, from http://livingtreasureslosalamos.org/default.asp

Lytras, M. D., Naeve, A., & Pouloudi, A. (2005). A knowledge management roadmap for e-learning: The way ahead. *International Journal of Distance Education Technologies, 3*(2), 68-75.

McLoughlin, C., & Oliver, R. (2000). Designing learning environments for cultural inclusivity: A case study of indigenous online learning at tertiary level. Electronic Version. *Australian Journal of Educational Technology, 16*, 58-72. Retrieved September 27, 2007, from http://www.ascilite.org.au/ajet/ajet16/mcloughlin.html

Merlyn, P. R., & Välikangas, L. (1998). From information technology to knowledge technology: Taking the user into consideration. *Journal of Knowledge Management, 2*(2), 28-35.

Mezirow, J. (1990). *Fostering critical reflections in adulthood: A guide to transformative and emancipatory learning.* San Francisco, CA: Jossey-Bass Publishers.

Moore, M. (1989). Three types of interaction. *The American Journal of Distance Education, 3*(2), 1-6.

Moore, M., & Kearsley, G. (2005). Distance education: A systems view. (2nd ed.). Belmont, CA: Thomson Wadsworth.

Na Ubon, A., & Kimble, C. (2002). Knowledge management in online distance education. *Proceedings of the 3rd International Conference Networked Learning 2002,* University of Sheffield, UK, March 2002, 465-473.

PBwiki. (2007). Retrieved September 7, 2007, from http://pbwiki.com/

Pettenati, M. C., Cigognini, E., Mangione, J., Guerin, E. (2007). Using social software for personal knowledge management in formal online learning. *Turkish Online Journal of Distance Education, 8*(3). Retrieved April 23, 2008, from http://tojde.anadolu.edu.tr/tojde27/index.htm

Ravitz, J., & Hoadley, C. (2005). Supporting change and scholarship through review of online resource in professional development settings. *British Journal of Educational Technology, 36*(6), 957-974.

Rogers, E. M. (1995). Diffusion of Innovations, 4th ed. New York, NY: The Free Press.

Salisbury, M. W. (2003). Putting theory into practice to build knowledge management systems. *Journal of Knowledge Management, 7*(2), 128-141.

Saxena, A. (2007). Knowledge management and its applications in distance education. *The Turkish Online Journal of Distance Education, 8*(4). Retrieved October 19, 2007, from http://tojde.anadolu.edu.tr/index.htm

Townley, C. T., Geng, Q, & Zhang, J. (2002). Bilateral team learning: Using distance technologies to enhance global education. *International Education, 32*(2), 19-48.

Wenger, E., McDermott, R., & Snyder, W. M. (2002). Cultivating communities of practice. Cambridge, MA: Harvard Business School Press.

Wiig, K. M. (1997). Knowledge management: Where did it come from and where will it go? *Expert Systems with Applications, 13*(1), 1-14.

KEY TERMS

Community: A purposeful group of people centered around a knowledge concept who collaborate through the use of knowledge management and social software tools to support a sustainable and innovative online course and to share learning experiences with person(s) outside of the group.

Individualization: A process in which differentiated instruction based on learners' needs and interests allows the learner to personalize the knowledge in a meaningful way.

Instructional Design: The systematic application of instructional content, technology and tools used to design an individualized, interactive and reflective online learning environment.

Interaction: An exchange of knowledge and ideas between learners, instructor, content and learning interface(s) that encourages sustainable community development and innovation.

Knowledge Management: The process of capturing, storing and distributing information across learning environments to improve the application of knowledge to a variety of social contexts, thus increasing its availability to others to increase innovation in the evolution of community development and learning.

Online Education: A dynamic learning format taught by means of the Internet in which learners and instructor interact through the use of several of technologies for the purpose of intentional learning.

Reflection: A process in which online participants (learners and instructors) and community members (former learners and experts in the field) observe and interpret the learning experience so that they can consistently adapt and improve the high quality instructional systems design.

Social Software: A combination of two or more online tools encouraging learning, interaction and community development between two or more people.

Chapter XIX
Using Social Software for Teaching and Learning in Higher Education

Petros Lameras
South East European Research Centre, Research Centre of the University of Sheffield and CITY College, Greece

Iraklis Paraskakis
South East European Research Centre, Greece & Research Centre of the University of Sheffield and CITY College, Greece

Philipa Levy
University of Sheffield, UK

ABSTRACT

This chapter focuses on discussing the use of social software from a social constructivist perspective. In particular, the chapter explains how social constructivist pedagogies such as collaborative learning and communities of practice may be supported by the adoption of social software tools. It begins by briefly discussing the social constructivist perspective considering certain pedagogies such as collaborative learning and communities of practice. Then, it explains how these pedagogies are reflected in actual practice by using a variety of social software tools such as discussion boards, blogs and wikis. Finally, the chapter presents the implications of using social software based on the impact of certain factors such as teachers' understandings of, and beliefs about, teaching in general. The purpose of this chapter is to support higher education practitioners in theory-informed design by distilling and outlining those aspects of social constructivism that addresses the use of social software tools. It is perceived that a gradual introduction of social software to institutional Virtual Learning Environments, with a strong focus on collaborative learning processes and engagement in online learning communities, will highlight the need for discursive tools, adaptability, interactivity and reflection.

INTRODUCTION

The diversity of perspectives on, and approaches to, the pedagogical use of social software can prove overwhelming to practitioners and researchers alike. In order to make sense of this, this chapter explains how social constructivist theories such as communities of practice and collaborative learning may be assist in the use of social software. This chapter aims to explain the different pedagogical responses to social software tools and social networks regarding specific characteristics of learning, which may inform practitioners in their use of such tools. This is particularly useful in the context of e-learning where higher educators and researchers seek a clear understanding of the affordances of social software and guidance on how to use and integrate these into their educational practice. This may draw practitioners' attention to the relationship between espoused theories and theory in use (Argyris and Schon, 1974) and also for acknowledging curriculum design as a social practice (Conole et al., 2004).

Teaching and learning using social software may require teachers to rethink their beliefs and approaches in order to develop patterns of learning that at least allow and preferably encourage collaboration as a process of planning, criticising and evaluating. This could also allow learners to personalise their learning within a framework where teachers may monitor their progress. In this context, a better articulation and mapping of different pedagogical processes, tools and techniques may provide a pedagogical approach that can be regarded as more consistent and with teachers' theoretical and practical perspectives for teaching and learning using social software. As Downes (2005) argues, educators and practitioners should recognise that social software is not a technical revolution but is about encouraging and enabling collaboration and participation through applications and tools that can support the social constructivist approach to learning. However, adopting teaching and learning activities with the use of social software in a way that promotes interaction and collaborative knowledge building does not mean that it will result in learning per se. These practices require from the teachers an awareness of how students learn and this adds an increased responsibility for teaching and learning. Twigg (1994) argues that many students are concrete-active learners, that is, they learn best from concrete experiences where they engage their senses, and their best learning experiences begin with practice and end with theory.

The purpose of this chapter is to support higher educators for theory-informed design by outlining current issues of social constructivism in a way that assists the use of social software tools but also taking into consideration that creating a network of interactions between the instructor and the students may not lead to effective communication and collaborative knowledge building. For example, the design of a group project may not necessarily lead to the desired learning outcome. At best, it would appear that learning benefits can be achieved under certain circumstances. Students have to contribute to the learning process by posting their thoughts and ideas to an online discussion because learning is an active process in which both the teacher and the students should participate if it is to be successful. Research by Sharpe et al., (2005) provides examples, from a learner scoping study, about the roles of the teacher and the learner for ensuring and enhancing the quality of instructional design and how this relates to effective online learning processes. The scoping study highlighted the holistic nature of students' experiences of learning and proposed that learning design should focus on students' motivations, beliefs and intentions and the meanings they attach to e-learning. For example, as is well known, collaborative learning may not suit everyone (Laurillard, 2002, Mason and Weller, 2001). So a plethora of questions remain about how to design online learning activities whose purpose is understandable by the students. The important issue to note, from research in teaching and learning, is that there may be contradictions between what teachers and students conceive as effective teaching. Highlighting such differences may be helpful in assisting teachers to design learning activities that are adjusted to students' needs. For example, Jones et al., (2004) used semi-structured interviews to compare the student and the teacher perspective of what is good teaching. Students emphasised effective feedback, teacher enthusiasm, encouragement and good organisation and direction for learning. Teachers mentioned these but gave less attention than students to feedback, but added that disciplinary knowledge and technical expertise are important for students' learning. Laurillard (2002) and Thomas et al., (2004) also identified the importance attached by students to feedback, as well as teacher availability and approachability.

This chapter continues by briefly explaining social constructivist theory. This is important because it allows pedagogies to be described and related to social constructivist theory in terms of the use of specific technological tools and resources. It then discusses pedagogies that could be mapped to a social constructivist perspective such as collaborative learning and the idea of communities of practice. A number of issues related to these pedagogies will be highlighted. Then it explains how these pedagogies may be reflected in practice by using a number of social software tools such as discussion boards, blogs and wikis. Social software could be defined as technologies for the social construction of knowledge that emphasise the design of teaching and learning activities which promote collaborative learning processes and group interactions. Finally, the chapter discusses emerging issues regarding the use of social software in educational contexts. It is perceived that a gradual introduction of social software in the institutional context with a strong focus on collaborative learning and the creation of online learning communities may encourage teachers to design learning tasks which afford the use of these tools while at the same time taking into consideration students' own perceptions of e-learning and how they use technology to learn more effectively.

RETHINKING PEDAGOGY FROM A SOCIAL CONSTRUCTIVIST PERSPECTIVE

The social constructivist perspective views learning as a social activity which is created by the process of conversation, discussion and negotiation (McConnell, 2002, Ernest, 1995). In addition, social constructivists argue that a learner may be able to understand concepts and ideas by teachers or peers who are more experienced. This collaboration between teacher and student may be achieved in learning activities that are situated in real-world contexts. From this perspective, meaning making is the process of sharing perspectives and experiences through collaborative processes and within communities of practice. Therefore, learning can be derived from meaningful discussions with other peers who have similar or different perspectives based on their own experiences.

An important context for thinking about social constructivism is in relation to particular learning processes that are described from two concepts: (1) Vygotsky's 'Zone of Proximal Development (ZPD)' (the term became part of mainstream thinking in pedagogy since the translation of his Mind and Society in 1978), and (2) 'Intersubjectivity' (Jonassen, 1999; Lave and Wenger, 1991). Vygotsky defined the ZPD as the distance between a learner's current conceptual development, as measured by independent problem solving, and the learner's potential capability, as measured by what can be accomplished under the assistance or in collaboration with more capable peers (Vygotsky, 1978). With practice and personal support, learners may increase their learning skills, until they can manage on their own (Cole, 1992). 'Intersubjectivity refers to the mutual understanding that has been achieved between students through effective communication. The social constructivist theme is reflected in the way in which learning occurs through the process of intersubjectivity in the Zone of Proximal Development. That is, learning occurs through negotiation of meaning and communication between students and teachers within a context of real-world activities. Peal and Wilson (2001) summarise the design of web-based tools as ZPDs by adopting the following features:

- Learning activities that are part of real or simulated activity systems, with close attention to the tools and interactions, characteristic of actual situations
- Structured interaction among participants
- Guidance by an expert
- The locus of control passes to the increasingly competent learners

At the same time, there is a wide range of pedagogies that can be mapped to a social constructivist perspective such as collaborative learning (McConnell, 2002) and the accounts of community facilitated by technology with social and situated views of learning. That is, the idea of communities of practice (Lave and Wenger, 1991).

Collaborative Learning as a Process of Interaction

Given the potential of more able peers to help less able ones, researchers have tried to identify the characteristics of collaborative learning. For example, Goodyear (2003) argues that collaboration may be viewed as a mechanism for causing interaction among students which may enable certain processes such as explanation, disagreement and social negotiation of meaning. Dillenbourg (1999) offered an account of collaborative learning processes in terms of developing ways to increase the probability that learning interactions will occur within an educational context (Figure 1).

One way to think about these mechanisms constructively is to consider how these situations can be designed for online learning activities and how these activities can generate interactions between students. At the same time, a key challenge is the question of how to use these mechanisms in order to empower learners to engage actively with the range of tools and resources of the online environment. For example, online discussions may provide learners opportunity for reflection through creating explanations and by posing alternative positions, where negotiation of meaning between

Figure 1. Situations, interactions, mechanisms and effects (Excerpted from Dillenbourg, 1999)

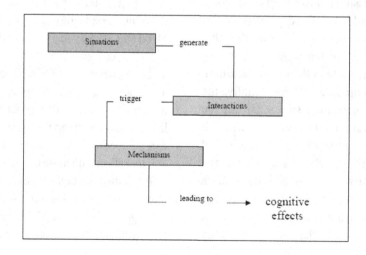

peers may occur. In addition, an alternative online activity such as a group-based task within an online learning environment, peers may share learning tasks for ensuring mutual engagement and cognitive load especially when students' skills within group are in advanced level In each case, however, less able peers in particular areas may develop their understandings by observing the more able ones in conducting particular learning activities. An interesting challenge is to think the types of situations that can create collaborative processes within learning communities where learners may give their own interpretations of different views. This might be encouraged by creating and engaging students in communities of practice.

Communities of Practice

The notion of community facilitated by technology have been explored by many researchers with social and situated views of learning and the idea of communities of practice in Computer Supportive Collaborative Learning (CSCL). Accounts of situated learning (e.g. Brown et al., 1989; Lave and Wenger, 1991; Wenger, 1998) have had a particular influence for e-learning. Wenger (1998) argues that issues of education should be addressed primarily in terms of identities and modes of belonging, and secondarily in terms of skills and information. This view regards pedagogy for e-learning not just in terms of procedures and techniques for supporting the construction of knowledge but in terms of their effects on the formation of identities (Mayes and Fowler, 1999). The essence of a community of practice is that, through a joint engagement in a particular activity, learners form identities and develop and share practices (Mayes and de Freitas, 2004). A community of practice has been defined by Wenger (1998) based on three aspects:

- What is about – as a joint enterprise as it is understood and continually renegotiated by its members

- How it functions – as a mutual engagement that binds members together into a social entity.
- What capability it has produced – the shared repertoire of communal resources members have developed over time, e.g. routines, sensibilities, artifacts and vocabulary.

Involvement is central here because it means making conscious commitment to a group. Shaffer and Anundsen (1993) refer to this as 'conscious community' and as described by Wenger (1998) this is a community that emphasises participants' needs for transformation and personal growth, as well as the social aspects of the community. In some instances these learning communities may be more interesting and stimulating because they involve participants with similar objectives and interests. This aspect may be a part of what differentiates community for social networking (e.g. Facebook, YouTube or My Space) and communities that nurture personal growth and development.

The attraction of applying communities of practice in higher education is whether or not students are motivated for conceptualising learning as a process of guided construction of knowledge. This means that teachers need to focus on the student's cognitive activity otherwise there will be no useful learning. For example, Rohde et al., (2007) proposed a design of practice-based courses where students created a community of practice. The online community's purpose was to facilitate the view of knowledge as a construction of students' online interactions within the community and remains within the virtual domain to be accessed, challenged and developed further by other members in the community. At the same time, Goodyear (2003) gives an account of communities of practice as knowledge-sharing by describing a cycle of learning, moving through phases of externalisation (of tacit knowledge) sharing, discussion, refinement and internalisation.

The design of online learning tasks is central here. Goodyear (2003) distinguishes between a task (what gets set by the teacher) and an activity (what follows as the learners' response to the task specified). A number of taxonomies of task types exist, and these can be useful for teachers to decide what specific tasks to set according to the desired software tools to be used. Paulsen (1995) has reviewed a wide range of e-learning and teaching techniques and has produced a taxonomy of online learning tasks. At the same time, in face-to-face mode these learning tasks may be accomplished through the use of simulations, group activities and small-group projects and by encouraging students to pursue topics of their own interest. A sense of community in the classroom may emerge from these activities which may allow students to create physical interactions.

USING SOCIAL SOFTWARE TOOLS FROM A SOCIAL CONSTRUCTIVIST PERSPECTIVE

Successful collaborative processes and the creation of online learning communities emerge and are shaped by their own members. The teacher as a member of that community may influence the structure and the character of the community but not the creation of that community. The teacher, therefore, may set up or modify learning tasks, select and design software tools that may assist to the emergence of the learning community where each student may customise these tools to meet their own needs. The design of these tools may

be modified to meet the requirements of a new learning task on which students are working. For example, the teacher has assigned an online collaborative learning task for students to share opinions and ideas. The teacher could initiate that particular task by designing supportive organisational forms and structures necessary for establishing an online social network. These supportive organisational forms may include social software tools for triggering students' action. Social software can be broadly defined as 'software that supports group interaction' (Owen et al., 2006). The most common type is likely to be discussion boards. However, applications like weblogs, and wikis are now widely used for teaching and learning. According to Owen et al., (2006) some of the key attributes of these tools, in relation to higher education, are that they:

- Deliver communication between groups
- Provide gathering and sharing resources
- Deliver collaborative collecting and indexing of information
- Enable communication between many people
- Support conversational interaction between individuals or groups ranging from real-time instant messaging to asynchronous collaborative teamwork spaces
- Support social feedback
- Deliver to many platforms as this is appropriate to the teacher, student and context

Table 1. Paulsen's taxonomy of online learning tasks

Techniques	Example methods
One-alone	Online databases; online journals; online applications wikis, blogs, social bookmarking; software libraries; online interest groups, social networking
One-to-one	Learning contracts; Apprenticeships; interviews, collaborative assignments, roleplays, wikis, blogs, social networking
One-to-many	Symposiums; lectures; role plays; interviews, wikis, blogs, social networking
Many-to-many	Discussion groups; simulations; games; debates; case studies; brainstorming; Delphi techniques; Forums; project groups, wikis, blogs, social networking

Weblogs are updatable personal websites, often used as personal journal, consisting of brief paragraphs of opinions, information and links, called posts (Anderson, 2006). Wiki software allows learners to easily upload content and easily edited by anyone who is allowed access (Owen et al., 2006; Anderson, 2006). One of the well-known examples is the online encyclopedia Wikipedia (http://www.wikipedia.org/). The principle behind the operation of Wikipedia is that a wiki may be regarded as a collaborative tool that may facilitate both the needs of a large group but also may be used as an asynchronous social tool for the particular needs of small groups (Owen et al., 2006). Flexibility, ease of use and open access are some of the many reasons why wikis and blogs are useful for group working.

This section will consider a range of social software tools such as discussion boards, blogs and wikis in relation to the two social constructivist perspectives: collaborative learning and communities of practice. The particular approaches proposed may provide, to teachers, a starting point for reflection on how collaborative learning and communities of practice may be mapped to teaching and learning using social software. However, there are a number of elements that determine the level of learning that can be achieved by using social software. These limitations may often be apparent to the design of learning activities because students may perceive their engagement, for example, into online learning communities differently often causing lack of engagement, interaction and participation. Social presence becomes a critical element in community building in a way that the instructor should empower students to participate in the community building and exploration of content (e.g. Goodyear, 2001; Ellis et al., 2007). Also, establishing guidelines as a starting point for collaborative processes in a group may serve as a means by which the group defines shared goals and purposes (e.g. Goodyear, 2007; Kanuka, 2007).

Using Social Software for Engaging in Collaborative Learning Processes

Collaborative learning may be instantiated in actual practice by using a number of different tools. For example, discussion boards and blogs may be used to create processes of collaboration and interaction by introducing online discussions through linking and posting information and resources. The interactive nature of online discussions assists in promoting discussion among learners by creating a forum for sharing opinions and ideas. By engaging students in online discussions, teaching and learning may be transformed from a one way instructional approach to a highly interactive approach to learning (Ellis et al., 2006). Additionally, reflection and reflective practice may be seen as one of the most valuable affordances that online discussions can provide. This is particularly useful when face-to-face discussions and online discussions complement each other. For example, the online discussion may be planned not just to be an 'add on' but to be an integral part of the learning environment. Therefore, by integrating blogs or discussion forums for engaging in online discussions into the teaching and learning flow of the classroom, students have the time to foster a habit of reflective practice, critical thinking and articulating online, which can subsequently further develop during in-class discussions.

Research findings show, that online discussions often focus on similar kinds of learning tasks such as the encouragement of participants to put their thoughts into writing in a way that other peers can understand, promoting self reflective dialogue and dialogue with others. That is, effective online discussions through the use of social software tools foster effective collaborative learning (Ellis et al., 2007). However, students may only achieve this deep reflection on the online postings made by other peers, if the purpose of the learning activity is understood by them (Ellis et al., 2004).

For the purpose of developing student's understanding, teachers should view the reflective practice as a part of an active learning structure, for the use of blogs and discussion boards, which facilitate the sharing of different viewpoints and ideas. This is central here, particularly for using blogs where a permanent record of a student's thoughts is provided for later students' reflection and debate, by automatically saving the messages posted in the discussions. This may create a network of interactions, which may form a social network. For example, if blogging activity is combined into two models which can function simultaneously then the particular application can be both user and content focused or a mix of either. The user - focused model may be designed for the purpose of interaction, sharing and formulating social networks. The content –focused model may be used for assigning learning content which can be written from a personal point of view, with students expressing their own range of interests, rather than on an assigned project or a course topic. This provides to students the ability to create their own content by adopting a research-based approach. For example, Britain (2004) argues that the teacher should gradually engage students in collaborative learning by primarily focusing on making explicit students' conceptions of the phenomenon in question which, in turn, they will determine their prior knowledge of that phenomenon. The second stage is to help students to be aware the level of knowledge they already have and this could be accomplished by engaging them in online discussions for exchanging opinions that would assist on experiencing other students' views on the same issue (e.g. McLoughlin and Luca, 2001). Interaction may occur throughout the students' group instead of between students and the teacher within the group setting and therefore, the teacher is acting as a group member who is contributing to the learning process thus, encouraging students to form different communities with different knowledge-building practices. Such communities may be

academic or vocational, at a first instance, and ideally students should recognise that both the creation and the application of knowledge within the community are well-understood and have value for the members (Goodyear, 2007).

Creating Communities of Practice With the Use of Social Software

Conceptualising the use of a blog from a content-focused approach, there is the possibility to build learner knowledge networks. That is, the design of a Knowledge Forum, as Scardamalia and Bereiter (2003) addresses it, aiming at supporting learners to pool ideas and reflecting to these by developing supportive arguments. In the form of content, like notes, a multimedia community knowledge space is created through students' different perceptions, models, theories, evidence and reference material in a shared space. Through this space, students may develop a collective responsibility for the solution of knowledge problems, and the teacher is assisting students to grow into that responsibility. The learning activity includes the development of ideas and explanations which then are shared with a group of peers. Then, refinement of these ideas is important as new ideas develop. In this way the use of a blog as a Knowledge Forum has the potential to include an interplay between socially defined knowledge and personal experience which is mediated by a membership of the group. This provides a learning situation that negotiates both an individual's experience, and the knowledge that the individual takes from, or brings to, the community. Consequently, the use of a blog as a Knowledge Forum supports the creation of communities from a focus of carrying tasks and activities to a focus on the continual improvement of ideas and creative problem solving (Scardmalia and Bereiter, 2003).

An important element for social software is linking as it may deepen the conversational nature and also the sense of immediacy (Anderson, 2006). From a user-focused perspective, the process of linking to different communities may lead to 'boundary crossing'. For example, through linking, students can be members of online learning communities that include other cultures, experiences and ages. By this way, students have the opportunity to move beyond their particular social community and enter other communities where new skills are developed with the assistance of more experienced members of the community. In particular, White (2006) argues that teachers may start thinking about strategic approaches to using blogs as a medium for community development. That is, in terms of (1) technology and design: the impact of blogging tools on the community and (2) the social architecture: locus of control, power, identity, interaction processes and the role of subject matter. White (2006) distinguishes blog based communities in three main patterns: The blog centric community, the central connecting topic community and the boundaried community.

The main difference between these kinds of blog based communities is based on locus of control power and identity. In blog centric communities the power is firmly held by the blog owners as they can set the rules and norms of engagement. The topic centric blog community's power and identity is distributed across the community because there is no technological platform and bloggers may select their own tool. In boundaried communities, blogs and blog readers are hosted on a single site or platform. Learners may become members of the community where are offered the opportunity to create a blog. Often boundaried communities have other social software tools such as discussion boards, instant messaging and wikis. Power in boundaried communities is held partly by the owner of the platform, who may impose rules but also is exercised by bloggers in terms of the frequency of posting and interest as measured by how many comments a blogger gets. An example of adopting a boundaried community for teaching and learning would be to design a learning activity where each student would have

the chance to log in a Virtual Learning Environment (VLE) where there would be collections of other students' blogs for the students to post their opinions and ideas for the issues discussed. This may lead to faster social connections and community building. However, these blogs are not replacing the forum instead they offer a new community activity because bloggers have more control of the message than in a forum in terms of controlling the pace of the postings and determining their relevance according to their own learning experiences. Therefore, blogs can be regarded as a more personal part of the VLE where the students reflect, criticise and control different posts based on their personal interests.

An interesting point made by White (2006) is that blog communities may take the form of a network since they are not bounded by the technology and may grow beyond the ability of an individual to keep track of the network. With the perspective of social architecture including the roles and forms of interaction within each type of blog communities, teachers may be able to design their blog community while taking into consideration the role of content or subject matter, their role as facilitators and the role of the technology. In essence, the view of online communities provided by White (2006) may form pedagogical approaches for designing and nurturing blog communities by distributing control, power and identity.

A strong element of this socio-cultural view of using blogs and other social software tools is online identity or social presence – what persons become when they are online and how they express that person in virtual space (Palloff and Pratt, 2007). For example, an introverted student, who tends to have more difficulty establishing presence in face-to-face teaching, may become more extroverted by establishing presence and interaction with other peers online. This notion of changing identity when interacting with technology may be caused by the fact that introverted students process information internally and are more comfortable spending time thinking about information before responding to it (Palloff and Pratt, 2007). Consequently, introverted students may have less difficulty creating a blog for exchanging opinions within a boundaried community where the establishment of a social presence may be easier than in-class. It can be argued, therefore, that the degree of social presence that may be developed within a boundaried community may be attributable to the particular technological tool in use. For example, introverted students may still be introvert when using a synchronous chat because it may be perceived as a "noisier" space where they have to post instantly their thought without having available time for reflection, but when they use a blog they may become more extrovert as they have a sense of control and time to reflect their arguments before posting. However, recent studies that investigated social presence have suggested that the medium does not affect the development of online presence. Instead of the particular tool, the way that the student interacts and behaves with other peers impacts on the development of online presence (Wenger, 1998; Polhemus, Shih, and Swan, 2000; Stein and Wanstreet, 2003).

Learning through an online community may not be accomplished only by designing online learning activities that promote interactions between a learner or learners and an environment that is carried out in response to a task with an intended learning outcome (Beetham, 2004) but by focusing also on the process of learning and on the learning activities that students carry out to develop understanding. Although the teacher is responsible for designing appropriate learning activities that facilitate the process of participation, interaction and expression of different opinions and ideas, students also have to contribute for achieving successful online learning activities. Therefore, in order for the students to be considered 'active' in an online community, they must not only access the online learning environment but they must post a comment of some sort. By

posting comments students are considered as active participants and as a result ideas can be collaboratively developed and socially negotiated.

This ability to collaborate and create meaning communally is a clear indicator that students are actively participating in the learning process. For example, an active student who participates and generates knowledge may be the one who gives substantive feedback for other students' ideas but also provides additional resources that other peers may want to review. This development may be considered as a successful learning outcome because the student is able to critically evaluate other students' comments and at the same time being able to gather additional learning resources that go beyond the material assigned, thus developing their skills and their confidence as researchers. At the same time, teachers may offer some guidelines for achieving minimal participation, making it more likely that the students will participate in the learning process. Palloff and Pratt (2007) note that this expectation of participation differs from face-to-face teaching and learning because the discussion can be dominated by more extroverted students giving the impression that the class is engaged.

The opportunity for reflection and the ability to think before responding to a post may help to create a level of participation and engagement that may be greater than a face-to-face discussion. For this reason, the instructor needs to be actively engaged in the process and motivating students to participate by posting interesting topics for accomplishing the desired learning outcome. This may encompass the development of a learning community and not just a social community where knowledge about the learning content can be understood and the ability for collaborative knowledge building can be achieved.

However, research studies reported that students may be uncomfortable to engage in online environments for openly criticizing each others work (MacDonald, 2003), engaging them in peer feedback (Ramsey, 2003) or shifting the power from the tutor to them (Crook, 2002). Sweeney et al., (2004) conducted open-structured interviews with 12 students in a blended course where some sessions were conducted face-to-face and some on discussion boards. Sweeney et al., (2004) concluded that there were students who perceived discussion boards as requiring reflection and hard work whereas others perceived them as offering freedom of speech and deep learning. These variations in students' perceptions may be related to students' understanding of their learning, the role of the learning environment and the activities that are engaged within that. Ellis and Calvo (2006) attempted to investigate these relations by exploring the student experience of learning through discussions in an undergraduate engineering subject. A quantitative approach was used by giving three questionnaires for providing a comprehensive investigation of the qualitative variation in students' experience. They suggested that if students do not understand how discussions could help them reflect on and revise their ideas, they tended not to approach face-to-face or online discussions in ways likely to improve their understanding. They conclude:

"It would also seem necessary to strengthen the relationship between the purpose of the discussions, whether online or face-to-face, in relation to the learning outcomes of the students… Without such strategies, poor approaches to discussions, negative perceptions of workload and a general lack of awareness of the value of discussions for learning will hamper the quality of learning experienced in discursive learning contexts." (p. 67-68)

IMPLICATIONS FOR USING SOCIAL SOFTWARE FOR TEACHING IN HIGHER EDUCATION

Since the use of social software promotes communication, interaction, sharing of resources and social feedback, it is difficult to talk about pedagogically driven practice in terms of using social software without investigating teachers' conceptions, beliefs and intentions of teaching, in order to sketch their main approaches to using social software. However, uptake and implementation does only depend on teachers' beliefs and intentions to using social software but also on students' conceptions of teaching and learning, their conceptions about the learning environment and their conceptions about the subject matter. Part of this section focuses on teachers' conceptions in terms of distilling the main outcomes they imply.

Kember (1997) identified five conceptions of teaching which could be located from a continuum, from a teacher-centered, content oriented conception of teaching to a student-centered and learning conception of teaching as follows:

- Teaching as imparting information
- Teaching as transmitting structured knowledge
- Teaching as an interaction between the teacher and the student
- Teaching as facilitating understanding on the part of the student
- Teaching as bringing conceptual change and intellectual development in the student.

It is apparent that the first two categories have practical implications for using social software. At a first instance these conceptions heavily rely on declarative conceptual knowledge, contemplative forms of analysis and use of textual representations (Barnett, 1997). Therefore, the aim is for the students to absorb predefined knowledge relevant to the discipline's objectives. The main kind of learning outcome associated with these conceptions is the ability to recall prior knowledge and use it for the construction of arguments or for problem solution more generally (Goodyear, 2003). On the contrary, the following three conceptions converge more with the pedagogical assumptions for using social software because the student is supported to handle with confidence concepts, theories and ideas and communicating them with peers and teachers. Also these conceptions encourage informed but critical action by understanding the power and limitations of the field as a resource for action (Barnett, 1997).

These conceptions of teaching may imply that the way social software tools are used depends on the educational beliefs and presumptions of teachers. This also implies that the use of social software is likely to have varied uptake and implementation because of differences in conceiving how these tools may be used between teachers and also between the educational presumptions inherent in these tools. Connected to this observation, teachers may rethink their conceptions, towards a more social constructivist approach for using social software. Teachers that wish to support the use of these tools may plan curriculum design as a social process by:

- Allowing learners to personalise their learning but in a framework that monitors their progress
- Collaborating with experts in a particular domain so students can participate in discussions and become knowledge creators
- Developing learning tasks that encourage collaboration and sharing of ideas
- Supporting the learning experience in terms of designing different learning tasks outside class environment
- Creating organisational structures and deploying appropriate tools for online learning communities to emerge.

These suggestions involve a detailed consideration of the nature of using social software, which may also influence teachers' conceptions of teaching in general. Therefore, for using social software teachers may need to decide what concepts, tasks and methods to introduce based on their conceptions of teaching and the demands of the curriculum. This suggests that particular beliefs and intentions for teaching may bring certain affordances and constrains to the use of social software. This indicates that there is a need for sustained and influential research to understand teachers' conceptions of using social software for teaching and learning.

Another important implication is the integration of social software tools into institutional Virtual Learning Environments (VLEs). Institutions support that these environments reflect the organisational reality. This means that a VLE provides the student with tools such as discussion boards, email, noticeboards, whiteboards, etc and connects the user to university libraries, resources, regulations and specific content such as assessment and modules. The argument is that since VLEs contain all this data, there is the potential to change the particular learning environment (such as the type of learning tasks, learning resources, type of tools, complexity of material, etc) to the student's preferences. However, practitioners now question whether the idea of a VLE can support the integration of social software tools (Anderson, 2006). In response to these concerns, Johnson et al., (2006) investigated the development of a Personalised Learning Environment (PLE) as having a significant effect in managing personal goals in the context of personal development planning and for introducing the integration of social software and e-portfolios.

CONCLUSION

This chapter explained how the social constructivist perspective can inform the use of social software. Certain pedagogies from a social constructivist approach were discussed including collaborative learning and communities of practice. Then, this chapter discussed how these pedagogies may be used for social software. This is particularly useful for mapping the social constructivist approach against specific characteristics of learning, which may enable teachers to design specific learning tasks for social software tools. This also may allow teachers to make the link between pedagogy and theory more explicit. It is perceived that using social software tools for helping students to engage in online discussions will promote collaborative learning and interactions amongst learners as well as reflective practice. Furthermore, providing the appropriate organisational structures and technological tools enable learners to develop online learning communities where the sharing of learning material and the construction of new ideas, with the help of more experienced peers, may lead to user-generated content. From a user-focused perspective, an important element of social software is linking which gives the opportunity to students to enter other communities, with different cultures and experiences to create new knowledge and skills. This may generate a network of interactions, which can result in the formation of a social network community. Personal identity and social presence are important for establishing internal dialogue for formulating responses which can be potentially different from how students may respond to face-to-face teaching and learning. The discussion and acknowledgement of these issues support the development of control, power and identity in the online community by designing pedagogically informed learning activities. However, we must acknowledge that designing such learning activities may not lead to intended learning outcomes because students' conceptions of teaching and learning and how they intend to engage in the online learning environment may vary.

Teachers' conceptions of teaching seem to be an important consideration for using social software from a social constructivist approach. Teachers may need to decide their teaching strategies (nature of learning tasks, curriculum design, teaching approaches etc), in terms of using social software, based on their particular understandings of the teaching process. This is particularly useful in the context of e-learning, because through teachers' conceptions of teaching, researchers could investigate the impact of factors such as individual perspectives, cultural and discipline differences in terms of using social software.

Further empirical research is needed to understand the role of social software from a pedagogical perspective by investigating how the use of these tools can support students' learning experiences. Social software tools are currently perceived as technologies that imply a different relationship between institutional boundaries and social forms (Jones, 2008) so further investigation is needed to see how current institutional VLEs can afford the opportunity of greater peer-based pedagogy to allowing more radical or diverse learning activities by integrating social software or whether it is preferable to rely on publicly available social software resources which can be used for teaching and learning.

REFERENCES

Anderson, P. (2006). *What is the Web2.0? Ideas, technologies and implications for education.* Available at: http://www.jisc.ac.uk/media/documents/techwatch/tsw0701.pdf [Accessed 5 April, 2007].

Argyris, C., & Schon, D. A (1974). *Theory in practice: Increasing professional effectiveness.* San Francisco, Jossey-Bass.

Barnett, R. (1997). *Higher Education: a critical business.* Buckingham, Open University Press.

Britain, S. (2004). *A Review of Learning Design: Concept, Specifications and Tools, a report for the JISC E-learning Pedagogy Programme, JISC.* http://www.jisc.ac.uk/uploaded_documents/ACF83C.doc [Accessed on 25th of April, 2006].

Brown, J. S., Collins, A., & Duguid, P. (1989). Educational Researcher. NBEET Commisioned Report No.28. In P. Candy, C. Crebert, G. O'Leary

(Eds.), J. *Australian Government Publishing Service, 18*, 32-42.

Cole, P. (1992). Constructivism revisited: A search for common ground. *Educational technology, 33*(2), 27-34.

Conole, G., Dyke, M., Oliver, M., & Seale, J. (2004). Mapping pedagogy and tools for effective learning design. *Computers and education, 43*, 17-33.

Crook, C. (2002). The Campus Experience of Networked Learning. In C. A. J. Steeples (Eds.), *Networked Learning: Perspectives and Issues.* London, Springer-Verlag.

Dillenbourg, P. (1999). What do you mean by collaborative learning? In P. Dillenbourg (Ed.), *Collaborative learning: Cognitive and computational approaches.* (pp. 1-19). Oxford: Elsevier.

Downes, S. (2005). E-learning 2.0. *eLearn Magazine.* Available at: http://www.elearnmag.org/subpage.cfm?section=articles&article=29-1 [Accessed 10 May, 2006].

Ellis, R. A., & Calvo, R. A. (2004). Learning through discussions in blended environments. *Educational Media International, 40*(1), 263-274.

Ellis, R. A., & Calvo, R. A. (2006). Discontinuities in university student experiences of learning through discussions. *British Journal of Educational Technology, 37*(1), 55-68.

Ellis, R. A., Goodyear, P., O'Hara, A., & Prosser, M. (2006). How and what university students learn through online and face-to-face discussions: conceptions, intensions and approaches. *Journal of computer assisted learning, 22*, 244-256.

Ellis, R. A., Goodyear, P., O'Hara, A., & Prosser, M. (2007). The university student experience of face-to-face and online discussions: coherence, reflection and meaning. *ALT-J, 15*(1), 83-97.

Ernest, P. (1995). The one and the many. In P. Steffe & J. Gale (Eds.), *Constructivism in education*

(pp. 459-524). Hillsdale, NJ: Lawrence Erlbaum Associates.

Goodyear, P. (2003). *Effective networked learning in higher education: notes and guidelines.* Available at: http://www.csalt.lancs.ac.uk/jisc/guidelines_final.doc. [Accessed 15th March, 2005].

Goodyear, P. (2007). Discussion, Collaborative Knowledge Work and Epistemic Fluency. *British Journal of Educational Studies, 55*(4), 351-368.

Goodyear, P., Salmon, G., Spector, M., Steeples, C., & Tickner, S. (2001). Competences for online teaching: A special report. *Educational Technology, Research and Development, 49*(1), 65-72.

Johnson, M., Hollins, P., Wilson, S., & Liber, O. (2006). *Towards a reference model for the personal learning environment. Proceedings of the 23rd annual ascilite conference: Who's learning? Whose technology?* Australia.

Jones, C. (2008). Infrastructures, institutions and networked learning. *Sixth International Conference on Networked Learning,* Halkidiki, Greece.

Jones, P., Miller, C., Packman, G., & Thomas, B. (2004). *Student and tutor perspectives of online moderation.* Welsh Enterprise Institute, University of Glamorgan.

Kanuka, H. (2008). Instructional Design and eLearning: A Discussion of Pedagogical Content Knowledge as a Missing Construct. *e-Journal of Instructional Science and Technology, 9*(2), http://www.usq.edu.au/electpub/e-jist/docs/vol9_no2/papers/full_papers/kanuka.htm [Accessed 20 of February, 2008].

Kember, D. (1997). A reconceptualisation of the research into university academics' conceptions of teaching. *Learning and Instruction, 7*(3), 255-275.

Laurillard, D. (2002). *Rethinking University Teaching.* London: Routledge.

Lave, J., & Wenger, E. (1991). *Situated learning.* New York: Cambridge University Press.

Mason, R., & Weller, M (2000). Factors affecting student satisfaction on a web course. Education at a distance. *Australian Journal of Educational Technology, 16*(2), 173-200.

Mayes, T., & De Freitas, S. (2004). Review of E-Learning Theories, Frameworks and Models. *JISC E-Learning Models Desk Study*. JISC: 43.

Mayes, T., & Fowler, C (1999). Learning Technology and Usability. *Interacting with Computers, 11*, 485-497.

McConnell, D. (2002). *Implementing computer supported cooperative learning.* London: Kogan-Page.

McDonald, J. (2003). Assessing online collaborative learning: process and product. *Computers & Education, 40*(4), 215-226.

McLoughlin, C., & Luca, J (2001). Quality in Online Delivery: What does it Mean For Assessment in E-Learning Environments. Meeting at the Crossroads. *Proceedings of the Annual Conference of the Australasian Society for Computers in Learning in Tertiary Education (ASCILITE)*: http://www.ascilite.org.au/conferences/melbourne01/pdf/papers/mcloughlinc2.pdf [Accessed on February 14th 2008].

Owen, R., Grant, L., Sayers, S., & Facer, K. (2006). Social sofware and learning. *FutureLab.* Bristol, UK. Available at: http://www.futurelab.org.uk/research/opening_education/social_software_01.htm [Accessed 20 January, 2007].

Palloff, R., & Pratt, K. (2007). *Building Online Learning Communities.* San Franscisco, Jossey-Bass.

Paulsen, M. (1995). *The online report on pedagogical techniques for computer-mediated communication.* Available: http://www.emoderators.com/moderators/cmcped.html [Accessed on 10th November 2006].

Peal, D., & Wilson, B. (2001). Activity theory and web-based training. In B. H. Khan (Ed.), *Web-based Training.* New Jersey: Educational Technology Publications.

Polhemus, L., Shih, L., Richardson, J., & Swan, K. (2000). *Building and Affective Learning Community: Social Presence and Learning Engagement.* Paper presented at the World Conference on the WWW and the Internet (WebNet) San Antonio.

Ramsey, C. (2003). Using virtual learning environments to facilitate new learning relationships. *International Journal of Management Education, 3*(2), 31-41.

Rohde, M., Klamma, M. J., & Wulf, V. (2007). Reality is our laboratory: communities of practice in applied computer science. *Behaviour & Information Technology, 26*(1), 81-94.

Scardamalia, M., & Bereiter, C. (2003). CSILE/knowledge forum. In A. Kovalchick, & K. Dawson (Eds.), *Educational and Technology: An Encyclopedia.* Santa Barbara, ABC-CLIO.

Shaffer, C., & Anundsen, K. (1993). *Creating Community Anywhere.* Los Angeles, CA: Tarcher/Perigee Books.

Sharpe, R., Benfield, G., Lessner, E., & De Cicco, E. (2005). *Final Report: Scoping Study for the Pedagogy Strand of the JISC e-learning Programme.* www.jisc.ac.uk/uploaded_documents/scoping%20study%20final%20report%20v4.1.doc [Acessed on 2 June, 2006].

Stein, D., & Wanstreet, C. (2003). Role of Social Presence, Choice of Online or Face-to-Face Group Format, and Satisfaction with Perceived Knowledge Gained in a Distance Learning Environment. *Midwest Research to Practice Conference in Adult, Continuing and Community Education*: http://alumni-osu.org/midwest/midwest%20papers/Stein%20&%20Wanstreet-Done.pdf [Accessed on 5th of May, 2006].

Sweeney, J., O'Donoghue, T., & Whitehead, C. (2004). Traditional face-to-face and web-based tutorials: A study of university students' perspectives on the roles of tutorial participants. *Teaching in Higher Education, 9*(3), 311-323.

Thomas, B., Jones, P., Packman, G., Miller, C. (2004). *Student perceptions of effective e-moderation: a qualitative investigation of e-college.* Wales: Networked Learning Conference.

Twigg, C. (1994). The Changing Definition of Learning. *Educom Review, 29*(4). http://educom.edu/web/pubs/reviewArticles/29422.html [Accessed on 15th of March 2005].

Vygotsky, L. S. (1978). *Mind in society: The development of higher psychological processes.* Harvard, Harvard university press.

Wenger, E. (1998). *Communities of Practice: Learning meaning and identity.* Cambridge: Harvard University Press.

White, N. (2006). *Blogs and community: launcing a new paradigm for online community.* Available at: http://kt.flexiblelearning.net.au/wp-content/uploads/2006/12/white.pdf [Accessed 15 December 2006].

Chapter XX
The Potential of Enterprise Social Software in Integrating Exploitative and Explorative Knowledge Strategies

Dimitris Bibikas
South East European Research Centre, Greece
Research Centre of the University of Sheffield and CITY College, Greece

Iraklis Paraskakis
South East European Research Center, Greece
Research Centre of the University of Sheffield and CITY College, Greece

Alexandros G. Psychogios
CITY College, affiliated Institution of the University of Sheffield, Greece

Ana C. Vasconcelos
The University of Sheffield Regent Court, UK

ABSTRACT

The aim of this chapter is to investigate the potential role of social software inside business settings in integrating knowledge exploitation and knowledge exploration strategies. These strategies are approached through the lens of dynamic capabilities, organisational learning and knowledge lifecycle models. The authors argue that while current enterprise Information Technology (IT) systems focus more on knowledge lifecycle processes concerning the distribution and application of knowledge, enterprise social software can support knowledge exploration strategies and leverage knowledge creation and validation procedures. We present secondary data from the utilisation of enterprise social computing tools inside two companies for that matter. The first case illustrates how social computing tools were deployed in an international bank, and the other presents the employment of these technologies in an international broadcasting company. The authors suggest that free-form and pre-defined structures can co-exist in bounded organisational environments, in which knowledge exploitation and knowledge exploration strategies can harmonically interact. This chapter concludes with some managerial implications and future research avenues.

INTRODUCTION

During the last decade, industry and scholarly communities have equally highlighted the importance of managing organisational knowledge and posited that intangible assets form a critical enterprise resource asset (Metaxiotis et al., 2005; Davenport and Prusak, 1998). Knowledge management has been previously associated with the exploitation and growth of the organisational knowledge assets (Davenport and Prusak, 1998) aiming at increased operational efficiency and continuous time-to-market improvement. Yet, recent developments associate knowledge strategies with the ability of the organisation to explore and identify critical changes of the external operating environment, ultimately renewing its internal knowledge base and core competencies (Bhatt et al., 2005). Hence, the mere existence of strong organisational resources and capabilities appear to be inadequate for obtaining long-term sustainable competitive advantage.

The term "Enterprise 2.0" promptly followed the widespread of the so-called "Web 2.0" and dominated the discourse surrounding the utilisation of business concepts in relation not only to enterprise information applications, but also to associated managerial approaches related to our post-industrial age (Bughin, 2008; Hamel, 2007). The use of the decimal point in the term implies a proposed discontinuity from previous forms of organisational contextures, emphasising on a suggested transformative role of social computing inside companies (e.g. wikis, blogs, podcasts, RSS (Really Simple Syndication), Instant Messaging, social bookmarking, etc) (McAfee, 2006). Now,

there is a heated debate between sceptics who argue that the term "Enterprise 2.0" has nothing to offer other than basic managerial selections regarding the utilisation of generic networked business applications (Stenmark, 2008), while supporters claim that the term conveys something new: a flexible and adaptable perspective to organisational knowledge strategies (Bibikas et al., 2008; Ip & Wagner, 2008; Kosonen & Kianto, 2008; Marfleet, 2008; Patrick & Dotsika, 2007; Coakes, 2006; McAfee, 2006) and a key driver towards the development of dynamic capabilities (Shuen, 2008). Has Enterprise 2.0 some actual meaning or the term should just be approached metaphorically? In this paper, we explore whether Enterprise 2.0 can provide strategic business value affecting key knowledge processes and adaptive capabilities of organizations.

The remaining of this chapter is structured in five parts: The first presents the research approach and study methodology. The next section explores knowledge exploitation and knowledge exploration strategies through the lens of dynamic capabilities theory. The third part presents some of the main characteristics of Enterprise 2.0 and investigates the potential of social software in the future of organisational information and knowledge management systems. We argue that these technologies can help towards the integration of exploitation and exploration knowledge strategies. The fourth session presents secondary data from the utilisation of enterprise social computing tools inside two multinational companies. Finally, suggestions and managerial implications are presented along with future research directions.

RESEARCH APPROACH

This article is an early exploratory study and employs a deductive qualitative research approach. It uses a combination of critical literature review on dynamic capabilities theory, knowledge lifecycle and organisational learning in order to conceptualise a model illustrating the potential role of enterprise social software in bridging knowledge exploitation and exploration strategies. Subsequently, this model is tested through secondary data from use cases of social computing inside two large organisations. Since empirical studies providing insights and concrete results on the use of social computing tools for knowledge management purposes are rare, a few anecdotal case studies present some early indications. This research was performed using a desk study method, exclusively using secondary sources. Desk research approaches are usually regarded as mere literature reviews in order for the researcher to be familiarised with background knowledge (Remenyi et al., 1998; Gill and Johnson, 1991). However, this chapter aims at having the desk study as the main method of research. The objective of this article is to adopt a deductive argument in order to conceptualise the role of enterprise social software in an integrated knowledge exploitation and knowledge exploration model. This model is later juxtaposed with secondary data of social software deployments inside organisations. Therefore, this chapter adopts a deductive desk research approach and involves the development of a theory that is subsequently subjected to a test (Collis and Hussey, 2003).

Through this preliminary exploratory investigation it is proposed that social software can be employed to support organisational knowledge exploration strategies. Yet, one cannot neglect the limitations of this particular approach and emphasise on the need to further investigate the suggested theoretical model to other companies and industry sectors, through primary data and field investigation methods.

EXPLOITATION AND EXPLORATION PERSPECTIVES OF KNOWLEDGE MANAGEMENT

Knowledge Exploitation and Exploration as Organisational Learning Strategies

Learning organisations are defined by Senge (1990) as places in which creative thinking is cultivated and continuous learning is fostered. Today's businesses face the challenge of continuous learning and usable knowledge generation in order to increase their responsive capabilities to market changes and advance their innovation outcomes. Therefore, current businesses – which in this chapter are approached as "learning organisations" – plan and implement various knowledge management strategies. Often these practices lay between two largely defined selections: knowledge exploitation and knowledge exploration (March, 1991; Liu, 2006). Knowledge exploitation strategies consist of organisational learning practices for the optimisation of existing processes and improvement of pre-existing knowledge assets. It mainly involves the deployment of resources the enterprise already holds on its possession (Sitkin et al., 1994). On the contrary, knowledge exploration strategies comprise organisational learning practices regarding the creation of new knowledge for the development of new products, services and processes. The latter often lead to the creation and addition of new resources and organisational knowledge assets (Sitkin et al., 1994). Knowledge exploitation reflects moderate yet definite and immediate returns on organisational performance by continuously adopting, synthesizing and applying current knowledge(Liu, 2006). On the contrary, the highly uncertain and unpredictable nature of knowledge exploration process reflects the capability of an organisation to create new core competences, by investing in flexibility, risk, experimentation and innovation (March, 1991; Liu, 2006).

There seems to be a tight link between organisational dynamic capabilities and the two abovementioned organisational knowledge management strategies (i.e. exploitation and exploration). Exploitation and exploration activities can be associated with key knowledge management processes that *create, validate, present, distribute* and *apply* knowledge-based resources of the firm through an iterative circle of change, renewal and exploitation (Bhatt, 2001; Nielsen, 2006). This dynamic interconnection between exploitation and exploration knowledge practices creates an iterative flow towards and from the firm's stock of knowledge-based resources. In particular, dynamic capabilities through knowledge exploration contribute to the organisational stock of knowledge – thus creating an "in-flow" stream to the firm's stock of knowledge. On the other hand, dynamic capabilities through knowledge exploitation practices utilise existing resources for the development of new products, services and procedures – thus creating an "out-flow" stream from the firm's stock of knowledge (Nielsen, 2006). Consequently, the knowledge lifecycle

refers to the phases of knowledge process management that an organisation utilises in order to learn, reflect and act upon available resources (Bhatt, 2001): a) *knowledge creation* can lead to the generation of innovative ideas and uncover hidden solutions to existing problems; b) the *knowledge validation* phase provides revision and reflection upon available organisational resources in order to investigate whether these intangible assts are in line with the current state of the art or outdated by more recent developments; c) *knowledge presentation* depicts the means of knowledge illustration in organisational settings through a variety of procedures, media, departments and work practices; d) the *knowledge distribution* process allows knowledge to be shared across organisational boundaries by means of interaction between available communication technologies, management techniques and people; e) *knowledge application* usually refers to the embodiment of available knowledge resources in the organisational value creating system through its products or processes.

Figure 1. The role of knowledge lifecycle in forming the dynamic capabilities

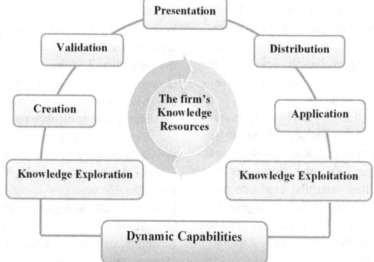

It is proposed that a vital aim of the knowledge lifecycle is to harmonise *knowledge exploration* and *knowledge exploitation*, where the five distinct stages of the knowledge process management appear to be an amalgamation of new knowledge formation (i.e. creation, validation and presentation procedures) with existing knowledge employment, iteration or removal (i.e. distribution and application) (Liu, 2006, Bhatt et al., 2005). The above figure (Figure 1) depicts the association of knowledge lifecycle with knowledge exploitation and exploration strategies in respect to organisational dynamic capabilities.

The Potential of Enterprise Social Software in Knowledge Exploration

It is argued that the use of a new breed of emerging collaborative environments in knowledge intensive organisations can facilitate knowledge work (Bibikas et al., 2008; Bughin, 2008; Ip & Wagner, 2008; McKelvie et al., 2007; Patrick & Dotsika, 2007; McAfee, 2006). These new digital environments for generating, sharing and refining knowledge are already popular on the Internet, where they are collectively labelled as "Web 2.0" technologies. Interestingly enough, these technologies are entering enterprise bounded environments for creating and sharing organisational knowledge (Bughin, 2008). Although "Web 2.0" technologies in organisational settings can be viewed from varying perspectives and can be referred to employing different names (i.e. social software, social computing, Enterprise 2.0, etc), their main general operations appear to be (McAfee, 2006):

- Search, to provide mechanisms for discovering information.
- Links, to provide guidance to knowledge workers in order to discover the needed knowledge and ensure emergent structure to online content.

- Authoring, to enable knowledge workers to share their opinions with a broad audience.
- Tags, to present an alternative navigational experience exploiting un-hierarchical categorisation of intranet content.
- Extensions, to exploit collaborative intelligence and recommend to knowledge workers contextually relevant content.
- Signals, to automatically alert knowledge workers for newly created and relevant content.

From a technological point of view these technological features are hardly new (i.e. search, links, metadata and signalling technologies – such as electronic mail – existed from the very beginning of the Internet), yet they are becoming more and more easy to use. Perhaps more importantly, they convey a novel perspective regarding the process of utilising enterprise information and developing knowledge management systems in organisations. Unlike the design of current technologies, where particular tools usually predefine their employment (i.e. presenting certain business rules and specific procedural requirements), enterprise social software can be abstracted from its practical use, in a manner that the tools are not directly defining their utilisation. However, these applications cannot be considered "social" as such. Rather they provide functionality in order for the social constructs of organisations (i.e. individuals, teams, units, customers, partners, etc) to engage in social activities (Bouman et al., 2008). As an example, a wiki application can be utilised from formal business policy documents editing to brainstorming and realising meeting agendas. Similarly, a blog can be employed from business project activities reporting to posting personal work-related thoughts and reflections. Therefore, the deployment of enterprise social software can be eventually emergent according to adapting needs, ideas, organisational policies etc. We argue that the "social" attribute of enterprise "Web 2.0" tools, the fact that by design are intended to provide for interaction and communication, presents an opportunity for enhancing explorative knowledge strategies.

Often the design of enterprise IT/KM systems focuses on rigid procedural tasks and routine information in a structured manner. In transactional or computational business information systems this is can be desirable (e.g. Enterprise Resource Planning, Management Information System, Business Intelligence, etc). Pre-defined categorisation of users, access rights management and specified up front roles together with process replication mechanisms are all vital functionalities of such enterprise information systems. Yet, these functionalities are – by design – more focused on knowledge distribution and application. They convey the embodiment of available organisational knowledge resources in the firm's products, services and procedures for the creation of a process-based unified work environment (Brynjolfsson & McAfee, 2007). However, social computing tools can enhance knowledge exploration strategies, leveraging knowledge creation, validation and presentation processes.

Knowledge Creation Process

Knowledge creation is essentially associated with individual creativity and innovation capabilities (Bhatt et al., 2005). An organisation can create new knowledge through the embodiment of a deeper level of understanding that occurs when individuals question their own and shared mental models (Guzman & Wilson, 2005; Metaxiotis et al., 2005). As Argyris and Schon (1978) point out, knowledge creation effectively takes place when there is a conflict between one's "espoused theory" (i.e. mental models concerning values, behaviour, leadership style, etc), and one's "theory-in-use" (i.e. what an individual actually does). Enterprise social software can act as a dynamic and emergent repository of digital content where contributions can be under circumstances widely

visible and persistent and invoke conversations and divergence of ideas and thoughts. The basic categorisation of user roles in enterprise social computing tools, as well as the absence of rigid structures of the knowledge resources which are meant to capture, in a sense can promote dissent or debate, or otherwise a conflict between one's "espoused theory" and "theory-in-use". These platforms through their conversation engagement functionality appear to compose a model for enhanced contextual understanding of the underlying philosophy of established organisational norms and routines: a critical process for achieving new knowledge creation (Bhatt et al., 2005; Argyris and Schon, 1978).

Knowledge Validation Process

As realities in the inner or outer organisational environment can be rapidly altered, knowledge validation process drives a continuous examination and supervision of available organisational knowledge assets (Bhatt, 2001). In this way outdated knowledge should be revised or discarded. Enterprise social software consists of digital environments which are initially freeform and largely avoid the "binary logic" of imposed roles, identities, workflows, or interdependencies. The social design element of these technologies can help generate flexible and experimenting practices inside businesses. Knowledge workers can be empowered to create, adjust and dismantle their processes across the organisation. McAfee (2006) calls the procedure of presenting "untested" knowledge using social computing tools and the subsequent dialectic examination and revision of such resources "knowledge episodes". Knowledge episodes are explained as the recordings of both the interactions of knowledge workers in a particular matter, as well as the actual output of their work practices (McAfee, 2006). The participatory design element of social computing tools as well as their initially freeform and loosely-structured character constitutes a promising element for element for maintaining both the relevance and currency of organisational knowledge.

Knowledge Presentation Process

With regards to the knowledge presentation process, enterprise social software can contribute to the development of a unified work place and co-exist with other corporate IT systems. The functionality of enterprise Web 2.0 software of creating widely and permanently visible content appears to promote an integrated presentation scheme of organisational knowledge resources, regardless of corporation location, media and work practice. The goal of universally visible and persistent content within the organisation can effectively reinforce the rigidities of existing organisational boundaries, actively promoting the exploration of new knowledge.

"Legacy" enterprise IT/KM systems jointly with enterprise social software seem to effectively leverage all activities of the knowledge lifecycle. Social computing tools can be used in order to promote knowledge creation and validation through open discussion, communication and ideas exchange. On the other hand, traditional business information systems can focus on process replication mechanisms, such as the knowledge distribution and application processes. Hence,

the combination of enterprise social software with existing corporate IT/KM systems can lead to an integrated view of the knowledge lifecycle process in organisational settings. This interaction of "legacy" IT systems and enterprise social computing in relation to the knowledge process management is depicted in the following figure. It presents the complementary role of enterprise social software in knowledge lifecycle and organisational learning in respect of dynamic capabilities formation.

Participative enterprise social software can co-exist with "legacy systems", such as Enterprise Resource Planning (ERP), Customer Relationship Management (CRM) and Human Resource Management (HRM) (Brynjolfsson & McAfee, 2007; McAfee, 2006). These business information systems will continue to play a major role in everyday organisational operations (payments, orders, expense submissions, etc). Decision-making processes should still be based on highly structured systems and processes leaded by knowledge-based assets and business objectives (Goh, 2005). Yet, in parallel to these business operations, we suggest that knowledge workers should utilise social software technologies in order for informal collaboration and person-to-person interaction to take place. Structured data and information from "legacy systems" can be communicated and con-

Figure 2. Integrating knowledge strategies with existing and social software technologies.

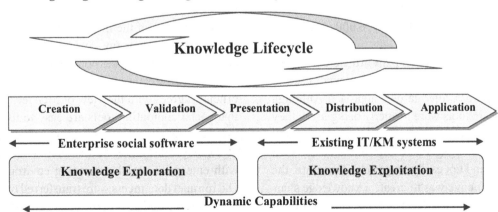

sistently available through emergent participative technologies. Free-form and pre-defined structure can co-exist in bounded organisational environments employing an integrated setting in which knowledge exploitation and knowledge exploration strategies can effectively interact.

In the following cases the reader is introduced to some examples of social software utilization inside business boundaries. The cases illustrate the generic attributes of enterprise social software as pointed by McAfee (2006):

- Digital environments in which content can be persistent and widely visible.
- Lightweight deployment, in the sense that they are easy to implement and use.
- Emergent categorization of content in an evolving and self-organizing manner.
- Based on SLATES functionalities (search, links, authoring, tags, extensions, and signals).
- Can provide widely accessible content on both the process as well as the final output of collaborative work practices.
- Reliant on social constructs of organizations (e.g. individuals, teams, networks, etc).

INTERNATIONAL BANK CASE

The international investment bank of the first case is established in Europe (London and Frankfurt) and provides a range of financial services. The company has approximately 6.000 employees internationally.

Employees of the company in different departments and geographical locations were used to working in a "walled garden" approach. Although groupware tools were formerly being used, they had only limited impact on content sharing and wider user engagement. Information was often isolated and not easily accessible. Therefore, the main challenge was to create a knowledge sharing digital environment without compromising

on security issues. The company started with internal wikis and blogs deployment. At the beginning only the IT department employees were using these applications. However, the aim was to transform these technologies into a central hub for all departments – technical and non technical – to participate. A bottom-up publicisation approach was selected, mainly through e-mails and word-of-mouth. The first encouraging results did not take long to appear. Employees from a wide variety of backgrounds and responsibilities started to follow and contribute to the internal wiki articles and blog postings. Previously undiscovered knowledge resources were starting to be revealed. Employees with different competences were starting to add value to various subjects outside their every-day tasks. This is in line with the view of McAfee (2006) in which enterprise social software can accumulate widely and permanently visible knowledge assets through flexible and experimentation practices. Also the participation empowerment of the internal wiki deployment in this case agrees with the view in which enterprise social software encourages knowledge workers to create, adjust and dismantle processes across the organisation (McAfee 2006). Ideas, solutions to problems and knowledge assets were generated from various employees from different departments, levels and geographical locations. This "demand-driven" operational model of social software could potentially invoke new organisational competencies and empower expertise creation.

As the users of the internal enterprise social tools grew the company decided to offer short and informal training sessions. The fact that the guidance to use of these tools was speedy and "unofficial" agrees with the view of McAfee (2006) that social computing tools are easy to use and they require only a little or no training at all.

Legacy technologies were soon after integrated with enterprise social computing environment. Old intranet documents were transferred on wiki articles and employees of the bank revised out of date contents. With the help of the wiki there have been a continuous examination and supervision of available organisational knowledge assets as the knowledge validation procedure asserts. In this way outdated knowledge was revised and updated or discarded accordingly.

Furthermore, the wiki was used in order to effectively present inter-departmentally information of various types. Allegedly, the employees found the use of the wiki for presentation purposes more effective than other applications. The functionality of enterprise Web 2.0 software of creating widely and permanently visible content appears to promote an integrated presentation scheme of organisational knowledge resources, regardless of corporation location, media and work practice. Also, using the wiki the employees had the opportunity to collaboratively create, validate and present knowledge assets, developing therefore iterations between the exploration stages of the knowledge lifecycle.

In this case, social computing tools facilitated the creation of an open environment where content was permanently and widely visible, with employees creating, validating and distributing knowledge assets asynchronously and in parallel. Management played a significant role. Executive staff was the first to explore the use of such tools. They transfer information from the intranet to wiki articles and championed the use of social computing tools for various purposes (e.g. presentations, reporting, briefings, etc). Moreover, management planed for future utilisation of social computing tools. Their vision was not only to expand the use of such tools inside the firewall, but also to develop a dedicated area outside the company's intranet for customers and partners in order to promote discussion and to collaboratively develop documentation. This scope agrees with the suggestion of Shuen (2008) that in order to develop and sustain dynamic capabilities organisations should connect and interact with other companies and generate open ecosystems for managing digital syndications.

INTERNATIONAL BROADCASTING COMPANY CASE

The broadcasting company of the second case is arguably one of the oldest and largest established broadcasting organisations world-wide. It is a multi-billion globalised corporation and offers many national television stations, international, national and local radio stations. Relationships and not static documents were seen as the essence of employees' daily knowledge work. The challenge in managing knowledge in such an organisation was to enhance its already relationship-based and conversational culture.

Contrary to the established approach of managing knowledge in such multifaceted and complex environments, the organisation did not select to deploy a large and expensive knowledge management system. What they focused on was the means by which they could facilitate relationship building and enhance conversational links among employees all over the world. Although that the company possessed centralised and formal directories with human resources and business information, they were rarely updated and did not reflect the dynamic connections between employees.

The organisation started experimentally to deploy social computing tools for the employees of all levels: blogs, wikis and social-networking tools. The first step in the social software deployment venture was the set up of fora and blogs. These tools were created with virtually no enforcement of work categorisation, output or structure. The ultimate goal was to empower flexibility, risk and experimentation. Employees of all levels used these tools for various reasons from setting up meetings and company excursions to discussing key strategy decisions. Blogs were deployed in a bottom-up fashion. Individuals, teams and executives that wished to create and maintain a blog, were free to do it with no other requirement except basic commitment to avoid unprofessional conduct. This implementation approach agrees with the view of McAfee (2006) that freeform and loosely-structured enterprise social computing tools, allow knowledge to eventually self-organise through day-to-day work practices.

The next step was to deploy company-wide internal wikis. The library department envisioned to generate a dynamic "knowledge base" in order to reflect the active relationships and linkages among business, units, teams and individuals inside the organisation. Although that an intranet infrastructure existed beforehand, the content was never updated in time and did not reflect the changes in the corporation. This would only happen if the information provided was easily updated from anyone inside the organisation. The library department should initiate the content creation procedure, yet the information had to be dynamically updated from members of all levels and departments. As a result, there were continuous iterations in which employees inside the organisation created, validated and presented knowledge assets in a collaborative and widely visible manner. The organisation had perhaps for the very first time a massive amount of knowledge assets created in a decentralised and speedy fashion. This outcome is aligned to what McAfee (2006) suggests on the facilitation capabilities of enterprise social software, i.e. that these tools can make experimentation procedures, interaction and knowledge exchange widely available inside organisations. This recorded output could eventually lead to the creation of new knowledge and novel organisational competences.

The corporation of this case proceeded with the utilisation of social computing tools for other purposes as well. Collaborative document editing and project management related tasks were also facilitated with the use of these technologies.

Again the role of the management played a key role. In this case executives started to use social computing tools and presented an early strategic intent, an act that gave the example to the corporation's units and individuals. Furthermore, these technologies were approached as a

long term competitive advantage for the company and not as a short term and merely tactical tools. Business and technology executives of the organisation envisioned from the early beginning creating an ecology of open and conversational digital spaces for all partner-companies, units, teams and individuals.

DISCUSSION

This chapter has explored the role of enterprise social software, not only as a novel perspective concerning the integration of knowledge exploitation and knowledge exploration strategies, but also its potential and a catalyst for effective dynamic learning capabilities leverage in corporate environments. It is argued that its demand driven and knowledge worker centric approach, allied with a capability to enable "on demand" knowledge management techniques offer the flexibility required to support the formation of knowledge exploration strategies (Bibikas et al, in press). At the same time, enterprise social software is amenable to integration with legacy systems that may already support well the exploitation of existing knowledge resources, leading in effect, to an approach that will enable to underlie the management of overall knowledge lifecycle activities in organisations.

There are practical managerial implications for the implementation of a strategy that encompasses this type of approach: in a first instance, this requires the adoption of an incremental process, starting with pilot and informal initiatives, allowing for collaboration and bottom-up process improvement; secondly, it entails the formation of an adaptive knowledge management strategy, based upon the study of existing formal and informal work practices of knowledge workers and their community interaction, as well as existing innovation process management activities; thirdly, there is the need for awareness towards a clear rationale for the allocation of resources for both exploitative and explorative activities. The direction and implementation of such strategies and the balance to be achieved needs to be contextual to the requirements of each organisation, depending upon environmental driving forces that affect it, such as policy, market and technology dynamism, as well as internal structures, know-how resources and culture. Further research, particularly at the empirical level, is required in order to identify how these balances are achieved, in a variety of organisational contexts, which strategies can effectively support them and how these new developments in enterprise social software can concretely underpin them.

REFERENCES

Argyris, C., & Schon, D. (1978). *Organisational Learning: A Theory of Action Perspective*. Reading, MA: Addison-Wesley.

Bhatt, G. D. (2001). Knowledge management in organizations: examining the interaction between technologies, techniques, and people. *Journal of Knowledge Management, 5*(1), 68-75.

Bhatt, G., Gupta, J. N. D., & Kitchens, F. (2005). An exploratory study of groupware use in the knowledge management process. *The Journal of Enterprise Information Management, 18*(1), 28-46.

Bibikas, D., Kourtesis, D., Paraskakis, I., Bernardi, A., Sauermann, L., Apostolou, D., Mentzas, D., & Vasconcelos, A. C. (2008). Organisational Knowledge Management Systems in the Era of Enterprise 2.0: The case of OrganiK. *In proceedings of the 2nd Workshop on Social Aspects of the Web (SAW 2008)*, held in conjunction with the 11th International Conference on Business Information Systems (BIS 2008), Innsbruck, Austria, May 2008.

Bibikas, D., Paraskakis, I., Psychogios, A. G., & Vasconcelos, A. C. (In press). Emerging enterprise social software knowledge management environments: Current practices and future challenges. *International Journal of Learning and Intellectual Capital*.

Bouman, W., Hoogenboom, T., Jansen, R., Schoondorp, M., de Bruin, B., Huizing, A. (2008). The Realm of Sociality: Notes on the Design of Social Software. University of Amsterdam, Netherlands. Sprouts: Working Papers on Information Systems, 8(1). http://sprouts.aisnet.org/8-1

Brynjolfsson, E., & McAfee, A. P. (2007). Beyond Enterprise 2.0. *MIT Sloan Management Review, 48*(3), 50-55.

Bughin, J. (2008). The rise of enterprise 2.0. *Journal of Direct, Data and Digital Marketing Practice, 9*, 251-259.

Coakes, E. (2006). Storing and sharing knowledge: Supporting the management of knowledge made explicit in transnational organisations. *The Learning Organization, 13*(6), 579-593.

Collis, J., & Hussey, R. (2003). *Business research: a practical guide for undergraduate and postgraduate students*. New York, NY: Palgrave Macmillan.

Davenport, T. H., & Prusak, L. (1998). *Working Knowledge: How Organizations Manage What They Know*. Boston, MA: Harvard Business School Press.

Gill, J., & Johnson, P. (1991). *Research Methods for Managers*. London: Paul Chapman.

Goh, A. L. S. (2005). Harnessing knowledge for innovation: an integrated management framework. *Journal of Knowledge Management, 9*(4), 6-18.

Guzman, G. A. C., & Wilson, J. (2005). The "soft" dimension of organisational knowledge transfer. *Journal of Knowledge Management, 9*(2), 59-74.

Hamel, G. (2007). *The Future of Management*. Boston, Massachusetts: Harvard Business School Press.

Ip, R., & Wagner, C. (2008). Weblogging: A Study of Social Computing and Its Impact on Organizations, *Decision Support Systems*, 45(2), 242-250.

Kosonen, M., & Kianto, A. (2008). Social Computing for Knowledge Creation? The Role of Tacit Knowledge. *In Proceedings of the 3rd Organization Learning, Knowledge and Capabilities Conference (OLKC 2008)*, Copenhagen, Denmark, 28-30 April 2008.

Liu, W. (2006). Knowledge Exploitation, Knowledge Exploration, and Competency Trap. *Knowledge and Process Management*, 13(3), 144-161.

March, J. (1991). Exploration and exploitation in organisational learning. *Organization Science*, 2, 71-87.

Marfleet, J. (2008). Enterprise 2.0 What's your game plan? What, if any, will be the role of the information. *Business Information Review*, 25(3), 152-157.

McAfee, A. P. (2006). Enterprise 2.0: The Dawn of Emergent Collaboration. *MIT Sloan Management Review*, 47(3), 21-28.

McKelvie, G., Dotsika, F., & Patrick, K. (2007). Interactive business development, capturing business knowledge and practice: A case study. *The Learning Organization*, 14(5), 407-422.

Metaxiotis, K., Ergazakis, K. & Psarras, J. (2005). Exploring the world of knowledge management: agreements and disagreements in the academic/practitioner community. *Journal of knowledge management*, 9(2), 6-18.

Nielsen, A. P. (2006). Understanding dynamic capabilities through knowledge management. *Journal of Knowledge Management*, 10(4), 59-71.

Patrick, K., & Dotsika, F. (2007). Knowledge sharing: developing from within. *The Learning Organization*, 14(5), 395-406.

Remenyi, D., Williams, B., Money, A., & Swartz, E. (1998). *Doing research in Business and Management: an introduction to process and Method*. London: SAGE Publications.

Senge, P. (1990). *The Fifth Discipline – The Art and Practice of The Learning Organization*, New York, NY: Doublebay.

Shuen, A. (2008). *Web 2.0: A Strategy Guide*. Sebastopol, CA: O'Reilly Media.

Stenmark, D. (2008). Web 2.0 in the business environment: The new intranet or a passing hype? *In Proceedings of the 16th European Conference on Information Systems (ECIS 2008)*, Galway, Ireland, June 9-11, 2008.

Sitkin, S. B., Sutcliffe, K. M., & Schroeder, R. G. (1994). Distinguishing control form learning in total quality management-A contingency perspective. *Academy of Management Review*, 19, 537–564.

References of Enterprise 2.0 Implementations

Weinberger, D. (2005). *The BBC's low-tech KM, KMWorld*, available at: http://www.kmworld.com/Articles/Column/David-Weinberger/The-BBC%E2%80%99s-low-tech-KM-14276.aspx, last accessed on 15/09/2008.

Semple, E. (2006). *Rise of the wiki. EI Magazine*, 3 (2), available at: http://www.eimagazine.com/xq/asp/sid.0/articleid.4E73DFF9-53B3-4FF1-BA27-E5127C5FD365/qx/display.htm, last accessed on 15/09/2008.

Socialtext, Dresdner Kleinwort Wasserstein Case Study, available at: http://socialtext.com/customers/case-studies/drkw/, last accessed on 15/09/2008.

KEY TERMS

Dynamic Capabilities: It is the firm's ability not only to exploit its existing resources and organisational capabilities, but also its ability to renew and develop its organisational capabilities.

Enterprise Social Software/Enterprise 2.0: The use of social computing tools in organisational settings.

Knowledge Exploitation: Knowledge exploitation strategies consist of organisational learning practices for the optimisation of existing processes and the improvement of pre-existing knowledge assets.

Knowledge Exploration: Knowledge exploitation can be viewed as the employment of organisational learning activities involving the employment of resources the firm already holds on its possession.

Organisational Capabilities/Core Competences: Critical knowledge assets that form the basis for products and services offered by the firm.

Chapter XXI
Personal Knowledge Management Skills for Lifelong-Learners 2.0

M. C. Pettenati
University of Florence, Italy

M. E. Cigognini
University of Florence, Italy

E. M. C. Guerin
University of Florence, Italy

G. R. Mangione
University of Florence, Italy

ABSTRACT

In this chapter the authors identify the Personal Knowledge Management (PKM) pre-dispositions, skills and competences of the current effective lifelong-learner 2.0. They derive a PKM-skills model centred on a division into basic PKM competences, associated with social software Web practices of create-organize-share, and Higher-Order skills (HO-skills), which identify enabling conditions and competences which favour the advanced management of one's personal knowledge (PK). To derive the PKM-skills model we addressed a survey to 16 interviewees who can be defined as expert lifelong-learners 2.0. The HO-skills branch out into four macro competences, identified as connectedness, ability to balance formal and informal contexts, critical ability and creativity.

INTRODUCTION

Managing our personal knowledge through the use of technologies is referred to as PKM - Personal Knowledge Management (Dorsey, 2000; Sorrentino & Paganelli, 2006) and is a key asset in our society. This concept has been widely studied (Frand & Hixon, 1999; Dorsey, 2000; Wright, 2005; Jarche, 2006) in keeping with its importance in the Knowledge Society. Personal knowledge managment (PKM), through interaction and sharing across members of a community, is the basis of an individual's social learning. Indeed, awareness and responsibility for personal knowledge (PK) do determine the effectiveness of the individual inside a learning, professional, practice, or enterprise community.

PKM is a process and a strategy for the proper use of technology tools to enhance learning-skills (O'Conner, 2002). Research into how children and young people become competent in using the Internet and other research tools highlights that the information literacy of young people has not improved despite widening access to technology (British Library & JISC, 2008; Katz & Macklin, 2007; Katz, 2006; Kvavik, 2005). Indeed, their apparent familiarity and competency with computers disguises some worrying issues (Lorenzo & Dziuban, 2006): little time is spent in evaluating information, either for relevance, accuracy or authority. Young people find it difficult to assess the relevance of the materials presented and often print off pages with no more than a surface level glance at the content. Moreover, young people have a poor understanding of their information needs and thus find it difficult to develop effective information search and retrieval strategies.

Acquiring PKM-skills is a complex and ongoing process that can be favoured by enabling conditions and internalization of suitable and effective practices and behavioural values. The present chapter delineates the multifaceted and fluid profile of the lifelong-learner which, in our conception of it, becomes the mental habitus and, simultaneously, the ideal training path for the learner who is very much aware of the knowledge and learning processes which are inherent in the concept of the Knowledge Society (EU-Commission, 2006).

The long-term current research aim focuses on teaching-methodology i.e., planning PKM-skills training for adults who are not expert lifelong learners (e.g. undergraduates). We believe it possible to develop training aimed at triggering processes so that digital and social literacy skills and competences can be gradually enriched, become internalized and personalized by non-expert subjects. Hence, this study examines the efficacious practices of expert learners in relation to Web 2.0 tools and environments. On the basis of a qualitative survey, our objective is to delineate a competence profile of the lifelong-learner 2.0 so as to identify a valid quality-training planning support-tool aimed at developing PKM-skills in non-experts. This PKM-skills model centres around basic competences and Higher-Order skills (HO-skills). It identifies enabling conditions and competences which favour effective management of one's PK (Mangione, Cigognini & Pettenati, 2007).

The research linked to the HO-skills model design is presented is in three main parts: (i) theoretical precepts and structure of the initial PKM-skills model; (ii) qualitative research to identify HO PKM-skills using a semi-structured survey to 16 expert lifelong-learners 2.0 defined as such based on their everyday PKM uses in their work; (iii) analysis of results in a model which restructures and advances our previous one (Mangione et al., 2007).

PART 1: BACKGROUND

Literacy and Skills for Knowledge Society Learners

Developing a PKM competence landscape (Martin, 2006a) helps prepare and orient Net-Generation learners (Oblinger & Oblinger, 2005) for a lifelong-learning culture which helps them perform better in the Knowledge Society.

Many terms used to denote concepts akin to PKM-skills include: literacy (UNESCO, 2002), information literacy (Irving & Crawford, 2007), media or multimedia literacy (Aviram & Talmi, 2004), e-skills (European e-Skills Forum, 2004), eLiteracy (Martin, 2003; 2006a-b), digital literacy and digital competences (Mayes & Flowes, 2006, Varis, 2005; Martin, 2006; Tornero, 2003: Buckingham, 2007). Several other terms recall concepts of PK, learning acquisition and management (PLE, PKM-skills and literacy) with respect to social networking environments in general (Dorsey, 2004; Sorrentino & Paganelli, 2006; Pettenati et al., 2007).

A mindset of lifelong-learner skills constitutes an essential tool to achieve the Lisbon Treaty objectives (2007). The "e-Skills" definition adopted in the European e-Skills Forum (2004) is linked only to an instrumental viewpoint. Shifting the discussion to more complex concepts of literacy and competences by adopting a more holistic approach is necessary. Based on our empirical research and resources cited from the literature, we believe that PKM-skills are necessary Knowledge Society learning-skills.

PKM-skills encompass a multifaceted set of abilities which differs from digital and information literacy (Martin & Ashworth, 2004; Martin, 2006b; Mayes & Flowes, 2006). Connectivism (Siemens, 2004; 2006) highlights the fact that, in social and relational aspects of knowledge construction, mastering technology is but one aspect of a set of more complex skills.

Kvavik's (2005) studies show that the "Net-Generation" uses technologies mainly for private and social purposes and highlights that there is a significant need for further training in the use of ICT to support learning-skills. Instead, in the learning and knowledge processes, the use of the network is still limited because of the lack of PKM-skills. Recent studies (Lorenzo & Dziuban, 2006; British Library & JISC, 2008) focus on the central use of social media – blogging, online social networking, creating all kinds of digital material – in many teenagers' lives. These practices and Internet uses are mainly related to their social and personal lives: these communication practices are highly interconnected and are undertaken especially with mobile devices.

Hence, the need to re-think the lifelong-learner's set of skills as a complex asset (Martin, 2003; Midoro, 2007; Hilton, 2006). Aspects of Reflection, Learning Management, Organizational skills, Net-working abilities (Dorsey, 2004) constitute key-assets which enable Internet users to become key-protagonists of their potential lifelong knowledge-acquisition experience.

Knowledge Society Lifelong-Learners

How can one define the figure moving in this knowledge and learning landscape? Warlick (2007) and Palfrey (2008) see the lifelong-learner as one who effectively avails of the Internet to enrich personal knowledge wherever (s)he perceives the need, be it in the area of learning, work, or leisure.

(S)He is engaged in an e-lifelong learning journey using Web-based resources and Web 2.0 tools (i.e., creating personal content, sharing it, and being involved in social networks), deploying a range of strategies to interconnect and relate to people and resources. This learning-itinerary involves informal learning-activities (Warlick, 2007). Informal e-learning contexts constitute the socio-technological educational system as it moves towards a more complete realization of the lifelong-learning experience which can enhance and enrich learners' personal and professional skills. We argue that a lifelong-learner is a multi-faceted, interconnected figure immersed in the Web 2.0 environment who needs an equally multifaceted and versatile set of skills intrinsic to the various re-elaborations of the knowledge and learning landscapes which (s)he constantly traverses.

To identify such a specific set of skills, this research avails of theoretical studies, the related literature (Peña-López, 2007; Palfrey, Gasser & Weinberger, 2007; Palfrey, in press), the authors' research and teaching experience, and the views of those who move through the Web based on the afore-shared meaning of lifelong-learner 2.0, i.e., "knowledge-technology" experts who tell-their-tale/s to the authors in the semi-structured interview presented in part two. This interview which required in-depth analysis of the direct experience of the afore-mentioned experts enabled us to deepen and develop our reflections and specify Web-usage practices in relation to the skills studied.

Before examining the results, it is useful to summarise our reflections in relation to PKM in general.

Basic and Higher-Order PKM-Skills

Table 1 summarizes the PKM-model skills and competences treated in previous works. The table shows two basic types of skills: (i) Basic skills i.e., fundamental to Knowledge creation-organisation-sharing on the Internet (Pettenati et al., 2007), and (ii) Higher-Order skills which are only developed experientially when one has acquired Web-usage awareness in social networking environments. In previous studies we hypothesized a methodological link between PKM-skills and learning-design (Pettenati et al., 2007a; Pettenati, Cigognini, Mangione & Guerin, 2007b; Cigognini, Mangione & Pettenati, 2007).

The above three PKM-skills macro-categories must be well-rooted in a HO set of PKM-skills which can better orient and favour a holistic approach to online-learning and knowledge construction. The Create-Organize-Share basic PKM-skills must be developed and applied emphasizing the aspects related to an augmented critical and creative vision of the use of the Web and its resources. The HO PKM-skills emerge as a result of a literature review in a previous study (Mangione et al., 2007) which is further developed (part 3) in light of the survey results presented in part 2.

Parts two and three present the survey and its results so as to identify and better describe the research construct (i.e., HO PKM-skills) charac-

teristics and practices through direct comparisons between lifelong-learner 2.0 experts' (i) opinions and (ii) identified efficacious uses.

PART 2: THE SURVEY

Aim

The experimental phase of the research requires: (i) comparison between the definition and the characteristics of the expert lifelong-learner 2.0., and (ii) refining of the PKM-skills model conceptual node using the HO practices and skills involved in Web usage. By translating these goals into research questions one can say that the initial part of the study answers the need to understand the specific characteristics (pre-dispositions, skills and competences) of the lifelong-learner 2.0. The remaining question is whether the uses related to the implementation of these skills constitute inherent skills.

Our Sample: Who are the Lifelong-Learner 2.0 Experts?

Based on our initial definition of expert lifelong-learner 2.0 (Part 1), 8 males and 8 females were interviewed. All interviewees are actively involved in the learning-knowledge contexts, and use social-networking applications intensively.

Interviewees were chosen following careful deliberation and consideration of their scientific and professional areas of study, their scientific publications, and their "Web-life" (blog, Facebook, multi-media sharing, etc.). Our sample includes five senior eLearning specialists, three junior elearning designers, one knowledge-based-software-developer, two researchers in sociology of technology-mediated social systems, one researcher in e-learning for languages, one researcher in public policy for development, one associate professor in experimental pedagogy, one deputy director of a university e-learning centre, and one senior ICT consultant.

Table 1. PKM basic and HO-skills (Mangione et al., 2007)

PKM-skills		
Higher-Order PKM-skills		
CRITICAL ABILITIES refer to the critical use of the network and its resources i.e., content evaluation and relations. Contents need to be evaluated for quality, accuracy, reliability and pertinence; network relations (subjects) need to be evaluated for competences, trustworthiness and reputation.	**ETHICAL ABILITIES** refer to the adoption of a code governing social-behaviour expectations within networked society. Assuming multiple context-dependent and also anonymous identities, demands proper solution definition for digital identities management, reputation management, and implementation of technological security in communication, content and relation management.	**CREATIVE ABILITIES** include mental processes involving new ideas/concepts generation, or new associations between existing ideas or concepts to solve problems, renew ideas, provide different views, build new knowledge etc.
Basic PKM-skills		
CREATE: *Editing* (e.g., digital information creation in multimedia formats); *Integrating* (post-processing of recordings, digital annotations, automatic abstracting, etc.); *Correlating* (make connections, draw diagrams, mind maps); *Managing content security issues* (manage privacy, Intellectual Property Rights, Digital Rights Management, etc.).		
ORGANIZE: *Searching & finding* (selecting search engines, querying search etc.); *Retrieving* (reading, managing cognitive overload etc); *Storing* (archiving, considering resource availability and accessibility, etc.); *Categorizing/classifying* (defining relations among pieces, use taxonomies and folksonomies, etc.); *Evaluating* (extracting meaning, attributing relevance, affecting trust levels).		
SHARE: *Publishing* (presenting relevant information, using appropriate publication channels, etc.); *Mastering knowledge exchanges* (being concise, using appropriate language, turn-taking, topic-focusing, etc.); *Managing contacts* (keeping profiles, contact, contexts and social-network representation, etc.); *Relating* (establishing connections, communicating through new media; understanding peers, using different languages, etc.); *Collaborating* (sharing tasks, working to common goals, etc.).		

The Survey: Characteristics and Network Practices of the Lifelong-Learner 2.0

All participants in our above-mentioned survey were contacted via e-mail using a semi-structured questionnaire.

Based on focus group methodology (Bailey, 1982), brainstorming, and workshop approaches (Metid Center, 2007), interviewees were asked to provide ten adjectives or key-words to compose their personal tag-cloud of adjectives that identifies the expert lifelong-learner 2.0. Based on their responses, interviewees were further asked to specify whether they:

1. innately possessed the characteristics identified by them,

2. had acquired these competences and skills through experience (personal or professional),

3. had learned these skills through previous training experiences (formal, informal, etc.).

The mental representations and opinions of our experts served as micro-theories which recall interpretative frameworks of social phenomena (Chandler & Lalonde, 1995; Norman & Schmidt, 2000). Thus, *the Naïve theories* expressed by interviewees vis-a-vis competences and skills employed in their Web practices became their cognitive structures to explain the social phenomena associated with social-software practices.

Analysis of the data thus obtained is based on the literature review and the authors' studies which permitted a priori identification of the macro investigation categories (Mangione et al., 2007). Our indepth analysis of the habits and practices of the critical, ethical and creative uses of the Web followed the first interview. The three skills were represented as three core assets. Highly talented respondents with those skills were identified by their natural pre-disposition in those skills and their documented (Web and other) use of the same. For each of the three single skills, these three experts were asked to formulate their own individual translation of the specific skill into "Web-life practices".

The data categorized by independent judges (Corbetta, 1999) resulted in a 90% inter-rater agreement supplemented by a negotiated discussion and agreement on the discordant elements. The frequency of each element considered varied from 6 to 14 values. For the purposes of agreement, the occurrences (and related synonyms) with less than six subjects in agreement were excluded from the model.

Some of the elements considered and condensed include analysis of the occurrences, Semantic coherence, and synonym selection. During data analysis we found the a-priori ethical category too broad to effectively describe all values. Hence, two distinct macro-categories were introduced as detailed hereafter.

PART 3: SURVEY RESULTS

The experts' responses to the open-ended request produced adjectives which could be referred indifferently to either skills or pre-dispositions. Analysis of the results permitted us to sub-divide the results into two groups: (i) skills and competences, and (ii) pre-dispositions, in accordance with the general definitions of these terms. For survey purposes, the pre-dispositions constitute the ingredients for "potential" skills & competencies development, and can subsequently evolve and develop under specific conditions within a suitable and facilitating environment.

The study proceeded by grouping, where possible, the different contributions based on Semantic affinity while trying to find a generalisation which respected the different levels of meaning.

It is plausible to assume that, though many pre-dispositions (openness, curiosity, passion-to-learn, etc.) may be cultivated, they are by nature as well as in meaning, innate or easily verifiable under certain conditions (availability of time and resources, a strong inherent inclination towards technology use, etc.). Hence, it is difficult for such pre-dispositions to be acquired or assimilated through training.

Given the relevance experts attributed to the natural pre-dispositions, these are synthesised and commented upon in the next section. However, greater attention is given to the skills and competences aspects since these elements can and need to be transformed into learning paths for the lifelong-learner 2.0, in accordance with our ultimate research goal.

Lifelong-Learner 2.0 Natural Pre-Disposition

The 16 respondents identified three broad-based factors which they considered to be essential "natural" or inherent characteristics or requirements which constitute the grassroots layer for the development and growth of the PKM-skills. These can be defined as

1. individual or self-related,
2. technology-related,
3. temporal-related factors.

When referring to the term "pre-dispositions" one should also consider the terms attitudes, aptitudes and inclinations. The Merriam-Webster online dictionary (2007) defines "attitude" as "a mental position with regard to a fact or state"; "a feeling or emotion toward a fact or state"; "an organism state of readiness to respond in a characteristic way to a stimulus (as an object, concept, or situation)".

1. Individual or self-related factors
    Within this concept (see Figure 1) we identify three further subsets: (a) openness to experi-

ence, (b) self-concept, and (c) self-regulation. Given the emergence of these subsets in our investigation it is worthwhile examining briefly how these findings find resonance in previous research and different domains.

a.   Openness to experience

Individuals or learners who demonstrate an openness to experience are those who show an open mentality to new ideas. This characteristic relates to the individual's intrinsic motivation. It includes curiosity, broad interests which indicate a passion-to-learn approach to the world of knowledge and learning through aspects of discovery and serendipity. Such individuals conceive of learning as an active, goal-seeking process (Van Rossum & Schenk, 1984) which inundates the being. Furthermore, it reflects the McCrea and Costa five-factor model of personality (1987) in which one factor i.e., openness to experience

relates to creativity. Costa and Mc-Crea (1987) found that interest in a variety of domains such as fantasy, aesthetics, feelings, actions and values was related to divergent thinking and other creativity measures. Likewise Martindale reached the conclusion that "creative cognition occurs only within a certain configuration of personality traits" (Martindale, 1989).

b.   Self-concept

In relation to self-concept we can identify extrinsic and intrinsic motivation at work. This subset is characterised by features such as ability to communicate, self-worth, self-value, being enterprising, extrovert in nature and serendipitous, together with the desire to emerge, discover and show independence of judgement. Such individuals are confident and willing to share and compare ideas and beliefs. They are also naturally energetic and imaginative.

Figure 1. Individual/self-related natural pre-disposition

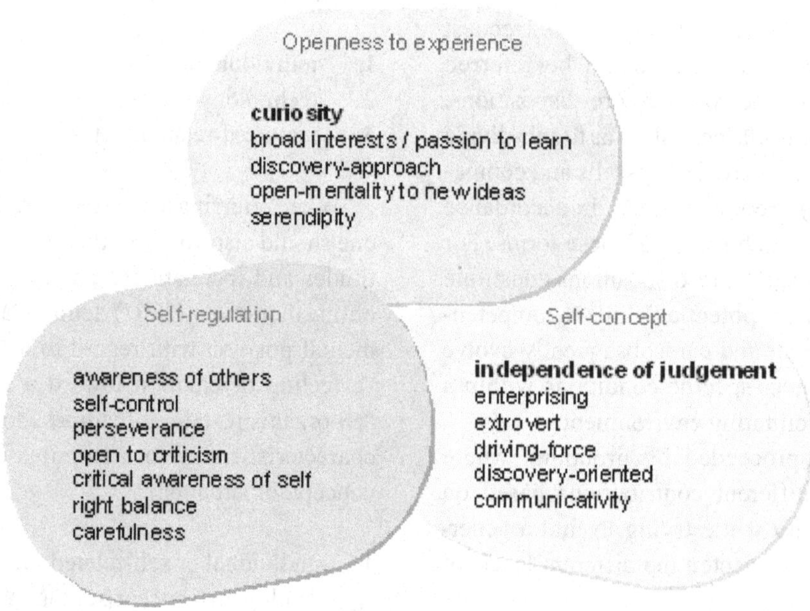

Openness to experience

curiosity
broad interests / passion to learn
discovery-approach
open-mentality to new ideas
serendipity

Self-regulation

awareness of others
self-control
perseverance
open to criticism
critical awareness of self
right balance
carefulness

Self-concept

independence of judgement
enterprising
extrovert
driving-force
discovery-oriented
communicativity

c. Self-regulation

The subset related to self-regulation includes concepts such as motivation and volition. It encompasses ideas such as openness to criticism, carefulness, self-control, critical awareness of self (this echoes Bateson's (1972) belief that the process of systemic adjustment requires a degree of self-awareness), awareness of others (otherness) and perseverance (commitment, constancy). Time and mental effort are also involved.

In line with motivation theory and research they consider motivation as comprising constructs and processes that affect decision making and choice with respect to an individual's goals. According to Boekaerts (1997), self-regulated learning is a powerful construct that allows researchers to describe the various components that are part of successful learning and to explain the reciprocal and recurrent interactions that occur between and among the different components, as well as to relate learning and achievement directly to the self, i.e., to a person's goal structure, motivation, volition, and emotion.

This highlights the importance of making learning-strategy education an essential part of the education process, which is basically what promoting and acquiring PKM-skills sets out to achieve.

2. Technology-related factors

The technology-related factor involves the idea of "connectness" within technology environments. It also includes the ubiquitous nature of modern technology, and as Prensky (2001) puts it "digital natives" and "digital immigrants". The importance of this technology-related factor is highlighted by the fact that the "digital natives" are the product of a world "populated" by telematic technologies all of which they use naturally, and as a result of which they "think and process information fundamentally differently" to previous generations. They are "ubiquitous" and continuously "connected". As lifelong-learners 2.0 they need is a learning approach that matches their natural pre-disposition. Given that future Learning needs to come to grips with the already existent and emerging issues related to learning, education (Guerin, 1998) needs to adjust its tack. The technology-oriented user or "digital immigrant" who has had to learn to be "connected" makes a constant effort to stay up-2-date in the technology enhanced world. It becomes all the more obvious why the development of PKM-skills is so necessary if future learners are to develop critical and creative abilities.

3. Temporal-related factors

The time factor assumes a pivotal importance in so far as it determines inclusion or exclusion based on the learner's temporal obligations and/or commitments. Without the opportunity to avail of time to dedicate to the aspect of "connectedness" it becomes extremely difficult to maximize the possibilities related to "Web presence". Thus, having time at one's disposal to spend in "connectedness" constitutes a specific characteristic of the lifelong-learner 2.0.

Competences and Skills for the Lifelong-Learner 2.0

The qualitative evaluation of the survey results permitted us to identify first and foremost three background enabling conditions which cannot be considered either natural pre-dispositions, or specific PKM-skills. These are:

1. having English skills; English is the Internet lingua franca.
2. being constraint-free: indicates the temporal and environmental condition which enables access to the Internet network
3. being ubiquitous and always online; means that there are no time/space boundaries. "People and information are just a click away" (Peña-López, 2007).

These conditions define a "foundation" on which skills & competencies of the effective lifelong-learner 2.0 should be acquired (see Fig. 2). Most interviewees describe the lifelong-learner 2.0 as already expert and highly competent in the basic PKM-skills as they were described in Part 1. These skills, which build on digital literacy skills, are simply the entrance point for the lifelong-learner 2.0 into the spiral of HO-skills and competencies (see Fig. 2).

Higher-Order Skills and Competencies

The experts identified a set of skills and competences which we grouped into four main categories: (1) connectedness, (2) ability to balance formal and informal contexts, (3) critical ability and (4) creativity. A detailed analysis follows hereafter.

The Lifelong-Learner 2.0 is Connected (Connectedness)

Almost all of the experts identified "being connected" as one of the fundamental skills of the lifelong-learner 2.0. Being connected does not have a technological meaning (such as that of the background identified in "being ubiquitous and always online"). Rather, it means being networked i.e., "being a connector": the "connector" is a subject who, thanks to his/her networked way of functioning, collaborates and interacts with the objective of constructing, developing and

maintaining social-networks (see Fig 2 top left quadrant). From this point of view, the connected subject needs to develop specific abilities to communicate effectively on the Web, and at the same time be balanced and aware of the idiosyncrasies – enabling and otherwise – of global communication. Some of the experts noted that the condition of "being connected" also draws on the connection of the subject with the off-line world.

In the framework of our survey, Fabio Giglietto commented on the three specific abilities which belong to the ethical issues of Web-life but which can profoundly influence the connectedness of the lifelong-learner 2.0:

1. behave on the Web as one behaves off-line: i.e., allow moral and ethical norms which govern our identity off-line, to prevail on the Web.
2. know you are one and accept being many: i.e., understand how the Web is not a space in which to construct new identities, but rather a space in which to experiment and organise one's identity, aware that each subject with whom one enters into contact through the Internet can develop a subjective and different idea of each other's identity: identity – especially if virtual – will of necessity be multiple.
3. managing one's own identity on the Web with the awareness of the tracks left in the digital world: i.e., being highly conscious of the permanence, replicability, searchability and accessibility to an unidentified public (Boyd, 2002) of all the tracks we leave on the Internet. Such a consideration is not obviously only a limitation for the lifelong-learner 2.0, but it also represents the opportunity to avail of the network-world interface and the frequently deffered times of online relations so as to offer a more meditated (since it is mediated) decomposition of our public-self[1]. The meanings of this reflection push in the direction of the knowing consideration of

Figure 2. Lifelong-learner 2.0 PKM-skills and competences

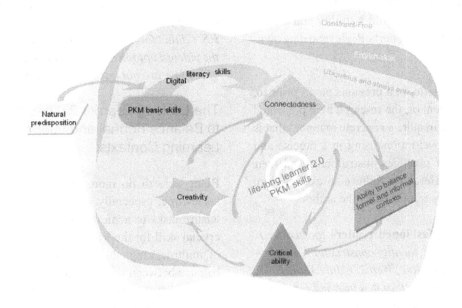

Figure 3. PKM higher-order skills

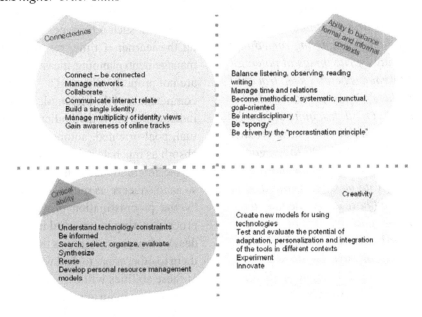

other important ethical/moral aspects such as the Respect/Protection/Management of resource privacy and visibility and of IPR (Intellectual Property Right) and data ownership.

Fabio Giglietto, in a previous post - prior to, and independent of, the research here presented – represented in quite a concrete manner what is expressed above: rationalising in a precise and direct manner practices, instruments and their applications. Hereafter follows an extract from this post freely translated by the authors:

Notice to old-fashioned readers *(posted by F. Giglietto) public[2], identity-construction[3], continuous partial attention[4], Web 2.0[5] July 12th, 2007 Even if I do believe that it is justified (or rather, necessary) to skip something in the information era in which information flows increase exponentially, and that frequently this loss is compensated for by the internal redundancy of the system, I would like to inform all those who read this blog through the RSS[6] feed, that they are missing something. Ever more frequently I write things of potential interest here[7], I take notes here[8], I keep traces of the books I read here[9], I post events in which I am interested here[10]. Of all this, quite obviously, there is no trace here[11]. For this I have created an omni-comprehensive post here[12] (aggregating everything including the blog with the sole exception of Twitter's private messages). Besides, in the About me[13] page I have added the link to the single feeds, to aggregate only one of the above services. Moreover, I am always using Facebook[14] more and more especially to understand its logic from the inside. The idea behind the application is bright and is making this environment a real aggregator of social-networks. At the moment I am aggregating all the information flows I produce to my Facebook profile. Therefore, another way to follow everything without the typical seriality of the feed and, at the same time, to visualize my contacts network and their contents is to invite me as a friend on Facebook.
P.S. I didn't forget the photos I publish here[15] and the videos I upload here[16]. But I think the majority of readers are not interested in them.*

The Lifelong-Learner 2.0 has the Ability to Balance Formal and Informal Learning Contexts

Being able to do more than one thing at the same time, especially combining job-training-leisure tasks to achieve a difficult balance is a crucial skill for the lifelong-learner 2.0. Instead of multi-tasking, the issue is rather finding a balance between the different learning contexts with which the learner can be confronted: the ability to balance the quality participation of the listener, observer/reader and author (see Fig. 2, top right quadrant).

As one of our experts observed, however, trying to find such a balance "can also play havoc on the learner if time, resources and relations management (planning, measuring and allocating) are not properly allocated"[17]. Hence, some basic competences of the lifelong-learner 2.0 have been indicated as: being methodical, systematic, punctual, goal-oriented, autonomous, "spongy"[18] (to absorb as much as possible, keeping the essence of the interactions with contents and relations so as to squeeze as much as necessary) and "led by the procrastination principle"[19] (capable of procrastinating in time and in relations so as "to deal with problems only as they arise — or leave them to other users to deal with). The acquisition of these abilities will permit the lifelong-learner 2.0 to define in an appropriate manner priorities and/or long-term strategies, and at one and the same time manage his active and passive role within the personalised knowledge construction paths.

The Lifelong-Learner 2.0 has Critical Ability

The adoption of a critical approach to the use of network resources (contents and relations) is closely related to the ability to evaluate their trustfulness and reputation. Being able to question oneself about the quality, accuracy, pertinence, up-to-dateness, reliability and/or reputation of a resource is certainly a basic mental attitude in an awareness approach to social networking environments (WSJ, 2007). Nonetheless, the issue highlighted by the expert lifelong-learner 2.0 interviewees lies not so much in the concentration of criteria related to reliability and validation of the sources, as in the capacity to collocate the resources with respect to a would-be context of use, i.e., in understanding what use such resources might be and how, thanks to which enrichments, integrations and collocations. The acquisition of this ability will permit the lifelong-learner 2.0 to be informed, search, select, organise, synthesise, evaluate and re-use resources and relations, while being aware of the limitations (technological and other) of each of them (see Fig. 2 bottom left quadrant).

An integral part of this skill means translating it into a method which can be fine-tuned by the learner in an ever more subjective manner and closely linked to his knowledge objectives. An example from one of the expert lifelong-learner 2.0 in the context of our survey is reported in the following blog-post extract[20]:

Critical abilities *(posted by A. Fini)*
My "information centre" (for retrieving NEW information) is set up mainly of two sources: the RSS feed and the email. There are of course other non-digital sources, such as newspapers, TV and books. I normally begin my daily working activity reading my email through a client-program. I use the client as a real archive, indexed by GoogleDesktop. In the mail I spot the newsletter, and I run through it. If there is something interest-
ing I open the news in my browser. The next step is the RSS reader. I use GoogleReader, which I have chosen after several jumps between desktop programs. I organise my feed in macro-categories among which I name "daily" those that contain the top 10 feeds I do read daily. The others ...I read them when I find the time. Obviously the daily feeds are not fixed, rather I modify them according to what I am more interest in. Of course also the other feeds are "variable" even if I adopt a growing logic structure, that is I seldom delete and more frequently I add new feeds (sigh..). Due to this gathering my reading is necessarily very quick: the post title is therefore very important to me; it may happen (it happened) that I discard a post only because it's heading was inappropriate ...
If I find something interesting, I generally open the post, I read more deeply and I follow the links. Sometimes I comment and, generally, I tag the post as "shared". In such a way the post appears also in the related box on the right of my blog page. This is a way to communicate to others that for me that post is relevant. In some cases I tag the post on del.icio.us[21]. The evaluation on the quality of the post is largely implicit, based on the authors' reputation but, in some cases, I go into more depth using focused search, especially to better understand the topic or verify hypothesis and links with my ideas or previous works. I do believe that RSS is the main tool [to stay updated] even if the natural constraint is the number of manageable feeds.

The Lifelong-Learner 2.0 is Led by Creativity

Creativity is undoubtedly an essential part of innovation and invention and is important in all professions. Creativity is also a mental attitude which needs to be nurtured; it is a mental habit through which to see the world: irony, humour, techniques and situations in which the mind finds the discordant perspective in the environment, creating the contrast which boosts intuition triggering the renewal of ideas and situations.

As one of our experts observed, creativity requires exploration (both structured and serendipitous), observation, linking and association to imagine unexpected and unusual combinations between the possible associations and links. This can be partly led and inspired by the techniques associated with lateral thinking (De Bono, 1970), but also conditioned by a personal pre-disposition to the Arts and to the habit of using writing both as a form of expression and as a means of communication. "Creativity is like building bridges between two banks in between which one is undiscovered: design, intuition, braveness and planning, old and new, known and unknown"[22].

Creativity in lifelong-learning is the ability to identify new models for the use of technologies in specific contexts as well as the ability to test and understand the functionalities of adaptation, personalization and integration of tools. Creativity provides concrete ways through which to play a creative role in one's knowledge construction path: interpreting, linking, proposing and experimenting new lifelong learning strategies.

CONCLUSION

We recognize PKM as being a critical asset in today's professions in which digital and analogical actions and expressions are closely intertwined. Performance in PKM requires specific skills and abilities. Here, we tried to provide a comprehensive overview of these skills so as to advance a holistic approach to learning and knowing. Among these we highlighted "Higher-Order skills " (i.e., connectedness, being able to balance formal and informal contexts, critical ability and creativity) in the use of network resources which are still poorly addressed at present. Future research involves identifying ways and means to develop these skills into an educational model, revising and integrating other approach as they emerge in relation to our initial one.

Our main purpose has been to understand whether such Higher-Order abilities are innate or should be learnt. Our conviction is that they should be taught by educational institutions through the development of specific educational modules or activities. The survey conducted with expert lifelong-learners 2.0 was thus chosen as a guiding method for this study so as to solve the critical aspects and increase the transfer of Higher-Order skills into practice at a more detailed level.

The results of this qualitative research which uses the opinions of expert subjects to develop an interpretative framework of social phenomena, pertains to the meta-cognitive studies area (Cornoldi, 1995). The input provided by the 16 experts enabled us to design and develop the PKM-skills acquisition model presented here. The research is now in a broader phase which also includes a validation phase with classroom implementation. This new phase has a further 23 subjects involved in semi-structured interviews for the purposes of model validation. It is hoped that the results of this second investigation will integrate and optimise the identified elements of the PKM-skills model and enable the translation of the elements thus far presented from a theoretical perspective, into efficacious teaching and learning strategies and scenarios.

ACKNOWLEDGMENT

The authors are grateful to the 16 expert lifelong-learners 2.0 who gave generously of their time to our undertaking. In line with the personal-disposition they described, the experts accepted with openness of mind and curiosity to discuss with us the themes treated in this chapter. We are grateful to the following for their thoughtful responses to our survey: Mario Rotta, Fabio Giglietto, Ismael Peña-López, Antonio Fini, Mitja Švab, Daniele Vistalli, Marco D'Alessio, Sarah Guth, Maria de Los Angeles Castro, Graziella Testaceni, Fortunato Sorrentino, Linda Giannini, Susanna

Sancassani, Gisella Paoletti, Chiara Fonio, and Simona Azzali.

REFERENCES

Aviram, R., & Talmi, D. (2004). Are you a Technocrat A Reformist Or a Holist? *eLearning Europa.* Retrieved on 1st, March 2008, from http://www.elearningeuropa.info/index.php?page=doc&doc_id=4965&doclng=6&menuzone=1

Bailey, K. D. (1982). *Metodi della ricerca sociale.* Bologna, Italy: Il Mulino.

Bateson, G. (1972). *Steps to an Ecology of Mind.* New York, USA: Ballantine.

Boekaerts, M. (1997). Self-regulated learning: a new concept embraced by researchers, policy makers, educators, teachers, and students. *Learning and instruction, 7*(2), 151–86.

Boyd, D. (2002). *Faceted Id/entity: Managing Representation in a Digital World.* Cambridge, MA: MIT Master's Thesis. Retrieved on 7th April 2008, from http://www.danah.org/papers/Thesis.FacetedIdentity.pdf

British Library & JISC (2008). *Information behaviour of the researcher of the future.* A ciber briefing paper, 11 January 2008. Retrieved on 7 April, 2008, from http://www.bl.uk/news/pdf/googlegen.pdf

Buckingham, D. (2007). Digital Media Literacies: rethinking media education in the age of the Internet. *Research in Comparative and International Education, 2*(1), 43-55.

Chandler, M. J., & Lalonde, C. E. (1995). Teorie ingenue della mente e del Sé. In L. O. Sempio, & A. Marchetti (Eds.), *Il pensiero dell'altro. Contesto, conoscenza e teorie della ment* . Milano, Italy: Raffaello Cortina.

Cigognini, M. E., Mangione, G. R., & Pettenati, M. C. (2007). *E-Learning design in (in)formal*

learning. TD - Tecnologie Didattiche 41(3), 55-58, Ortona, Svizzera: Menabò Edizioni.

Commission of the European Communities (2006). *Key Competences for Lifelong Learning.* Recommendation the European Parliament and the Council of 18 December 2006. *Official Journal of the European Union* (2006/962/EC), L394/10-18.

Corbetta, G (1999). *Manuale di metodologia della ricerca sociale.* Bologna, Italy: Il Mulino.

Cornoldi, C. (1995). *Metacognizione e apprendimento.* Bologna, Italy: Il Mulino.

Di Fraia, G. (2004). *eResearch: Internet per la ricerca sociale e di mercato.* Bari, Italy: Laterza.

De Bono, E. (1970). *Lateral thinking : creativity step by step.* New York, USA: Harper & Row.

Dorsey, P. (2000). *Personal Knowledge Management: educational framework for global business.* Tabor School of Business, Millikin University. Retrieved on 7 April, 2008, from http://www.millikin.edu/pkm/pkm_istanbul.html

Dorsey, P. (2004). *What is PKM? - Overview of Personal Knowledge Management.* Millikin University. Retrieved on 7 April, 2008, from http://www.sacw.cn/What%20is%20PKM.html

European eSkills Forum (2004). *eSkills for Europe: towards 2010 and beyond: synthesis report*, European Commission, DG Enterprise and Industry, September 2004.

Frand, J., & Hixon, C. (1999). *Personal Knowledge Management : Who, What, Why, When, Where, How?* December 1, 1999. UCLA University. Retrieved on 7th April 2008, from http://www.anderson.ucla.edu/faculty/jason.frand/researcher/speeches/PKM.htm

Guerin, E. M. C. (1998). Technology and Pedagogical Content: Are They Really Hand in Hand? *Proceedings of EDEN 1998 Conference, Universities in a Digital Era: Transformation, Innovation and Tradition-Roles and Perspectives of Open and Distance Learning*, 390-393, EDEN Annual Conference, University of Bologna, Italy, 24-26 June 1998.

Hilton, J. (2006). The future for higher education: Sunrise or perfect storm. *EDUCAUSE Review, 41*(2), 58-71. Retrieved on 7th April 2008, from http://www.educause.edu/ir/library/pdf/erm0623.pdf

Irving, C., & Crawford, J. (2007). *A National Information Literacy Framework Scotland.* Glasgow Caledonian University, ILS Report Project. Retrieved on 7 April, 2008, from http://www.caledonian.ac.uk/ils/framework.html

Jarche, H. (2006). *My PKM System, blog post and comment.* 29th August 2006. Retrieved on 7 April, 2008, from http://www.jarche.com/?p=865

Katz, I. R., & Macklin, A. S. (2007). Information and communication technology (ICT) literacy: Integration and assessment in higher education. *Systemics, Cybernetics and Informatics, 5*(4), 50-55. Retrieved on 7 April, 2008, from http://www.iiisci.org/Journal/CV$/sci/pdfs/P890541.pdf

Katz, R. N. (2006). The ECAR study of Undergraduate Students and Information Technology 2006. Retrieved on 7 April, 2008, from http://www.educause.edu/ir/library/pdf/EKF/EKF0607.pdf

Kvavik, R. B. (2005). Convenience, communications and control: How students use technology. In D. Oblinger & J. Oblinger (Eds), *Educating the Net Generation*, 7.1-7.20. Washington, DC: EDUCAUSE. Retrieved on 7 April, 2008, from http://www.educause.edu/educatingthenetgen

Lorenzo, G., & Dziuban, C. (2006). *Ensuring the Net-Generation is net savvy.* Washington, DC: EDUCAUSE. Retrieved on 7 April, 2008, from http://www.educause.edu/ir/library/pdf/ELI3006.pdf

Mangione, G. R., Cigognini, M. E., & Pettenati, M. C. (2007). Favouring a Critical, Creative and Ethical Use of the Network Resources Through Web 2.0 Applications. Proceedings from *Towards a Social Science of Web 2.0 Conference*, 5 -6 September 2007, University of York, UK. Retrieved on 7 April, 2008, from http://www.york.ac.uk/res/siru/Web2.0/cigognini.htm

Martin, A., & Ashworth, S. (2004). Welcome to the Journal of eLiteracy!. *Journal of eLiteracy, 1*(1), 2 – 6. Retrieved on 7 April, 2008, from http://www.jelit.org/11/

Martin, A. (2006a). The Landscape of Digital Literacy. *DigEuLit project.* Glasgow. Retrieved on 7 April, 2008, from http://www.digeulit.ec.

Martin, A. (2006b). Literacies for the digital age: preview of Part 1. In A. Martin & D. Madigan (Ed.), *Digital literacies for learning*, (pp. 3-25). London, Uk: Facet Publishing.

Martindale, C. (1989). Personality, situation, and creativity. In J. A. Glover, R. R. Ronning, & C. R. Reynolds (Eds.), *Handbook of creutivdy* (pp. 211-232). New York, USA: Plenum.

Mayes, T., & Fowler, C. (2006). Learners, learning literacy and pedagogy of e-learning. In A. Martin & D. Madigan (Ed.), *Digital literacies for learning*, (pp. 107-123). London, UK: Facet Publishing.

McCrea, R. R., & Costa, P. T. Jr. (1987). Validation of the five-factor model of personality across instruments and observers. *Journal of Personality and Social Psychology, 66*, 574-83.

Merriam-Webster Online Dictionary (2007). Definition of " attitude". Retrieved on 7th April 2008, from http://www.merriam-Webster.com/

Metid Center (2007). *Workshops on Web 2.0 in the classroom.* Politecnico of Milan, Retrieved on 7 April, 2008, from http://www.sidelab.com/workshops.htm

Midoro, V. (2007). Quale alfabetizzazione per la società della conoscenza? *TD - Tecnologie*

Didattiche, 41(2), 47-54, Ortona, Svizzera: Menabò Edizioni.

Norman G. R., & Schmidt, H. G. (2000). Effectiveness of problem-based learning curricula: theory, practice and paper darts. *Medical Education, 34*(9), 721–728.

Oblinger, D., & Oblinger J. (2005). *Educating the Net Generation.* EDUCASE. Retrieved on 7 April, 2008, from http://www.educause.edu/content. asp?PAGE_ID=5989&bhcp=1

O'Conner, M. (2002). *Personal Knowledge Management (PKM).* Millikin University Report. Retrieved on 7 April, 2008, from http://www. millikin.edu/Webmaster/pkm/

Palfrey, J. (2008). *Born Digital: Understanding the First Generation of Digital Natives (Hardcover).* New York, USA: Basic Books.

Palfrey, J., Gasser, U., & Weinberger, D. (2007). Digital Born. *John Palfrey. From the Bercam Center at haverval Law School.* Retrieved on 7 April, 2008, from http://blogs.law.harvard.edu/ palfrey/2007/10/28/born-digital/

Peña-López, I. (2007). Skills of an expert knower 2.0/leaner 2.0. *ICTlogy.* Retrieved on 7 April, 2008, from http://ictlogy.net/20071107-skills-of-an-expert-knower-20leaner-20/

Pettenati, M. C., & Cigognini, M. E. (2007). Social networking theories and tools to support connectivist learning activities. *International Journal of Web-Based Learning and Teaching Technologies (IJWLTT), 2*(3), 39-57, July-September 2007, Idea Group Inc.

Pettenati, M. C., Cigognini M. E., & Sorrentino, F. (2007a). Methods and tools for developing personal knowledge management skills in the connectivist era. Proceedings from *EDEN 2007 Conference NEW LEARNING 2.0? Emerging digital territories Developing continuities, New divides,* EDEN 2007 Annual Conference, 13-16 JUNE, 2007, Naples, Italy.

Pettenati, M. C., Cigognini, M. E., Mangione, G. R., & Guerin, E. (2007b). Use of Social software for knowledge construction and management in formal online learning. *Turkish Online Journal of Distance Education (TOJDE), 8*(3). Retrieved on 7th April 2008, from http://tojde.anadolu.edu.tr/

Prensky, M. (2001). Digital Natives, Digital Immigrants. *On the Horizon, NCB University Press, 9*(5).

Siemens, G. (2004). Connectivism: A Learning Theory for the Digital Age. *eLearnSpace.* Retrieved on 7th April 2008, from http://www. elearnspace.org/Articles/connectivism.htm

Siemens, G. (2006). *Knowing knowledge.* Retrieved on 7 April, 2008, from http://www. knowingknowledge.com/

Sorrentino, F., & Paganelli, F. (2006). *L'intelligenza distribuita. Ambient Intelligence: il futuro delle tecnologie invisibili.* Trento, Italy: Erickson.

Tornero P. (2003). *Understanding Digital Literacy Promoting Digital Literacy.* Final report EAC/76/03.

Treaty of Lisbon (2007). Taking Europe into the 21st century. Key document of Treaty of Lisbon, European Web portal. Retrieved on 7 April, 2008, from http://www.consilium.europa.eu/cms3_fo/ showPage.asp?id=1296&lang=en&mode=g

UNESCO (2002). Recommendations addressed to the United Nations Educational Scientific and Cultural Organization - UNESCO. Youth Media Education. Seville, 15-16 February 2002.

Van Rossum, E. J., & Schenk, S. M. (1984). The Relationship between Learning Conception, Study Strategy and Learning Outcome. *British Journal of Educational Psychology, 54*(1) 73-83.

Varis, T. (2005), New Literacies and e-Learning Competences. *elearningeuropa.info directory.* Retrieved on 7 April, 2008, from http://www.elearningeuropa.info/directory/index. php?page=doc&doc_id=595&doclng=6

Warlick, D. (2007). *Life long learners 2.0. Who writes the blog 2 Cents Worth?* Blog post Retrieved on 7 April, 2008, from http://repairman.wordpress.com/2007/07/09/lifelong-learner-20/

Wright, K. (2005). Personal knowledge management: supporting individual knowledge worker performance. *Knowledge Management Research & Practice, 3*, 156-165.

WSJ (2007). The Good, the Bad, And the 'Web 2.0'. *The Wall Street Journal online.* Retrieved on 7 April, 2008, from http://online.wsj.com/article/SB118461274162567845.html?mod=Technology

KEY TERMS

Connectedness: Being networked, being a Web connector, collaborating and interacting for the purpose of building, developing and maintaining social networks.

Creativity: A mental process involving the generation of new ideas or concepts, or new associations between existing ideas or concepts.

Digital Literacy: The ability to read, write and interact across digital social networks.

Lifelong-Learner 2.0 (Learner 2.0): A connected (networked) lifelong-learner capable of balancing formal and informal learning contexts who has the critical ability to evaluate online resources and contacts and the ability to use such resources to empower his creativity in his PKM.

Personal Knowledge Management (PKM): The act of managing one's personal knowledge through technologies.

PKM Basic Skills: Basic skills related to the use of social software organized around three main competencies create-organize-share to favour the effective management of one's personal information.

PKM Higher-Order Skills: Competences going far beyond the basic skills of information management, which constitute the distinctive assets in one's PKM: connectedness, ability to balance formal and informal contexts, critical ability, creativity.

Pre-Dispositions: A habit, a preparation, a state of readiness, or a tendency to act in a specified way.

Skills & Competences: The learnt capacity or talent to effectively perform some task.

ENDNOTES

1. "It is also true that different pieces of the mosaic of our personality must permit, once reunited, an acceptable and true definition of ourselves: the pieces represent our heteronyms , "light" versions of ourselves." (Federico Bo, in Comment n. 4 to the previously cited post by F. Giglietto).
2. http://larica-virtual.soc.uniurb.it/nextmedia/taxonomy/tags/social/publicy/
3. http://larica-virtual.soc.uniurb.it/nextmedia/taxonomy/tags/individual/identity-construction/
4. http://larica-virtual.soc.uniurb.it/nextmedia/taxonomy/tags/individual/continuous-partial-attention/
5. http://larica-virtual.soc.uniurb.it/nextmedia/taxonomy/tags/nextmedia/Web-20/
6. http://feeds.feedburner.com/nextmedia
7. http://twitter.com/account/archive
8. http://www.connotea.org/user/fabiogiglietto
9. http://www.anobii.com/people/fg/
10. http://upcoming.yahoo.com/user/13492/
11. http://feeds.feedburner.com/nextmedia
12. http://feeds.feedburner.com/fg-meta
13. http://larica-virtual.soc.uniurb.it/nextmedia/about-me/

14 http://www.facebook.com/p/Fabio_Giglietto/500798146

15 http://www.flickr.com/photos/f-g/

16 http://www.youtube.com/user/fabio.giglietto

17 http://ictlogy.net/20071107-skills-of-an-expert-knower-20leaner-20/

18 http://sciaradelfuoco.blogspot.com/2007/11/vita-da-spugna.html

19 http://ictlogy.net/20071107-skills-of-an-expert-knower-20leaner-20/

20 http://eduspaces.net/anto/Weblog/214056.html

21 http://del.icio.us/antonf

22 Mario Rotta, commenting on the survey questions.

Chapter XXII
Reconceptualising Information Literacy for the Web 2.0 Environment?

Sharon Markless
King's College, London, UK

David Streatfield
Information Management Associates, UK

ABSTRACT

This chapter questions whether the shift from the Web as a vehicle for storing and transmitting information to the new Web as a series of social networking environments, requires significant changes in how students interact with information when they are studying within a formal learning environment. It explores the origins and growth of the idea of information skills development, the translation of this work into frameworks and sequential models and the adaptation of these models to take account of changes in information storage and transmission brought about by the Internet. The chapter then examines the changing contexts and changes in learning being brought about by the Web 2.0 environment and questions whether adjustment of existing information literacy models is a sufficient response to deal with these changes. We conclude that although Web 2.0 developments are not fundamentally undermining the nature of teaching and learning they do provide important possibilities for more effective information literacy development work. A non-sequential framework is offered as a contribution to supporting HE students when seeking to obtain, store and exploit information simultaneously in the informal social world of Web 2.0 and in their formal academic discipline.

THE RISE OF INFORMATION SKILLS

In the early 1980s a spate of books appeared in the UK containing a new term in the title: 'information skills'. This term was the brainchild of a working party concerned about school pupils' competence in *"using libraries, exploring references and making notes"* (Marland, 1981, p7) and arose out of the Schools Council's desire to explore what a curriculum for a changing world might comprise. The working party report asserted that *"Individuals today have an increasing need to be able to find things out...never before have our lives depended so much on our ability to handle information successfully"* (Marland, 1981, p9). Narrow concerns about library skills and user education were replaced by a focus on students' problems in finding and using information to tackle assignments and conduct their research within a formal learning environment. This intervention was due to the interest in these skills by educationalists, who, working alongside librarians, ensured wider adoption for information skills and a clearer place for the concept within the learning process.

However, despite this development and the appearance of a number of books exploring the place of information skills in learning (see, for example, Markless and Lincoln, 1986, and Wray, 1985) the concept of information skills was far more widely accepted by librarians than by teachers. This resulted in heavy emphasis on competence in resource use and on finding information.

MODELS OF INFORMATION SKILLS

From the outset writers wanted to show the need for students to develop these 'new' information skills. The issue was presented as one of skills deficit and consequently led to a plethora of information skills frameworks and models, spelling out what students should be able to do. (Many of these models were later 'rounded up' and described by Loertscher and Woolls, 2002.) Model constructors conceived the requisite process as tying together distinct elements of information-related behaviour into a logical, sequential process which could then be taught (e.g. Marland, 1981; Brake, in Markless and Lincoln 1986).

An important retrospective review of these models and frameworks (Eisenberg and Brown, 1992) concluded that

"while each author may explain this process with different terms ... all seem to agree on the overall scope and the general breakdown of the process ... it appears that the various process models are more alike than different and it may be possible and desirable to begin speaking about a common process approach to library and information skills instruction." (p. 7)

The approach to information skills as a 'common process' to be applied to library research and information handling unfortunately tended to result in a disregard for the context of learning. Skills were perceived as generic; the sequential process outlined in the models was to be adopted at all ages and across different subjects. The process formed a 'curriculum' to be taught to students and applied by them whenever necessary. This view was hardly challenged in the early world of information skills although research on information behaviour in context and on critical thinking skills was calling into question the whole notion of easy transfer, which is also a well-established assumption in mainstream education (Perkins and Salomon, 1992).

Perhaps the most influential of these generic information skills models was advanced as the Big6. This model was created by Eisenberg and Berkowitz (1990); it was widely disseminated in book form and continues to be heavily promoted in the USA and internationally through their website and through an extensive programme of workshops. We will use this Big6 framework as the basis of our critique for the remainder of this chapter because it is one of the frameworks most widely used in USA and UK schools to support information skills teaching and because its authors were amongst the first to integrate ICT into information skills in a distinct and transparent manner.

THE BIG SIX SKILLS™ APPROACH

The main elements of this model are outlined below:

1. Task Definition: (determine the purpose and need for information)
    Define the problem
    Define the information requirements of the problem
2. Information Seeking Strategies: (examining alternative approaches to acquiring the appropriate information to meet needs)
    Determine the range of possible resources
    Evaluate the different possible resources to determine priorities
3. Location and Access: (locating information sources and information within sources)
    Locate sources (intellectually and physically)
    Finding information within resources
4. Use of Information: (using a source to gain information)
    Engage (e.g. read, hear, view) the information in a source
    Extract information from a source
5. Synthesis: (integrating information drawn from a range of sources)
    Organize information from multiple sources
    Present information
6. Evaluation: (making judgements based on a set of criteria)
    Judge the product (effectiveness)

Judge the information problem-solving process (efficiency)
Eisenberg and Berkowitz (1990)

It is not surprising that when the concept of information skills was new, and people sought to understand its scope, frameworks such as the Big6 were widely adopted. They provided a foundation on which to build learning activities and assessment. Would such frameworks survive intact into the 'information age' of ICT?

THE SHIFT TO INFORMATION LITERACY: A BROADER VIEW?

With the advent of Worldwide Web and the extensive accompanying investment in ICT in educational institutions of all kinds, concerns about students' ability to find and use information grew exponentially and a new vocabulary began to emerge in formal education - that of information literacy. The notion of information literacy developed in the USA in the 1980s in response to a move towards more active learning in universities and the concomitant need to move away from terms implying passive instruction (Martin, 2006). Use of the term expanded considerably in the 1990s (Bawden, 2001) and has gained some worldwide influence, leading to a declaration by UNESCO (2003) stressing the global importance of information literacy within the information society. A parallel growth in the UK has seen the term widely adopted in academic libraries and national educational bodies (but with most school libraries until now still preferring to focus on information skills - Streatfield and Markless, 2007).

Did the new term signify any fundamental change in thinking or signal a new characterisation of the skills or processes previously called information skills? National Information Literacy Standards in Australia (CAUL, 2001) and the USA

(ACRL, 2000) echoed much of what was in the earlier process models, as did the information literacy model proposed in the UK by the Society of College, National and University Libraries (1999). Despite the fact that 'literacy' is a problematic and contested concept (it has been variously described as encompassing notions of functional competence and skills, of sets of wider cognitive abilities, and as part of a contextualised approach to learning in its social and economic context - Bowden, 2001), information literacy was usually reduced in presentation to a series of skills, procedures and technicalities. This inhibited approach attracted some criticism for being too mechanistic and some writers moved towards a conceptualization that includes attitudes, underpinning knowledge and meta-cognitive abilities (Kuhlthau, 1988; Bruce, 1997). Although Kuhlthau recognised the importance of student attitudes and emotions in her information process model, these elements have not been integrated into other process models - although the commentaries accompanying these models usually refer in some way to motivation and attitudes.

INFORMATION SKILLS AND THE INTERNET

In this phase of its development, the Internet was viewed primarily as a new information storage and delivery system for which existing information skills frameworks could simply be expanded or adapted to take account of the growth in access to information via the Internet. Eisenberg and Johnson (1996) exemplified this view when they explicitly integrated ICT into the Big6 Skills model, saying that

Students need to be able to use computers flexibly, creatively and purposefully... (they) should be able to use the computer as part of the process of accomplishing their task. (p. 2)

During the 1990s, the creators of the Big6 confidently extended the model to include student use of ICT when solving learning problems. They claimed that various computer and information technology skills were integral parts of the Big6 Skills. This claim was sustained as their model continued to be implemented in schools across the USA and the UK (Eisenberg and Berkowitz, 2000). Adherents of this and other process models confidently asserted that the basic principles of information seeking and use, derived from years of watching and helping students to interact with print-based information, remained unchallenged.

We have chosen to exemplify current process models by citing the Big6 when looking at whether the concept of information literacy needs to be repackaged or reconceptualised because:

- the model crystallizes the general process approach favoured until now and serves as an adequate exemplar of the model-driven approach
- it serves our purpose because it was the only model advanced until recently that systematically encompasses the ICT dimension
- It is still currently being used and promoted in that form.

The Big6 framework is useful for this purpose because it is a systematic and widely adopted model. Our comments should not be construed as an attack on this particular framework.

EXAMINING THE PROCESS MODELS

What are the assumptions underpinning the Big6 and similar models and what are their main characteristics?

- A sequential view of the process of student research, conceived as a series of logical steps

- Use of prescriptive language to convey an 'ideal approach' to information-seeking and use (e.g. "After students determine their priorities for information-seeking they must locate information from a variety of sources"; "once the information problem has been formulated, the student must consider all possible information sources and develop a plan for searching"). This approach is commonplace in this period, despite the warning offered a decade earlier by Tabberer and Altman (1986) about the danger of idealising study behaviour and promoting 'the right way to ...' They stressed that success came by diverse routes and as a result of different choices made in different situations. They warned that students did not always gain much by being confronted with 'the ideal' because there is a range of influences that prevent adoption of 'best behaviour'.
- The process models were designed to support information skills teaching (i.e. to provide a 'curriculum' for the teachers and a pathway to be followed by students when doing their research).
- A particular and limited conception of information-related behaviour is represented in these models, with much emphasis on information seeking, location and access. Use of information is reduced to determining relevance and extracting pertinent items of information (by taking notes or resorting to cut and paste). The words knowledge, understanding and making sense of, seldom occur in these models, nor does the idea of creating one's own viewpoint. The apparent assumptions are that this shortcoming will be addressed in the subject teaching or that the acts of extracting and organising relevant information will themselves stimulate the construction of meaning. What happens instead is frequently cut and paste activity leading to more or less unintentional plagiarism. In these models, synthesis is not about transforming information to encapsulate new knowledge
- Overall they present ways to support teaching ("innovative instructional methods") designed to provide a framework to guide teachers or librarians when preparing appropriate activities or tasks for their students.

These models reflected the main uses conceived for the Web in this period as a vehicle for storing and transmitting information.

INFORMATION LITERACY AND WEB 2.0: CHANGING THE CONTEXT, CHANGING THE LEARNING?

The 'orthodoxy' of information skills within formal learning environments, as enshrined in the Big6 Model, is being increasingly challenged. Recent research into information literacy is moving away from technological processes and skills-based models, recognising the complexities inherent in finding and using information. A more experiential perspective that recognises the contextual and affective elements of information literacy is emerging (Williams and Wavell, 2007). Two complementary developments have influenced this shift in focus: greater interest amongst information literacy researchers and practitioners in the processes of learning (especially theory about variation in learning and constructivist approaches); and an electronic environment that is increasingly being shaped by its users.

Have traditional views of information literacy really been rendered obsolete? Does learning through Web 2.0 require different skills and abilities? Are a new range of cognitive and meta-cognitive strategies needed to learn effectively within the Web 2.0 environment? Or, does the Web 2.0 environment provide tools that enable teachers to engage students more effectively in well-established learning processes than could be achieved hitherto?

In our view, learning is not fundamentally different within Web 2.0, nor does the 'new' social software change the basic processes of learning. Where Web 2.0 has made a difference is in making it easier to engage with some aspects of learning that were previously difficult to address (for example, real collaboration and groupwork, peer critique, hearing students' authentic voices and construction of new knowledge). None of these important aspects of effective learning are new: all can be found in the education literature of the 20th Century, from Dewey to Ausubel, and from Vygotsky to Marton. However, despite their importance, few of these elements have found their way into information literacy models or practice.

When the Worldwide Web was primarily a vehicle for storing and delivering information it was easy to portray information literacy as an ordered sequence of skills to be *transmitted* to students, whilst ignoring other approaches to learning. Web 2.0 effortlessly undermines this approach with its disregard for authority, hierarchy and order and its focus on the voice of the individual and on ever changing constructed groups. Any contemporary approach to information literacy must consider how to engage more effectively with learners, by understanding these multiple aspects of how they can learn.

Before we examine in a little more detail some of these key elements of learning and their relationship to information literacy and social software, we need to note two other factors that may influence this relationship: the reluctance of individuals and institutions to change; and the ways in which the 'Google generation' of 'digital natives' may interact with information and learn in new and different ways. What are the key elements of learning as they relate to information literacy and social software? Some at least of these key elements are:

1. Reluctance to change (institutions and teachers)

Faced with the unfamiliar challenge of a new world of social networking, some education institutions have tended to react in a predictably conservative way by blocking access to elements such as Face book and Second Life. As a result of such embargos, as well as a reluctance by teachers to engage with this new world, students are frequently operating in different electronic environments during formal learning from those in their out of hours experience (especially in schools). This makes teaching of information literacy more problematic.

To somewhat over-dramatize the dilemmas created: as a teacher, how can you fully engage with students in helping them to exploit information if you don't have easy access to what may constitute their major sources of information? Or, from a student perspective, why should you bother to engage with all this 'information literacy stuff' if your perception is that all you have to do to get the information and help that you need, is to resort to your social networks? When you are away from the institution, if you can effortlessly manipulate multi-media information to build your own web pages, why jump through what might be seen as sterile and irrelevant information literacy hoops when you are in formal learning mode? Again, as the world of Web 2.0 becomes increasingly sophisticated, the version of ICT encountered in formal learning is likely to appear ever more limited and pedestrian.

2. Digital natives and others
    "Future students in higher education belong to a generation that has grown up with a PC mouse in their hands, a TV remote control, a mobile phone, an i-pod, a PDA and other electronic devices for communication and entertainment ... computer games, the Internet, MSN, wikis and blogs being an integral part of their lives" (Veen, 2007, p.1). Prensky has labelled these young people

'digital natives' and has asserted that they now exhibit different characteristics from their forbears (the digital immigrants) due to the extent of their exposure to technology in all its forms.(Prensky, 2001). He claims that changes in activity during development may result in different neural wiring via processes of 'neuro-plasticity'; a view recently echoed by Martin Westwell of the Institute for the Future of the Mind (2007). Both advocates assert that current students have much better visual skills, do better at visual-spacial tests, are able to deal with lots of information at once, and can process this information and make decisions quickly. On the other hand, this generation of students may have shorter attention spans, be easily distracted, may not maintain focus well when interrupted and may have less ability to reflect on topics than the previous generation. Veen (2007) adds to this list of differences, talking about non-linear learning behaviour; clicking and zapping to deal with information overload; using exploratory approaches to new situations; and becoming experienced at problem solving at a young age. "We now have a new generation with a very different blend of cognitive skills than its predecessors – the digital natives." (Prensky, 2001)

As a result of Web 2.0 developments, we can also anticipate that 'digital natives' may have different social skills.. This is because the Internet is increasingly used for socialisation rather than just information-seeking, with even those seeking information often doing so via peer groups. Westwell claims that more people use Second Life and Facebook than use Google. Whether or not we believe all these claims, Oblinger and Oblinger (2005) have forecast that the next generation of students entering higher education will be digitally literate, highly Internet-familiar, connected via networked media, used to immediate responses, and preferring experiential learning.

This generation will be highly social: they will prefer to work in teams and will crave interactivity in image-rich environments as distinct from text-intensive environments.

Where does this leave traditional information literacy, with its focus on using libraries and finding primary sources, its reliance on laborious sequential steps and its scant reference to collaboration or to multi-media resources? If Westwood and others are correct, their picture of our 'new' students implies that not only have they gained from their early digital experiences but they have also lost in terms of opportunities for reflection and 'slow-learning'. This picture of gains and losses calls into question the widespread claims that elements of Web 2.0 (wikis etc.) automatically help to develop meta-cognitive skills. However, it is also interesting to note that traditional information literacy frameworks do not emphasise reflection and its role throughout learning.

WEB 2.0, INFORMATION LITERACY AND FORMAL LEARNING

Where do all these changes leave information literacy? How might traditional models of information literacy need to be altered to accommodate the experience and expectations of students within formal education? Where does Web 2.0 fit in?

- The sequential view of skills deployment is now being questioned. Learning tasks make a range of different demands on students, which call into question the notion of applying the same series of steps to meet all these demands. Observations of pupils from 5-18 in schools and students in further education colleges show that they seldom follow the prescribed sequence (Streatfield and Markless, 1994; Moore, 1997; Markless and Streatfield, 2000). Formal studies of information-seeking behaviour in universities again challenge this premise (Foster, 2006).

To be fair, most of the process models that are set out in steps are accompanied by some form of caveat recognising or even advising that it is not necessary to follow the prescribed sequence. However, there is usually little help offered on how to use the model in a non-sequential way, with the result that the framework tends to be taught as a sequence. The desire to inflict sequences on students is remarkably resilient in the world of information literacy. Even writers who are responding to the Web 2.0 environment tend to present a sequence of processes to be learned in order to become 'information fluent' (e.g. the five-stage process of Jukes (2007): asking questions; accessing data; analysing and authenticating information; applying it to real-life problems; assessing product and process). This approach takes no account of the influence of context on any sequence, the influence of learners' cognitive styles, or the need to make sense of any information and transform it into knowledge.

In addition, a core characteristic of Web 2.0 tools is that they transfer power, ownership and authority to the participants. This inevitably gives people license to design their own routes through learning tasks in any way that suits them. Finding information is less likely to involve systematic information seeking than, for example, interest groups, peer web pages or social bookmarking.

These observations lead to the key question - can the Big6 or any similar information literacy model be adapted to take account of how students actually find and use information, especially in the Web 2.0 environment?

- Although the importance of learning as construction is recognised within the rhetoric of information skills pedagogy and "Information literacy is often seen as the school library version of constructivism" (Moore,

2005 p.3), much of the observed planning and practice[1] suggests heavy reliance on transmission, learner practice, and feedback, all heavily structured into manageable segments and strongly 'teacher' controlled (that is, the classic behaviourist approach). Early voices such as Kuhlthau's (1993), which present information-seeking as a process of seeking meaning, were at first largely ignored in practice. In recent years there have been intensified efforts to ensure that people who are teaching information literacy adopt constructivist approaches (e.g. Todd, 2001). Limberg (2007) asserts that to learn is not to receive knowledge and information, but is about changing the relationship between a person and the world. She claims that information-seeking is too often focussed on teaching technical procedures and on fact-finding rather than on students formulating authentic questions and constructing their own positions. The concept of authenticity is central to Limberg's ideas on information literacy. Contrived questions and tasks, designed solely to meet externally imposed assessment and with no other consequences for the student, will not engage and motivate students. Without a real and personal interest, students will be satisfied with the superficial answer, the first 'hit', or 'good enough' information. There is no incentive to go beyond using technical skills to collect facts.

Again, the latest outputs from the USA-based Center for International Scholarship in School Libraries (Kuhlthau and others, 2007) focus on the concept of 'guided inquiry' as the basis for teaching and learning of information skills. The main characteristics of guided inquiry are:

- active engagement by students in the learning process

- students building on what they already know
- high levels of reflection
- a recognition of the importance of social interaction and of students' different ways of learning
(Kuhlthau and Todd 2007)

All these are recognisable characteristics of learning as construction (see, for example, Papert and Harel, 1991). There is little doubt that constructivist approaches are particularly suited to Web 2.0 tools. In this environment, students can construct artefacts such as video presentations, blog entries and wiki pages both individually and collaboratively. Teachers can join in with collaborative editing and can scaffold students' work. It seems likely that the constructivist approach to teaching and learning so well supported by Web 2.0 tools may finally lead to information literacy teaching becoming more attuned to how students learn.

If constructivist principles are used to inform and guide information literacy work, students will be required to develop a repertoire of strategies that are conspicuously absent from most information literacy models. This will involve:

- reflection: the ability to reflect constructively and to use that reflection in planning for their own development
- evaluation of the processes undertaken as well as of the products of their study
- making sense (deep understanding) of the information that they obtain, linked to the ability to transform the information to reflect their own emerging views

We do not think that these aspects of learning can simply be grafted onto existing frameworks or inserted after any particular element of a linear, sequential model. They are part of an iterative process of learning not well represented in existing information literacy frameworks.

THE IMPORTANCE OF CONTEXT

The importance of context in relation to information behaviour is well established (e.g. Streatfield and Wilson, 1980; Dervin, 1992; Ingwersen and Jarvelin, 2005). Context in information-related behaviour is recognised as multi-dimensional: with different facets reflecting features of the task; characteristics of the learner; and features of the system. Louise Limberg observed in a conference presentation that "Influential studies have abandoned the idea of information literacy as a set of generic skills applied anywhere. Information literacy is not generic but should be seen as social practice …" (Limberg, 2007). Looking at secondary schools, Williams and Wavell (2007) warned that if we are trying to to develop pupils' information literacy we cannot ignore content in favour of technicalities and procedures - if we do so, we will get trivial learning outcomes. Nevertheless, as we have already noted, information literacy advocates have persisted in offering generic skills development frameworks that take little no account of context.

How can the importance of context be reflected in an information literacy framework? We believe that a different type of framework is needed; one that moves away from offering a list of abilities to be taught or applied in an unvarying sequence, irrespective of context.

Alongside the challenge of producing an appropriate information literacy framework we face another problem: how can we teach information literacy in ways that respect the influence of context? Current views on skills development (e.g. Luke, 2006; Williams and Wavell, 2006) assert that if students are to develop their information-related skills through assignments there is a need for:

- Authentic tasks that are recognised as relevant by the students (tasks that have meaning to students on a personal or academic level; not contrived to allow them to practice particular skills)

- Immersion in authentic contexts (realistic environments, current information drawn from the real world, engagement with real world problems and concerns)
- High quality tasks related to current academic work (e.g. asking students to conduct critical evaluation of sources to construct a position for an essay, rather than offering general guidance on evaluating information)
- Learning embedded in the relationships, values and discourse of the learning community (inherently social)
- Timely teacher interventions in order to move learners on at transition points in their work

Web 2.0 can once again be a powerful support for increasing authenticity and enabling the deployment of information literacy strategies in a variety of meaningful contexts. The possibility of a public platform for their work may help students to take more seriously the underlying information literacy processes involved in producing that work.

STUDENT REFLECTION

If we are to take context into account when deciding on information literacy strategies, this immediately introduces the concept of variation. Bowden and Marton (1998) argued that not only do students need to experience variation in order to learn, but they must also explore variation by comparing and analysing their experiences. To do this, students need to:

- actively engage in discussion and reflection about finding and using information in order to uncover variation in their conceptions
- confront variation in their own experience and in the experience of others.
(Based on Bruce, 2007, pp. 51-52)

Since at least the 1970s, reflection has been seen as a mainstay of learning and this concept has found its way into many models of learning (e.g. Kolb, 1975; Schon, 1983).

Reflection is a particularly important element in developing the processes underpinning learning and is therefore potentially important in any systematic approach to information literacy. Reflection is taken for granted in most models of information literacy or placed at the very end of the process. This approach in not likely to enable the development of the meta-cognitive strategies necessary to perform problem-solving with information. It is likely to be difficult to integrate reflection into existing information literacy frameworks in any meaningful way (see the discussion about constructivism above). The possibilities for learning provided by Web 2.0 may provide a way forward. For example, peer critique and the collaborative production of artefacts may automatically stimulate reflection. If not, engagement in these processes should provide opportunities for a more formal emphasis on reflection as part of information literacy teaching.

COLLABORATIVE LEARNING

Collaborative learning has long been seen as a desirable process: for example, groupwork is a key element of training courses for teachers in all sectors. Web 2.0 tools have turned many students into sophisticated social networkers via YouTube, Facebook, blogs and discussion boards (Ipsos MORI, 2007). The same tools can also be used to facilitate collaboration in formal learning settings, whether the focus is on creating specific interest groups, building learning communities or enabling the collaborative production and editing of artefacts.

Collaborative learning requires many skills of communication and interaction, but does it make fundamentally different information literacy demands on learners than those made when individually finding and using information? There is little in recent research to indicate that this is the case (Williams and Wavell, 2007; Kuhlthau, 2007). The influence of context (subject, learner characteristics and teacher expectations) is not just about whether students are working individually or in groups to find and use information. At the same time, Web 2.0 can be seen as working counter to collaboration through increased personalisation of learning paths. Overall, this aspect of Web 2.0 raises important issues in the wider context of approaches to learning by providing increased scope for a variety of activities. It may offer valuable avenues for the teaching of information literacy but does not seem to fundamentally affect the information handling skills required.

LEARNERS' EXPECTATIONS OF INFORMATION

Web 2.0 inevitably raises questions of ownership and authority of information. It is an environment in the course of creation by its participants. These participants individually and collaboratively generate content in a form, format and structure that best suits their own needs and preferences. This process works well when the primary focus is on participation in social networks or developing personal interests. However, it can create major difficulties when the same processes are applied in formal learning. Keen (2007) claims that we are diving headlong into an age of mass mediocrity because of the absence of gatekeeper expertise and the increase in user-created content. This view is echoed by Gorman in his Britannica Blog (2007) which identifies an erosion of traditional respect for authenticity and expertise in a world in which everyone is an expert "ignorant of the knowledge they will never acquire and the rich world of learning that search engines cannot currently deliver to them."

Most students should be able to operate both in the social world of web 2.0 and in more formal learning environments (even before we take account of the growing presence of academic interests and institutions on Web 2.0). However, to operate effectively in formal learning environments, student autonomy may have to give way to recognised academic authority. Students' preferred use of Wikipedia and social bookmarking, alongside their facility in creating new 'knowledge' through remixing text, image and audio, or through the collaborative creation and editing of web pages may come into conflict with the necessity to conform to academic norms of using externally-validated information. Students will not be able to simply replicate their social/leisure on-line behaviour when engaging in formal academic tasks. Information literacy should help in this arena: traditional information literacy models do focus on evaluating sources of information, on considering authority and credibility. Such an emphasis should raise students' awareness of the problems associated with following their own preferences and concentrating on their own perspectives. A new balance may need to be drawn between encouraging students to use the range of pathways to information that are open to them in Web 2.0 and ensuring that they have the ability to choose the most appropriate for academic study.

However, do we also need to respond more positively to students' expectations of information? Should the information literacy field legitimise elements of students' preferred information-related behaviour? For example, should we ensure that information literacy frameworks encompass such concepts as 'good enough' information, trial and error, and peer 'expertise' rather than focusing primarily on a set of competencies that appear to be designed to turn all learners into systematic researchers, regardless of the task context?

DOES FINDING INFORMATION REALLY MATTER ANY MORE?

One question likely to worry traditional information literacy proponents is whether there will be a continuing need for skills in information seeking, given an information world in which search engines are become increasingly sophisticated and in which Web 2.0 offers a range of enticing alternatives to systematic searching. According to Carol Kuhlthau (2007) what is important in the 21ˢᵗ century is the ability to use information for problem-solving **not** "the technology of finding."

IS A NEW MODEL OF INFORMATION LITERACY NEEDED TO MEET THE CHALLENGE OF WEB 2.0?

We are not convinced that the Web 2.0 environment on its own necessitates the development of new sets of abilities for finding and using information. It does, however, move learning into new directions (e.g. increased collaboration, more authentic tasks, peer critique, non-linear aapproaches to information). In doing so, learning with Web 2.0 tools should put increasing pressure on proponents of information literacy to move in the direction of well recognised learning principles and practices. In particular, information literacy can be enhanced in a formal learning environment by exploiting some possibilities offered through Web 2.0 tools:

- Enhanced group work and shared tasks
- Cooperative creation of multi-media artefacts
- Collaborative editing and critiquing
- Searching for information (e.g. using social bookmarking and folksonomies)
- Organising information in new ways (e.g. using tagging)

- Increasing authenticity of work by presenting ideas to others in a more public space and using a wider range of media
- Providing 'just-in-time' scaffolding to support students
- Facilitating student reflection using records of individual and group processes and providing virtual contemplative spaces

None of these aspirations are new to formal education but some have been difficult to achieve hitherto without the benefits of advances in Web 2.0.

If the information literacy community is prepared to design materials, activities and support mechanisms based on the opportunities offered by Web 2.0, can they adapt existing information literacy frameworks to scaffold their work? Is a framework needed at all to enable information literacy development in formal education settings?

Any model or framework will be flawed because it cannot fully take account of the influence of context on information use or the problems inherent in producing any generic view of information literacy. However, whilst doing research and development work in many further and higher education institutions and schools, we have found that staff and students want to put some sort of framework in place. They want a public statement that clarifies what is encompassed by information literacy; a guide to support curriculum planning; and something that students can refer to when doing research and tackling academic tasks.

The following framework (Markless and Streatfield, 2007) was originally designed to address problems being encountered by the University of Hertfordshire. The University was trying to develop an institution-wide approach to supporting students when finding and using information in an electronic environment. At first it was thought that an existing framework could be used or adapted to meet the needs of staff and students. However, consideration of the issues explored in this chapter made the shortcomings of such an approach apparent. We concluded that many of the traditional information literacy models had been built on a series of assumptions about learning and information behaviour that were problematic and that the increasing use of Web 2.0 threw these assumptions into stark relief. We therefore needed to offer a different solution that is more in keeping with the changing learning environment.

The solution offered is essentially a framework to support student choice in learning rather than information literacy teaching. The framework is designed to enable students to get help where and from whom they need it rather than to usher them through a regimented programme of information skills development. Some of the individual elements of the framework hark back to those designed in the 1980s and 90s. The skills and strategies included are not all new, although we have moved away from a heavy emphasis on systematic searching. In addition this framework is designed to be approached and used differently from traditional frameworks such as the Big6. The drivers behind our approach are student choice and reflection to support effective learning rather than laying out a sequence of steps to be taught.

During three key stages (which do tend towards the sequential) students *choose* which strategy to adopt at different points in their research. Help and guidance is available for each of the key elements. Importantly, if one avenue fails students can go back to the big picture and choose another route; they are not trapped in a sequence that they are expected to follow. The framework is designed for students to construct their own problem-solving approaches to finding and using information, either individually or collaboratively. The impact of context on learning should lead students to make different choices about which strategies to employ and which skills to draw on depending upon the nature of the task they are addressing and the wider social context in which they are operating. The framework is designed

to take advantage of technological developments that allow individuals to make choices, navigate between options and then save their search paths for future reflection.

The framework that we designed drew on two research-based published models, a non-linear model of information-seeking behaviour[2] devised by Allen Foster (2004; 2006) and a model of information and critical literacies offered by Ross Todd (2001). Foster worked with academics to show the fallacies inherent in the assumption that researchers looked for information using a fixed sequence of steps. Todd's overview of information literacy emphasised transformation and construction of knowledge because he wanted to encourage students to stop interpreting research tasks or assignments merely as processes of collecting information. Instead they are encouraged to think in terms of forming their own perspectives, creating new insights and presenting their own authentic voices.

Our new framework builds on these ideas as well as addressing some of the concerns discussed earlier in this chapter. It is presented below as a series of figures.

Figure 1 provides students with an overview of what is involved with finding and using information. It was important to avoid the trap of presenting information literacy as a series of steps (anything between 5 and 12 stages in many traditional frameworks. The Big6 actually contains 12 steps as there are two stages in each of the 6 main elements of the framework.) Students can choose to engage in any one of the 3 main elements depending on the nature of the academic task they are tackling.

Figures 2, 3 and 4 are what the students see when they click on the relevant box in figure one. There is no set path through any of these figures; if the student is at the beginning of a project they may look at figure two and decide that the best place to begin is with networking. If they click on networking they will get some ideas about who they might contact and how they might work with

Figure 1.

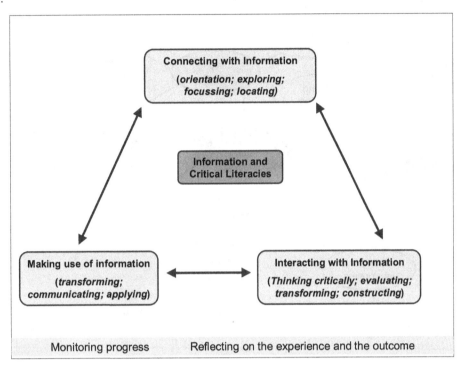

Figure 2.

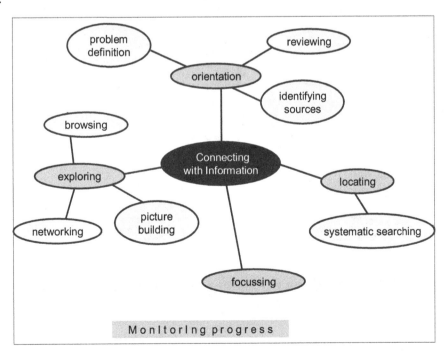

Figure 3.

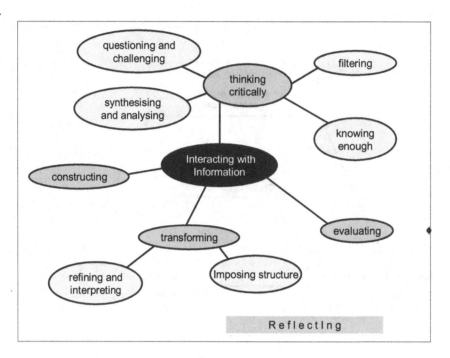

Figure 4.

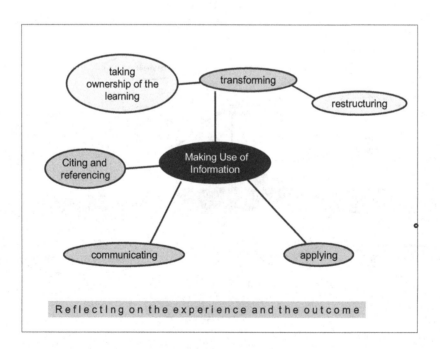

peers. Equally, a student might decide to begin with problem definition. Again, this element is populated with activities, ideas and advice about how to analyse a problem. Whatever path a student or group of students decides to take through this framework they are offered on-line support at the point of need. They are also encouraged to save their path so that they can see how they worked through a particular assignment - the choices they made. Students compare their chosen paths with those of their peers and consider which have been most effective. They can also review their approaches across a number of different tasks to see whether and how they have adapted their approach to the context. Encouraging reflection on the process of learning was an important element in our design of a non-sequential framework.

Where our framework is being used, each element is being populated with material designed by both academic staff and librarians. The framework itself has stimulated some useful collaborative work between staff interested in specific elements most relevant to their discipline. Their aim is to provide support for students who want to use a particular information skill or strategy in the course of their academic work without dictating a path through that work.

This framework is very much a work in progress. It is being tested at universities in the UK and Spain and is currently being translated into Arabic. The real test for this framework will be if students do not see it as a straightjacket, constraining their normal interactions with information, but find it useful no matter what the information environment in which they are working.

CONCLUSION

The traditional information skills models (such as the Big6) that grew out of early interest in enhancing the use of libraries and text-based resources tended to be based on a simplistic view of learning and information behaviour. These models served a purpose in introducing students to the formal world of academic information and, as such, continued to be of use when responding to the arrival of the Internet in its original conception as an information storage and transmission vehicle. However, the shift in focus towards ever greater information access through the Internet combined with greater attention to teaching and learning of information literacy based on constructivist education principles, has led to the traditional information skills approaches being increasingly questioned.

The changes being brought about by the advent of Web 2.0 have served both to provide a further challenge to traditional approaches to information literacy and potential solutions to some of the inherent problems in traditional approaches. The value of teacher-led, text-focussed, sequential models must now be in question because they are based on very un-web 2.0 propositions. Instead, the social networking possibilities offered by Web 2.0 provide fresh opportunities for supporting social learning, including peer information seeking, evaluation, critique of strategies and capturing of processes when helping students to engage with information literacy development. Accordingly, a new framework is tentatively offered here as an alternative to the Big6 and similar models, with the intention of allowing students to construct and revisit their own paths to information discovery, organisation, sense-making and exploitation in the evolving world of Web 2.0.

REFERENCES

Association of College and Research Libraries (ACRL) (2000). *Information literacy competency standards for higher education.*

Bawden, D. (2001). Information and digital literacies: a review of the concepts. *Journal of Documentation, 57*(2), 218-259.

Bowden, J., & Marton, F. (1998). *The university of learning: beyond quality and competence in higher education.* London: Kogan Page.

Bruce, C. S. (1997). *The seven faces of information literacy.* Adelaide: Auslib Press

Bruce, C. S., Edwards, S., & Lupton, M. (2007). Six frames for information literacy education: A conceptual framework for interpreting the relationships between theory and practice. In S. Andretta, (Ed.), *Change and challenge: information literacy for the 21ˢᵗ century.* Adelaide: Auslib Press.

Council of Australian University Libraries (2001). *Information literacy standards.* Canberra: CAUL

Dervin, B. (1992). From the mind's eye of the user: the sense-making qualitative-quantitative methodology. In J. D. Glazier & R. R. Powell (Eds.), *Qualitative Research in Information Management.* Englewood, CO: Libraries Unlimited.

Eisenberg, M. B., & Berkowitz, R. E. (1990). *Information problem-solving: the Big Six skills approach to library and information skills instruction.* New Jersey: Ablex Publishing Corp.

Eisenberg, M. B., & Johnson, D. (1996). Computer skills for information problem-solving: learning and teaching technology. In *context ERIC Digest 1996, 4*

Eisenberg, M. B., & Berkowitz, R. E. (2000). *Teaching information and technology skills: The Big6 in secondary schools.* New Jersey: Ablex Publishing Corp.

Eisenberg, M. B., & Brown, M. K.(1992). Current themes regarding library and information skills instruction: research supporting and research lacking. *SLMQ 20*(2) (Winter) http://archive.ala.org/aasl/SLMR/slmr_resources/select_eisenberg.html

Foster, A. E. (2004). A non-linear model of information seeking behavior. *J. of the American Society for Information Science and Technology, 55*(3), 228-237.

Foster, A. E. (2006). A non-linear perspective on information seeking. In A. Spink & C. Cole (Ed.), *New directions in human information behaviour.* New York: Springer.

Gorman, M. (2007). *The Siren Song of the Internet Part 2.* http://www.britannica.com/blogs/2007/06/the-siren-song-of-the-internet-part-ii/

Ingwersen, P., & Jarvelin, K. (2005). *The turn: integration of information seeking and retrieval in context.* New York: Springer

Ipsos MORI (2007). *Student expectations study: key findings from on-line research and discussion evenings held in June 2007 for the Joint Information Systems Committee JISC.*

Jukes, I. A. (2007). *Born to be wired: NetSavvy and communication literacy for an information age.* web.mac.com/iajukes/thecommittedsardine/Presentations.html [Accessed 15 December 2007]

Keen, A. (2007). *The cult of the amateur: how today's Internet is killing our culture and assaulting our economy.* London: Nicholas Brealey.

Kolb, D. A., & Fry, R. (1975). Towards an applied theory of experiential learning. In C. Cooper (Ed.), *Theories of group processes.* London: John Wiley.

Kuhlthau, C. C. (1988). Developing a model of the library search process: cognitive and affective aspects. *RQ* (Winter) (pp.232-242).

Kuhlthau, C. C. (2007). From information to meaning: confronting the challenges of the 21ˢᵗ century. Keynote paper presented at *Information: interactions and impact conference*, Aberdeen June.

Kuhlthau, C. C. (1993). *Seeking meaning: a process approach to library and information services.* Norwood, NJ: Ablex; [Second edition published 2004].

Kuhlthau, C. C., & Todd, R. J. (2007). Guided inquiry: a framework for learning through school libraries in 21st century schools. http://cissl.scils. rutgers.edu/guided_inquiry/characteristics.html [accessed 21 December 2007]

Kuhlthau, C. C., Caspari, A. K., & Maniotes, L. K. (2007). *Guided inquiry: learning in the 21st century.* New York: Libraries Unlimited Inc.

Limberg, L. (2007). What matters: shaping meaningful learning through teaching information literacy Presentation at *Information: interactions and impact conference*, Aberdeen June.

Loertscher, D. V., & Woolls, B. (2002). *Information literacy: a review of the research. A guide for practitioners and researchers* 2nd Edition Salt Lake City: Hi Willow Publishing.

Luke, A. (2006). On critical literacy: learning to question texts and discourses Keynote paper at *Bridging the Gap* Conference Yokohama November

Markless, S., & Lincoln, P. (Eds.) (1986). *Tools for learning* British Library R and D Report 5892 London: British Library Board.

Markless, S., & Streatfield, D. R. (2000). *The really effective college library.* Library and Information Commission Research Report 51 Twickenham, Middx. IMA for the LIC.

Markless, S., & Streatfield, D. R. (2007). Three decades of information literacy: Redefining the parameters. In S. Andretta (Ed.), *Change and challenge: information literacy for the 21st century.* Adelaide: Auslib Press.

Marland, M. (Ed.) (1981). *Information skills in the secondary curriculum: the recommendations of a Working Group sponsored by the British Library and the Schools Council.* London: Methuen Educational

Martin, A. (2006). Literacies for the Digital Age. In A. Martin & D. Madigan (Eds.), *Digital literacies for learning.* London: Facet Publishing.

Moore, P. (1997). Teaching information problem solving in primary schools: an information literacy survey. *J of Contemporary Educational Psychology, 20*, 1-31.

Moore, P. (2005). An analysis of information literacy education worldwide in School. *Libraries Worldwide, 11*(2), 1-23.

Papert, S., & Harel, I. (1991). *Constructionism.* New Jersey: Ablex Publishing Corp.

Perkins, D. N., & Salomon, G. (1992). Transfer of learning. In *International encyclopedia of education,* 2nd edition. Oxford, Pergamon Press.

Oblinger, D., & Oblinger, J. (Eds.) (2005). *Educating the net generation.* Educause. www.educause. edu/educatingthenetgen/

Prensky, M. (2001). Digital natives, digital immigrants. *On the Horizon, 9*(5) (October) www. markprensky.com/writing/Prensky%20-%20Dig ital%20Natives.%20Digital%20Immigrants%20-%20Part1.pdf [Accessed 21 December 2007]

Schon, D. (1983). *The reflective practitioner.* New York: Basic Books.

Society of College, National and University Libraries (1999). *Seven pillars of information literacy.* http://www.sconul.ac.uk/activities/inf_lit/sp/model.html [Published 1999; re-published 2004 - viewed December 21 2007]

Streatfield, D. R., & Markless, S. (2007). Information literacy. In J. H. Bowman (Ed.), *British librarianship and information work 2001-2005.* Aldershot, Hampshire: Ashgate 2007 (pp. 413-430)

Streatfield, D. R., & Markless, S. (1994). *Invisible learning? The contribution of school libraries to teaching and learning. Report on ... a research project* Library and Information Research Report 98 London: British Library.

Streatfield, D. R., & Wilson, T. D. (1980). *The vital link: information in social services departments.*

London: Community Care and the Joint Unit for Social Services Research.

Tabberer, R., & Altman, J. (1986). *Study and information skills in schools.* London: British Library.

Todd, R. (2001). Transitions for preferred futures of school libraries. Keynote paper to International Association of School Libraries (IASL) Conference, Auckland, Symposium. http://www.iasl-slo.org/virtualpaper2001.html [Accessed 15 December 2007]. [Since developed by Professor Todd in various conference papers and presentations].

UNESCO (2003). *Conference report of the information literacy Meeting of Experts.* Prague, September.

Veen, W. (2007). Homo Zappiens and the need for new education systems. Paper presented at the 2nd international convention *New Millennium Learners: Schools, ICT and learning* Florence. March

Westwell, M. (2007). Bending minds: how technology can change the way we think. Keynote paper presented at *Information: interactions and impact conference*, Aberdeen June.

Williams, D., & Wavell, C. (2006*). Untangling spaghetti? The complexity of developing information literacy in secondary schools,* Scottish Executive, Web publication of research report.

Williams, D., & Wavell, C. (2007*).* Making connections: the nature and impact of information mediation in the development of information literacy in schools. Paper presented at *Information: interactions and impact conference*, Aberdeen June.

Wray, D. (1985). *Teaching information skills through project work.* London: British Library.

KEY TERMS

Constructivist Learning: Learning as an individual or social act of construction, leading to sense-making and the building of meaning.

Information Literacy: A set of abilities for seeking and using information in purposeful ways related to task, situation and context. (Limberg, 2007)

Information Skills: The sets of skills and competencies required to find and use information, usually in a formal education context.

ENDNOTES

[1]   This observation is based on our experience over twenty years of observing information skills/ literacy lessons and examining lesson plans.

[2]   Although Foster describes his model as non-linear, it may be more helpful to regard it as a non-sequential model

Chapter XXIII
Pedagogical Responses to Social Software in Universities

Catherine McLoughlin
Australian Catholic University, Australia

Mark J. W. Lee
Charles Sturt University, Australia

ABSTRACT

Learning management systems (LMS's) that cater for geographically dispersed learners have been widely available for a number of years, but many higher education institutions are discovering that new models of teaching and learning are required to meet the needs of a generation of learners who seek greater autonomy, connectivity, and socio-experiential learning. The advent of Web 2.0, with its expanded potential for generativity and connectivity, propels pedagogical change and opens up the debate on how people conceptualize the dynamics of student learning. This chapter explores how such disruptive forces, fuelled by the affordances of social software tools, are challenging and redefining scholarship and pedagogy, and the accompanying need for learners to develop advanced digital literacy skills in preparation for work and life in the networked society. In response to these challenges, the authors propose a pedagogical framework, Pedagogy 2.0, which addresses the themes of participation in networked communities of learning, personalization of the learning experience, and learner productivity in the form of knowledge building and creativity.

INTRODUCTION

In contrast to earlier e-learning efforts that simply replicated traditional models of learning and teaching in online environments, social software, together with other components of the Web 2.0 (O'Reilly, 2005) movement, offer rich opportunities to move away from the highly centralized industrial model of learning of the past decade, towards achieving individual empowerment of learners through designs that focus on collaborative, networked communication and interaction (cf. Rogers, Liddle, Chan, Doxey, & Isom, 2007; Sims, 2006). Hilton (2006) discusses how a number of "disruptive forces" are shaping the future of higher education. These include: the unbundling of content; the shift from "provider push" to "demand pull;" the arrival of ubiquitous access to information and services; and the rise of the "pure property" view of ideas that is incongruent with the Web 2.0 philosophy and spirit of collaboration and sharing.

For the purposes of the current discussion, the focus is on social software that enables participation, collaboration, personalization, creativity, and generativity, as these are arguably the key elements of what it means to be educated in a networked age (Bryant, 2006). Social software tools are a defining characteristic of Web 2.0, and many are already being widely used to support learning. For example, one of the most basic social software tools, the Weblog (blog), has been a resounding success in many colleges and universities, used to facilitate reflective writing and the building of e-Portfolios (Ganley, 2004; Richardson, 2006a). With the rich and varied functionality of social computing in mind, together with its "always on" culture and participatory attributes, it is useful to consider the potential value adding of these new and emerging tools and technologies for millennial learners.

HOW SOCIAL SOFTWARE TOOLS IMPACT ON LEARNING AND WAYS OF KNOWING

The affordances of Web 2.0 are now making learner-centered education a reality, with collaborative writing tools (wikis, Google Docs & Spreadsheets), media sharing applications (Flickr, YouTube, TeacherTube), and social networking sites (MySpace, Facebook, Friendster, Ning) capable of supporting multiple communities of learning. These tools enable and encourage informal conversation, dialogue, collaborative content generation, and the sharing of information, giving learners access to a wide raft of ideas and representations of knowledge.

The attributes and affordances of the new software tools and services also make possible an expanded repertoire of online behavior, distributed collaboration, and social interaction. Mejias (2005, p. 1) observed that "... social software can positively impact pedagogy by inculcating a desire to reconnect to the world as whole, not just the social part that exists online," referring to the isolating and decontextualized experience of much text-based traditional education. Many social software applications straddle the virtual and real social worlds, as they entail both online and offline interactions and visual/verbal connectivity. These new affordances are being harnessed for knowledge sharing, development of ideas, and creative production, while allowing for personal sense making and reflection.

There are also associated changes in what and how people learn, and the ways in which they access information. Knowledge is no longer controlled and stable, but open to interpretation, modification, and re-creation by anyone, anywhere. The traditional macro-structures of the disciplines are being replaced by dynamic microstructures created by networked individuals working collaboratively. These communication networks are able to link people and summon the "wisdom of crowds" (Surowiecki, 2004), so that the collective intelligence of groups can be harnessed to generate ideas that are fresher, richer, and more sophisticated than the contributions of individual users. Lindner (2006) quotes Parkin (2005), who observes: "it's not content or even context, but process that gets us going" (p. 31), indicating that participating, doing, and experiencing rather than knowing what or where, and creating knowledge rather than consuming it, is the new mindset and *modus operandi* of learners, online communities, and the knowledge economy at large. All in all, we have an environment in which digital technology and the flow of information are paramount, and in which "learning to learn" (know-how) is now far more important than memorizing explicit knowledge and facts (know-what).

Implications for the Design of Learning Environments

The expansion and growth in popularity of Web 2.0 services and the increased prevalence of user-generated content have implications for learning environments in higher education, and are already influencing pedagogical choices and approaches (Williams & Jacobs, 2004). In what can be described as a user-driven revolution, there is a shift away from the production of Web content by traditional, "authoritative" sources, towards content is that is generated by the users themselves. In academia, these users are students and they now have the tools, spaces, and skills to contribute ideas and publish their views, research, and interpretations online. It is important to remember that these tools can also be used in combination and engage people through communication, co-production, and sharing. Through these activities, social and cognitive benefits accrue to both individuals and to the community of users who support and take part in them (Boyd, 2007; Barsky & Purdon, 2006).

For example, course content and learning resources can come from many sources, and this is partly a result of the ease with which social software can be used to create, share, augment, tag, and upload content. In what has been described as a "rip, mix, and burn culture" and a "digital democracy," all participants can become creators of content (Goodman & Moed, 2006; Hughes & Lang, 2006; Lamb, 2007). In academia, this means moving beyond the confines of learning management systems (LMS's) and tapping into a wider pool of expertise, to include community-generated learning resources (Eisenstadt, 2007; Lamb, 2007). These changes are having a profound and immediate effect on the learning landscape, and on the nature of literacies and skills required of learners, as many authors and researchers have recently noted (Eisenstadt, 2007; Berg, Berquam, & Christoph, 2007; Lankshear & Knobel, 2007). As students engage with social technologies and begin to generate and re-mix content, share it with a global audience, and connect to a wide range of communities, their expectations for "always-on" services and relevant, participatory, interactive flexible learning experiences expand and become drivers of change in higher education (Milne, 2007; Tynan & Barnes, 2007).

Nevertheless, challenges remain for higher education institutions in terms of how they will manage change, and set up physical infrastructures and spaces for learners (Bleed, 2001; JISC, 2006; Australian Learning & Teaching Council, 2008) to maximize networking and knowledge exchange. In the United Kingdom in particular, research on the applications of social software is informing innovative approaches to education in all sectors, and is driving a strong agenda for personalization of curricula and the foregrounding of lifelong learning skills, innovation, and creativity as desirable learning outcomes (Owen, Grant, Sayers, & Facer, 2006).

RETHINKING PARADIGMS: LEARNING AS KNOWLEDGE CREATION

Before investigating the transformative impact of social software tools on existing practice and pedagogy, a conceptual overview of emerging practices in higher education, grounded in explanatory theoretical frameworks, will signpost changes that are already prevalent. A number of terms and metaphors signal the change from traditional pedagogies to more active forms of teaching and learning engagement, where learners have greater levels of agency, social connectedness, and autonomy.

How we conceptualize learning evokes a number of possible scenarios or metaphors. Sfard (1998), for example, distinguished between two metaphors of learning, the acquisition metaphor and the participation metaphor. The former represents a view of learning that is mainly a process of acquiring chunks of information, typically delivered by a teacher. An alternative model, according to Sfard, is the participation metaphor, which sees learning as a process of participating in various cultural practices and shared learning activities. In order to keep pace with knowledge-building processes that are emerging in the Web 2.0 era, it now appears to be necessary to go beyond the acquisition and participation dichotomy. The knowledge creation metaphor of learning (Paavola & Hakkarainen, 2005) mirrors the societal shift towards a networked knowledge age, in which creativity, originality, and the capacity to gain knowledge from networks are highly valued. The concept builds on common elements of Bereiter's (2002) theory of knowledge building, Nonaka and Takeuchi's (1995) model of knowledge creation, and Engeström's (1987, 1999) theory of expansive learning. The "trialogic" nature of the knowledge creation metaphor reminds us that learning is an intensely social activity, as ideas are generated with others in the community through mutual exchange, contribution, and sharing of ideas.

Applying the Metaphor: Students as Knowledge Producers

Students, enabled by social software tools, are capable of being both producers and consumers ("prosumers") of knowledge, ideas, and artifacts. As newcomers to a community of practice, they not only engage in "legitimate peripheral participation" (Lave & Wenger, 1991) to develop their own mastery of knowledge and skills through interaction with experts such as their instructors, but also have a responsibility to play a part in the continued advancement of the community's existing body of knowledge, as they move toward full participation in the socio-cultural practices of this community (Lee, Eustace, Hay, & Fellows, 2005). In a knowledge building community, members are managers or "curators" of its knowledge artifacts (Eustace & Hay, 2000; Lee, et al.,, 2005), intent on making responsible decisions in addition to generating novel and innovative contributions to benefit the community as a whole.

"Knowledge creation" and "knowledge building" are now terms that are applied in management, corporate organizations, and institutions of higher learning that value innovation and creativity (Leadbeater, 2006; Nonaka & Toyama, 2003). The knowledge construction paradigm can be appropriately applied to learning environments where digital tools and affordances enable engagement in self-directed activities, and learners have freedom and choice to move beyond mere participation in communities of inquiry to become active creators of ideas, resources, and knowledge artifacts.

LEARNING THROUGH AND WITHIN COMMUNITIES AND NETWORKS

In the Web 2.0 era, new and dynamic forms of community are emerging that are self-directed and open to a global audience. These offer new forms of social and intellectual engagement to students, often based on sharing objects and artifacts, in what has been termed "object-centered sociality" (Engeström, 2005). Flickr allows the posting and sharing of photos and commentary; social bookmarking (Furl, del.icio.us) allows people to connect through shared metadata and user-driven tagging of Web-based resources; social writing platforms enable collaborative writing and editing, asynchronous creation of text, and personal written commentary. Social networking practices also enable the creation of virtual communities based on shared motives and/or common interests, leading to powerful forms of relationship building. Such social, informal experiences are very often the foundation of learning (Gee, 2003). Social software tools tend to prioritize the individual, as anytime, anyplace connectivity is the primary driver; however, these tools also motivate the individual to link personal interests to broader social networks, thereby situating responses and contributions within a dynamic community that provides feedback and reciprocity (Owen, et al., 2006). These new agendas are already impacting significantly on the reconceptualization of pedagogies and practices in future environments.

Contemporary learning environments for the profession, for industry, and for society in general must therefore take into account the networked nature of knowledge, opportunities afforded by teamwork, and the importance of participation in knowledge generation in technology-rich environments (van Weert, 2006). A theory that has emerged to describe the social, interconnected, and community-based characteristics of learning in contemporary times is connectivism. In the words of its originator, George Siemens (2005): "Personal knowledge is comprised of a network, which feeds into organizations and institutions, which in turn feed back into the network, and then continue to provide learning to individual. This cycle of knowledge development (personal to network to organization) allows learners to remain current in their field through the connections they have formed" (p. 7).

Connectivism strives to overcome the limitations of behaviorism, cognitivism, and constructivism. It synthesizes salient features and elements of several educational, social, and technological theories and concepts to create a new and dynamic theoretical construct for learning in the digital age. In connectivism, learning is the process of creating connections between nodes to form a network, a view that is congruent with the ways in which

people engage in socialization and interaction in the Web 2.0 world through social networking sites and the "blogosphere." As in the knowledge creation metaphor, connectivism acknowledges the centrality of learning through the generation of ideas, supported by social activity, enabled by personal networks, interactivity, and engagement in experiential tasks.

In summary, current educational and social research is making an increasingly strong case for the conceptualization of learning as a networked, collaborative, and social activity, supported by a range of ICT affordances, including those provided by the new wave of social software tools (Mejias, 2005; Brown & Duguid, 2000). The importance of integrating digital resources and social software tools stems from the fact that such resources are part of the knowledge society and economy, and are beoming more and more tightly woven into how we communicate, think, and generate knowledge and ideas in everyday life. In an era in which changes to higher education are set against the backdrop of the digital age and Web 2.0 revolution, fueled by high connectivity and ubiquitous, demand-driven access to information and services, we are witnessing broader societal and technological trends mirrored in the growth of paradigms of active learning in ways that compel us to expand our vision of pedagogy.

NEW CONCEPTUALIZATIONS OF PEDAGOGY THAT RESONATE WITH WEB 2.0

Emerging paradigms conceive of learners as active participants or co-producers of knowledge rather than passive consumers of content, and learning is seen as a participatory, social process supporting personal life goals and needs. To provide an overview, Table 1 describes emerging conceptualizations of pedagogy inspired and enabled by Web 2.0 and social software, along with their associated values and principles. These terms signal changes in pedagogy from teacher controlled,

Table 1. Terms indicating innovative conceptualizations of learning

Term	Author	Principles
Network learning	Polsani (2003)	A form of education whose site of production is the network, i.e. that enables lifelong and life-wide learning processes through connections and access to networks where there are multiple layers of information and knowledge.
e-learning 2.0	Downes (2005)	Learning content is created and distributed in a very different manner to "e-learning 1.0." Rather than being composed, organized, and packaged, content is syndicated, much like a blog post or podcast. It is aggregated by students, using their own personal tools and applications. From there, it is remixed and repurposed with the student's own individual learning needs in mind.
social learning 2.0	Anderson (2007)	Learning is essentially social and dialogic and moves beyond didactic modes to learner engagement with social tools. Courses must be negotiated and tap into wider social pools of knowledge, as student control and freedom are part of lifelong learning for the 21st century.
micro-learning	Hug, Lindner, and Bruck (2006); Lindner (2006)	A new paradigm that involves learning through relatively small learning units and short-term learning activities. Micro-learning processes often derive from interaction with micro-content, which involves small chunks of learning content and flexible technologies that can enable learners to access them easily, anywhere, on demand and on the move. In a wider sense, it describes the way in which informal and incidental learning and knowledge acquisition are increasingly occurring through micro-content, micro-media, or multitasking environments, especially those that are based on Web 2.0 and mobile technologies.
nano-learning	Masie (2005, 2006)	An analogue of nano-technology. Similar to micro-learning, in emphasizing the trend towards the atomization of learning beyond the learning object (Menell, 2005) to comprise personalized smaller units of information that can be learned and recombined. This enables greater relevance for learners as well as allowing for just-in-time learning.
University 2.0	Barnes and Tynan (2007)	A new generation of universities using social networking technologies, where pedagogy is reframed to meet the needs of millennial learners and connect them to wider social networks. The key idea is to start with the connections students have made through informal learning in their day-to-day lives.
Curriculum 2.0	Edson (2007)	Curriculum is negotiated, personalized, and driven by learner needs. It is based on providing learners with skills in managing and accessing knowledge, and allowing them to take control of their own learning pathways.

prescriptive, and didactic modes to learner-driven social, collaborative, and participatory approaches to task design and learner engagement.

If we consider and compare the conceptualizations of learning depicted in Table 1 to the narrow, transmissive approaches that are often adopted in higher education, a number of discontinuities become apparent. The big change is occurring in e-learning paradigms where new tools and software enable students to create, share, and showcase their own ideas and content, for example through e-Portfolios, podcasting, and blogging.

The learner is conceptualized as mobile, active, and engaging with peers in collaborative knowledge generation. Downes (2005) notes that social software tools allow learning content to be created and distributed in ways that move beyond pre-packaged course content consumed by students, promoting the view that learning and the content associated with it involve highly creative processes on the part of both students and teachers.

Arguing along similar lines, Boettcher (2006) suggests that there is a need to carefully re-evaluate the role of content in courses, particularly in a higher education climate in which the value of textbooks and prescribed content is being questioned (Moore, 2003; Fink, 2005), and in which the open source and open content movements (Beshears, 2005; Massachusetts Institute of Technology, 2008; *MERLOT*, 2008) are gaining momentum. Today's younger students perceive little value in the absorption or rote learning of factual information, given the accessibility and ease of use of search engines and Web-based reference sites such as Google and Wikipedia (Berg, et al., 2007). Instead, the real educational value lies in the facilitation of a learning experience in which the students are empowered to create content for themselves and for others.

PEDAGOGY 2.0: A FRAMEWORK FOR INNOVATION

Evidence suggests that the boundaries of current pedagogies are being stretched and challenged by the potential offered by social software applications for dynamic, user-generated content, while pervasive computing and wireless networking tools ensure constant connectivity and promote participation in communities of learning and practice. With social software, there is a recognizable shift to include both formal and informal spaces for learning, and the tools afford greater learner autonomy and flexibility, as the learning experience becomes more personalized and responsive not only to the learners themselves, but also to their future needs in a knowledge based-society.

Earlier in this chapter, the importance of access to and use of social software tools and services was emphasized as these are integral to communicating, networking, and generating new ideas in the knowledge society. The need for pedagogical innovation is urgent and immediate. As Richardson (2006b) remarks: "In an environment where it's easy to publish to the globe, it feels more and more hollow to ask students to 'hand in' their homework to an audience of one.

When we're faced with a flattening world where collaboration is becoming the norm, forcing students to work alone seems to miss the point. And when many of our students are already building networks far beyond our classroom walls, forming communities around their passions and their talents, it's not hard to understand why rows of desks and time-constrained schedules and standardized tests are feeling more and more limiting and ineffective" (para. 10).

The authors therefore propose a framework for innovative teaching and learning practices, *Pedagogy 2.0*, which capitalizes on the core energies and affordances of Web 2.0, while facilitating personal choice, collaboration and participation, as well as creative production. These overlapping elements are depicted in Figure 1.

Pedagogy 2.0 is envisioned as an overarching concept for an emerging cluster of practices that advocates learner choice and self-direction, and engagement in flexible, relevant learning tasks and strategies. Though it is intended neither as a prescriptive framework, nor a technology-driven mandate for change, it distills a number of guidelines characterizing effective learning environments, such as choice of resources, tasks, learning supports, and communication modalities. Each of the core elements, i.e., the three P's of personalization, participation, and productivity, can be applied to teacher and student roles and enables transformation and extension of current practices.

Participation as an Element of Pedagogy 2.0

More engaging, socially-based models for teaching and learning are needed to replace the traditional, "closed classroom" models, which place emphasis on the institution and instructor. A defining feature of Pedagogy 2.0 is that, alongside the increased socialization of learning and teaching, there is a focus on a less prescriptive approach, and greater emphasis on teacher-student partnerships

Figure 1. Key elements of Pedagogy 2.0

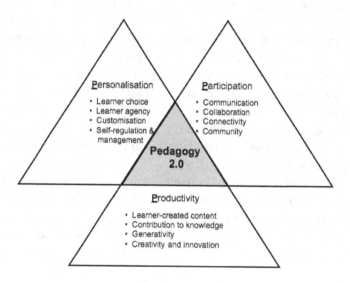

in learning, with teachers as co-learners. As such, this element of Pedagogy 2.0 is reflective of the "participation model of learning" (Sfard, 1998), as opposed to the "acquisition" model.

While the use of popular social software technology in itself is of value in motivating learners, the tools also allow learners to engage deeply with their peers, instructors, other subject-matter experts, and with the wider community. The additional connectivity achieved by linking tools, people, and data is part of an emerging global network or "architecture of participation" (O'Reilly, 2005; Barsky & Purdon, 2006). Pedagogy 2.0 therefore adds a further dimension to participative learning by increasing the level of socialization and collaboration with experts, community, and peer groups, and by fostering connections that go beyond the walls of the classroom or institution.

Personalization as an Element of Pedagogy 2.0

The notion of personalization is not entirely new to educators and is often linked to the term "learner-centered" education, a desirable state where learners know how to choose and make decisions relating to their personal learning needs. However, there continue to be significant gaps and differences in espoused and enacted constructivist pedagogies (Lim & Chai, 2008). By harnessing digital technologies and social software tools, a number of key areas pivotal to the development of personalization through teaching are summarized by Green, Facer, Rudd, Dillon, and Humphreys (2005). According to them, pedagogy must:

- Ensure that learners are capable of making informed educational decisions;
- Diversify and recognize different forms of skills and knowledge;

- Include learner-focused forms of feedback and assessment.

For many students, the ability to socialize and study online already affords them a high level of personalization, as they can access resources aligned to their own needs and interests. In addition, Web 2.0 and social software tools enable choice and allow learners to make decisions about which tools best suit their goals and needs for connection and social interaction. Apart from choosing which resources and sites to subscribe and contribute to, which tools to use, and how and where to use them, we are witnessing a shift in the modalities of expression that are now available. Text alone is not always preferred mode of communication, as Web-based multimedia production and distribution tools incorporating rich audio (podcasting, Skype), photo (Flickr), and video (vodcasting, YouTube) capabilities are growing. Research attests to a growing appreciation of the learner's control over the whole learning process, with evidence suggesting that we can improve learning effectiveness by giving the learner control over, and responsibility for, his/her own learning. This is the foundation for such approaches as problem-based and inquiry-based learning (Desharnais & Limson, 2007), and is central to the grand vision of Pedagogy 2.0, where learners have the freedom to decide how to engage in personally meaningful learning.

One of the interesting developments in e-learning is the on-going discussion around the notion of Personal Learning Environments (PLE's). According to Siemens (2007), a PLE is "... a collection of tools, brought together under the conceptual notion of openness, interoperability, and learner control. As such, they are comprised of two elements – the tools and the conceptual notions that drive how and why we select individual parts" (para. 2). Moving on from LMS's, the PLE concept represents the latest step towards an alternative approach to e-learning. Unlike LMS's that take a course-centric view of learning, PLE's are learner-centric (Attwell, 2007). Instead of promoting centralized, instructor-controlled learning and relying on LMS's to deliver pre-packaged materials and activities, Pedagogy 2.0 challenges university and college teachers to harness the many resources that exist outside the formal spaces of the institution, to create opportunities for authentic learning that are relevant to learners personally, and to capitalize on the interests and digital competencies that learners already possess.

Productivity as an Element of Pedagogy 2.0

The knowledge creation metaphor of learning (Paavola & Hakkarainen, 2005) acknowledges that students are also capable of creating and generating ideas, concepts, and knowledge, and in the Web 2.0 era, the importance of encouraging and enabling this form of creativity and productivity is of vital significance. Educators are beginning to realize that instructor-supplied content has limitations, particularly if it pre-empts learner discovery and research, and active student involvement in the knowledge creation process. The importance and value of student-generated content, or student performance content (Boettcher, 2006) is becoming increasingly apparent.

For example, in recent years, the e-Portfolio (Love, McKean, & Gathercoal, 2002; Abrami & Barrett, 2005; Stefani, Mason, & Pegler, 2007) has emerged as popular strategy for capturing and organizing student-generated content, which, in addition to completed project/assignment work or deliverables, may also incorporate successive drafts of solutions, descriptions of mistakes made, or evidence of difficulties encountered. Such artifacts document the process of engaging in an authentic problem-based learning experience, and are representative of the complexity and "messiness" of an experience. Student-generated content may also include synchronous and asynchronous computer-mediated communication (CMC) discourse such as chat logs and discussion board postings, reflective writing in the form of diaries or blogs, summaries, and reviews, created by students working individually or in teams.

A few examples will illustrate the new forms of knowledge creation and productivity enabled by social software tools. Learners can now engage in creative authorship by being able to produce and manipulate digital images and video clips, tag them with chosen keywords, and make this content available to their friends and peers worldwide through Flickr, MySpace, and YouTube. Other individuals write blogs and create wiki spaces where like-minded individuals comment on, share and augment these sources, thereby creating a new genre of dynamic, self-published content. This outpouring of information and digital user-generated content between peers has been dubbed "personal publishing" (Downes, 2004). This trend stands in stark contrast to the control culture of education, where pre-packaged content and teacher-designed syllabi dominate, thereby denying students choice and autonomy in shaping their own learning trajectories. The challenge for educators is to enable self-direction, knowledge building, and learner control by providing options and choice while still supplying the necessary structure and scaffolding.

CURRENT EXAMPLES OF PEDAGOGY 2.0

Pedagogy 2.0 can be demonstrated by a number of exemplary practices by tertiary teachers at various institutions worldwide, as shown in Table 2. The 3 P's of Pedagogy 2.0 are exhibited by the examples in a variety of different ways. For example, to support his course in General Psychology at the University of Connecticut, Professor David B. Miller (2006, 2007) hosts weekly informal discussions with students following each week's lectures. During these discussions, students are able to seek clarification on the course material

and talk about it in greater depth, while interacting and actively exploring and discussing issues not covered during the lecture that are of interest and relevance to the group (participation). The discussions are recorded and made available to other members of the class as a series of podcasts for individual listening at a convenient time and place (personalization). The process of creating and participating in the discussions becomes a form of student-generated content (productivity). All students in the cohort are welcome to submit questions in advance of the discussion via email; these questions, as well as those asked by students who attend in person, are answered during the discussion.

In another example, at the University of North Carolina at Pembroke (UNCP), Dr. Kenneth Mentor's courses make use of a wiki-based encyclopedia, with the goal being for students to create and maintain articles or entries on a variety of subjects related to law, criminal justice, sociology, and criminology. In previous courses, Mentor's students created Web pages as class assignments. The *Online Encyclopedia of Criminal Justice* (2007) project extends those efforts in two notably powerful ways: using a wiki enables the student-generated content to be readily shared in virtual "public spaces" and with a broader audience beyond the walls of the classroom, and the wiki's ease of use enables students to create substantial amounts of content within a short timeframe (productivity). In addition to generating and entering initial content, students also perform the roles of editing, revising, and organizing the content, which becomes part of the shared pool of resources accessible to all learners. The learning experience and activities are personalized in that students have a great deal of autonomy and choice in determining when, where, and how to contribute to the collection of information on the wiki, as well as in deciding which topics or entries to create, read, add to, and/or modify (personalization). Although UNCP students initially wrote all site content, the site is now available for educators to

Table 2. Examples of Pedagogy 2.0 in tertiary teaching and learning

Reference/ author	Institution and Country	Description of technology use	Key pedagogical features
Read (2005)	Drexel University, USA	Drexel distributed iPod Photo players to their Education freshmen in September 2005. Read (2005) reported there were plans for a variety of learner-centered applications, including but not limited to having students record study-group sessions and interviews, as well as having them maintain audio blogs to connect with administrators and peers during the work experience semester.	Peer-to-peer learning; distributed intelligence approach
Lee, Chan, and McLoughlin (2006)	Charles Sturt University, Australia	Second year undergraduate students take charge of producing talkback radio-style podcasts to assist first year students undertaking a unit of study that the former group previously completed.	Learner-centered instruction; student-generated content
Evans (2006)	Swathmore College, USA	Students studying a literature course read short passages aloud and record them as podcasts, as well as creating separate podcasts discussing the passage they chose and its relationship to other material.	Development of digital and social competencies
Miller (2006, 2007)	University of Connecticut, USA	Three types of podcasts are used to support a General Psychology course: • *iCube podcasts* – Informal discussions with students following each week's lectures; • *Precasts* – Short enhanced podcasts previewing material prior to each lecture; • *Postcasts* – Short post-lecture podcasts containing re-explanations of selected concepts.	Blending of formal and informal learning; mobile, ubiquitous learning
Frydenberg (2006)	Bentley College, USA	Students in an introductory information technology class work in pairs or groups to produce vodcasts to teach topics from the course schedule to their peers.	Peer teaching; reciprocal learning
Edirisingha, Salmon, and Fothergill (2006)	University of Leicester, United Kingdom	Students make use of "profcasts," i.e. material designed to support learning distinct from that which is facilitated through structured on-campus or e-learning processes alone. e.g., weekly profcasts to supplement online teaching through updated information and guidance.	Extended learning, enrichment and extension activities; personalization of learning content
Kukulska-Hulme (2005)	Open University, United Kingdom	Students studying German and Spanish courses in distance mode use digital voice recorders and mini-camcorders to record interviews with other students and with native speakers, as well as to create audio-visual tours for sharing with their peers.	Peer-to-peer learning; student-generated content using mobile devices
McCarty (2005b, 2006); Sener (2007a)	Osaka Jogakuin College, Japan	Students are interviewed by their instructor, perform roles, and/or present their own creations, in contribution to the instructor's bilingual podcast feed and blog targeted to those studying Japanese or English as a foreign language. The podcast episodes cover Japanese culture, history, folklore, and comparative religions, as well as contemporary social issues such as the education system and the rights of minorities in Japan.	Role play and audio recording of students' own creations and interpretations of social and educational issues
McCarty (2005a); Sener (2007a)	Matsuyama Shinonome College, Japan	As part on an intensive course on translation, students from two East Asian cultures (Chinese and Japanese) participate in a recorded discussion in which they are asked to explain five proverbs in English as well as in their native language.	Cross-cultural collaborative work using student-generated content
Sener (2007b)	University of North Carolina at Pembroke, USA	A wiki-based encyclopedia is maintained by students, the goal being to create entries on a variety of subjects related to law, criminal justice, sociology, and criminology.	Student-generated content, collaborative writing, organizing and editing of content

continued on following page

345

Table 2. continued

Reference/ author	Institution and Country	Description of technology use	Key pedagogical features
Wenzloff (2005); Richardson (2006a)	Macomb Independent School District, Michigan, USA	Social bookmarking is used to compile and share resources with teacher training participants / student teachers. The instructor also subscribes to the RSS feeds of his pre-service teachers' Furl sites, to see what they are reading as well as their comments about the sites.	Resource-based and collaborative learning
Lin, Li, Hu, Chen, and Liu (2007)	National Central University, Taiwan	Students enrolled in an introductory computer science course make use of a wiki to provide assistance and support to one another as they learn introductory programming concepts and techniques. They form project groups, taking on roles that model "real-world" software development teams to produce a computer game that is "marketed" to the rest of the class. During the course of the software development project, the wiki serves as a repository for managing and sharing knowledge and reflections on experiences, and as a mechanism for submitting deliverables.	Community of learning; peer support and mentoring; authentic learning and assessment
Chan, Frydenberg, and Lee (2007)	Charles Sturt University, Australia and Bentley College, USA	Undergraduate students studying first year (freshman) level introductory information technology subjects at Charles Sturt University and Bentley College work in teams consisting of a mixture of students from each institution. Each team is given the task of collaboratively producing a short podcast, to be recorded over the voice over Internet Protocol (VoIP) tool Skype (i.e. a "Skypecast"), in which members discuss issues of relevance to topics that are common to the curricula at both institutions.	Cross-cultural, Internet-mediated collaborative learning and exchange
Helms (2007b); D. Helms, personal communication	Mt. San Jacinto College, USA	Students use the social networking site Ning to create Web 2.0-based web sites to teach others about the dangers associated with drug use and abuse. Working in groups, they each take on one of four roles: Web Designer, Multimedia Designer, Researcher, and Copyrighter. The instructor assigns each group with a specific drug to research and provides "job descriptions" for each of the four roles. The instructor produces a sample Ning site for students to view as an example of the possibilities of the medium (Helms, 2007a). Students also use the blogging and threaded discussion features of Ning to engage in constructive and reflective discourse	Authentic, inquiry-oriented, and project-based learning, with an emphasis on student-generated content (The instructor also employs a form of modeling in the use of a sample Ning site.)
Chao (2007)	Bowling Green State University, USA	Wikis were used by students in a project-based software engineering course. The students used the wiki to support and augment collaborative software development activities, including but not limited to project planning, requirements management, test case management, and defect tracking, as well as the development of user documentation. While the instructor and the students were fully aware that there were a number of Computer-Aided Software Engineering (CASE) tools designed specifically for the above activities, the fact that wikis are available free of charge, combined with their ease of use and flexibility, made them an ideal choice for supporting the dispersed student project teams in this course.	Collaborative learning, authentic learning, project-based learning
Mateer (2008)	The Pennsylvania State University, USA	Dirk Mateer uses YouTube to support his teaching of Economics at Penn State University. Mateer digitizes his lectures, which involve a range of interactive learning approaches, and publishes them on his "Teaching Economics with YouTube" (Mateer, 2007) channel. In addition, he encourages students to find, view, and share with others a variety of freely available video clips provided by other YouTube users.	Multi-modal, peer-to-peer and collaborative learning

use for class assignments, and users outside the institution are allowed to register and contribute (Sener, 2007b). In this way, Mentor's students are active participants not only in the context of the course they are studying, but also in a wider, professional, academic community that transcends the walls of the classroom and institution in which they are based (participation).

POTENTIAL PROBLEMS AND PITFALLS IN IMPLEMENTING PEDAGOGY 2.0

It must be recognized that the implementation of a Pedagogy 2.0 approach is not without its issues and challenges. For example, although the advent of Web 2.0 and the open content movement significantly increases the volume of information available to students and exposes them to a raft of ideas and representations, many higher education students currently lack the competencies necessary to navigate and use the overabundance of information available, including the skills required to locate quality sources and assess them for objectivity, reliability, and currency (Windham, 2005; Katz & Macklin, 2007). In a recently published EDUCAUSE Learning Initiative (ELI) white paper, it is recommended that students develop sound information literacy skills in effectively finding, evaluating, and creating information. Additionally, beyond search and retrieval, information is contextualized, analyzed, visualized, and synthesized, which involves complex critical thinking skills (Lorenzo & Dziuban, 2006; Jenkins, 2007). Fortunately, many of the examples presented earlier demonstrate that in combination with appropriate strategies, social software can also serve as levers for such critical thinking and meta-cognitive development (e.g. Sener, 2007b; Lee, et al., 2006).

Furthermore, in fostering learning processes that encourage the production and use of student-generated content, there is still a need for account-ability and recognition of authoritative sources of information. As seen in this chapter, content supplied by experts such as teachers and textbook authors is but one of many resources available to assist students in developing knowledge and skills, and may have limitations, particularly if it pre-empts learner exploration and discovery, and active student involvement in the knowledge creation process. At the same time, in their desire to engage in emerging forms of collaborative scholarship and self-expression, students must be made aware of the expectations from the point of view of academic integrity. Practices such as "mix, rip, and burn" raise questions about the importance of originality, and give rise to concerns about copyright, ownership, and intellectual property, which must be carefully addressed by educators and educational institutions. There is also a need for quality assurance mechanisms to maximize the validity and reliability of student-generated content. Moving away from teacher-centered models of evaluation and assessment, the review, editing, and quality assurance of content can be done collaboratively and in partnership with learners, while simultaneously drawing on input from the wider community (i.e. "wisdom of crowds").

A further challenge is that educators may not be fully aware of the potential and range of social software tools, and may need opportunities for professional development to reveal how Web 2.0 applications can support teaching and assessment in meaningful and authentic ways. In addition, teachers who adopt social software tools need to do so not merely to appear conversant with the tools, but to integrate the tools into sound pedagogical strategies in order to add value to existing courses, and facilitate authentic exchange and dialogue with and among students. They must be wary of the fact that they may feel unwelcome in their students' online social networks and communities. Although there may be attempts by teachers to co-opt the technologies students use of communication and entertainment, such attempts may be perceived by students as intrusions into "their space" (Mazer, Murphy, & Simonds, 2007).

CONCLUSION: FUTURE LEARNING LANDSCAPES INFORMED BY PEDAGOGY 2.0 PRINCIPLES

Pedagogy 2.0 offers the potential for transformational shifts in teaching and learning practices, whereby learners can access peers, experts, the wider community, and digital media in ways that enable reflective, self-directed learning. While the adoption of social software tools may provide opportunities to meet the increasingly diverse needs of institutions and learners, they may also be used to support both local communities and wider professional contexts, facilitating both lifelong and life-wide learning.

These next-generation practices provide an opportunity for higher education institutions to look at wider implementation issues around technical infrastructure, but they must also address pedagogical challenges such as the integration of informal learning experiences, the limitations of existing physical and virtual learning environments, and the personalization of learning experiences. There may be a culture shock or skills crisis when "old world" educators are confronted with the expectation of working in unfamiliar environments and scenarios, and with tools with which they lack expertise and confidence. For these reasons, there is a need to make time for talking, awareness raising, and discussion of what pedagogic approaches and tools best target the desired learning outcomes.

In summary, Web 2.0 and social software tools promote autonomy and increased levels of socialization and interactivity, while enabling user-controlled, peer-to-peer knowledge creation and network-based inquiry. There are signs of optimism that existing Pedagogy 2.0 practices, by capitalizing on the three P's of personaliza-

tion, participation, and productivity, will result in a learning landscape and a diverse range of educational experiences that are socially contextualized, engaging, and community based. However, obstacles and barriers remain. Can teachers, whose traditional frame of reference is formality, understand how informal learning can take place through social networking and beyond the formal spaces of classrooms, libraries, and laboratories? Can they extend these formal spaces to link with dynamic and open communities that are constantly sharing, revising, and creating new ideas? Can academia, with its established legacy of transmissive pedagogy, rise to the challenge and affect the kind of teaching revolution and changes that are both necessary and inevitable in the new age? The goal is to facilitate learning, be less prescriptive, and be open to new media, tools, and strategies, while nurturing innovation and creativity, independent inquiry, and digital literacy skills. This can be achieved by employing the new tools, resources, and opportunities that can leverage what our students do naturally – socialize, network, and collaborate. Overall, for the principles of Pedagogy 2.0 to be realized, institutional and sector-level change is needed to dissolve educational silos and to equip educators with the skills and facilities that make it possible to be responsive to learner needs, while encouraging learners to become active partners in creating educational pathways that will give them the skills and competencies needed to be successful in the networked age.

In describing the wave of social and technological changes affecting higher education, Hilton (2006) uses two competing metaphors to depict the challenges of the Web 2.0 era: "a perfect storm, born from the convergence of numerous disruptive forces … [and] the dawn of a new day, a sunrise rife with opportunities arising from these same disruptive forces" (p. 59). Taking a positive view, the authors of the present chapter believe that change is imminent. Student-driven demand, coupled with a new approach to pedagogy that leverages the flexibilities and creative options of Web 2.0 and social software tools, can and is already beginning to make the teaching and learning process much more dynamic, creative, and generative. As evidenced in Table 2, there is a great deal of innovation and experimentation with social software on an international scale, and many educators are transforming their pedagogy to create learning experiences that are participatory, personalized, and geared to the production of digital knowledge artifacts by learners. Pedagogy 2.0 therefore enables new pathways to learning with peers and connections to the wider community to flourish, and makes active, self-directed, self-managed learning a reality. Clearly, success in the knowledge economy demands that we leverage the educational value of social software tools to promote student-generated content and digital competencies that allow learners to develop their critical thinking, knowledge-building, and creative skills.

REFERENCES

Abrami, P. C., & Barrett, H. (Eds.), (2005). Special Issue on Electronic Portfolios. *Canadian Journal of Learning Technology, 31*(3).

Anderson, T. (2007). *Social Learning 2.0.* Keynote paper presented at ED-MEDIA 2007 World Conference on Educational Multimedia, Hypermedia, & Telecommunications, Vancouver, BC, June 25-29. Retrieved June 27, 2007, from http://www.slideshare.net/terrya/educational-social-software-edmedia-2007/

Attwell, G. (2007). Personal learning environments: the future of e-learning? *eLearning Papers, 2*(1). Retrieved December 11, 2007, from http://www.elearningeuropa.info/files/media/media11561.pdf

Australian Learning & Teaching Council. (2008). *Places and spaces – for learning.* Retrieved July 2, 2008, from http://www.altc.edu.au/carrick/go/home/grants/pid/398

Barnes, C., & Tynan, B. (2007). The adventures of Miranda in the brave new world: learning in a Web 2.0 millennium. *ALT-J, Research in Learning Technology, 15*(3), 189-200.

Barsky, E., & Purdon, M. (2006). Introducing Web 2.0: social networking and social bookmarking for health librarians. *Journal of the Canadian Health Libraries Association, 27*(3), 65-67.

Berg, J., Berquam, L., & Christoph, K. (2007). Social networking technologies: a "poke" for campus services. *EDUCAUSE Review, 42*(2), 32-44.

Bereiter, C. (2002). *Education and mind in the knowledge age.* Hillsdale, NJ: Erlbaum.

Beshears, F. M. (2005). Viewpoint: The economic case for creative commons textbooks. *Campus Technology*, October 4. Retrieved March 10, 2007, from http://campustechnology.com/articles/40535/

Bleed, R. (2001). A hybrid campus for the new millennium. *EDUCAUSE Review, 36*(1), 17-24.

Boettcher, J. V. (2006). The rise of student performance content. *Campus Technology*, February 28. Retrieved January 10, 2007, from http://www.campustechnology.com/article.aspx?aid=40747

Boyd, D. (2007). The significance of social software. In T. N. Burg & J. Schmidt (Eds.), *BlogTalks reloaded: Social software research & cases* (pp. 15-30). Norderstedt, Germany: Books on Demand.

Brown, J., & Duguid, P. (2000). *The social life of information.* Boston: Harvard Business Press.

Bryant, T. (2006). Social software in academia. *EDUCAUSE Quarterly, 29*(2), 61-64.

Chan, A., Frydenberg, M., & Lee, M. J. W. (2007). Facilitating cross-cultural learning through collaborative Skypecasting. In J. J. Ekstrom (Ed.),

Proceedings of the 2007 ACM Information Technology Education Conference (SIGITE'07) (pp. 59-66). New York: ACM.

Chao, J. (2007). Student project collaboration using wikis. In *Proceedings of the 20th Conference on Software Engineering Education & Training (CSEET'07)* (pp. 255-261). Los Alamitos, CA: IEEE Computer Society.

Desharnais, R. A., & Limson, M. (2007). Designing and implementing virtual courseware to promote inquiry-based learning. *Journal of Online Learning and Teaching, 3*(1), 30-39.

Downes, S. (2004). Educational blogging. *EDUCAUSE Review, 39*(5), 14-26.

Downes, S. (2005). e-*learning 2.0. ELearn*, October. Retrieved January 11, 2006, from http://www.elearnmag.org/subpage.cfm?section=articles&article=29-1

Edirisingha, P., Salmon, G., & Fothergill, J. (2006). *Profcasting: a pilot study and a model for integrating podcasts into online learning.* Paper presented at the Fourth EDEN Research Workshop, Castelldefels, Spain, October 25-28.

Edson, J. (2007). Curriculum 2.0: user-driven education. *The Huffington Post*, June 25. Retrieved December 10, 2007, from http://www.huffingtonpost.com/jonathan-edson/curriculum-20-userdri_b_53690.html

Eisenstadt, M. (2007). Does e-learning have to be so awful? (Time to mashup or shutup). In J. M. Spector, D. G. Sampson, T. Okamoto, Kinshuk, S. A. Cerri, M. Ueno, & A. Kashihara (Eds.), *Proceedings of the 7th International Conference on Advanced Learning Technologies (ICALT'07)* (pp. 6-10). Los Alamitos, CA: IEEE Computer Society.

Engeström, J. (2005). *Why some social network services work and others don't – Or: the case for object-centered sociality*. Retrieved July 23, 2008, from http://www.zengestrom.com/blog/2005/04/why_some_social.html

Eustace, K., & Hay, L. (2000). A community and knowledge building model in computer education. In A. E. Ellis (Ed.), *Proceedings of the Australasian Conference on Computing Education (ACCE'00)* (pp. 95-102). New York: ACM.

Evans, L. (2006). *Using student podcasts in literature classes*. Retrieved January 23, 2007, from http://www.academiccommons.org/ctfl/vignette/using-student-podcasts-in-literature-classes

Engeström, Y. (1987). *Learning by expanding.* Helsinki, Finland: Orienta-Konsultit Oy.

Engeström, Y. (1999). Innovative learning in work teams: analysing cycles of knowledge creation in practice. In Y. Engeström, R. Miettinen, & R.-L. Punamäki (Eds.), *Perspectives on Activity Theory* (pp. 377-404). Cambridge, England: Cambridge University Press.

Fink, L. (2005). Making textbooks worthwhile. *Chronicle of Higher Education*, September 16. Retrieved March 10, 2007, from http://chronicle.com/weekly/v52/i04/04b01201.htm

Frydenberg, M. (2006). Principles and pedagogy: the two P's of podcasting in the information technology classroom. In D. Colton, W. J. Tastle, M. Hensel, & A. A. Abdullat (Eds.), *Proceedings of ISECON 2006* (§3354). Chicago, IL: AITP. Retrieved November 27, 2006, from http://isedj.org/isecon/2006/3354/ISECON.2006.Frydenberg.pdf

Ganley, B. (2004). Images, words, and students finding their way. *Bgblogging* [Weblog], October 11. Retrieved October 25, 2007, from http://mt.middlebury.edu/middblogs/ganley/bgblogging/2004/10/images_words_and_students_find.html

Gee, J. P. (2003). *What video games have to teach us about learning and literacy.* New York: Palmgrave.

Goodman, E., & Moed, A. (2006). *Community in mashups: the case of personal geodata.* Paper presented at the 20th ACM Conference on Computer Supported Cooperative Work, Banff, AB, November 4-8. Retrieved March 19, 2008, from http://mashworks.net/images/5/59/Goodman_Moed_2006.pdf

Green, H., Facer, K., Rudd, T., Dillon, P., & Humphreys, P. (2005). *Personalisation and digital technologies.* Bristol, England: Futurelab. Retrieved October 23, 2007, from http://www.futurelab.org.uk/resources/documents/opening_education/Personalisation_report.pdf

Helms, D. (2007a). *Drug use and abuse.* Retrieved November 2, 2007, from http://druguseandabuse.ning.com/

Helms, D. (2007b). *Group project.* Retrieved November 2, 2007, from http://www.msjc.edu/hs/hs123_group_project.html

Hilton, J. (2006). The future for higher education: sunrise or perfect storm. *EDUCAUSE Review, 41*(2), 58-71.

Hug, T., Lindner, M., & Bruck, P. (Eds.). (2006). *Microlearning: emerging concepts, practices, and technologies after e-learning. Proceedings of Microlearning 2005: Learning & working in new media.* Innsbruck, Austria: Innsbruck University Press.

Hughes, J., & Lang, K. (2006). Transmutability: digital decontextualization, manipulation, and recontextualization as a new source of value in the production and consumption of culture products. In *Proceedings of the 39th Annual Hawaii International Conference on System Sciences (HICSS'06)* (§ 165a). Los Alamitos, CA: IEEE Computer Society.

Jenkins, H. (2007). *Confronting the challenges of participatory culture: media education for the 21st Century.* Chicago, IL: MacArthur Foundation. Retrieved January 4, 2007, from http://www.digi-tallearning.macfound.org/atf/cf/%7B7E45C7E0-A3E0-4B89-AC9C-E807E1B0AE4E%7D/JENKINS_WHITE_PAPER.PDF.

Joint Information Systems Committee. (2006). *Designing spaces for effective learning: a guide to 21st century learning space design.* London, England: Joint Information Systems Committee. Retrieved July 2, 2007, from http://www.jisc.ac.uk/media/documents/publications/learningspaces.pdf

Katz, I. R., & Macklin, A. S. (2007). Information and communication technology (ICT) literacy: integration and assessment in higher education. *Systemics, Cybernetics and Informatics, 5*(4), 50-55. Retrieved November 17, 2007, from http://www.iiisci.org/Journal/CV$/sci/pdfs/P890541.pdf

Kukulska-Hulme, A. (2005). *The mobile language learner – now and in the future.* Plenary session delivered at the Fran Vision till Praktik (From Vision to Practice) Language Learning Symposium, Umeå, Sweden, May 11-12. Retrieved February 3, 2006, from http://www2.humlab.umu.se/video/Praktikvision/agnes.ram

Lamb, B. (2007). Dr Mashup; or, why educators should learn to stop worrying and love the remix. *EDUCAUSE Review, 42*(4), 12-25.

Lankshear, C., & Knobel, M. (2007). Researching new literacies: Web 2.0 practices and insider perspectives. *e-Learning, 4*(3), 224-240.

Lave, J., & Wenger, E. (1991). *Situated learning: legitimate peripheral participation.* Cambridge, England: Cambridge University Press.

Leadbeater, C. (2006). *The ten habits of mass innovation.* London, England: NESTA. Retrieved November 3, 2007, from http://www.nesta.org.uk/assets/pdf/ten_habits_of_mass_innovation_provocation_NESTA.pdf

Lee, M. J. W., Chan, A., & McLoughlin, C. (2006). Students as producers: second year students' experiences as podcasters of content for first year undergraduates. In *Proceedings of the 7th IEEE Conference on Information Technology Based Higher Education and Training (ITHET'06)* (pp. 832-848), Sydney, NSW: University of Technology, Sydney.

Lee, M. J. W., Eustace, K., Hay, L., & Fellows, G. (2005). Learning to collaborate, collaboratively: an online community building and knowledge construction approach to teaching computer supported collaborative work at an Australian university. In M. R. Simonson & M. Crawford (Eds.), *Proceedings of the 2005 AECT International Convention* (pp. 286-306). North Miami Beach, FL: Nova Southeastern University.

Lim, C. P., & Chai, C. S. (2008). Teachers' pedagogical beliefs and their planning and conduct of computer-mediated classroom lessons. *British Journal of Educational Technology, 39*(5), 807-828..

Lin, C.-H., Li, L.-Y., Hu, W.-C., Chen, G.-D., & Liu, B.-J. (2007). Constructing an authentic learning community through Wiki for advanced group collaboration and knowledge sharing. In J. M. Spector, D. G. Sampson, T. Okamoto, Kinshuk, S. A. Cerri, M. Ueno, & A. Kashihara (Eds.), *Proceedings of the 7th International Conference on Advanced Learning Technologies (ICALT'07)* (pp. 342-344). Los Alamitos, CA: IEEE Computer Society.

Lindner, M. (2006). Use these tools, your mind will follow. Learning in immersive micromedia and microknowledge environments. In D. Whitelock & S. Wheeler (Eds.), *The next generation: Research proceedings of the 13th ALT-C conference* (pp. 41-49). Oxford, England: ALT.

Lorenzo, G,. & Dziuban, C. (2006). *Ensuring the net generation is net savvy.* Washington, DC: EDUCAUSE. Retrieved July 10, 2007, from http://www.educause.edu/ir/library/pdf/ELI3006.pdf

Love, D., McKean, G., & Gathercoal, P. (2002). Portfolios to Webfolios and beyond: levels of maturation. *EDUCAUSE Quarterly, 25*(2), 29-37.

Mazer, J. P., Murphy, R. E., & Simonds, C. J. (2007). I'll see you on "Facebook": The effects of computer-mediated teacher self-disclosure on student motivation, affective learning, and classroom climate. *Communication Education, 56*(1), 1-17.

Masie, E. (2005). *Nano-learning* [Podcast transcript]. Retrieved July 2, 2006, from http://www.masieWeb.com/component/option,com_alphacontent/Itemid,122/section,9/cat,29/task,view/id,1321/

Masie, E. (2006). Nano-learning: miniaturization of design. *Chief Learning Officer, 5*(1), 17.

Massachusetts Institute of Technology. (2008). *MIT OpenCourseWare.* Retrieved June 2, 2008, from http://ocw.mit.edu/

Mateer, G. D. (2007). *Teaching Economics with YouTube.* Retrieved March 3, 2008, from http://www.youtube.com/dmateer

Mateer, G. D. (2008). *Teaching with YouTube: an economist's guide to free Web-based content.* Paper presented at the 2008 American Economic Association Conference, New Orleans, LA, January 4-6. Retrieved March 3, 2008, from http://www.aeaWeb.org/annual_mtg_papers/2008/2008_669.pdf

McCarty, S. (2005a). Similar proverbs in Chinese, Japanese, and English? *Japancasting* [Weblog]. Retrieved March 10, 2007, from http://stevemc.blogmatrix.com/:entry:stevemc-2005-09-01-0000/

McCarty, S. (2005b). Spoken Internet to go: popularization through podcasting. *The JALT CALL Journal, 1*(2), 67-74.

McCarty, S. (2006). *Japancasting* [Weblog]. Retrieved December 3, 2006, from http://stevemc.blogmatrix.com

Mejias, U. (2005). A nomad's guide to learning and social software. *The Knowledge Tree: An e-Journal of Learning Innovation, 7.* Retrieved November 10, 2006, from http://knowledgetree. flexiblelearning.net.au/edition07/html/la_mejias. html

Menell, B. (2005). Atomization of learning (Beyond the learning object). *Learning 2.0,* [Weblog], November. Retrieved January 8, 2006, from http://learning20.blogspot.com/2005/11/atomization-of-learning-beyond.html

MERLOT. (2008). Retrieved February 19, 2008, from http://www.merlot.org/

Miller, D. B. (2006). Podcasting at the University of Connecticut: enhancing the educational experience. *Campus Technology*, October 18. Retrieved April 10, 2007, from http://campustechnology. com/news_article.asp?id=19424&typeid=156

Miller, D. B. (2007). *iCube.* Retrieved April 10, 2007, from http://icube.uconn.edu/

Milne, A. J. (2007). Entering the interaction age: implementing a future vision for campus learning spaces. *EDUCAUSE Review, 42*(1), 12-31.

Moore, J. W. (2003). Are textbooks dispensable? *Journal of Chemical Education, 80*(4), 359.

Nonaka, I., & Takeuchi, H. (1995). *The knowledge-creating company: how Japanese companies create the dynamics of innovation.* New York: Oxford University Press.

Nonaka, I., & Toyama, R. (2003). The knowledge-creating theory revisited: knowledge creation as a synthesizing process. *Knowledge Management Research and Practice, 1*(1), 2-10.

Online Encyclopedia of Criminal Justice. (2007). Retrieved November 15, 2007, from http://cjencyclopedia.com

O'Reilly, T. (2005) *What is Web 2.0: design patterns and business models for the next generation of software.* Retrieved December 15, 2006, from http://www.oreillynet.com/pub/a/oreilly/tim/ news/2005/09/30/what-is-Web-20.html

Owen, M., Grant, L., Sayers, S., & Facer, K. (2006). *Social software and learning.* Bristol, England: Futurelab. Retrieved April 11, 2007, from http://www.futurelab.org.uk/resources/ documents/opening_education/Social_Software_report.pdf

Paavola, S., & Hakkarainen, K. (2005). The knowledge creation metaphor – An emergent epistemological approach to learning. *Science and Education, 14*(6), 535-557.

Polsani, P. R. (2003). Network learning. In K. Nyíri (Ed.), *Mobile learning: essays on philosophy, psychology, and education.* Vienna, Austria: Passagen Verlag.

Read, B. (2005). Drexel U. will give free iPods to students in School of Education. *The Chronicle of Higher Education*, March 2. Retrieved May 8, 2005, from http://chronicle.com/free/2005/03/ 2005030203n.htm

Richardson, W. (2006a). *Blogs, wikis, podcasts, and other powerful tools for classrooms.* Thousand Oaks, CA: Sage.

Richardson, W. (2006b). The new face of learning: the Internet breaks schools walls down. *Edutopia*, October. Retrieved November 3, 2007, from http://www.edutopia.org/new-face-learning

Rogers, P. C., Liddle, S. W., Chan, P., Doxey, A., & Isom, B. (2007). Web 2.0 learning platform: harnessing collective intelligence. *Turkish Online Journal of Distance Education, 8*(3), 16-33.

Sener, J. (2007a). *Podcasting student performances to develop EFL skills.* Retrieved March 10, 2007, from http://www.sloan-c-wiki.org/ wiki/index.php?title=Podcasting_Student_Performances_to_Develop_EFL_Skills

Sener, J. (2007b). *University of North Carolina at Pembroke – cjencyclopedia.com: Online Encyclopedia of Criminal Justice.* Retrieved March 10, 2007, from http://www.sloan-c-wiki.org/wiki/index.php?title=University_of_North_Carolina_at_Pembroke_--_cjencyclopedia.com:_Online_Encyclopedia_of_Criminal_Justice

Sfard, A. (1998). On two metaphors for learning and the dangers of choosing just one. *Educational Researcher, 27*(2), 4-13.

Siemens, G. (2005). Connectivism: a learning theory for the digital age. *International Journal of Instructional Technology and Distance Learning, 2*(1), 3-10.

Siemens, G. (2007). PLEs – I acronym, therefore I exist. *elearnspace: learning, networks, knowledge, technology, community* [Weblog], April 15. Retrieved November 1, 2007, from http://www.elearnspace.org/blog/archives/002884.html

Sims, R. (Ed.). (2006). Online distance education: new ways of learning; new modes of teaching? [Special issue]. *Distance Education, 27*(2).

Stefani, L., Mason, R., & Pegler, C. (2007). *The educational potential of e-Portfolios: supporting personal development and reflective learning.* Abingdon, England: Routledge.

Surowiecki, K. (2004). *The wisdom of crowds.* New York: Doubleday.

van Weert, T. J. (2006). Education of the twenty-first century: new professionalism in lifelong learning, knowledge development ,and, knowledge sharing. *Education and Information Technologies, 11*(3/4), 217-237.

Wenzloff, J. (2005). *Furl, furled, furling: social on-line bookmarking for the masses.* Retrieved July 10, 2007, from http://www.classroomhelp.com/workshop/Furl_Guide.pdf

Williams, J. B., & Jacobs, J. (2004). Exploring the use of blogs as learning spaces in the higher education sector. *Australasian Journal of Educational Technology, 20*(2), 232-247.

Windham, C. (2005). The student's perspective. In D. G. Oblinger & J. L. Oblinger (Eds.), *Educating the Net Generation* (pp. 5.1-5.16). Washington, DC: EDUCAUSE.

KEY TERMS

Architecture of Participation: A term that describes the nature of innovation in the open source movement, whereby individuals can share, create, and amend software, thereby participating in the creation of improved forms of software. This can help turn a good idea, tool, or application into a best-quality product as many users and developers can adapt, change, and improve it.

Collective Intelligence: A form of intelligence that results from the cooperation, collaboration, and/or competition of a large number of individuals. *See also* wisdom of crowds.

Connectivism: A "learning theory for the digital age" developed by George Siemens, based on an analysis of the limitations of behaviourism, cognitivism, and constructivism. It employs a network with nodes and connections as a central metaphor for learning. In this metaphor, a node may be any entity, whether tangible or intangible, that is able to be connected to other nodes, including but not limited to information, data, feelings, and images. Learning is seen as the process of creating connections between nodes to form a network.

E-Portfolio: An electronic collection comprising self-assembled evidence demonstrating a learner's knowledge, skills, and abilities, including learner-generated artifacts in multiple media forms that showcase both the products and processes of learning. e-Portfolios are excellent tools for facilitating students' reflection on their own learning, as well sas serving a variety of purposes in assessment (including recognition of prior learning) within an academic course or program. Lifelong e-Portfolios are also increasingly being used for professional purposes such as certification/accreditation and career advancement (e.g. promotion).

Knowledge Creation Metaphor of Learning: Unlike theories that emphasize learning as knowledge acquisition (the acquisition metaphor) and as participation in a social community (the participation metaphor), this third metaphor foucses on mediated processes of knowledge creation that have become especially important in a knowldge society. This view focuses on mediated processes of knowledge creation that have become especially important in a knowledge society.

Learning Management System: *See* LMS.

LMS: Learning Management System. An integrated suite of software tools designed to manage learning interventions. Commercial examples are Blackboard and WebCT, although many open source alternatives, such as Moodle and Sakai, exist. In addition to the provision of online learning content and activities and the facilitation of online assessment, LMS's typically support a range of administrative functions including learner enrollment, workflow, records management (e.g. reporting of assessment results/outcomes), and resource management (e.g. instructors, facilities, equipment).

Object-Centered Sociality: A term coined by the Finnish sociologist Jyri Engeström to describe the phenomenon whereby shared objects are the means by which people connect to each other to form social relationships and networks. According to this concept, links are created not just between people, but between people and objects, or around objects. Engeström claims that the problem with some social networking services is that they focus solely on people and links, ignoring the objects of affinity that those linked people share. He invokes the concept of "object-centered sociality" to explain how the inclusion of shared objects including but not limited to photos, URLs, and events can enhance online social networking.

Pedagogy 2.0: Digital tools and affordances call for a new conceptualization of teaching that is focused on participation in communities and networks, personalization of learning tasks, and creative production of ideas and knowledge. McLouglin and Lee's concept of Pedagogy 2.0 is a response to this call. It represents a set of approaches and strategies that differs from teaching as a didactic practice of passing on information; instead, it advocates a model of learning in which students are empowered to participate, communicate, and create knowledge, exercising a high level of agency and control over the learning process.

Personal Learning Environment: *See* PLE.

Personal Publishing: A process in which an individual actively produces his/her own content and information and publishes it on the World Wide Web. For example, the maintenance of a personal blog as an online diary is an instance of personal publishing. *See also* user-generated content.

PLE: Personal Learning Environment. A system, application, or suite of applications that assists learners in taking control of and managing their own learning. It represents an alternative approach to the LMS, which by contrast adopts an institution-centric or course-centric view of learning. Key PLE concepts include the blending of formal and informal learning, participation in social networks that transcend institutional boundaries, as well as the use of a range of networking protocols (RSS, peer-to-peer [P2P], Web services) to connect systems, resources, and users within a personally-managed space. *See also* LMS.

Prosumer: A portmanteau formed by contracting word "producer" with the word "consumer," signifying the blurring of the distinction between the two roles in today's knowledge economy.

Student-Generated Content: Content that is produced by students, often for sharing with peers or a wider audience on the Internet, as distinct from instructor-supplied content such as course notes and textbooks. It is arguable that the main benefits to be gained from student-generated content lie in the process of content creation and knowledge construction, as opposed to the end product itself. *See also* user-generated content.

User-Generated Content: A term that refers to Web-based content created by ordinary people or users, e.g. pictures posted on Flickr or encyclo-pedia entries written in Wikipedia. Such "Read-and-Write" applications are key characteristic of the Web 2.0 movement, which encourages the publishing of one's own content and commenting on or augmenting other people's. It differs from the "Read-Only" model of Web 1.0, in which Web sites were created and maintained by an elite few. *See also* personal publishing.

Wisdom of Crowds: A concept that relates to the aggregation of information in groups and communities of individuals. It recognizes that the innovation, problem-solving, and decision-making capabilities of the group are often superior to that of any single member of the group. The term was used as the title of a book written by James Surowiecki, published in 2004. *See also* collective intelligence.

Chapter XXIV
Knowledge Media Tools to Foster Social Learning

Alexandra Okada
The Open University, UK

Simon Buckingham Shum
The Open University, UK

Michelle Bachler
The Open University, UK

Eleftheria Tomadaki
The Open University, UK

Peter Scott
The Open University, UK

Alex Little
The Open University, UK

Marc Eisenstadt
The Open University, UK

ABSTRACT

The aim of this chapter is to overview the ways in which knowledge media technologies create opportunities for social learning. The Open Content movement has been growing rapidly, opening up new opportunities for widening participation. One of the Open Educational Resources (OER) initiatives is the OpenLearn project, launched by the Open University, which integrates three knowledge media technologies: Compendium, FM and MSG. In this chapter, the authors analyse some examples, which show how these tools can be used to foster open sensemaking communities by mapping knowledge, location and virtual interactions. At the end, they present some questions and future horizons related to this research.

INTRODUCTION

Due to the widespread use of new technologies, people have greater access to information, interaction at distance and knowledge reconstruction than ever before. Open learning materials, online libraries, electronic journals and collective repositories are part of a larger movement to create a public online space providing open high-quality content in different formats such as hypertext, image, sound and video. The Open Educational Resources (OER) movement has also been opening up new opportunities for widening participation (Willinsky, 2006; Dholakia, King & Baraniuk, 2006; Downes, 2006; O'Mahony & Ferraro, 2003; Open Source Initiative, 2007).

The Open University UK's OpenLearn Project, for instance, is a large scale project that makes a selection of higher education learning resources freely available on the internet. OpenLearn, which is supported by William and Flora Hewlett Foundation, was launched in October 2006 and in eighteen months released over 5,400 learning hours of the OU's distance learning resources for free access and modification by learners and educators under the Creative Commons license (OpenLearn, 2006). OpenLearn also offers three knowledge media tools: Compendium (knowledge mapping software), MSG (instant messaging application with geolocation maps) and FM (Web-based videoconferencing application).

This chapter introduces these three OpenLearn technologies and presents examples about the use and integration of these tools to promote social learning. During its first year and a half there are 50,000 registered users in OpenLearn, over 1,000,000 unique visitors to the site, over 1,000 video meetings booked, 1,377 Compendium Knowledge Map downloads and 17,000 MSG users.

Our current work is to investigate how these tools can be applied to foster open sensemaking communities (Buckingham Shum, 2005a) around the OERs, that is, the interpretative work that must take place around any resource for learning to take place. How can these technologies be used to support this critical activity in an OER context when learners must find and engage with peers themselves, if they do not wish to study alone?

"Open sensemaking communities" refer to open and self-sustaining communities that construct knowledge together from an array of environmental inputs (Buckingham Shum, 2005a; Weick, 1995). Thousands of open communities can be found on Facebook, MySpace, Orkut, Flickr, Yahoo groups, Google Groups, Moodle etc. However, there are some challenging issues for an "open community" (Reagle, 2004) to turn into an "open sensemaking community"(Buckigham Shum, 2005a). Participants must literally reflect upon information (Brooks & Scott, 2006) and "make" sense together by giving shape or modelling diverse ideas through significant representations (Buckingham Shum and Okada, 2008). They need transform their abstract thoughts about what is being learned into their personal framework - "knowledge objects" (Entwistle, 1995) and into "collective representations of knowledge" (Nonaka and Takeuchi, 1995). The term knowledge object is used *to describe the essence of these quasi-sensory experiences of aspects of understanding*", through structures of thinking paths or summaries of integrated body of knowledge produced by a student (Entwistle, 1995:50). However, the "making" of a "shared artefact" to express the emerging, collective view of the problem/solution is an important distinction. Sensemaking is a *mutually negotiated understanding*" (Weick, 1995:4). It means interpreting and representing plausible narratives about the world collectively. Through sensemaking, externalising one's understanding clarifies one's own grasp of the situation, as well as communicates it to others — literally, *the making of sense* (Weick, 1995: 4). An example of open sensemaking community is a community of open source software's developers. They learn with each other by representing and sharing understanding about the content, programming code, and also the process. They construct their set of principles and practices by themselves which facilitate access and quality to the design and production of their products and knowledge.

In higher education, how can knowledge media technologies be used by online learners interested in learning with their social network? How can they represent and share meanings together constructed from what they are studying? In the next sections, we present ways in which Compendium, FM and MSG have been used by participants of an OpenLearn Community. Based on these examples, we analyse some benefits and also their difficulties of using knowledge media tools for social learning and for fostering open sensemaking communities.

BACKGROUND

Information and Communication technologies have been promoting the rapid and flexible dissemination of open content and educational resources. There are currently many open content initiatives offering free access to learning materials on the Web. However, one of the main challenges for online learners is not only to be able to access free high quality content; they also need to be able to capture, organise, discuss and make sense of it including the deluge from search engines, news feeds, digital libraries, blogs and emails in order to construct meaning from this ocean of available information and opinions (Okada and Buckingham Shum, 2006).

The simple access to information does not necessarily mean understanding. In order to develop understanding, students need to be engaged in higher order thinking which operates beyond mere exposure to factual or conceptual information. Understanding means going beyond the information given to make inferences, connections and explanations. "*Understanding is not mere knowledge of facts but inference about why and*

how, with specific evidence and logic – insightful connections and illustrations." (Wiggins and McTighe, 2005:86).

In contrast to "information technologies" whose purpose is to deliver data structured through different media and representations, "knowledge technologies" aim to support learners to interpret those representations and construct their understanding together (Buckingham Shum, 2005a). Interpretation means the process of assessing information to construct personal meaning. It is making an implicit idea "x", explicit as "y". (Jonassen, Beissner and Yacci, 1993). Understanding involves being able to explain meanings and apply it in different contexts (Wiggins and McTighe, 2005).

The term "knowledge media tools" introduced by the Knowledge Media Institute KMi at the Open University UK means technologies to support the processes of generating, understanding and sharing knowledge using several different media, as well as understanding how the use of different media shape these processes. KMi considers that "media-rich learning experiences based on constructivist models of education are the key for ownership of understanding". Knowledge media technologies empower individuals - schoolchildren, adult learners, or corporate employees and their managers - to create their own content, to represent understanding and reconstruct their own knowledge. Learners need to develop their critical authorship rather than being merely recipients of information. Through these tools, users can research topics, collect information, discuss the content, manipulate digital media, categorise and structure meanings and publish their reconstructed thinking and knowledge on the Web (Eisenstadt and Vincent, 1998:ii). Knowledge Media Tools are designed to assist users in giving form to their ideas as they evolve from ill-formed, inchoate structures to more formal, rigorously organised expressions and foster their own "open sensemaking communities" (Buckigham Shum, 2005b).

Contemporary approach on education consider learning as a process that is developed through dialogue (Vygotsky, 1962; Bakhtin, 1981). Learners construct their understanding through dialogic interactions with peers, teachers and learning materials. A critical discussion scaffolded by a learning community enables participants make sense of what they are learning. They internalise new meanings from significant dialogues developed interpersonally to form new understandings intrapersonally in their ZPD - zone of proximal development (Vygotsky, 1962).

Sensemaking is enacted through the interaction of explicit and tacit knowledge (Nonaka and Takeuchi, 1995) from individuals to groups (Cook and Brown, 1999). Tacit knowledge is highly personal and hard to communicate to others. *"We know more than we can tell"* Polanyi(1967:4). In contrast, explicit knowledge is easily stored, expressed and reused (Nonaka, 1991). Sensemaking is a process shaped not only by tacit knowledge - what people have in their mind, but also explicit knowledge – from interactions with their social and physical world (Cook and Brown, 1999).

The spiral of collective building of knowledge (Nonaka and Takeuchi, 1995) shows that, students need to learn to connect their own ideas with the other people's and knowledge from different domains to their own experiences (combination). They need to make sense of their own selected network of information, generate questions, critical arguments and pursue their reasoning to some coherent conclusion or outcome (internalisation). Students also need to know how to represent their insights, reflections, interpretations through images, sound, words, even maps, (externalisation) and share their thinking with their community (socialisation) using knowledge media tools.

Knowledge technologies have a role to play in this process, and the focus must move from simply capturing and storing knowledge to supporting learning and sharing understanding (Finerty, 1997; Ruggles, 1998; Sumner et al, 1998). Social tools designed for educational use support and engage individuals to learn together by eliciting their implicit knowledge based on their individual and collective needs (Anderson, 2007). In this context, knowledge media tools can be used to engage learners to (see figure1a):

1. Externalise their implicit knowledge by representing what they have in their minds through modelling, mapping and writing it down in forums, chats, Web videoconference or knowledge mapping tools.
2. Combine explicit knowledge by connecting different perspectives, adding new meanings, tagging or categorising best examples.
3. Internalise explicit knowledge by accessing, analysing, questioning and interpreting codified knowledge
4. Socialise implicit knowledge by sharing new experiences, observing, brainstorming and opening new opportunities for feedback.

Table 1, which is based on the examples presented in this chapter, summarises the role that some knowledge media technologies (Compendium, FM and MSG) can play in order to construct knowledge collectively.

Compendium, FM and MSG can be used to externalise their ideas, combine different viewpoints, internalise new concepts and socialise new meanings. However, there are some challenges in order to leverage the spiral of knowledge to foster collective sensemaking from individual to groups.

•   Could these tools help a learner identify and bridge a gap for sensemaking? *"Sense-making moment is the point in time-space when a person experiences a gap while moving through time-space. (...) The person bridges this gap by experiencing questions and muddles that lead them to construct bridges consisting of ideas, thoughts, emotions, feelings, hunches and memories"* (Naumer, Fisher and Dervin, 2008:3).

Figure 1a. Spiral of the collective building of knowledge(Nonaka and Takeuchi, 1985)

Table 1. Knowledge media tools integrated in the OpenLearn project

	Compendium a hypermedia mapping tool	FM a web videoconferencing application	MSG an instant messaging application
Externalisation	Represent reasoning through knowledge maps.	Present and discuss ideas through web video conferencing.	Point out opinions and feedback through instant messaging.
Combination	Connect ideas, concepts, argument, and web resources.	Connect questions, feedback, comments from different media (text, audio, urls, graphs).	Connect location, social presence and social awareness.
Internalisation	Visualise, reflect and analyse connections in order to develop better interpretation.	Replay the discussion in order to reflect on and analyse the content.	Access the chat history to recall answers, solutions and insights.
Socialisation	Share knowledge maps by downloading editing and uploading them again.	Share FM events, taxonomy system in order to search and find events.	Share relevant content from instant messages by copying and pasting it in a forum, a FM session or a knowledge map.

- How do learners use these tools to create and share representations around some problem they need to understand? *"Sensemaking is the way people go about their process of collecting, organising and creating representations of complex information sets, all centered around some problem they need to understand"* (Russel, Jeffries and Irani, 2008:1).

- In what ways learners can apply these tools to identify common conflicts, clarify new concepts and negotiate a consensual understanding together in virtual learning environments? *"Learners are not naturally likely to argue spontaneously with each other, at least with respect to the subjects that they have not been in contact with yet and sometimes, interpersonal conflicts or individual contradictions are not sufficient to provoke the incidence of argumentation"* (Okada, 2005: 85). In order to make sense together by developing a consensual agreement through argumentative dialogue, learners need to identify a common problem (e.g. conflicts) by mastering concepts from theories that support their opinion and personal experiences (figure1b).

CASE STUDY

"CoLearn - Comunidade de Pesquisa sobre Aprendizagem Colaborativa " (Community of research about Collaborative Learning) is a Community of OpenLearners from Portuguese-speaking Countries <http://colearn.open.ac.uk> in the OpenLearn – LabSpace. LabSpace is an open area in the OpenLearn for users creating and sharing materials, and running their com-

munities. CoLearn's participants are educators and academic students whose interests focus on exploring knowledge media tools to facilitate collaborative learning. Based in different countries, they use FM to meet online, learn together and create OER. Their discussions are focused on diverse open learning issues such as game based environments, knowledge media and social software. Compendium Knowledge Maps are created on e-democracy, thinking skills and information literacy. Through MSG, they can see who is online, ask questions and get answers quickly. By exchanging instant messages, they can discuss problems with tools, share additional information on the Web, such as OER, knowledge maps, Web videoconferences and papers' URL about what they are studying.

Figure2 shows the Labspace area of this community, and some information about one of its OpenLearners, "Lila" and her social learning network. On the left, there are three blocks: MSG Instant Messaging, FM and Knowledge Maps.

Figure 1b. Argumentative dialogue for sensemaking in collaborative learning environments (Okada, 2005: 88)

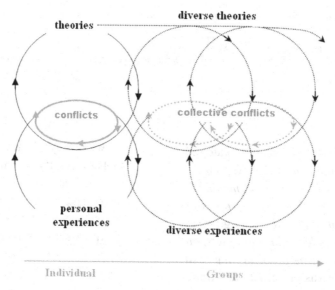

Figure 2. CoLearn - Community of Portuguese Language Countries in the OpenLearn

In the MSG block, she can chat with 93 fellows from her list of 1419 contacts. She can also locate them in her MSG Google map. In this picture, we can see that she is one of the 17.041 OpenLearn users, in which 414 are online. Lila can access 11 FM Web-conferences for replaying. She can also browse or download a list of 62 knowledge maps.

On the right, in Lila's Personal Profile, we can see that she is registered in six OpenLearn communities, and her interests are focused on information literacy, digital games applied to education, open learning, culture, society and media, knowledge media tools and knowledge mapping for learning design. As an OpenLearn user, Lila can access all her forum posts, her learning journal and activity reports.

Whenever Lila is logged, she can chat with her peers through MSG, book a video meeting, manage and edit her events. She can download

and install the Compendium software tool for knowledge mapping in order to create and share maps within her communities.

MAPPING KNOWLEDGE WITH COMPENDIUM

Compendium <http://www.compendiuminstitute. org> is a software tool for visual thinking, used to connect ideas, concepts, arguments, Websites and documents. The purpose of the Compendium application is to manage information, model problems, and map argumentation discussions. It can be used as an individual or group tool to develop new ideas, goals, logical concepts and collaborative scenarios. A key feature of Compendium is its ability to categorise information. It offers a set of different types of "nodes": question, idea, pro, con, reference, note, decision, list and maps views. This node classification allows one to better organise the structure of the map and understand the argumentation discussion more easily.

Figure 3 shows a map created by an Open-Learn user from the CoLearn community also interested in Information Literacy. It illustrates how to use Compendium to organise ideas and arguments:

1. Drag and drop a question-icon ⍰ from the palette and type a question.
2. Create new nodes: ◯ for answers, concepts or data; ⚒ for arguments, choices or possibilities; ✚ for supporting arguments; ━ for counterarguments. If you want to make connections, by clicking the right button of the mouse over the icon, drag the arrow and drop it onto the other icon.
3. Pictures, sites and documents from the Web can be added into this map by dragging and dropping the media resource.

4. A number superimposed on a node (e.g. 2) means that it appears in more than one map. The same idea can play roles in multiple contexts and conversations which can be linked. When the mouse is over the number you will see all maps related to that node.
5. User-defined keyword tags [T] can be annotated onto nodes to help when searching for related material across multiple maps, and include comments [*].

CoLearn community has been using Compendium to create knowledge mapping applied to studying an OER together, sharing new references and describing the meaning of concepts.

Knowledge Maps as a Strategy for Studying an OER Together

Knowledge Mapping can be used as a strategy to study online learning materials (Buckingham

Figure 3. Compendium's user interface for linking issues, ideas and documents

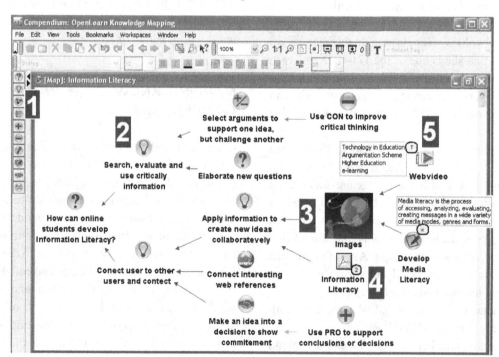

Shum and Okada, 2008). Figure 4 shows an OpenLearn participant who used Compendium to select key sentences from the OpenLearn Unit "Information Literacy" in the LabSpace and from other Websites such as WikipediA and flickr. By dragging and dropping the content into their maps, she collected relevant pieces of information from different sources. She externalised her interpretation graphically by combining their own comments, bringing arguments and raising new questions. She could identify concepts that they did not understand (e.g. what does it mean?) and also "recognise where there is information gap" (e.g. what competencies are they talking about?).

By socialising a map within their communities, their fellows interested in the same topic can browse it, visualise and reinterpret keypoints, access Web resources, download it and combine

new contributions in order to internalise new meanings. They can also discuss about its content (questions, ideas and arguments) in a video meeting, MSG or forum.

Knowledge Maps as a Strategy for Sharing New References

Figure 5 shows a Compendium map to collect and share relevant information source, which was created by another openlearner interested in "Media Literacy". It shows interesting Websites and offers complementary references related to "Information Literacy". This Webmap with nine online references was accessed by other participants for downloading, editing and new uploading. Participants interested in this topic used these references to compare Media Literacy

Figure 4. Compendium's user interface for linking issues, ideas and documents

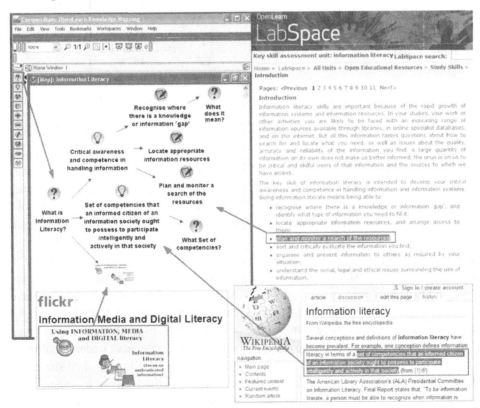

Figure 5. Studying the arts and humanities through a web map, http://labspace.open.ac.uk/file.php/1801/ knowlegde_maps/1165338042/abujokas.html

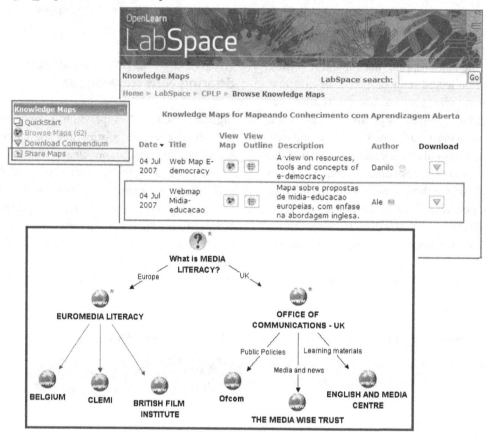

in the UK and their countries. These references were used to support new ideas, answer questions related to Media Literacy and raise new issues, concepts and arguments. Web maps can be described as hybrid way of mapping in the sense that learners can integrate diverse objects of their own – concepts, links, personal documents, organizers - and progressively evolve these maps into concept maps (Zeiliger and Esnault, 2008).

Knowledge Maps as a Strategy for Describing the Meaning of Concepts

Figure 6 shows how Compendium was used to describe the meaning of a new concept. This concept map indicates several keywords that were collected from different sources and connected to explain what information literacy means. Other openlearners can access this map, visualise how the concept information literacy was interpreted and access the reference sources by clicking in the icons. They can also download this map to represent new viewpoint and new ways to make sense of this concept by adding examples, resources, case studies and new keywords.

Concept maps is an effective way to represent and contrast learners' understanding of various concepts by allowing they share and build knowledge individually or in groups (Canas and Novak 2008). Through concept mapping learners

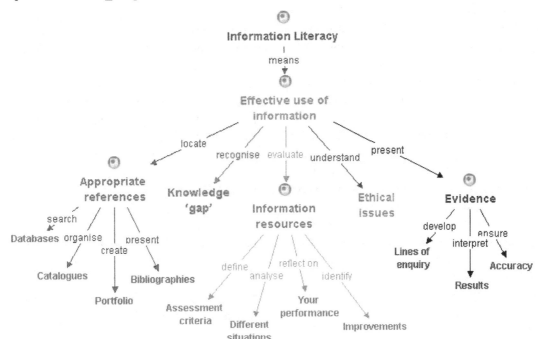

Figure 6. Studying the arts and humanities through a web map, http://labspace.open.ac.uk/file.php/1456/kmap/1199906929/il_cmap.html

make sense of new concepts by structuring their thinking and connecting their prior knowledge (Novak, 1998).

MSG: AN INSTANT MESSAGING APPLICATION WITH GEOLOCATION

Social presence can stimulate group awareness and the building of collective knowledge in online communities. Presence has evolved from just being 'online' or 'offline' to a range of preferences such as availability or location (Chakraborty, 2002). Websites, such as 'The World as a Blog', released in 2003, can provide real time blogging activity and the blogger's physical location, represented as a dot on the earth (Maron, 2003). This approach can be extended in communities of practice having a common knowledge objective,

where members located in different parts of the world can support each other, and where knowledge use and reuse has a specific impact upon their evolution. Wenger (1998) described communities of practice as the interplay of four fundamental dualities: participation vs. reification, designed vs. emergent, identification vs. negotiability and local vs. global. Location and social presence display an aspect of the users' context, contributing to collective understanding.

MSG is a Web application for instant messaging that allows users to contact fellow OpenLearn users. It is an evolution of BuddySpace (Vogiazou, et al., 2005) that acts like a 'personal radar' that shows who is online and where. A key advantage of MSG over other instant messenger systems (e.g. MSN Messenger, AIM, GTalk etc) is the full integration into all OpenLearn units — meaning that throughout the site (e.g. in discussion forums) users can see who is currently online and can immediately 'click to chat' to the poster of a relevant forum message. Groups of contacts are automatically generated in MSG based on the courses users have enrolled on, enhancing in this way the creation of a sense of community with common knowledge goals and interests.

MSG also offers a presence map which allows users to find out where fellow users are located geographically and gives the same presence information and click-to-chat functionality as given in the OpenLearn units. The markers on the map are automatically clustered to avoid markers overlapping and obscuring each other. Clicking on a marker shows all the users at that location with their presence status and click to chat option if they are online. Additionally, users can easily search for users, update their own location and filter the map markers based on the groups and courses they have enrolled on.

MSG, as Strategy for Finding Peers to Learn Together

Open learning can be sometimes a lonely experience. OpenLearners are located in different countries, access a course at different times and start from different areas. How can they find fellow students studying the same course when they are logged in the LabSpace? Figure7 shows that Lila can contact her fellow students from the Google Map on the left bar (MSG Block) or from any Webpage in the Labspace such as the discussion. By keeping an eye out for the green and yellow 'presence status icons' throughout LabSpace, e.g. next to user names in a discussion forum, she can just click on it to chat directly to the person (eg. Beto), even if she has not yet launched MSG.

If Lila, who lives in Rio, wants to find her peers who are in Sao Paulo and online, she can then access the MSG Presence Maps. Figure 10

Figure 7. The MSG block where you can click on contacts and chat with them

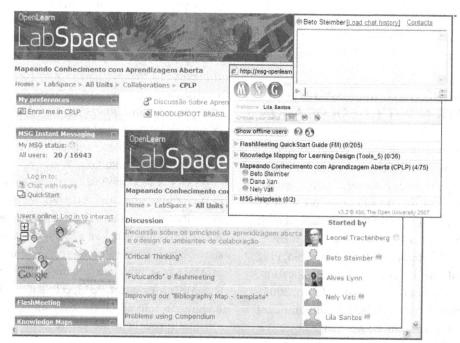

shows that through the map, Lila can view who is currently online in Sao Paulo by clicking on the marker over Sao Paulo.

The box on the right in figure8 indicates that Lila is online, she received 8 new MSG messages and by clicking in this hyperlink she can read the content. She can update her current location and also hide in case she does what to show it. She can search her fellows by name, locality or groups. Each group represents an OpenLearn course that she has enrolled on. She has 4 groups which shows the quantity of people logged in and online. For instance, in the group "FM QuickStart" there are 205 users and one is online. Lila can also contact people in Portugal and ask how they have been using knowledge media tools.

Figure 9 shows Lila from Rio de Janeiro chatting with Nely from Lisbon. Nely was searching the FM and used MSG to find a solution for her problem ("Hi Lila! I am looking for the FM Website…") and her fellow Lila helped her answering her question ("See this url http://fm-openlearn. open.ac.uk"). In this case MSG is useful to bridge quickly a gap that can be important in a more complex activity to develop understanding or foster the spiral of knowledge.

MSG, as Strategy for Mapping Social Presence

Presence is an indispensable social software function, featuring in instant messaging, video-conferencing and ambient video awareness tools. In Biocca et al (2001), presence is described as 'being there in other places' and 'being there with other people'. Mapping social presence in open sense making communities can give insights by providing geo-locations of the individuals who may be relevant with specific knowledge areas and can provide advice to others.

In instant messaging systems, a set of presence attributes may include time, context, availability, location, activity etc. A great variety of software supporting group interaction and location based social software applications, from providing awareness of friends being in vicinity to online community sites, helping users meet other users with similar interests. In the case of OpenLearn,

Figure 8. Multiple groups of MSG contacts

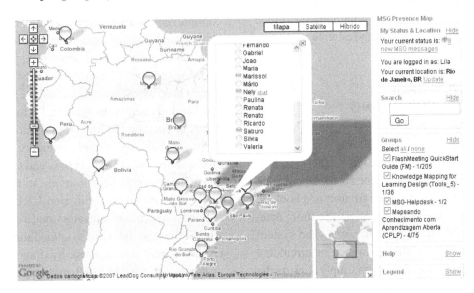

Figure 9. MSG displaying the availability of contacts of the same course worldwide

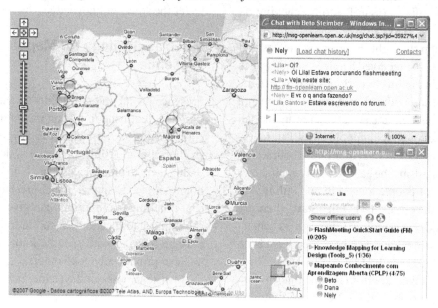

MSG maps the location of members of the same community of practice, representing in this way the geo-location and impact of collective intelligence related to a specific course. In this way, the users can obtain a list of contacts, who may provide peer support during learning activities. Through MSG OpenLearners can identify the availability of contacts throughout the globe related to a specific learning resource.

FM: A WEB-BASED VIDEOCONFERENCING APPLICATION

FM (fm-openlearn.open.ac.uk) is a desktop videoconferencing tool, integrated in the OpenLearn environment. Any OpenLearn user can book an online video meeting and select the time, date, duration and number of attendees. The system generates a URL, which can then be circulated to the meeting attendees, who simply click on the link to gain access to the videoconference.

FM as Strategy for Social Learning through Group Discussion

The FM live communication tool allows learners to externalise their implicit knowledge into explicit knowledge by presenting their ideas during a video meeting either through the foreground communication channel (broadcast) or through the background channel (text chat). The application provides a 'push-to-talk', simplex audio system, allowing only one person to broadcast at any one time. Those who wish to talk can raise a symbolic hand and queue, whilst waiting for their turn to come, or click on the 'interrupt' button.

In the mock up example in Figure 10, Leo is broadcasting, while Luci is next and Carla is the last in the queue. Other communication channels in FM include a text chat function, URL sharing, a voting system, mood indicators, and a whiteboard which allows participants to upload slides, reflect on the content and annotate by drawing shapes or write text, visible to all participants. In this

Web videoconferencing there are people from UK, Portugal and Brazil. While Lia from UK is explaining in English the graphics generated by FM, Leda is answering questions in the chat in Portuguese and translating important key ideas from English to Portuguese. All participants can visualise the graphs, interpret the content, ask questions and give feedback through different media: text, sound, audio, graphic and icons. In this way, users make sense by combining explicit knowledge from different media.

FM as Strategy for Individual Learning by Replaying the Discussion

FM events can be recorded and their replay, called FM Memo™, can be annotated, edited and

discussed with their community or viewed by other people in the world. The replay is browsed by navigating through the names of the attendees on the right, or via the timeline on the bottom of the window, representing the length of each broadcast, with different colours to distinguish between participants. In this way, the FM Live Communication tool engages learners in internalising explicit knowledge through the replay function; users can replay the recording of the discussion in order to reflect upon it and analyse the content.

The example shown in Figure 11 portrays the replay of the broadcasts of 6 attendees from different cities in Brazil and Portugal. The whiteboard presents the purpose of their meeting, which is to discuss about technology and pedagogical methods applied to higher education. The time

Figure 10. FM extract from CoLearn community

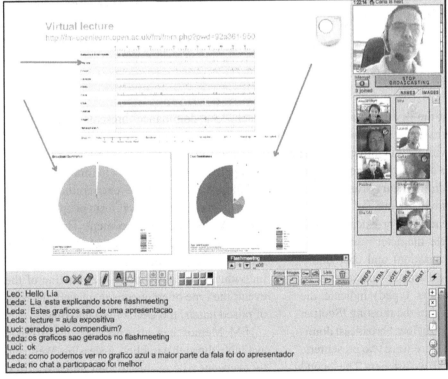

Lia: "FM offers 3 graphs. The first graph is a time line, which shows who, when and how long was broadcasting. The other graph shows the broadcast and chat dominance.

Gio: "What is the role of these graphs?"

Luci: "Can any participant access these graphs?"

Figure 11. FM is a web videoconferencing application offering instant online meetings.

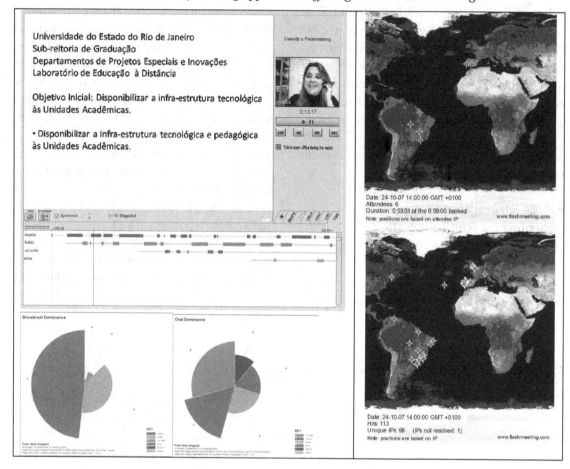

line below shows that the first two participants started to talk and the two following attendees in this list participated with their comments during the middle and at the end of this meeting. The other two attendees did not start broadcasting, they were probably only listening.

Automatically generated broadcast dominance diagrams (circle diameter=turns taken, circumference=total duration) and chat dominance diagrams (circle diameter=messages sent, circumference=characters typed) indicate the attendees' participation in the meeting (Scott et al, 2007). The first graph below, "broadcast dominance", confirms that there were two presenters, two active attendees and two listeners. The second

graph, "chat dominance" presents almost similar participation among the six participants.

The meeting minutes are available online, providing different information in order to enhance the understanding of the event, remind attendees of what was discussed, or inform people who did not attend of the meeting content. The metadata generated after each meeting include the chat log, the number of attendees, a linear visualisation of individual broadcasts along the timeline of the event, the type of emoticons displayed, the time of raised hands, the URLs fired and others.

FM Memos can also be shared and made available through a publicly accessible Webpage for everyone who wishes to view and learn from them, enhancing in this way the collective knowledge of new, reusable learning objects. In less than two years of existence, the FM-OpenLearn folksonomy hosts around 100 public events. In this perspective, the FM Live Communication encourages learners to socialise implicit knowledge by sharing their video meetings, allowing other learners to search and find events related to their interests and build knowledge through social awareness. Around 10 public events have been attended by the CoLearn community, such as series of interactive seminars held by experts on Moodle, video lectures on a variety of topics such as information literacy, elearning games and knowledge media tools. Amongst the rest of events, there are also Web-casts of conferences,

Figure 12. A FM map in Compendium representing Games webconference

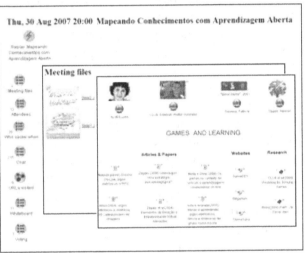

Figure 13. Keeping track of who spoke when

interviews of e-learning experts, moderated project meetings, peer-to-peer student meetings and many others. These different kinds of events may contain different communication patterns, which can be interpreted in different sense-making representations, be it knowledge maps of the meeting or visualisations of the event shape.

In FM, the metadata produced after each meeting can be used to interpret the event in different ways. For example, the IP resolutions of FM users include information about the use of the tool by different communities. Using people's IP addresses, their location can be plotted on a world map. In this way, maps can be generated to show the distributions of users for both the attendance of live meetings and replay access. For example, the IP resolution of the users connected to the live meetings shows how the tool is being used to connect people from the same social network or community of practice, while the IP resolution of the users viewing a public replay shows the learning impact of the event reuse in different parts of the world.

In Figure11 the map on the top shows 6 unique IP addresses from Brazil and Portugal that were connected to this live video meeting in the Co-Learn community, while the map below shows the truly global use being made of FM recordings during the same month, with 113 unique IPs viewing FM recordings around the world, representing in this way the impact of the knowledge included in the replays of virtual events and transferred to hundreds of individuals around the world.

FM and Compendium as Strategy for Constructing Collective Knowledge

The FM Memos generate a set of metadata, available in XML format. This XML can be imported into Compendium and turned into knowledge maps as we can see in a virtual meeting about digital games applied to education. These maps can enhance the understanding of the event, as they include temporal and conceptual connec-

tions amongst all event elements, such as who attended the meeting and who spoke when (Fig. 12 and 13), the URLs visited and the whiteboard images or interactions (Fig. 14 and 15), text chat logs, annotations, votes and keywords. All these elements are nodes automatically linked in a knowledge map, which can be used to assist the replay users in structuring, acquiring and reconstructing the knowledge transferred during the discussions and argumentations in the meeting (Okada et al, 2008). In this way, learners can internalise explicit knowledge of the community into implicit knowledge. The nodes are actually links back to the original replay as well; therefore a way of traversing the replay through different categories of indexed timestamps.

The knowledge maps of different kinds of FM events may differ in that they may present different map structures. For example, seminars can present richer maps in terms of URLs, broadcasts and chat logs, as they are more interactive events, involving the active participation of several attendees. Virtual lectures, on the other hand, with a main presenter broadcasting and her virtual audience interacting with chat, may include poorer argumentation between individual nodes. The structuring of the FM replay information in maps allows the users to browse the different parts of the event, based on the different event elements, such as individual broadcasts, annotations, URLs shared etc. Mapping the knowledge transferred in a virtual meeting enhances the combination of explicit knowledge in the form of questions, feedback and comments from different media.

DISCUSSION

In this initial study, the use of Compendium, FM and MSG was introduced around OERs, providing learners and educators with some strategies to foster open sensemaking communities. Table 2 shows a summary about how these knowledge

Figure 14. Mapping the URLs visited along with their time during the event

Figure 15. Mapping questions, ideas, pros and cons discussed on the webconference

media tools can be useful to develop understanding from individuals to groups.

The combination of knowledge media tools for knowledge mapping, presence and live collaboration can assist learners in identifying and bridging gaps, developing and sharing representations around the same problem, tackling common problems and negotiating a consensual understanding. Learners can identify gaps by raising simple questions via instant messaging and visualising questions addressed for the first time and concepts without connections through hypermedia mapping. New questions can be raised during a live videoconferencing session.

Table 2. Knowledge media tools for open sensemaking communities

	How these tools help learners to	Compendium hypermedia mapping	FM a web videoconferencing	MSG Instant messaging
I N D I V I D U A L	identify a gap	Visualising questions not addressed and concept without connections	Raising questions through broadcasting, chat or Flashboard and unknown concepts	Raising simple questions through instant messaging.
	bridge a gap	Selecting relevant information resources	Getting peers' feedback through smiles, vote, chat or broadcasting E	Contacting who knows the answer for simple problems that need to be solved quickly
	develop and share representations around some problem	Bringing significant information in their maps and uploading the files in their community.	Preparing slides or Compendium maps and sharing them in WhiteBoard	Identifying simple problems that can be discussed in MSG
G R O U P S	identify common conflicts	Visualising questions and gaps in other's maps	Voting or highlighting in the WhiteBoard issues that the group are interested in	Meeting peers who are helpful to raise significant issues
	negotiate a consensual understanding	Mapping FM discussions representing the groups' argumentation around problems	Discussing Compendium Maps of previous meetings, which represents the groups' understanding, in the Whiteboard	Meeting participants who are helpful to solve problems

Relevant resources organised in knowledge maps can help bridge gaps in sensemaking, while learners can locate and communicate with people who know the answer to simple problems via instant messaging and can get instant feedback in a videoconference through broadcasting, text chat, voting and emoticons.

Knowledge media tools can encourage the development and sharing of representations around a common problem. Learners can discuss simple problems via the MSG instant messaging tool and bring significant information in the knowledge maps, which can be accessed by their community, or prepare maps and slides to be shared in the whiteboard during a live video meeting.

Common conflicts can be tackled through visualising questions and gaps in fellow learners' maps, or finding contacts who may be helpful with the identifying problems via instant messaging, or through voting and highlighting issues in the whiteboard. The process of making sense is induced by issues that create discontinuity in the flow of experience engaging learners to collective interpretations (Weick, 1979).

Finally, consensual understanding can be negotiated by identifying contacts though MSG groups and maps, who may be able to solve problems. Moreover, the mapping of virtual discussions represent the groups' argumentation around problems and the discussion of Compendium maps of previous meetings via the FM whiteboard represent the group understanding.

In this case study, we analysed some examples, which show how these tools can be used to foster open sensemaking communities by mapping knowledge, location and virtual interaction. The sensemaking process in online environments can be developed by connecting sequences of enactment, selection and retention (Weick 1979) via knowledge media tools. In enactment, learners actively construct meaning by rearranging and labelling raw data into equivocal data to be interpreted in their maps or synchronous conversations . In selection, learners identify meanings that can clarify equivocal data by overlaying their prior knowledge or past interpretations as templates to the current experience. Compedium, FM and MSG can be used to provide explanations of what is going on. In retention, the community stores the products (maps, Webconferences and messages) of successful sensemaking that learners may retrieve in the future.

In this pilot study, it is important to stress this work will be extended through quantitative and qualitative research. A Web survey with follow-up interviews will soon be conducted about the uses of these knowledge media tools in the OpenLearn project. Although there are significant number of members registered, it is not yet possible to see widespread of open sensemaking communities around OER. Previous surveys indicated that individuals come to OpenLearn primarily for accessing the free OERs. It is not surprising that they do not as a rule share knowledge objects — or indeed, engage in a lot of collaborative learning activities. In order to start their communities, **they need to find peers with similar interests and have** social and intellectual commitment to learn content and tools together. Disseminating strategies and ways to apply these tools to foster open sensemaking communities may engage OpenLearn users in collaborative learning.

CONCLUSION AND FUTURE RESEARCH

Knowledge media technologies mark a profound shift in developing products, creating new strategies for learning, and sharing knowledge. Learners move from simply following information, instructions and tasks to discussing them, making sense of them, reconstructing and sharing meanings collectively with anyone in the world with similar interests. OpenLearn indicates a new way to interact and construct knowledge collaboratively from individual learners to social groups (Aigrain, 2003) and from global networks

to local communities (Anderson, 2007). It offers an environment to actively support individual learners, educators and self-organising communities through the integration of Compendium, FM and MSG. In order to enhance social learning, these knowledge media tools can be used to:

- Create awareness that the user is part of a community
- Build new learning objects, leaving them open for sharing, reuse and remixing
- Manage personal or group information by dragging and dropping in any document or Website (a form of 'visual e-portfolio');
- Manage knowledge and learning by charting questions, ideas, and arguments as they arise;
- Share learning pathway maps over resources; to work through revision question templates;
- Browse or construct knowledge maps associated with learning resources and literatures, or dialogue maps which add value to online meetings.
- Identify social roles and improve individual behaviour and social interactions in open sense making communities
- Build knowledge through social awareness

The number of knowledge media technologies' users has been rising in this first year and a half of OpenLearn Project. During this period, the OpenLearn project has engaged a critical mass of over more than 1,000,000 users, taking advantage of the OER to learn at their pace and time. Our future research focuses on how students and educators can use the knowledge media tools as open sensemaking tools to foster their social learning networks and contribute to the open learning resources movement by developing their learning materials and new pedagogical strategies. Open Educational Resources, knowledge media tools and open sensemaking communities are essential to promote open learning mainly if OpenLearners can take part in this movement as active participants by valuing their authorship.

REFERENCES

Aigrain, P. (2004). The individual and the collective in open information communities. *16th BLED Electronic Commerce Conference*, (pp. 9-11). Retrieved on January, 17, 2007 from < http://opensource.mit.edu/papers/aigrain3.pdf >.

Anderson, T. (2007). Reducing the Loneliness of Distant Learner Using Social Software. *Open and Distance Learning Conference*. Retrieved on January, 17, 2007 from < http://www2.open.ac.uk/r06/conference/TerryAndersonKeynoteCambridge2007.pdf >

Biocca, F., Burgoon, J., Harms, C., & Stoner, M. (2001). Criteria and Scope Conditions for a Theory and Measure of Social Presence. *Presence 2001 Conference*, Philadelphia.

Brooks, F., & Scott, P. J. (2006). Knowledge work in nursing and midwifery: An evaluation through computer mediated communication. *International Journal of Nursing Studies, 43*(1), 83-97.

Buckingham Shum, S. (2005a). From Open Content Repositories to Open Sensemaking Communities. *Conference on Open Educational Resources*, Logan, Utah (Sept. 2005).

Bucking Shum, S. (2005b). *Knowledge Technologies in Context*. Open University Press.

Canas, A., & Novak, J. (2008). Concept Mapping Using CmapTools to Enhance Meaningful Learning. In A. Okada, S. Buckingham Shum, & T. Sherborne (Eds.), *Knowledge Cartography: software tools and mapping techniques*. London: Springer-Verlag.

Chakraborty, R. (2002). *Presence: A Disruptive Technology*. Jabber Conf 2001 presentation, Denvor.

Cook, S. D. N., & Brown, J. S. (1999). Bridging Epistemologies: The Generative Dance between Organizational Knowledge and Organizational Knowing. *Organization Science*, 10(4), 381-400.

Dholakia, U. M., King, J. W., & Baraniuk, R. (2006). What Makes an Open Education Program Sustainable? *The Case of Connexions*. Retrieved on January, 17, 2007 from www.oecd.org/dataoecd/3/6/36781781.pdf

Downes, S. (2006). *Models for Sustainable Open Educational Resources*. Retrieved on January, 17, 2007 from http://www.downes.ca/cgi-bin/page.cgi?post=33401.

Eisenstadt, M., & Vincent, T. (1998). *The Knowledge Web: Learning and Collaborating on the Net*. London: Kogan Page.

Entwistle, N. (1995). Frameworks for understanding as experienced in essay writing and in preparing for examination. *Educational Psychologist*, 30(1), 47.

Finerty, T. (1997). Integrating learning and knowledge infrastructure. *Journal of Knowledge Management,1*(2), 98-104.

Jarman, S. (2005). *Open Content Initiative Application to The William and Flora Hewlett Foundation*. Retrieved on January, 17, 2007 from http://www.open.ac.uk/openlearn/__assets/06sngpqpwminsmwxov.pdf

Jonassen, D., Beissner, K., & Yacci, M. (1993). Structural Knowledge: Techniques for Representing, Conveying, and Acquiring Structural Knowledge. Lawrence Erlbaum Assoc Inc

KMI Knowledge Media Institute (2006). Open Sense Communities. Retrieved on January, 17, 2007 from http://kmi.open.ac.uk/projects/osc/index.html

Maron, M. (2003). *the World as a Blog*. Retrieved on January, 17, 2007 from http://brainoff.com/geoblog/

Naumer, C., Fisher, K., & Dervin, B. (2008). *Sense-Making: A Methodological Perspective.* Paper presented at the CHI 2008, Florence, Italy. ACM.

Nonaka, I., & Takeuchi, H. (1995). *The Knowledge-Creating Company.* New York, NY: Oxford University Press.

Okada, A., Buckingham Shum, S., & Sherborne, T. (2008, forthcoming). *Knowledge Cartography: software tools and mapping techniques.* London: Springer.

Okada, A., & Buckingham Shum, S. (2006). Knowledge Mapping With Compendium in Academic Research And Online Education. 22nd ICDE World Conference, 3-6 Sept. 2006, Rio de Janeiro [www.icde22.org.br]

Okada, A. (2005). The Collective Building of Knowledge in Collaborative Learning Environments. In T. Roberts (Org.), *Computer-Supported Collaborative Learning in Higher Education.* 1 ed. Idea Groups. London, v. 1, p. 70-99.

O'mahony, S., & Ferraro, F. (2003). Managing the boundary of an 'Open' project. Retrieved on January, 17, 2007 from http://opensource.mit.edu/papers/omahonyferraro.pdf

Open Source Initiative (2007). Retrieved on January, 17, 2007 from http://www.opensource.org/

Openlearn (2006). Retrieved on January, 17, 2008 from http://www.open.ac.uk/openlearn/home.php

Polanyi, M. (1967). *The Tacit Dimension.* New York: Anchor Books.

Reagle, J. (2004). Open content communities. *M/C: A Journal of Media and Culture, 7.* Retrieved on January, 17, 2008 from <http://journal.media-culture.org.au/0406/06_Reagle.rft.php>

Rogers, E. M. (1995). *Diffusion of Innovations.* New York: Free Press.

Ruggles, R. (1998). The state of the notion: knowledge management in practice. *California Management Review, 40*(3), 80-89.

Russel, D., Jeffries, R., & Irani, L. (2008). *Sensemaking for the rest of us.* Paper presented at the CHI 2008, Florence, Italy. ACM.

Salwen, M. B., & Stacks., D. W. (Eds.) (1997). *An Integrated Approach to CommunicationTheory and Research.* Mahwah, JF, Erlbaum.

Scott, P. J., Tomadaki, E., & Quick, K. (2007). The Shape of Live Online Meetings. *International Journal of Technology, Knowledge and Society, 3.*

Sumner, T., Domingue, J., & Zdrahal, Z. (1998). *Enriching representations of work to support organisational learning.* Milton Keynes: Open University, Knowledge Media Institute (Tech Rep No KMI-TR-60).

Vogiazou, I.T., Eisenstadt, M., Dzbor, M. & Komzak, J. (2005, March). From Buddyspace To CitiTag: Large-Scale Symbolic Presence For Community Building And Spontaneous Play. *Proceedings Of The ACM Symposium On Applied Computing.*

Weick, K. (1979). *The Social Psychology of Organizing.* 2nd. ed. New York: Radom House.

Weick, K. (1995). *Sensemaking in Organizations.* Thousand Oaks, CA: Sage Publications.

Wiggins, G., & Mctighe, J. (2005). *Understanding by design,* 2nd ed. Alexandria, VA: Association for Supervision and Curriculum Development.

Wenger, E. (1998). *Communities of Practice: Learning, Meaning, and Identity* (pp. 318). Cambridge: Cambridge University Press.

Willinsky J. (2006). The access principle: the case for open access to research and scholarship. Cambridge: MIT Press.

KEY TERMS

Knowledge Mapping: A technique for organising knowledge, which aims to facilitate the creation and communication of knowledge through graphical representations. Beyond the mere transfer of facts, knowledge mapping aims to further create or transfer insights, experiences, attitudes, values, interpretations, perspectives, understanding, and predictions by using various complementary visualisations.

Knowledge Media Technologies: Means tools to support the processes of generating, interpreting and sharing knowledge using several different media, as well as understanding how the use of different media shape these processes.

Open Educational Resources: Educational materials and resources offered freely and openly for anyone to use and under creative commons licenses, which allows users re-mix, improve and redistribute on the Web.

Open Learning: A learning method for the knowledge acquisition based on open educational resources, free technologies and online communities. Open learning aims to allow participants self-determined, independent and interest-guided learning. It has been also offering opportunities for collaborative study and social learning.

Open Sensemaking Communities: Refer to open and self-sustaining communities that construct knowledge together by interpreting, reconstruct their understanding together and literally "making of sense" from an array of environmental inputs.

Peer-to-Peer Networks: Typically used for connecting people via largely ad hoc connections. Such networks are useful for many purposes, such as social and open learning, sharing content files containing audio, video, data or anything in digital format and realtime data.

Social Learning: Refers to the acquisition of social competence that happens primarily in a social group, virtual learning environments or online communities. Social learning depends on group dynamics, people with similar interests and disposition for studying together.

Social Presence or Co-Presence: Terms used in virtual learning, which refer to the ability of learners to project their personal characteristics into the online community by presenting themselves as 'real people' through the media of communication: picture, profile and via the "sense" of being with others.

Chapter XXV
A Critical Cultural Reading of "YouTube"

Luc Pauwels
University of Antwerp, Belgium

Patricia Hellriegel
Lessius University College, Belgium

ABSTRACT

This chapter looks into YouTube as one of the most popular Social Software platforms, challenging the dominant discourse with its focus on community formation and user empowerment. On the basis of an analysis of the steering mechanisms embodied in the infrastructure as well as empirical observations of YouTube's content fluctuations during a period of time, insight is provided into the embedded cultural values and practices and into the nature of the ongoing negotiation of power and control between the YouTube controllers (owners, designers, editors) and the "prosumers". This exploratory study is theoretically inspired by Michel de Certeau's ideas of utilization as a productive activity involving strategic and tactical behaviour. Methodologically the model for 'hybrid media analysis' (Pauwels 2005) is taken as a point of departure for analysing various aspects of the Website's platform (including structure, design, hyperlinks, imagery, topics and issues). This model is geared towards decoding the multimodal structure of Websites and their social and cultural significance.

QUESTIONING DOMINANT DISCOURSES ON WEB 2.0, SNS AND YOUTUBE

In the dominant discourse about Web 2.0 and 'Social Software' in particular, it is often suggested that this major next step in Web related development - as complacently claimed by the number 2.0 - represents a truly revolutionary development in the on-line world. The most distinctive features in this regard are the so-called 'social' aspects attributed to the set up of the 2.0 applications and to its resulting user practices.

Marked differences with 'Web 1.0' applications are the clear shift from desktop to the Web with the effect that everything created is already on line and can be shared immediately (Rhie 2000); the fact that the programming code is often released[1], thus allowing anyone to refine, rethink and add functionality; and finally the fact that applications are in general easy to use and available for free, and as such within the reach of many.

Also with respect to the 'content' and the related practices of use, there is a strong 'social' focus. Interacting with peers is a key part of many Web 2.0 applications and of social networking sites in particular. Social Networking Sites (SNS) can be described as *'Websites that allow individuals to construct a public or semi-public profile within the system and formally articulate their relationship to other users in a way that is visible to anyone who can access their profile'* (Boyd & Ellison 2007). Next to the personal information and connections displayed in the on-line profiles, many a SNS also contains other types of content uploaded by users, e.g. on *Bebo.com,* self-written stories, poems and books are available, on *MySpace.com* one can listen to free music and through YouTube, people share short videos. This form of Do-It-Yourself content production and sharing is considered by some the very essence of Web 2.0. The growing popularity of this practice is considered to have far reaching consequences (Gillmor 2006, p.$_{XV}$):

Grassroots journalism is part of the wider phenomenon of citizen generated media production of a global conversation that is growing in strength, complexity and power. When people can express themselves they will. When they can do so with powerful yet inexpensive tools, they take to the new media realm quickly. When they can reach a potentially global audience, they literally can change the world.

While there is hardly anything new about on-line content being generated by non-professional users (cf. the fairly common practice of setting up homepages or family Websites using prefabricated templates, Pauwels 2008) or Web-users communicating/interacting with each other, Web 2.0 offers a platform to the average individual through which a vast number of people can be reached in a very interactive way and requiring few technical skills or financial resources.

Examples like Wikipedia are readily used to illustrate a newly acquired autonomy for users in creating self-organizing collaborates which arise bottom-up, liberated from control (Leadbeater 2007):

The power of mass creativity is about what the rise of the likes of Wikipedia and YouTube, Linux and Craigslist means for the way we organize ourselves, not just in digital businesses but in schools and hospitals, cities and mainstream corporations. My argument is that these new forms of mass, creative collaboration announce the arrival of a society in which participation will be the key organizing idea rather than consumption and work. People want to be players not just spectators, part of the action, not on the sidelines.

In this quite up-beat discourse about Web 2.0, the focus is clearly on the 'citizen' users: their control over content and development of technology and the way users interact on line with their peers. This 'user-centeredness' also dominates current research on YouTube. (i.e. Fonio et. al. 2007, Harp & Tremayne 2007, Lange 2007, Webb 2007).

At odds with this general idea of user-empowerment and autonomy is the fact that the Web 2.0 user-practices reside in a relatively small number of Websites controlled by powerful gatekeepers. Of all Web 2.0 applications, particularly the popularity of SNSs stands out. Over the last two to three years a more or less stable top ten has emerged.

Figures indicate that these top SNS's reach up to 45 percent of today's active Web users.[2]

The number of unique *monthly* visitors to YouTube alone can be estimated at 55 to 75 million and over 65,000 videos are claimed to be uploaded to the site each day. Some sources rank *MySpace* as the most visited Website world-wide, surpassing even the Google search engine[3]. To sustain this kind of traffic, these Websites have to be powered by organisations with ample financial means. *YouTube* (launched April 2005) was acquired by *Google* in 2006 for $1.65 billion, and *MySpace* at present is part of the *Murdoch* media conglomerate *News Corp*. The direct revenue for all three of these SNSs stems from on-line advertising, and SNS advertising has a lot of exposure on a Website with hundreds of thousands of visitors a day. But perhaps even more interesting is the vast amount of collectable user data available (i.e. personal details, links and on-site surfing behaviour) to fuel the marketing machine.

THEORETICAL GROUNDING, RESEARCH FOCUS AND METHODOLOGICAL FRAMEWORK

Theoretical Grounding

We interpret Websites as cultural artefacts which can be 'read' as dynamic media texts interacting with a sometimes very active 'user' base. From different strands of media and communication studies the notion has emerged that embedded in any media text is an 'inscribed reader' or 'implied audience' (Hall 1980) for which a 'preferred reading' is constructed by the producer of the text. However, while *'the discourses of particular examples of media content are often designed or inclined to control, confine or direct the taking of meaning',* the reader may 'resist' the sender's desired response' (McQuail 2000, p.350).

But, the terms 'reader', 'receiver', 'consumer' or even the more activity-suggesting term 'user'

aren't fully adequate for expressing the centrally important productive activity of the typical 'prosumer' (a contraction of the terms 'producer' and 'consumer' to indicate the active role the users play in creating content) of YouTube. These prosumers provide the core content (posted bits of videos and other types of reactions) and thus embody the 'raison d'être' of this type of Website.

To better grasp the implications of this mixed or multi-sided 'production', it is useful to recall Michel de Certeau's ideas around 'practices of consumption', which in his view are determined by the difference or similarity between the production of an artefact and the 'secondary production' hidden in the process of its utilization (de Certeau 1994, p. 476). YouTube is in this sense clearly characterised by a joint and secondary production of meaning caused on one side by a predetermined framework, and on the other by the productive practices of utilization by both its Web controllers and the highly divergent population of consumers (visitors) and prosumers (contributors). Of further value for our analysis of a social software application as a cultural space, is de Certeau's distinction between two logics of action, which he calls the 'tactical' and the 'strategic', terms which he uses in ways quite distinct from their military sense. De Certeau asserts that: *'The space of the tactic is the space of the other. Thus it must play on with a terrain imposed on it and organized by the law of a foreign power'* (de Certeau 1994, p. 36-37). The 'foreign power' for the YouTube user is the strategically constructed infrastructure and the imposed rules of conduct as well as the controlling practices exercised by the Website's gatekeepers. According to de Certeau, the strategic player has authority, dedicated resources, seeks to perpetuate and grow and usually benefits from homogenising its audiences. The tactical player lacks these characteristics, doesn't seek to compete with the institution or take over power, but primarily seeks to fulfil his or her needs behind an appearance of conformity. Faced with a product and a set of 'rules of the game', tactical players may enrol in gentle forms of subversion to make the offered products, services and space more 'habitable' and function better to fulfil their needs (de Certeau 1994). De Certeau's powerful ideas as developed in his book 'The Practice of Everyday Life' (1994, originally published in French as *L'invention du quotidien. Vol. 1, Arts de faire'* (1980)) pre-date the digital, networked era and yet seem to find their most vivid expression in present day practices of cybersociety.

Research Focus

In this article we examine YouTube as a prominent representative (both in popularity and in set-up) of the Web 2.0 applications, with the aim of uncovering the strategic infrastructure and gate-keeping activities of the YouTube owners and the 'room for manoeuvring' of the prosumer. Emphasis therefore lies on issues of power, control and mutual influence as manifested in a social software application that is advertising itself as offering broadcasting power to 'you', or in other words to anyone. This research focus can be summarized in the following questions:

- Which cultural traits (e.g. values and norms) are embedded in the YouTube platform and manifested through interventions by Website controllers / gatekeepers? Does an ideal user/preferred reading emerge and how is this profile being constructed and maintained?
- How do the users deal with the imposed directives, constraints and control mechanisms? Is there a breach apparent between goals and aspirations of the gatekeepers and those of the prosumers, and how is this manifested?

So in de Certeau's terminology we are primarily analysing the strategic and tactic interaction between YouTube as an institutional player vis-à-vis the varied group of users (visitors and prosumers). While a static view or snapshot of the form and content of YouTube may already reveal much of the embedded culture of the infrastructure, a diachronic observation of the practices and behaviours from both sides offers further insight into how the complex cultural discourse manifests itself.

Methodological Framework

Social Networking Sites – and YouTube in particular – are complex and dynamic media texts that do not easily disclose their hybrid ways of cultural meaning production. To approach the multimodal complexity of Websites from a cultural angle, we deploy the 'Hybrid Media Analysis Model' (Pauwels 2005) which was developed from of an interest to culturally decode the multimodal structure of family Websites (Pauwels 2002; 2008) and the ambition to counter the dominant verbal bias in analysing Computer Mediated Communication. This model proposes a number of possibly significant 'cultural indicators or parameters' of Websites as expressed by words, pictures, design features, navigational or narrative strategies. It starts with an analysis of the 'Web internal level', which is focused on discovering embedded cultural values and norms in the overall structure of Websites, their design features, navigational structures, content categories, the point(s) of view they embody, topics and views expressed (or significantly absent) in text, images and audio, the construction of the 'implied' or preferred audience, the linkages to other sites as indications of ideological or other types of affiliation, etc. But it also deals with issues related to the broader context of production and consumption. With respect to the analysis of the production side, the model looks at the cultural meanings that can be attributed to the larger technical, social, economical and political infrastructure of the Websites under study and also suggests an approach to reach the Website owners' intentions and sought/received gratifications.

Finally the model tries to include the audience or users of the Websites under study, which often proves to be a very cumbersome aspect of this type of research, since the majority of users of many types of Websites remain hard to identify and contact.

Many aspects of the Hybrid Media Analysis Model are used in this study to uncover the basic interplay of the YouTube infrastructure and the gate-keeping practices of its owners vis-à-vis the ways the prosumers are dealing with those practices. We discuss the findings from these analyses in the following sections.

A CRITICAL ANALYSIS OF YOUTUBE

Intertextuality and Intermedia Context

YouTube as an on-line phenomenon is to be situated and understood in the broader context of media such as television, newspapers, Websites, and finally as a very particular member of the family of Web 2.0 applications and SNSs. This media context influences the way the Website is 'shaped' as well as the way it is understood and used by the prosumers. YouTube subscribes to a framework of conventions through which the site is presented and recognized as a social networking and video sharing site: the main building blocks are personal profile pages and there are features available to establish and display relations with other users. This set-up is similar to on-line dating sites in the late nineties, now combined with chat, forum and file sharing functions. A snapshot from the Internet Archive reveals that YouTube indeed started out as an on-line dating site, but quickly repositioned itself as a more general video repository, thus widening its potential market.

By now the SNS has established itself as a genre within Web 2.0 applications and users are likely to have specific expectations when accessing the site. The extent and nature of these expectations depends on individual experiences and familiarity with the Internet in general, including similar and dissimilar Websites.

The Look of Things: Design, Identity and Metaphor

On the whole the YouTube design appears to be highly structured (see Figure 1). There are only a couple of lively, dynamic elements and only limited use of bright or pastel colours. The background is white, putting maximum focus on the content represented by stills of the available videos. Striking elements in the design are the rounded corners, and the 'mirror' (subtle reflections of objects and words), 'shading' (representing the effect of shade to add the illusion of depth) and 'gradient' (a blending of shades from light to dark or from one colour to another) effects. These features give the Website an overall polished, fresh look, a reference perhaps to the newness of the Web 2.0. The design elements identifying YouTube reappear frequently in other Web 2.0 applications and are described and discussed on the Internet as 'design 2.0'.[4]

These visual design elements (i.e. 'mirror' effects, rounded corners) have no specific meaning attached to them in isolation and could just as well be used in any Website or even other media. But their systematic and joint occurrence within a group of Websites which share other functionalities and features, co-defines the meaning generated by the entirety (Lacey 1998, p.36). Through these particular design choices, YouTube subscribes to the aesthetic conventions of what has developed into an identifiable design style. The overall design as such functions as a signet advertising and underlining an association with the concept of Web 2.0. How effective this signet is, again depends on the visitor's familiarity with the signs and symbols of this design style and how it will evolve. Web design, after all, is fluid and ever changing. A more widespread use

Figure 1. Excerpt of YouTube design, (source: YouTube.com, 21/11/2007)

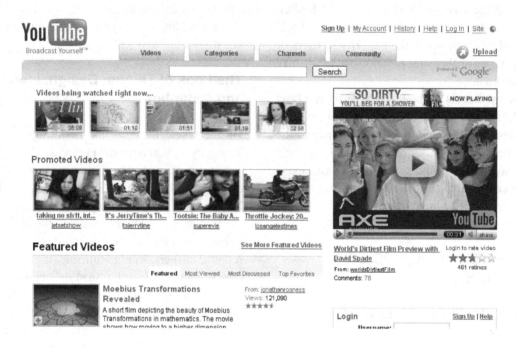

of the described features on Websites in general, for example, could loosen the link with Web 2.0. applications

Although research has shown that Web users are attentive to the overall design of a Website i.e. use it as a measure for trustworthiness (Cyr & Haizley 2004, p.1200), the issues of whether and how Website design style (as part of a frame of reference) is used to construct meaning still needs to be researched further.

Content Categorizing: Establishing and Resisting Cultural Preconceptions

A limited number of categories are offered for posting videos on YouTube. Apart from the category *News & Politics,* they are all located in the domain of leisure, entertainment and consumer goods, i.e. *Autos & Vehicles*, *Pets & Animals* or *Sports*. Several country/language options are available to users, with a translation of menu and titles. The

particular ranking of the categories is also relative to the selected country (see Table 1).

Each country option is accompanied by an icon of the respective national flag. *USA* was available previously, but is now quite literally replaced by the default option *Global*. A comparison of the particular position (highest, lowest) of the categories per country yields some interesting differences: *News & Politics* ranks very low in the category list for most countries, but is listed number one for *France*; while *Pets & Animals* are top of the list for *Brazil* and *Italy,* they rank at the very bottom for *Poland*. The *Global* category rankings are identical to those of the other native English speaking regions: *UK, Australia, New Zealand, Canada* and *Ireland*.

These predefined categories and their ranking by YouTube, embody preconceptions of what the site is to be used for or most likely to be used for in the different countries. Apart from differences in ranking and slight Semantic changes in their translation (e.g. the French *Voyages et Nature*

Table 1. Top (1-3) and bottom (10-12) video category ranking per country, (source: YouTube.com, 27/09/2007)

Rank	Global	Japan	Brasil	Poland	France
1	Autos & Vehicles	Entertainment	Pets & Animals	Gadgets & Games	News & Politics
2	Comedy	Gadgets & Games	Entertainment	Film & Animation	(Pets &) Animals
3	Entertainment	Comedy	Sports	People & blogs	Entertainment
10	Pets & Animals	Music	People & blogs	Comedy	Autos & Vehicles
11	Sports	Autos & Vehicles	Autos & Vehicles	News & Politics	How to & DIY
12	Travel & Places	Travel & Places	Travel & Places	Pets & animals	Travel & Places

instead of *Travel & Places*) the categories are more or less the same throughout all versions of YouTube and represent, or even impose, an Anglo-Western cultural stance. This observation is further substantiated by a comparison with the Japanese video-sharing Website *EbiTV.jp*. This latter site was probably inspired by YouTube in terms of look and features, but there are some remarkable (cultural) differences, especially in terms of categories. *Food,* for instance, is a separate category as well as *Art* (with video topics ranging from receptions to martial arts), and there are two categories devoted to children: the 'how-to' category *Education,* and the category *Child,* where parents can post funny videos. The category *Other* is not so remarkable in itself, were it not for the depiction of an ageing couple to represent it (see Figure 2). In Western culture, this image is more likely to be used for issues related to the elderly, rather than for a miscellaneous category.

However, the predefined categories are often but a façade for the actual content of YouTube. Via added tags and specific keywords in the title, a video can be found by those looking for content on a certain topic, regardless of how much it strays from the category in which it was placed. Videos stirring religious discussion are, for example, in no way absent from YouTube and a search on a controversial topic such as 'anorexia' yields more

than 7,000 videos classified under (the relatively apt) 'People & Blogs', but also under 'Music' or 'News and Politics'. Yet again it is culturally significant that no separate categories are being created for important issues such as 'Health' and 'Religion'. Analysing these omissions in the categories may offer further information on the kind of cultural discourse that YouTube wants to foster. Users may ignore the labels they are forced to make a selection from, and upload content that doesn't match the selected category. YouTube may allow this to happen while still deciding not to draw extra attention to these (often somewhat controversial) issues by granting them a separate category. On the other hand this may all be part of the YouTube strategy: allowing very diverse content in very plain and innocent looking cat-

Figure 2. The miscellaneous category 'Other', represented by a picture of an elderly couple, (source: http://www.EbiTV.jp, 27/11/2007)

egories so as to yield the widest attraction for visitors and participants.

The personal profiles are also highly structured in YouTube, as in most SNSs. Detailed personal (name, age, location) and professional information can be entered and hobbies and interests described. Each user has to choose what is called an 'account type'. These predefined account types loosely define the content of their videos. Some account types are very concrete e.g. *Politician*, *Comedian* and *Musician*, others are less clear such as *Director*, *YouTuber* and *Guru*. Account types can be further categorized by choosing a 'style' (see Figure 3), e.g. *Beauty*, *Educational*, *Financial*, *Relationships*, *Spiritual*. In these account types again fixed ideas of what the site is to be used for are embedded, but the less strictly

defined accounts (particularly *Guru*) leave room for innovation or ambiguity.

The centrally controlled subdivision of You-Tube content and the resulting rigid structure also has roots in the fact that large-scale Websites such as this are database driven. When setting up such a Website, the first step is to design the database structure. Information architects map out what information needs to be stored. In a database, every piece of information is broken down to the smallest meaningful unit and is subsequently labelled. By linking and combining the stored data units, Websites are generated dynamically. This inclination to structure, pre-define and pre-label all Website content is reflected in the Website's interface.

Figure 3. Excerpt of a personal profile of a YouTube user. The chosen account type is 'Director' and the style 'Variety'. The background-image is a picture uploaded by the user, (source YouTube.com, 27/11/2007)

Choices on the personal pages are offered to users so that they can 'profile' themselves, but looking at the type of information requested, it is evident that these data are particularly valuable for target marketing (whereby the online advertisements are selected to meet the needs of specific market segments identified by their surfing behaviour). Users who are aware of this threat or simply value their privacy, may try to gain more control over their personal profiles by evading the constraints, or by using the provided means and space for unintended purposes e.g. providing mock descriptions and information. This is a common practice on SNSs as illustrated by a recent study on MySpace, which yielded a dubiously high number of centenarians (Thelwall 2007, p. 10-11). The options to personalize the look of a *channel* (a term used by YouTube to denote the personal pages which users can create to upload their videos and manage their personal contacts) are limited. The most effective way to personalize your channel is to insert a background image, an option chosen by many. Within these boundaries, the channels are claimed and used as a tool for impression management and self-representation.

Staying Tuned to YouTube: Linking Strategies and Tactics

YouTube's set-up encourages linking to other YouTubers via their channel. To this end there are a number of predefined options on offer. Users can display links to favourite videos, friends and subscribers or to their received comments. This feature is important to users on SNSs as a means to establish themselves as a 'popular' member of the on-line community. Research on *Facebook,* for example, found that users with a high number of friends were perceived to be more popular, self-confident and attractive (Kleck 2007).

Conversely, YouTube restricts the posting of external links on the site: it is, for example, not allowed to include links in the text comments.

Often users successfully circumvent these restrictions by embedding links directly into their videos or by disguising them in text comments so they cannot be detected automatically. This restriction is partly a measure to prevent spam on the site, although it appears to be inefficient in this respect based on the volume of spam which still reaches the site.

External links are also unwanted since they lead users away. In fact, YouTube reverses this process by using links as a tool to draw visitors in. This is realized by allowing anyone to embed videos in other Websites, without breaking the link with YouTube. You can watch the videos from the other Websites, but the YouTube logo remains clearly visible and YouTube itself is only one click away.

Whose Tube? Alleged Purposes, Preferred Audiences and Embedded Points of View

On top of allowing and encouraging users to link to each other, YouTube actively tries to create a sense of community. Examples are abundant, but the video posted by the founders of YouTube, shortly after the company was acquired by Google in 2005, is particularly explicit in this regard.

Much effort is put into constructing the 'it's all for the community'-idea. The take-over by Google is presented as not about commerce, but about the user, to ensure them an even better service. Another example is the on-line 'fact-sheet'. Here it is stressed that there are no 'no-go'-areas. The users are put on a level of equality with the YouTube management and are even invited behind the scenes to help develop functionality:

YouTube is an open community and encourages users to send in their thoughts and comments about their experiences on the site. YouTube understands that each and every user makes the site what it is and welcomes them to get involved to help create new features and be a part of new developments on the site.

This community sense is affirmed to stimulate users' engagement, but at the same time it is a way for YouTube to enhance their functionality by tapping into free labour. Reverting to Althusser's theory of interpellation it can be argued that the users are 'hailed' into a discourse where 'them' and 'we' are phased out and 'us' is pushed to the forefront. Interpellation implies an active response from the addressees who 'recognize' the 'system of representations' (images, myths, rituals, ideas or concepts) and thereby subject themselves to the presented state of affairs (Althusser 1999, In: Evans & Hall, p.320-323).

Examples in YouTube of prosumers identifying with the imposed discourse are abundant. In many of the user-generated videos the audience is addressed as 'YouTubers' or 'YouTube community' and whole threads of videos and text comments are dedicated to discussing issues of 'the community', such as flaming (Lange 2007), or are aimed at setting up joint initiatives e.g. the 'free hugs' campaign (videos of people giving out free hugs in cities all over the world in an effort to counter social indifference).

Althusser also stated that most 'subjects' do not react to or question the imposed ideology because they are unaware of the matter (Althusser 1999, In: Evans, p.321). Web 2.0 users, however, seem very sensitive to discrepancies between actions and discourse. Prosumers aware of inconsistent measures, such as channels and videos being deleted, can lead to user-centred discourse turning against YouTube, forcing the gatekeepers to adhere to their professed principles. Some prosumers have already reacted against these covert practices by posting a video addressing the issue[5]. Other 2.0 Websites (*Digg.com* and *Flickr.com*) have had to deal with harsh user reactions forcing the platform owners to reinstall deleted content[6]. Until now, however, YouTube seems to have evaded a large-scale user rebellion.

Since August 2006, the basic lay-out and content of YouTube's main page have changed very little. The clear links at the top of the main page offering more explanation about the concept and workings of the site, however, have been relocated since then. This information is now hidden deeper in the site, confirming that YouTube targets an audience that is Internet savvy and accustomed to surfing and contributing user-generated content to Websites. The available country/language options support the assumption that YouTube is trying to attract a broad and increasingly international audience. Although currently they are still chiefly targeting the U.S. market: the user demographics on the section reserved for advertisers are US figures only and the fill out form for interested organizations exclusively lists U.S. states.

The growing involvement of YouTube in the U.S. presidential elections (2008) is somewhat surprising for a Website otherwise entertainment and leisure oriented. A YouTube sub-site 'YouChoose '08' has even been created for this purpose and YouTube is collaborating with CNN in the organization of televised debates. Although the political subject matter differs from other YouTube content, it is incontestable that the debates obtain a high level of media coverage around the world. In addition it has been found that U.S. citizens are increasingly using the Internet to gather political information (Madden 2007). The percentage has even doubled since 2002 and on-line video is playing an important part:

Political video content currently garners about the same number of viewers as those who say they watch or download movies and television shows on line; 15% of Internet users say they have sought out political video content on line, and 2% report doing this on a typical day. (Madden 2007, p.16).

In the light of this evolution, YouTube's efforts to be involved in US politics are less surprising. They just seem to be tapping into a growing market of on-line political communication left unattended up till now by other SNSs.

Navigational Options and Strategies in the Construction of Popularity and News Worthiness

YouTube holds a large collection of video materials supplied by its prosumers. A basic structure overlays the site allowing the users to find their way through the millions of 'video' and 'channel' pages. The main entry point is the homepage from which four main options are accessible: 'videos', 'categories', 'channels' and 'community'. All these pages offer a selection of videos based on different parameters. The selection for 'video' and 'channels' is based on popularity and time (e.g. *'Most viewed/Today'*) but the videos featured on the remainder of these pages are hand-picked by 'YouTube editors'.

Next to this main menu there is a search box. The search function is fairly basic especially when considering that Google also powers a leading and highly sophisticated Internet search engine. There is no 'Advanced Search' such as on Google.com which would allow narrowing detailed searches down with a combination of parameters. The absence of such advanced search options may encourage users to opt for YouTube's predefined selections instead. Especially those who are merely browsing the site, may be prompted to consult pre-selected videos such as *'Most viewed/All times'*.

Eye-catching features on the Web page also have the potential to influence users in the choices they make, for example content at the top of a page leaps more into view and elements emphasized by size, colour or framing attract users' attention. YouTube employs several of these elements to steer visitors (e.g. a coloured box with a 'pick of the day' or a video shown much larger than the others on the homepage) with the effect that certain content is favoured (see Figure 4).

This self-reinforcing cycle of popularity combined with (purposely) embedded steering or 'priming' mechanisms sheds a different light on the matter of whether the popularity of videos can indeed be seen as a reflection of the public taste, as is readily assumed and therefore unquestioned by some researchers (e.g. Harp & Tremayne 2007, p.20).

We studied some examples to further explore the possible effects of the way the user is directed through YouTube. For three days, we tracked the viewing numbers reported for videos featured at the top left of the main page (1st level), the 'pick of the day' on the categories page (2nd level) and at the top left of the categories 'Music' and 'News and Politics' (3rd level). It immediately became clear that the videos prominently featured on these pages experienced a large increase in viewings within the first three days (see Table 2). This indicates that YouTube has a considerable influence on which videos are viewed and become popular. The same mechanism of self-reinforcement comes into play in other ways. If a video receives many views (and the owner's channel attracts more visitors in consequence), it is also shown at the top of the pages 'videos' and 'channels' and obtains even more exposure.

These figures (Table 2) are of particular interest now that journalists are starting to use YouTube as a source for news, an increasing trend, for example, in Flanders (Belgium). Over the last few years, Flemish newspapers have started mentioning the site with increasing frequency. A closer look at the context reveals a shift from referring to and describing YouTube as an Internet 'phenomenon' (mainly concerning the Websites popularity and the take-over by Google clearly marked by the sudden increase in references to the site in December 2006: see Table 3), to using YouTube videos as a source for articles. Also noteworthy is that the popularity of a video is consistently referred to and used as a legitimization of news worthiness of the selected item.

With respect to the increasing popularity of YouTube with journalists another factor should be considered: the opaque nature and origin of the videos. The home-made or self made format seems to enjoy an aura of authenticity, a way of

Figure 4. 'Pick of the day' video under the main menu option 'category', portrayed larger and in a coloured box to attract attention, (source: YouTube.com, 07/08/2007)

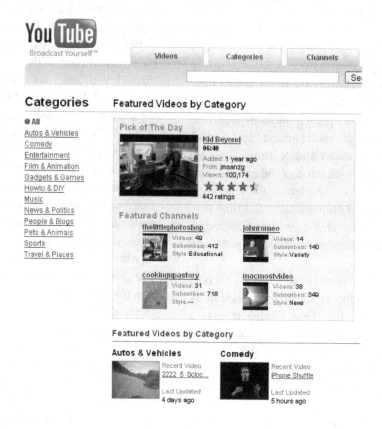

Table 2. Number of views reported by YouTube for prominently located videos

Selected sample of videos	Number of clicks from main page	Views day 1	Views day 2	Views day 3
Main page	0	46,326	507,567	704,666
Categories	1	3,384	43,931	removed from page
Category 'music'	2	7,463	9,893	10,902
Category 'news & politics'	2	27	18,823	42,914

production considered less prone to influences of government or commercial corporations, and one through which dissenting opinions can be voiced to a large audience, thus realizing a form of grass-roots journalism. While this may be true in many cases, the deceptive potential lies in the ease with which this 'home-made' type of video can be mimicked and used for manipulative purposes (Palser 2006). In YouTube, several of such videos have already been uncovered as not being what they pretend to be. One example is the anti-Hillary *'Vote Different'* ad. The video is

Table 3. Types of References to YouTube in Flemish newspapers, (source: http://www.mediargus.be, 27/09/2007)

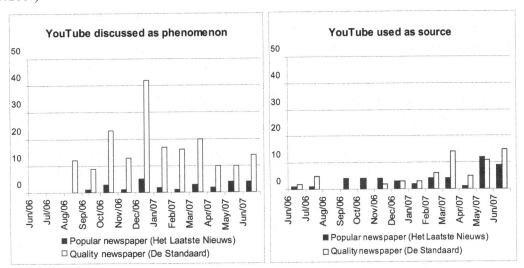

based on an old Apple commercial and portrays *Hillary Clinton* as Big Brother. By now different versions have received over 4 million views on YouTube in addition to being featured in television news world-wide. The biggest surge in interest was prompted by the discovery that the creator of the ad was an employee of the *Barack Obama* presidential campaign.

The combination of the many gate-keeping and priming strategies successfully exercised by YouTube, the dubious nature and origin of some of the video materials and the increased use of the Website as a reliable source for news all call for further research. For example, taking a closer look at YouTube's growing involvement in the U.S. presidential elections campaign (2008) and the ensuing media coverage could unearth hitherto overlooked steering processes that could have powerful consequences far beyond YouTube's virtual boundaries and audiences.

User-Generated Content: Research Opportunities into Video Form and Content

There is an enormous variety of videos available on YouTube in terms of themes covered, origin of the material, levels of production expertise and technologies that have been used: vlogs, home-made movies shot by camcorders or mobile phones, videos mimicking or parodying TV-formats, etc. Also popular are the (mostly illegal) snippets of televised content such as music videos, movies, TV-series or sports events. Legal actions against YouTube from copyright holders lead to restricting the length of any video to a maximum of 10 minutes. Users again evade this measure by posting their videos in consecutive parts. YouTube also offers a *Video Toolbox* with tips and guidelines on camera-work, lighting, manipulating time, adding music etc. for creating on-line video. This guide is a mixture of a selection of videos created by

YouTubers (on the topic of how to create a video for YouTube) and information supplied by YouTube itself. YouTube also recently released *the Remixer*, a tool that allows you to remix your old videos by rearranging sequences, adding graphic elements and transitions or choosing different audio tracks. The limitations to videos imposed by YouTube and the supplied tips and tools are an aspect to consider when studying the content and form of videos posted by users on the site.

Keeping this in mind, the collection of DIY videos available still offers an unmatched and freely available repository for research. A careful analysis of both the filmic aspects (the visual statements as expressed through numerous parameters) and the profilmic aspects (the depicted events, the performances of actors, so everything that happens in front of the camera) may provide answers to a myriad of interesting questions regarding issues like self-representation, media literacy, political awareness, media power, media convergence, performances of social class, gender and race etc.

Most parameters and levels of analysis applicable to the macro-level of YouTube's infrastructure and policies may also be applicable to the micro-level of individual videos: we can analyse points of view (e.g. often a first person media approach in self recorded footage: see Figure 5), the cultural meaning (values, inspirations, tokens of affiliation) embedded in the form (framing, camera-movements, editing, narrative structure), the construction of an implied audience, modes of address etc.

Processes of selection and re-contextualisation of movie and television content are employed as vehicles to highlight painful issues or criticize current events and the way they are presented by

Figure 5. Self-made video in the 'People & Blogs' category typical 'first-person media' style, (source YouTube.com, 27/11/2007)

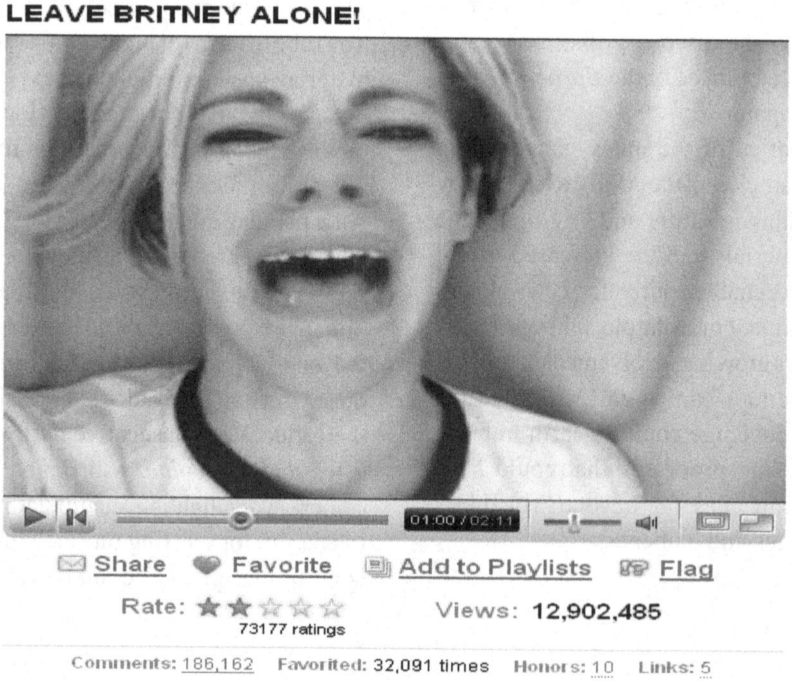

mainstream media. One prominent example is the racist 'rant' of the actor and stand-up comedian Michael Richards during a live show in a small club which was filmed by mobile phone and posted on the Internet. YouTubers immediately responded by posting parodist fragments from the actor's work in the popular TV series *'Seinfeld'*. In the wake of the incident all television appearances were also collected on YouTube and lead to hefty discussions and opinions aired through text comments, video responses, video blogs should be explained somewhere what they are and parodying videos. At the time of writing (September 2007), this had resulted in 4,706 entries for *'Michael Richards'* on YouTube. Such reactions also point to the urgent need for a more qualified discussion of the many complex ethical issues regarding rapidly evolving on-line practices, as cyberspace hitherto largely seems to escape the ethical standards that are commonly observed in offline situations (Pauwels 2006, p. 365-369)

On the matter of intertextuality at this level, it is also interesting to consider how YouTube video formats are influencing other media. Some are tapping directly into the Website's success e.g. magazines printing weekly YouTube video reviews or television shows, covering solely YouTube videos (e.g. *The Fizz*[7] hosted by popular video bloggers).

But YouTube's influence on other media could stretch further than mere incorporation in those media. New formats emerging on the site could find their way to TV and film. Some 'YouTubers' for example are integrating several of the Website's interactive possibilities (from video-responses to text comments and links) into their videos. From this a type of 'series'[8] has evolved whereby users actively contribute to the scenario and content. Evolutions like this could bring new life to interactive TV. As a result of the popularity of YouTube-like videos lasting only a few minutes, the concept of 'bite-size media' or 'snack-size entertainment' is now emerging which might

be a stimulus to reconsider TV-formats such as TV-series or reports in terms of length.

CONCLUSION

This exploratory case-study of YouTube started from the premise of a perceived conflict between the general user-centred discourse about Web 2.0, the particular set-up of the Web 2.0 platforms and the practices of utilization.

In applying the 'hybrid media model' (Pauwels 2006) we looked at such things as YouTube's position in relation to other media, its overall structure and design as cultural markers; the ratio behind the predefined video categories; the specific structure and possible purposes of the personal profile pages; concrete manifestations of the professed 'sense of community'; embedded points of view; the efforts to set and maintain standards for the video content, and the reasons behind the available internal/external link options. These aspects have in turn been compared with the on-site user practices and user-generated content. We also touched on actual and potential effects of the YouTube phenomenon on the wider offline world of politics and media.

Important to note about many Web 2.0 applications – and SNSs such as YouTube in particular – is the highly heterogeneous and multi-actor production of cultural meaning as it resides in both form and content. On one side there is the Website's imposed and constantly monitored platform with predefined options and categories and rules of engagement, and on the other, a vast and heterogeneous base of users, many of which could better be addressed as 'prosumers' as they take an active part in the production of the core content of the Website. By observing the 'behaviour' of both users and platform owners as expressed in choices and changes with respect to the content and organization of the Website over a set period of time, we have acquired some insight into the subtle or at times open grappling between the owners' and the users' goals and needs in a way that may be more reliable than asking the parties involved.

Apart from the strategically built set-up of the Websites which embodies already a set of values and goals, the Website controllers also have a number of strategic tools to further promote desired behaviour (e.g. by highlighting certain types of contents) and prohibiting or discouraging undesired practices (through censoring, removing or demoting particular types of content).

An Anglo-Western cultural stance does seem to emerge from the available video categories and their country relative ranking notwithstanding the effort to customize the site for different countries. The 'personal' space on YouTube is also strongly pre-fabricated and as a result strongly biased toward constructing a preferred audience (of potential consumers). Users are encouraged to make use of links within YouTube via prominently available options, but external links, that would move visitors away from YouTube, are restricted. YouTube actively participates in constructing the image of the collaborate of users being in control, or at least on an equal footing with the platform producers. But the pre-moulded personal space, the presented (and 'significantly missing') options and embedded steering mechanisms question the notion of user-empowerment and autonomy often related to the Web 2.0.

However, looking carefully at what was happening on site on a daily basis, we could assert that YouTube's users and in particular its active prosumer base continuously engage in boundary bending activities to tactically counter the restrictions imposed by the infrastructure and the controlling authorities. These active users regularly deploy tactical behaviour to subtly resist the power being exercised from above. At times they even openly contest actions of the Website owners that go against the 'social' spirit of Web 2.0 (e.g. unilateral censorship exercised by YouTube's management), forcing the YouTube authorities to

'walk the talk'. Indications of these mild forms of resistance or subversion can be found in tactical user practices such as: circumventing imposed link restrictions or providing mock descriptions and information to avoid becoming an easy marketing target and/or retaining anonymity. New practices and video formats continuously emerge from the community of users resulting in very rich collections of videos that critically or sometimes bluntly or coarsely, re-appropriate and re-contextualise media artefacts and events.

We have tried here to critically examine YouTube's dominant and largely self-professed discourse around 'community sense' and 'user empowerment', and added to that a view of a marketing driven enterprise that is unequivocally into money making through constructing a space where individuals define themselves as easy marketing targets. We also highlighted the subtle struggle for power and control between owners and users as well as pointing at possible effects of cultural mainstreaming or ideological reproduction.

Yet it would be a mistake to replace a one-sided, narrow view on user empowerment with an equally skewed and undifferentiated one of crash commercialism or cultural propaganda. YouTube, and other Web 2.0 applications demonstrate a very complex phenomenon that may serve many purposes, some of which could have been foreseen by the originators and many which could not have been predicted and are still beginning to take shape. We have tried to make a modest start with a cultural analysis of the different features and practices of YouTube, to identify emerging effects of this phenomenon.

However, further research is needed to grasp the many multifaceted functions and effects of this on-line activity, the messages and strategies within the individual videos, on its users and on society at large. This kind of research should involve many aspects and levels of inquiry, and necessitate the further development of adequate theories and above all more refined methodologies for scrutinizing the multimodal and multi-leveled nature of on-line artefacts, processes and interactions.

REFERENCES

Althusser, L., (1999). Ideology and idelogical state apparatuses (notes towards an investigation. In Evans & Hall, (Eds.), *Visual culture: The reader,* (pp. 412). Sage Publications.

Barker, C. (2000) Cultural Studies: Theory and Practice, Sage Publications Ltd, London.

Boyd, D. & Ellison, N. (2007) Social Network Sites: Definition and Conception, URL (consulted 17 September 2007). http://www.danah.org/papers/worksinprogress/SNSHistory.html

Certeau, M. (1984). *The Practice of Everyday Life.* S. Rendall (Trans.). University of California Press, Berkeley originally published in French as *L'invention du quotidien. Vol. 1, Arts de faire'* (1980).

Fonio, C., Giglietto, F., Pruno, R., Rossi, L., & Pedrioli, S. (2007). *Eyes on You: analyzing user generated content for social science.* Paper presented at the Towards a Social Science of Web 2.0 conference, York, UK.,URL (consulted 17 September 2007): http://larica-virtual.soc.uniurb.it/nextmedia/wp-content/uploads/2007/09/eyes_on_you.pdf

Gillmor, D. (2006). We the Media: Grassroots Journalism By The People, For the People, O'Reilly Media, URL(consulted 4 October 2007). http://www.oreilly.com/catalog/wemedia/book/index.csp

Hall, S. (1980). Encoding/Decoding. In S. Hall, D. Hobson, A. Lowe, & P. Willis (Eds.), Culture, media, language (pp. 128-138). Hutchinson, London.

Harp, D. M., & Tremayne, M. (2007). *Programmed by the People: The Intersection of Politi-cal Communication and the YouTube Generation.* Paper presented at 57th Annual Conference of the International Communication Association San Francisco, CA.

Kleck, C. A. (2007). *The company you keep and the image you project: putting your best face forward in on-line social networks.* Paper presented at 57th Annual Conference of the International Communication Association San Francisco, CA.

Lacey, N. (1998). *Image and Representation: Key Concepts in Media Studies.* MacMillan Press Ltd, London.

Lange, P. (2007). *Commenting on Comments: Investigating Responses to Antagonism on You-Tube.* Paper presented at Society for Applied Anthropology Conference Tampa, Florida,URL (consulted 17 September 2007). http://Web3.cas.usf.edu/main/depts/ANT/cma/Lange-SfAA-Paper-2007.pdf

Leadbeater, C. (2007). We-Think, URL (consulted 17 September 2007): http://www.wethinkthebook.net/home.aspx

Madden, M. (2007). On-line Video: PEW Internet and the American Life Project. Washington, DC.: PEW Research Center for People and the Press, URL (consulted 29 January 2008): http://www.pewinternet.org/PPF/r/219/report_display.asp

McQuail, D. (2000). *McQuail's Mass Communi-cation Theory.* London: Sage Publications.

Palser, B. (2006). Artful disguises: sultans of spin masquerade as amateurs on citizen media Web sites. *American Journalism Review*, Issue October/November 2006, URL (consulted 31 July 2007): http://www.ajr.org/Article.asp?id=4215
Pauwels, L. (2002). Families on the Web. In D. Newman (Ed.), *Sociology: Exploring the Archi-tecture of Everyday Life* (pp. 231-235). Fourth Edition, Thousand Oaks, CA: Pine Forge. P.

Pauwels, L. (2005). Websites as visual and mul-timodal cultural expressions: opportunities and issues of on line hybrid media research. Media, culture & society, 27(4), 604-613.

Pauwels, L. (2006). Ethical Issues of On-line (Visual) Research. *Visual Anthropology, 19*(3-4), 365-369. Taylor & Francis.

Pauwels, L. (2008). A Private Visual Practice Going Public? Social Functions and Sociological Research Opportunities of Web-based Family Photography. *Visual Studies, 23*(1), 34-49. Routledge.

Rhie, K. (2000). From Desktop to Webtop: Achieving True Computing Freedom, Anytime, Anywhere. *Proceedings of the AACE WebNet conference*, Chesapeake, VA, URL (consulted 29 January 2008): http://www.editlib.org/index. cfm?fuseaction=Reader.ViewAbstract&paper_id=6328&from=NEWDL

Thelwall, M. (2007). *Social networks, gender and friending: An analysis of MySpace member profiles*. Paper presented at the Towards a Social Science of Web 2.0 conference, York, UK, URL (consulted 29 January 2008): http://www.scit.wlv. ac.uk/~cm1993/papers/MySpace_d.doc

Webb, M. (2007). Music analysis down the (You) tube? Exploring the potential of cross-media listening for the music classroom. *British Journal of Music Education, 24*(2), 147-164.

KEY TERMS

Hybrid Media Analysis Model: 'Hybrid Media Analysis Model' (Pauwels 2005) which was developed from of an interest to culturally decode the multimodal structure of Websites proposes a number of possibly significant 'cultural indicators or parameters' of Websites as expressed by words, pictures, design features, navigational or narrative strategies. It starts with an analysis of the 'Web internal level', which is focused on discovering embedded cultural values and norms

in the overall structure of Websites, their design features, navigational structures, content categories, the point(s) of view they embody, topics and views expressed (or significantly absent) in text, images and audio, the construction of the 'implied' or preferred audience, the linkages to other sites as indications of ideological or other types of affiliation, etc. But it also deals with issues related to the broader context of production and consumption.

Prosumer: A contraction of the terms 'producer' and 'consumer' and as such referring to the fact that in contemporary media the role of producers and users are often mixed. Alvin Toffler coined the term "prosumer" when he predicted that the role of producers and consumers would begin to blur and merge. In social software environments the more active users (as opposed to the mere 'lurkers') typically engage in the production of content. Some see the term 'prosumer' as a short for 'professional consumer'.

Social Networking Sites: Social Networking Sites (SNS) are Web based **social network services** focused "on building online communities of people who share interests and activities, or who are interested in exploring the interests and activities of others." (source: Wikipedia)

Strategic and Tactic Interaction: These terms refer to Michel De Certeau's distinction between 'two logics of action' linking "strategies" with institutions and structures of power, while "tactics" are utilized by individuals to create space for themselves in environments defined by strategies. Applied to Social Software the 'strategic' space is enacted by the Web site controllers and the set up which embodies already a set of values and goals, while the active users develop tactical behavior to counter the restrictions imposed by the infrastructure and controlling authorities.

Web 2.0: "Web 2.0 is a term describing changing trends in the use of World Wide Web technology and Web design that aims to enhance creativity, secure information sharing, collaboration and functionality of the Web. Web 2.0 concepts have led to the development and evolution of Web-based communities and its hosted services, such as social-networking sites, video sharing sites, wikis, blogs, and folksonomies. The term became notable after the first O'Reilly Media Web 2.0 conference in 2004. Although the term suggests a new version of the World Wide Web, it does not refer to an update to any technical specifications, but to changes in the ways software developers and end-users utilize the Web". (source: Wikipedia)

YouTube: YouTube is a video sharing Website where users can upload, view and share video clips. YouTube was created in February 2005 by three former PayPal employees and contains a wide variety of user-generated video content, including movie clips, TV clips and music videos, as well as amateur content such as videoblogging and short original videos. In 2006, Google Inc. acquired the company.(source: Wikipedia).

ENDNOTES

[1] See for example the extensive list of API's on line available at http://www.programmableWeb.com/apis/directory (consulted 17 September 2007)

[2] Figures on line available at: http://www.nielsen-netratings.com/pr/pr_060511.pdf (consulted 17 September 2007)

[3] Hitwise US Top 20 Websites August, 2007. On line available at: http://www.hitwise.com/datacenter/rankings.php (consulted 17 September 2007)

[4] See for example: Coles, S. (2006) The Logo's of Web 2.0. [on line] Available at: http://www.fontshop.com/fontfeed/archives/the-logos-of-Web-20; Faulkner, T. (2007) The state of Web 2.0 design. [on line] Available at: http://valleywag.com/tech/jakob-nielsen/the-state-of-Web-20-design-260583.php; Hunt, B. (2007) Design 2.0: Current Web style. [on line] Available at: http://www.Web-designfromscratch.com/current-style.cfm; Mittermayr, R. (2006) Web 2.0 Design... in a nutshell. [on line] Available at: http://mittermayr.wordpress.com/2006/02/03/20-culture/ (consulted 17 September 2007)

[5] Examples include the videos: *'Bring YoungTubersUnited AND Jesari Back'* available on line at: http://www.youtube.com/watch?v=isHYOXUzXwM and *'The video that got Nick Gisburnes account deleted'* available on line at: http://www.youtube.com/watch?v=6GO3kfw8bHU (consulted 17 September 2007)

[6] See: Greenberg, A. (2007) 'Digg's DRM Revolt' Forbes.com on line available at: http://www.forbes.com/technology/2007/05/02/digital-rights-management-tech-cx_ag_0502digg.html) and Arrington, M. (2006) 'Facebook Users Revolt, Facebook Replies' Techcrunch.com [on line] Available at: http://www.techcrunch.com/2006/09/06/facebook-users-revolt-facebook-replies/ (consulted 17 September 2007)

[7] See: thefizz.tv, broadcasted on DIRECTV The 101.

[8] See for example: I, http://www.youtube.com/user/ichannel

Chapter XXVI
The Personal Research Portal

Ismael Peña-López
Universitat Oberta de Catalunya, Spain

ABSTRACT

The author of this chapter proposes the concept of the Personal Research Portal (PRP) – a mesh of social software applications to manage knowledge acquisition and diffusion – as a means to create a digital identity for the researcher, an online public notebook and personal repository, and a virtual network of colleagues working in the same field. Complementary to formal publishing or taking part in events, and based on the concept of the e-portfolio, the PRP is a knowledge management system that enhances reading, storing and creating at both the private and public levels. Relying heavily on Web 2.0 applications – easy to use, freely available – the PRP automatically implies a public exposure and a digital presence that enables conversations and network weaving without time and space boundaries.

INTRODUCTION

In a *Knowledge* Society, the main problem knowledge workers[a] have is invisibility: if people don't know that you know, and people are not aware of what you know, you are not. In a *Network* Society, the main problem that nodes have is being kicked off the network: you are worth what you contribute, if you don't contribute, you are not worth a dime.

Digital technologies have forever changed the way knowledge is disseminated and accessed, in at least two crucial ways. First, diffusion procedures (publishing, broadcasting, etc.) have been getting infinitely easier and cheaper for those digitally initiated (the 'digerati'), but still remain surprisingly arcane for the ones on the dark side of the digital divide, less digitally literate and, thus, less prone to benefit from all the advantages of '*online casting*'. Second, intellectual property rights – and their trade – have seen their basements dynamited by the fact that a digital copy has certain characteristics of a public good insofar as it is a copy and as such can be duplicated and disseminated. Under this approach, the tension between 'coffee for all' and private property has caused an increasing strengthening of copyrights with a parallel adoption of new licenses aimed for the maximum spreading and sharing of content.

In view of this scenario, researchers, scholars and civil society organizations from developed and developing countries[b], are pressing governments and institutions to foster Open Access (OA) for their documentation: this means that documents are 'digital, online, free of charge, and free of most copyright and licensing restrictions' (Suber 2005a). OA can be considered a way to achieve universal reach of research diffusion at inexpensive and immediate levels[c]. Most OA efforts have been aimed at the institutional level, devoting little energy to what the individual can do to contribute to this goal. Even though there are some valid reasons for this imbalance, there is ample opportunity for the individual to make a difference.

The philosophy and tools around the web 2.0 seem to bring clear opportunities so that these people, acting as individuals, can also contribute, to build a broader personal presence on the Internet and a better diffusion for their work, interests or publications. A Personal Research Portal, fostered and built individually, with the help of Web 2.0 applications and services, helps bringing into the spotlight underrepresented researchers and subjects, such as researchers from developing countries, junior experts or vanguard disciplines and topics not yet into the mainstream scholarly landscape and academic publishing systems. Indeed, the nature of ICTs – and the Internet in particular – do open a new landscape for knowledge exchange not necessarily mediated alone by institutions.

This paper aims to explore how individuals can contribute to the diffusion of research in the OA paradigm by means of social software and web 2.0 technologies. The example of the Personal Research Portal – a concept more than an artifact – can contribute to making knowledge more accessible to other researchers, but also provides a model by which international research networks might be fostered. In detail, the paper analyzes how the PRP can contribute to creating an 'online identity', how this identity can help to create a network and how digital publishing is the currency of this network.

A Background Note on the Open Access Paradigm and Open Access for Development

Before entering the core of our article, we would like to expand a little bit the fact that access to knowledge is crucial for the development of research and, hence, for the progress of the society. In 2002 the Open Society Institute initiated the Budapest Declaration, supported by a group of scholars and seconded since then by thousands of signatories. The Declaration states:

Open access to peer-reviewed journal literature is the goal. Open access to peer-reviewed journal literature is the goal. Self-archiving (I.) and a new generation of open-access journals (II.) are the ways to attain this goal (Budapest Open Access Initiative 2002).

This set the basis of OA was later complemented by the Bethesda Statement on Open Access Publishing (2003) and the Berlin Declaration on Open Access to Knowledge in the Sciences and Humanities (2003), with the aim to both give some definitions and commitments related to the OA paradigm. The transposition to a developing world framework took place in Brazil more than three years later with the Salvador Declaration on Open Access: the developing world perspective (2005) and was revisited at the Bangalore Declaration: A National Open Access Policy for Developing Countries (2006). As stated by Suber and Arunachalam (2005) "[f]or researchers in developing countries, OA solves two problems at once: making their own research more visible to researchers elsewhere, and making research elsewhere more accessible to them". Of course, this statement does not only apply to developing countries.

Most of these manifestos emphasized the role of institutions in fostering OA, being the main target scientific journals. But, in Peter Suber's words (2005) "OA archiving is even more promising than OA journals. It is less expensive, allows faster turnaround, and is compatible with publishing in conventional journals". Hence, OA archiving's "key benefit for developing country scientists is that global participation could take place without further delay" (Chan and Kirsop, 2001). As some literature shows[d], open archiving usually happens at the institutional level, at "'Institutional archives', administered by universities or research institutes for members of their community" (Chan et al. 2005). The initially identified benefits of open archiving – cost, immediacy, flexibility – can play havoc with by the institutional procedures, where dedicating personnel to new initiatives is expensive, tempos are slow and bureaucracy inflexible. Indeed, institutional repositories might still be isolated, not contributing to a researcher's visibility or content availability.

Ironically, even having gone open the problem might persist: researchers still need broad access to knowledge, high visibility and network weaving at low costs and highest flexibility to cope with the speed of times.

THE PERSONAL RESEARCH PORTAL

The approach we here want to present is closely related to the concept of e-portfolio, but not from the learner's point of view but the researcher's:

An e-portfolio is a digitized collection of artifacts, including demonstrations, resources, and accomplishments that represent an individual [...].

This collection can be comprised of text-based, graphic, or multimedia elements archived on a Web site or on other electronic media. (Lorenzo and Ittelson, 2005).

E-portfolios are usually associated with students and teaching rather than with researchers, their main goal being for students to gather and present their work for assessment; therefore the term 'personal research portal' (PRP) is introduced here as an alternative, whereby its main goal is to act as a knowledge 'gatherer', contributing to

1. Increased access to international research output
2. Enhanced access to research generated by non-mainstream disciplines or experts
3. Promotion of institutional research output
4. Improved citation and research impact
5. Improved access to subsidiary data, and
6. A strongly facilitated peer review[e]

To achieve this, the PRP should be a low cost, highly flexible virtual space, which supports:

*   Hosting a repository for personal production, with public aim, with past and present (work in progress) information and documentation, being everything linked to and fro;
*   Gathering digital resources, news, general information and materials on the same platform, accessible from each and every computer with an Internet connection;
*   Self-archiving and self-publishing research results, including the ongoing research, reflections, doubts, findings – avoiding waits and delays;
*   Informing what one knows and that one knows
*   Increase one's visibility, enable networking and knowledge sharing (Peña-López et al., 2006)

All in all, the PRP tracks the 'read-think-write' routine performed by scholars and scientists involved in research. The big difference with publishing is that the PRP should not only keep record of stock knowledge –formal knowledge that lasts or should last – but also keep record of flow knowledge – non-structured knowledge that is not intended to stay for long because it is devoted to foster exchange[f].

As it happens with Personal Learning Environments, there is not such a thing as *the* PRP, but *many* PRPs could potentially be built from a mesh of different applications to fit the concept. We nevertheless believe that the core set of applications of a PRP are as follows:

- A static web site with personal and professional information, drawing the researcher's profile;
- A blog, where to note news, reflections and most 'flow' knowledge arising from readings, research results and hypotheses;
- A blogroll, understood as both a live reader for the researcher and a live bibliography of bookmarks for the community;
- A wiki, where 'stock' knowledge is stored but allowing it to evolve along time and with the collaboration of third parties;
- A bibliographic manager, with online access to all or most records;
- A personal repository to (self-archivee) published papers and (self-published) preprints, working papers, presentations, syllabuses, etc.;
- Other tools such as social bookmarking tools, file stores (image, sound, video), and so forth; and.
- RSS feeds for each and every dynamic page

In other words, the PRP can be imagined as a lifetime personal web space "magnificiently equipped (with software, communication, search, and multimedia tools), beehive[ly]-configured [...]"

that possesses sufficient organizational plasticity to accommodate the user's developmental capacities and needs across a lifetime" (Cohn & Hibbits, 2004). From a researcher's point of view, these capacities and needs are related with their inputs (readings, conversations), transformation processes (reflections, peer reviews), and outputs (communications, preprints, papers).

There are notwithstanding two caveats to be made. First, this individual reporting alternative is in no way a substitute to the stated ways of institutional OA publishing, but a complementary one that has some exclusive characteristics only attainable by this means. Second, along the same line, this is in no way a substitute for mainstream ways of publishing and validating scientific outcome but, again, a complementary one. We will deal about this issue later on.

A Background Note on Social Software, the Web 2.0 and DIY Web Technologies

In the last years new, user-friendly web tools have appeared which moreover are often interconnected in such a way that communication and collaboration can take place. 'Social software' – blogs and content management systems, wikis, message boards – actually finds itself embedded in a wider concept, the Web 2.0, based on contribution enhanced by and taking place in the World Wide Web, easiest online publishing and simultaneously creating a network of both content and authors.

Another important feature of these 'do-it-yourself' web technologies is that they are usually licensed under free software licenses – so they can be installed and used for free – or/and are hosted by a provider that allows free use – often sponsoring the service through advertising. In either case, the cost for the user is restricted to a personal computer connected to the network, while the benefits are significant.

These cheap and accessible technologies:

- Provide a way for researchers and experts to easily share, make public, diffuse their findings;
- Make all information published this way easily available to anyone;
- Help tracking the author of a specific content or an idea;
- Enhance the creation of communities, where the more everyone joins a community, the richest it becomes.

The high level of economic sustainability of the PRP model is one of the main highlights. Besides the required tools, the cost of hosting services for those aiming to install free software applications to be run under their own domain is constantly decreasing. In fact, some of these services are even free, hosted in institutions (e.g. universities) or supported by advertising. Being one of the major problems that researchers face is lack of necessary funding (Brooks et al., 2005), decentralized web 2.0 tools as described above can contribute to alleviating this aspect, by providing an alternative means for researchers to circumvent costly infrastructures and formal institutions, yet allowing them join international research communities, access relevant information and make results known..

Three barriers stand in the way of widespread usage of this model in a development context. First, infrastructure: while affordable and easy access to ICTs and the Internet are pending issues around the globe, public libraries or civic centers increasingly provide free or low cost access, as do private telecentres. Although an in-depth analysis of these issues goes beyond the scope of this paper, it is worth stressing that web 2.0 technologies demand relatively low computing power (in terms of both hardware and software). A second major barrier is user capacity, which is often limited in some countries and age segments, in part due to the limited exposure to ICTs as described above. Computer skills are however increasingly addressed in political programmes,

and moreover, web 2.0 applications and social software are designed for non-technological users. Thus, even with a relatively low level of digital, technological and informational literacy can a user achieve interesting results and foster a 'conversation' (Levine et al.,1999) among peers and scholars. Third, dissimilar cultural backgrounds and different mother tongues affect the ease of knowledge flow on online fora, but this aspect extends beyond ICT-enabled interaction; moreover, precisely the adaptability of web 2.0 technologies can stimulate the formation of local communities, providing a way by which this problem can be circumvented.

A PERSONAL RESEARCH PORTAL PROTOTYPE

So what does a PRP look like? What does it involve? The underlying principle is that "instead of building new applications from scratch, [...] it makes sense to concentrate in the future on systematic combinations of existing Open Source tools for learning and competency development" (Kalz, 2005). In this light, the design and implementation process is as interesting as the goal:

The combination of e-portfolios, social networks and weblogs may have immense benefits for the learner. These tools and the ethos behind them enhance the prospect for deep learning. Creation of a learning landscape where learners engage in the whole process both academically and socially should increase the opportunity to build one's learning instead of just being the recipients of information (Tosh & Werdmuller, 2004).

A 'one minute handbook' on how to build a Personal Research Portal would include the following components:

- *Domain and hosting*: A domain name is automatically associated with specific content and its managers and contributes to the 'digital identity' of the owner, as discussed above. Hosting allows autonomous tools to be integrated into the portal, in terms of services, shape, contents and so forth; it also helps to retain autonomy and even property rights on what is uploaded to the site.

- *Content management*: Static pages and most of the dynamic ones can be built using a content management system (CMS). Drupal or Joomla are open source varieties of such systems, with the advantage that they also feature blogs. Reversely, WordPress is a blog engine that can also be used as CMS. Alternative tools are e-portfolio applications such as Elgg and OSPI.
- *Collaborative tools*: In terms of collaborative tools, the options are clear: if the expected output is content, a wiki is probably the best option. If the goal is the process, the debate itself, then discussion fora are required. Appropriate applications might include Mediawiki or TikiWiki – for the wiki – and phpBB – for the message board.
- *Bibliographical tools*: While different bibliographic managers are available, there is little consensus in terms of the best bet. However, Refbase and BibCiter fit the PRP purpose: both are web based and have RSS output. EPrints and Open Journal Systems work well for self-archiving and self-publishing, respectively.
- *Social software*: Many other applications exist to share bookmarks, photos and slide-shows, podcasts, vodcasts, etc. Most of them are online services provided – and hosted – by third parties. An important consideration when choosing such tools is their capacity to import and export a user's data and the ease by which they can be linked in a PRP.
- RSS: 'Really Simple Syndication' (RSS) is an alternative means of accessing the vast amount of information that now exists on the World Wide Web. Instead of the user browsing websites for information of interest, the information is sent directly to the user (source: epolitix.com). In any case, RSS output, as the glue of such portals (Kalz, 2005) is a must.

When connectivity is not available and a user intends to work predominantly 'locally', XAMPP[g] makes it possible to (re)install all these social software applications – in fact the whole PRP – on a hard drive or a USB pen drive. Indeed, it can work as a backup for our PRP and/or make it portable across different operating systems.

We suggest visiting the experiences of George Siemens[h], Stephen Downes[i], Helen Barrett[j] or the authors'[k] to see what we consider good examples of a PRP.

DIGITAL IDENTITY

As we have already said, one of the main problems that researchers is invisibility. This invisibility has at least two major consequences:

- Minimum awareness and recognition of their findings, fields of work, interests even existence
- Difficult access to mainstream publishing circuits, in part due to the former point

In order for researchers and their work to be recognized in academic and practitioner circles at the international level, their visibility needs to be enhanced. Setting up a PRP can thus be understood, at a primary level, as the creation of a personal home page that builds "a virtual identity insofar as it flags topics, stances and people regarded by the author as significant" (Chandler, 1998). Notwithstanding, this digital identity – or the researcher's presence in the Net – is juxtaposed to the identity shown by author-ship in paper journals and conference speeches, complementing each one the other one. While the later is strongly tied to a handful of concepts exposed in a determinate paper, the digital identity should give further information on the following aspects:

- The owner's identity (who am I);
- The owner's activities and interests (what do
- The owner's achievements (what have I done);
- The owner's contact details (where am I).

If mainstream systems – congresses, journals, seminars – act as diffusion hubs for offline identities, search engines, portals, third parties' blogs and institutional pages, signature files in e-mails (specially when placed in discussion lists and message boards) act as diffusion hubs for online identities.

Nevertheless, there are, in our opinion, two main differences among both channels:

- The higher potential reach of online media;
- The *always* up to date information provided by PRPs: If managed properly, PRPs can show the latest news about a researcher's institutional affiliation, can include recent research trends and so on. In fact, if updated pages use RSS feeds and are correctly meta-tagged, human intervention is not necessary for the changes to be echoed in specific search engines and feed aggregators.

Overall, the main component of a PRP should be evolving, up-to-date information of one's own. Search engines, are web 2.0-friendly and award high rankings to dynamic pages with rich and focused content. Descriptions about one's research and interests, side-by-side to documents and other materials – as we will now see – and links to and from other people with similar interests enhances the possibility of being found under specific keywords. This information can be created through static pages by means of simple HTML documents or, better, using a CMS – or CMS-like features from other applications such as blogs. The blogroll can play a significant part in terms of linking and networking.

Reading, Live Storing and the Public Notebook: Reinforcing Digital Identity

The research process generally involves extensive note taking, as highlights of what has been read, reflections that arise after the reading or simply as a record of the fact that something has been read. Social software empowers researchers in such a way that their notes can be "published to the World Wide Web as a way to 'display and reflect on their learning' to an audience that is broader than just their classmates" (Ittelson, 2001). Moreover, "[knowledge] only works if each person makes links as he or she browses, so writing, link creation, and browsing must be totally integrated. If someone discovers a relationship but doesn't make the link, he or she is wiser but the group is not" (Berners-Lee 2000).

Such a digital notebook – in the shape of a blog, an important part of the PRP – allows the process of reading, writing, analysis, reflection and learning to be fully public: "Eventually, there will be publications in scholarly outlets, but there are both more immediate and more long lasting benefits. In the near term, ideas can be more readily implemented, data automatically collected" (Piccoli et al., 2000). Another immediate consequence of this way of working is that "less knowledge [is] left behind" (Cohn & Hibbits, 2001), as a live digital store is created each day, a store that is categorized, searchable and fully accessible.

The PRP here "represents a space where the relationship between memory and promise, the link between past and future is made possible", understood the past as Derrida's 'trace' and the future as Ricouer's 'promise'. Hence, a factual driven dynamic identity takes place by tracking the evolving researcher. To understand more about this dynamic identity, we should go on with the way the researcher builds their own wengerian trajectory by creating new knowledge in the framework of their community[1].

This identity is reinforced by the fact that content is categorized – tagged – according to specific keywords. And, besides the fact that categorization (and 'searchability', as everything is online) can be useful to the researcher, full accessibility is the key: not only data and information are accessible everywhere and everywhen to the owner or creator of the PRP, but also to other researchers. In view of enhancing accessibility to knowledge and visibility, this can make a difference. Through its inherent characteristic of immediacy, a PRPs provide access without filters and without waits: the PRP becomes a digital store of resources, news and current events, general information, academic materials and state of the art research. It should be noted that in some countries Internet censorship can obscure this aspect; however, this is a political problem rather than a technological or conceptual one, and so goes beyond the scope of this paper.

Joining the blog as a collector of 'flow' knowledge, 'stock' knowledge can be stored to the PRP by means of a wiki – allowing all sorts of content interlinking, tagging and categorizing – or uploading files to the server, being the aim increasing the information available as a whole and enabling collaboration: "personal skills and experience are just the sort of thing which need hypertext flexibility. People can be linked to projects they have worked on, which in turn can be linked to... [etc.]" (Berners-Lee, 2000).

In this context, bibliographic tools are also worth exploring. Their purpose is to organize one's references and to ease the task of citation. Some varieties of bibliographic tools are web applications, installed on a web server and run on web browsers. This allows not only managing but publishing one's references and bibliographies.

This feature reinforces building one's digital identity by allowing cross-referencing in a body of knowledge which includes the owner of the PRP, and providing more rigour to the content shared on a PRP. A side effect is, indeed, and increased attraction for search engines which implies a better visibility on the Internet.

WRITING AND TAKING PART IN THE CONVERSATION: NETWORK BUILDING

Social software is all about meeting colleagues, exchanging impressions and collaborating. Interconnecting PRPs capitalize on this capacity by taking advantage of automated linking methods.

Of the different software varieties and perhaps even more than search engines, RSS feeds are the ones that make really possible knowledge sharing in real time. RSS feeds allow subscription – that can be selective through tags –, syndication and aggregation to new knowledge created around the world. On the other hand, RSS fosters community building in many other ways: refbacks, pingbacks and trackbacks are surely the easiest – for they are mostly automatic – way to interconnect different PRPs. While these methods contain implicit technological linking, all linkback types require an explicit conceptual linking among different researchers that takes place when one writes about the work of another one that usually reads.

"Sometimes it feels as though the discussion concerns two different nodes. The 'eportfolio' used for final assessment / job seeking where the emphasis is on the product(s) and then the 'e-portfolio' used for reflection, deep learning, knowledge growth and social interaction where the emphasis lies on the process" (Tosh & Werdmuller, 2004). It is the latter that interests us over all: citation on a PRP using social software encourages social interaction, albeit driven by technology. Social networking can further be reinforced by comments on others' PRPs or the creation of 'Friend of a friend' (FOAF)[m] files and blogrolls. Specially these last two shape a virtual research network around the PRP and, actually, around its creator. And again, the extension of this behavior among other scholars enables the 'invisible' researchers being present in the relevant (virtual) fora, being known by other investigators and meeting for the first time investigators unknown to them. The PRP can, potentially, "seamlessly link individuals to larger communities, thereby facilitating interpersonal connectivity versus fostering social isolation" (Cohn & Hibbits, 2001).

In fact, "web pages are a form of asynchronous communication, […]" and can "mediatively interact[] with other people in [one's] absence... " (Chandler, 1998). Indeed, collaboration can occur, "reducing contact time while also increasing the quality of contact time" (Roberts et al., 2005). From this perspective, PRPs "can help people to define their own success through reflection with evidence often *enhanced with peer or mentor commentary*" (Roberts et al., 2005, emphasis added). Of course, such a peer review is not the habitual double-blind review that most journals follow, and possibly lacks some of the goodness of this kind of system. On the other hand, this open peer accompanying boosts networking and collaboration far beyond anonymous readers. A higher exposure makes that:

hypotheses [can be] more easily tested, thus reducing the cost associated with research ventures and increasing productivity. Similarly new researchers can quickly be integrated into ongoing projects and make contributions to the research or production engines […]. In the long term, the external visibility of the web-based research engine will promote a shift in organizational culture toward a more open and cooperative environment where knowledge augmentation and sharing are instrumental to individual learning and organizational development. In such a culture research engine

participants will benefit from increased collaboration with qualified colleagues both within and outside the institution. (Piccoli et al., 2000)

Overall, to take part of the conversation one must speak: the blog is, probably, a perfect tool to make one's voice be heard. Mutatis mutandis, commenting and linking is the way to let others know they have been listened to. Even if collective blogs are widely used, for collaborative work wikis or online office suites might become better tools in the near future. Of course, no conversation takes place by only speaking, so a feedreader will also become a perfect companion to one's blog.

SELF-ARCHIVING, SELF-PUBLISHING

"Whilst the fundamental technical difference between the medium of speech and that of writing is that writing is automatically recorded, web pages introduce another key feature: what is written on a web page (and stored on a web-server) is automatically published" (Chandler, 1998). As mentioned above, some researchers face tough barriers to do such publishing. A tool like the PRP can help address this problem in different ways.

First of all, self-archiving of preprints and published works in a personal repository is an evident purpose for the PRPs to fulfil. Of course this does not solve the problem of access to journal publishing itself, but it does solve access to published works, both the access for researchers to content of mainstream journals and access to unpublished or non-mainstream content, often out of literature databases and indices because of their nature. A PRP will act, then, as a repository for these papers, so the output of the PRP owner can easily be found at a glance and easily consulted. "This complete openness may be an anathema to archivists and cataloguers as it abandons all attempts to control the system, but it was suggested that such an approach could greatly facilitate short term uptake [of knowledge]" (Roberts et al., 2005).

"Anathemic" or not, self-publishing goes one step further still in terms of challenging the faculty establishment, because it avoids peer review. Even so, self-publishing has its value, providing an opportunity for publication of interesting work that might otherwise remain unpublished, including peer-reviewed that might never see the light[n]. In this train of thought, works that need no review – newsletters, bulletins, opinion columns, datasets – or works that have already been reviewed – working papers, theses and other kind of dissertations – can obtain formal identifiers (ISSN or ISBN) and be published on a PRP without violating academic standards or other publishing norms. Under an open license, their publishing will contribute to increase the visibility of the author, shaping a digital identity, enriching the content of the site, making it more appealing to users and search engines and, all in all, helping any kind of research to have its place in the academic arena.

In the long run, an increased legitimacy of open access science can be expected, as its openness implies higher exposure and higher transparency in the whole reviewing and publishing process. Also, self-archiving and self-publishing undoubtedly increase the amount of scholarly literature available. The fact that the content lies on a personal repository also contributes in the strengthening of the researcher identity and network.

STATE OF THE SITUATION AND FUTURE TRENDS

As White (2007) has recently shown, there is still little but already significant use of some tools – wikis, social bookmarking, social networking, file sharing, RSS feeds, discussion forums and blogs – that are used for study or work[o], being the blog the most important among them. Even

if there is an evident age divide, it seems to be diminishing among scholars and, indeed, new generations will bring along with them the mastering of these tools.

Despite the digital divide which still restrains researchers at the digital competences level from capitalizing fully on the possibilities provided by these tools, virtual communities have demonstrated their potential for bridging capacity divides, whereby technology stewardship take place naturally, nonhierarchically yet nonchaotically. The philosophy of openness and contribution of the Web 2.0 paradigm is thus helping to bridge the same skills divide that it also contributed to create.

More than just a matter of being published, or participating in knowledge communities, it is a matter of empowering the individual with (digital) means to master their learning and research process, and the fruit of it. "Discourse technologies are among the principal means by which we reproduce the artefacts of our culture. Culture is built of contexts[.] Novel discourse technologies enabled by ICT [...] are increasingly important components of the contexts of our culture" (Roberts, 2006).

The creation of a digital identity is a means of empowerment, contributing to gaining control over one's life, but also participating equally in a globalized knowledge society. "Through [a] paper, through its form, the activity of research is dominant. [The researcher] cannot stop there, however. The act of undertaking research cannot be disengaged from the subject of research, or from the beliefs of the researcher" (Roberts, 2006). As such, the PRP – or whatever construct we made up – is, overall, an e-inclusion device. Provided there are infrastructures and skills to use them – the essential preconditions to play the game – it is possible to create a constructivist Internet where, multidirectionally, everyone and everything contributes to create a vast and public knowledge for progress.

CONCLUSION

Besides institutional efforts, we absolutely believe that there is a place for individual initiatives to try and bridge the biases and unbalances in the weight that researchers and research topics have in the international arena. And these initiatives have a perfect companion on social software tools.

As we have tried to explain, the main benefits of the Personal Research Portal are as follows:

- Build a digital identity – or a digital presence on the World Wide Web – that relies on a 'live' curriculum, and that is shaped not explicitly but through the content that 'wraps' and shapes this identity. The openness of the whole process makes it also easy for the researcher to be better positioned before search engines.
- Improve the amount of information and explicit knowledge that is available to anyone. Indeed, not only the quantity is enhanced, but the accessibility of it all: digital technologies reduce publishing costs, make content easier to find and, if the information architecture is properly designed (e.g. provides RSS feeds), makes it possible that the information actively finds the correct person, and not the contrary.
- The Personal Research Portal improves the way knowledge is managed by their owner. On one hand, it constitutes a real and public e-portfolio where all output can be stored, categorized, searched through and retrieved from anywhere. On the other hand, technology makes it also possible that this content is interlinked in many ways, thus enriching the content itself.
- Last, but not least, the Personal Research Portal contributes in building a semantic web where people and content are related one to each other. This fact helps building the researcher's network as personal and professional relationships are made explicit,

be it deliberately, by taking part in the 'conversation', or unintentionally, mediated by content and technology.

Among the main challenges that this model still faces, here are the most relevant ones:

- The digital divide at the infrastructures level makes it difficult for people with little resources to maintain the required hardware, software or connectivity quality to properly access or maintain a fully online construct as a Personal Research Portal.
- Likewise, the digital divide at the skills level is also an important barrier to overcome. And not only technological and informational illiteracies, that limit the actual access to Information and Communication Technologies, but also a minimum level of *e-awareness* to understand the possibilities and benefits of such technologies.
- Reputation and reviewing systems in the digital world still need some tweaking. While some initiatives have brought more transparency to the traditional reviewing system, and the so-called 'wisdom of crowds' have proven extraordinarily useful in specific communities (e.g. free software developers), the tested benefits of double-blind peer review has yet to find its transposition in the virtual arena.
- Tied to reputation systems, the 'infoxication' caused by the huge – and rising – amounts of information available does demand urgent solutions to distinguish relevant from irrelevant content. Even if social software has provided some interesting initiatives (e.g. social bookmarking), there still is a lot of work to be done.

Undoubtedly, the future will be digitally enhanced. Only by taking the best of both 'worlds' – the digital and the analogue one (if such a difference makes any sense) – can science respond to the requirements of society. Knowledge workers need to understand the possibilities of new technologies to increase their research output, make it broadly available, connect with other experts and, over all, bring the knowledge back to the society. Challenges are many, but they can only be overridden by looking behind with yesterday's learnings.

REFERENCES

Bangalore Declaration: A National Open Access Policy for Developing Countries. (2006). *Declaration signed in the Workshop on Electronic Publishing and Open Access*. Bangalore: Indian Institute of Science. Retrieved February 01, 2007 from http://www.ncsi.iisc.ernet.in/OAworkshop2006/pdfs/NationalOAPolicyDCs.pdf

Berlin Declaration on Open Access to Knowledge in the Sciences and Humanities. (2003). *Berlin: Max Plank Society*. Retrieved February 01, 2007 from http://oa.mpg.de/openaccess-berlin/berlin_declaration.pdf

Berners-Lee, T. (2000). *Weaving the Web*. New York: HarperCollins.

Bethesda Statement on Open Access Publishing. (2003). Chevy Chase: Peter Suber. Retrieved April 15, 2007 from http://www.earlham.edu/~peters/fos/bethesda.htm

Brooks, S., Donovan, P., & Rumble, C. (2005). Developing Nations, the Digital Divide and Research Databases. In *Serials Review*, (31), 270–278. London: Elsevier. Retrieved August 23, 2006 from http://www.sciencedirect.com/science?_ob=MImg&_imagekey=B6W63-4HGD78H-1-1&_cdi=6587&_user=4016542&_orig=search&_coverDate=12%2F31%2F2005&_sk=999689995&view=c&_alid=468268740&_rdoc=1&wchp=dGLzVlz-zSkWA&md5=aecc01d0d6d23db59291893f2c3665cb&ie=/sdarticle.pdf

Budapest Open Access Initiative. (2002). *Declaration after the Open Society Institute meeting* in Budapest December 1-2 2001. Budapest: Open Society Institute. Retrieved February 08, 2007 from http://www.soros.org/openaccess/read.shtml

Cape Town Open Education Declaration. (2007). *Cape Town: Open Society Institute*. Retrieved February 05, 2008 from http://www.capetown-declaration.org/read-the-declaration

Chan, L., & Kirsop, B. (2001). Open Archiving Opportunities for Developing Countries: towards equitable distribution of global knowledge. In *Ariadne,* (30). Bath: UKOLN. Retrieved February 01, 2007 from http://www.ariadne.ac.uk/issue30/oai-chan/

Chan, L., Kirsop, B., & Arunachalam, S. (2005). Open Access Archiving: the fast track to building research capacity in developing countries. In *SciDev.Net*, November 2005. London: SciDev. Retrieved April 25, 2006 from http://www.scidev.net/open_access/files/Open%20Access%20Archiving.pdf

Chandler, D. (1998). *Personal Home Pages and the Construction of Identities on the Web*. [online document]. Retrieved January 18, 2007 from http://www.aber.ac.uk/media/Documents/short/webident.html

Cohn, E. R., & Hibbits, B. J. (2004). Beyond the Electronic Portfolio: A Lifetime Personal Web Space. In *Educause Quarterly, 4*, 7-10. Boulder: Educause. Retrieved April 12, 2007 from http://www.educause.edu/ir/library/pdf/EQM0441.pdf

Ittelson, J. (2001). Building an E-dentity for Each Student. In *Educause Quarterly, 4*, 43-45. Boulder: Educause. Retrieved April 12, 2007 from https://www.educause.edu/ir/library/pdf/EQM0147.pdf

Kalz, M. (2005). Building Eclectic Personal Learning Landscapes with Open Source Tools. *Conference proceedings for the Open Source for*

Education in Europe, Research & Practise conference. Heerlen: Open University of the Netherlands. Retrieved April 14, 2007 from http://www.open-conference.net/viewpaper.php?id=16&cf=3

Kirsop, B., & Chan, L. (2005). Transforming Access to Research Literature for Developing Countries. In *Serials Review*, (31), 246-255. London: Elsevier. Retrieved February 01, 2007 from http://hdl.handle.net/1807/4416

Levine, F., Locke, C., Searls, D., & Weinberger, D. (1999). *The Cluetrain Manifesto*. New York: Cluetrain.

Lorenzo, G., & Ittelson, J. (2005). *An Overview of E-Portfolios*. ELI Paper 1: 2005. Boulder: Educause Learning Initiative. Retrieved July 26, 2005 from http://www.educause.edu/ir/library/pdf/ELI3001.pdf

Paton, S. (2005). *In Search of the Knowledge Worker. Labour Process Conference 2005*. Glasgow: University of Strathclyde. Retrieved April 29, 2008 from http://www.hrm.strath.ac.uk/ILPC/2005/conf-papers/Paton.pdf

Peña-López, I., Córcoles, C., & Casado, C. (2006). El Profesor 2.0: docencia e investigación desde la Red. In *UOC Papers*, (3). Barcelona: UOC. Retrieved October 10, 2006 from http://www.uoc.edu/uocpapers/3/dt/esp/pena_corcoles_casado.pdf

Peña-López, I. (2006). Position Paper for the Bazaar Seminar Hey Dude, Where's My Data? In *ICTlogy*, (37). Barcelona: ICTlogy. Retrieved October 24, 2006 from http://ictlogy.net/review/?p=471

Piccoli, G., Ahmad, R., & Ives, B. (2000). Knowledge management in academia: A proposed framework. In *Information Technology and Management, 1*(4), 229-245. Hingham: Kluwer Academic Publishers. Retrieved May 09, 2006 from http://www.springerlink.com/index/M56672931049044P.pdf

Raymond, E. S. (1999). *The Cathedral & the Bazaar*. (revised edition: original edition 1999). Sebastopol: O'Reilly.

Roberts, G., Aalderink, W., Cook, J., Feijen, M., Harvey, J., Lee, S., & Wade, V. P. (2005). *Reflective learning, future thinking: digital repositories, e-portfolios, informal learning and ubiquitous computing*. Briefings from the ALT/SURF/ILTA Spring Conference Research Seminar. Dublin: Trinity College. Retrieved April 12, 2007 from http://www.surf.nl/download/ALT_SURF_ILTA_white_paper_2005%20(2).pdf

Roberts, G. (2006). "MyWORLD e-Portfolios: Activity and Identity". In *Brookes eJournal of Learning and Teaching, 1*(4). Oxford: Brookes University. Retrieved April 12, 2007 from http://www.brookes.ac.uk/publications/bejlt/volume1issue4/perspective/roberts.pdf

Rossi, P. G., Pascucci, G., Giannandrea, L., & Paciaroni, M. (2006). L'e-Portfolio Come Strumento per la Costruzione dell'Identità. In *Informations, Savoirs, Décisions, Médiations*, (25), art.348. La Garde: Université du Sud Toulon-Var. Retrieved April 12, 2007 from http://isdm.univ-tln.fr/PDF/isdm25/RossiPascucciGiannandreaPaciaroni_TICE2006.pdf

Salvador Declaration on Open Access: the developing world perspective. (2005). *Declaration signed in the International Seminar Open Access for Developing Countries*. Salvador: BIREME/PAHO/WHO. Retrieved February 01, 2007 from http://www.eifl.net/docs/Dcl-Salvador-OpenAccess-en.pdf

Suber, P. (2005). *Open Access Overview*. Retrieved April 28, 2005 from http://www.earlham.edu/~peters/fos/overview.htm

Suber, P., & Arunachalam, S. (2005). Open Access to Science in the Developing World. In *World-Information City*, October 17, 2005. Tunis: WSIS. Retrieved February 01, 2007 from http://www.earlham.edu/~peters/writing/wsis2.htm

Tosh, D., & Werdmuller, B. (2004). *Creation of a learning landscape: weblogging and social networking in the context of e-portfolios.* [online document]. Retrieved April 14, 2007 from http://eduspaces.net/dtosh/files/7371/16865/Learning_landscape.pdf

White, D. (2007). *Results of the 'Online Tool Use Survey' undertaken by the JISC funded SPIRE project.* Oxford: David White. Retrieved March 19, 2007 from http://tallblog.conted.ox.ac.uk/index.php/2007/03/16/some-real-data-on-web-20-use

KEY TERMS

Blogroll: Is the list of blogs that a *blogger* usually reads or specially likes. A dynamic list – as tastes and subjects change along time – it can be understood as an explicit representation of one's personal network of colleagues (reciprocal or not) and interests.

Comments: in this chapter, with *comments* we refer to the feature that some blogs and news sites have to write your reflections on a piece of content. In formal frameworks, these comments are usually signed and include a link to the commenter's web site. In the *blogosphere*, post-to-post and comment-to-post are rich ways in which exchange of ideas and debate take place.

E-Awareness: a part of digital literacy, we think of e-awareness as the most conceptual and strategic of digital skills. It can be defined as the ability to understand the *real* impact of the changes brought by the Information Society in one's context. At another level, e-Awareness would also imply foreseeing and anticipating such changes, either to avoid or smooth their impact, or to benefit from them by adapting one's behaviour.

Feed Readers: are applications that, from a user's point of view, work in very similar ways as e-mail readers do. They 'ask' a (subscribed) web site for new content and display it to the user if new content is found. The main benefit is that the user needs not browsing each and every web site and guess what the new content is.

Linkbacks, Pingbacks, Trackbacks and Refbacks: Linkbacks (general term for three methods: pingbacks, trackbacks and refbacks) help website owners to be aware of who has linked to their site. In our case, these methods are relevant to engage in the 'conversation' and discover people interested in the subjects dealt with in a PRP.

Open Science and Open Research: often treated as synonyms, Open Science is a movement that promotes open access to content by digital means, the use of free software / open source applications to conduct research and the free availability of data sets (open data) used in this research. Besides philosophical considerations, many authors have stated evidence of better performance and more benefits for researchers being 'open'. The PRP is fully in line with this way of thinking, as it promotes maximum transparency and sharing.

RSS: usually based in XML technologies (though not only), an RSS feed is a content format that, among other things, tells machines – not humans – when a website was updated and what the new content is.

Web/Remote vs. Local Technologies: Web 2.0 applications are, by definition, hosted in web servers (i.e. not in a desktop) that are remotely accessed through a web browser. This usually implies permanent connection to the Internet. Nevertheless, some of these applications can be used locally (i.e. in a desktop or laptop) by replicating the installed setup of a web server (this is what XAMPP does – see note vii). This allows content being accessible without an Internet connection and, in some cases, to synchronized it with the remote database once the connection is re-established.

ENDNOTES

[a] For both an introduction about knowledge workers and the distinction between information, knowledge and the different kinds of knowledge being, please see Patton (2005). In our case, we will be using most times information and knowledge as quite synonyms,

[b] A very interesting summary on OA for Development can be found in Chan et al. (2005).

[c] See for instance Chan et al. 2005

[d] For an interesting overview, see, for instance, Kirsop and Chan (2005)

[e] Adapted from Chan et al. (2005).

[f] These definitions adapted from Peña-López (2006).

[g] XAMPP is an Apache distribution that can be installed in one's desktop. In other words, this means that web applications – such as blogs, wikis and other Web 2.0 applications – can be run offline in a web browser.

[h] http://elearnspace.org

[i] http://downes.ca

[j] http://electronicportfolios.com

[k] http://ICTlogy.net

[l] These quotations and more about the concepts by Derrida, Ricoeur and Wegner can be found at Rossi et al. (2006).

[m] "Friend Of A Friend (FOAF) is an XML standard that allows website owners to define who they are as well as their relationships with other website owners – effectively creating a wide area social network" (Tosh & Werdmuller, 2004). Again, the point is not technology but the social networking uses.

[n] Think, for instance, of working papers or drafts for research projects that actually went through a peer review that, institutionally, lack of publishing interest, but that can provide useful insight about the reflections and making off that, later on, ended coming up with interesing results.

[o] It is relevant to notice that, as the sample of the survey mostly belonged to Oxford University, it is probably not wrong to understand "work" as "academic work" or "work performed by scholars". Even if this work is not research, what is relevant in this case is not the use but the user, and the fact that he or she is skilled in these tools.

Chapter XXVII
Ambient Pedagogies, Meaningful Learning and Social Software

Andrew Ravenscroft
London Metropolitan University, UK

Musbah Sagar
London Metropolitan University, UK

Enzian Baur
London Metropolitan University, UK

Peter Oriogun
American University of Nigeria, Nigeria

ABSTRACT

This chapter will present a new approach to designing learning interactions and experiences that reconciles relatively stable learning processes with relatively new digital practices in the context of social software and Web 2.0. It will begin with a brief position on current educational articulations of social software before offering some theoretical pointers and methodological perspectives for research and development in this area. The authors will then explain how an ongoing initiative in advanced learning design has developed notions of "ambient learning design" and "experience design" to address these issues and describe a new methodology for developing digital tools that incorporate these concepts. This approach is exemplified through ongoing work within an initiative in Digital Dialogue Games and the InterLoc tool that realises them. Finally, the implications this work has for future trends in designing for inclusive, highly communicative and engaging learning interactions and practices for the digital age are discussed.

INTRODUCTION

One of the problems with recent educational articulations of social software and Web 2.0 is the misalignment of social practices that are ostensibly oriented towards and motivated by 'interest' with those that are oriented towards and motivated by 'learning'. This has been demonstrated in many ongoing projects, such as those supported by the UK JISC (Joint Information Systems Committee), although there is little mature research in this area as yet. Whilst these purposes and the practices they entail are not mutually exclusive, they often involve different processes of meaning making. In learning situations there is usually a defined or identifiable context, that may be organised or emergent, which involves some management, structure or scaffolding. This operates as an 'interaction narrative', and is usually required to promote suitable sorts of thinking, collaborative meaning making and content assimilation and generation that corresponds to learning. In other words, whilst specific practices such as personal content creation and expression, communication, media sharing, multimodal dialogue and social networking are relevant to communities of interest and learning, these will usually be orchestrated differently in both. And furthermore, understanding these differences is important if we want to harmonise interest driven informal learning with more formal learning activities, given that all these activities are now increasingly performed within the same digital landscape. So a question we are tackling in this Chapter is: What forms of contextualisation and support are needed with more open and social software to stimulate, catalyse and realise meaning making that corresponds with attested notions of learning through social interaction and dialogue?

Based on substantial previous work emphasising the centrality of dialogue in learning (e.g. Vygotsky, 1978; Mercer, 2000; Ravenscroft, 2001, Wegerif, 2007) and particularly in the context of promoting productive conceptual change (e.g. Hartley, 1998; Ravenscroft and Pilkington, 2000) we hold that a key component in social networking and communication for learning will be the quality, educational efficacy and general value of the dialogue and media-rich interaction between digital interlocutors. Indeed, it may be the case that the degree of learning that occurs with open and social software corresponds to the quality of the multimodal dialogues that are being performed. But how can we design for these inclusive and valuable multimodal learning dialogues? Or more generally: how can we embrace and exploit the opportunities offered by open digital technologies to support contemporary approaches to dialogue, thinking and meaning making in ways that support new and relevant learning practices? When we start to unpack these questions we have to address some additional emphases that characterise contemporary digital practices, such as participation and collaboration, and the production of shared and yet more provisional knowledge representations.

The remainder of this Chapter will present theoretical pointers, a research and development perspective, and a specific approach and methodology to design that aims to address these questions. This work is based on the notion that we will typically need to introduce some appropriate organisation and structure to direct learning whilst 'working with' students developing digital literacies. Or for learning we will usually need some pedagogically derived and 'managed openness' to support meaningful learning practices We will then show how this approach is realised through an ongoing initiative in Digital Dialogue Games.

BACKGROUND

Before launching into contemporary approaches to designing learning interaction for the digital age it is useful to consider what fundamental learning processes and practices at which we are looking to emphasise and foster meaningful learning experiences. In considering this challenge Ravenscroft, Wegerif and Hartley (2007) have recently argued for a re-conceptualisation of 'learning dialogue' through developing and synthesising notions of *dialectic* and *dialogic*. Their arguments that are relevant to this article are summarised below.

Dialectic and Learning

The dialectic that was used by Socrates (470-399 BC) during what has become known as 'the Socratic method' is one of the earliest recorded educational approaches, which is also receiving considerable attention in contemporary education through computer-mediated tutorial approaches used by Bjork (2001). Hegel (1770-1831) turned dialectic into a more abstract notion of a dynamic logic proceeding from thesis to antithesis and then synthesis. Hegel's approach rested on a coherence theory of truth, where the truth relies not on a single proposition but a whole system of propositions, and only within this complete system can contradictions be recognised and falsity removed. Similarly, the process of synthesis preserves the rational and removes the irrational but then also provides another thesis that can become the subject of the same triadic process, and so on. So for Hegel, although "The true is the whole", this is a developing whole that develops through contradiction. Applying Hegel's dialectic Marx argued that culture and consciousness arise as 'tools' in the dialectic interaction between humans and nature. Vygotsky took this as a model of how an individual consciousness is formed through the internalisation of tools. So Vygotsky's (1978) theory of the development of higher mental processes can remain a foundation and inspiration for approaches to technology enhanced learning that emphasise collaborative, argumentative and reflective discourses, along the lines that have

been emphasised by Mercer (2000), Ravenscroft (2001, 2004) and Wertsch (1991). However, we now need to take full account of the mediational power offered by new and evolving digital tools and semiotic systems.

Dialogic and Learning

Bakhtin (1986), a contemporary of Vygotsky, argued that dialectic had become over formalised and we needed to return to real dialogues because logic itself has no meaning, holding that it is only the clash of different voices that gives meaning. So he opposed what he called 'Hegel's monological dialectic' with his notion of dialogic that refered to the interanimation of real voices where there is no necessary 'overcoming' or 'synthesis' (Wegerif, 1999). Following Wertsch the socio-cultural approach has tended not to recognise this and combine together two notions of mediation, Vygotskys account of mediation by tools including words as sign-tools (dialectic) and Bakhtin's account of mediation by the voices and perspectives of others (dialogic). While mediation by tools is not incompatible with mediation by the perspective of the other person and both happen in education, it is important to point out that these are different kinds of mediation, that can be conceived as different dimensions, or features, of the dialogue process. For each participant in a dialogue the voice of the other is an outside perspective that includes them within it. The boundary between subjects is not therefore a demarcation line, or an external link between self and other, but an inclusive 'space' within which self and other mutually construct and re-construct each other. So, as emphasised by Wegerif (2006), a dialogic approach to learning considers that the main mechanism for learning is taking the perspective of another in a dialogue, where the dialogue is an end to be valued in itself as perhaps the most important goal of education. Recently, Wegerif (2007) has argued powerfully for this perspective to 'expand the spaces of learning' through digital technologies and emphasised that it's not just the use of explicit reasoning but the ability to change one's mind and see things from a new perspective that is essential for learning.

Dialectic or Dialogic? Relative Dimensions for Learning Dialogue and Meaning Making

Ravenscroft, Wegerif and Hartley (2007) also questioned the relationship between these two characterisations of dialogue. Do they work together or in opposition? The work of Ravenscroft and his colleagues in designing dialogue games for conceptual change in science (e.g. Ravenscroft & Hartley, 1996; Ravenscroft & Pilkington, 2000; Ravenscroft & Matheson, 2004) has shown that an argumentative and dialectical approach was needed for a student and tutor to achieve a synthesis around a correct conceptual understanding of the physics of motion. In contrast Wegerif (2006) has argued and demonstrated that in some circumstances, especially when dealing with younger children and those with emotional and behavioural problems, a more dialogic approach, with its emphasis on 'taking the perspective of another' is more important than progression towards some sort of synthesis around a common understanding. So considering their previous work collectively, they argued that dialectic and dialogic are two relative dimensions that are not in opposition, as they focus on different yet equally important features of the dialogue process relevant to learning. Dialectic emphasises the epistemic and cognitive dimensions of learning that are realised through social processes that occur when an appropriate dialogic state is established. Dialogic emphasises emotional and interpersonal dimensions, or the sort of 'relationships' and 'intersubjective orientations' (Habermas, 1991) that enable the spaces where learning can happen. These are a complementary emphasis. The desire to reason

to progress towards a rational synthesis does not have to override the need to understand others, and likewise, the desire to understand others does not have to override that pragmatic need to reach a rational consensus that links to purposeful action in a context. The two will always interplay and vary in emphasis based on what is wanted from a learning situation.

"To paraphrase Kant (Kant, 1781/1982, A 51/ B75): dialectic without dialogic is blind (as in machine cognition), dialogic relations without dialectic is empty of content (as in the mother child couple): it is through their union that new shared understandings can arise." Ravenscroft, Wegerif and Hartley (2007), p 47

Contemporary Contexts for Learning

An essential point that is entailed by the argument made above is that through social and more open technologies we are creating new spaces and contexts which have the potential for dialectic and dialogic learning through new and developing digital literacies. These contexts can often be conceived as 'democratic spaces' that are either generated or populated by the users, whose relationships mediate learning as much as the processes and tools that are in play. These contexts are clearly creating new forms of intersubjective orientations where learning can happen, that are shaped through open participation, collaboration, multimodal language, the provisionality of representations and could potentially contribute, generally, to a more 'democratic epistemology'. So drawing together the relations we have introduced in connection with dialogue, thinking and the potentially empowering role of social software - our position is similar to that of Friere (2001).

"To think correctly implies the existence of subjects whose thinking is mediated by objects that provoke and modify the thinking subject. Thinking

correctly is, in other words, not an isolated act or something to draw in isolation but an act of communication...For this reason, a correct way of thinking is dialogical not polemical." (Friere, 2001, p 42-43)

So in embracing these new (social software) contexts and possibilities, our position also aligns with what tends to be called 'egalitarian dialogue', which foregrounds the assessment of contributions in terms of the validity of the arguments presented rather than according to any power positions of those who advocate them. The remainder of this article will attempt to demonstrate how we can design to support well attested and fundamental approaches to thinking, learning and meaning making through exploiting learners developing digital literacies and practices. Where a key question is: how can we create or support, through design, the pedagogical contexts that realise contemporary forms of learning and digital meaning making? A first step in this process is identifying a suitable research and development perspective that is capable of working in harmony with the rapid evolutions in technologies and related practices that typify the digital age.

DESIGN-BASED RESEARCH FOR CONTEMPORARY LEARNING INTERACTION AND PRACTICE

A central tenet of design-based research, relevant to the work described in the rest of this article, is:

*The challenge of design-based research is in flexibly developing research trajectories that meet our dual goals of refining locally valuable innovations and developing more globally usable knowledge for the field. (*Design Based Research Collective, Educational Researcher, 2003, p.7).

In the context of the work described in the rest of this article, the locally valuable innovations we will consider are digital dialogue games (Ravenscroft and McAlister, 2006a, Ravenscroft, 2007) and the InterLoc (Collaborative *Inter*action through scaffolding *Loc*utions) tools that implement them (Ravenscroft & McAlister, 2006b, Ravenscroft, Sagar and Baur, 2007). The latter of these is described and discussed later. More generic insights about the dialogue processes required for learning and conceptual development have been provided through discourse analysis and dialogue modelling methods that are embodied by these tools or led to their development, along with the evaluations of the delivered designs (e.g. Ravenscroft 2000; Ravenscroft and Matheson, 2002; McAlister, Ravenscroft and Scanlon, 2004b; Ravenscroft, McAlister & Baur, 2006).

But a key additional argument for adopting design-based research in our digital age is that it can allow us to fully articulate the role of technology as a mediating tool for social and intellectual development, rather than seeing technology as the organisational 'means' to deliver traditional learning. Given the increasingly pervasive nature of technology, an approach which considers design-based research within a sociocultural scientific frame (e.g. Vygotsky, 1978; Wertsch, 1991; Engestrom, 1987) is particularly powerful for investigating and promoting contemporary learning. This stance emphasises the mediating role of technological tools and social relationships that these tools may operate within or give rise to in the context of contemporary learning practices. So this perspective is particularly relevant to the development of dialogue and social software and the ways these are articulated within the learning landscape.

Following this approach and building on their discourse analysis work (e.g. Pilkington, 1999) Ravenscroft and Pilkington (2000) developed the methodology of "investigation by design" (hereafter IBD) to investigate educational dialogue and design models that support reasoned discourse leading to conceptual change and development. This method combines discourse analysis and other dialogue game techniques (e.g. Levin and Moore, 1977; MacKenzie, 1979; Walton, 1984) to specify models that can be implemented as digital tools. These game designs and tools are developed through modelling key social and pragmatic level features of effective dialogue interaction, such as the roles of the interlocutors (e.g. learning manager, facilitator, player), the ground rules for commitment and turn-taking, and the type of speech-acts (Searle, 1969) that may be performed (e.g. assertion, question, challenge). The dialogue games that are developed, whilst sharing the same categories of features (e.g. pre-defined goals, numbers of players, roles, moves and rules, etc.) are distinctive in terms of the actual configurations of these features. They are also different in terms of the particular learning problems they address (e.g. critical, creative or exploratory dialogue) and the learning processes they support whilst retaining certain 'family resemblances' (Wittgenstein, 1953). The methodology has been successfully used to design a number of digital dialogue game tools (e.g. DIALAB, CoLLeGE, CLARISSA, AcademicTalk and InterLoc) that, along with a more detailed explanation of the IBD and dialogue game approach, are given in Ravenscroft (2007). This educationally and socially derived definition and articulation of games is justified in some detail and contrasted with 'video-game' approaches (e.g. Prensky, 2001; Gee, 2003) in Ravenscroft and McAlister (2006a), and our conception of dialogue games is illustrated in some detail later in this Chapter, in the sections that demonstrate how our InterLoc tool realises them. This technology creates contexts and process-oriented learning designs to support and scaffold collective inquiry, critical thinking and collaborative argumentation through the orchestration of social games that are performed synchronously amongst small groups

(of 4 – 8 students). These environments are inclusive and personalised, and yet, also provide structuring and scaffolding, through pre-defined features and rules of interaction - that follow well-established pedagogical frameworks derived from sociocultural and dialogue theory that were referred to earlier. This and earlier dialogue game tools, such as AcademicTalk, have been used and evaluated in a range of Higher Education contexts, from ODL to campus-based institutions (e.g. see Ravenscroft, 2007 for a review).

The latest tools have been produced through a refinement of the IBD methodology. This has involved introducing new concepts of 'ambient pedagogy' (realised through ambient learning designs) and 'experience design' whilst also considering recent research into more personalised approaches to learning design that are suitable for the technology enabled learner (Ravenscroft and Cook, 2007) and their widespread use of social software. So the IBD approach has been extended to support the design of contemporary learning practices that are suitable for social, inclusive and participative approaches within the social software and Web 2.0 landscape. In essence, this has represented an elaboration of pedagogical process design into a more experiential pedagogical practice and context design. However, to signal any potential misconceptions, note that our approach to design needs to be considered within a broader frame than the existing family of social software and conceptions of Web 2.0. Our emphasis on designing highly inclusive, social and collaborative learning is intended to harmonise with developing digital literacies in the context of social software rather than being predicated upon their specific aims and functionality, that can be quite narrow (e.g. based around social networking and media sharing). To clarify this position we will demonstrate how this perspective and methodology is being applied within our ongoing multi-partner dialogue game initiative (see www.interloc.org). This 'serious gaming' approach is inclusive, social and collaborative, and yet focussed on the fundamental need to structure and scaffold learning dialogues that support types of thinking and meaning making that are relevant within the digital landscape and conveyed through the production of a 'collaborative text'. These texts (see Figures 2 and 3 later) are more formal than records of unstructured Chat or dialogue that is typical in conferencing software, and yet are less formal – in terms of textual representation - than a typical wiki or blog, and they are significant in that they capture 'live thinking'. So they can provide unique intermediary representations between collaborative thinking and thoughtful writing. Our approach is also motivated by research that has highlighted the difficulty of supporting truly engaging, critical and reasoned learning dialogue (McAlister, Ravenscroft and Scanlon, 2004a,) combined with the potential of new technologies to help remedy this (e.g. Wegerif, 2007). Note also that this approach does not deny the value of social software as platforms for generating and sharing diverse ideas and media. It instead, attempts to harmonise with these practices and yet manage and coordinate them along pedagogical lines in ways that lead to more focussed and coherent interaction and meaning making that aligns with learning. In a sense, the current dialogue game approach is a way of generating and capturing thinking on the net in ways that realise and satisfy accepted ambitions for learning that also 'sits with' more informal and media driven digital practices with social software.

Ambient Pedagogy and Experience Design

In succinct terms: ambient pedagogy holds that the structure or scaffolding supporting the learning interaction is 'behind the scenes' and yet also implicit in the digital practice that is supported; and, 'experience design' emphasises that the learning occurs through the production of an experiential context, in contrast to foregrounding

the management of instruction and pedagogical or learning design. Of course we are not saying that we should literally aim to directly design experiences, instead the term is meant to be interpreted more circumspectly, as 'design that aims to give rise to a particular type of learning experience', that bears some significant similarities with other, typically less formal activities with social software.

Our initial design principles that represent this approach are:

1. Realise digital naturalism: Build on and integrate with developing social software and practices that are familiar to learners, so their educational interaction 'feels like' a natural digital practice.

2. Consider proximal practices: Support highly social, communicative, relevant and engaging experiences that are in harmony with learners' commonplace informal digital behaviour.

3. Emphasise semi-formal activities that reconcile organisational and personal activities and requirements (or constrain interaction for a purpose).

4. Provide flexible, open and yet configurable experiences, or 'managed and structured openness'.

5. Make the complex simple: Design interfaces that incorporate narrative and contingent features, so users only experience the interactions and contexts that are relevant to them. In other words, do not expose the full complexities of the machine, but instead emphasise the experiences that functionalities give rise to.

Note that this approach should not be considered as a simple 'layer above' conventional notions of learning design, but instead considered as a philosophy incorporated into the learning and interaction design process. The following sections demonstrate how these principles are articulated through a design based research initiative in digital dialogue games for learning.

DIGITAL DIALOGUE GAMES: A DESIGN-BASED APPROACH TO DIGITAL LEARNING DIALOGUE

Our Dialogue Game approach has proven efficacy for a range of learning problems and contexts, as documented in a range of research projects over the past ten years that are summarised in Ravenscroft (2007). It is currently realised through the Open Source tool, called InterLoc that realises the dialogue games through creating and organising a suitable learning context and mediating learning processes through supporting a structured practice and a unique method of collaborative text production. This approach has been supported through three successive multi-partner projects over the past three years (see www.interloc.org). The current project that is supported by the UK JISC and has partners at London Metropolitan University, UK Open University, Universities of Exeter and Teesside and, Queen Mary (University of London).

InterLoc3: Attractive, Inclusive and Reusable Learning Dialogues

Our current dialogue game technology, Interloc3, embodies the need to reconcile learners developing digital literacies with the well-established requirements for reasoned and purposeful dialogue. Specifically, through incorporating the notions of 'ambient pedagogy' and 'experience design' we have provided a managed and yet attractive and inclusive learning context and experience that provides a structured, collaborative and engaging learning practice. This practice, in turn, allows learners to incorporate media and generate text and content that are relevant and valuable through linking their digital dialogue to their thinking and

the production of collaborative and personalised texts or knowledge assets. So this practice aims to link learners interest-driven, and typically media-centric behaviours, to more learning-driven dialogue and textual practices. There is also the incorporation of multimodal and multimedia aspects into learning interactions to further enrich the learning experience.

In brief, InterLoc3 is Web-technology with low barriers to participation that is easily used and deployed to address relatively generic learning problems and opportunities. So it is pedagogically inclusive and technically pervasive[1]. In the pedagogical sense, it is inclusive because its ease of operation means that virtually any learner or tutor is capable of using it to support digital learning dialogues and linking these to related learning and pedagogical practices. In the technical sense, it is pervasive because it is easily deployed, is cross platform, and is flexible and extensible. The way that these features are operationalised in the InterLoc3 design and the practices it supports are given later, after briefly describing the technical model that implements them.

Technical Model and Realisation

To address these requirements (above) in the context of a distributed and collaborative application involved the development of a new methodology involving four related layers:

1. Client-server architecture, based on Jabber messaging protocol (sophisticated Open Source messaging protocol);
2. JAVA application programming (for sophisticated learning and interaction design);
3. HTML interface (for a natural and attractive user-experience);
4. Client deployed through Web-start technology (for flexible and robust deployment, e.g. from within institutional infrastructures).

Further details of how the design is technically realised is given in Ravenscroft, Sagar and Baur (2007a). Adopting this development approach and methodology allowed us to develop a sophisticated Web-technology that is easily deployed and feels like a typical 'Web experience'. The design was derived, ostensibly, from two different and yet typical Web-experiences; the first being the use of the Web in the normal sense of the word - such as Web browsing, social networking etc., and the second based on the use of Instant Messaging applications.

The way in which the interface design has taken into account the experience most Web users have with Instant Messaging applications (IM software) is shown in Figures 1 and 3. Users who are familiar with applications like MSN, Yahoo and Skype find using InterLoc extremely easy since the interaction builds on these experiences. As an example, IM users expect to be presented with a simple login page which requires the input of usernames and passwords before gaining access and being presented with content. While logged in, users expect to view the status (online/offline) of their friends (other users) and to be able to communicate informally with them (InterLoc provides an informal chat feature to support this aspect). Also, the layout of the dialogue window (the main venue where the communication between participants is taking place) has typical layout where an upper part is used to present the communication that's taking place (the actual contributions) and a lower part allows the player to enter their contributions to the discussion. InterLoc3 was designed to take into account such subtle layout and design familiarity with 'similar' applications to accommodate the realisation of its design. This allows new users to quickly learn the 'interaction basics' that allow them to increase the sophistication of their dialogue game practices in a cumulative way.

InterLoc3: Interface Design for Organising and Playing the Dialogue Games

Essentially, through following the methodology above InterLoc3 incorporates the same proven pedagogy as previous dialogue game tools (e.g. Interloc1, see Ravenscroft and McAlister 2006b), but has re-engineered this into the Web-technology that realises ambient pedagogy and experience design, so it is more pervasive, intuitive and attractive than previous designs that made their learning design more explicit. Put simply, InterLoc3 makes its complex learning and interaction designs look and feel simple.

Roles and Setting the Learning Context

Users of InterLoc are assigned one of three roles, namely Learning Manager, Facilitator or Player. The Learning Manager, who is usually a tutor, takes the initiative to set the context for the dialogue games through assigning the roles, selecting any preparatory materials, deciding on a specific dialogue game and setting a question, or questions, that seed the game. Once the users login - using the username and password that has been assigned to them - they are presented with the interfaces that reflect the rights for their role and the functionality that is specific to their role. So for the players - logging in takes them to a realisation of the context and (ambient) learning design that has been set up for them. This is typically a number of preparation materials and media along with the particular dialogue game that has been selected or configured for them. This demonstrates how InterLoc provides the means to realise flexible, open and yet configurable learning experiences.

A user with a Facilitator role sees the same interfaces presented to players in addition to being able to broadcast a message to all players to

Figure 1. The activity screen

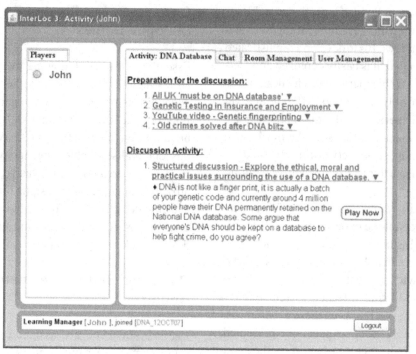

manage the synchronous game. Figure 1 shows an Activity screen for a discussion topic about using and storing DNA. Here John is a Learning Manager because he has access to Room Management and User Management in addition to having Activity and Chat screens – that are available to all user roles

The above example shows how the contextual aspects of the ambient pedagogy are set through linking the preparation tasks to a suitable dialogue game. This activity uses four preparation tasks associated with the topic of DNA testing, but the Learning Manager could use more or less depending on the preparation requirements. Most dialogue games require such preparation, to give the learners sufficient prior knowledge and understanding, or grounding, to perform an engaging and meaningful dialogue game. The second part of the screen displays the actual question, which seeds this dialogue game entered through

selecting the "Play Now" button. Typically players will perform the preparation asynchronously, in advance of the scheduled game activity, in their own time. The bottom window pane displays the participant's role and status.

Playing the Dialogue Game

The interface in Figure 2 shows how each player performs the dialogue game. They can either Contribute to the current state of the developing dialogue through selecting "Make Contribution" or Reply to a specific previous contribution by selecting "Reply". Contributing to the dialogue places a response at the bottom of the display and Replying indents the responses below the specific contribution that is replied to - in a threaded way. This model contains affordances that achieve a balance of 'keeping the dialogue moving forward' whilst allowing reflective asides and specific re-

Figure 2. The Interloc3 Interface: Realising ambient pedagogy and experience design

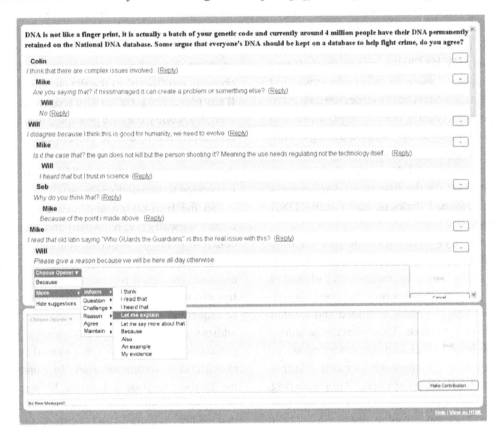

sponses to previous contributions. So players need to distinguish whether they are "Contributing" to the developing dialogue (using the large reply bar at the bottom), typically responding to the latest 'state of the dialogue', or replying to a specific previous contribution (by selecting "Reply" next to each contribution). Also, all contributions or replies are made using the pre-defined Move categories (Inform, Question, Challenge etc.) and the specific locution openers ("I think…", "I disagree because…", "Let me elaborate…" etc.) that have to be used to perform the dialogue. Similarly, rules about the legitimate and logical responding openers, based on the specific Openers that are replied to, are offered selectively - but these can be overridden to select the full range of options

through selecting "More". For example Figure 2 shows a player called Seb[2] deciding to access the full range of moves and openers through selecting "More" instead of using "Because…" - which is the prompted response to the "Please give a reason…" opener.

This interface shows how the adoption of html, CSS and common design colours and idioms (e.g. threading, menu operation and expansion boxes) ensures the dialogue game experience is attractive and 'feels like' a typical and intuitive Web experience and realises our principles of 'Realise digital naturalism'. Similarly, it operationalises the principle of 'Consider proximal practices' through supporting a style of interaction that builds on students experiences with technologies like MSN and Skype.

Figure 2 also shows how the structuring and scaffolding works. It shows Seb replying to a previous contribution by Will – who has requested a reason for a position offered by Mike. So Seb has responded to Will's Challenging move of "Please give a reason…" using an Informing move "Let me explain…" and is about to enter the content of his response. Even this brief excerpt, which was taken from a user-test performed during a workshop with members of the Learning Technology Research Institute (LTRI), most of whom were using InterLoc for the first time, demonstrates coherent reasoned dialogue about using DNA technology.

This activity started with all players watching a video about Genetic fingerprinting on YouTube, which was the third preparation activity listed in Figure 1. Figure 2 shows how the question that seeds the dialogue game is bolded and located at the top of the screen. This interchange shows how in addition to the Challenge described above the dialogue game approach supports features such as a clarification requests - "Are you saying that?…", reasoned disagreements - "I disagree because…", various probing questions – "Is it the case that?…", "Why do you think that?…", and referring to evidence – "I read that…". So it should also be clear how this learning and interaction design is semi-formal in nature, in that is supports a scholarly practice that is realised in an engaging way and linked to the types of digital assets that students may frequently use for either informal or formal learning.

Turn-Taking and 'Listening'

To ensure the dialogues remain coherent a turn-taking model is employed, that is shown in Figure 3, which allows each player to 'hold the floor' whilst making a response, which is automatically signalled to the other players, 'blocks out' other responses to the same contribution and generally allows the dialogue to be logically and coherently displayed and managed. So this feature is a good exemplification of our principle of 'Make the complex simple', as without it we would have confusing dialogues and a confusing representation of them. This also means that players don't 'rush' to make their contributions, and instead observe and 'listen' to the developing dialogue. If any player holds the turn for too long (e.g. more than 90 seconds) they are prompted to Contribute or Cancel, and of course players can always attend to another contribution if the specific one they wanted to reply to is in the process of being responded to by another player.

So the turn-taking and awareness features ensure logically (i.e. reasoned) and sequentially coherent dialogue is performed and sequential incoherence (e.g. that is experienced with chat) is avoided. This leads to a more considered, reflective and thoughtful dialogue. Note that problems of sequential and semantic incoherence that are addressed by the InterLoc design are significant problems in virtually all other tools that support synchronous communication. In contrast this mechanism realises a balance between fairly managed dialogue and a 'pace of interaction' that leads to thoughtful and yet 'forward moving' dialogue. In Figure 3 we can see what Colin and the other players observe when Seb is making the response referred to in Figure 2. which 'locks out' the Contribution input field for the selected reply for all players of the game until he has finished.

To summarise the interchange in Figure 2 and 3, which although brief, demonstrates how collaborative arguments, and texts, are developed through InterLoc. Colin initiates the dialogue (about storing and using DNA) using "I think…" to assert that there are complex issues involved. Mike replies to this using "Are you saying that…" to probe what these complex issues might be, which Will then disagrees with by saying "No". Will then contributes using "I disagree because…" to explain he's in favour of using DNA technology because it shows 'evolution in humanity'. Mike then replies to this using "Is it the case that…" to question and suggest that its not the technology itself but the people using it that need regulating. Will replies to this with "I heard that…" to acknowledge Mike's point but affirm his own position. Seb then contributes using "Why do you think that…" to question the points made by Mike, who refers him to previous contributions and uses "I read that…" to elaborate his position in terms of "Who GUards the Guardians". This stimulates Will to reply to Mike's contribution, using "Please give a reason…" to press Mike to clarify his position, who then does so using "Let me explain…". A number of previous papers (McAlister, Ravenscroft and Scanlon, 2004a; Ravenscroft and McAlister, 2006a, 2006b) give a considerable number of longer and more varied dialogue game interactions along with their analysis and evaluation.

Saving, Replaying and Reusing the Dialogues

As the content of the dialogue games can be saved as a html file – it forms a valuable learning resource that contains a collaborative, structured and semi-formal textual argument. This may be used as personal notes, the pre-cursor to an essay or assessment exercise, or as content that could be posted to another forum, a blog or a wiki. The html format can de replayed using a standard text to speech translator, such as the one freely available with the Opera browser. This provides an accessible 'replay' facility that can be performed after the dialogue games so that players can decide whether to further manipulate or edit the generated content. Of course, this replay facility

Figure 3. Turn-taking and listening

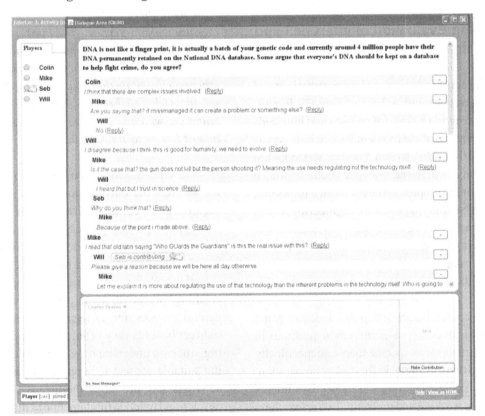

could be performed via a Web-enabled mobile phone. This flexibility, across platform, device and modality also demonstrates our principles of 'Realise digital naturalism' and 'Consider proximal practices'.

Amending the Pre-Defined Dialogue Games

Note that all the textual contents contained in the Menus that realise the dialogue games are read in from xml files and so can be easily edited and amended, to provide flexible configuration of the ambient learning design. So the Learning Manager can choose to modify particular Move categories, alter the wording of the Openers or alter some of the rules of the interaction in ways they think will fit their pedagogical purposes. Ongoing work with early adopters is making this process easier, through the development of a dialogue game editing tool.

Ongoing Evaluation of InterLoc3 and Preliminary Findings

There are currently ongoing implementations and evaluations of InterLoc3 across four HE Institutions, involving a range of courses and hundreds of students, so at the moment we can only report some early findings from London Metropolitan University, where the dialogue game approach was initially adopted and used by two tutors and 53 students studying software engineering within the Department of Computing. This total number of students was divided into twelve groups based at two campuses, which accounted for approx 75% of the total cohort of students studying this module.

The course leader set up the dialogue game activities covering pre-examination questions in 'formal methods for specification' and specifically included two reading tasks for student preparation. So in this context the aim was to 'get the students thinking, working and revising'. Two researchers

from the project and the course tutor (who are co-authors of this article) observed the student groups, as these initial trials were performed in a computing lab. In a de-briefing interview within a month of these sessions the tutor made the following comments that give a flavour of the anticipated impact of InterLoc and what the student experience might be:

"But with Interloc, what's different is once students engage with it they realise it's different and they have to think about what they are doing and that is the difference. They are not just uploading things or downloading things they have to read something and understand whatever they have read. And while they are within the InterLoc sessions they realise that they need to think about what they've got to do before they do it. "

and,

"The main thing is that they are thinking while they are within InterLoc. The thinking that they are doing is slightly different from their normal thinking. In as much as they are thinking about other people within the group: everybody's thinking about what each other's thinking, about what's going on, which is very, very important. So it's almost like meta-thinking activity."

One clear finding from these initial studies was that the introduction of this innovation requires more contextualisation than originally anticipated, precisely because it is a practice that as the quotes above indicate, whilst clearly beneficial and important, is not typical of the 'instruction and assessment' nature of conventional teaching. So the dialogue game activities need careful introduction in terms of the direct and indirect benefits they offer, in terms of improving students understanding of a topic, generating suitable content to support related learning activities and, providing the means for them to develop and practice fundamental skills of critical thinking and collective inquiry. Also, the process of 'question-setting' performed by the Learning Manager to seed the dialogue games cannot be underestimated and needs careful thought. In brief, although InterLoc3 is so far being successfully deployed and adopted in this exemplar context, it has to be conceived of holistically, as a practice that needs to be contextualised within a wider pedagogical and technological context, and ideally built into the broader learning designs (e.g. courses).

FUTURE TRENDS

Interestingly, it was over twenty years ago that we were promised a revolutionary cyber-reality, most famously characterised by William Gibson's (1984) Neuromancer. Then both Scientists and Science Fiction writers predicted the spread of an all-encompassing cyberspace that would tear apart our conventional notions of reality, replacing them with a virtual reality that would drastically change the way we learn, think and behave. But as far as our work and the explosion in social software has shown it has not happened in this way. The work reported in this article suggests that we are not creating a new landscape for 'e-learning' or 'learning in cyberspace', but instead we are supporting hyper-interactions that are fundamentally human. In this sense the internet is a landscape that provides the technologies that can catalyse, scaffold and amplify learning processes and re-shape learning practices. So contemporary learning will inevitably involve the close interplay of minds, machines and practices.

Hyper-Interactions for Learning

Our work that has been reported in this article demonstrates how specially designed tools, such as InterLoc, support the sort of collaborative thinking and collective inquiry, through blending dialectical and dialogic dialogue, in ways that are virtually impossible to achieve in more naturalistic ways. Studies of our dialogue games have demonstrated how they: empower learners to engage in 'thinking conversations'; scaffold the development of dialogue and reasoning skills; and, promote inclusive and fairly balanced dialogue practices. Also in some of our studies the students frequently commented that these dialogue games were better than face-to-face dialogues for a number reasons, and especially because some were particularly enthusiastic about being given a 'voice' in critical discussions in ways that overcame significant emotional and social barriers that they had previously experienced. So this clearly demonstrates what we have called 'hyper-interactions for learning', where the technological mediation enables the sort of relationships, dialogue and thinking to be developed and realised that could not have been, or would be very difficult to achieve, without this specialised social software.

CONCLUSION

We accept that the ideas, approach and technologies that are reported in this article, along with the synthesis we attempt, are somewhat ambitious. But they represent a serious attempt to reconcile 'classical' learning practices, such as the development of thinking, reasoning and discussion skills, with the opportunities offered by more open, inclusive and social software - and the developing digital practices that these support. It is early days in this initiative, as the educational and epistemological implications that are entailed by emerging digital practices with social software have arisen very much 'from under the radar', and so academic institutions are trying hard to assimilate their significance. Implicit in the argument that has been developed in this Chapter is a call, through design, to re-focus on fundamentals of learning, through reclaiming notions like 'thinking', 'meaning making', 'understanding' and 'collaborative inquiry'. It is strange that when compared with a lot of the current terminology of learning technology, that has tended to be dominated by somewhat mechanistic and content-centric terms like 'managed learning environments', 'delivering learning', 'content repositories' and such like these more fundamental terms seem somewhat fanciful and alien. But it's also reassuring that when we think of designing future learning practices through embracing more open and social software we have the opportunity to focus on these fundamental human processes. This can be achieved through setting up or promoting new contexts, conditions and catalysts for meaningful learning, as an alternative to using technology to emphasise more sophisticated ways to 'teach'.

ACKNOWLEDGMENT

The authors are very grateful to the many colleagues who have significantly contributed to this line of work. In particular, all members of the Dialogue Game project teams at London Metropolitan University, UK Open University, Exeter University, Oxford University, Queen Mary (University of London), University of Teesside and Bolton University, see www.interloc.org. Recent work on InterLoc tool has been carried out with the support of the UK Joint Information Systems Committee (JISC) "Capital Programme". The content of this paper does not necessarily reflect the position of the JISC, nor does it involve any responsibility on the part of the JISC.

REFERENCES

Bakhtin, M. (1986). *Speech Genres and Other Late Essays.* (Austin: University of Texas.)

Bork, A. (2001). Tutorial learning for the new century. *Journal of Science Education and Technology, 10*(1), 57–71.

Digital Dialogue Games for Learning Website. http://www.interloc.org/, accessed 13 December 2007.

Design-based research collective (2002). Design-Based Research: An Emerging Paradigm for Educational Inquiry. *Educational Researcher, 32*(1), 5-8.

Engstrom, Y. (1987). *Learning By Expanding: An Activity Theory Approach To Developmental Research.* Helsinki, Orienta-Konsultit.

Friere, P. (2001). *Pedagogy of freedom – ethics, democracy and civic courage*, Lanham, MD: Rowman and Littlefield.

Gee, J. P. (2003). *What video games have to teach us about learning and literacy.* Macmillan.

Gibson, W. (1984). *Neuromancer.* Harpercollins.

Habermas, J. (1991). *The Theory of Communicative Action, 1.* Cambridge: Polity Press.

Hartley, J. R. (1998). Qualitative reasoning and conceptual change: computer based support in understanding science. In R. G. F. Winkels & B. Bredeweg (Guest Eds.), *Interactive Learning Environments. Special Issue on The Use of Qualitative Reasoning Techniques in Interactive Learning Environments, 5*(1 and 2), 53-64.

Joseph, D. (2004). The Practice of Design-Based Research: Uncovering the Interplay Between Design, Research, and the Real-World Context. *Educational Psychologist, 39*(4), 235-242.

Levin, L. A., & Moore, J. A. (1977). Dialogue-Games: Metacommunication Structures for Natural Language Interaction. *Cognitive Science, 1*(4), 395-420.

Mackenzie, J. D. (1979). Question-begging in non-cummulative systems. *Journal of Philosophical Logic, 8,* 117-133.

McAlister, S., Ravenscroft, A and Scanlon, E. (2004a). Combining interaction and context design to support collaborative argumentation using a tool for synchronous CMC, *Journal of Computer Assisted Learning: Special Issue: Developing dialogue for learning* 20/3, 194-204.

McAlister, S., Ravenscroft, A., & Scanlon, E. (2004b). Designing to promote improved online educational argumentation: an evaluation study, In *Networked Learning 2004*. Banks et al. Lancaster and Sheffield Universities, (pp. 541-548).

Mercer, N. (2000). *Words and Minds: how we use language to think together.* London: Routledge.

Prensky, (2001). *Digital Game-Based Learning.* McGraw-Hill Education.

Ravenscroft, A. (2001). Designing e-learning interactions in 21C: Revisiting and re-thinking the role of theory. *European Journal of Education: Special edition on On-line Learning, 36*(2), 133-156.

Ravenscroft, A. (2007). Promoting Thinking and Conceptual Change with Digital Dialogue Games, *Journal of Computer Assisted Learning (JCAL), 23*(6), 453-465.

Ravenscroft, A. (2004). Towards highly communicative eLearning communities: Developing a socio-cultural framework for cognitive change. In Land, R and Bayne, S. (Eds.) *Cyberspace Education*, Routledge, Chapter 9, (pp. 130-145).

Ravenscroft, A. (2000). Designing Argumentation for Conceptual Development, *Computers and Education, 34*, 241-255. Elsevier Science Ltd.

Ravenscroft, A., & Cook, J. (2007). New Horizons in Learning Design. In H. Beetham & R. Sharpe (Eds.), *Rethinking pedagogy for the digital age: Designing and delivering e-learning* (pp. 207-218).Routledge.

Ravenscroft, A., McAlister, S., & Baur, E. (2006). *Development, piloting and evaluation of Inter-Loc: An Open Source tool supporting dialogue games in education.* Final Project Report to UK JISC (Joint Information Systems Committee), Bristol, UK.

Ravenscroft, A., & Pilkington, R. M. (2000). Investigation by Design: Developing Dialogue Models to Support Reasoning and Conceptual Change. *International Journal of Artificial Intelligence in Education: Special Issue on Analysing Educational Dialogue Interaction: From Analysis to Models that Support Learning*, 11(1), 273-298.

Ravenscroft, A., & McAlister, S. (2006a). Digital Games and Learning in Cyberspace: A Dialogical Approach, *E-Learning* Journal, Special Issue of *Ideas in Cyberspace 2005 Symposium*, 3(1), 38-51.

Ravenscroft, A., & McAlister, S. (2006b). Designing interaction as a dialogue game: Linking social and conceptual dimensions of the learning process. In C. Juwah, (Ed.), *Interactions in Online Education: implications for theory and practice* (pp 73-90). Routledge.

Ravenscroft, A., Sagar, M., & Baur, E. (2007). Cross-institutional implementation and evaluation of digital dialogue games for inclusive and personalised learning. *Annual Report to UK Joint Information Systems Committee (JISC),* November 2007.

Ravenscroft, A., Wegerif, R. B., & Hartley, J.R. (2007). Reclaiming thinking: dialectic, dialogic and learning in the digital age, British *Journal of Educational Psychology Monograph Series, Learning through Digital Technologies* , Underwood., J & Dockrell, J. (Guest Eds), Series II, Issue 5, (pp 39-57).

Searle, J. R. (1969). *Speech Acts: An essay in the philosophy of language.* Cambridge University Press.

Vygotsky, L. (1978). *Mind and society: The development of higher psychological processes.* Cambridge, MA: Harvard University Press.

Walton, D. (1984). *Logical Dialogue-Games and Fallacies.* Lanham: University Press America.

Wittgenstein, L. (1953). *Philosophical Investigations,* translated by G.E.M. Anscombe, Blackwell, Oxford, UK.

Wertsch, J. V. (1991). Voices of the mind: A sociocultural approach to mediated action. London: Harvester Wheatsheaf.

Wegerif, R. (2006). A dialogic understanding of the relationship between CSCL and teaching thinking skills. *International Journal of Computer Supported Collaborative Learning, 1*(1), 143-157.

Wegerif, R. B. (2007). *Dialogic, Education and Technology: Expanding the Space of Learning.* New York: Springer-Verlag.

KEY TERMS

Advanced Learning Design: This is an approach to learning design which accepts that contemporary learning is becoming more personalised, social and emergent - rather than the outcome of highly structured and pre-planned institutional practices.

Ambient Pedagogy: An approach to pedagogy and learning design that foregrounds the experiences that are produced through the realisation of the pedagogy, that is present but 'behind the scenes', in a learning situation. So this contrasts with approaches that focus on and externalise the structural complexities of the learning design. Instead, here there is a deliberate effort to render the complexities of learning designs into accessible learning practices that are performed 'naturally'.

Dialectic: An approach to dialogue which holds that knowledge and understanding develops through 'rational argument' and 'reasoned inquiry', with an emphasis on the clarification of meaning.

Dialogic: An approach to dialogue which holds that knowledge and understanding develops in a dynamic and relational way, through a process that involves the continuous development of descriptions, or re-descriptions, that arise from being able to 'adopt the perspective of another' in a dialogue.

Digital Dialogue Games for Learning: A well attested approach to learning through dialogue that is organised and managed according to computer-mediated social games (such as InterLoc above) that are performed synchronously amongst small groups.

InterLoc: A 'state of the art' Web-technology that implements digital dialogue games for reasoned dialogue, collaborative inquiry and learning.

Investigation by Design (IBD): A methodology for investigating and modelling educational dialogue in ways that: identify and examine the dialogue features and processes that are in play; and, provides specifications that can be implemented as digital tools.

Meaningful Learning: An approach to learning which emphasises the human social and cognitive processes that are in play, such as 'thinking', 'meaning making', 'understanding' and 'collaborative inquiry', and articulates the value of knowledge representations in these terms. So this term foregrounds the processes that give rise to the, usually collaborative, development of knowledge and understanding, in contrast to approaches that locate meaning and knowledge ostensibly within media and content.

432

ENDNOTES

1   Note that here we use the term 'pervasive' to give recognition to the fact that this technology can be used on any Web-enabled platform and from within institutional infra-structures, which currently is not common for an application with InterLoc's level of complexity.

2   Note that the actual names have been anonymised but the gender retained.

Chapter XXVIII
Interactivity Redefined for the Social Web

V. Sachdev
Middle Tennessee State University, USA

S. Nerur
University of Texas at Arlington, USA

J. T. C. Teng
University of Texas at Arlington, USA

ABSTRACT

With the trend towards social interaction over the Internet and the mushrooming of Web sites such as MySpace, Facebook and YouTube in the social computing space, practitioners and researchers are motivated to explain the sudden surge in user interest. The authors propose that interactivity is an important and appropriate subject of investigation to shed light on this explosion in social media use. Based on a review of the extant literature, they justify the use of interactivity for addressing research questions motivated by this new phenomenon. In particular, they propose a redefinition of interactivity for the social computing domain and term it Social Computing Interactivity (SCI). The authors suggest possible operationalizations of the dimensions of SCI and explore theory bases which would inform a study of their relevance in predicting the continued growth of social computing.

INTRODUCTION

The recent explosion in the individual use of websites such as MySpace, Facebook, YouTube and others, has generated a lot of buzz in the media.

This buzz has not been without valid reason, as is evidenced by the amount of traffic these sites draw and the valuation being assigned to these companies, without any significant revenue streams to justify those valuations (e.g., Google acquisition

Table 1. Usage and growth of some social Websites

Website	Unique U.S. users (Sept.2007, Millions)	Growth from previous year (percent)
MySpace	68.1	23
Facebook	30.6	129
Flickr	13.1	90
Bebo	4.4	83
Imeem	3.2	1,590

Source: Businessweek, November 5, 2007 (pp. 24)

of YouTube for $1.6 billion and Microsoft's investment of $240 million in Facebook). The number of users visiting these sites as well the growth rate they exhibit is staggering (see Table 1).

Given the extraordinary success of these sites, it behooves us to address the following questions:

a. What is the motivation for users to participate in social computing?
b. What will it take for these sites to retain existing users and attract new ones?

However, before we attempt to answer these questions, it is pertinent to define social computing and have some sense of how popular it is.

Social Computing

According to Schuler (1994), social computing refers to any type of computing where software serves as an intermediary for a social relation. However, his conceptualization is very broad and he includes in it the instance when the government devises policies involving software development. A good definition from the IBM Social Computing Group (IBM n.d.) is given below.

"Social computing refers to systems which support the gathering, representation, processing and dissemination of social information, that is, information which is distributed across social collectivities such as teams, communities, organizations, cohorts and markets." (IBM n.d.)

We define social computing as computing where the user takes an active role in the process, often creating content or modifying the computing environment, and the computing experience extends from the individual to the social. In order to make our conceptualizations relevant, we limit the scope of our analysis to websites, and exclude applications such as e-mail and independent instant messaging applications. We expect our research to extend to mobile computing too, since the distinctions between the computer and the phone are becoming hazy.

Current Trends

According to a recent report by Forrester Research (Li 2007), 48% of US adult online consumers participate in activities such as publishing blogs/webpages, uploading video to YouTube and other sites, commenting on blogs, posting reviews, using social networking sites, or simply consuming user generated content. This increase in interest in social computing is supported with some web traffic statistics. According to a February 2007 report from Hitwise (Prescott 2007), the top twenty social networking websites accounted for 4.9% of Internet Traffic in September 2006, a growth of 96% over September 2005. YouTube.com was the 26th most popular website on the internet in

September 2006 (Prescott 2007). YouTube traffic alone comprises approximately 20% of all HTTP traffic, or nearly 10% of all bandwidth usage on the Internet (Ellacoya Networks 2007). While the traffic statistics above indicate a high level of user activity, there are few sites, if any, that have a viable business model. However, because many of these websites are not very capital intensive until they reach a certain scale of traffic, there is a proliferation of clones of popular sites such as MySpace and YouTube.

Given the statistics above, it is important to find out the reason behind this tremendous increase in use of these websites. Based on our review of literature in Human Computer Interaction (HCI) and Computer Mediated Communication (CMC), we propose that Interactivity, with our suggested extensions, is an appropriate concept to study in an effort to shed light on the success of these websites. Interactivity has been conceptualized in many different ways depending on the perspective taken by the researchers and the context involved. We propose a redefinition of the interactivity construct and justify its salience as an important independent variable to study in line with our objectives above. We define the dimensions of interactivity or SCI, as we label it, and justify our additions to the dimensions popular in extant literature.

Contributions of this Research

This conceptualization of interactivity will provide a theoretical grounding for further investigations into the likely impact of interactivity on user behavior on social websites or while interacting with social software. It will provide a platform from which we propose to conduct empirical investigations toward answering an important question about the role SCI can play in explaining the unprecedented success of social computing. While we will not evaluate the psychometrics of the dimensions of interactivity proposed in this article, we will provide an evaluation of extant

literature on the existing operationalizations and provide guidance on their adaptation for social interactivity.

The rest of the article is structured as follows. First, we review the importance of interactivity as a predictor variable in several contexts. Then we review the extant literature on different perspectives on interactivity, focusing primarily on the CMC literature, as it is the most appropriate foundation for our work. Our research is also informed by relevant studies in psychology, sociology and human-computer interaction (HCI). We highlight the need for extension of the concept and define the dimensions of SCI and suggest adaptations to existing definitions. Finally, we provide guidance on operationalizing the constructs and suggest theory bases which would inform a study of their relevance in predicting the continued growth of social computing.

BACKGROUND

Interactivity has been an important construct in several fields of research such as marketing, communication, human computer interaction (HCI) and computer mediated communication (CMC). Given this diverse theoretical background there have been several competing and complementary conceptualizations of interactivity. While the concept of interactivity has attracted a fair share of attention, the disparate literature on interactivity has also been the subject of much discussion (Downes and McMillan 2000; Yadav and Varadarajan 2005; Kiousis 2002). We review this literature to establish the importance of interactivity as an independent variable and create a foundation for the redefinition of the concept in the context of social computing.

In a study on interactive advertisements, Cho and Leckenby (1999) found that the level of perceived interactivity was positively associated with attitude toward the product as well as with the intention to purchase. Wu (1999) found that perceived interactivity was positively associated with the user's attitudes towards the website. Likewise, Teo et al. (2002) found that increased level of interactivity on a website has positive effects on user's perceived satisfaction, effectiveness, efficiency, value, and overall attitude towards the website. Ghose and Dou (1998) found that greater interactivity is associated with Internet presence sites being counted as 'top sites'. Other research has considered the relationship of interactivity to choice difficulty (Ariely 2000), online navigation experience (McMillan and Hwang 2002; Novak et al. 2000), and processing of online advertisements (Liu and Shrum 2002; Stewart and Pavlou 2002). This representative review indicates the importance of the business to customer (B2C) aspect of communication in which the literature is based. However, this line of research ignores the current trend in social websites, where the emphasis is on user-user interaction, rather than just user-medium interaction or user-firm interaction. Since the central concern in the field of computer mediated communication (CMC) is the mediated enablement of user-user interaction, we anchor our research in the rich body of literature in that field.

Early research in CMC indicated that it was low in social presence, which was defined as the user's perception of the ability of the means of communication to marshal and focus the presence of communicating subjects (Short et al. 1976). This observation was consistent with the 'cues filtered out'(CFO) perspective (Culnan and Markhus 1987), as well as with the views on media richness (Daft and Lengel 1986) and limited social cues (Kiesler et al 1984). However, this notion has been contradicted in research that builds on the foundations of the social information processing view (Walther 1992). The central theme of the latter perspective is that the level or richness of communication enabled by CMC is not only determined by the medium or the technology but may be contingent on other factors, such as the time spent in the interaction or the expectation of

future interaction. The findings of some research studies contradict the results from early experiments in the 'cues filtered out' tradition, suggesting that CMC may be able to support effective interpersonal interactions partly due to the ability to optimize self-presentation, assuming there is an opportunity for repeated interactions (Walther and Burgoon 1992, Walther 1996).

With the applications available today on the web, CMC has moved beyond the realm of the 'text' interface. The increased level of interactivity afforded by these applications requires a deeper level of analysis as well as a redefinition of the notion of interactivity to make it germane to the context of social computing. We examine the various perspectives on interactivity below and then propose our redefinition.

Perspectives on Interactivity

Interactivity has been conceptualized in many different ways depending on the perspective taken by the researchers and the context involved. Kiousis (2002) provides an excellent review of the disparate conceptualizations of interactivity and conflicting results in extant research. For example, they mention that the operationalization of levels of interactivity as a function of the technological features (Schneiderman 1992) is in stark contrast to its operationalization as a perceptual report from the users (Newhagen et al 1995). Kiousis posits that interactivity has been defined with regard to technological properties, communication context, and user perceptions of interactivity. In addition to providing an excellent review of the multiple definitions of interactivity, Kiousis provides his own, which we quote below:

"Interactivity can be defined as the degree to which a communication technology can create a mediated environment in which participants can communicate (one-to-one, one-to-many, and many-to-many), both synchronously and asynchronously, and participate in reciprocal

message exchanges (third-order dependency). With regard to human users, it additionally refers to their ability to perceive the experience as a simulation of interpersonal communication and increase their awareness of tele-presence." (Kiousis, 2002, p.372)

Yet another context-specific definition of interactivity for electronic marketplaces, proposed by Yadav and Varadarajan (2005), reads as follows:

"Interactivity in the electronic marketplace is the degree to which computer mediated communication is perceived by each of the communicating entities to be (a) bidirectional, (b) timely, (c) mutually controllable, and (d) responsive." (Yadav and Varadrajan, 2005, p.593)

Both the definitions above propose a composite definition of interactivity based on the underlying dimensions identified by the authors. The definition by Yadav and Varadarajan (2005) is very appropriate for an extension to our context of social computing. A detailed review of the empirical work on interactivity, including several excellent meta analyses of the concept (McMillan and Hwang 2002; Tremayne 2005; Kiousis 2002), suggests three dominant perspectives: a) Interactivity as the users perception; b) as a function of the properties of the medium, and c) as a process of message exchange or interaction

with the message/medium. For the sake of brevity, only an overview of the conceptualizations is presented below. See Table 2 for a summary of the research.

Interactivity as a Perception

Earlier conceptualizations focused on interactivity as properties of the medium or the affordances. However, with empirical work showing that individual perception of the features was more important than the presence of the features themselves; this approach has gained ground (Kiousis 1999; McMillan 2000; McMillan and Hwang 2002; Wu 1999). These perceptions were measured using different operationalizations of interactivity, such as control (Steuer 1992), interpersonal communication (Kiousis 1999), awareness of telepresence (Kiousis 1999), and responsiveness (Wu 1999).

Interactivity as Properties of the Medium or Technology

The traditional thinking on interactivity promoted it as a function of the features of the medium, sometimes as a gradient, with more features implying more interactivity. Prominent among them were Ha and James (1998) who identified five characteristics of interactivity and Novak et al. (2000) who focused on time required for interaction. Ghose and Dou (1998) listed twenty three

Table 2. Different conceptualizations of interactivity

	Control	Communication	Responsiveness
Perception	Steuer 1992 Wu 1999, 2000 Liu&Shrum 2002 McMillan 2002	Kiousis 1999 Liu and Shrum 2002 McMillan 2002	Wu 1999, 2000 Steuer 1992 Coyle&Thorson 2001 Liu&Shrum 2002
Property	Jensen 1998 McMillan 2000	Massey & Levy 1991 Heeter 1989 McMillan 2000	Novak et al. 2000
Process	Williams et al. 1988 Yadav & Varadrajan 2005	Rafaeli 1988 Ha and James 1998	

site characteristics and evaluated which ones were most often found in a sample of 'Internet Presence Sites' and related them to a site being classified as a 'top site' in the rankings from Lycos, a search engine. McMillan (1999) used site features as indicators of interactivity, using the six dimensions proposed by Heeter (1989): complexity of choice available, effort users must exert, responsiveness to the user, monitoring information use, ease of adding information and facilitation of interpersonal communication. Clearly, the results/findings of these studies suggest a multidimensional conceptualization of interactivity.

Interactivity as Process of Message Exchange or Interaction with Message/Medium

The classical definition of interactivity, which is cited very often in the communication literature, was proposed by Rafaeli (1988). According to him,

"Interactivity is an expression of the extent that in a given series of communication exchanges, any third (or later) transmission (or message) is related to the degree to which previous exchanges referred to even earlier transmissions." (Rafaeli, 1988, p.111)

This definition completely ignores the technological factors included in earlier conceptualizations. Here the focus is on the exchange of messages and implies that the messages in a sequence should relate to each other. Another prominently cited definition was proposed by Willams et al. (1988) which was "the degree to which participants in a communication process have control over, and can exchange roles in, their mutual discourse" (p. 10). In a similar vein, Cho and Leckenby (1999) measured interactivity as the process of interaction with an advertisement.

SOCIAL COMPUTING INTERACTIVITY

As the literature review above indicates, interactivity is a multi-dimensional construct. It has been studied as a media characteristic, as a perceptual variable, and as a process of message exchange (Tremayne 2005). In consonance with current research (Wu 1999; Sohn & Lee 2005), we conceptualize Social Computing Interactivity (SCI) as a perceived measure with multiple dimensions. Further, rather than restricting the definition to a particular kind or groups of software, we keep the definition independent of technology, but relevant to the context of social software use, which is the domain of interest in our study.

Since many conceptualizations of interactivity propose dimensions of control, responsiveness and reciprocal communication, we consider these three dimensions the core dimensions of interactivity and retain them in our redefinition of the concept. However, we argue that the 'social' aspect of the social computing phenomenon is not addressed by these dimensions. Motivated by Ma and Agarwal's (2007) research, we propose three other dimensions, namely, social presence, self-presentation and deep profiling. These constructs were originally proposed in the context of participation in online communities. The authors highlight the importance of identity communication and subsequent verification in traditional non-mediated interaction and extend this argument to online community participation. They discuss technology artifacts, the use of which promotes identity verification. We adapt these for our context, and opine that the issue of identity communication is salient even for individual users engaged in social computing (not necessarily in a group or a community). Furthermore, since the dimensions of identity communication and verification have been shown to be a prerequisite for effective interaction (Ma and Agarwal, 2007), it seems appropriate to include them in our definition of interactivity.

In keeping with the definitions reviewed above, we define SCI as *"the degree to which the interaction (user-medium and user-user) is perceived to: a) enable control; b) exhibit responsiveness; c) enable reciprocal communication and social presence; and e) provide capabilities for self-presentation and deep profiling".*

As argued correctly by Sohn and Lee (2005), the dimensions of perceived interactivity should not be integrated into one score, since that dilutes the investigation into the differential impacts of these individual dimensions. So, instead of determining a single composite score and evaluating a medium for levels of interactivity on a gradient, we suggest that these dimensions should be independently measured before their relationships with suitable outcome variables are studied. We define the dimensions below:

Control

The literature review above highlighted a formulation of interactivity as the degree of control afforded by the medium. This has been conceptualized in several ways:

1. Control over navigability, content or pace (Sohn and Lee 2005).
2. 'The extent to which users can participate in modifying the form and content of a mediated environment in real-time" (Steuer 1992 p.84). Though this is the definition of interactivity, it is referring to the users' control over the form and content of the medium.
3. Control over the communication process (Yadav and Varadrajan 2005).
4. "the degree to which participants in a communication process have control over, and can exchange roles in, their mutual discourse is called interactivity" (Williams et al. 1988, p. 10).

Since we propose to conceptualize the dimensions as perceptions and keep them independent

of the characteristics of the medium, the definition proposed by Steuer (1992) is used as the basis. He conceptualized three dimensions of interactivity, namely, speed, range, and mapping. Here the concept of range is most pertinent for our needs. We quote the definition here

"The range of interactivity is determined by the number of attributes of the mediated environment that can be manipulated, and the amount of variation possible within each attribute" (Steuer 1992 pp. 86)

When considered from the perspective of the number of attributes manipulated, control over the form of some social software, such as a social networking website, would include attributes such as the layout or the colors. The higher the number of attributes that the user can modify, the greater the degree of control. It is important to reiterate that we do not enumerate the attributes that can be modified to get a measure of controllability for the medium; instead, we will rely on the perceptions of the user. Control over the content of such a site would involve content that the users can put in there, the content they that want to see from their friends' pages, or content from third party services (such as photos, music, stock prices, weather etc) using RSS feeds.

The sources cited above offer alternatives for scale creation for measuring this variable, but we propose that the scale used by Liu and Shrum (2002), with appropriate modifications to capture the ability of the user to control the content, layout, colors and other personalization options.

Responsiveness

This dimension captures the element of time it takes for the medium to respond to user action and the possibility of response as well. The speed of response was central to Steuer's (1992) definition of interactivity. Coyle and Thorson (2001) also state that quick transitions between a user's actions and the consequent outcome make a website interactive. Wu(1999) concluded that navigation and responsiveness are two dimensions to measure interactivity of websites. Liu and Shrum (2002) use a term called "Synchronicity", which refers to the degree to which a user's input and its attendant response is simultaneous.

Since social computing is focused on user-generated content, this dimension becomes very important. The users are no longer just browsing casually or doing information search. They are interacting actively with the medium, to change its form or content, and communicating with other users. Besides the speed of response, we also include the probability of response in this definition. Therefore, lower interactivity results if the user interacts with the interface and does not get a response.

For measuring responsiveness, we would again recommend using the scale by Liu and Shrum (2002) as the base and incorporate an item measuring the speed of response when the user is customizing the website to her needs, since that is an important activity on these websites.

Reciprocal Communication

The ability of a medium to provide two-way communication is central to the definition of interactivity. Massey and Levy (1999) opine that providing user's with communication tools such as chat rooms and bulletin boards enable "interpersonal interactivity". According to Heeter (1989), facilitation of interpersonal communication is one of the dimensions of interactivity. McMillan (2002) uses the dimensions of control and direction of communication to identify four different types of interactivity.

We conceptualize reciprocal communication as the enablement of user-to-user and user to website communication. User to user communication could be one to one, one to many and many to many. This may be explicit in the form of Blog posts and comments (one to many), chat rooms

(one to many), bulletin boards (one to many), instant messaging, notes on a friends 'wall' on Facebook.com (one to one and one to many), etc. It could also be more implicit in terms of providing feedback to other users such as ratings on user content, such as the model in Digg.com or rating a user's video uploaded on Youtube.com. User to website communication would be enabled by providing easy options to provide feedback on the site content or features to the site administrators. Many of these websites develop features iteratively based on user feedback. If the site administrators make it evident that they are accepting feedback and making changes, users are likely to rate the website higher on reciprocal communication.

Since the construct is tapping two dimensions of user to user and user to website communications and the resulting construct is a result of the rating of the website on these two dimensions, we propose that this construct should be operationalized as a formative construct. For items measuring the user to website communication capability, Liu and Shrum (2002) would be an appropriate source and we recommend development of new items to measure the user to user communication capability.

Social Presence

This construct along with the next two, Self-presentation and Deep Profiling, have been adapted from Ma and Agarwal (2007) along with suitable modifications to make them relevant to our context. As mentioned earlier, Short et al. (1976) define social presence of a medium as the user's perception of the ability of the means of communication to marshal and focus the presence of communicating subjects. They define this as a subjective quality of the medium, with varying levels in different communication media. These levels are based on the ability of the media to transmit information about facial expression, direction of looking, and nonverbal cues. However, this perspective is based on the assumption that the benchmark for CMC is traditional face-to-face communication and thus CMC has been considered low in social presence (Short et al. 1976). Walther (1992) countered this argument and proposed the social information processing viewpoint, where he proposed that the level of presence afforded by a media cannot be measured using the features of the medium. Instead, the perception of the users dictates the level of presence. He also reviews literature which contradicts the 'low social presence' view of CMC and says that presence may be a function of the context, user characteristics, and purpose of use of the media as well. For a detailed discussion of the varied conceptualizations of presence, the reader is referred to Gunawardena (1995) and Biocca et al. (2003).

A more relevant and contextual definition was proposed by Ma and Agarwal (2007) for a construct called virtual co-presence. Building on the conceptualization by Biocca et al. (2003), they defined it as the feeling of being together in a virtual environment in the context of users in an online community. According to Biocca et al. (2003, pp.456-457), these 'others' whose co-presence is of interest to the user are "primarily technologically mediated representations of other humans or forms of intelligence including mediated representations of remote humans via text, images, video, 3D avatars..."

So, this presence could be human or artificial. The definition used by Ma and Agarwal (2007) considers interactivity, speed of interaction, and vividness as factors that enable perceptions of virtual co-presence. Since we are conceptualizing social presence as a dimension of interactivity we need to avoid this broad definition. We want to capture the ability of the medium to simulate co-presence, in terms of sensory awareness of the other (Goffman 1959), and the perception that the others react to the focal user (Heeter 1992). Hence, we define social presence as the degree to which users perceive the physical existence of others and the perception of the extent of interaction with the other user(s). .

Since this construct taps into two dimensions, we propose that this construct should be formative. Diamantopoulos and Winklhofer (2001) proposed guidelines regarding the creation and validation of the formative indicators, which is appropriate for this construct and the other formative constructs we propose. Though the items created by Ma and Agarwal (2007) for these constructs followed these guidelines, the context for their research was user's knowledge contribution in two specific online communities. In our context, the role of these constructs in influencing the perception of relatedness with other users is most important and hence we recommend a modification of the items accordingly.

Self-Presentation

Ma and Agarwal (2007) propose this construct and define it as "a process to communicate one's identity, helping others form a more sophisticated and accurate understanding of "Who am I?""(p. 50). According to them, self-presentation can be achieved through the use of signatures, screen names, avatars (virtual representations, sometimes animated), personal profiles, and web pages or personal photographs, among others. The authors discuss the psychological processes involved in non technology-mediated interactions from the perspective of Attribution theory(Heider 1958), which contends that people use available social information to judge the personality and identity of others. This communication of identity is a first step in any new interaction (Goffman 1967). Since people with shared interests or tastes are more likely to communicate and build relationships (Newcomb 1961), identity communication will enable discovery of such people. Though the authors use this construct in the context of online community members, we propose that this conceptualization is equally valid for an individual user using social websites, even if it is not a formal online community.

Ma and Agarwal (2007) formulate this as a formative construct and we propose the same and recommend the items used by them as suitable for our context, with minor modifications.

Deep Profiling

Ma and Agarwal (2007) contend that availability of artifacts such as rankings, feedback, detailed archives of user contributions, and 'Who did what' features are examples of deep profiling artifacts. Deep profiling, along with the earlier two dimensions of social presence and self-presentation, enables efficient identity communication. These artifacts provide a context which assists in reducing attribution differences arising due to the rarity of cues afforded by CMC. In contrast to self-presentation, where it is the initiative of the user to use the features, deep profiling features are more under the control of the system, often dependent on the use of such features (e.g., feedback mechanisms) by other users. Since these mechanisms allow for users to evaluate other users and form perceptions, they are a prerequisite for effective interaction. Hence, we include deep profiling as another dimension of interactivity.

In addition to self-presentation and social presence, we also conceptualize deep profiling as a formative construct, rather than reflective as was done by Ma and Agarwal (2007). In the original study, the items were measuring a user's

Table 3. Constructs and their operationalizations

Construct	Formative/Reflective
Control	Reflective
Responsiveness	Reflective
Reciprocal Communication	Formative
Social Presence	Formative
Deep Profiling	Formative
Self Presentation	Formative

perceptions of what information about her was being viewed or considered by the other users while interacting with her. In our context, the perspective is about the ease of finding information about another user who is the subject of a possible interaction. Hence the language of all the items needs to be modified. For example, instead of the item "I think that other people have read my previous posts", we would recommend an item "I can easily read the earlier posts of other users". The list of constructs and the appropriate operationalization is presented in Table 3 below.

FUTURE RESEARCH

In the discussion above, we have proposed three new dimensions of interactivity to represent the richer and more complex social software that we see today. In order to confirm these dimensions of interactivity, we call for exploratory research to develop and validate scales for the dimensions and to study the impact of the various dimensions of SCI on the use of social computing websites. While there are several theoretical lenses that could be used to illuminate the relationship between SCI dimensions and use of these websites, we mention only some relevant theory bases here.

One prominent theory in the communication and advertising literature is the use and gratifications perspective. This perspective focused on the psychological orientation of the receiver/user of the communication and thus proposed an alternative to the predominant emphasis that was placed on the sender and the message in mass communication research until the 1970s. It offers the explanation that people consume different types of media, be it newspapers, television, radio or the Internet, because of the gratification they get out of their use. In a review of the literature on the use of this perspective to explain Internet use, LaRose and Eastin (2004) found that several studies explained very little variance in Internet use. They went on to propose additional constructs based on social cognitive theory (Bandura 1986) to better explain Internet usage. The use and gratifications theory base seems very appropriate to investigate the impact of the interactivity dimensions on gratifications obtained, which in turn may help explain the surge in social computing.

On a related note, there is a well developed theory or rather a collection of mini-theories in psychology called the Self Determination Theory (SDT) that was proposed by Deci and Ryan (1985, 2000). This set of theories examines the concepts of intrinsic and extrinsic motivation, the effects of social contexts or environmental factors on intrinsic motivation, and the concept of basic psychological needs and their relationship to psychological health and well-being. They propose that all humans have some basic psychological needs - autonomy, competence and relatedness - and fulfillment of these needs is positively associated with higher levels of self-determined motivation, which subsequently leads to persistent behavior. If the dimensions of interactivity are considered to be the factors that the users are exposed to while using a particular website, then these dimensions could be hypothesized to fulfill certain needs. For example, a greater ability for self-presentation on the website might be associated with a higher level of relatedness perception, where relatedness is defined as the desire to feel connected to significant others.

CONCLUSION

In this article, we reviewed the importance of interactivity and proposed it as an important research construct in the context of social computing. We highlighted the major conceptualizations of interactivity and discussed the rationale for its redefinition. This traditional definition of interactivity is extended by adding three new dimensions, thus evolving a six-dimensional view of interactivity that is likely to be more useful in understanding issues pertaining to social computing. Further,

we provided direction on operationalizing the constructs. Finally, we suggest some theoretical lenses to evaluate the impact of these dimensions of interactivity on the use of social software. The validation of this multi-dimensional model of interactivity relevant for the social computing domain as well as the development of theory-based models investigating the impact of SCI on the use of these websites would provide a useful conceptual platform for pursuing research in this rich and complex area of social computing.

REFERENCES

Amabile, T. M. (1985). Motivation and creativity: Effects of motivational orientation on creative writers. *Journal of Personality and Social Psychology, 48*(2), 393-399.

Anderson, R., Manoogian, S. T., & Reznick, J. S. (1976). The undermining and enhancing of intrinsic motivation in preschool children. *Journal of Personality and Social Psychology, 34*(5), 915-922.

Ariely, D. (2000). Controlling the information flow: effects on consumers' decision making and preferences. *Journal of Consumer Research, 27*(2), 233-248.

Bandura, A. (1986). *Social foundations of thought and action: a social cognitive theory*. Englewood Cliffs, NJ: Prentice-Hall.

Biocca, F., Harms, C., & Burgoon, J.K. (2003). Toward a more robust theory and measure of social presence: review and suggested criteria. *Presence: Teleoperators & Virtual Environments, 12*(5), 456-480.

Cho, C. H., & Leckenby, J. D. (1999). Interactivity as a measure of advertising effectiveness: antecedents and consequences of interactivity in web advertising. *Proceedings of the 1999 Conference of the American Academy of Advertising*, (pp. 162-179).

Coyle, J. R., & Thorson, E. (2001). The effects of progressive levels of interactivity and vividness in web marketing sites. *Journal of Advertising, 30*(3), 65-77.

Culnan, M. J., & Markus, M. L. (1987). Information technologies. *Handbook of Organizational Communication: An interdisciplinary perspective,* (pp. 420-443).

Daft, R. L., & Lengel, R. H. (1986). Organizational information requirements, media richness and structural design. *Management Science, 32*(5), 554-571.

Deci, E. L., & Ryan, R. M. (1985). *Intrinsic motivation and self-regulation in human behavior.* New York: Plenum Press.

Deci, E.L., & Ryan, R.M. (2000). The "What" and "Why" of goal pursuits: Human needs and the self-determination of behavior. *Psychological Inquiry, 11*(4), 227-268.

Diamantopoulos, A., & Winklhofer, H. M. (2001). Index construction with formative indicators: an alternative to scale development. *Journal of Marketing Research, 38*(2), 269-277.

Downes, E. J., & McMillan, S. J. (2000). Defining interactivity. *New Media & Society,* 2(2), 157-179.

Eastin, M. S., & LaRose, R. (2000). Internet self-efficacy and the psychology of the digital divide. *Journal of Computer-Mediated Communication,* 6(1), 25-56.

Ellacoya Networks. (2007). Ellacoya data shows web traffic overtakes peer-to-peer (p2p) as largest percentage of bandwidth on the network.

Ghose, S., & Dou, W. Y. (1998). Interactive functions and their impacts on the appeal of internet presences sites. *Journal of Advertising Research, 38,* 29–43.

Goffman, E. (1959). *The presentation of self in everyday life.* New York: Doubleday.

Goffman, E. (1967). *Interaction ritual: Essays on face-to-face interaction.* Garden City, NY: Doubleday.

Gunawardena, C. (1995). Social presence theory and implications for interaction and collaborative learning in computer conferences. *International Journal of Educational Telecommunications,* 1(2), 147-166.

Heeter, C. (1989). Implications of new interactive technologies for conceptualizing communication. In J. L. Salvaggio & J. Bryant (Eds.), *Media use in the information age: Emerging patterns of adoption and computer use* (pp. 217-235). Hillsdale, NJ: Lawrence Erlbaum Associates.

Heider, F. (1958). *The psychology of interpersonal relations.* New York: Wiley.

IBM. *What is social computing?* Retrieved July 7, 2007, from http://www.research.ibm.com/SocialComputing/SCGFAQs.htm#WhatIsSocialComputing.

Kiesler, S., Siegel, J., & McGuire, T. (1984). Social psychological aspects of computer-mediated communication. *The American psychologist, 39*(10), 1123-1134.

Kiousis, S. (2002). Interactivity: A Concept Explication. *New Media & Society, 4*(3), 355-383.

LaRose, R., & Eastin, M. S. (2004). A social cognitive theory of internet uses and gratifications: toward a new model of media attendance. *Journal of Broadcasting & Electronic Media, 48*(3), 358-377.

Li, C. (2007) *Social technographics.* Available at: http://blogs.forrester.com/charleneli/2007/04/forresters_new_.html

Liu, Y., & Shrum, L. J. (2002). What is interactivity and is it always such a good thing? Implications of definition, person, and situation for the influence of interactivity on advertising effectiveness. *Journal of advertising, 31*(4), 53-65.

Ma, M., & Agarwal, R. (2007). Through a glass darkly: Information technology design, identity verification, and knowledge contribution in online communities. *Information Systems Research, 18*(1), 42-67.

Massey, B. L., & Levy, M. R. (1999). Interactive online journalism at English-language web newspapers in Asia. *Gazette, 61*(6), 523-538.

McMillan, S. J. (2002). A four-part model of cyber-interactivity: Some cyber-places are more interactive than others. *New Media and Society, 4*(2), 271-291.

McMillan, S. J. (1999). Health communication and the internet: Relations between interactive characteristics of the medium and site creators, content, and purpose. *Health Communication, 11*(4), 375-390.

Mcmillan, S. J., & Hwang, J. S. (2002). Measures of perceived interactivity: An exploration of the role of direction of communication, user control, and time in shaping perceptions of interactivity. *Journal of Advertising, 31*(3), 29-43.

Newcomb, T. M. (1961). *The acquaintance process.* Holt, Rinehart and Winston.

Newhagen, J. E., Cordes, J. W., & Levy, M. R. (1995). Nightly@ nbc. com: Audience scope and the perception of interactivity in viewer mail on the internet. *Journal of Communication, 45*(3), 164-75.

Novak, T. P., Hoffman, D. L., & Yung, Y. F. (2000). Measuring the customer experience in online environments: A structural modeling approach. *Marketing Science, 19*(1), 22-42.

Prescott, L. (2007). *Hitwise US Consumer Generated Media Report, Feb 2007.*

Ryan, R. M., & Deci, E. L. (2000). The darker and brighter sides of human existence: Basic psychological needs as a unifying concept. *Psychological Inquiry, 11*(4), 319-338.

Ryan, R. M., & Deci, E. L. (2000a). Intrinsic and extrinsic motivations: Classic definitions and new directions. *Contemporary Educational Psychology, 25*(1), 54-67.

Ryan, R. M., & Deci, E. L. (2000b). Self-determination theory and the facilitation of intrinsic motivation, social development, and well-being. *American Psychologist, 55*(1), 68-78.

Schuler, D. (1994). Social computing. *Communications of the ACM, 37* (1), 28-29.

Short, J., Williams, E., & Christie, B. (1976). *The social psychology of telecommunications.* London: Wiley.

Sohn, D., & Lee, B. (2005). Dimensions of interactivity: Differential effects of social and psychological factors. *Journal of Computer-Mediated Communication, 10*(3).

Stewart, D. W., & Pavlou, P. A. (2002). From consumer response to active consumer: measuring the effectiveness of interactive media. *Journal of the Academy of Marketing Science, 30*(4), 376-396.

Stromer-Galley, J. (2004). Interactivity-as-product and interactivity-as-process. *The Information Society, 20*(5), 391-394.

Teo, H., Oh, L., Liu, C., & Wei, K. (2003). An empirical study of the effects of interactivity on web user attitude. *International Journal of Human-Computer Studies, 58*(3), 281-305.

Tremayne, M. (2005). Lessons learned from experiments with interactivity on the web. *Journal of Interactive Advertising, 5*(2).

Vallerand, R. J. (1997). Toward a hierarchical model of intrinsic and extrinsic motivation. *Advances in experimental social psychology, 29*, 271-360.

Vallerand, R. J., Fortier, M. S., & Guay, F. (1997). Self-determination and persistence in a real-life setting: Toward a motivational model of high school dropout. *Journal of Personality and Social Psychology, 72*(5), 1161-1176.

Walther, J. B. (1992). Interpersonal effects in computer-mediated interaction: a relational perspective. *Communication Research, 19*(1), 52-90.

Walther, J. B., & Burgoon, J. K. (1992). Relational communication in computer-mediated interaction. *Human Research Communication, 19*(1), 50-88.

Walther, J. B. (1996). Computer-mediated communication: impersonal, interpersonal, and hyperpersonal interaction. *Communication Research, 23*(1), 3-43.

Williams, F., Rice, R. E., & Rogers, E. M. (1988). *Research methods and the new media.* Collier Macmillan.

Wu, G. (1999). Perceived interactivity and attitude toward website. *Proceedings of the 1999 Conference of the American Academy of Advertising,* (pp. 254-262).

Yadav, M. S., & Varadarajan, R. (2005). Interactivity in the electronic marketplace: an exposition of the concept and implications for research. *Journal of the Academy of Marketing Science, 33*(4), 585.

KEY TERMS

Control: The perception of control over the form of and content on a website.

Deep Profiling: The perception of availability of information about users on a website.

Reciprocal Communication: The perception of enablement of user to user and user to website communication.

Responsiveness: The perception of the speed of response during a user interaction with a website and the probability of that response.

Self Presentation: The perception of the ability to project one's identity on the website.

Social Computing Interactivity: The degree to which the interaction (user-medium and user-user) is perceived to: a) enable control; b) exhibit responsiveness; c) enable reciprocal communication and social presence; and e) provide capabilities for self-presentation and deep profiling.

Social Presence: The degree to which users perceive the physical existence of others and the perception of interaction with the other user(s).

Chapter XXIX
Transliteracy as a Unifying Perspective

Sue Thomas
De Montfort University, UK

Chris Joseph
De Montfort University, UK

Jess Laccetti
De Montfort University, UK

Bruce Mason
De Montfort University, UK

Simon Perril
De Montfort University, UK

Kate Pullinger
De Montfort University, UK

ABSTRACT

Transliteracy might provide a unifying perspective on what it means to be literate in the 21st Century. It is not a new behaviour but has been identified as a working concept since the internet generated new ways of thinking about human communication. This chapter defines transliteracy as "the ability to read, write and interact across a range of platforms, tools and media from signing and orality through handwriting, print, TV, radio and film, to digital social networks" and opens the debate with examples from history, orality, philosophy, literature, ethnography and education. The authors invite responses, expansion, and development. See also http://www.transliteracy.com

PREFACE

When I look straight forward I can see that I'm flying. I have a dramatic pair of bat wings but they don't help me fly; they just look neat. When I focus on what I can hear, though, it is a radio and it is broadcasting a debate about whether David Beckham should change his mind about moving to the United States of America to play football[a]. If I listen really carefully, I can hear the fan of my computer and a cat breathing as it sleeps. In front of me, to my right and left are shelves of books, a digital camera, mp3 player and a cup of coffee. There's a newspaper on the table to my left and, somewhere outside, it sounds as if a group of students are discussing Big Brother. This is my world and it's probably not that dissimilar to yours, gentle reader - if "reader" is an appropriate term for who you are.

We live in a world of multiple literacies, multiple media and multiple demands on our attention. Each of these is complete in itself yet we do not experience them individually, we synthesize and mould them to our needs. Each of us, every day, is involved in staggering acts of comprehension and production. It's only a few thousand years since we sat around fires telling stories to hold back the night using nothing more than sound and gesture. What we do now may draw on technologies that could not have been predicted just a few generations ago yet, we argue, what we do now is not fundamentally different from what we did then. In this chapter, we explore a new concept - "Transliteracy" - which is both very old and brand new and may help us shed light on how we, as human beings, communicate. To do so we are going to shift literacy away from its original association with the medium of written text and apply it as a term that can refer to any kind of medium. And then we're going to go across and beyond literacy to transliteracy.

WHAT IS TRANSLITERACY?

Transliteracy is the ability to read, write and interact across a range of platforms, tools and media from signing and orality through handwriting, print, TV, radio and film, to digital social networks.

As a behaviour, it is not new – indeed it reaches back to the very beginning of culture – but it has only been identified as a working concept since the internet allowed humans to communicate in ways which seem to be entirely novel. As a notion, it grew to fruition during discussions among the Production and Research in Transliteracy (PART) Group at the Institute of Creative Technologies (IOCT), De Montfort University. It is a good example of open source thinking between diverse collaborators, and in this chapter we offer up the idea of transliteracy for further development. Some of the ideas discussed here were first mooted in an article for First Monday in December 2007 (Thomas, 2007).

The word 'transliteracy' is derived from the verb 'to transliterate', meaning to write or print a letter or word using the closest corresponding letters of a different alphabet or language. This of course is nothing new, but transliteracy extends the act of transliteration and applies it to the increasingly wide range of communication platforms and tools at our disposal. From early signing and orality through handwriting, print, TV and film to networked digital media, the concept of transliteracy calls for a change of perspective away from the battles over print versus digital, and a move instead towards a unifying ecology not just of media, but of all literacies relevant to reading, writing, interaction culture and education, both past and present. It is, we hope, an opportunity to cross some very obstructive divides.

Our use of the term transliteracy is pre-dated by the plural 'transliteracies', which evolved at the Transcriptions Research Project directed by

Professor Alan Liu in the Department of English at the University of California at Santa Barbara. (Transliteracies project, 2007). In 2005, Liu developed and formalized the Transliteracies Project, researching technological, social, and cultural practices of online reading. Sue Thomas attended the first Transliteracies conference and came away inspired to develop her own understanding of transliteracy in its broadest sense.[b] As a result, the Production and Research in Transliteracy (PART) group was formed in 2006. PART is a small group of researchers based in the Faculty of Humanities but researching in the Institute of Creative Technologies. The IOCT, which opened in 2006, undertakes research work in emerging areas at the intersection of e-Science, the Digital Arts, and the Humanities. It comprises an interdisciplinary laboratory at the heart of an infrastructure grid connecting significant research centers across the university and providing a faculty-neutral space for the development of transdisciplinary projects. It is, therefore, the ideal cultural medium for transliterate practice. As well as analyzing transliteracy in general terms, the PART group also observes, responds to, and advises transdisciplinary projects within the IOCT, where the concept has become embedded in the discourse of the Institute.

Everyone in the PART group has worked closely with writing, computers and the internet for various lengths of time, several of us for over twenty years. We have been deeply engaged with questions about the impact of computers on lit-

Figure 1. Image of a "publish button" from the blogspot interface

eracy (and upon the literary). Is the internet really changing the ways in which we read, write, and think? Is the book truly dead? Is anything being lost in the frantic rush to get online? What has happened to the idea of literary value?

Many people seem to feel that they should have a preference between the analogue and the digital, as if the situation really were so polarized. For example, in 2005 English literary critic Mark Lawson revealed his high state of anxiety about the web on BBC TV when, whilst interviewing Tim Berners-Lee, founder of the World Wide Web, he referred repeatedly to pornography, identity theft and commercialism, exclaiming "Because of your invention, I was able to look up every article written by or about you quickly and easily. But at the same time, I was sent several unsolicited links to porn sites. I have to accept that someone in Mexico may have stolen my identity and now be using it. Is the latter absolutely worth paying for the former?" ("Berners-Lee on the read/write web", 2007). And in 2007, in an article for *The Observer*, Nick Cohen – a columnist asked to be a judge on the "Blooker Prize" ("The Lulu Blooker Prize 2007", 2007) – reflected largely positively on blogs and publishing on demand. Yet he still felt compelled to note that the internet "allows millions to drone on in blogs that no one but their friends will read," (Cohen 2007). This use of the pejorative word "drone", and the implication that writing something only your friends will read makes the work worthless, demonstrates Cohen's misunderstanding of the medium. In a transliterate world, the 'publish' command on a blog refers to a technical operation and is not related to any kind of value judgement or any relationship to the publishing industry.

TRACING TRANSLITERACY

It is important to outline the ways in which transliteracy differentiates from "media literacy", defined by Ofcom as – "the ability to access, understand and create communications in a variety of contexts" (Ofcom, 2003). Our thinking is that because it offers a wider analysis of reading, writing and interacting *across* a range of platforms, tools, media and cultures, transliteracy does not replace, but rather contains, "media literacy" and also "digital literacy", defined by Gilster as "the ability to understand and use information in multiple formats from a wide range of sources when it is presented via computers," (Gilster, 1997, p.1) . "Convergence" is another term which has become widely used, especially by the media and gaming worlds, but it is enormously broad. In 2001 MIT scholar Henry Jenkins wrote "Part of the confusion about media convergence stems from the fact that when people talk about it, they're actually describing at least five processes" (Jenkins, 2001). He lists these types of convergence as technological, economic, social or organic, cultural, and global, concluding that "these multiple forms of media convergence are leading us toward a digital renaissance - a period of transition and transformation that will affect all aspects of our lives" (Jenkins, 2001). Transliteracy is, perhaps, the literacy of this process. However, it is important to note that transliteracy is not just about computer-based materials, but about all communication types across time and culture. It does not privilege one above the other but treats all as of equal value and moves between and across them.

In 1964, Marshall McLuhan saw the process Jenkins describes as occurring increasingly via technology, proposing that "in this electric age we see ourselves being translated more and more into the form of information, moving towards the technological extension of consciousness," (McLuhan, 1964, p.63). Walter Ong, writing in 1982 about the relationship between literacy and orality, also approached the matter from the point of view of linear progressive change: "The shift from orality to literacy and on to electronic processing engages social, economic, political, religious and other structures," (Ong, 1982, p.3).

The concept of media ecology developed by McLuhan, Ong, Postman and others is certainly closely related to transliteracy. The difference lies in transliteracy's insistence upon a lateral approach to history, context and culture, its interest in lived experience, and its focus on interpretation via practice and production. It is characteristic of our deliberations that we do not view digital media as part of a linear historical progression, but see them as manifestations of other similar modes of communication. In our view, the ecology of transliteracy is both global and historical.

Howard Rheingold's work on the history of cooperation is useful in elucidating a context for transliteracy. In *Technologies of Cooperation*, he speculates on the nature of the very earliest collectives:

Humans lived as hunter–gatherers in small, extended family units long before they lived in agricultural settlements. For most of that time, small game and gathered foods constituted the most significant form of wealth—enough food to stay alive. At some point, larger groups figured out how to band together to hunt bigger game. We don't know exactly how they figured this out, but it's a good guess that some form of communication was involved, and however they did it, their banding-together process must have solved collective-action problems in some way: our mastodon-hunting ancestors must have found ways to suspend mistrust and strict self-interest long enough to cooperate for the benefit of all. It is unlikely that unrelated groups would be able to accomplish huge game hunting while also fighting with each other. (Saveri et al, 2005, p.3)

Eventually, around forty thousand years ago, there was enough leisure time for such communities to record their activities on the walls of their caves. And just five thousand years ago, they began to write: "The first forms of writing appeared as a means of accounting for the exchange of commodities such as wine, wheat, or sheep—and the taxation of this wealth by the empire. The master practitioners of the new medium of marks on clay or stone were the accountants for the emperors and their priest-administrators. When writing became alphabetic (claims McLuhan), an altogether new kind of empire, the Roman Empire, became possible." (ibid.)

Across this long stretch of cultural time, five millions years of human communication, the privileging of reading and writing as primary defining literacies begins to seem somewhat out of scale. As Rheingold writes: "[w]hat we are witnessing today is [thus] the acceleration of a trend that has been building for thousands of years. When technologies like alphabets and Internets amplify the right cognitive or social capabilities, old trends take new twists and people build things that never could be built before." (ibid.)

REALLY NEW MEDIA

Some kinds of media certainly do seem to be entirely new. In February 2007, Kate Pullinger and Sue Thomas, with their students on the Online MA in Creative Writing and New Media at De Montfort University, collaborated with Penguin Books on the innovative Million Penguins Wikinovel project. ("amillionpenguins.com", 2007). Described as "a global experiment in new media writing," [c]it is a collaboratively-written fiction in which anyone could contribute to a text and also edit the work of others, producing an evolving piece of writing supplemented by a vast document history of previous changes. By the end of the experiment 80,000 unique visitors had viewed a work which had grown to over 50,000 words and which had been written, edited, spammed and vandalized by 1,500 people (Ettinghausen 2007a). Penguin Digital Publisher Jeremy Ettinghausen wrote at the opening of the wiki: "The buzz these days is all about the network, the small pieces loosely joined. About how the sum of the parts is greater than the whole. About how working together and join-

ing the dots serves the greater good and benefits our collective endeavors." (Ettinghausen, 2007) It was clear from early on that the success of A Million Penguins lay not in the literary quality of the 'novel' (which was agreed to be variable, to say the least) but in the generation of a smart mob (to use Rheingold's term) of largely anonymous authors and editors who came out of nowhere within hours of the project's launch and worked together intensively for a month to grow something creative from the blank screen of an empty wiki. Originally developed by Ward Cunningham in 1994, wiki software such as that which powers "Wikipedia" has given rise to a genuinely new form of collective literary behavior which has no historical parallel and which only became possible via recent technological innovation.[d]

Transliteracy is an inclusive concept which bridges and connects past, present and, hopefully, future modalities. The chitchat of a blog is, perhaps, not dissimilar to campfire stories after a day's hunting. The literacies (digital, numerate, oral) may be different, but the transliteracies (social, economic, political) often transect them in similar ways, depending on cultural context. For example, in recent years we have begun to switch from searching for information in encyclopedias, indices and catalogues to querying the kinds of data collections that existed before books – that is to say, we are asking each other. Via millions of message boards and chatrooms we ask each other for advice about health problems, moral dilemmas, or what to cook for dinner. We share those answers, elaborate upon them, and, in so doing, we aggregate them so that others unknown to us can use them. As Bush and Tiwana write: '[u]nlike knowledge repositories, which follow a people-to-documents model, knowledge networks are inherently people-to-people,' (Bush and Tiwana, 2005, p.70). Today, even large corporations are recognizing that knowledge which cannot easily be classified or stored can often be accessed via individuals and then synthesized through peer-to-peer networks and conversations.

It would seem that transliteracy may be synonymous with collective or participatory modes of production, and this would be a fruitful area for future research.

The philosopher Bernard Stiegler suggests that past technologies have always involved a change in our phenomenological experience of the world. Transliteracy engages with new innovations in participatory media even as it recognizes that part of what such media enables is a recovery of an older plurality of literacies with possibly ancient provenances. Stiegler's work draws attention to the degree to which theorizing about technology is often polarized between anxiety and euphoria. His response is to refuse to distance technology from life; and to suggest that human individuation and technology have always had a transductive relationship. Our sense of transliteracy is informed by such a relationship.

However, despite these recovered practices, textual literacy has become so ingrained in Western society that it has reached the point of invisibility. But humans have only been using reading and writing for a very short time in our history, so how else do we communicate? Transliteracy pays attention to the whole range of modes and to the synergies between them to produce a sense of a 'transliterate lifeworld' in constant process. A lifeworld is the combination of physical environment and subjective experience that makes up everyday life. Each individual's lifeworld is personal to them, as Agre and Horswill describe:

Cats and people, for example, can be understood as inhabiting the same physical environment but different lifeworlds. Kitchen cupboards, window sills, and the spaces underneath chairs have different significances for cats and people, as do balls of yarn, upholstery, television sets, and other cats. Similarly, a kitchen affords a different kind of lifeworld to a chef than to a mechanic, though clearly these two lifeworlds may overlap in some ways as well. A lifeworld, then, is not just a physical environment, but the patterned ways

in which a physical environment is functionally meaningful within some activity. (Agre and Horswill, 1997, node 3)

The transliterate lifeworld is highly subjective, diverse and complicated. It is not one kind of place, but many – an ecology which changes with the invention of each new media-type. Yet a story is always still a story, whether it's told whilst walking down the street, printed in a book, or Twittered across the internet.

So what are the "patterned ways" of the complex lifeworld of transliteracy and how are they meaningful? Transliteracy happens in the places where different things meet, mix, and rub together. It is an interstitial space teeming with diverse lifeforms, some on the rise, some in decline, expressed in many languages in many voices, many kinds of scripts and media. It is a world where print has a place, but not the only place.

WRITING AND READING ARE NOT ENOUGH

The philosopher Socrates, who eschewed learning to read and write in a culture where such practices were unusual, believed that the fixed nature of writing limits thought and enquiry. In The Phaedrus we read that in 370BC Socrates asserted writing was an aid "not to memory, but to reminiscence" providing "not truth, but only the semblance of truth." Readers would, he said, "be hearers of many things and will have learned nothing; they will appear to be omniscient and will generally know nothing; they will be tiresome company, having the show of wisdom without the reality," (274e-275b).

It is interesting to place Socrates' complaints about reading and writing alongside the charge of graphocentrism currently being leveled at Western agencies engaged in trying to colonize societies such as those found in the Brazilian rainforests.

Marilda Cavalcanti writing about the Brazilian Rainforest Asheninka tribe observes:

...the Asheninka traditional form of education (includes) planting rituals (and) living in communion with nature [ ] school and schooling are thus just (a small) part of the whole discussion on public policies. [ ] As the indigenous teachers say all the time, they are teachers full time, all day long wherever they are. They go hunting and fishing with their students and their families. (2004, p.320)

The Asheninka recognize the importance of literacy but not its supremacy, and just as Socrates assigned the task of writing down his words to Plato, so the Asheninka assign the use of literacy to certain nominated individuals:

As our traditional system of life does not internally depend on writing, we are educating just a few people to make contact with other societies. We are also educating teacher researchers to record our history, to get them involved in our present political organisation, to get them to help us maintain the cultural world of the people, making the old and young people aware and opening up an issue of reflection about writing so that we don't override our culture. Through school, we also work with drawings and maps regarding territorial control because for us it's new to work within a delimited territory. (Cavalcanti, 2004, p.322)

The reference to territories correlates with eco-philosopher David Abram's explanation of the Dreaming songs of Australian aborigines and of their connection to actual features of the landscape. These stories are inextricably linked to specific locations providing, Abram suggests, "an auditory mnemonic (or memory tool) - an oral means of recalling viable routes through an often harsh terrain," (Abram, 1997, p.175) in which "just as the song structure carries the memory of

how to orient in the land, so the sight of particular features in the land activates the memory of specific songs and stories" (ibid). Robert Lawlor writes that:

In the Aboriginal world view, every meaningful activity, event, or life process that occurs at a particular place leaves behind a vibrational residue in the earth, as plants leave an image of themselves as seeds. The shape of the land - its mountains, rocks, riverbeds, and waterholes - and its unseen vibrations echo the events that brought that place into creation. Everything in the natural world is a symbolic footprint of the metaphysical beings whose actions created our world. As with a seed, the potency of an earthly location is wedded to the memory of its origin. (Lawlor, 2007)

Abram adds:

'Given this radical interdependence between the spoken stories and the sensible landscape, the ethnographic practice of writing down oral stories and disseminating them in published form, must be seen as a peculiar form of violence, wherein the stories are torn from the visible landforms and topographic features that materially embody and provoke them.'[e]*(Abram, 1997, p.177)*

Today we still exercise that "peculiar form of violence" in, for example, annotating and mashing up Google maps to achieve similar topographical connections with stories. In the transliterate lifeworld, a Flickr image is understood not as an isolated event but in conjunction with the user's knowledge about what a Flickr page is; what prompted that person to post it, and why sixteen people left comments. It's not just a photo-collecting technology, but the equivalent of the tree in a Dreamtime story - another kind of "sensible landscape" marked with "vibrational residues" which the transliterate user can pick up and "read".

GOING ACROSS AND BEYOND

There has been much discussion among the authors about whether the 'trans' prefix is there to signify a going 'beyond', or a moving 'across'. Certainly to think in terms of the latter is immediately to acknowledge that we are talking about *literacies* plural – otherwise there would be no necessity to move *across*. A visual metaphor for the liminal qualities of transliteracy we are trying

to articulate here can be found in the following image from the British poet and collagist Alan Halsey (2005).

The title of the series this plate comes from also serves our purpose: this work is called "This Problem of Script: Essays in textual analysis" (Halsey, 2005) and therefore overtly references the hegemony of print-based literacy whilst at the same time challenging it in the images that make up the essay. What makes the image a use-

Figure 2. "This Problem of Script"

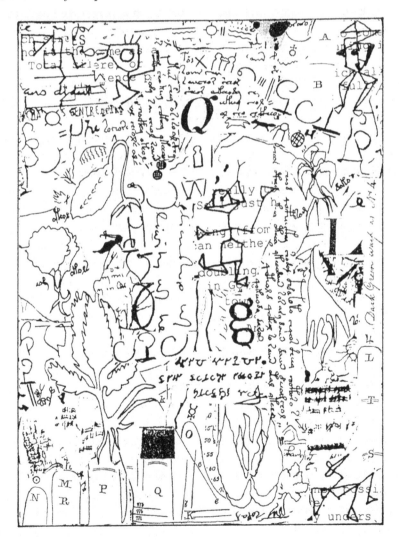

ful analogy to the experience of transliteracy is our inability to rest in it; our inability to focus and establish an anchor; to resolve the problem of script by isolating a hierarchy of discourse that will enable us to prioritize one level of representation over another in order to make sense of the piece. Do we read it left to right? Up or down? Top to bottom? And why does this work compel us to describe what we are doing as 'reading' in inverted commas? Halsey's 'essay' is a compendium of differing types of inscription – pictographs, hieroglyphs, diagrams, maps, staves, fonts, letters, words, severed phrases – it places under re-view the primacy of fixed-print; it re-places script back into a heritage of dialogue between word, image and sound that has always been there in earlier cultures, but that has been masked by the dominance of a print-anchored literacy. As such, transliteracy is both a concept and a practice productively situated in a liminal space between being a new cognitive tool and the recovery of an old one.

The "patterned ways" of transliteracy are multiple, varied, and often physical. A sense of how it feels to hold a feather quill, chisel a stone, type on a keyboard, or take a photograph, is important and helps connect the material product – a letter, photo, etc – to the means of production. For those fond of 2.0 expressions, perhaps this is Physicality 2.0. And then there is the issue of cognition. Behaviours hitherto seen as dysfunctional, such as dyslexia, attention deficit disorder, and even synaesthesia, may actually be useful literacies in less textual environments like computer games (and, indeed, real life) which privilege multimodality over fixed-type print. It appears that flexibility is certainly an essential part of being transliterate. As just a small example, travel to other countries often introduces us to minor differences in cultural practices which demand constant adjustment. Although this can sometimes be stressful, it can also be enjoyable as the visitor increases their level of transliteracy in the new environment. A willingness to embrace the new

might be an essential feature of transliteracy because its opposites, fear and reluctance to learn, are powerful inhibitors to the acquisition of new skills, and skills play an important role in transliterate practice. Many technologies are not new but simply innovative applications of established processes, new tools for old behaviours demanding adjustments to existing skills. As already noted, the way we converse online in chat rooms is often not dissimilar from the way we talk face to face. And a hypertext story, with its many diversions and elaborations, could be eerily similar in form to the telling of family holiday memories. There are more similarities between modes than may be at first apparent, and the technological skills involved are often simple to acquire if the user is positively inclined to attempt them.

NETWORKING THE BOOK

Kate Pullinger and Chris Joseph engage with transliteracy via writing and multimedia design. They have collaborated on several digital fiction projects, including "The Breathing Wall" (Pullinger, Schemat and Joseph, 2004), a novel that responds to the reader's rate of breathing, and the multi-episode online interactive novel "Inanimate Alice" (Pullinger and Joseph, 2007). While work on Alice continues, Pullinger and Joseph are embarking on a new project to create 'Flight Paths', a networked work of fiction:

I have finished my weekly supermarket shop, stocking up on provisions for my three kids, my husband, our dog and our cat. I push the loaded trolley across the car park, battling to keep its wonky wheels on track. I pop open the boot of my car and then for some reason, I have no idea why, I look up, into the clear blue autumnal sky. And I see him. It takes me a long moment to figure out what I am looking at. He is falling from the sky. A dark mass, growing larger quickly. I let go of the trolley and am dimly aware that it is getting away from me but I can't move, I am stuck there in the middle of the supermarket car park, watching, as he hurtles toward the earth. I have no idea how long it takes – a few seconds, an entire lifetime – but I stand there holding my breath as the city goes about its business around me until...

He crashes into the roof of my car.

The car park of Sainsbury's supermarket in Richmond, southwest London, lies directly beneath one of the main flight paths into Heathrow Airport. Over the last decade, on at least five separate occasions, the bodies of young men have fallen from the sky and landed on or near this car park. All these men were stowaways on flights from the Indian subcontinent who had believed that they could find a way into the cargo hold of an airplane by climbing up into the airplane wheel shaft. No one can survive this journey. "Flight Paths" seeks to explore what happens when lives collide – the airplane stowaway and the fictional suburban London housewife, quoted above. This project will tell their stories; it will be a work of digital fiction, a networked book, created on and through the internet. The project will include a web iteration that opens up the research process to the outside world, inviting discussion of the large array of issues the project touches on. As well as this, Pullinger and Joseph will create a series of multimedia elements that will illuminate various aspects of the story. This will allow them to invite and encourage audience-generated content, opening up the project to allow other writers and artists to contribute texts – both multimedia and more traditional – images, sounds, memories, ideas. At the same time, Pullinger will write a print novel which will act as a companion piece to the project overall.

"Flight Paths" will actively engage with many of the questions that are raised by the concept of a transliterate production. Those questions include: what are the possibilities for new narrative forms? How do we "write to be seen" or "write to be heard" when creating multimedia narratives, and can we imagine writing to be smelled, tasted, felt? What are the effects of collective authorship across multiple forms? At what point does multimedia – "a combination of different media which function next to each other and remain clearly discernable" (Van de Poel, 2005, p.8) become intermedia – "an integrative combination of different media [such that] the usual frames and structure of the different media are affected and influenced by each other?" (ibid.)

Cultural production is often analyzed from one of two perspectives:

- the how (practical issues of media and digital literacy, particularly access to and use of the tools and skills of production) or
- the why (social, economic and cultural determinants).

A transliterate analysis would consider both of these, and more: for example, the shift in emphasis from static monologue to dynamic dialogue suggested by participatory narratives; the practices and politics of collaboration, particularly when many geographically and linguistically spread authors collaborate simultaneously; and the existence of a "group creativity" or "intelligence", perhaps as an emergent property of individual creativities or intelligences.

The concept of the networked book of non-fiction is not new and there is a long history of new media fiction works that include user-generated content. But there are very few fiction projects that from the earliest, research phase attempt to harness participatory media and audience generated content in the way that "Flight Paths" will, with its sensitivity to the complex multimodal toolbox of the transliterate reader.

As we have seen, transliteracy involves being able to read, write and interact across multiple modes. It opens up a perspective on pre-digital multimodality in the same way that hypertext theorizing (e.g. Bolter 2001, Landow 2005) opened up a perspective on textual footnotes and indices as pre-digital hypertext. This characterization of transliteracy deliberately refuses to presuppose any kind of offline/online divide; indeed it posits a complete interpellation of one by the other within everyday life, what might be whimsically called a cultural Google Gears[f] combining both online and offline functionalities.

In 2005, the Institute for the Future of the Book (IF:book) conducted a thought experiment in which they proposed that if Marx and Engels had published the Communist Manifesto today and posted it to the web it would attract a global networked multimedia conversation of articles, blog posts, YouTube video, and audio podcasts. Critiques of the manifesto could be accessed in relation to all the others instead of existing as "isolated islands which at best can reference each other but which are not connected in the way we might imagine in the networked world." In March 2007 IF:book Director Bob Stein reported that the Amazon.com page for the Communist Manifesto now provides a linked citation list of 2,061 books which reference it. (Stein, 2007) And that is without the accretion of all the accumulated reader comments and recommendations at Amazon. Today, on the internet at least, the Manifesto is not just a book you can read in the bath[g] but an entire networked body of many media, including no doubt real meetings in real places, as always. And the conversation continues to grow. Indeed, the IF:book blog post, and now this chapter too, are part of it.

TRANSLITERATE READING

Dene Grigar's web fiction "Fallow Field" is an example of how the online environment easily foregrounds multimodality (Grigar, 2004). Grigar situates the story within an agricultural scenario where digging, flowing, and cultivating signal both the plot and the reader's procedural harvesting of the narrative. Just as the narrator swats flies and

bypasses empty fields in search of succulent corn and herself, so the reader wends her way through sounds, images, words, and links. Marcus Bastos describes Grigar's narrative approach as one where "[t]he overlapping of physical and digital, among other things, problematize the existence of clear borders or, at least, defy traditional categorizations of 'natural' and 'artificial'," (Bastos et al, 2007, para 2) and so too must the transliterate reader take these elements into account. Grigar's emphasis on junctures, crossroads, and choices discourages notions of concrete conclusions by highlighting the "liminal spaces between" (ibid.). The how and the why, like form and content, are inextricably intertwined. The role assigned to the reader in such a fiction is an example of what we mean by transliteracy: the reader is required to understand how the aural (in the form of music, sound effects, the narrator's voice), visual (images and text) and interactive modes function simultaneously. Without recognizing how these various modes play against and with one another the reader risks grasping only part of the plot.

However, material does not have to be digital to be multimodal. For example, according to Cavalcanti, the culture of the Asheninka tribe is learned and passed on via an interwoven accretion of images and stories.

Everything we use has a story; each drawing has a long and comprehensive story. Each drawing which is passed from one generation to another is our writing; each little symbol has an immense story. As one learns a drawing, one learns its origin, who taught it, who brought it to us. (p.322)

Transliteracy is, of course, inextricable from social practice, and social researchers have an influential part to play by investigating from two directions – transliteracy as a cultural phenomenon, and as a lens through which to examine society and culture. On one hand, it is the kind of literacy we require to be able to simultaneously attend to multiple media and modes of

Figure 3. Screen shot from fallow field

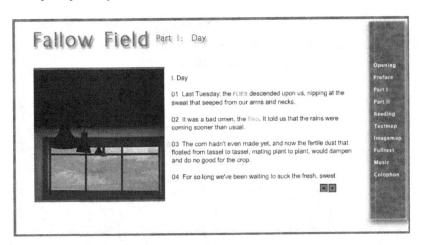

communication: the literacy of the 'trans'. On the other, it also refers to that kind of literacy we use to apply the literacies of one mode or medium to another one: transliteration. This dual nature of transliteracy implies that it can be employed to understand communication both diachronically (over time) and synchronically (at the same time). Diachronically, it helps us understand, for example, how the practice of blogging might draw upon non-digital methods of combining modes in handwritten media or how personal blogs relates to diaries and journals. Synchronically, it can help us see how multiple media and modes of communication are used in relation to each other at the same time. As an example of the former, the image below from *Time Magazine* shows Al Gore sitting at his desk while surrounded by various media each of which has different modal affordances.[h] A transliterate perspective can help us understand how these modes and media relate.

Gore appears to be paying attention primarily to his computer but is surrounded by various non-digital media: books, flip charts, articles, a television and so on. Naturally there may be some staging involved but what we see here is something that perhaps many of us recognize from our working practices; at any time we may be able to shift attention or position in the room in order to reorient ourselves. In a blog entry about this photo, the author annotates the image and relates it to Bolter and Grusin's notion (1999) of the "hypermediated work environment", noting that "[t]he method in which the information is delivered changes the way we understand it," (Übernoggin, 2007) which is to reprise the McLuhanesque assertion that the medium is the message. In this case Gore's workspace is saturated with multiple media delivering information: even the frog on the wall can be read as a medium which conveys a message about threats to the environment.[i] A transliterate perspective encourages us to see this image holistically. Gore's room is not hermetically sealed, presumably, so there are elements in the scene which are invisible in the still photograph: sounds from outside, smells and so on. Other people will have been in the room and traces of their activities may be relevant, even the fact that the room appears to be a sprawling, chaotic mess indicates a certain set of behaviours. Al Gore's lifeworld may be embodied, in part, by that office:

Figure 4. Photograph of Al Gore sitting at his desk

what to an outsider may seem to be disorder may well be rather more structured.

EVERYDAY LIFE IN A TRANSLITERATE WORLD

The ways in which people manage different media and modes of communication in their everyday lives is of great interest to the transliteracy researcher. In his 1981 paper "The Ethnography of Literacy", ethnographer John Szwed called for research into the "social meaning of literacy" on the grounds that "…the stunning fact is that we do not fully know what literacy is. The assumption that it is simply a matter of the skills of reading and writing does not even begin to approach the fundamental problem: what are reading and writing for?" (Szwed 1981, p.14). The emergence of Web 2.0 technologies since then has only intensified this challenge, and transliteracy encourages

us to adapt Szwed's statement and ask: what are "Reading 2.0" and "Writing 2.0" for?[j]

Writing in 1998, Bruce Mason argued that "research into computer-mediated communication (CMC) has begun to challenge much of the scholarship in the orality and literacy debate," (p.306). This is not to suggest that transliteracy is restricted to Web 2.0 but, rather, to suggest that we can use the plethora of new media devices and affordances to view what might be ancient practices in a twenty-first century light. It should be possible to adapt Szwed's call for ethnographies of literacy into an examination of "… the roles these abilities play in social life; the varieties of reading and writing available for choice; the contexts of their performance; and the manner in which they are interpreted and tested, not by experts but by ordinary people in ordinary activities". We need ethnographies of transliteracy, studies of its social, cultural and power relationships and of its networked vernacular from the perspectives of those who live and work within it.

CHALLENGES TO EDUCATION

According to the Institute for the Future, transliteracy is a 'disruptive innovation' which presents challenges that will shape the way we think of teaching and learning in the context of the open economy. In their view, 'developing transliterate creative production practices and communication across multiple platforms represents a sensory and cultural explosion that will frame new kinds of experience and knowing.'[k] In a 2007 report 'The Future of Learning Agents' they propose that 'transliterating social and creative life implies new social and political understandings as new relations of creative production emerge. Collective authorship and collective intelligence are modes of active learning and discovery that present new dynamics between individuals and groups with respect to knowledge. Roles of authority and expertise shift when information and experience are created and aggregated in blogs, chat, and online group discussions lists. Ownership of content in a remix context, and for a public audience, present new ways of understanding ideas, knowledge, people, and perspectives.'[l] This is borne out in the work of researchers like Marc Prensky, who wrote in 2007: 'While some teachers do embrace the kids' technological world, those teachers who are fearful of being unable to engage a generation of students used to technological advances often attribute their own failures, such as the loss of control implied in integrating tools that they know relatively little about, to untruths such as lack of attention span and Attention Deficit Disorder on the part of students. In exchange, students observe their teachers' lack of fluency with modern tools, and view them as 'illiterate' in the very domain the kids know they will need for their future – technology.'[m]

The Institute for the Future proposes that 'to avoid a dysfunctional disconnect between teachers and students, the education community must correct the current asymmetry in the classroom around media literacy' and, as Stephen Downes points out, learning must be understood to be taking place everywhere, not just in the institution: 'the learning environment is, in essence, the removal of the classroom entirely from the learning, and the use instead of whatever environment the learners happen to find themselves in.' (Downes, 2004).

CHALLENGES TO THE WORKPLACE

In May 2007 the authors invited forty people from academia, business and the arts to a Transliteracy Colloquium. Selected for their fluency with new media, we hoped they would help us open up new avenues of thought and transliteracy and its applications in their particular fields. Their feedback enabled us to expand our vision and presented us with further challenges and ideas.

For example, Microsoft National Technology Officer Jerry Fishenden observed that the digital age will change everything: "There remains much talk of a "digital divide" - but we have so long grown accustomed to a world in which there is a "literacy divide" it is not often mentioned. The move to the digital era could be as democratizing as the birth of the printing press was in the fifteenth century. It will bring the ability to capture and share human experiences, learning and entertainment in far more intuitive ways than the age of literacy allowed." [n]

Roland Harwood, of the UK National Endowment for Science, Technology and the Arts, saw applications for transliteracy in his work to develop business innovation: "All innovation is fundamentally collaborative. With increasing specialization in business and academia in recent years, this has led to an increasing need for organizations and individuals to develop wider, more open networks, partnerships and trusted communities to share ideas and to innovate. In particular, a powerful source of innovation is to collaborate across traditional boundaries, be they organizational, disciplinary or geographic. Therefore, much of the discussion centered upon how can we communicate effectively and build trust across these disparate communities. Technology definitely has a major role to play in supporting these boundary-disrupting collaborations, but perhaps there is a need to further develop most peoples' 'transliteracy' skills." ᵒ

And English scholar Dr Ruth Page, of the University of Central England, responded to the proposition that collaboration could be a quality of transliteracy: "I see the relationship between transliteracy and collaboration as one of mutual and dialectic enabling, rather than as one being a defining property of the other. I questioned whether one could be transliterate on your own? Surely you can? Similarly collective behavior need not be transliteracy. Instead, I think the collective (Web 2.0) nature of communication is both a by-product and a cause of transliteracy."ᵖ

Transliteracy is essentially an open source idea. Much more research is needed to reveal its potential and the authors are necessarily limited by their own fields of expertise. We are keen to encourage further development by researchers in other areas who may see synergies with their own work and wish to develop their own take on transliteracy. We see potential applications everywhere - in e-learning and education; cultural networks; business, commerce and manufacturing; social science, politics and economics; transdisciplinary studies; philosophy and anthropology; the arts, and many other fields. Transliteracy is already embedded in the curriculum for students on the DMU Online MA in Creative Writing and New Media and the transdisciplinary IOCT Master's Programme, and there is interest in developing it for primary and secondary curricula. We would be interested to hear of proposals to add it to other syllabi at all levels of education.

ACKNOWLEDGMENT

This paper profited hugely from the input of many people, online via our blogs and their own, and offline at the Institute of Creative Technologies at De Montfort University. We have also benefited from conversations with IOCT Visiting Professor and PART researcher Howard Rheingold, and with students on the Online MA in Creative Writing and New Media. In addition, we wish to acknowledge the contributions of Howard Rheingold and Professors Andrew Hugill and Mohammad Ibrahim in their presentations at the Transliteracy Colloquium, May 2007. Many ideas in this chapter were heavily influenced by participants at that colloquium and we wish to thank each participant for their freely offered time, insights and criticisms, all of which have helped to strengthen this paper. Thanks also to colleagues at various seminars and conferences where we have presented our early thinking on transliteracy, and to the UK Higher Education Academy English Subject Centre for its interest and support from the very beginning. A special acknowledgement must go to Professor Alan Liu and his Transliteracies Project team at the University of California Santa Barbara for their 2005 conference *Research in the Technological, Social, and Cultural Practices of Online Reading*, without which this work would not have begun.

REFERENCES

Agre, P. & Horswill, I. (1997). Lifeworld Analysis. *Journal of Artificial Intelligence Research* Volume 6, pp. 111-145, and at http://www-2.cs.cmu.edu/afs/cs/project/jair/pub/volume6/agre97a-html/lifeworlds.html.

Abram, D. (1997). *The Spell of the Sensuous: Perception and Language in a More-Than-Human World*. New York: Vintage.

"amillionpenguins.com" Retrieved June 20, 2007 from http://www.amillionpenguins.com/wiki/index.php/Main_Page.

Bastos, M., Grigar, D., & Rodgers, T. (2007). Dene Grigar and Tara Rodgers: LEAD - Wild Nature and Digital Life Chat Transcripts. *Leonardo Electronic Almanac* 15. 1 – 2, at http://leoalmanac.org/resources/lead/digiwild/dgrigartrodgers.asp, accessed 20 June 2007.

"Berners-Lee on the read/write web." Retrieved June 20, 2007, from http://news.bbc.co.uk/1/hi/technology/4132752.stm.

Bolter, J. D. (2001). *Writing Space: Computers, Hypertext, and the Remediation of Print.* Mahwah, NJ: Lawrence Erlbaum Associates.

Bolter, J. D., & Grusin, R. (1999). *Remediation: Understanding New Media.* Cambridge, MA: MIT Press.

Bush, A. A., & Tiwana, A. (2005). Designing Sticky Knowledge Networks. *Communications of the ACM*, 48(5).

Cavalcanti, M. C. (2004). It's Not Writing by Itself that is Going to Solve our Problems': Questioning a Mainstream Ethnocentric Myth as Part of a Search for Self-sustained Development. *Language and Education*, *18*(4), 317–325 and at http://www.multilingual-matters.net/le/018/le0180317.htm, accessed 20 June 2007.

Cohen, C. (2007). Meet Colby Buzzell, a king among blookers. *Guardian Unlimited* at http://www.guardian.co.uk/commentisfree/story/0,,2073619,00.html, accessed 20 June, 2007.

Downes, S. (2004). From Classrooms to Learning Environments: A Midrange Projection of E-Learning Technologies. *College Quarterly, 7*(3).

Ettinghausen, J. (2007). About this Blog. *A Million-Penguins.com Blog*, at http://amillionpenguins.com/blog/?page_id=2, accessed 20 June 2007.

Ettinghausen, E. (2007a). A Million Thanks. *A Mil-lionPenguins.com Blog*, at http://amillionpenguins.com/blog/?p=28, accessed 21 June 2007

Gilster, P. (1997). *Digital Literacy.* NY: John Wiley and Sons.

Grigar, D. (2004). Fallow Field: A Story in Two Parts. *Iowa Review Web, volume 7,* at http://www.uiowa.edu/~iareview/tirweb/feature/grigar/fallowfield/fallow_field_opening.html, accessed 20 June 2007.

Grigar, D. (2004a). Preface: Fallow Field: A Story in Two Parts, 2004. *Iowa Review Web*, 7, at http://www.uiowa.edu/~iareview/tirweb/feature/grigar/fallowfield/fallow_field_preface.html, accessed 20 June 2007.

Halsey, A. (2005). This Problem of Script: Essays in Textual Analysis. *Marginalien.* Hereford: Five Seasons Press.

Jenkins, H. (2001). Convergence? I diverge. *Technology Review*, (June), p. 93, and at http://www.technologyreview.com/Biztech/12434/, accessed 23 June 2007

Landow, G. P. (2005). *Hypertext 3.0: Critical Theory and New Media in an Era of Globalization.* Baltimore, MD: John Hopkins University Press.

Lawlor, R. (2007). Voices of the First Day: Awakening in the Aboriginal Dreamtime. at http://www.didgeridoos.net.au/dreamtime%20stories/Index%20dreamtime%20stories.html, accessed 20 June 2007.

McLuhan, M. (1964). *Understanding Media.* London: Routledge.

Mason, B. L. (1998). E-Texts: The Orality and Literacy Issue Revisited. *Oral Tradition*, *13*(2), 306-29.

Ofcom (2003). Media Literacy Audit - Report on adult media literacy. at http://www.ofcom.org.uk/advice/media_literacy/medlitpub/medlitpubrss/medialit_audit/, accessed 20 June 2007.

Ong, W. J. (1982). *Orality and Literacy*. London: Routledge.

Plato "The Phaedrus," trans. by Alexander Nehamas and Paul Woodruff. In John M. Cooper (editor), *Plato: Complete Works*, Indianapolis, IN: Hacket Publishing, (1997).

Prensky, M. (2007). How to Teach With Technology -- keeping both teachers and students comfortable in an era of exponential change. *BECTA's Emerging Technologies for Learning*, 2, 4.

Pullinger, K., Schemat, S., & Joseph, C. (2004). The Breathing Wall. CD-ROM and at http://www.thebreathingwall.com, accessed 20 June 2007.

Pullinger, K., & Joseph, C. (2007). "Inanimate Alice," at http://www.inanimatealice.com/, accessed 20 June 2007.

Saveri, A., Rheingold, H., & Vian, K. (2005). *Technologies of Cooperation*. Palo Alto: Institute for the Future and at http://www.rheingold.com/cooperation/Technology_of_cooperation.pdf, accessed 20 June 2007.

Stein, R. (2007). Amazon starts to close the loop. at http://www.futureofthebook.org/blog/archives/2007/03/amazon_starts_to_close_the_loo.html, accessed 21 June 2007

Szwed, J. (1981). The Ethnography of Literacy. In M. F. Whiteman (Ed.), *Writing: The Nature, Development and Teaching of Written Communication*. Baltimore, MD: Lawrence Erlbaum, pp.13-24.

"The Lulu Blooker Prize 2007". Retrieved June 20, 2007 from http://www.lulublookerprize.com.

Thomas, S. et al. (2007). Transliteracy: Crossing divides. *First Monday*, *12*(12). Available at: http://www.uic.edu/htbin/cgiwrap/bin/ojs/index.php/fm/article/view/2060/1908.

Transliteracies Project: Research in the Technological, Social, and Cultural Practices of Online Reading. (2007). Retrieved June 20, 2007 from http://transliteracies.english.ucsb.edu/category/research-project.

Übernoggin (2007). Hypermediated Work Environments. *Übernoggin* at http://ubernoggin.com/?p=18, accessed 20 June 2007.

Van de Poel, J. (2005), Intermediality Reinterpreted. at http://www.ethesis.net/worlds/worlds_contence.htm, accessed 20 June 2007.

ENDNOTES

[a]   Soccer, for our North American readers.

[b]   Her conference report can be read at Sue Thomas, Transliteracy – Reading in the Digital Age, English Subject Centre Newsletter Issue 9 - November 2005 http://www.english.heacademy.ac.uk/explore/publications/newsletters/newsissue9/thomas.htm, accessed 21 June 2007.

[c]   Press release, available at http://www.dmu.ac.uk/news_events/news/current/wiki_novel.jsp, accessed 20 June 2007.

[d]   There are indirect parallels which are occasionally drawn such as "round robins" or games in which each author writes the next section of the story. In a wiki, the authors work to add, revise, delete and otherwise edit comment and, unless the wiki is "locked" there is never a final text just the text that there happens be now.

[e]   Of course, it is impossible to ignore the fact that Plato did exactly this when he transcribed the conversation between Socrates and Phaedrus as it was taking place under a plane-tree by the banks of the Ilissus.

[f]   An open source browser extension that lets developers create web applications that can run offline. Available at http://gears.google.com/, accessed 20 June 2007.

[g]   The ubiquitous quality test of equating a good book with being able to read it in the

bath is guaranteed to infuriate these authors whenever it appears. See, for example, Jess Laccetti, "Digitise or Die: a personal reflection," at http://www.hum.dmu.ac.uk/blogs/part/2007/04/digitise_of_die_a_personal_ref.html, accessed 20 June 2007.

[h] http://www.time.com/time/photogallery/0,29307,1622338_1363003,00.html

[i] The tree frog is a common symbol of biodiversity.

[j] We do not propose to define these terms here and now. Indeed it is unclear whether the terms have any meaning.

[k] From an internal research report on the future of learning agents prepared by Institute for the Future, November, 2007

[l] IBID.

[m] Prensky, M. (2007). How to Teach With Technology -- keeping both teachers and students comfortable in an era of exponential change. *BECTA's Emerging Technologies for Learning*, 2, 4.

[n] http://ntouk.com/?view=plink&id=284, accessed 20 June 2007.

[o] http://blogs.nesta.org.uk/innovation/2007/05/trust_technolog.html, accessed 20 June 2007.

[p] http://digitalnarratives.blogspot.com/2007/05/transliteracy-colloquim.html, accessed 20 June 2007.

Chapter XXX
Bridging the Gap Between
Web 2.0 and Higher Education

Martin Weller
The Open University, UK

James Dalziel
Macquarie University, Australia

ABSTRACT

This chapter looks at some of the areas of tension between the new social networking, Web 2.0 communities and the values of higher education. It argues that both the granularity of formal education and the manner in which the authors formalise learning are subject to change with the advent of digital technologies and user generated content. The gap between higher education and Web 2.0 could be bridged by, amongst other approaches, a sort of flickr for learning design, which allows users to share activities and sequences, thus meeting the diverse needs of learners and utilising the best of social networking approaches.

INTRODUCTION

The rise of internet technologies that can be grouped under the web 2.0 heading has generated a good deal of interest in education, as witnessed by the number of conferences that now have web 2.0 or related approaches as a main theme, the number of educational technology bloggers, and the interest of commercial web 2.0 start-up companies such as TeachThePeople.com.

This is because the popularity of sites such as flickr, facebook, MySpace, wikipedia, etc is interesting of itself, in terms of what drives users to these sites and why they keep returning. But more significantly it is their potential as tools to facilitate learning that has caused much discussion. Their implications for learning can be summarised as:

- Technology – with most universities now possessing a virtual learning environment (VLE) (OECD 2004, Barro and Burillo, 2006), the extent to which some of the technologies could form a learning environment has been discussed. For example Downes (2007) highlights Facebook's educational heritage, and Kemp and Livingstone (2006) have integrated the virtual world SecondLife with the Moodle VLE.

- User generated content – wikipedia is the most famous example, but through formats such as blogs, podcasts, vlogs, wikis, slideshare (shared presentations), splashcasts (video clips that combine different media formats), screencasts (slideshows with synchronised audio), and webcasts there is a good deal of material that is both useful for students, and is generated by them.

- Pedagogy – learning as it occurs in web 2.0 communities tends to be informal, and socially oriented. If we look at open source software communities as an example of where learning takes place in such communities there are a number of differences with higher education. For example, these communities are very flexible where roles are not stagnant. Although hierarchies and formalised roles exist, they are not as rigid, with advancement or promotion through meritocracy, with a selection of individuals earning the right to make decisions based on merit or past contributions. A number of researchers, such as Bacon & Dillon (2006) have suggested that open source communities might serve as an example for future educational structures and processes.

- Content and resources – there are a variety of educational sites offering a range of resources. These include open educational resource repositories such as MITs Open-CourseWare and the Open University's Openlearn project, and also audio and video lectures and talks through providers such as iTunesU. Students thus have access to a wide diversity of high quality material to supplement their studies.

- Philosophy – this is probably the most significant, and one we will explore further below. There is a fundamental difference between the principles that the web 2.0 world enshrines and those within higher education. At its simplest this can be summarised as bottom up versus top down.

The last point in the above list suggests that there are differences between the cultures and values found in the web 2.0 community and those in higher education. It is worth examining these in more detail as they hold the key to the central question, both of this article and for education as whole, which is how do we bridge the gap between these two worlds? In this chapter we wish to explore some of the differences, consider their implications for higher education and lastly to map possible benefits for the learner that such approaches may have on to the existing higher education structures, through the process of learning design.

DIFFERENT CULTURES

Firstly, let us examine the values of the web 2.0 community. Web 2.0 can be seen as both a set of technologies (such as the use of particular programming languages) and also a set of values. In his essay 'What is web 2.0?' Tim O'Reilly (2005) sets out a number of key features. The first of these principles is the notion of web as platform. This was an idea that first surfaced with much of the initial dot.com hype. That didn't come to pass, but O'Reilly suggests a crucial difference this time around, which is personified by Google. Whereas Netscape was based around a software product, Google is based around a service. He summarizes it thus:

In each of its past confrontations with rivals, Microsoft has successfully played the platform card, trumping even the most dominant applications. Windows allowed Microsoft to displace Lotus 1-2-3 with Excel, WordPerfect with Word, and Netscape Navigator with Internet Explorer.

This time, though, the clash isn't between a platform and an application, but between two platforms, each with a radically different business model: On the one side, a single software provider, whose massive installed base and tightly integrated operating system and APIs give control over the programming paradigm; on the other, a system without an owner, tied together by a set of protocols, open standards and agreements for cooperation.

Another principle, and one that has relevance for education, is that of 'harnessing collective intelligence'. Wikipedia is an obvious example here, as are sites such as Flickr, YouTube, 43Things, etc. This ability to harness what James Suriowecki (2005) calls the wisdom of crowds is partly what sets aside successful e-commerce sites such as e-bay and Amazon. This seems to be one of the key principles, that the actions of users when interacting with a site (selecting content, commenting, tagging, voting, etc) collectively adds value that benefits all users. The technology or site therefore needs to be set up so that it encourages participation. This shift to co-ownership of information and technology challenges the conventional hierarchical model found in traditional broadcast media.

In terms of software development web 2.0 applications operate a much more evolutionary model, continually adding new features and monitoring the use of these. Because the applications are all delivered online this can be achieved without the need for a major update and release of software. O'Reilly suggests that

Users must be treated as co-developers, ... The open source dictum, "release early and release often" in fact has morphed into an even more radical position, "the perpetual beta," in which the product is developed in the open, with new features slipstreamed in on a monthly, weekly, or even daily basis....

Another principle is that of lightweight programming models. The key to these models are that systems are often loosely coupled, (at least from the user's perspective) rather than tightly integrated. This facilitates the 'perpetual beta' model and also means that tools and services from other providers can be easily assimilated to make the overall system more powerful. The approach is summarized as 'innovation in assembly', whereby value is added by assembling a number of different components together in a useful manner. This may have been achieved through hardware previously, for example, Dell computers assemble components to produce PCs that suit a user's needs. With the sort of lightweight programming models now in practice, the same approach can be applied to tools and services.

There are a number of key features to web 2.0 approaches then. The first of these is democracy, in that participation and governance is the result of the collective. The second is that a bottom-up approach drives content generation, description and discovery. And, from the educational perspective, the third is that they are socially oriented.

Now let us compare these with the values that are enshrined in higher education practices. While not always in direct conflict, there are a number of clashes. For instance, education is a hierarchically arranged system, with Professors, Lecturers, part-time support staff and students.

Education places a high priority on quality assurance of the content (where content can be physical resources such as books and journal articles, and also events such as lectures). It achieves this through a largely top-down process of review (for example of journal articles) and formal assessment (such as exams and course approval processes) which effectively act as filters to participation in the process. Much of education can be seen as a process of enculturation into academic practice, for instance a PhD student is not only conducting research in to their subject, but learning *how* to be a researcher and publish academic material.

This is in marked contrast to web 2.0 which removes all barriers to participation, and then uses popularity, user tagging, and metrics such as number of links and quotes to an article to filter for quality and appropriateness. Weinberger (2007) refers to the process as 'filtering on the way out'. In education, this filtering is done on the way in, through the process of peer review, standardised measures of quality (such as the Research Assessment Exercise in the UK), and the enculturation process mentioned above. Web 2.0 removes all this prefiltering, so that anyone is free to publish, but then adds in a suite of tools and metrics to help users search through the content and judge its quality. For example, blogs can be listed in the blog directory Technorati, which provides an 'authority' ranking, which is calculated by the number of unique blogs linking to your blog, and their respective authority. This works on the assumption that the more times a blog is linked to, then the greater it's reliability, and particularly if those doing the linking have a good reputation. Combined with search, metrics such as authority are then used to do some of the filtering on the way out.

There are a number of other areas of conflict between higher education and web 2.0. For instance the perpetual beta approach to software development reveals a fundamentally different belief as to how not only software, but any project should develop. Weller (2007) argues that

"Most higher education institutions will favour rigorous, consultative approaches when developing or adopting software with the specification process taking months and maybe years to complete, with the intention that the system will be in place for a suitably lengthy period. Such an approach does not match well with the faster, loose knit, rapid turnover mentality of the web 2.0 approach."

Perhaps most significantly is the belief in education that there is a right way to do things, that essentially the educator holds the knowledge about how the students should learn and provides the pathway. In web 2.0 diversity and personalisation are championed. However, can this miscellaneous approach apply to education? There has been a shift towards more constructivist approaches in education recently which acknowledge the role of the individual's experience in the learning process, but the key function of education remains to overcome Meno's paradox, which states 'how can I inquire about something which I don't know anything about?' (e.g. Laurillard 2001). It is this need to maintain the structure and guidance, while embracing some of the principles of web 2.0 which a learning design based approach may be able to address, and which we will examine later in this paper.

WEB 2.0 CRITICS

Any movement that gains as much publicity and generates as much hype as web 2.0 is bound to attract a range of critics. Some are merely concerned that it is an over-used and misleading term, for example, Hirschorn (2007) says that "Like 'push,' 'social media' is a functional advance pimped out as a revolution."

Perhaps most prominent amongst these has been Andrew Keen, who argues against the quality of user generated content. The cult of the amateur he says *"worships the creative amateur: the self-taught filmmaker, the dorm-room musician, the unpublished writer. It suggests that everyone—even the most poorly educated and inarticulate amongst us—can and should use digital media to express and realize themselves."*

On the Encyclopaedia Britannica web site, Michael Gorman (2007a) takes this argument further stating that the difference between traditional sources of information (such as encyclopaedias) and online information is

"the authenticity and fixity of the former (that its creator is reputable and it is what it says it is), the expertise that has given it credibility, and the scholarly apparatus that makes the recorded knowledge accessible on the one hand and the lack of authenticity, expertise, and complex finding aids in the latter."

Authenticity and reliability lies at the heart of the problem for Gorman, who argues that only through top down processes can these be assured:

"The task before us is to extend into the digital world the virtues of authenticity, expertise, and scholarly apparatus that have evolved over the 500 years of print, virtues often absent in the manuscript age that preceded print."

This concern over the quality and reliability of content is one that is pertinent to education and frames many educators' response to web 2.0. For example, many will find themselves in agreement with Gorman (2007b) when he asks

"Do we entrust the education of children to self-selected "experts" without any known authority or credentials? Would any sane person pay fees to take university courses that are taught by people who may or may not be qualified to teach such a course?"

And on wikipedia, the best example of online user generated content Gorman (2007c) adds

"A few endorse Wikipedia heartily. This mystifies me. Education is not a matter of popularity or of convenience—it is a matter of learning, of knowledge gained the hard way, and of respect for the human record. A professor who encourages the use of Wikipedia is the intellectual equivalent of a dietician who recommends a steady diet of Big Macs with everything."

What the argument between the critics and the proponents seems to be about is *process.* For the critics the top-down, official metrics and measure approach to authenticity is the best way to produce high quality resources. For the proponents, the bottom up, distributed process is more powerful.

In terms of the power of distribution we have an analogy in the process of open source software. Eric Raymond's (2000) maxim of 'given enough eyeballs, all bugs are shallow' sums up the benefits of the distributed approach. There is no debate about the quality of the software produced through open source communities, including some of the most robust and widely used software in use today such as Apache, Linux, Open Office, etc. Wheeler (2007) uses quantitative data to make the case for open source software from the perspectives of market share, reliability, performance, scalability, security and cost, where open source solutions nearly always outperform proprietary ones.

The question then is whether a similar distributed approach can be applied to domains other than software development. There are undoubtedly areas where the top-down centralised approach is necessary, for example it is difficult to imagine a feature film being produced through a distributed model. Wikipedia is the best example of user generated content, where the process of creating entries is performed through careful negotiation and dialogue between contributors.

In objective tests wikipedia has been found to be as reliable as Britannica (Giles 2005) (and it even contains a list of entries with errors in Britannica http://en.wikipedia.org/wiki/Wikipedia: Errors_in_the_Encyclop%C3%A6dia_Britannica_that_have_been_corrected_in_Wikipedia). After this study was completed the errors identified in wikipedia were fixed within a few days, whereas Britannica had to wait until the next round of publication to address theirs. This at least demonstrates that distribution as process can work in creating complex content other than software. As with open source software, the contributers to wikipedia may be 'experts' in their own field, but the means by which they have acquired this expertise is irrelevant, that is they are not required to have particular credentials *before* they can contribute, but rather they are judged on the quality of their contribution.

THE GRANULARITY OF EDUCATION

The digitisation of content and its frictionless distribution on a global scale is challenging many of the assumptions we have about the format of content and the underlying business models that support these. Often these are so ingrained in our view of the content and its related businesses that we do not even recognise them as assumptions.

Prior to digitisation, all content was bound up in its physical form. That is, you had to buy or obtain, the physical copy of a book, CD or DVD. Evans and Wurster (1999) argue that previously a product and its information were bound together and therefore forced to follow the same business models. For example to find out which books are on sale in a bookstore you have to physically walk past the products. But online these two elements – the product and its information – are unbundled and free to follow different models.

The business models of content industries followed the demands of this physical form – CDs require production, packaging, storage, distribution and retail. The record company and record stores are thus a logical necessity in a market for music CDs. But with the digitisation of content many of these demands disappear. MP3s can be distributed freely online, they do not require production (in the physical format sense), or a distribution network. There are also a number of computer based 'studio' software packages that mean the production, mixing, and overlaying of tracks is much easier and cheaper.

What web 2.0 adds to this process is the removal of the filtering function performed by intermediaries, which previously were a necessary part of the model. Prior to the internet, artists could make tapes or CDs of their own music and try and bypass the record companies, but they lacked a significant distribution network. With the advent of the internet they had access to a potential global distribution method, but they lacked the promotion and a means of people finding their music. With web 2.0 content discovery is facilitated through services such as LastFM and iTunes. Here users can create playlists, recommend artists and tracks, and add favourites. In addition, data mining finds similar artists and songs by monitoring user behaviour (like book recommendations in Amazon), so that in LastFM for example, a user can enter an artist's name and will be played a series of songs by artists that are deemed similar. Thus the filtering process of the record companies is also removed.

This leads to some profound implications for content industries, including newspapers, television, music, film, etc. For instance in the music industry, record companies are beginning to be disintermediated, with artists (e.g. Radiohead) offering free downloads of their albums.

It also changes the nature of our relationship to content. Weinberger (2007) says of music

"For decades we've been buying albums. We thought it was for artistic reasons, but it was really because the economics of the physical world

471

required it: Bundling songs into long-playing albums lowered the production, marketing, and distribution costs ... As soon as music went digital, we learned that the natural unit of music is the track."

As we shall see in a later section, education has some similarities with content industries, but also some significant differences. However, it is worth considering whether we hold similar assumptions about the granularity of education as we held about the granularity of music, which would be subject to change with digitisation of content and provision of online services. Higher education, as we normally conceive of it, is typified by the undergraduate degree course. This takes 3-4 years continuous study, comprises a number of modules, has regular exam and assessment sessions, is taught face to face, and students are assessed in terms of the knowledge they demonstrate of the taught modules. There are, of course, variations to each of these elements – study can occur at a distance, it can be part-time, assessment can be portfolio and continuous, there can be breaks in study, etc. But each of these adaptations is usually mapped on to the existing, standard model. They represent modifications to it, not replacements.

However, it may be that many of these assumptions are bound up in the economic models that have their roots in the physical aspects of education. For example, if you are requiring students to come to a physical campus, then it makes sense to bundle all their modules in to a short time span to minimise inconvenience and to manage staff time. If the assessment is then based on an exam, it similarly follows that you package this up into one event. These restrictions have then moulded what we deem to constitute a higher education experience, but like the album, perhaps this packaging is merely a product of the physical format, not a 'natural' means of structuring it. Even when courses have moved online, they have usually followed similar conventions in terms of length and assessment.

The digitisation of content, and perhaps more significantly, dialogue and collaboration, means that the type of learning event we can include and assess now changes. It is not just the standard lecture, but can include student reflective writing on their learning through video, blogs, podcasts, etc. It can also include discussions between learners, in the form of asynchronous text forums, recorded virtual meetings, instant messaging transcripts, etc. So the type of content we assess the student's understanding of changes, which will inevitably have consequences for the way we assess it. The formal exam or multiple choice question bears little relationship to the student's experience when connected to such a range of media.

As well as altering *what* is assessed, the frequency and *nature* of assessment is subject to change also, which we will address in the next section.

THE TOPOGRAPHY OF FORMALITY

Just as we think of learning being bundled into a convenient course package, so we think of the formalisation of learning being grouped into large chunks. Informal learning is difficult to recognise and accredit, and is thus often overlooked in favour of formal education. There is an intrinsic paradox with informal learning – in order to reward and recognise it, then it needs to be formalised in some manner. This can be through an accredited programme, the use of portfolios to demonstrate competency, or diagnostic tests.

If we were to consider the formalisation of learning as a topology then currently it is a flat plain with a few high peaks, rather like skyscrapers in a desert, representing courses. The learner traverses this topology over their lifetime, most of it spent on the flat plain, with no easy access to formal recognition, and is then requested to climb large peaks of formality, such as a postgraduate course. This bears little resemblance to how they actually learn, which will have some peaks, but will be more evenly distributed.

In the online world however, this topology could be subject to considerable change. The peaks become shallower, but more frequent, so it is more akin to an archipelago. In this model, the digitisation of content and interaction mentioned in the previous section allows users to gather evidence of informal learning on a daily basis. They may then choose to bundle this into a formally recognised event, for example by having their portfolio assessed, or engaging in a 'micro-course' which demonstrates their ability in a given area, or by creating a meta-document of their own, for example a reflective blog post that draws on the different pieces of evidence.

Ironically this is actually how educators conduct their professional lives. An educator may engage in a research project and they will formalise this learning through conference presentations or journal articles. They will bundle together recent experience into published text books, or project reports, with a number of informal steps along the way, such as class discussions, departmental seminars, work in progress conference papers, etc. In this respect the academic profession has a number of recognised means of formalising learning. Many other professions and individuals do not have such readily available and acknowledged means of unifying recent learning and experience.

THE THREAT TO HIGHER EDUCATION

Higher education has many similarities to content and broadcast industries, such as book publishing and the music industry. As we saw in a previous section, the digitisation of content and the use of the internet as a distribution method is having profound implications for these industries. They are essentially faced with two choices:

1. Find ways of maintaining the publisher model, by managing the rights and use of content through a combination of technological and legal controls.
2. Find new business models that give away content but build and sell services around it.

The struggle between these two modes of operating will define content industries over the next five to ten years. As George Siemens (2007) puts it

"Consumers, like learners will in the future, have a dramatically different relationship with content than they have had in the past. Textbook publishers, journals, and other content-centric industries need to take heed of these lessons and adjust before they become the next statistic."

However, education is also unlike these businesses in many ways. Much of the 'content' of higher education, be it books or journal articles, has always been readily, if not freely available. Noam (1995) suggests that there are three main university functions:

"Scholarly activity, if viewed dispassionately, consists primarily of three elements: to create knowledge and evaluate its validity; to preserve information; and to pass it on to others."

These can broadly equate to research, librarianship and teaching. If we accept the web 2.0 argument then both the creation and evaluation of knowledge includes those outside the remit of the university, although a good deal of research is still likely to be best performed by universities. The preservation of information could also be argued to be more of a function performed by Google, or digital archive projects such as the Internet archive, than universities. This leaves teaching of Noam's three main functions. However, the establishment of a number of open educational resource (OER) initiatives such as MIT's Open CourseWare and the Open University's openlearn project, then even that is subject to weakening. If one extends the definition of content to the lecture or tutorial then the challenge to education does resemble those faced by content industries to an extent, in that learners can find freely available content online, for example lectures from Stanford via iTunesU.

So, with the net providing the content and the technology the quote in *Schindlers List* comes to mind, when Itzhak Stern asks of Schindler "Let me understand. They put up all the money. I do all the work. What, if you don't mind my asking, would you do?" Increasingly this is a question that students will ask of HE, but more importantly which it should ask of itself.

But Noam's three functions are probably too restrictive. To these we can add:

- Guidance – this is perhaps the strongest service that higher education offers (and also one of the most difficult to 'market'). As more content becomes available, the value of guidance and skill development becomes more important, not less. The role of educators shifts from being a content provider to a content interpreter or skills developer. Through a framework (which conventionally one might think of as the course, but it needn't necessarily be structured this way), the educator provides activities, guidance and support enabling learners to find, interpret, use and analyse content.
- Social – the student cohort which consists of individuals learning the same things at the same time, with the same experience, is a powerful motivating factor for many students.
- Convenience and coordination – although it is possible to be an autodidact with less effort than was required of the one depicted

in Sartre's *Nausea*, university courses still offer a degree of convenience as someone knowledgeable (the educator) has assembled (and produced) the right set of resources, structured them into a meaningful pathway, coordinated access to a range of resources (articles, books, peers, laboratory equipment) and managed the timetable.
- Accreditation – this is the valuable service held by higher education. It accredits education in a format that is widely recognised by employers and others e.g. the Bachelor's degree. Holding a near-monopoly on formal accreditation has enabled universities to resist competition from other providers, however, in a world where services are modularised, then accreditation may be vulnerable to predation from other providers. Offering accreditation of other forms of learning and experience may be one means of providing alternative revenue streams. This happens to an extent in some sectors, for example IT certifications for networking, with some universities now delivering externally developed programs of study, such as the Cisco networking courses.

BRIDGING THE GAP

Having looked at the different cultures in higher education and web 2.0 and some of the potential conflicts we can now ask how we might bridge the gap between these two seemingly diverse worlds. We will concentrate on the possible role learning design could play, as an illustration of how education may need to adapt, but other bridging techniques would undoubtedly be required, for example the development of appropriate technologies.

We are using the term learning design in its broadest sense here, and not the specific IMS specification. As such it can be taken to mean the process and underlying design of a learning sequence or activity. It is thus roughly synonymous with lesson, or pedagogical planning and instructional design. A learning design then can be in a variety of formats, including a template document, case studies, formal activity sequences, and visual representations.

Over recent years there has been a commendable effort to make educational content freely available, through initiatives such as open access, MIT's opencourseware, learning object repositories such as MERLOT and the Open University's openlearn project. It may still be too early to assess the success of such initiatives, and although some of the statistics are impressive, for example 1 million visitors per month for MIT's open courseware in 2005 (MIT 2005) as yet they have not had the scale of impact on higher educational practice that had been hoped for.

The reasons for this are undoubtedly numerous, including cultural factors such as academics attitude towards reuse and institutional recognition of teaching. It seems likely that one contributory factor is that education is more than content. As we observed in an earlier section, much educational content has always been available. The value that educators provide is in the process of scaffolding learners through content. This becomes a more valuable service when the range and quality of content increases dramatically.

If we look at the issues raised in this paper we can now suggest how a learning design focused approach can help resolve many of them:

- Meno's paradox – learners still often seek guidance and structure. For some subjects they are satisfied with creating this structure themselves, for example by finding resources such as blog postings, tutorials, articles, podcasts and video clips. For other subjects, particularly when the subject is itself complex, or the learner feels less confident of the subject area, then providing a scaffolding structure (which has been created by someone more knowledgeable in the subject) is essential to help the learner build concepts and skills in a robust manner.

- Granularity of learning – in the section on granularity, we argued that the size of educational unit we commonly recognise has been largely determined by physical factors. If learning designs were created and shared by a community of users, what might be thought of as a Flickr for learning designs, and these could be run by individuals, or by groups of interest, then many of the restrictions on size which derive from a hierarchical, centralised model disappear. We looked at the music industry as an analogy, and in education perhaps a more relevant model is that of blogging. Prior to the advent of blogs, the type of academic output was usually limited to books or journal articles. The granularity of these was partly driven by the economics of publishing, as Shirky (2003) argues: "Analog publishing generates per-unit costs - each book or magazine requires a certain amount of paper and ink, and creates storage and transportation costs. Digital publishing doesn't. Once you have a computer and internet access, you can post one weblog entry or one hundred, for ten readers or ten thousand, without paying anything per post or per reader. In fact, dividing up front costs by the number of readers means that content gets *cheaper* as it gets more popular, the opposite of analog regimes." With the advent of blogging, academics (as well as many other bloggers) have found the format liberating, so that blog posts can vary in size from small links with comments to full essays.

- Topography of formality – as with granularity, a set of user generated learning designs allows users to bundle their recent experience together into a course which can be formally recorded more frequently. This would be possible not only because the monopoly of formality is removed from universities, but also because a distributed model of learning design production is the best way to attack the long tail (Anderson 2006) of possible learner interests. If a user wants to find small courses to formally accredit their understanding of highland knitting patterns, history of Sydney in the 1960s or anthropology amongst football fans, then most current formal providers will not meet their requirements, but a sufficiently distributed pool of user generated designs might.

- Web 2.0 quality – much of the concern educators have around web 2.0 is of the quality, and how it can be assured. A set of user generated learning designs could go someway to addressing this by providing a pedagogical structure around resources, and those resources are then changeable. Users can see who has created any given learning design, so some designers may be trusted more than others, rather like sellers and buyers on eBay gain reputational status by recommendations from other users. Similarly, users will be able to comment on designs, thus providing information and context for other users. However, by allowing users to create and select learning sequences it is necessary to accept some of the bottom-up metrics mentioned previously, as the 'filtering on the way in' approach currently used in education is replaced by filtering on the way out. This is necessary to encourage participation.
- Personalisation – if a learning design pool reached a sufficient critical mass, then users will be able to select designs that are appropriate to them in a number of different ways: subject area, style of learning, level, range of resources, duration, assessment method, etc. However, it may be that for some subject areas, particularly those that have a professional body such as medicine, that personalisation is not a desired goal, as they wish to maintain a core set of common knowledge.

CONCLUSION

Learning designs potentially offer a means of overcoming some of the cultural differences between web 2.0 and higher education. They can do this in a number of ways, but ostensibly they provide a means of maintaining the structure, guidance and formality required of higher education, whilst simultaneously embracing the user generated, distributed and personalised approach found in web 2.0.

Although some means of achieving this have been suggested, such as a site for sharing designs and an unbundling of the accreditation function from universities, there are a number of significant obstacles that would need to be overcome. The first of these would be the provision of appropriate tools, which are easy to use and simple to understand. The IMS Learning Design specification is too complex for most users to adopt, as it requires an understanding of the specification, the nature of roles and XML code. If it is to be used, it requires tools that 'hide' much of this complexity from user. The most popular example of such a tool, which can conform to the specification, but does not depend on it, is LAMS (Learning Activity Management System). This has an easy to use visual interface, and does not require specialist knowledge. At the LAMS community (Dalziel 2006) over 200 LAMS learning sequences have been uploaded for others to share. While not many sequences are reused, it seems that users tend to take existing sequences as the basis, or inspiration for creating their own sequences.

At the Open University (OU), the argument mapping software Compendium has been adapted to act as a learning design tool. Again, the tool is easy to use, (although unlike LAMS it is a design only tool, not a runtime delivery system also), with a visual interface, which allows users to easily create activity sequences. The tool incorporates a number of context sensitive information aids, helping users with examples of new technologies, or application of pedagogy (Conole, forthcoming). Early trials with the software have been positive with course teams at the OU designing activities in a collaborative setting.

However these tools represent only an initial step in creating the range of easily shared designs that would be necessary to bridge the gap in the manner suggested. As well as further development of such tools, what would be required is for them to be embedded in a cultural context that provides the motivation to create and share designs. With many successful web 2.0 sites, such as Flickr and YouTube the motivation to share and create is driven partly by social factors such as recognition, and ego. The threshold to participation is also sufficiently low that there is little 'cost' to the user in participating and they can easily vary the level of their involvement.

Learning differs from the content of such sites in being a more complex and nebulous activity. The same motivational factors could still be used however, particularly if a system for sharing designs reaches a critical mass, so the tipping point of participation seen in other web 2.0 services is reached. This could be achieved through an initial seeding of such a system from a global consortium of universities, who as an extension to the current Open Educational Resource (OER) initiatives, begin to share not just learning content, but learning designs. When setting up the LAMS community Dalziel (2005) set out nine principles for its design, which would help address some of the pitfalls seen with learning object repositories. From our perspective the most relevant of these are:

- learning activity as focus rather than content,
- community focus rather than repository focus,
- resources can be easily adapted and
- resources are easy to share.

These four principles in particular would be key to the success in using a learning design approach to help bridge the gap between web 2.0 and higher education.

REFERENCES

Anderson, C. (2006). *The Long Tail: How Endless Choice Is Creating Unlimited Demand*. Random House.

Bacon, S., & Dillon, T. D. (2006). The potential of open source approaches for education. *Futurelab report* http://www.futurelab.org.uk/resources/publications_reports_articles/opening_education_reports/Opening_Education_Report200

Barro, S., & Burillo, P. (dir.) (2006). Las ICTs en el sistema universitario español (2006): un análisis estratégico. *CRUE.* http://www.crue.org/UNIVERSITIC2006/Analisis%20Estrategico.pdf

Conole, G. (forthcoming). Using Compendium as a tool to support the design of learning activities. In A. Okada, S. Buckingham Shum & T. Sherborne (Eds.), *Knowledge cartography – software tools and mapping techniques.* http://kmi.open.ac.uk/projects/kc-book/.

Dalziel, J. (2006). *The design and development of the LAMS Community.* Available at http://www.lamscommunity.org/dotlrn/clubs/educational-community/lamsresearchdevelopment/forums/message-view?message_id=311748

Downes, S. (2007). Places to go: Facebook. *Innovate,* 4(1) http://innovateonline.info/index.php?view=article&id=517&action=article

Evans, P., & Wurster, T. (1999). *Blown to bits: How the New Economics of Information Transforms Strategy.* Harvard Business School Press.

Giles, A. (2005). Internet encyclopaedias go head to head. *Nature, 438,* 900-901. http://www.nature.com/nature/journal/v438/n7070/full/438900a.html

Gorman, M. (2007a). The sleep of reason. *Britannica blog* http://blogs.britannica.com/blog/main/2007/06/web-20-the-sleep-of-reason-part-i/

Gorman, M. (2007b). Jabberwiki: The educational response part 1. *Britannica blog.* http://blogs.britannica.com/blog/main/2007/06/jabberwiki-the-educational-response-part-i/

Gorman, M. (2007c). Jabberwiki: The educational response part 2. *Britannica blog,* http://blogs.britannica.com/blog/main/2007/06/jabberwiki-the-educational-response-part-ii/

Hirschorn, M. (2007). The web 2.0 bubble. *The Atlantic,* http://www.theatlantic.com/doc/200704/social-networking

Keen, A. (2007). *The Cult of the Amateur: How Today's Internet Is Killing Our Culture and Assaulting Our Economy.* Nicholas Brealey Publishing

Kemp, J., & Livingstone, D. (2006). *Putting a second life "metaverse" skin on learning management systems.* http://www.sloodle.com/whitepaper.pdf

Laurillard, D. (2001). *Rethinking University Teaching: A Conversational Framework for the Effective Use of Learning Technologies.* Routledge.

MIT (2006). *2005 Program Evaluation Findings Summary.* http://ocw.mit.edu/ans7870/global/05_Eval_Summary.pdf

Noam, E. M. (1995). Electronics and the Dim Future of the University. *Science, 270,* 13 October 1995, 247-249

O'Reilly, T. (2005). *What is Web 2.0?: Design Patterns and Business Models for the Next Generation of Software* http://www.oreillynet.com/pub/a/oreilly/tim/news/2005/09/30/what-is-web-20.html

OECD (2005). E-learning in Tertiary Education: Where Do We Stand? *Education & Skills 2005,* 2005(4), 1–293.

Raymond, E. (2000). *The Cathedral and the Bazaar.* http://catb.org/~esr/writings/cathedral-bazaar/cathedral-bazaar/index.html

Shirky, C. (2003). *Fame vs Fortune: Micropayments and Free Content.* http://www.shirky.com/writings/fame_vs_fortune.html

Siemens, G. (2007). *Relationships and content.* http://www.elearnspace.org/blog/archives/003078.html

Suriowecki, J. (2004). *The Wisdom of Crowds: Why the Many Are Smarter Than the Few and How Collective Wisdom Shapes Business, Economies, Societies and Nations.* Little, Brown.

Weinberger, D. (2007). *Everything is miscellaneous: The power of the new digital disorder.* Times books.

Weller, M. J. (2007). *Virtual Learning Environments: Using, choosing and developing your VLE.* Routledge.

Wheeler, D. (2007). *Why Open Source Software / Free Software (OSS/FS, FLOSS, or FOSS)? Look at the Numbers!* http://www.dwheeler.com/oss_fs_why.html

Chapter XXXI
Destructive Creativity on the Social Web:
Learning through Wikis in Higher Education

Steve Wheeler
University of Plymouth, UK

ABSTRACT

The use of group oriented software, or groupware, encourages students to generate their own content (McGill et al, 2005) and can foster supportive and dynamic communities of learning (Shaikh & Macauley, 2001). One form of open architecture groupware known as the Wiki is freely available online in several versions, and enables tutors to quickly set up online spaces which can be edited by students, at any time and from any location. Online social spaces of this nature can be used to encourage creative writing and to engage students in critical discourse through focused discussion, but Wikis also have disruptive potential and can cause dissent and disharmony within the group. This chapter aims to highlight some uses of the wiki as a social writing tool, reporting on student perceptions of the limitations and benefits. The chapter also focuses on the tension between creative and destructive uses of wikis and concludes by offering recommendations on the effective use of wikis in mainstream higher education. The use of interview data gathered from a study conducted with a group of student teachers in 2007 is included to support the key messages of this chapter.

'You can't make an omelette without breaking eggs'

THE EMERGENCE OF THE SOCIAL WEB

In recent years the social Web has emerged as a distinct and significant reiteration of the World Wide Web and is focussed more on people than on content. Predominantly known as 'Web 2.0', the social Web offers an emerging set of tools that afford exciting new opportunities in education and according to some commentators, places the Web back where it was originally intended to be – in the hands of the people (Kamel Boulos, Maramba & Wheeler, 2006).

The advent of Web 2.0 is particularly apposite for today's net generation students, whose desire is to interact with online resources, broadcast themselves and create their own content. This shift in emphasis is a result of a need to deepen the social dimensions of the Web, and to circumvent long standing problems of usability. A potentially useful and relevant Website can be marred when some piece of vital information is missing, inaccurate or out of date. The natural reaction is to wish that the content can be edited or added to so that the site can be improved. Most Web 1.0 sites have the tendency to be 'sticky', meaning that they are content secure and can only be updated by the Webmaster or owner. There are issues here of ownership and control, where for some time, the content of sites was controlled centrally. Web 2.0 signifies a shift away from central to community ownership, where individuals can alter the content of Web pages (O'Reilly, 2004). One social tool, known as the wiki, enables visitors to change the content on a Web page, participate in discussion with other users and create new links to other resources. Wikis are an important aspect of the social Web – an open network type architecture that enables users to participate in creating and occasionally destroying Web based artefacts.

IMPACT ON PEDAGOGY

Although relatively new, the exponential and rapid growth of the social Web is beginning to impact upon post-compulsory education, compelling some academics and teachers to repurpose key aspects of course development and delivery. For example, the social affordance of multiple-user generation of content is challenging previously accepted mores, not least the traditional primacy of the tutor role. Students are beginning to take greater responsibility for their own learning, whilst the role tutors have enjoyed as the sole source of specialist knowledge is rapidly waning.

It is not only the role of the teacher that is being challenged. Popular Websites such as Wikipedia are premised on the principle that all users have the freedom to generate their own content, and this presents a significant challenge to the traditional status of knowledge. Moreover, the exponential upsurge in student activity on extra-institutional social networking sites such as MySpace and FaceBook raises the stakes in the teaching and learning game. Not all students are ready to generate their own course content and learning materials, but increasing numbers are familiar with the concept of a shared digital space and they pursue it with vigour. Student reactions will vary, but recent studies report that students of all ages comment positively about content generation using wikis (Richardson, 2006; Wheeler, Yeomans & Wheeler, 2008).

There is little doubt that the social Web is making a significant impact on traditional forms of pedagogy by promoting a stimulating and creative environment where readers can become writers, and consumers can become contributors (Kamel Boulos, et al, 2006). For the first time, all users are able to exploit the capability of Web 2.0 tools to air their message to a world wide audience. The 'read/write Web' exhibits an openness and accessibility that enables users to become their own producers, directors, publishers or broadcasters. Popular social networking tools such as Bebo,

YouTube, Flickr and MSN owe their phenomenal success largely to freely downloadable and richly participatory elements.

Another popular Web phenomenon is the posting of online diary entries known as Web logging or 'blogging'. Bloggers aim to regale a potential audience of millions with their thoughts, whilst budding photographers or videographers similarly wish to demonstrate their prowess through the use of images to depict their thoughts in videoblogging or 'vlogging'. At the time of writing, pop groups are gaining fame not for their television appearances or radio airplay, but for entering the popular music charts solely on the basis of their sales of music downloads over the internet. Prominent politicians are exploiting the power of social networking tools to reach large sections of the electorate for minimal cost (BBC, 2008). A more comprehensive review of the social Web can be found in the musings of Web 2.0 champion Tim O'Reilly (2004).

VLE VS. PLE

Social software encourages activities that have democracy and freedom from institutional influence at their heart. There is a tension between the personalisation the social Web offers and the regimentation that is often promoted by institutional systems such as the virtual learning environment (VLE). In its short lifespan, the VLE has wrought several significant changes in education, but inevitably, it will be supplanted by personal learning environments (PLEs: cf. Wilson, 2007). PLEs offer students many advantages over VLEs such as the ability to quickly create online spaces that can be moulded to meet their individual needs, learning orientations and personal preferences. Students who enjoy the practice of mixing their own play-lists using music downloads and iPods for example, appreciate the opportunity to express their creativity and enjoy the freedom to design unique and personal digital spaces. Mobile tech-

nologies, wireless systems, open source software, and other liberating ambient media have quickly established themselves as important components of the instant access communication culture of western youth. The freedom from time and place constraints such technologies bring is cherished by the latest generation of undergraduates. For many of the current crop of students, it seems that institutional control over the learning process is often rejected in favour of the more self directed, autonomous forms of learning available in Web 2.0 tools (Wheeler, 2007a). Indeed it is probable that PLEs are already superceding VLEs as the most important Web tools in education, given that both wikis and blogs are replacing the more expensive features found in commercially available systems (Sauer et al, 2005).

PERSONALISED LEARNING ENVIRONMENTS

A long running debate about the effectiveness of media and technology to influence learning has been sustained by the likes of Kozma (1994) and Clark (1994), but choice of delivery technology remains crucial to the success of any programme. Although it displays a natural orientation toward independent use, tutors who manage education at a distance have a unique opportunity to tap into the power and potential of social software. In so doing, they can facilitate student centred activities that go beyond the superficial content delivery typical of many Web sites, to engage and challenge. Social Web tools transcend the somewhat stilted and linear 'managed learning environment' approach established throughout much of further and higher education, providing an architecture of participation that encourages students to engage in non-hierarchical communities of practice. The term 'personalised learning environment' is now used to describe the use of individually tailored social Web software in higher education.

WIKI: THE ARCHITECTURE OF COLLABORATION

The notion of space is being radically redefined through the widespread adoption of digital technologies in education (Curtis, 2004). Significantly, the opportunity to share a digital space with others for the purposes of collaboration, dialogue and debate causes individuals to reformulate their own identities (Owen, Grant, Sayers & Facer, 2006). Tim O'Reilly's introduction of the term 'Web 2.0' and his declaration that it is the 'architecture of participation', have together heralded a new phase in which the democratic, chaotic and 'always under construction' nature of the present day Web takes precedence (O'Reilly, 2004). Web 2.0 – the 'social Web' – is characterised by its ability to take many forms and guises, but the common feature all Web 2.0 tools share is the capability to draw like-minded people together to share ideas, debate, create, vote and otherwise engage in a culture of participation. Central to the future success of this architecture of participate is a tool known as the wiki.

Wikis are part of the variegated and ever growing set of sociable software applications. They are essentially Websites holding content which can be typically edited by anyone. Wikis extend many exciting opportunities for tutors to provide dynamic, collaborative and sociable learning environments for students. The word wiki derives from the Hawaiian phrase 'wiki wiki' which means 'quick' or 'to hurry' (Ebersbach, Glaser & Heigl, 2006). Wiki pages are certainly quickly created, easily edited and expanded, and place content quality control firmly into the hands of the user group.

Wikis often contain content that has been generated in informal settings and outside of the boundaries of the institution, so it is debatable to what extent universities and colleges can, and should attempt to manage them. Wikis quickly evolve into shared knowledge repositories as communities aggregate their contributions over a period of time (Godwin-Jones, 2003) and the effect of 'wisdom of crowds' is an emergent property. Collaborative learning has long been a touch stone of online education, but has proved somewhat elusive to date, partly due to the 'stickiness' or immutability of most Web based delivery. The use of social software such as the openly editable wikis, free form blogs and automatic alerting of changes through Really Simple Syndication (RSS) or Atom feeds, may provide the best opportunities yet to realise online collaborative learning, providing teachers and institutions are willing to relinquish a certain amount of control.

THE WIKI AS A COGNITIVE TOOL

Immersing students in richly collaborative learning environments where they are able to create, mix, modify and extend their own knowledge yields positive learning outcomes. Such environments have been called 'mind tools' (Jonassen, Peck & Wilson, 1999) because they are able to extend cognitive abilities such as memory, recall, reasoning and critical thinking skills beyond normal capabilities, using the software as a kind of knowledge repository. Wikis can store the learning community's projects, ideas and work in progress, making it constantly accessible to group members, as and when they need it (Wheeler, Yeomans & Wheeler, 2008).

Wikis offer users a 'blank slate' upon which they can express their ideas, build a text over time, and collaborate with others in the generation of narratives. The provisionality of the wiki pages also facilitates a sense of the ephemeral – that nothing is permanent and that mistakes can be made without recrimination. Wikis are best used as long term repositories of ideas, resources and long term projects and are less useful in the generation of quick solutions or completed works. The notion that the wiki can be used as an extension of the capabilities of the human mind is becoming more popular, as a means to develop critical thinking skills, create social writing spaces and as a storage space for evolving ideas and processes. For any tutor wishing to enhance the learning experience and provide open access to learning resources, the wiki may provide the ideal mind tool.

THE NEED FOR SOCIAL PRESENCE

Solo engagement with technology has been shown to be generally less fruitful than learning conducted in a richly social environment (Jonassen et al, 1999). More often than not, contemporary learning is now achieved within a community context (Lemke, 2002). If used correctly, the social Web can offer a community focused learning environment, providing students with communication tools and virtual contacts that emulate but do not replace co-presence. Face to face learning environments are obviously preferred by most students (Simonson, 1999) but when students are separated from their parent institutions through distance, problems can arise.

Many students report a sense of 'coldness' in environments where communication is technologically mediated (Rice, 1993) and the warmth of human contact is often perceived to be lacking from many online learning environments (Wallace, 1999). Students need to sense that they are not merely interacting with an impersonal technology, but that a human presence exists at the 'other end' as social presence. This is the student's perception that s/he is communicating *with* people *through* the technology (Short, Williams & Christie, 1976). Such perceptions encourage many distance learners to persist in their studies (Wallace, 1999) and a correlation has been identified between perceptions of social presence and online interaction (Tu & McIsaac, 2002).

Where learning is mediated through technology some students feel socially isolated and require a higher level of social presence. Where high levels of social presence are in evidence, students express greater satisfaction with their learning experiences and tend to achieve better learning outcomes (Richardson & Swan, 2003). Even where rich social cues are reduced, the kind of interactions that occur between learners and their peers has been shown to increase perceptions of social presence (Gunawardena, 1995). Rich and meaningful communication, immediacy of responses from tutor and students, and a common sense of purpose within the community of learners are all key features that contribute toward stronger perceptions of social presence (Wheeler, 2007b). Wikis are socially rich in nature, enabling collaborative dialogue and promoting peer review (Trentin, 2008) so can provide these features, but they are not problem free. They can also scaffold meaningful learning tasks that can be undertaken co-operatively, regardless of the geographical location of the learners, or the times in which they are able to access the online space.

OWNERSHIP AND CONFLICT

A number of destruction metaphors are associated with the use of Web 2.0. Verbs such as burning, ripping, mashing and mixing connote that all things change, nothing is safe from deletion, modification or re-purposing on the social Web and the wiki is particularly susceptible to this constant change process. This is highlighted in the words of the Wetpaint wiki strap line – 'always a wet canvass'. When faced with Wikipedia and other open architecture spaces, students are sometimes uncomfortable with the ease by which their work can be deleted or modified by others. A recent study by the author with a group of teacher trainees unearthed some interesting responses from students faced with the prospect of having their work deleted or edited. One male first year education student said:

'If anyone changes my page, I'll kill them! It's odd I do feel a slight ownership to my page.'

Another first year female education student remarked:

'I think I will cry if anyone changes my page!!!'

Students tend to hold the view that their ideas remain 'theirs' once they have been posted to the wiki. Indeed, tacitly the ideas do remain their own. Intellectual property is a contentious area, particularly within the internet domain, and should be discussed with students prior to their use of wikis in a formalised learning context. Ultimately students should realise that once the 'send' button is clicked, their ideas then become available and visible to the other space users and are then vulnerable to editing, adulteration or even deletion. A first year student of education saw the use of the wiki as a means of learning from others. He showed more acceptance of the volatile nature of the wiki page:

'I'd be more than happy for my input to be changed, fed back on etc. If my knowledge is lacking, then others can inform me.'

Another student, a mature student studying at postgraduate level for his teaching qualification saw the need for a change of opinion about ownership of ideas:

'Two personal concerns I had were firstly that my comments could be judged by others, and so I would want to be confident of the content I would submit, and secondly, a big change in my views of ownership is also required - anyone can edit my information. This is both exciting but also requires a 'letting go' of what I submit'.

Disagreements often observed between student users over the contested ground of wiki content confirms that the ownership of ideas can be problematic (Wheeler et al, 2008). Further, unless group members can agree on the form

and style of content of work they place on wiki pages, an endless series of 'modification wars' can result. Where groups meet regularly face to face, this kind of conflict can often be obviated amicably, but the same may not be true for learner groups who rarely meet or who are separated by distance. Ultimately, the potentially destructive capability of wikis can militate against social connections and relationships. Intellectual property has historically been an important issue for some individuals – one over which legal battles have been fought and in which friendships have been damaged irreparably.

Students who are rooted in old ways of thinking about learning may fail to appreciate community ownership of knowledge and heated exchanges leading to discord can ensue, but that these can be beneficial if managed effectively (Kanuka & Anderson, 1998). Intellectual property – the 'I thought of this idea and it's mine' mentality which is often a minefield many academics must navigate – must begin to assume less import in shared community spaces than it has in previous educational paradigms. The wiki is changing all this, because in this kind of collaborative learning, outcomes are achieved by the group through a process of negotiation, and are not always as emotive or critical. However, teachers need to accept that students can and do argue, and should consider their strategies in managing this process so that the outcomes are as positive as possible.

THE CREATIVE/DESTRUCTIVE PROCESS

For any teacher intending to use wikis, a key management strategy will be to balance creativity and destructiveness against learning outcomes – for the benefit of all of the actors. It has been acknowledged that online social exchanges can lead to discord just as easily as they can result in agreement, and that discord in itself may positively support the construction of knowledge (Kanuka & Anderson, 1998).

One recommended approach is to encourage students to work within their own designated wiki spaces and then 'join up' their contributions using hyperlinking later in the process. However, it should be acknowledged that compartmentalising 'shared spaces' in this way can be counterproductive to collaborative learning and will certainly frustrate some students who wish to work together. Another solution is to get all students to agree beforehand that modification and deletion of all postings is permissible, and that all should agree to work toward improving the entire content of their wiki space. Yet reaching such an agreement may be tortuous, or may fail entirely if judicious editing becomes too severe for some to bear. Ultimately, wiki users need to realise that their shared space is open and free for the entire community to use and contribute toward, and that the creative/destructive process is cyclical and iterative (Wheeler & Kamel Boulos, 2007). Whatever the sensibilities of such agreements or *modus operandi*, it is clear that the mashing and mixing of content will continue to gather pace because the very nature of social software dictates that it be open and accessible to all.

There are other issues related to the creative/ destructive process: some students report that the anonymity of wiki content creation denies them recognition for their hard work. Tutors are able to follow contributions using onboard tracking tools, but in the open wiki space contributions are not visibly attributable. To discover what has been created or changed by whom, tutors would need to access the 'history' tool for each page to determine sources, and this takes time. One second year male undergraduate student in a recent study (Wheeler et al, 2008) complained:

'I don't like the fact that it's anonymous. I want credit for what I have done'.

TUTOR INTERVENTION

Generally most students accept that all content is volatile, and that certain content will be removed or altered to ensure it is accurate and relevant to the user community. It is incumbent on tutors and moderators of wikis to ensure that contributions are not potentially offensive or illegal, but they should only intervene when absolutely essential. There have been very few isolated occasions when tutors have been required to intervene to remove offending items, but students have complained when their content has been removed. Issues that arise include the posting of illicit or otherwise undesirable content onto the wiki. This may include the posting of hyperlinks to pornographic, violent or racist Websites, but in most cases, students have simply posted images or texts within the space which the university would deem inappropriate or unacceptable.

However, removal of student generated content should be seen as a last resort, when no other option will suffice. The underlying ethos of the wiki resides within is its open and democratic nature, and the right of all users within the community to freely voice their opinions or publish their ideas. The tension arises as a result of the cleavage between democratic and open Web authoring and the more rigid policies and regulations of the parent institution. Therefore tutors wishing to tap into the potential of wikis as cognitive tools will need to maintain the openness of the wiki in fine balance against the occasional need for intervention and censorship.

EVOLVING WIKI CULTURE

There is something distinctly feral about wikis. Despite the relentless criticism of their effectiveness in presenting relevant and accurate information (Keen, 2007), they continue to inspire, but beneath the surface, within the social layer of knowledge production, there lurks a primitive and ruthless mien. This may best be observed when speculative or inaccurate content is posted to a Wikipedia page. Such a post is rarely left for long before someone either removes it or tags it as 'needing a quote', or 'in dispute'. These are processes that are familiar to all Wikipedians. Should a contributor be seen to be deliberately posting inaccurate, objectionable or otherwise undesirable content to a wiki space, they are often excluded from access to editing in future by other members of the group using the space. Thereby the wiki community self regulates its content and the behaviour of its members.

Within the emerging culture of wiki authoring there are several approaches to the management of content generation. These include 'mergism' – where the best content from disparate sources is mashed together to create a newer, better item; 'deletionism' – in which all 'bad' items must be removed as quickly as possible to maintain encyclopaedic standards; and 'eventualism' – the long term view of the wiki where all is a 'work in progress' and eventually, over a sufficient period of time, the content will develop into something of true value. This evolutionary metaphor is extended into 'Darwikianism' – a belief that the fittest – that is the most accurate and relevant entries – will survive and grow, whilst weaker entries will be sought out by the community of users and deleted, or modified to make them stronger. This 'wisdom of crowds' approach appears to be the most dominant in for example, Wikipedia. In evolutionary terms, only the fittest (or in this case the most accurate) content does actually survive.

New wiki pages tend to grow exponentially when they are first created, as authors scramble to produce useful, incisive and current information for their pages. After a short while, however, most wiki pages have been observed to 'slow down' and eventually reach equilibrium, because there is simply no new material left to add. The use of an evolutionary metaphor to describe this aspect in the life cycle of a wiki can be useful in another way. When wikis have served their usefulness, they simply become extinct – that is, no-one adds any more content or visits tail off.

CREATIVE WRITING IN WIKIS

How can the preceding commentary be applied in a learning context? One useful outcome of student generated content activities can be the development of creative writing through peer collaboration. Recent experiments by publishing houses have yielded a patchwork of results, ranging from entire novels created by mass online authorship; to fragmented and incoherent ramblings. Although the quality of many of these products may be questionable, the inventive nature and creativity often shines through. However, it should also be noted that creative writing and academic writing are two different things.

In a recent study at the author's university, 35 student teachers were asked to use a wiki space for one complete term as an integrated part of their studies. Activities took place predominantly in the classroom, but also transgressed into other settings such as home and work placement, in a distributed format. One mature female postgraduate student recognised the creative potential of the wiki as a means of expression:

'...started off feeling frustrated and incompetent, but process of learning and creativity involved made me feel engaged and excited.'

Academic writing in a typical university undergraduate course demands critical engagement, and wikis are yet to be proved as digital tools fit for purpose in the development of such a skill.

CRITICAL THINKING SKILLS AND WIKIS

There is evidence from the recent study that some students developed healthier critical thinking skills through their engagement with learning through the wiki. A male second year education student reported that although the wiki activities had not improved his writing skills, he had noticed an improvement in his ability to apply critical analysis to his studies:

'I think I am now developing a healthier critical and analytical writing style thanks to the wiki. Looking at other people's opinions and findings has helped me to question what's in front of me, and I have found myself researching certain areas further to see if all opinions are the same.'

Another female second year student identified improvement in her ability to focus on key aspects of her studies. Referring to the capability of the wiki to compartmentalise topics and themes, she wrote:

'Using the wiki has made writing much more focused on a part of a topic ..., rather than getting confused trying to tackle the topic as a whole.'

A WIKI ACTIVITY FRAMEWORK

There is a spectrum of wiki activities that can be used to encourage critical thinking in writing. In order to rationalise activities within such an open and collaborative space, it is prudent to identify a framework within which activities can be defined. Perhaps one of the most useful frameworks is offered by Gunawardena, Lowe and Anderson (1997) in which five phases of knowledge construction within shared, collaborative learning environments were identified:

- Phase 1: The sharing or comparing of information;
- Phase 2: Discovery and exploration of dissonance and inconsistency among ideas, concepts or statements by different participants;
- Phase 3: Negotiation of meaning and co-construction of knowledge;
- Phase 4: Testing and modification of proposed synthesis or co-construction;
- Phase 5: Phrasing of agreement, statements and applications of newly constructed meaning.

Several activities have been used often in recent online wiki based learning with trainee teachers and it is possible to locate these within the phases proposed by Gunawardena and her colleagues.

The first simple activity has been used both as a warm-up exercise for new groups, and as a means of familiarising students with the topography of the wiki space. Students are asked to introduce themselves with a few words about their personal interests and background. They are also asked to post an image which they think best represented themselves. A mix of photographs, cartoons and images of inanimate objects or animals is the result. This activity is a Phase 1 activity, and involves minimal social interchange.

The second activity becomes more socially interactive, tasking students to define the boundaries of their activities within the wiki space. The group is asked to decide on what they consider to be the key rules of the space, acceptable and unacceptable behaviour when using the wiki. This has now become known popularly as 'wikiquette'. This represents a Phase 2 task, in that it explores differences of opinion and encourages the group to ultimately reach some kind of consensus about how they will behave within the shared online learning space. Discussion tools are used for this dialogue, and ultimately, students post their wikiquette decisions onto a prominent page within the wiki.

One activity promotes critical engagement by tasking students to find 'gold dust' resources online which they consider indispensible to their studies. Alongside the hyperlink they post an annotated commentary on why the resource is so important, whilst other students are invited to inspect the resource and provide additional or alternative commentary. This represents co-construction of knowledge in the peer group, which is a Phase 3 activity.

One phase 4 activity which taps into testing and modification of proposed co-construction is introduced in week 3 of the programme of study. The exercise requires small groups to research a single topic and then populate a wiki page with explanatory text, images and hyperlinks to resources related to their topic.

The above wiki activities can be seen as a thread of separate, but increasingly complex social writing activities. They require the students to engage in individual research, with increasingly deeper levels of critical evaluation. As the tasks progress they become more socially and critically demanding, with students working within a team to construct an online 'shop window' of their findings on which they must eventually reach some level of consensus. The tasks facilitate collaborative writing and critical thinking within a shared space, and as they progress elicit deeper amounts of critical engagement, co-ordination and co-operative dialect between members of the space.

THE 'HIDDEN AUDIENCE' EFFECT

Over the course of the development of wiki pages, students must decide what to include and exclude, how to present it, and whether to 'tag' their pages using key words. The choice of key words is an important activity in itself, requiring students to distil the essence of the page in a semblance of précis. If pages are tagged, they become increasingly visible to search engines, so attracting more external visitors to the site. Such online activity can be tracked using hit counters, and shown to the students to alert them to the possibility that they have a 'hidden audience'. Interestingly, students have commented that such surveillance, although somewhat daunting for a few, has the function of encouraging them to improve their presentational skills and take more care over the accuracy of the sources they are quoting.

One female first year education student reported:

'I have to concentrate more on my spelling and grammar so that it makes sense for the person who is reading it, which is really challenging and I have to read the paragraph multiple times before posting it!'

A male student in the same group highlighted a feature of the wiki used in the study which made him more vigilant over his own writing:

'Wiki has no spelling or grammar functions, so I have to pay more attention to what I write.'

Some wikis do of course have spell checking tools, so the statement must be taken in context. A female first year student discovered the importance of referencing sources after a time working on the wiki:

'...my referencing has improved through using the wiki, as it has made me realise how important it is to state where you got your information from initially.'

Students reported that regular writing enables them to discover a more critical side to themselves. Similar to those engaged in 'blogging, they report that their use of the wiki has encouraged them to be better writers and ultimately, more skilful communicators. One female first year education student said:

'Writing on the wiki is a challenging activity which involves much thought about the length and structure of sentences...'

Another male student wrote:

'I think my writing has become more thought provoking. I'm now thinking at a higher level than I normally would.'

STUDENT PERCEPTIONS OF THE WIKI

Reactions to the wiki activities have been mixed. Some students enjoy structured activities as they provide boundaries within which they can operate which leave room for risk-taking and experimentation within a psychologically safe environment. Others prefer the chaotic and inchoate nature of the wiki, and see the blank pages as a canvass on which to paint their ideas in their own style. A male postgraduate education remarked:

'The ways that people are encouraged to research various areas and post their findings is the major success for me. Being able to recommend Websites, references etc. without coming across as pompous or pushy is great'.

Some students are less keen on using the wikis for a variety of reasons. Some view the use of the wiki as an extra task or chore they have to perform to comply with the programme requirements. Others dislike the wiki in principle, viewing it as a duplication of normal effort in learning. One male postgraduate student argued:

'I am not sure exactly how the Wiki has helped me so far. I think the tasks in themselves are ok but it's the further parts to evidence that get more and more complicated each week that I find rather annoying. It seems a crafty way of multiplying our work load, quite frankly. You can probably

guess from my comments that I am not a fan of the Wiki'.

Some students were keen to test the boundaries of the wiki, in terms of its enhanced capabilities for communication. A female postgraduate student thought that there were several benefits brought by the wiki that were communication centred:

'The key benefits are finding out information about others on the course, interesting articles, books of interest, ideas and a forum to discuss everything really. It is also quite nice when you see a message that has to be read. The final thing I would like to say is the wiki encourages others on our course to communicate to each other and in a way that you wouldn't do in email. I find it interesting'.

Another postgraduate student agreed about the positive outcomes of the wiki:

'As regards benefits, it is helping us fulfil [the course] requirements, improving our IT skills and making us think which can't be a bad thing. It can also be a great way to share information which our peers can access easily. I will have to use it a bit more to decide on limitations, I'm sure I will think of some though, and when I do I will e mail you with my pearls of wisdom'.

CONCLUSIONS

Today, social software applications are continuing to rise in popularity due to the democratic and free nature of the social Web. The attraction extends to the ability of users to create and repurpose content and form in ways which are most appealing to them. The students featured in this sample, if representative of a wider population of young undergraduates, reveal a number of key issues surrounding the use of wikis in higher education. Young people in particular are gravitating more toward communication and sharing using social networking tools, and such activities prepare them to participate in formalised study using social software. As evidenced in some of the preceding comments from students, a certain amount of disconcertion and readjustment may be expected where students share and co-edit the same space on a wiki. Students tend to dislike their work being edited or deleted by their peers, and some feel that the anonymity of the form denies them appropriate recognition. However, although such activities appear to be destructive, when viewed over a period of time, group based generation of content on wikis can be both creative and fulfilling, with long lasting and positive learning outcomes.

REFERENCES

BBC News Online (2007). *The Arctic Monkeys' Stellar Rise.* Retrieved 30 June, 2008 from: http://news.bbc.co.uk/1/hi/entertainment/5319434.stm

BBC News Online (2008). *PM Launching Online Question Time.* Retrieved 30 June, 2008 from: http://news.bbc.co.uk/1/hi/uk_politics/7407650.stm.

Clark, R. E. (1994). Media will never influence learning. *Education Technology Research and Development, 42*(2), 21-29.

Ebersbach, A., Glaser, M., & Heigl, R. (2006). *The wiki concept: Web collaboration.* Springer-Verlag: Berlin.

Godwin-Jones, R. (2003). Emerging technologies: Blogs and wikis: environments for on-line collaboration. *Language Learning & Technology, 7*(2), 12-16.

Gunawardena, C. N. (1995). Social presence theory and implications for interaction and collaborative learning in computer conferences. *International Journal of Educational Telecommunications, 1*(2/3), 147-166.

Jonassen, D. H., Peck, K. L., & Wilson, B. G. (1999). *Learning with Technology: A Constructivist Perspective.* Upper Saddle River, NJ: Merrill Prentice Hall.

Kamel Boulos, M. N., Maramba, I., & Wheeler, S. (2006). Wikis, blogs and podcasts: a new generation of Web-based tools for virtual collaborative clinical practice and education. *BMC Medical Education, 6*(41). [Online at: www.biomedcentral.com/1472-6920/6/41] Accessed 30 November, 2006.

Kanuka, H., & Anderson, T. (1998). Online social interchange, discord and knowledge construction. *Journal of Distance Education* [Online at: http://cade.icaap.org/vol13.1/kanuka.html] (Retrieved 13 November, 2007).

Keen, A. (2007). *The Cult of the Amateur: How Today's Internet is Killing Our Culture and Assaulting Our Economy.* London: Nicholas Brealey.

Kozma, R. B. (1994). Will media influence learning? Reframing the debate. *Education Technology Research and Development, 42*(1), 7-19.

Lemke, J. (2002). Becoming the village: Education across lives. In G. Wells & G. Claxton (Eds.), *Learning for life in the 21st Century: Sociocultural perspectives on the future of education.* London: Blackwell.

Levy, Y. (in press). Comparing dropouts and persistence in e-learning courses. *Computers & Education, 48*, 185-204.

McGill, L., Nicol, D., Littlejohn, A., Grierson, H., Juster, N., & Ion, W. (2005). Creating an information-rich learning environment to enhance design student learning: challenges and approaches. *British Journal of Educational Technology, 36*(4), 629-642.

Moore, M. G., & Kearsley, G. (1996). *Distance Education: A Systems View.* Belmont, CA: Wadsworth.

O'Reilly, T. (2004). Open Source Paradigm Shift. [Online at: http://tim.oreilly.com/articles/para-digmshift_0504.html] (Retrieved 15 February, 2007).

Owen, M., Grant, L., Sayers, S., & Facer, K. (2006). *Opening Education: Social Software and Learning.* Bristol: Futurelab. [Online at: www.futurelab.org.uk/research] (Retrieved 20 November, 2006).

Rice, R. E. (1993). Media appropriateness: Using social presence theory to compare traditional and new organisational media. Cited in Stacey, E. (2002) Social presence online: Networking learners at a distance. In D. Watson & J. Anderson (Eds.), *Networking the Learner: Computers in Education.* Boston, MA: Kluwer Academic Press.

Richardson, J. C., & Swan, K. (2003). Examining social presence in online courses in relation to students' perceived learning and satisfaction. *Journal of Asynchronous Learning Networks, 7*(1), 68-88.

Richardson, W. (2006). *Blogs, Wikis, Podcasts and other Powerful Web Tools for Classrooms.* Thousand Oaks, CA: Corwin Press.

Sauer, I. M., Bialek, D., Efimova, E., Schwartlander, R., Pless, G., & Neuhaus, P. (2005). Blogs and Wikis are valuable software tools for communication within research groups. *Artificial Organs, 29*(1), 82-89.

Shaikh, A. N., & Macauley, L. (2001). Integrating groupware technology into a learning environment. *Association for Learning Technology Journal (ALT-J), 9*(2), 47–63.

Short, J., Williams, E., & Christie, B. (1976). *The Social Psychology of Telecommunications.* London: John Wiley and Sons.

Simonson, M. (1999) Equivalency theory and distance education. *Tech Trends, 43*(5), 5-8.

Trentin, G. (2008). Using a wiki to evaluate individual contribution to a collaborative learning project. *Journal of Computer Assisted Learning,* 10.1111/j.1365-2729.2008.00276.x

Tu, C-H and McIsaac, M. (2002). The Relationship of Social Presence and Interaction in Online Classes, *The American Journal of Distance Education, 16*(3), 131-150.

Wallace, P. (1999). *The Psychology of the Internet.* Cambridge: Cambridge University Press

Wheeler, S., & Boulos, M. (2007). Mashing, Burning, Mixing and the Destructive Creativity of Web 2.0: Applications for Medical Education. *Electronic Journal of Communication, Information and Innovation in Health, 1*(1), 27-33.

Wheeler, S. (2007a). Something wiki this way cometh: Evaluating open architecture software as support for nomadic learning. In I. Bo & A. Szucs (Eds.), *Proceedings of EDEN 2007 Annual Conference*, Naples, Italy. 13-16 June.

Wheeler, S. (2007b). The Influence of Communication Technologies and Approaches to Study on Transactional Distance in Blended Learning. *ALT-J: Research in Learning Technology, 15*(2), 103-117.

Wheeler, S., Yeomans, P., & Wheeler, D. (2008). The good, the bad and the wiki: Evaluating Student Generated Content as a Collaborative Learning Tool. *British Journal of Educational Technology, 39*(6), 987-995.

Wilson, S. (2007). *The personal learning environments blog.* Retrieved 30 June, 2008 from: http://zope.cetis.ac.uk/members/ple

KEY TERMS

Collaborative Learning: Learning activities that encourage group work and co-operation between students.

Darwikianism: A belief that the fittest – that is the most accurate and relevant entries – will survive and grow, whilst weaker entries will be sought out by the community of users and deleted, or modified to make them stronger.

Post Compulsory Education: In the UK, all students who are over the age of 14. Also synonymous with lifelong learning.

Social Networking: In this sense, Websites designed to connect people together who have common interests.

Social Presence: The perception that individuals are brought closer through the use of technology.

Wiki: An editable Website.

Wikipedia: One of the first and most popular wiki encyclopaedia sites.

Wikiquette: Acceptable behaviour and use of wikis which are generally agreed by all users.

Chapter XXXII
Presence in Social Networks

Scott Wilson
University of Bolton, UK

ABSTRACT

This chapter describes the mechanisms of presence in social networks and presents an ontology that frames the purpose, content, methods of production and methods of consuming presence information. The concept of presence in social networks has been steadily evolving along with the Internet. Recognised as an essential feature of all instant messaging services from the IRC onwards, mechanisms for constructing and consuming presence information have become more elaborate, with the addition of more sophisticated mechanisms for producing, consuming and representing presence. A model for systems that offer presence services is developed, and this enables a number of future trends to be identified.

INTRODUCTION

In the context of social networks the term "presence" has a number of distinct meanings. Commonly within the literature of virtual environments, the discussion of presence is concerned with the personal experience of being present; that is, the "perceptual illusion of nonmediation" (Lombard and Ditton, 1997). However, there is also the sense in which presence is about the exposure of personal states and the awareness of the states of others, a usage which derives from the indicators of online presence and availability

found in various kinds of social software tools, particularly instant messaging.

The concept of presence in social networks has been steadily evolving along with the Internet. Recognised as an essential feature of all instant messaging services from IRC[1] onwards, mechanisms for constructing and consuming presence information have become more elaborate, with the addition of more sophisticated mechanisms for presence production and representation.

The earliest forms of presence awareness in the Internet age seem to have taken as their inspiration the LED indicator schemes of the Internet hardware itself, routers and switches, where a green LED indicates that a device has been connected to the network, and orange indicates connected but has communication problems. This 'physically connected' way of looking at online presence is embedded in the assumptions of the earlier presence mechanisms of IRC and AOL Instant Messenger, with its concepts of "Online" versus "Away". However, as we discuss later, the concept of "presence" at the social level is more complex, and has subverted the meaning of the original indicator states.

Many presence technologies remain within the context of the laboratory or art experiment, however there is a trend in social networks for presence to be seen as an essential part of 'being in the network', with new services emerging with a specific focus on presence, such as Twitter, Jaiku and Explode. The "buddy list", once the preserve of instant messaging, is now a common feature of social networking applications, with "buddy icons" of currently online users decorating the pages of many "Web 2.0" websites.

In this chapter we examine the meaning of presence, the technologies for producing and consuming it, and construct the ontology of this exciting but often neglected aspect of social computing.

THE MEANING OF PRESENCE

What is the Message?

There is a possible 'cultural divide' in the use of technologies such as instant messaging as being fundamentally either messaging applications or presence applications (Boyd, 2005). For advocates of the presence perspective, presence is not a means for identifying opportunities for communication, presence *is* the communication; the availability and state of the participants in the network is the message.

For example, while the ostensible purpose of the presence mechanism in a service such as Skype is to indicate availability for communication, the way in which the presence indication is made is also content in its own right; it also provides a communication channel at a different level from that of a full two-way conversation. Services such as Skype, AOL Instant Messenger, and MSN have long offered the "custom away message" or "mood message" to augment the meaning of the standard availability metadata. The "mood message" typically appears alongside the availability graphic as a short piece of text (see Figure 1.)

These messages provide a surprisingly rich mechanism for communication, and its therefore not surprising that new forms of "micro blogging" have emerged that extend this property, such as Twitter.

The Purpose of Presence

Why do agents expose presence information to others? While individual motivations may vary considerably, an overview of the available literature suggests a few possible categories of purpose:

Managing attention and interruption is a core concern of the business perspective on presence, evident in the work on concepts of bounded deferral (e.g. Achloptas and Horvits, 2005) and interruption (e.g., Dabbish and Kraut, 2004). Presence offers a way for workers to assess the interruptability of colleagues based on an awareness of their current context.

Facilitating casual interactions is a less studied but equally valid purpose of presence. In this case, rather than manage interruptions, presence can instead be used to encourage more communication, exposing the communications availability of people in the network and reducing the coordination required to initiate communications.

Figure 1. Example of Mood Message in Skype

Presence can also provide a **sense of activity in an interaction space**. Rather than have an instrumental role, presence can relate an ambience related to a space or context, such as the number of colleagues or friends online, or their level of engagement or activity within the context.

Presence can be used to **facilitate team or group self-awareness**, either as a side effect of its use for managing interruptions and facilitating casual interactions, or as a main effect in its own right. By presenting together the presence information for a group of people, or in some cases collating those presences into a single presence "signal", a sense of identity and coherence may be amplified.

Presence also **supports self-expression**, enabling individuals to present themselves to others through their choice of graphical avatars, screen names, and mood messages.

In any particular situation several purposes may be applicable to any given presence message.

Semantics of Presence

From the implementation of presence technologies in applications such as social networks, instant messaging and VoIP systems, we can readily identify some basic categories of presence information as the basis for a set of presence semantics:

Network availability. Is the user's device on the network? In synchronous systems such as instant messaging this typically means whether the client application is in a state where it is communicating with the network. In asynchronous web-based systems such as social networking websites, this may be a heuristic of session context; that is, whether the user has an active session.

Communication availability. Is the user willing to enter communication? In many messaging applications this was simply the absence of an "away" state. Skype extended this with "not available" and "do not disturb" states for negative availability, as well as "skype me" for positive availability. The addition of these communication states to the network availability allows for a number of combined states to be propagated; the ramifications of what "online, not available" versus "online, away" means in Skype, for example, has been largely left to users to figure out. One pattern that seems reasonably common is to use the "away" state to convey not that user is unavailable for communication, but is instead available to communicate with some people – such as close friends and colleagues – but not others.

Emotional context. What is the emotional state of the user? This is explicitly visible in Skype as the "mood message" feature, and can also be seen in other services, such as LiveJournal, and to some extent in FaceBook with its "status message" feature, although this is more often used to communicate an activity context (q.v.).

Activity context. What is the user doing? While communication availability states can convey whether or not a user is interruptable, they do not give any indication of what it is that is occupying their attention. Activity context states convey what are user is doing. The "mood message" feature of Skype can be used to propagate activity context instead of moods; the Facebook "status message" feature by contrast is primarily aimed at propagating an activity context, but can also be used for emotional context (Figure 2). Micro-blogging services such as Twitter can also be characterized as propagating activity context presence information.

Beyond these common categories found in current systems, there are also some more specialized categories that can be found in some services:

Location. Where is the user? With the addition of geo-locating services, presence information can also include geographical information. Less formally, a generic "away message" or "mood message" can convey a sense of where the user is. Some social networking tools, such as Plazes, specialize in using geo-located presence information.

Needs and desires. What does the user want or need? While such information can be part of generic presence information, there are also specialized applications that make use of presence information about user desires; for example, the Nokia Sensor application can broadcast dating-style profile information over short-range Bluetooth networks.

Figure 2. Status messages in Facebook

Identity projection. Who is the user, and why might I care? Some of the earliest "hacks" of presence information were concerned with projecting the identity of the user, for example an early addition to the Apple iChat application was to automatically replace the away message with the music the user was listening to at the time in iTunes. In most presence systems an image is propagated along with other status information (generally referred to as a graphical avatar, or "gravatar") that offers a means of self-expression for users.

Awareness of Presence

People can become of aware of presence information in different ways:

Interruptions occur where presence information disturbs the consumer's current activity. For example, an alert message coming up on screen. Few, if any, presence mechanisms generate true interruptions. Instead, it is more typical for presence information to result in an interruption of the presentity; for example, in response to a presence state changing to "available", the consumer initiates messaging with the presentity.

Ambient awareness engages the consumer in a more subtle fashion, with presence information integrated into the environment through media that is intended to either influence the overall state of the consumer, or to attract attention only where there is sudden change in the presence information being conveyed. For example, an ambient presence display might show slow colour changes where there is a "normal" level of team activity context presence information, and rapidly flickering changes where there is an abnormally high level of activity to attract the user's attention.

Situated awareness places the presence information within a context relevant to the information, For example, the placement of communication availability presence information within the context of the instant messaging buddy list.

PRODUCING AND CONSUMING PRESENCE

In any system involving presence, there are three key concerns:

- *What* entity is being presented
- How is the entity's presence *produced?*
- How is it *consumed?*

The "what is being presented" question concerns the nature of presented entities (often contracted to "presentities"). At one level this is the question of what type of entity is being presented in the real world; for example, a human user or some sort of automated system such as an agent or a "point of presence" systems such as a specific node or terminal. At another level this is the question of how an entity presents itself – how it is named and identified, whether it is associated with particular representations. Representation is a problematic concept in regards to presence; it could be argued whether presence systems present an entity, or present information on behalf of an entity. That is, the answer to the question of what presence information actually *represents* is ambiguous.

The production of presence concerns how the presence information of an entity is produced, so that it can be propagated to other nodes in the network. The methods for the production of presence can be split into two categories: *explicit* and *passive* cues. Explicit cues involve the intervention of the entity to make a statement about their presence, such as selecting a value or entering a piece of text to display. Passive cues involve the use of sensors to automatically produce presence information, such as network connection sensors and activity measurement.

Finally, the consuming of presence concerns how other nodes in the network access presence information. These can vary widely, from the "Buddy List" indicators found in most messaging systems to innovative ambient technologies.

Presentities

In most presence technologies, the entity whose presence is being broadcast (the *presentity*) is typically an identity of a person, linked to a profile in the network. For example, the presence mechanisms of Facebook, Moodle, Skype and so on offer a graphical avatar and a name for the presentity that are linked to the user's profile.

However, in some cases the presentity may not correspond to the identity of a person, but to a non-human agent or other entity. For example, in enterprise instant messaging systems such as Akeni[2], a presentity can be offered for a business function that represents a pool or team of staff that support the function. Only on initiating communication is a specific user identity determined from the pool. This is used typically to offer customer support, and is the synchronous equivalent of the support@company.com generic email address, where messages are forwarded to an available operator.

Producing Presence

Passive Cues

Passive cues are collected from users and their environment in order to construct presence information for distribution in the network. In the software environment this might involve the deployment of various kinds of listeners that propagate events in response to particular stimuli. However, there are also presence production methods that take passive cues from the physical environment, although these are not used in any commonly used systems or social networks.

Network listeners are the most basic kind of listener that most networks could not operate without; this enables the network to determine whether the device a user uses to communicate their presence is connected to the network. In instant messaging this typically follows a publish-subscribe and event propagation pattern, using protocols such as XMPP (XML Messaging and Presence Protocol) or SIMPLE (Session Initiation Protocol for Instant Messaging and Presence Leveraging Extensions). For example, in a typical messaging application, when a user selects a new status, the client application sends a presence notification message to the server, which then sends the message to each subscriber to that user (typically, everyone who has the user on their "buddy list"). In other kinds of social software network listeners have to follow a slightly different model. In web applications this is typically based on the management of the browser session state, and is rather less accurate than dedicated presence protocols.

System capability listeners are a more advanced type of network listener found in instant messaging and VoIP systems. These are needed to propagate information needed to support communication options, such as whether the user has a video camera plugged in to support video chat. These listeners generate a notification to the network as the system capabilities of the user's client are modified. At a more basic level, most networks that rely on specialized client software and protocols transmit client version details to assess compatibility with other users and services.

Application task listeners extend outside any client application the user may be using to connect to the network, and instead listen to the status of other applications they may be using. For example, a number of tools enable instant messaging and VoIP clients to listen to currently-playing media in iTunes and other media players; this information can then be propagated as a custom away message or mood message. This might be extended to inspecting the state of particular documents or processes as a kind of simple workflow listener (q.v.). For example, in the study by Fogarty, Lia and Christensen (2004), availability of users was estimated by combining information from the user's calendar, information from the computer on its location, and speech detection via access to the computer's built-in microphone.

Workflow listeners are a specialised type of application task listener that propagates information related to the state of the presentity's workflow. For example, a workflow listener attached to a business process might set the communications availability of the participants in the transaction to reduce interruptions to the task. Alternatively, a workflow listener may propagate workflow state changes as presence messages to help generate transcripts and reports.

Physical sensors extend beyond the network and into the presentity's environment, transducing the environmental measurements into types of presence information. For example, the Nimio ambient device discussed later in this chapter converts the input from a range of motion and sound sensors into activity presence information. In other work sensors in the environment have been used to generate activity context and communication availability presence information. In a project at Carnegie Mellon University (Fogarty, Lia and Christensen, 2004), speech detection sensors were used to track availability. In another study in Sweden a physical sensor – in this case, a video camera – was used to capture a physical "sign in" board at the entrance to a laboratory, and convert this into location presence information (Rafael, 2001). The range of physical sensors with the potential to generate presence information is very large indeed, and includes motion, pressure, noise, speech, temperature, audio, video, posture, and so on. A study by Hudson et. al, (2003) used a very wide range of sensors to try to predict interruptability, apparently with some success. However, despite all the research, to date very few presence systems make use of physical sensors outside the laboratory.

Psychophysiological interfaces extend beyond other kinds of physical sensors and interact directly with the presentity, measuring their physiological characteristics to infer psychological states. At its most extreme this could include MRI or PET scanning. More practically this can include eye-tracking scanners or systems that interpret facial expressions from video capture.

Explicit Cues

Explicit cues offer direct intervention by the user in setting their presence information. Typically this involves selecting a particular type of status or entering some text into a program to create status information.

Away messages typically offer a predefined list of status messages that describe the communication availability of the presentity. The early away message systems, such as early versions of AOL Instant Messenger and ICQ had a fixed list of status messages; later systems added custom messages; these custom messages mutated into the more freeform presence status system Skype calls a *mood message*.

Mood messages are a means of offering usually quite freeform presence information. Although the name suggests this is for emotional context, the mood message format can also be used for other types of presence information, including task context and communication availability.

One of the issues of using explicit cues as it requires the direct intervention of the user to express their presence. This can lead to presence information becoming stale: mood messages can remain for months after they are no longer relevant, for example "having a great Valentine's!" status messages that continue to show up in July. In addition, as users engage in more systems and networks that use presence information, the number of explicit cues needed grows. To counter this latter issue, tools have started to emerge that enable presence information to be broadcast to multiple systems simultaneously. For example, the MoodBlast[3] application can set mood and away messages in several networks, including Skype, Twitter, and Facebook (Figure 3).

Mapping Production Mechanisms To Presence Semantics

Given the set of presence categories, and the set of production cues, we can construct a simple map of their relationships (Figure 4).

Consuming Presence

Ambient Awareness Technologies

The ways in which presence is 'consumed' place a particular stress upon ambient awareness, and much recent work on consuming presence has had origins either in the world of ambient art

Figure 3. Moodblast broadcasts the users explicit cues to multiple systems

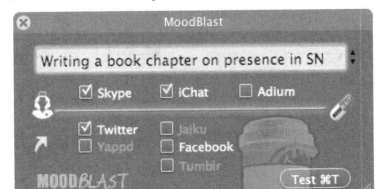

(e.g., Beale, 2005) or management attention (e.g. Achloptas, D., Horvits, E., (2005)) where ambient awareness and management of interruption is a topic of interest for the improvement of coordination efficiency. Ambient art can be used to convey mood, activity, presence and other ambient information in a way that doesn't demand full attention (Beale, 2005).

In the art and design domain, there have been a number of efforts to construct ambient information appliances that use a concept of presence.

Joanna Brewer's "Nimio" device (see Figure 5.) is a translucent pyramid that is designed to enhance awareness within a closely collaborative workgroup (Brewer, Williams, and Dourish, 2005). Nimio uses embedded sensors to measure an overall 'activity level' based on sound and movement, and coloured LEDs to reflect the activity level across the other pyramids. There are also special effects possible through shaking the pyramids or moving them close together.

Mauricio Melo's "Networked Emoticon Device" (Melo, 2005) is one of several devices that are aimed at sharing mood information using ambient displays. The NED is a very small device with lighted emoticons indicating the mood of a particular person (see Figure 6.)

As well as these experimental designs, products using ambient forms and presence indicators have started to appear. The Nabaztag, or "Smart Rabbit" is a commercial product that uses a number of mechanisms to share presence with other rabbit "friends" (see Figure 7.) For example, two Nabaztag owners can "pair" their rabbits, after which any movement made to the ears of one rabbit is reflected by the other. The movement can be both a simple signal of "I'm here" or could have a more complex meaning within a shared code, e.g. "left ear means I'm bored, call me. Right ear means I miss you, but have nothing much to say". Nabaztag also has various LEDs that can cause spots to light up in different colours.

Figure 4. Map of relationships between presence categories and production methods

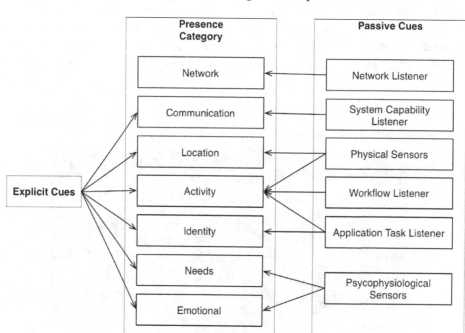

Figure 5. Nimio, an ambient awareness device

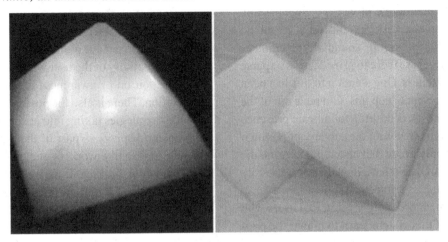

Figure 6. Networked emoticon device

These ambient presence awareness devices all rely on the power of subtle messages using very limited 'content'. The use of subtle cues such as colour, movement, and lighting enable information to enter the awareness of the user in a way that does not immediately compel attention or gener- ate interruption. Where the cues have contextual importance (e.g., you're waiting for the Nimio to flash red, indicating your team have arrived in the office with coffee) then they can easily 'surface' to draw attention.

By contrast, messaging software tends to be shoved under a pile of work, metaphorically speaking, on the desktop, and only the audio cues (e.g. the "plip-plop" sound Skype emits as buddies arrive) are there to provide a very sparse kind of awareness. One solution to this has been the use of presence 'pop ups' that poke out of the bottom of the users desktop to indicate presence changes; compared with the subtlety of Nimio it seems not only crude, but also to undermine the ambient awareness effect altogether by constantly prompting the user to pay attention. However, it would seem, anecdotally at least, that users who make use of this system learn to ignore the pop-ups after a while.

In some respects ambient displays and devices are not a good fit with the affordances of human attention mechanisms. In general, the constant low-level stimulation offered by ambient information displays should result in attention inhibition effects; stable objects in the field of attention have

a tendency to fade over time as far the perceiver is concerned. (See, for example, Simons & Chablis, 1999). However, it is entirely possible that ambient technologies may have more subtle effects on the mood and activity of the user without necessitating attention on or awareness of the source of stimulation. There is also the possibility of user's attention strategies taking into account scanning of ambient displays as part of their general behaviour, rather like workers glancing out of the window while thinking or between tasks.

In Dabbish & Kraut's (2004) experiments on awareness displays, it was found that abstract representations of activity context and availability were more effective than the simplified representations used in instant messaging, which offer availability states in too coarse a timeframe, and more sophisticated systems that proved to be a distraction for users. Designing effective ambient solutions for consuming presence would appear to present a considerable design challenge. How

Figure 7. Nabaztag, the "Smart Rabbit"

can a system snythesize the various dimensions of presence information into a succinct, yet useful, abstract representation?

Communication Technologies

There is a wide range of synchronous communication technologies (also known as instant messaging systems) available today that consume presence information. Skype, AOL Instant Messenger, MSN, Yahoo and iChat are some obvious examples from the desktop. There are also web-based communication systems with similar features, such as Meebo.

All of these systems have several key recurring patterns in their implementation of presence, which can be traced in their evolution back to the earliest instant messaging applications such as ICQ.

Instant messaging systems tend to offer presence information in the form of a list of users associated with a graphical avatar and a status icon; this was first termed by AOL a "Buddy List", and this term has stuck for a wide range of instant messaging systems. The Buddy List provides an index of known presentities and their current state, displaying their graphical avatar for easy identification. Status icons in the earlier systems tended to follow a "traffic light" system, with red indicating the presentity is not connected, amber connected but unavailable, and green for available. As mentioned earlier in this chapter, the pattern of these lights is also a possible harking back to the physical connection indicators on Internet routers, which have a similar use.

Social Networks

Social networks such as Facebook have also become presence consumers. Lacking many of the synchronous capabilities of dedicated messaging systems, nonetheless some of these applications also make use of a type of "buddy list" displays for presence awareness. However, recently on social networks there has been a shift away from placing "buddy list" displays quite so prominently as in the past, instead offering a "feed" or "river" of status updates.

Rather than offering the current status of a presentity, these feeds aggregate the history of presence notifications from the user's connections. This form of presence offers a convenience for asynchronously connected users, as the history of presence state changes offers a more appropriate way of "catching up" than a single synchronous state.

For example, Facebook offers presence in several different ways:

1. An "online now' option on the Friends menu displays the friend profile information for friends who have interacted recently with the Facebook system.
2. The "mini-feed" widget on the user's profile page displays a feed of events including recent profile updates by friends
3. The "status updates" option of the Friends menu displays a feed containing only the status updates of friends
4. The profile page of each user has a status message subtitle displayed by the user's name.

Social networks have evolved unique forms of presence consuming technologies that are better adapted for asynchronous interaction than the "buddy list". Less useful for coordinating conversations, these methods instead amplify self-expression and enable more sophisticated monitoring of the sense of activity among friends.

Microblogs

Taking the "feed" approach one stage further, services such as Twitter[4] (see Figure 8) and Jaiku[5] have created a new "microblog" format that treats status messages as an end in itself. These services encourage users to create very short activity updates that can then be aggregated by others using regular RSS technology.

Using these services, presence information is produced using a fairly normal text entry mode, either from a web browser or a mobile phone via SMS. The presence information is displayed on a user's profile as a list of entries, latest first. This presence feed is also available to be consumed as an RSS feed, or via a dedicated "widget" that can be displayed within a social networking site such as Facebook, or on a "normal" personal blog page. The widget displays a similar feed view to the main website.

Categorising Presence-Consuming Techniques

There is considerable potential variety in the ways systems offer presence for consumption by users and systems. However, several common patterns can be identified.

Status icons indicate one or possibly two dimensions of presence information in a small graphic (e.g. Skype status icons).

Graphical avatars offer a representation of the presentity, and can convey presence information through the state of the image; this may be greyed out or faded to indicate network availability, an approach to conveying presence information explored by Tyman and Huang (2003). The avatar itself is used for projecting identity.

Subtitles provide a means of supplementing a display with a short text message containing presence information. This may convey emotional context (e.g. the Skype mood message), or activity context (e.g. Facebook status).

Feeds offer a continuous stream of presence-related information, rather than a single updated display such as a status icon. Twitter is an example of this; Facebook also offers presence information as a feed. Feeds can make use of existing feed interoperability specifications such as RSS and

Figure 8. Twitter, a microblog service

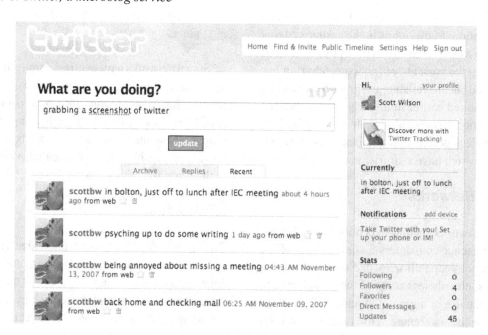

Atom to broaden the context in which presence information occurs.

Abstract representations of presence information translate the meaning of the information into a very different form for consumption. Nimio and Nabaztag are examples of this type of approach, translating activity context states into colour and motion.

Composite representations combine multiple types of presence information into a single abstract cue. Some ambient experiments such as Nimio fall within this category, as does the work of Dabbish and Kraut (2004).

Interactions With Nonhuman Agents

In addition to human consumers, there is also the area of nonhuman agents consuming and responding to presence messages. One area of particular focus has been in exploring the bounded deferral approach to information awareness. In this model, messages from agents for a user are deferred while the user is in a state where they do not want to be interrupted. The messages are delayed until either the user enters a state where they can be interrupted, or a maximum delay time is reached (the *deferral boundary*).

An example of this approach is a Microsoft study focussing on bounded deferral using a "busy state" explicit cue (Achloptas & Horvitz, 2005). This study found that patterns in user's states could be used to construct interruption policies for machine agents.

TOWARDS AN ONTOLOGY OF PRESENCE

In this chapter we have presented several dimension of presence that we can use as the basis of a specialized ontology within the domain of presence technologies. This ontology is defined as the interaction of the methods of production and consumption of presence information, which

consists of both semantics and purpose. A presence technology may therefore be described as employing one or more *production methods* that *produces* presence information with particular *semantics*, *for* one or more *purposes*, which is then made available *using* one or more *consumption methods*.

This model exists within the overall simple domain model for presence, as illustrated in Figure 9. Note that this domain model uses UML model semantics.

Combining the variables of purpose, semantics, production methods and consumption methods identified in the earlier sections results in a simple ontology for presence. This is illustrated in Figure 10. Note this figure uses a Topic Map representation rather than UML.

We can use this ontology to create statements that describe the presence offerings of social software and other systems, for example:

"Skype offers the Mood Message feature, a Presence Subsystem that implements the Production Method Explicit Cue, which produces Semantics of Emotional Context, for the Purposes of Facilitating Casual Interactions and Supporting Self Expression, using the Consumption Method Subtitle."

When represented formally (e.g. using OWL[6]) it then becomes possible to ask a knowledge base questions such as "which *Systems* Facilitate Casual interactions *using* Feeds?"

It is possible to then use this ontology to map the approaches taken by some of the presence systems described in this chapter; this is summarized in Table 1, below, and as a topic map using the same ontology (Figure 11). This topic map only shows the utilized connections between the nodes in the ontology; this shows the extent to which the space of possible configurations for presence subsystems defined by the ontology is largely unexplored in current systems.

Figure 9. Domain model of presence systems

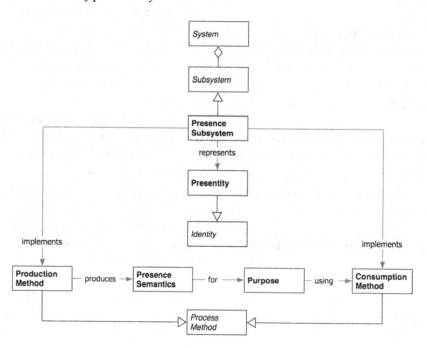

Figure 10. Presence ontology expressed as a topic map

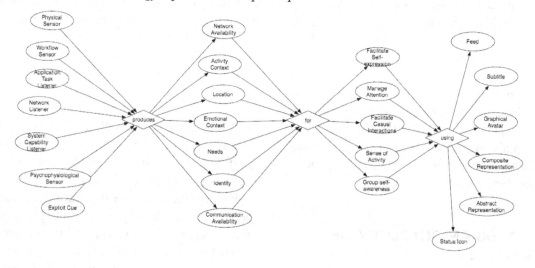

FUTURE TRENDS

While efforts at **standardising** synchronous messaging have largely stumbled, as competing instant messaging networks try to keep their mar-kets captive, new forms of presence consumption such as presence activity feeds are enabling more flexible ways of working with presence information using existing interoperability standards such as RSS and Atom. Google's OpenSocial project

Figure 11. Topic map of presence technologies

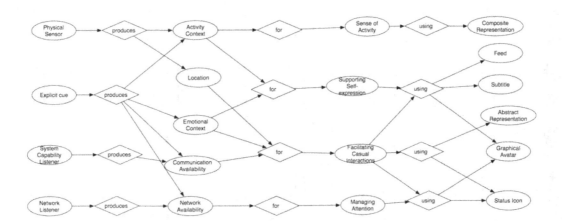

is an example of this trend, providing a way for social networks to expose feeds of activity status in a standard way to third-party widgets and services (Safuto, 2007). This form of presence is better suited to asynchronous connectivity than the buddy list found typically in messaging applications, and will become just as ubiquitous in social networks until the next "big idea" in presence technology comes along.

Going hand in hand with interoperability is **ubiquity**; as more presence systems are able to expose presence information in ways which are open and repurposable, presence information becomes another sharable commodity just like blog posts and social bookmarks, and can appear in many different forms in different places.

While so far **ambient presence** technologies have been used quite extensively in the field of digital art, there hasn't yet been mainstream uptake of this technology. However as presence information becomes interoperable and ubiquitous, abstract ambient representations of presence will start to emerge in surprising forms in more everyday settings.

Presence production will increasingly be part of everyday practice. There has been a very clear trend towards producing richer presence information through explicit human production and away from employing automated methods of producing presence. This seems in some ways counter to the general trend in computer systems. For example, a CNET report in 2004 quoted representatives from Siemens and Microsoft stating that automatically and intelligently assessing presence information from multiple sources was a prerequisite for useful presence information, especially in a business setting (Becker, 2004). However, the trend away from automated production is very clear from an observation of the uptake of presence systems in Facebook, Twitter and Skype, and the lack of traction for automatic production using sensors despite the large research base.

Rather than turning around, this trend is likely to continue, with only new forms of passive presence production potentially breaking this pattern. New forms of automated presence production may take their cues from the social network, and the activity and connection formation within it,

Table 1. Categorising presence technologies using the ontology

System	Presence Subsystem	Production Method	Presence Semantics	Purpose	Consumption Method
Skype	Mood Message	Explicit cues	Emotional context	Facilitate Casual Interactions Supporting Self Expression	Subtitle
	Status Message	Network listener Explicit cues	Network availability Communication availability	Manage attention and interruption	Status icon
	Video availability	System Capability Listener	Communication availability	Facilitate Casual Interactions	Status icon
IChat	Status Message	Network listener Explicit cues	Network availability Communication availability Emotional context	Manage attention and interruption Facilitate casual interactions	Status icon Graphical avatar Subtitle
	Video availability	System Capability Listener	Communication availability	Facilitate Casual Interactions	Status icon
	Audio availability	System Capability Listener	Communication availability	Facilitate Casual Interactions	Status icon
Facebook	Status Message	Explicit cues	Activity context Emotional context	Facilitate casual interactions Supporting self-expression Supporting group self-awareness	Subtitle Feed
Twitter		Explicit cues	Activity context Emotional context	Supporting Self-expression	Feed
Nimio		Physical Sensors – sound, movement	Activity Context	Sense of activity in interaction space	Composite
Networked Emoticon Device		Explicit cues	Emotional context	Supporting self-expression	Status Icon

continued of following page

Table 1. continued

System	Presence Subsystem	Production Method	Presence Semantics	Purpose	Consumption Method
Jaiku		Explicit cues Physical sensor (mobile GPS)	Activity context Emotional context Location	Supporting Self-expression Facilitate casual interactions	Feed
Moodle	Online Users	Network Listener	Network Availability	Facilitate casual interactions	Graphical Avatar
Nabaztag		Explicit cues (waggling the ears)	Activity context Emotional context Communication availability	Facilitate casual interactions	Abstract
Dabbish & Kraut's experiment		Application Listener	Activity context (workload)	Manage attention and interruption	Abstract

instead of using sensors aimed at individuals. For the most part presence production will continue to be a personal action that will increasingly be part of everyday practice in operating in social networks.

The **ontology** described in this chapter also identified that a large part of the available space of the presence domain is currently unused by present systems. This potentially identifies a wide range of new presence applications that can be developed and tested. In particular the

CONCLUSION

Presence is a fundamental component of the online experience, and while it originated to some extent within the specific demands of instant messaging networks, the concepts and technologies of presence have become embedded within social networks and other online systems. The development of new networks that have presence as a primary purpose – Twitter and Jaiku – reinforces the notion that the current and next phase of development of social network technology has a central role for presence. Experiments in ambient art and new technologies for producing and consuming presence, together with the emergence of more open, interoperable and ubiquitous presence systems, opens the possibility for more creative and sophisticated ways of making use of presence both online and also in physical space.

While the social effects of presence may run deep, the mechanisms of presence do lend themselves to a relatively simple ontology that can be used to position presence technologies in relation to the existing landscape.

REFERENCES

Achloptas, D., & Horvits, E. (2005). *Principles of bounded deferral for balancing information awareness with interruption.* Microsoft Research.

Retrieved 12th November, 2007 from http://research.microsoft.com/~horvitz/bounded_deferral.pdf

Beale, R. (2005). Ambient art: information without attention. In *11th International Conference on Human-Computer Interaction*. Lawrence Erlbaum Associates, Inc (LEA), Las Vegas, Nevada, USA. Retrieved 12th November, 2007 from http://www.cs.bham.ac.uk/~rxb/Online%20papers/Ambient%20art.pdf

Becker, D. (2004). Beware of geeks bearing "presence". CNET News, March 16th, 2004. Retrieved 12th November, 2007, from http://www.news.com/2100-1012_3-5173464.html.

Boyd, D. (2005). *Cultural divide in IM: Presence vs. communication*. Retrieved 12th November, 2007 from http://www.zephoria.org/thoughts/archives/2005/02/13/cultural_divide_in_im_presence_vs_communication.html

Brewer, J., Williams, A., & Dourish, P. (2005). Nimio: An ambient awareness device. In *Proceedings of CSCW 2005*. Retrieved 12th November, 2007, from http://www.ics.uci.edu/~johannab/papers/brewer.williams.dourish.ecscw2005.pdf

Dabbish, L., & Kraut, R. E. (2004). Controlling Interruptions: Awareness Displays and Social Motivation for Coordination. In *Proceedings of the 2004 ACM conference on Computer Supported Collaborative Work*, 182-191. ACM, New York.

Fogarty, J., Lia, J., & Christensen, J. (2004). Presence versus availability: the design and evaluation of a context-aware communication client. *International Journal of Human-Computer Studies, 61*(3), 299-317. Elsevier.

Horvitz, E., Apacible, J., & Subramani, M. (2005). Balancing Awareness and Interruption: Investigation of Notification Deferral Policies. In *User Modeling 2005*, (pp. 433-437). Heidelberg: Springer.

Hudson, S., Fogarty, J., Atkeson, C., Avrahami, D., Forlizzi, S.K., Lee, J., & Yang, J. (2003) Predicting human interruptibility with sensors: a Wizard of Oz feasibility study. In *Proceedings of the SIGCHI conference on Human factors in computing systems,* April 05-10, 2003, Ft. Lauderdale, Florida, USA

Lombard, M., & Ditton, T. (1997). At the heart of it all: The concept of presence. *Journal of Computer-Mediated Communication, 3*(2). Retrieved 12th November, 2007 from http://jcmc.indiana.edu/vol3/issue2/lombard.html

Melo, M. (2005). "Web Are You? Networked Emoticon Device". *Mauricio Melo Design*. Retrieved 12th November, 2007, from http://www.mauriciomelo.com/contents/interact05.htm

Rafael, M. L. G. (2001). *Sensing the presence of others in a work environment. Design and implementation of an awareness system: SIBO* (Sign-in Board Online). Masters thesis, Royal Institute of Technology, Stockholm. Retrieved 12th November, 2007, from ftp://ftp.nada.kth.se/IPLab/TechReports/IPLab-191.pdf

Safuto, R. (2007). *Why do we need OpenSocial?* Retrieved 12th November, 2007 from http://blog.awakenedvoice.com/2007/11/05/why-do-we-need-open-social/

Tyman, J., &Huang, E. M. (2003). Intuitive visualizations for presence and recency information for ambient displays. In *Proceedings of the SIGCHI conference on Human factors in computing systems*, Ft, Lauderdale.

KEY TERMS

Buddy List: A common recurring pattern of presence consuming technology found in instant messaging systems for exposing the *presence* of multiple *presentities* known to the user.

Explicit Cues: A mechanism for the production of presence information about a presentity that involves direct personal intervention, typically typing a short message to be displayed as a subtitle or in a feed, or of selecting a status from a vocabulary of possible states.

Microblogging: A form of blogging that involves the production by *explicit cues* of short activity updates, rather like a *mood message*, that can be consumed by others as a presence "feed".

Mood Message: A common recurring pattern of presence involving a subtitle or similar used to express the emotional context, activity, or identity of a *presentity*, produced using *explicit cues*.

Passive Cues: The use of listeners and sensors in the physical or virtual environment to produce presence information for a *presentity*.

Presence: The discourse, practices and technologies supporting the exposure of the states of *presentities* such that those states can be perceived by other agents in the network.

Presentity: An identity, e.g. of a person or agent, which produces presence information and about which presence information can be consumed. Presentities contextualize presence information by associating it with an identity; the identity can be projected using graphical avatars, "buddy names", and through the presence information itself, such as mood messages, subtitles, and activity context information.

ENDNOTES

[1]   Internet Relay Chat. One of the earliest forms of instant messaging, developed in 1998.

[2]   http://www.akeni.com/

[3]   http://blog.circlesixdesign.com/download/moodswing/

[4]   http://www.twitter.com

[5]   http://www.jaiku.com/

[6]   Web Ontology Language. See http://www.w3.org/TR/owl-features/

Compilation of References

"amillionpenguins.com" Retrieved June 20, 2007 from http://www.amillionpenguins.com/wiki/index.php/Main_Page.

"Berners-Lee on the read/write web." Retrieved June 20, 2007, from http://news.bbc.co.uk/1/hi/technology/4132752.stm.

"The Lulu Blooker Prize 2007". Retrieved June 20, 2007 from http://www.lulublookerprize.com.

Abbott, C. (1999). *The Internet, text production and the construction of identity: Changing use by young males during the early to mid 1990s.* Unpublished PhD, King's College, University of London, London.

Abbott, C. (2001). Some young male Website owners: the Technological Aesthete, the Community Builder and the Professional Activist. *Education, Communication and Information, 1*(2), 197-212.

Abbott, C. (2005). Towards Digital Impartiality: learning from young people's online literacy practices. In R. Kupetz & G. Blell (Eds.), *Fremdsprachenlernen zwischen Medienverwahrlosung und Medienkompetenz* (pp. 31-41). Frankfurt: Peter Lang.

Abbott, C., & Seale, J. (2007). Methodological issues in researching online representations: production, classification and personal web space. *International Journal of Research & Method in Education, 30.*

Abram, D. (1997). *The Spell of the Sensuous: Perception and Language in a More-Than-Human World.* New York: Vintage.

Abrami, P. C., & Barrett, H. (Eds.) (2005). Special Issue on Electronic Portfolios. *Canadian Journal of Learning Technology, 31*(3).

Abrams, D., & Hogg, M. A. (2001). Collective identity: Group membership and self-conception. In M. A. Hogg & S. Tinsdale (Eds.), *Blackwell handbook of social psychology: Group processes* (pp. 425-460). Malden, MA: Blackwell.

Ach, N. (1910). *Uber den willensakt und das temperament. [On the will and temperament].* Leipzig, Germany: Quelle & Meyer.

Achloptas, D., & Horvits, E. (2005). *Principles of bounded deferral for balancing information awareness with interruption.* Microsoft Research. Retrieved 12th November, 2007 from http://research.microsoft.com/~horvitz/bounded_deferral.pdf

Affordance. (2007). In *Wikipedia.* http://en.wikipedia.org/wiki/Affordance Accessed 17.08.07.

Agre, P. & Horswill, I. (1997). Lifeworld Analysis. *Journal of Artificial Intelligence Research* Volume 6, pp. 111-145, and at http://www-2.cs.cmu.edu/afs/cs/project/jair/pub/volume6/agre97a-html/lifeworlds.html.

Aigrain, P. (2004). The individual and the collective in open information communities. *16th BLED Electronic Commerce Conference,* (pp. 9-11). Retrieved on January, 17, 2007 from < http://opensource.mit.edu/papers/aigrain3.pdf >.

Akgün, A. E., Lynn, G. S., & Byrne, J. (2003). Organizational learning: A socio-cognitive framework. *Human Relations, 56*(7), 839– 868.

Albert, S., & Thomas, C. (2000). A new approach to computer-aided distance learning: the 'Automated Tutor'. *Open Learning, 15*(2), 141-150.

Alexander, B. (2006, March/April). Web 2.0: A New Wave of Innovation for Teaching and Learning? *EDUCAUSE Review,* 41(2), 32–44. www.educause.edu/apps/er/erm06/erm0621.asp?bhcp=1, (11/10/2007).

Allen, C. (2004). *Tracing the Evolution of Social Software.* www.lifewithalacrity.com/2004/10/tracing_the_evo.html, (04/26/2008).

Allen, S. (2005). *The missing link in alternative certification: Teacher identity formation.* Available [Online]: www.umbc.edu/llc/llcreview/2005/The_Missing_Link.pdf, Retrieved on 25 August 2006

Almas, A. G., & Nilsen, A.G. (2006). *ICT competencies for the next generation of teachers.* Formatex. Online. Accessed 20.04.08.

Amabile, T. M. (1985). Motivation and creativity: Effects of motivational orientation on creative writers. *Journal of Personality and Social Psychology, 48*(2), 393-399.

Amabile, T., Hadley, C. N., & Kramer, S. J. (2002, August). "Creativity Under the Gun," Special Issue on The Innovative Enterprise: Turning Ideas into Profits. *Harvard Business Review,* 80(8), 52–61.

Amiot, C., de la Sablionniere, R., Terry, D., & Smith, J. (2007). Integration of social identities in the self: Toward a cognitive developmental model. *Personality and Social Psychology Review, 11,* 364-368.

Amitay, E., Har'El, N., Sivan, R., & Soffer, A. (2004). *Web-a-Where: Geotagging Web Content.* Paper presented at the ACM SIGIR conference on Research and development in information retrieval.

Anderson, C. (2006). *The Long Tail: How Endless Choice Is Creating Unlimited Demand.* Random House.

Anderson, C. (2006). *The long tail: Why the future of business is selling less of more* (1st ed.). New York: Hyperion.

Anderson, P. (2006). *What is the Web2.0? Ideas, technologies and implications for education.* Available at: http://www.jisc.ac.uk/media/documents/techwatch/tsw0701.pdf [Accessed 5 April, 2007].

Anderson, P. (2007). *What is Web 2.0? Ideas, technologies and implications for education.* JISC Technology and Standards Watch, Feb. 2007. Bristol: JISC. Retrieved October 25, 2007 from http://www.jisc.ac.uk/media/documents/techwatch/tsw0701b.pdf

Anderson, R., Manoogian, S. T., & Reznick, J. S. (1976). The undermining and enhancing of intrinsic motivation in preschool children. *Journal of Personality and Social Psychology, 34*(5), 915-922.

Anderson, T. (2001). The hidden curriculum of distance education. *Change Magazine, 33*(6), 29-35.

Anderson, T. (2006). Higher education evolution: Individual freedom afforded by educational social software. In M. Beaudoin (Ed.), *Perspectives on the Future of Higher Education in the Digital Age.* (pp. 77-90). New York: Nova Science Publishers.

Anderson, T. (2007). Reducing the Loneliness of Distant Learner Using Social Software. *Open and Distance Learning Conference.* Retrieved on January, 17, 2007 from < http://www2.open.ac.uk/r06/conference/TerryAndersonKeynoteCambridge2007.pdf >

Anderson, T. (2007). *Social Learning 2.0.* Keynote paper presented at ED-MEDIA 2007 World Conference on Educational Multimedia, Hypermedia, & Telecommunications, Vancouver, BC, June 25-29. Retrieved June 27, 2007, from http://www.slideshare.net/terrya/educational-social-software-edmedia-2007/.

Anderson, T., (2007). Learning with Networks. Retrieved 25th April 2007, from http://terrya.edublogs.org/2007/03/28/46/.

Annand, D. (2007). Re-organizing universities for the information age. *International Review of Research in Open and Distance Learning, 8*(3). Retrieved April 11, 2008, from http://www.irrodl.org/index.php/irrodl/article/view/372/956

Anstey, M., & Bull, G. (2006). *Teaching and learning multiliteracies: Changing times, changing literacies.* Kensington Gardens: International Reading Association and Australian Literacy Educators' Association.

Archer, S. L. (1989). The status of identity: Reflections on the need for intervention. *Journal of Adolescence, 12*, 345-359.

Ardichvili, A., Page, V., & Wentling, T. (2003). Motivation and barriers to participation in virtual knowledge-sharing communities of practice. *Journal of Knowledge Management, 7*(1), 64-77. Retrieved April 2007 from http://www.emeraldinsight.com/Insight/ViewContentServlet?Filename=Published/EmeraldFullTextArticle/Articles/2300070105.html

Argyris, C., & Schon, D. (1978). *Organisational Learning: A Theory of Action Perspective.* Reading, MA: Addison-Wesley.

Argyris, C., & Schon, D. A (1974). *Theory in practice: Increasing professional effectiveness.* San Francisco, Jossey-Bass.

Ariely, D. (2000). Controlling the information flow: effects on consumers' decision making and preferences. *Journal of Consumer Research, 27*(2), 233-248.

Arora, S., Geppert, C. M., Kalishman, S. et al. (2007) Academic health center management of chronic diseases through knowledge networks: Project ECHO. *Acad Med., 82*(2), 154-60

Arrington, M. (2007). Diig surrenders to mob. *Tech Cruch,* Retrieved May 2007 from http://www.techcrunch.com/2007/05/01/digg-surrenders-to-mob/

Ashforth, B. R., & Mael, F. (1989). Social identity theory and the organization. *Academy of Management Review, 14*(1), 20-39.

Association of College and Research Libraries (ACRL) (2000). *Information literacy competency standards for higher education.*

Association of Graduate Recruiters. (1995). *Skills for graduates in the 21st century.* Cambridge: The Association of Graduate Recruiters.

Attwell, G. (2007). *Personal learning environments - future of elearning?* Retrieved June 16, 2007, from http://www.elearningpapers.eu/index.php?page=doc&doc_id=8553&doclng=6

Attwell, G. (2007). Personal learning environments: the future of e-learning? *eLearning Papers, 2*(1). Retrieved December 11, 2007, from www.elearningeuropa.info/files/media/media11561.pdf

Attwell, G., & Elferink, R. (2006). *Next Generation Learning and Personal Learning Environments.* Paper presented at Alt C conference, Edinburgh, September, Symposium #733 - "E-learning, Social Software and Competence Development.

Australian Flexible Learning Systems (2007). Social software and its contribution to teaching and learning - a report by Australian Flexible Learning Framework (part ii). Online. Accessed 19.04.08 http://www.masternewmedia.org/news/2007/05/24/social_software_and_its_contribution.htm

Australian Learning & Teaching Council. (2008). *Places and spaces – for learning.* Retrieved July 2, 2008, from http://www.altc.edu.au/carrick/go/home/grants/pid/398.

Aviram, R., & Talmi, D. (2004). Are you a Technocrat A Reformist Or a Holist? *eLearning Europa.* Retrieved on 1st, March 2008, from http://www.elearningeuropa.info/index.php?page=doc&doc_id=4965&doclng=6&menuzone=1

Backstrom, L., Huttenlocher, D., Kleinberg, J., & Lan, X. (2006). *Group formation in large social networks: Membership, growth, and evolution.* Paper presented at the KDD '06, Philadelphia, USA.

Bacon, S., & Dillon, T. D. (2006). The potential of open source approaches for education. *Futurelab report* http://www.futurelab.org.uk/resources/publications_reports_articles/opening_education_reports/Opening_Education_Report200

Bagozzi, R. P., & Dholakia, U. M. (2006). Antecedents and purchase consequences of customer participation in small group brand communities. *International Journal of Research in Marketing,* 23(1), 45-61.

Bailey, K. D. (1982). *Metodi della ricerca sociale.* Bologna, Italy: Il Mulino.

Bailey, T., & Noyelle, T. (1988). *New technology and skill formation: Issues and hypotheses.* New York: Conservation of Human Resources.

Baker, S., & Green, H. (2005). Blogs will change your business. *Business Week,* May 2, (pp. 43-51).

Bakhtin, M. (1986). *Speech Genres and Other Late Essays.* (Austin: University of Texas.)

Bakhtin, M.M. (1986/1978). Speech genres and other late essays. In C. Emerson & M. Holquist (Eds.). Austin, TX: University of Texas Press.

Bakker, P. (1999, October). Reinventing Roots: New media and national identity. *Second Expert Meeting on Media and Open Societies.* (pp. 21-23). Amsterdam, The Netherlands.

Ballagas, R., Rohs, M., & Sheridan, J. G. (2005). *Sweep and Point & Shoot: Phonecam-Based Interactions for Large Public Displays.* Paper presented at the CHI 2005.

Bandura, A. (1986). *Social foundations of thought and action.* Englewood Cliffs, NJ: Prentice-Hall.

Bandura, A. (1986). *Social foundations of thought and action: a social cognitive theory.* Englewood Cliffs, NJ: Prentice-Hall.

Bandura, A. (1997). *Self-Efficacy: The Exercise of Control.* New York: Freeman.

Bandura, A. (1997). *Self-Efficacy.* New York: W. H. Freeman and Company.

Bandura, A. (2001). Social cognitive theory: An agentic perspective. *Annual Review of Psychology, 52,* 1-26.

Bandura, A. (2006). Towards a psychology of human agency. *Perspectives on Psychological Science, 1*(2).

Bangalore Declaration: A National Open Access Policy for Developing Countries. (2006). *Declaration signed in the Workshop on Electronic Publishing and Open Access.* Bangalore: Indian Institute of Science. Retrieved February 01, 2007 from http://www.ncsi.iisc.ernet.in/OAworkshop2006/pdfs/NationalOAPolicyDCs.pdf

Baraniuk, R. G. (2007). *Challenges and opportunities for the Open Education Movement: A Connexions case study.* White paper, Rice University. http://mitpress.mit.edu/catalog/item/default.asp?ttype=2&tid=11309

Baraniuk, R. G., & Cervenka, K. (2002). *Connexions white paper: Building communities and sharing knowledge.*

Bargh, J. A., & McKenna, K. Y. A. (2004). The Internet and social life. *Annual Review of Psychology, 55,* 573-590.

Barker, C. (2000) Cultural Studies: Theory and Practice, Sage Publications Ltd, London.

Barnes, C., & Tynan, B. (2007). The adventures of Miranda in the brave new world: learning in a Web 2.0 millennium. *ALT-J, Research in Learning Technology, 15*(3), 189-200.

Barnes, K., Marateo, R. C., & Ferris, S. P. (2007). Teaching and Learning with the Net Generation. *Innovate, 3*(4). Retrieved November 5th 2007, from: http://innovateonline.info/index.php?view=article&id=382&action=article

Barnett, R. (1997). *Higher Education: a critical business.* Buckingham, Open University Press.

Barnett, R. (2000). *Realising the University in an Age of Super Complexity.* Buckingham: Society for Research into Higher Education and Open University Press.

Barnum, C., & Markovsky, B. (2007). Group membership and social influence [Electronic Version]. *Current Research in Social Psychology, 13,* 1-38, from http://www.uiowa.edu/~grpproc

Barrass, S. & Fitzgerald, R.N. (2008). Social software: Piloting MyToons as a digital learning community for teaching new media. Paper to be presented at ED-MEDIA 2008 - World Conference on Educational Multimedia, Hypermedia & Telecommunications, June 30-July 4, 2008, Vienna, Austria.

Barro, S., & Burillo, P. (dir.) (2006). Las ICTs en el sistema universitario español (2006): un análisis estratégico. *CRUE*. http://www.crue.org/UNIVERSITIC2006/Analisis%20Estrategico.pdf

Barron, T. (2000). *A Smarter Frankenstein: The Merging of E-Learning and Knowledge Management.* Retrieved April 11, 2007, from http://www.learningcircuits.org/aug2000/barron.html

Barsky, E., & Purdon, M. (2006). Introducing Web 2.0: social networking and social bookmarking for health librarians. *Journal of the Canadian Health Libraries Association, 27*(3), 65-67.

Barth, F. (1969). *Ethnic groups and boundaries: The social organization of cultural difference.* Oslo, Norway: Universitetsforlaget.

Bar-Yam, Y. (1997). *Dynamics of Complex Systems.* Addison-Wesley.

Bassi, L. J. (1997). Harnessing the power of intellectual capital. *Training and Development, 21*(12), 422-431.

Bastos, M., Grigar, D., & Rodgers, T. (2007). Dene Grigar and Tara Rodgers: LEAD - Wild Nature and Digital Life Chat Transcripts. *Leonardo Electronic Almanac* 15. 1 – 2, at http://leoalmanac.org/resources/lead/digiwild/dgrigartrodgers.asp, accessed 20 June 2007.

Bateson, G. (1972). *Steps to an Ecology of Mind.* New York, USA: Ballantine.

Bawden, D. (2001). Information and digital literacies: a review of the concepts. *Journal of Documentation, 57*(2), 218-259.

Bawden, D., Holtham, C., & Courtney, N. (1999). Perspective on information overload. *Aslib Proceedings, 51*(8), 249-255.

Baym, N. K., & Zhang, Y. B. (2004). Social interactions across media: Interpersonal communication on the Internet, telephone and face-to-face. *New Media & Society, 6*(3), 299-318.

BBC News (2007) Google opens up social networking. Retrieved on 13th Nov 2007 from http://news.bbc.co.uk/1/hi/technology/7070815.stm.

BBC News Online (2007). *The Arctic Monkeys' Stellar Rise.* Retrieved 30 June, 2008 from: http://news.bbc.co.uk/1/hi/entertainment/5319434.stm

BBC News Online (2008). *PM Launching Online Question Time.* Retrieved 30 June, 2008 from: http://news.bbc.co.uk/1/hi/uk_politics/7407650.stm.

Beale, R. (2005). Ambient art: information without attention. In *11th International Conference on Human-Computer Interaction.* Lawrence Erlbaum Associates, Inc (LEA), Las Vegas, Nevada, USA. Retrieved 12th November, 2007 from http://www.cs.bham.ac.uk/~rxb/Online%20papers/Ambient%20art.pdf

Bebo, Inc. (2008). *About Bebo.* Retrieved April 21, 2008, from http://www.bebo.com/StaticPage.jsp?StaticPageId=2517103831

Bebo, Inc. (2008). About Bebo. Retrieved April 21, 2008, from http://www.bebo.com/StaticPage.jsp?StaticPageId=2517103831

Becker, D. (2004). Beware of geeks bearing "presence". CNET News, March 16th, 2004. Retrieved 12th November, 2007, from http://www.news.com/2100-1012_3-5173464.html.

Beer, D. (2006). The pop-pickers have picked decentralised media: the fall of Top of the Pops and the rise of the second media age. *Sociological Research Online, 11*(3). Accessed 04/09/2007.

Behavioral Diabetes Institute (2006). *How medium is a medium apple.* Web page http://www.behavioraldiabetes.org/stories.html. Last accessed September 16th 2007

Beldarrain, Y. (2006). Distance education trends: Integrating new technologies to foster student interaction and collaboration. *Distance Education, 27*(2), 139-153.

Beldarrain, Y. (2006). Distance education trends: Integrating new technologies to foster studentinteraction and collaboration. *Distance Education, 27*(2), 139-153.

Bennis, W., & Ward Biederman, P. (1998). None of us is as smart as all of us. *IEEE Computer, 31*(3), 116–117.

Bereiter, C. (2002). *Education and mind in the knowledge age.* Hillsdale, NJ: Erlbaum.

Bereiter, C., & Scardamalia, M. (1996). Rethinking learning. In D. R. Olson & N. Torrance (Eds.), *The Handbook of Education and Human Development* (pp. 485-513). Cambridge, MA: Blackwell Publishers.

Berg, J., Berquam, L., & Christoph, K. (2007). Social networking technologies: A 'poke' for campus services. *Educause Review,* March/April, 32-44.

Berg, J., Berquam, L., & Christoph, K. (2007). Social networking technologies: a "poke" for campus services. *EDUCAUSE Review, 42*(2), 32-44.

Berger, P. L., & Luckmann, T. (1966). *The Social Construction of Reality: A Treatise in the Sociology of Knowledge.* Garden City, NY: Anchor Books.

Berki, E., & Cobb-Payton, F. (2005). Work-Life Balance and Identity in a Virtual World: Facts, Tensions and Intentions for Women in IT. In H. Isomäki, & A. Pohjola, (Eds.), *Lost and Found in Virtual Reality: Women and Information Technology.* University of Lapland Press: Rovaniemi.

Berki, E., Isomäki, H., & Jäkälä, M. (2003, June). Holistic Communication Modelling: Enhancing Human-Centred Design through Empowerment. D. Harris, V. Duffy, M. Smith, & C. Stephanidis (Eds.), *Cognitive, Social and Ergonomic Aspects, Vol 3 of HCI International,* (pp. 22-27). University of Crete at Heraklion, (pp. 1208-1212). Lawrence Erlbaum Associates Inc.

Berki, E., Isomäki, H., & Salminen, A. (2007). Quality and Trust Relationships in Software Development. The Proceedings of E. Berki, J. Nummenmaa, I. Sunley, M., Ross, & G. Staples (Eds.), *Software Quality in the Knowledge Society Software Quality Management XV,* (pp. 47-65). BCS: GB, Swindon.

Berlin Declaration on Open Access to Knowledge in the Sciences and Humanities. (2003). *Berlin: Max Plank Society.* Retrieved February 01, 2007 from http://oa.mpg.de/openaccess-berlin/berlin_declaration.pdf

Berners-Lee, T. (2000). *Waeving the web: The original design and ultimate destiny of the world wide web.* New York, USA: Harper Collins.

Berners-Lee, T. (2000). *Weaving the Web.* New York: HarperCollins.

Berners-Lee, T. (2000). *Weaving the Web.* San Francisco, Harper.

Beshears, F. M. (2005). Viewpoint: The economic case for creative commons textbooks. *Campus Technology,* October 4. Retrieved March 10, 2007, from http://campustechnology.com/articles/40535/.

Bethesda Statement on Open Access Publishing. (2003). Chevy Chase: Peter Suber. Retrieved April 15, 2007 from http://www.earlham.edu/~peters/fos/bethesda.htm

Beuschel, W. (2003). From Face-to-Face to Virtual Space – The importance of informal aspects of communication in virtual learning environments. In U. Hoppe, B. Wasson, & S. Ludvigsen (Eds.), *Computer Support for Collaborative Learning (CSCL 2003) – Designing for Change in Networked Learning Environments* (pp. 229-238). Bergen/Norway.

Bhatt, G. D. (2001). Knowledge management in organizations: examining the interaction between technologies, techniques, and people. *Journal of Knowledge Management, 5*(1), 68-75.

Bhatt, G., Gupta, J. N. D., & Kitchens, F. (2005). An exploratory study of groupware use in the knowledge management process. *The Journal of Enterprise Information Management, 18*(1), 28-46.

Bibikas, D., Kourtesis, D., Paraskakis, I., Bernardi, A., Sauermann, L., Apostolou, D., Mentzas, D., & Vasconcelos, A. C. (2008). Organisational Knowledge Management Systems in the Era of Enterprise 2.0: The case of OrganiK. *In proceedings of the 2nd Workshop on Social Aspects of the Web (SAW 2008),* held in conjunction with the 11th International Conference on

Business Information Systems (BIS 2008), Innsbruck, Austria, May 2008.

Bibikas, D., Paraskakis, I., Psychogios, A. G., & Vasconcelos, A. C. (In press). Emerging enterprise social software knowledge management environments: Current practices and future challenges. *International Journal of Learning and Intellectual Capital.*

Biggs, J. (1999). *Teaching for quality learning at university.* Buckingham, UK: SRHE and Open University Press.

Bijker, W. (1999). *Of Bicycles, Bakelites and Bulbs: Towards a Theory of Sociotechnical Change.* Cambridge: MIT Press.

Bikson, T. K., & Law, S. A. (1994). *Global preparedness and human resources: College and corporate perspective's.* Santa Monica, California: Rand Corporation, Institute on Education and Training.

Bilandzic, M., Foth, M., & De Luca, A. (2008, Feb 25-27). *CityFlocks: Designing Social Navigation for Urban Mobile Information Systems.* Paper presented at the ACM SIGCHI Designing Interactive Systems (DIS), Cape Town, South Africa.

Bintz, W. P., & Dillard, J. (2007). Teachers as reflective practitioners: Examining teacher stories of curricular change in a 4th grade classroom. *Reading Horizons, 47*(3), 203-228.

Biocca, F., Burgoon, J., Harms, C., & Stoner, M. (2001). Criteria and Scope Conditions for a Theory and Measure of Social Presence. *Presence 2001 Conference,* Philadelphia.

Biocca, F., Harms, C., & Burgoon, J.K. (2003). Toward a more robust theory and measure of social presence: review and suggested criteria. *Presence: Teleoperators & Virtual Environments, 12*(5), 456-480.

Birchmeier, Z., Joinson, A. M., & Dietz-Uhler, B. (2005). Storming and forming a normative response to a deception revealed online. *Social Science Computer Review, 23*, 108.

Biswas R. (2007a). *User driven healthcare model to answer present day patient physician needs.* Paper presented at the meeting of the IEEEP2407 working group, London, UK.

Biswas, R. (2003). Patient networks and their level of complexity as an outcome measure in clinical intervention. BMJ rapid response to Edwards N, Clinical networks. *British Medical Journal 2002, 324*(63).

Biswas, R., Maniam, J., Lee, E. W. H., Das, P. G., Umakanth, S., Dahiya, S. et al (2008b press). User driven healthcare- Answering multidimensional information needs in individual patients utilizing post EBM approaches: An operational model. J Eval Clin Pract. (2008a press)

Biswas, R., Martin, C., Sturmberg, J., Shankar, R., Umakanth, S., Shanker, S. et al, (2008a press). User driven healthcare- Answering multidimensional information needs in individual patients utilizing post EBM approaches: A conceptual model. J Eval Clin Pract. (2008apress)

Biswas, R., Umakanth, S., Strumberg, J., Martin, C. M., Hande, M. & Nagra, J. S. (2007b). The process of evidence-based medicine and the search for meaning. *Journal of Evaluation in Clinical Practice, 13*, 529–532.

Blackledge, A. (2002). The discursive construction of national identity in multilingual Britain. *Journal of Language, Identity, and Education, 1*(1), 67-87.

Blanchard, A., & Horan, T. (1998). Virtual Communities and Social Capital. *Social Science Computer Review, 16*(3), 293-307.

Bleed, R. (2001). A hybrid campus for the new millennium. *EDUCAUSE Review, 36*(1), 17-24.

Bleiklie, I. (2004). Diversification of higher education and the changing role of knowledge and research. *UNESCO Forum Occasional Paper Series.* Paper No 6. Retrieved June 15, 2006, from http://unesdoc.unesco.org/images/0014/001467/146736e.pdf

Blood, R. (2005). www.rebeccablood.net/essay/weblog_history.html, (01/30/2006).

Blood, R. (2006). Weblogs: A History and Perspective. *Rebecca's Pocket.* 07 September 2000. 25 October 2006. Retrieved 21st May 2008 from http://www.rebeccablood. net/essays/weblog_history.html.

Boekaerts, M. (1997). Self-regulated learning: a new concept embraced by researchers, policy makers, educators, teachers, and students. *Learning and instruction, 7*(2), 151–86.

Boettcher, J. V. (2006). The rise of student performance content. *Campus Technology*, February 28. Retrieved January 10, 2007, from http://www.campustechnology. com/article.aspx?aid=40747.

Boezerooy, P. (2003). *Keeping up with our neighbours: ICT developments in Australian higher education.* Retrieved November 11, 2007 from http://www.surf. nl/en/download/Australian_book.pdf.

Bolter, J. D. (2001). *Writing Space: Computers, Hypertext, and the Remediation of Print.* Mahwah, NJ: Lawrence Erlbaum Associates.

Bolter, J. D., & Grusin, R. (1999). *Remediation: Understanding New Media.* Cambridge, MA: MIT Press.

Bonnet, M. (1997). Computers in the classroom: Some values issues. In A. McFarlane (Ed.), *Information technology and authentic learning* (pp. 145-159). London: Routledge.

Bork, A. (2001). Tutorial learning for the new century. *Journal of Science Education and Technology, 10*(1), 57–71.

Bosma, H. A., Graafsma, T. L., Grotevant, H. D., & de Levita, D. J. (1994*). Identity and Development: An Interdisciplinary Approach.* Sage Focus Editions, Vol. 172. Thousand Oaks: SAGE.

Bosworth, A. (2006). *Healthcare information matters.* (web page: last downloaded:August 25th) http://google-blog.blogspot.com/2006/11/health-care-information-matters.html

Bouffard, T., Bouchard, M., Goulet, G., Cenoncourt, I., & Couture, N. (2005). Influence of achievement goals and self-efficacy on students' self-regulation and per-formance. *International Journal of Psychology, 40*(6), 373-384.

Bouman, W., Hoogenboom, T., Jansen, R., Schoondorp, M., de Bruin, B., Huizing, A. (2008). The Realm of Sociality: Notes on the Design of Social Software. University of Amsterdam, Netherlands. Sprouts: Working Papers on Information Systems, 8(1). http://sprouts.aisnet.org/8-1

Bowden, J., & Marton, F. (1998). *The university of learning: beyond quality and competence in higher education.* London: Kogan Page.

Bowen, H. R. (1996). *Investment in Learning: The Individual and Social Value of Higher American Education.* New Jersey: Transaction Publishers.

Boyd, D. & Ellison, N. (2007) Social Network Sites: Definition and Conception, URL (consulted 17 September 2007). http://www.danah.org/papers/worksinprogress/SNSHistory.html

Boyd, D. (2002). *Faceted Id/entity: Managing Representation in a Digital World.* Cambridge, MA: MIT Master's Thesis. Retrieved on 7th April 2008, from http://www. danah.org/papers/Thesis.FacetedIdentity.pdf

Boyd, D. (2005). *Cultural divide in IM: Presence vs. communication.* Retrieved 12th November, 2007 from http://www.zephoria.org/thoughts/archives/2005/02/13/cultural_divide_in_im_presence_vs_communication. html

Boyd, D. (2006). A blogger's blog: exploring the definition of a medium. *Reconstruction* 6.4. Retrieved 21st May 2008 from http://reconstruction.eserver.org/064/boyd/shtml

Boyd, D. (2007). The significance of social software. In T. N. Burg & J. Schmidt (Eds.), *BlogTalks reloaded: Social software research & cases* (pp. 15-30). Norderstedt, Germany: Books on Demand.

Boyd, D. (2007). The Significance of Social Software. In Th. Burg & J. Schmidt (Eds.), *Blog Talks Reloaded. Social Software – Research and Cases.* Norderstedt: Books on demand.

Boyd, D. (in press 2008). Why Youth (Heart) Social Nework Sites: The Role of Networked Publics in Teenage Social Life. In D. Buckingham (Ed.), *Identity*. MIT Press.

Boyd, d. m., & Heer, J. (2006). *Profiles as conversation: Networked identity performance on Friendster*. Paper presented at the Hawai'i International Conference on System Sciences (HICSS-39), Kauai, HI.

Boyd, D.M. (2007). The significance of social software. In T. N. Burg & H. Schmidt (Eds.), *BlogTalks reloaded. Social software: Research & cases* (pp. 15-30). Herstellung: Books on Demand GmbH, Norderstedt.

Bransford, J., Derry, S., Berliner, D., & Hammerness, K. (2005). Theories of learning and their roles in teaching. In L. Darling-Hammond & J. Bransford (Eds.), *Preparing teachers for a changing world: What teachers should learn and be able to do* (pp. 40-87). San Francisco CA: Jossey-Bass.

Brewer, J., Williams, A., & Dourish, P. (2005). Nimio: An ambient awareness device. In *Proceedings of CSCW 2005*. Retrieved 12th November, 2007, from http://www.ics.uci.edu/~johannab/papers/brewer.williams.dourish.ecscw2005.pdf

Brin, S., & Page, L. (2000). The Anatomy of a Large-Scale Hypertextual Web Search Engine. from http://www-db.stanford.edu/pub/papers/google.pdf

Britain, S. (2004). *A Review of Learning Design: Concept, Specifications and Tools, a report for the JISC E-learning Pedagogy Programme, JISC*. http://www.jisc.ac.uk/uploaded_documents/ACF83C.doc [Accessed on 25th of April, 2006].

British Library & JISC (2008). *Information behaviour of the researcher of the future*. A ciber briefing paper, 11 January 2008. Retrieved on 7 April, 2008, from http://www.bl.uk/news/pdf/googlegen.pdf

Brooks, F., & Scott, P. J. (2006). Knowledge work in nursing and midwifery: An evaluation through computer mediated communication. *International Journal of Nursing Studies, 43*(1), 83-97.

Brooks, S., Donovan, P., & Rumble, C. (2005). Developing Nations, the Digital Divide and Research Databases. In *Serials Review,* (31), 270–278. London: Elsevier. Retrieved August 23, 2006 from http://www.sciencedirect.com/science?_ob=MImg&_imagekey=B6W63-4HGD78H-1-1&_cdi=6587&_user=4016542&_orig=search&_coverDate=12%2F31%2F2005&_sk=999689995&view=c&_alid=468268740&_rdoc=1&wchp=dGLzVlz-zSkWA&md5=aecc01d0d6d23db59291893f2c3665cb&ie=/sd-article.pdf

Brown, A. (1987). Metacognition, executive control, self-regulation, and other more mysterious mechanisms. In F. E. Weinert & R. H. Kluwe (Eds.), *Metacognition, motivation, and understanding* (pp. 65-116). Hillsdale, NJ: Lawrence Earlbaum Associates.

Brown, A. L. (1992). Design experiments: Theoretical and methodological challenges in creating complex interventions in classroom setting. *The Journal of the Learning Sciences, 2*(2), 141-178.

Brown, B., Chalmers, M., Bell, M., Hall, M., MacColl, I., & Rudman, P. (2005, 18-22 September 2005). *Sharing the square: Collaborative Leisure in the City Streets*. Paper presented at the Proceedings of the Ninth European Conference on Computer-Supported Cooperative Work, Paris, France.

Brown, J. (2007). *Web 2.0*. Retrieved September 28, 2007, from http://www.judybrown.com/tools.html

Brown, J. S. (1998). Research that reinvents the corporation. In *Harvard Business Review on Knowledge Management*. (pp. 153-180). Boston, MA: Harvard Business School Press.

Brown, J. S. (1999). Learnig, working and playing in the digital age. Retrieved May 25, 2004, from http://serendip.brynmawr.edu/sci_edu/seelybrown/

Brown, J. S., & Duguid, P. (1991). Organizational learning and communities of practice: towards a unified view of working, learning and innovation. *Organization Science, 2*(1) 40-57.

Brown, J. S., Collins, A., & Duguid, P. (1989). Educational Researcher. NBEET Commisioned Report No.28. In P. Candy, C. Crebert, G. O'Leary (Eds.), J. *Australian Government Publishing Service, 18*, 32-42.

Brown, J. S., Collins, A., & Duguid, P. (1989). Situated cognition and the culture of learning. *Educational Researcher, 18*(1) 32-42.

Brown, J. S., Collins, A., & Duguid, P. (1989). Situated cognition and the culture of learning. *Educational Researcher, 18*(1), 32-42.

Brown, J., & Duguid, P. (2000). *The social life of information*. Boston, MA: Harvard Business Press.

Bruce, C. S. (1997). *The seven faces of information literacy*. Adelaide: Auslib Press

Bruce, C. S., Edwards, S., & Lupton, M. (2007). Six frames for information literacy education: A conceptual framework for interpreting the relationships between theory and practice. In S. Andretta, (Ed.), *Change and challenge: information literacy for the 21st century*. Adelaide: Auslib Press.

Bruening, T. H., Scanlon, D. C., & Hodes, C. (2001). *The status of career and technical education teacher preparation programs*. National Research Center for Career and Technical Education. Retrieved April 7, 2006, from http://www.nccte.org/publications/infosynthesis/r&dreport/Status_of_CTE/Status%20of%20CTE.html

Bruner, J. (1997). *The culture of education*. Cambridge, MA: Harvard University Press.

Bruns, A., & Jacobs, J. (2006). *Uses of blogs*. New York: Peter Lang Publishing.

Brusilovsky, P., Chavan, G., & Farzan, R. (2004). Social Adaptive Navigation Support for Open Corpus Electronic Textbooks. Paper presented at the AH 2004, Eindhoven.

Bryant, L. (2003). *Smarter, Simpler Social: An introduction to online social software methodology*. Headshift. Retrieved Nov. 2005 from http://www.headshift.com/moments/archive/sss2.html.

Bryant, T. (2006). Social software in academia. *EDUCAUSE Quarterly, 29*(2), 61-64.

Brynjolfsson, E., & McAfee, A. P. (2007). Beyond Enterprise 2.0. *MIT Sloan Management Review, 48*(3), 50-55.

BSCW (2008). public.bscw.de/de/about.html, (04/26/2008).

Bucking Shum, S. (2005b). *Knowledge Technologies in Context*. Open University Press.

Buckingham Shum, S. (2005a). From Open Content Repositories to Open Sensemaking Communities. *Conference on Open Educational Resources*, Logan, Utah (Sept. 2005).

Buckingham, D. (2007). Digital Media Literacies: rethinking media education in the age of the Internet. *Research in Comparative and International Education, 2*(1), 43-55.

Budapest Open Access Initiative. (2002). *Declaration after the Open Society Institute meeting* in Budapest December 1-2 2001. Budapest: Open Society Institute. Retrieved February 08, 2007 from http://www.soros.org/openaccess/read.shtml

Bughin, J. (2008). The rise of enterprise 2.0. *Journal of Direct, Data and Digital Marketing Practice, 9*, 251-259.

Burgess, J., Foth, M., & Klaebe, H. (2006, Sep 25-26). *Everyday Creativity as Civic Engagement: A Cultural Citizenship View of New Media*. Paper presented at the Communications Policy & Research Forum, Sydney, NSW.

Burke, J. & Reitzes, C. (1981). The Link between Identity and Role Performance. *Social Psychology Quarterly, 44*(2), 83-92.

Burnett, R. (2002). Technology, learning and visual culture. In I. Snyder (Ed.), *Silicon LIteracies: Communication, Innovation and Education in the Electronic Age* (pp.141-153) London: Routledge / Taylor & Francis Group.

Burrell, J., & Gay, G. K. (2002). E-graffiti: evaluating real-world use of a context-aware system. *Interacting with Computers, 14*(4), 301-312.

Bush, A. A., & Tiwana, A. (2005). Designing Sticky Knowledge Networks. *Communications of the ACM, 48*(5).

Bush, V. (1945). As we may think. *The Atlantic Monthly.* www.theatlantic.com/doc/194507/bush/, (01/27/2006).

Camp, L. J. (2004). Digital Identity. *IEEE Technology and Society Magazine.* (pp. 34-41).

Campbell, H. (2004). Challenges created by online religious networks. *Journal of Media and Religion, 3*(2), 81-99.

Campbell, H. (2005). Who's got the power? Religious authority and the Internet. *Journal of Computer-Mediated Communication, 12*(3).

Canas, A., & Novak, J. (2008). Concept Mapping Using CmapTools to Enhance Meaningful Learning. In A. Okada, S. Buckingham Shum, & T. Sherborne (Eds.), *Knowledge Cartography: software tools and mapping techniques.* London: Springer-Verlag.

Candy, P. (1991). *Self-direction for lifelong learning.* San Francisco: Josey-Bass Inc.

Cape Town Open Education Declaration. (2007). *Cape Town: Open Society Institute.* Retrieved February 05, 2008 from http://www.capetowndeclaration.org/read-the-declaration

Carlson, C. N. (2003). Information overload, retrieval strategies and Internet user empowerment. In L. Haddon (Eds.), *Proceedings The Good, the Bad and the Irrelevant (COST 269), 1*(1), 169-173. Helsinki (Finland).

Caruso, J. B., & Salaway, G. (2007). *The ECAR Study of Undergraduate Students and Information Technology, 2007* (September 2007). EDUCAUSE Center for Applied Research Key Findings. Retrieved November 21, 2007 from http://connect.educause.edu/library/abstract/TheECARStudyofUnderg/45076.

Carver, C., & Schier, M. (2002). Control processes and self-organization as complementary principles underlying behavior. *Personality and Social Psychology Review, 64*(4), 304-315.

Casey, C. (2006). Virtual ritual, real faith: The re-virtualization of religious ritual in cyberspace. *Online-Heidelberg Journal of Religions on the Internet, 2*(1).

Casey, M. E., & Savastinuk, L. C. (2007). *Library 2.0: The librarian's guide to participatory library service.* Medford, N.J.: Information Today Inc.

Castells, M. (1996). *The Rise of the Networked Society.* Oxford: Blackwell Publishers Ltd.

Caswell, T., Henson, S., Jensen, M., & Wiley, D. (2008). Open content and open educational resources: Enabling universal education. *International Review of Research in Open and Distance Learning, 9*(1). Retrieved April 11, 2008, from http://www.irrodl.org/index.php/irrodl/article/view/469/1009

Cavalcanti, M. C. (2004). It's Not Writing by Itself that is Going to Solve our Problems': Questioning a Mainstream Ethnocentric Myth as Part of a Search for Self-sustained Development. *Language and Education, 18*(4), 317–325 and at http://www.multilingual-matters.net/le/018/le0180317.htm, accessed 20 June 2007.

Cayzer, S. (2004). Semantic Blogging and Decentralized Knowledge Management, *Communication of the ACM, 47*(12), 47-52.

Cellan-Jones, R. (2007). How to make friends on Facebook. Retrieved 29th May 2007 from http://news.bbc.co.uk/go/pr/fr/-/1/hi/technology/6699791.stm.

Center for Remediation Design (1992). Survey of *Basic Skills Remediation Practices in JTPA Youth.*

Certeau, M. (1984). *The Practice of Everyday Life.* S. Rendall (Trans.). University of California Press, Berkeley originally published in French as *L'invention du quotidien. Vol. 1, Arts de faire'* (1980).

Cetron, M. (1988). *Seventy-one trends that may affect entrepreneurial education for future world markets.* Arlington, Virginia: Forecasting International Ltd. (ERIC Document Reproduction Service No. ED 294 041)

Chakraborty, R. (2002). *Presence: A Disruptive Technology*. Jabber Conf 2001 presentation, Denvor.

Chan, A., Frydenberg, M., & Lee, M. J. W. (2007). Facilitating cross-cultural learning through collaborative Skypecasting. In J. J. Ekstrom (Ed.), *Proceedings of the 2007 ACM Information Technology Education Conference (SIGITE'07)* (pp. 59-66). New York, NY: ACM.

Chan, L., & Kirsop, B. (2001). Open Archiving Opportunities for Developing Countries: towards equitable distribution of global knowledge. In *Ariadne,* (30). Bath: UKOLN. Retrieved February 01, 2007 from http://www.ariadne.ac.uk/issue30/oai-chan/

Chan, L., Kirsop, B., & Arunachalam, S. (2005). Open Access Archiving: the fast track to building research capacity in developing countries. In *SciDev.Net*, November 2005. London: SciDev. Retrieved April 25, 2006 from http://www.scidev.net/open_access/files/Open%20Access%20Archiving.pdf

Chan, T., Corlett, D., Sharples, M., Ting, J., & Westmancott, O. (2005). Developing interactive logbook: A personal learning environment. In *Proceedings of the ieee international workshop on wireless and mobile technologies in education*. Washington, DC, USA: IEEE Computer Society Press.

Chandler, D. (1998). *Personal Home Pages and the Construction of Identities on the Web*. [online document]. Retrieved January 18, 2007 from http://www.aber.ac.uk/media/Documents/short/webident.html

Chandler, M. J., & Lalonde, C. E. (1995). Teorie ingenue della mente e del Sé. In L. O. Sempio, & A. Marchetti (Eds.), *Il pensiero dell'altro. Contesto, conoscenza e teorie della ment*. Milano, Italy: Raffaello Cortina.

Chao, J. (2007). Student project collaboration using wikis. In *Proceedings of the 20th Conference on Software Engineering Education & Training (CSEET'07)* (pp. 255-261). Los Alamitos, CA: IEEE Computer Society.

Chattopadhyay, P., George, E., & Lawrence, S. (2004). Why does dissimilarity matter? Exploring self-categorization, self-enhancement, and uncertainty reduction. *Journal of Applied Psychology, 89*(5), 892-900.

Cheverst, K., Davies, N., Mitchell, K., Friday, A., & Efstratiou, C. (2000). *Developing a Context-aware Electronic Tourist Guide: Some Issues and Experiences*. Paper presented at the CHI 2000, Netherlands, April 2000.

Cho, C. H., & Leckenby, J. D. (1999). Interactivity as a measure of advertising effectiveness: antecedents and consequences of interactivity in web advertising. *Proceedings of the 1999 Conference of the American Academy of Advertising*, (pp. 162-179).

Christakis, N. A. (2004). Social networks and collateral health effects. *BMJ, 329*(7459), 184-5.

Christensen, C. M. (1997). *The Innovator's Dilemma*. Harvard Business School Press. ISBN 0-87584-585-1.

Christensen, C. M., Baumann, H., Ruggles, R., & Sadtler, T. M. (2006). Disruptive Innovation for Social Change. *Harvard Business Review*.

Christenson, L., & Menzel, K. (1998). The linear relationship between student reports of teacher immediacy behaviors and perceptions of state motivation, and of cognitive, affective and behavioral learning. *Communication Education, 47*, 82-90.

Cigognini, M. E., Mangione, G. R., & Pettenati, M. C. (2007). *E-Learning design in (in)formal learning. TD - Tecnologie Didattiche 41*(3), 55- 58, Ortona, Svizzera: Menabò Edizioni.

Cilliers, P. (1998). *Complexity and Postmodernism. Understanding Complex Systems*. London: Routledge.

Clark, R. E. (1994). Media will never influence learning. *Education Technology Research and Development, 42*(2), 21-29.

Clary, E. G., Snyder, M., Ridge, R. D., Copeland, J., Stukas, A. A., Haugen, J., & Miene, P. (1998). Understanding and assessing the motivation of volunteers: A functional approach. *Journal of Personality and Social Psychology, 74*(6), 1516-1530.

Cleine, M., & Darcy, C. (2006). Blogging and professional learning. In B. Doecke, M. Howie & W. Sawyer (Eds.), *Only connect: English teaching, schooling and community* (pp. 166-178). Kent Town SA: Wakefield Press.

Coakes, E. (2006). Storing and sharing knowledge: Supporting the management of knowledge made explicit in transnational organisations. *The Learning Organization, 13*(6), 579-593.

Coates, T. (2005). An addendum to a definition of Social Software. *Plasticbag.org (blog)* Retrieved October 12, 2007, from http://www.plasticbag.org/archives/2005/01/an_addendum_to_a_definition_of_social_software/

Cobb, P., Confrey, J., diSessa, A., Lehrer, R., & Schauble, L. (2003). Design experiments in educational research. *Educational Researcher, 32*(1), 9-13.

Cobcroft, R., Towers, S., Smith, J., & Bruns, A. (2006). *Literature review into mobile learning in the university context.* Brisbane: QUT.

Code, J., & Zaparyniuk, N. (this volume). Social identities, group formation, and the analysis of online communities. In S. Hatzipanagos & S. Warburton (Eds.), *Handbook of Research on Social Software and Developing Community Ontologies.* New York, NY: IGI Publishing.

Cohen, C. (2007). Meet Colby Buzzell, a king among blookers. *Guardian Unlimited* at http://www.guardian.co.uk/commentisfree/story/0,,2073619,00.html, accessed 20 June, 2007.

Cohn, E. R., & Hibbits, B. J. (2004). Beyond the Electronic Portfolio: A Lifetime Personal Web Space. In *Educause Quarterly, 4*, 7-10. Boulder: Educause. Retrieved April 12, 2007 from http://www.educause.edu/ir/library/pdf/EQM0441.pdf

Cole, P. (1992). Constructivism revisited: A search for common ground. *Educational technology, 33*(2), 27-34.

Coleman, W. D., & Williges, R. C. (1985). Collecting detailed user evaluations of software interfaces. *Proc. Human Factors Society: Twenty-Ninth Annual Meeting,* Santa Monica, CA, (pp. 204-244).

Coleman. (1988). Social capital and the creation of human capital. *American Journal of Sociology, 94*, 95-120.

Coll, R. K., & Zegwaard, K. E. (2006). Perceptions of desirable graduate competencies for science and technology new graduates. *Research in Science & Technological education, 24*(1), 29-58.

Collings, A., Joseph, D., & Bielaczyc, K. (2004). Design research: Theoretical and methodological issues. *Journal of the Learning Sciences, 13*(1), 15-42.

Collis, J., & Hussey, R. (2003). *Business research: a practical guide for undergraduate and postgraduate students.* New York, NY: Palgrave Macmillan.

Commission of the European Communities (2006). *Key Competences for Lifelong Learning.* Recommendation the European Parliament and the Council of 18 December 2006. *Official Journal of the European Union* (2006/962/EC), L394/10-18.

Conger, J. A. (1993). The brave new world of leadership training. *Organizational Dynamics, 21*(3), 46-58.

Connelly, M., & Clandinin, J. (1988). *Teachers as curriculum planners: Narrative experience.* **New York: Teachers College Press.**

Conole, G. (forthcoming). Using Compendium as a tool to support the design of learning activities. In A. Okada, S. Buckingham Shum & T. Sherborne (Eds.), *Knowledge cartography – software tools and mapping techniques.* http://kmi.open.ac.uk/projects/kc-book/.

Conole, G., Dyke, M., Oliver, M., & Seale, J. (2004). Mapping pedagogy and tools for effective learning design. *Computers and Education, 43*(1), 17-33.

Conole, G., Dyke, M., Oliver, M., & Seale, J. (2004). Mapping pedagogy and tools for effective learning design. *Computers and education, 43*, 17-33.

Conrad, C., & LaPointe, D. (October 2007). Wikis: Collaborative by Nature or Design? *Poster session at the South Central Chapter of the Medical Library Association Annual Conference.* Albuquerque, NM.

Conway, S., & Sligar, C. (2002). *Unlocking knowledge assets.* Redmond, WA: Microsoft   Press.

Cook, S. D. N., & Brown, J. S. (1999). Bridging epistemologies: The generative dance between organisational knowledge and knowing. *Organization Science, 10*(4), 381-400.

Cook, S. D. N., & Brown, J. S. (1999). Bridging Epistemologies: The Generative Dance between Organizational Knowledge and Organizational Knowing. *Organization Science*, 10(4), 381-400.

Corante (2004). www.corante.com/many, (06/20/2004).

Corbetta, G (1999). *Manuale di metodologia della ricerca sociale.* Bologna, Italy: Il Mulino.

Cordery, J., Sevastos, P., Mueller, W., & Parker, S. (1993). Correlates of employee attitudes toward functional flexibility. *Human Relations, 46*(6), 705-707.

Corno, L. (1993). The best laid plans: Modern conceptions of volition and educational research. *Educational Researcher, 22*(2), 17-22.

Corno, L. (2001). Volitional aspects of self-regulated learning. In B. Zimmerman & D. Schunk (Eds.), *Self-regulated learning and academic achievement* (Vol. 191-225). Mahwah, NJ: Lawrence Earlbaum Associates.

Corno, L., & Kanfer, R. (1993). The role of volition in learning and performance. *Review of Research in Education, 19*, 301-341.

Cornoldi, C. (1995). *Metacognizione e apprendimento.* Bologna, Italy: Il Mulino.

Council of Australian University Libraries (2001). *Information literacy standards.* Canberra: CAUL

Courtney, N. (2007). *Library 2.0 and beyond: innovative technologies and tomorrow's user.* Westport, Conn.: Libraries Unlimited.

Coyle, J. R., & Thorson, E. (2001). The effects of progressive levels of interactivity and vividness in web marketing sites. *Journal of Advertising, 30*(3), 65-77.

Creative Commons, San Francisco, CA. Retrieved April 12, 2008, from http://creativecommons.org/

Creed, T. (1996). Extending the Classroom Walls Electronically. In William Campbell and Karl Smith (Ed.), New Paradigms for College Teaching. Edina, MN: Interaction Book Co.

Cretchley, P. (2007). Does computer confidence relate to levels of achievement in ICT-enriched learning models? *Education and Information Technologies archive, 12*(1), 29-39.

Crook, C. (2002). The Campus Experience of Networked Learning. In C. A. J. Steeples (Eds.), *Networked Learning: Perspectives and Issues.* London, Springer-Verlag.

Csikszentmihalyi, M. (1998). Creativity: Flow and the psychology of discovery and invention. *Perennial*, June 1997.

Culnan, M. J., & Markus, M. L. (1987). Information technologies. *Handbook of Organizational Communication: An interdisciplinary perspective*, (pp. 420-443).

Cunningham, S., Tapsall, S., Ryan, Y., Stedman, L., Flew, T., & Bagdon, K. (1998). *New Media and Borderless Education.* Canberra: AGPS.

Dabbish, L., & Kraut, R. E. (2004). Controlling Interruptions: Awareness Displays and Social Motivation for Coordination. In *Proceedings of the 2004 ACM conference on Computer Supported Collaborative Work*, 182-191. ACM, New York.

Daft, R. L., & Lengel, R. H. (1986). Organizational information requirements, media richness and structural design. *Management Science, 32*(5), 554-571.

Dalsgaard, C. (2006). Social software: E-learning beyond learning management systems. *European Journal of Open, Distance and E-learning, 2*. Retrieved October 17, 2007, from http://www.eurodl.org/materials/contrib/2006/Christian_Dalsgaard.htm

Dalziel, J. (2006). *The design and development of the LAMS Community.* Available at http://www.lamscommunity.org/dotlrn/clubs/educationalcommunity/lamsresearchdevelopment/forums/message-view?message_id=311748

Davenport, T. H. (2005). *Thinking for a living*. Boston, MA: Harvard Business School Publishing.

Davenport, T. H., & Prusak, L. (1998). *Working Knowledge: How Organizations Manage What They Know*. Boston, MA: Harvard Business School Press.

Davis, J. (2002). *The experience of bad behavior in online social spaces: A survey of online users*, internal paper of Microsoft Social Computing Group, available at http://research.microsoft.com/scg/papers/Bad%20Behavior%20Survey.pdf, last accessed 4/29/2008.

Dawson, K. M. (2007) Blog Overload. *The Chronicle of Higher Education*. Retrieved November 6th 2007, from: http://chronicle.com/jobs/news/2007/01/2007013001c/careers.html.

De Angeli, A., Sutcliffe, A., Hartmann, J. (2006). *Interaction, usability and aesthetics: What influences users' preferences? DIS 2006 Conference Proceedings, ACM*, (pp. 271-280).

De Bono, E. (1970). *Lateral thinking : creativity step by step*. New York, USA: Harper & Row.

de Witt, C. (2006). *Hybride Lernarrangements in der universitären Weiterbildung*. Das Beispiel Educational Media. www.medienpaed.com/03-1/dewitt03-1.pdf, (01/20/2006).

Dean, B. (2007). *The challenge of creating a continuous learning culture: Linking the value chain between higher education and corporate learning*.

Deci, E. L., & Ryan, R. M. (1985). *Intrinsic motivation and self-regulation in human behavior*. New York: Plenum Press.

Deci, E.L., & Ryan, R.M. (2000). The "What" and "Why" of goal pursuits: Human needs and the self-determination of behavior. *Psychological Inquiry, 11*(4), 227-268.

DeFillippi, R. J., & Arthur, M. B. (1994). The boundary-less career: A competency-based perspective. *Journal of Organizational Behaviour, 15*(4), 307-324.

Delors, J. (1996). *Learning: the Treasure Within*. Report to UNESCO of the International Commission on Education for the Twenty-first Century. Paris: UNESCO.

Demos (2006). *Digital curriculum: Their Space*. Retrieved June 2, 2007 http://www.demos.co.uk/projects/digitalcurriculumproject/overview.

Denzin, N., & Lincoln, Y. (eds). (1994). *Handbook of Qualitative Research.* **Thousand Oaks, CA: Sage**

Derlega, V. J., & Chaikin, A. L. (1977). Privacy and self-disclosure in social relationships. *Journal of Social Issues, 33*(3), 102-115.

Dervin, B. (1992). From the mind's eye of the user: the sense-making qualitative-quantitative methodology. In J. D. Glazier & R. R. Powell (Eds.), *Qualitative Research in Information Management*. Englewood, CO: Libraries Unlimited.

Desharnais, R. A., & Limson, M. (2007). Designing and implementing virtual courseware to promote inquiry-based learning. *Journal of Online Learning and Teaching, 3*(1), 30-39.

Design-based research collective (2002). Design-Based Research: An Emerging Paradigm for Educational Inquiry. *Educational Researcher, 32*(1), 5-8.

Dewey, J. (1937) *Experience and education.* **New York: MacMillan.**

Dewey, J. (1938). *Experience and education*. New York: Macmillan.

DfES. (2005). *Harnessing Technology: Transforming learning and children's services*. London: DfES.

Dholakia, U. M., Bagozzi, R. P., & Pearo, L. K. (2004). A social influence model of consumer participation in network- and small-group-based virtual communities. *International Journal of Research in Marketing, 21*(3), 241-263.

Dholakia, U. M., King W. J., & Baraniuk, R. (2006). What makes an open educational program sustainable? The Case of Connexions. *OECD-CERI papers.*

Dholakia, U. M., King, J. W., & Baraniuk, R. (2006). What Makes an Open Education Program Sustainable? *The Case of Connexions.* Retrieved on January, 17, 2007 from www.oecd.org/dataoecd/3/6/36781781.pdf

Dholakia, U. M., Roll, S., & McKeever, J. (2005). Building community in Connexions. *Market Research Report for Connexions Project*, Rice University, January.

Di Fraia, G. (2004). *eResearch: Internet per la ricerca sociale e di mercato.* Bari, Italy: Laterza.

Diamantopoulos, A., & Winklhofer, H. M. (2001). Index construction with formative indicators: an alternative to scale development. *Journal of Marketing Research, 38*(2), 269-277.

Dickey, M. (2004). The impact of web-logs (blogs) on student perceptions of isolation and alienation in a web-based distance-learning environment. *Open Learning, 19*(3), 279-291.

Dieberger, A. (1995). Providing spatial navigation for the World Wide Web. In A. U. Frank & W. Kuhn (Eds.), *Spatial Information Theory, Proceedings of Cosit '95* (pp. 93-106). Semmering, Austria: Springer.

Dieberger, A. (1997). Supporting Social Navigation on the World-Wide Web. *International Journal of Human-Computer Studies, special issue on innovative applications of the Web, 46*, 805-825.

Dieberger, A. (2003). Social Connotations of Space in the Design for Virtual Communies and Social Navigation. In K. Höök, D. Benyon & A. J. Munro (Eds.), *Designing information spaces: The social navigation approach* (pp. 293-313). London: Springer.

Digital Dialogue Games for Learning website. http://www.interloc.org/, accessed 13 December 2007.

Dillard, M., Andonian, L., Flores, O., Lai, L., MacRae, A., & Shakir, M. (1992). Culturally competent occupational therapy in a diversely populated mental health

setting. *American Journal of Occupational Therapy, 46*(8), 721-726.

Dillenbourg, P. (1999). What do you mean by collaborative learning? In P. Dillenbourg (Ed.), *Collaborative learning: Cognitive and computational approaches.* (pp. 1-19).. Oxford: Elsevier:.

Dillenbourg, P., & Schneider, D. (1995). Mediating the mechanisms which make collaborative learning sometimes effective. *International Journal of Educational Telecommunications, 1*(2-3), 131-146.

Dix A., Levialdi S., & Malizia A. (2006). Semantic halo for collaboration tagging systems. In S. Weibelzahl & A. Cristea (Eds.), *Proceedings of Workshop held at the Fourth International Conference on Adaptive Hypermedia and Adaptive Web-Based Systems (AH2006). Workshop on Social Navigation and Community-Based Adaptation Technologies* (pp. 514-521), Lecture Notes in Learning and Teaching, Dublin: National College of Ireland.

Donath, J. (1999). Identity and deception in the virtual community. In M. A. Smith & P. Kollock (Eds.), *Communities in cyberspace* (pp. 29-59). London, UK: Routledge.

Donath, J. S. (1999). Identity and deception in virtual community. In P. Kollock & M. Smith (eds.). *Communities in Cyberspace* (pp. 29 – 59). London: Routledge.

Donath, J., & Boyd, D. (2004). Public displays of connection. *BT Technology Journal, 22*(4), 71-82.

Dorsey, P. (2000). *Personal Knowledge Management: educational framework for global business.* Tabor School of Business, Millikin University. Retrieved on 7 April, 2008, from http://www.millikin.edu/pkm/pkm_istanbul.html

Dorsey, P. (2004). *What is PKM? - Overview of Personal Knowledge Management.* Millikin University. Retrieved on 7 April, 2008, from http://www.sacw.cn/What%20is%20PKM.html

Dourish, P., & Chalmers, M. (1994). *Running Out of Space: Models of Information Navigation.* Paper presented at the HCI'94.

Downes, E. J., & McMillan, S. J. (2000). Defining interactivity. *New Media & Society,* 2(2), 157-179.

Downes, S. (2004). Educational blogging. *EDUCAUSE Review, 39*(5) 14-26.

Downes, S. (2004). From Classrooms to Learning Environments: A Midrange Projection of E-Learning Technologies. *College Quarterly, 7*(3).

Downes, S. (2005). *E-learning 2.0.* Retrieved February 3, 2006, from http://www.elearnmag.org/subpage.cfm?section=articles&article=29-1

Downes, S. (2005). E-learning 2.0. *eLearn Magazine.* Available at: http://www.elearnmag.org/subpage.cfm?section=articles&article=29-1 [Accessed 10 May, 2006].

Downes, S. (2005). e-*learning 2.0. ELearn*, October. Retrieved January 11, 2006, from http://www.elearnmag.org/subpage.cfm?section=articles&article=29-1.

Downes, S. (2006). *Models for Sustainable Open Educational Resources.* Retrieved on January, 17, 2007 from http://www.downes.ca/cgi-bin/page.cgi?post=33401.

Downes, S. (2006). Networks versus Groups. Talk at Future of Learning in a Networked World event in Auckland, video retrieved Oct 2007 from http://video.google.com/videoplay?docid=-4126240905912531540

Downes, S. (2007). *Learning networks in practice.* Retrieved April 5, 2008, from http://partners.becta.org.uk/page_documents/research/emerging_technologies07_chapter2.pdf

Downes, S. (2007). Models for sustainable open educational resources. *Interdisciplinary Journal of Knowledge and Learning Objects, 3,* 29-4.

Downes, S. (2007). Places to go: Facebook. *Innovate, 4*(1) http://innovateonline.info/index.php?view=article&id=517&action=article

Dron, J. Social software and the emergence of control. In *ICALT 2006:* Retrieved June 2007 from doi.ieeecomputersociety.org/10.1109/ICALT.2006.293.

Dron, J. (2006). On the stupidity of mobs. Paper presented at the WBC 2006, San Sebastian.

Dron, J. (2007). *Control and Constraint in E-Learning: Choosing When to Choose.* Hershey, PA: Information Science Pub.

du Plessis, J. (2007). Syllabu*s for 632 Digital Competencies for Information Professionals.* Online. Accessed 01.10.07. http://web.sois.uwm.edu/632%20duPlessis/Document/index.asp?Parent=163.

Du, H. S., & Wagner, C. (2007). Learning with weblogs: enhancing cognitive and social knowledge construction. *IEEE Transactions of Professional Communication, 50*(1), 1-16.

Dubé, L., Bourhis, A., & Jacob, R. (2005). The impact of structuring characteristics on the launching of virtual communities of practice. *Journal of Organizational Change Management, 18*(2), 145-166.

Duguid, P. (1989). Situated cognition and the culture of learning. *Educational Researcher, 18*(1) 32-42.

Duranti, A., & Goodwin, C. (Eds.). (1992). *Rethinking context: Language as an interactive phenomenon.* Cambridge, UK: Cambridge University Press.

Durkheim, E. (1912). *The elementary forms of the religious life.* English translation by Carol Cosman: 2001, Oxford: Oxford University Press.

Eagleton, T. (2006) Your thoughts are no longer worth a penny. *Times Higher Education Supplement. 10*[th] *March 2006.*

Earnshaw, R., Guedj, R., van Dam, A., & Vince, J. (2001). *Frontiers of Human-Centred Computing, Online Communities and Virtual Environments.* Springer, London.

Eastin, M. S., & LaRose, R. (2000). Internet self-efficacy and the psychology of the digital divide. *Journal of Computer-Mediated Communication, 6*(1), 25-56.

Ebersbach, A., Glaser, M., & Heigl, R. (2006). *The wiki concept: Web collaboration.* Springer-Verlag: Berlin.

Edelson, D. C. (2002). Design research: What we learn when we engage in design. *Journal of the Learning Sciences, 11*(1), 105-121.

Edirisingha, P., Salmon, G., & Fothergill, J. (2006). *Profcasting: a pilot study and a model for integrating podcasts into online learning.* Paper presented at the Fourth EDEN Research Workshop, Castelldefels, Spain, October 25-28.

EdNA (2007). *EdNA.* Available online at http://www.edna.edu.au/edna/go/highered/hot_topics/pid/2019 Web 2.0 resources.

Edson, J. (2007). Curriculum 2.0: user-driven education. *The Huffington Post*, June 25. Retrieved December 10, 2007, from http://www.huffingtonpost.com/jonathan-edson/curriculum-20-userdri_b_53690.html.

EDUCAUSE *Learning Initiative & The New Media Consortium.* (2007). *The Horizon Report.* Retrieved February 15, 2008 from http:// http://www.nmc.org/pdf/2008-Horizon-Report.pdf.

Efimova, L., & Fiedler, S. (2004). Learning webs: Learning in weblog networks. In P. Kommers, P. Isaias & M. B. Nunes (Eds.), *Proceedings of the IADIS International Conference Web Based Communities 2004* (pp. 490-494). Lisbon, Portugal: IADIS Press.

Eigner, C. (2004). Wenn Medien zu oszillieren beginnen. In: Eigner, C. et al. (Eds.): *Online-Communities, Weblogs und die soziale Rückeroberung des Netzes* (pp. 115-125). Graz/Austria.

Eisenberg, M. B., & Berkowitz, R. E. (1990). *Information problem-solving: the Big Six skills approach to library and information skills instruction.* New Jersey: Ablex Publishing Corp.

Eisenberg, M. B., & Berkowitz, R. E. (2000). *Teaching information and technology skills: The Big6 in secondary school*s. New Jersey: Ablex Publishing Corp.

Eisenberg, M. B., & Brown, M. K. (1992). Current themes regarding library and information skills instruction:

research supporting and research lacking. *SLMQ 20*(2) (Winter) http://archive.ala.org/aasl/SLMR/slmr_resources/select_eisenberg.html

Eisenberg, M. B., & Johnson, D. (1996). Computer skills for information problem-solving: learning and teaching technology. In *context ERIC Digest 1996, 4*

Eisenstadt, M. (2007). Does e-learning have to be so awful? (Time to mashup or shutup). In J. M. Spector, D. G. Sampson, T. Okamoto, Kinshuk, S. A. Cerri, M. Ueno, & A. Kashihara (Eds.), *Proceedings of the 7th International Conference on Advanced Learning Technologies (ICALT'07)* (pp. 6-10). Los Alamitos, CA: IEEE Computer Society.

Eisenstadt, M., & Vincent, T. (1998). *The Knowledge Web: Learning and Collaborating on the Net.* London: Kogan Page.

Ellacoya Networks. (2007). Ellacoya data shows web traffic overtakes peer-to-peer (p2p) as largest percentage of bandwidth on the network.

Ellis, R. A., & Calvo, R. A. (2004). Learning through discussions in blended environments. *Educational Media International, 40*(1), 263-274.

Ellis, R. A., & Calvo, R. A. (2006). Discontinuities in university student experiences of learning through discussions. *British Journal of Educational Technology, 37*(1), 55-68.

Ellis, R. A., Goodyear, P., O'Hara, A., & Prosser, M. (2006). How and what university students learn through online and face-to-face discussions: conceptions, intensions and approaches. *Journal of computer assisted learning, 22*, 244-256.

Ellis, R. A., Goodyear, P., O'Hara, A., & Prosser, M. (2007). The university student experience of face-to-face and online discussions: coherence, reflection and meaning. *ALT-J, 15*(1), 83-97.

Ellison, N., Steinfield, C., & Lampe, C. (2007). The Benefits of Facebook "Friends:" Social Capital and College Students' Use of Online Social Networks. *Journal of Computer Mediated Communication, 12*(4)

Retrieved Aug. 2007 from http://jcmc.indiana.edu/vol12/issue4/ellison.html

Emirbayer, M., & Mische, A. (1998). What is agency? *American Journal of Sociology, 103*(4), 962-1023.

Engeström, J. (2005). *Why some social network services work and others don't – Or: the case for object-centered sociality.* Retrieved July 23, 2008, from http://www.zengestrom.com/blog/2005/04/why_some_social.html.

Engeström, Y. (1987). *Learning by expanding.* Helsinki, Finland: Orienta-Konsultit Oy.

Engeström, Y. (1987). *Learning by expanding.* Helsinki: Orienta-konsultit.

Engeström, Y. (1999). Innovative learning in work teams: analysing cycles of knowledge creation in practice. In Y. Engeström, R. Miettinen, & R.-L. Punamäki (Eds.), *Perspectives on Activity Theory* (pp. 377-404). Cambridge, England: Cambridge University Press.

Engeström, Y., Engeström, R., & Vähäaho, T. (1999). When the center does not hold: The importance of knotworking. In S. Chaiklin, M. Hedegaard & U. J. Jensen (Eds.), *Activity theory and social practice: Cultural-historical approaches* (pp. 345-374). Aarhus, DK: Aarhus University Press.

Engstrom, Y. (1987). *Learning By Expanding: An Activity Theory Approach To Developmental Research.* Helsinki, Orienta-Konsultit.

Entwistle, N. (1995). Frameworks for understanding as experienced in essay writing and in preparing for examination. *Educational Psychologist, 30*(1), 47.

Erickson, T. (1996). *The World Wide Web as Social Hypertext.* Retrieved 03.05.2007, 2007, from http://www.pliant.org/personal/Tom_Erickson/SocialHypertext.html.

Erickson, T., & Kellogg, W. A. (2000). Social Translucence: An Approach to Designing Systems that Support Social Processes. *ACM Transactions on Computer-Human Interaction, 7*(1), 59-83.

Eriksen, T. E. (2001). *Tyranny of the Moment: Fast and Slow Time in the Information Age.* Pluto Press, London, UK.

Erikson, E. (1977). *Toys and reasons: Stages in the ritualization of experience.* New York: Norton.

Erikson, E. H. (1963). *Childhood and society (2nd Ed.).* New York, NY: Norton.

Erikson, E. H. (1980). Identity, youth, and crisis. In. New York, NY: Norton.

Ernest, P. (1995). The one and the many. In P. Steffe & J. Gale (Eds.), *Constructivism in education* (pp. 459-524). Hillsdale, NJ: Lawrence Erlbaum Associates.

Erpenbeck, J., & Heyse, V. (1999). *Kompetenzbiographie - Kompetenzmilieu - Kompetenztransfer* (No. 62). Berlin: Arbeitsgemeinschaft Betriebliche Weiterbildungsforschung, e.V.

Erpenbeck, J., & Rosenstiel, L. v. (Eds.). (2007). *Handbuch Kompetenzmessung.* Stuttgart, Germany: Schäffer-Poeschel.

Erstad, O. (2005). *Conceiving digital literacies in schools - Norwegian experiences.* Proceedings of the 3rd International workshop on Digital Literacy, 1-10. Online. Accessed 30.04.08. ftp.informatik.rwth-aachen.de/Publications/CEUR-WS/Vol-310/paper01.pdf

Espinoza, F., Persson, P., Sandin, A., Nyström, H., Cacciatore, E., & Bylund, M. (2001). *GeoNotes: Social and Navigational Aspects of Location-Based Information Systems.* Paper presented at the Ubicomp 2001: Ubiquitous Computing, International Conference.

Ettinghausen, E. (2007a). A Million Thanks. *AMillionPenguins.com Blog*, at http://amillionpenguins.com/blog/?p=28, accessed 21 June 2007

Ettinghausen, J. (2007). About this Blog. *AMillionPenguins.com Blog*, at http://amillionpenguins.com/blog/?page_id=2, accessed 20 June 2007.

European eSkills Forum (2004). *eSkills for Europe: towards 2010 and beyond: synthesis report*, European

Commission, DG Enterprise and Industry, September 2004.

Eustace, K., & Hay, L. (2000). A community and knowledge building model in computer education. In A. E. Ellis (Ed.), *Proceedings of the Australasian Conference on Computing Education (ACCE'00)* (pp. 95-102). New York, NY: ACM.

Evans, L. (2006). *Using student podcasts in literature classes*. Retrieved January 23, 2007, from http://www. academiccommons.org/ctfl/vignette/using-student-podcasts-in-literature-classes.

Evans, P., & Wurster, T. (1999). *Blown to bits: How the New Economics of Information Transforms Strategy*. Harvard Business School Press.

Facebook, Inc. (2008). *About Facebook*. Retrieved April 21, 2008, from http://www.facebook.com/about.php

Facebook, Inc. (2008). About Facebook. Retrieved April 21, 2008, from http://www.facebook.com/about.php

Farmer, J. (2006). Blogging to basics: how blogs are bringing online learning back from the brink. In A. Bruns & J. Jacobs (Eds.), *Uses of Blogs* (pp. 91-103). New York: Peter Lang.

Feinstein, A., & Horwitz, R. (1997). Problems in the "Evidence" of "Evidence-based Medicine". *American Journal of Medicine 1997, 103*(6), 529-535.

Festinger, L., Pepitone, A., & Newcomb, T. (1952). Some consequences of de-individuation in a group. *Journal of Abnormal and Social Psychology, 47*, 382-389.

Fiedler, S. (2003). Personal webpublishing as a refective conversational tool for self-organized learning. In T. Burg (Ed.), *BlogTalks* (pp. 190-216). Norderstedt, Germany: Books on Demand.

Fiedler, S. (2004). Introducing disruptive technologies for learning: Personal Webpublishing and Weblogs. In L. Cantoni & C. McLoughlin (Eds.), *Proceedings of Ed-Media 2004* (pp. 2584-2591). Lugano, Switzerland: Association for the Advancement of Computing in Education (AACE).

Fiedler, S. (2008). The notion of personal learning environments reconsidered (in press).

Fiedler, S., & Sharma, P. (2004). Seeding conversational learning environments: Running a course on personal webpublishing and weblogs. In T. Burg (Ed.), *BlogTalks 2.0* (pp. 271-294). Norderstedt, Germany: Books on Demand.

Fiedler, S., & Sharma, P. (2005). Navigating personal information repositories with weblog authoring and concept mapping. In S.-O. Tergan & T. Keller (Eds.), *Knowledge and information visualization* (pp. 302-325). Berlin: Springer.

Fiedler, S., Fitzgerald, R.N., Lamb, B., Pata, K., Siemens, G., & Wilson, S. (April 2007). *Proceedings from World Conference on Educational Multimedia, Hypermedia and Telecommunications* 2007. Chesapeake, VA: AACE.

Filerman, G. L.(1994). Health Care and Education Reform: The Time to Manage for Change Is Yesterday. *Educational Record, 75*(1), 47-51.

Finerty, T. (1997). Integrating learning and knowledge infrastructure. *Journal of Knowledge Management, 1*(2), 98-104.

Fink, L. (2005). Making textbooks worthwhile. *Chronicle of Higher Education*, September 16. Retrieved March 10, 2007, from http://chronicle.com/weekly/v52/i04/04b01201.htm.

Finn, B. (Chair) (1991). *Young People's Participation in Postcompulsory Education and Training: Report of the Australian Education Council Review Committee*. Australian Publishing Service, Canberra.

Fischer, G. (2006). *Distributed intelligence: extending the power of the unaided, individual human mind*. In C. Augusto (Ed.), AVI (pp. 7–14). ACM Press.

Fischer, G., & Scharff, E. (1998). Learning technologies in support of self-directed learning. *Journal of Interactive Media in Education, 98*(4). Retrieved June 16, 2004, from http://www-jime.open.ac.uk/98/4/

Fisher, M., & Baird, D. E. (2005). Online learning design that fosters student support, self-regulation, and retention. *Campus-Wide Information Systems, 22*(2), 88-107.

Fisher, S. G., Hunter, T. A., & Ketin Macrosson, W. D. (1997). Team or Group? Managers' Perception of the Differences," Journal of Managerial Psychology,, 12(4), 232-243.

Flavell, J.H. (1979). Metacognition and cognitive monitoring: A new era of cognitive developmental inquiry. *American Psychologist, 34*, 906-911.

Foerster, H. v. (1999). Triviale und nicht-triviale maschinen. In A. P. Schmidt (Ed.), *Der wissensnavigator. Das lexikon der zukunft* (pp. 102). Stuttgart: Deutsche Verlagsanstalt.

Fogarty, J., Lia, J., & Christensen, J. (2004). Presence versus availability: the design and evaluation of a context-aware communication client. *International Journal of Human-Computer Studies, 61*(3), 299-317. Elsevier.

Fonio, C., Giglietto, F., Pruno, R., Rossi, L., & Pedrioli, S. (2007). *Eyes on You: analyzing user generated content for social science.* Paper presented at the Towards a Social Science of Web 2.0 conference, York, UK.,URL (consulted 17 September 2007): http://larica-virtual. soc.uniurb.it/nextmedia/wp-content/uploads/2007/09/ eyes_on_you.pdf

Forsberg, M., Höök, K., & Svensson, M. (1998). *Design Principles for Social Navigation Tools.* Paper presented at the UI4All, Stockholm, Sweden.

Foster, A. E. (2004). A non-linear model of information seeking behavior. *J. of the American Society for Information Science and Technology, 55*(3), 228-237.

Foster, A. E. (2006). A non-linear perspective on information seeking. In A. Spink & C. Cole (Ed.), *New directions in human information behaviour.* New York: Springer.

Foth, M., Odendaal, N., & Hearn, G. (2007, Oct 15-16). *The View from Everywhere: Towards an Epistemology for Urbanites.* Paper presented at the 4th International Conference on Intellectual Capital, Knowledge Manage-

ment and Organisational Learning (ICICKM), Cape Town, South Africa.

Fox, J. (2007). Quoted in 'Networking Sites: Professors -keep out'. *The Independent,* 18th October 2007, Retrieved November 15th 2007, from: http://student.independent. co.uk/university_life/article3068385.ece

Frand, J., & Hixon, C. (1999). *Personal Knowledge Management : Who, What, Why, When, Where, How?* December 1, 1999. UCLA University. Retrieved on 7th April 2008, from http://www.anderson.ucla.edu/faculty/ jason.frand/researcher/speeches/PKM.htm

Franklin, T., & Van Harmelen, M. (2007). *Web 2.0 for content for earning and eaching in igher ducation.* Bristol: JISC. Retrieved December 15, 2007 from http://www.jisc.ac.uk/media/documents/programmes/ digitalrepositories/web2-content-learning-and-teaching. pdf.

Freeman, L.C. (2000). Social network analysis: Definition and history. In A. E. Kadzin (Ed.), *Encyclopedia of Psychology*, 7, 350-351. Washington, DC: American Psychological Association.

Freire, P. (1985). Towards a pedagogy of the question: Conversations with Paulo Freire. *Journal of Education, 167*(2), 7-21.

Freire, P. (1993). *Pedagogy of the Oppressed.* New York: Continuum.

Friedman, T. L. (2006). *The world is flat: The globalized world in the twenty-first century* (Updated and expanded ed.). Camberwell, Vic.: Penguin.

Friendster, Inc. (2008). *About Friendster.* Retrieved April 21, 2008, from http://www.friendster.com/info/ index.php

Friere, P. (2001). *Pedagogy of freedom – ethics, democracy and civic courage,* Lanham, MD: Rowman and Littlefield.

Frijda, N. H. (1986). *The emotions.* Cambridge: Cambridge University Press.

Fröhlich, P., Simon, R., Baillie, L., Roberts, J. L., Murry-Smith, R., Jones, M., et al. (2007). *Workshop on Mobile Spatial Interaction*. San Jose, CA, USA.

Fry, K. (2001). E-learning markets and providers: Some issues and prospects. *Education and Training, 43*(4/5), 233-239.

Frydenberg, M. (2006). Principles and pedagogy: the two P's of podcasting in the information technology classroom. In D. Colton, W. J . Tastle, M. Hensel, & A. A. Abdullat (Eds.), *Proceedings of ISECON 2006* (§3354). Chicago, IL: AITP. Retrieved November 27, 2006, from http://isedj.org/isecon/2006/3354/ISECON.2006. Frydenberg.pdf.

Ganley, B. (2004). Images, words, and students finding their way. *Bgblogging* [weblog], October 11. Retrieved October 25, 2007, from http://mt.middlebury.edu/middblogs/ganley/bgblogging/2004/10/images_words_and_students_find.html.

Garrett, J. J. (2003). *The elements of the user experience: User centred design for the web*. London: Easy Riders..

Garrison, D.R., & Anderson, T. (2003). *E-Learning in the 21st century*. London: Routledge.

Gauvain, M. (2001). Cultural tools, social interaction, and the development of thinking. *Human Development, 44*(2-3), 126-143.

Gaver, W. W. (1996). Affordances for interaction: The social is material for design. *Ecological Psychology, 8*(2), 111-129.

Gecas, V. (2003). Self-agency and the life course. In J. T. Mortimer & M. J. Shanahan (Eds.), *Handbook of the Life Course*. New York, NY: Kluwer Academic Publishing/Plenum Publishers.

Gee, J. P. (2000). Communities of Practice and the New Capitalism. *The Journal of the Learning Sciences, 9*(4), 515-523.

Gee, J. P. (2003). *What video games have to teach us about learning and literacy*. New York: Palgrave MacMillan.

Gee, J. P. (2003). *What video games have to teach us about learning and literacy*. New York, NY: Palmgrave.

Gee, J. P. (2003). *What video games have to teach us about learning and literacy*. Macmillan.

Gefter, A. (2006). This is your space. *New Scientist, 191*(2569), 46-48.

Georgiadou, E., Hatzipanagos, S., & Berki, E. (2005). Resource-Based Learning and Teaching: Concerns, Conflicts, Consensus, Community. G. A. Dafoulas, W. Bakry-Mohamed, & A. Murphy (Eds.), *e-Learning Communities International Workshop Proceedings*. Jan 3, Cairo. (pp. 89-95). Middlesex University Press: London.

Gergen, K.J. (1984). Theory of the self: Impasse and evolution. In L. Berkowitz (Ed.), *Advances in experimental psychology* (Vol. 17, pp. 49-115). New York, NY: Academic.

Gertz, C. (1973/2000). *The interpretation of cultures.* New York, NY: Basic Books.

Ghose, S., & Dou, W. Y. (1998). Interactive functions and their impacts on the appeal of internet presences sites. *Journal of Advertising Research, 38*, 29–43.

Gibson, J. J. (1986). *The ecological approach to visual perception*. Boston: Houghton Mifflin.

Gibson, W. (1984). *Neuromancer*. Harpercollins.

Giddens, A. (1990). *The Consequences of Modernity.* Cambridge, UK: Polity Press.

Giddens, A. (1990). *The Consequences of Modernity.* Cambridge: Polity Press.

Giddens, A. (1991). *Modernity and Self-Identity: Self and Society in the Late Modern Age.* Cambridge: Polity Press.

Gilbert, J.K. (2006). On the nature of "context" in chemical education. *International Journal of Science Education, 28*(9), 957-976.

Giles, A. (2005). Internet encyclopaedias go head to head. *Nature, 438*, 900-901. http://www.nature.com/nature/journal/v438/n7070/full/438900a.html

Giles, J. (2006). Internet encyclopaedias go head to head. Retrieved 24.07.2007, 2007, from http://www.nature.com/news/2005/051212/full/438900a.html.

Gill, J., & Johnson, P. (1991). *Research Methods for Managers*. London: Paul Chapman.

Gillmor, D. (2006). We the Media: Grassroots Journalism By The People, For the People, O'Reilly Media, URL(consulted 4 October 2007). http://www.oreilly.com/catalog/wemedia/book/index.csp

Gilster, P. (1997). *Digital Literacy*. NY: John Wiley and Sons.

Giustini, D. (2006). How web 2.0 is changing medicine. *British Medical Journal 2006, 333*, 1283-4

Glasersfeld, v. E. (1995). *Radical constructivism: A way of knowing and learning*. London: Falmer Press.

Godwin-Jones, R. (2003). Emerging technologies: Blogs and wikis: environments for on-line collaboration. *Language Learning & Technology, 7*(2), 12-16.

Godwin-Jones, R. (2006). Emerging Technologies: Tag Clouds in the Blogosphere: Electronic Literacy and Social Neworking. *Language Learning & Technology, 10*(2), 8-15.

Goffman, E. (1959). *The presentation of self in everyday life*. New York: Doubleday.

Goffman, E. (1959/1997). Self-presentation. In C. Lemert & A. Branaman (Eds.), *The Goffman Reader*. Malden, MA: Blackwell.

Goffman, E. (1967). *Interaction ritual: Essays on face-to-face interaction*. Garden City, NY: Doubleday.

Goffman, E. (1986) (Repr.) *Stigma: Notes on the Management of Spoiled Identity*. Harmondsworth: Penguin Books.

Goh, A. L. S. (2005). Harnessing knowledge for innovation: an integrated management framework. *Journal of Knowledge Management, 9*(4), 6-18.

Golbeck, J. (2007). The dynamics of Web-based social networks: Membership, relationships, and change. *First Monday, 12*(11), 1-15.

Golder, S. A., & Huberman, B. A. (2005). *The Structure of Collaborative Tagging Systems*.

Golder, S., & Huberman, B. A. (2006). Usage Patterns of Collaborative Tagging Systems. *Journal of Information Science, 32*(2), 198-208.

Goodfellow, R. (2005). Virtuality and the shaping of educational communities. *Education, Communication & Information, 5*(2).

Goodman, E., & Moed, A. (2006). *Community in mashups: the case of personal geodata*. Paper presented at the 20th ACM Conference on Computer Supported Cooperative Work, Banff, AB, November 4-8. Retrieved March 19, 2008, from http://mashworks.net/images/5/59/Goodman_Moed_2006.pdf.

Goodyear, P. (2003). *Effective networked learning in higher education: notes and guidelines*. Available at: http://www.csalt.lancs.ac.uk/jisc/guidelines_final.doc. [Accessed 15th March, 2005].

Goodyear, P. (2007). Discussion, Collaborative Knowledge Work and Epistemic Fluency. *British Journal of Educational Studies, 55*(4), 351-368.

Goodyear, P., Salmon, G., Spector, M., Steeples, C., & Tickner, S. (2001). Competences for online teaching: A special report. *Educational Technology, Research and Development, 49*(1), 65-72.

Google. (2007). Google searches more sites more quickly, delivering the most relevant results. *Our Search: Google Technology* Retrieved 27.04.2007, from http://www.google.com/technology/

Goos, M., & Cretchley, P. (2004). Teaching and learning mathematics with computers, the internet, and multimedia. In B. Perry, G. Anthony, & C. Diezmann (Eds.), *Research in mathematics education in Australasia 2000-2003* (pp. 151-174). Flaxton, Queensland: Post Pressed.

Gorman, M. (2007). *The Siren Song of the Internet Part 2*. http://www.britannica.com/blogs/2007/06/the-siren-song-of-the-internet-part-ii/

Gorman, M. (2007a). The sleep of reason. *Britannica blog* http://blogs.britannica.com/blog/main/2007/06/web-20-the-sleep-of-reason-part-i/

Gorman, M. (2007b). Jabberwiki: The educational response part 1. *Britannica blog*. http://blogs.britannica.com/blog/main/2007/06/jabberwiki-the-educational-response-part-i/

Gorman, M. (2007c). Jabberwiki: The educational response part 2. *Britannica blog*, http://blogs.britannica.com/blog/main/2007/06/jabberwiki-the-educational-response-part-ii/

Gow, K. & Chant, D. (1998). Australian Supervisors and Recruits: Closing the gap in understanding each others' viewpoints. *Journal of Constructivist Psychology, 11*(4), 309-332.

Gow, K. & Gordon, R. (1998). What constitutes a capable manager? *Capability Network Newsletter.*

Gow, K. & McDonald, P. (2000). Attributes required of graduates for the future workplace. *Journal of Vocational Education and Training, 52*(3), 373-394. (ERIC Document Reproduction Service No EJ617391)

Gow, K. (1995a). Are school leavers themselves the best resource in the transition from school to work? *Journal of Applied Social Behaviour, 1*(2), 40-49.

Gow, K. (1995b). In and out. Entry-level competencies for school leavers and university graduates. *Australian Training Review,* Sept/Oct/Nov. 15-16.

Gow, K. (1996a). Coaching: the link between school, community and the workplace. *Australian Journal of Career Development, 5*(3), 22-26.

Gow, K. (1999-2000). Entrepreneurial and virtual competencies. *VOCAL: Australian Journal of Vocational Education and Training in Schools, 2* (1), 32-34.

Gow, K. (1999a). *Competencies required of graduates in the 21ˢᵗ Century.* Paper presented at the UNESCO Conference, December, Bangkok.

Gow, K. (1999b). *The Delors Report and graduate competencies.* Keynote Address at the Post Compulsory Educators Conference, August, Adelaide.

Gow, K. (1999c). *Cross-cultural competencies for counsellors in Australasia.* Culture, Race and Community. International Conference, Melbourne, 19-21 August.

Gow, K. (2001a). *Impact of Globalisation and Technology on Teaching and Learning: The Good, The Bad, And The Challenging.* Paper presented at the International Conference on Education. Manila, Philippines, July 1-5.

Gow, K. M. (1995c). *Unless you become as effective coaches, they will not enter into the realm of committed workers.* Paper presented at the "Learning to Earning" International Conference. Port Douglas, 30 September - 6 October, 1995. (ERIC Document Reproduction Service No. ED 389835).

Gow, K. M. (1992). *Reconciling school leavers' expectation about work with those of their employers.* Unpublished doctoral dissertation, University of Queensland, Brisbane.

Gow, K. M. (1994). Recruithood: Smoothing the Transition. *Journal of Applied Social Behaviour, 1*(1), 29-44.

Gow, K. M. (1999d). *A University for the Rural Poor in the Third World.* Paper presented at the World Education Fellowship Conference, Launceston, Tasmania. 30th Dec- 4ᵗʰ Jan. (ERIC Document Reproduction Service No. ED 426232)

Gow, K., & Birch, A. (2006). Do Employers and Secondary School Stakeholders View the Core Skills as Important? *Canadian Journal of Career Development, 5*(1), 28-33.

Gow, K., Litchfield, K. & Sheehan, M. (2002). Delineating Professional Competencies for Sociologists and other Health Social Scientists. *Journal of Applied Health Behaviour, 4* (1&2), 21-30.

Gow, K., Litchfield, K., Sheehan, M. & Fox, T. (1998). *How Academic Sociologists rate the importance of generic and specialist competencies. (*ERIC Document Reproduction Service No. *ED 426685)*

Gow, K.M. (1996b). *Is capability a function of competencies required of the more experienced worker?* Applying capability to the workforce. Paper presented at the Second Conference of the Australian Capability Network, Brisbane, 5-6 December.

Gow. K. M. (1995) The Transition from school leaver to effective worker. *Social Sciences Monographs (2).* (ERIC Document Reproduction Service No. ED397259)

Granovetter, M. (1973). The strength of weak ties: A network theory revisited. *American Journal of Sociology, 78*, 1360-1380.

Granovetter, M. (2004). The impact of social structure on economic outcomes. *Journal of Economic Perspectives, 19*(1), 33-50. Retrieved May 2007 from http://www.leader-values. com/Content/detailasp?ContentDetailID=990

Granovetter, M. S. (1973). The strength of weak ties. *American Journal of Sociology, 78*(6), 1360-1380.

Green, H., Facer, K., Rudd, T., Dillon, P., & Humphreys, P. (2005). *Personalisation and digital technologies.* Bristol, England: Futurelab. Retrieved October 23, 2007, from http://www.futurelab.org.uk/resources/documents/opening_education/Personalisation_report.pdf.

Greenberg, R. (2007). *Diabetes Stories website* http://www.diabetesstories.com/. Last accessed September 16th 2007

Gregorio, J. (2003). Stigmergy and the World-Wide Web. Retrieved 13/12/2003, 2003, from http://bitworking. org/news/Stigmergy/

Griffin, A. (2003). 'I am a teacher - Oimigod!' The construction of professional knowledge for the beginning English teacher. In B. Doecke, D. Homer & H. Nixon (Eds.), *English teachers at work: Narratives, counter narratives and arguments* (pp. 312-325). Kent Town, SA: Wakefield Press in association with AATE.

Grigar, D. (2004a). Preface: Fallow Field: A Story in Two Parts, 2004. *Iowa Review Web*, 7, at http://www. uiowa.edu/~iareview/tirweb/feature/grigar/fallowfield/ fallow_field_preface.html, accessed 20 June 2007.

Grigar, D. (2004). Fallow Field: A Story in Two Parts. *Iowa Review Web, volume 7,*at http://www.uiowa. edu/~iareview/tirweb/feature/grigar/fallowfield/fallow_field_opening.html, accessed 20 June 2007.

Grimes, R. (1994). *The beginnings of ritual studies.* Columbia, SC: University of South Carolina Press.

Gross, B. M. (2004). *Multiple email addresses: A socio-technical investigation.* Paper presented at the First Conference on E-mail and Anti-Spam (CEAS), Mountain View, CA.

Grossman, L. (2006). *Best invention YouTube.* Retrieved June 27, 2007 from http://www.time.com/time/2006/techguide/bestinventions/inventions/youtube.html.

Gruber, T. R. (1993). A Translation Approach to Portable Ontology Specifications. *Knowledge Acquisition, 5*(2), 199-220.

Grunwald Associates. (2007). Creating *& Connecting: Research and Guidelines on Online Social and Educational Networking.* Washington: National School Boards Association. Retrieved Sept.2007 from http://files.nsba. org/creatingandconnecting.pdf.

Guerin, E. M. C. (1998). Technology and Pedagogical Content: Are They Really Hand in Hand? *Proceedings of EDEN 1998 Conference, Universities in a Digital Era: Transformation, Innovation and Tradition-Roles and Perspectives of Open and Distance Learning*, 390-393, EDEN Annual Conference, University of Bologna, Italy, 24-26 June 1998.

Guess, A. (2007). Well, if they're already using it... *Inside Higher Ed.* Retrieved October 29, 2007 from http://insidehighered.com/layout/set/print/news/2007/10/25/educause.

Gunawardena, C. (1995). Social presence theory and implications for interaction and collaborative learning in computer conferences. *International Journal of Educational Telecommunications, 1*(2), 147-166.

Gunawardena, C. N. (1995). Social presence theory and implications for interaction and collaborative learning in computer conferences. *International Journal of Educational Telecommunications, 1*(2/3), 147-166.

Gunawardena, C. N., Linder-VanBerschot, J. A., LaPointe, D., Barrett, K., Mummert, J., Cardiff, M. S., et al. (2007). *Learning Transformations through Cross-Cultural E-Mentoring: Perspectives from an Online Faculty Development Forum.* Paper presented at the Seventh International Transformative Learning Conference, October 23-26, 2007, Albuquerque, New Mexico.

Gusfield, J. (1978). *Community: A Critical Response.* New York: Harper & Row

Guskey, T. R. (2002). Professional development and teacher change. *Teachers and Teaching: Theory and Practice, 8*(3/4), 381-390.

Guzman, G. A. C., & Wilson, J. (2005). The "soft" dimension of organizational knowledge transfer. *Journal of Knowledge Management, 9*(2), 59-74.

Habermas, J. (1991). *The Theory of Communicative Action, 1.* Cambridge: Polity Press.

Hager, P., Holland, S., & Beckett, D. (2002). *Enhancing the learning and employability of graduates: The role of generic skills. Round Table Business Higher education.* B-Hert Position Paper No.9, July, 16 pp. Melbourne, Australia.

Hall, S. (1980). Encoding/Decoding. In S. Hall, D. Hobson, A. Lowe, & P. Willis (Eds.), Culture, media, language (pp. 128-138). Hutchinson, London.

Halsey, A. (2005). This Problem of Script: Essays in Textual Analysis. *Marginalien.* Hereford: Five Seasons Press.

Hamel, G. (2007). *The Future of Management.* Boston, Massachusetts: Harvard Business School Press.

Hamm, S. (2005). Linux, Inc. BusinessWeek, January 31, (p. 60).

Hammerness, K., Darling-Hammond, L., & Bransford, J. (2005). How teachers learn and develop. In D.-H. Linda & J. Bransford (Eds.), *Preparing teachers for a changing world: What teachers should learn and be able to do* (pp. 358-389). San Francisco CA: Jossey-Bass.

Han, S., Ahn, Y., Moon, S., & Jeong, H. (2006). Collaborative Blog Spam Filtering Using Adaptive Percolation Search. *WWW2006 Workshop on the Weblogging Ecosystem,* Retrieved Oct. 2007 from http://www.blogpulse.com/www2006-workshop/papers/collaborative-blogspam-filtering.pdf

Handy, C. (1996). *Beyond certainty: The changing worlds of organizations.* Boston, MA: Harvard Business School Press.

Haney, C., Banks, W. C., & Zimbardo, P. G. (1973). A study of prisoners and guards in a simulated prison. *Naval Research Review, 30,* 4-17.

Hanley, G. (2005). MERLOT: Enabling open education. *Presentation at the COSL Conference,* Utah State University, Logan, UT.

Harbutt, K. (2007). Students strive to avert virtual epidemic. *Education Times, 15*(11), 15.

Hargittai, E. (2002). Second-Level Digital Divide: Differences in People's Online Skills. *First Monday, 7*(4). Retrieved April 2007 from http://www.firstmonday.org/issues/issue7_4/hargittai/

Hargreaves, A. & Fink, D. (2006). *Sustainable leadership.* San Francisco: Jossey-Bass.

Harmelen, M. v. (2008). Design trajectories: Four experiments in ple implementation. *Interactive Learning Environments, 16*(1), 35-46.

Harp, D. M., & Tremayne, M. (2007). *Programmed by the People: The Intersection of Political Communication and the YouTube Generation.* Paper presented at 57th Annual Conference of the International Communication Association San Francisco, CA.

Harri-Augstein, S., & Thomas, L. (1991). *Learning conversations: The self-organised way to personal and organisational growth.* London: Routledge.

Harste, J. (2003). What do we mean by literacy now? *Voices from the middle, 10*(3), 8-12.

Hartley, J. R. (1998). Qualitative reasoning and conceptual change: computer based support in understanding science. In R. G. F. Winkels & B. Bredeweg (Guest Eds.), *Interactive Learning Environments. Special Issue on The Use of Qualitative Reasoning Techniques in Interactive Learning Environments, 5*(1 and 2), 53-64.

Hartmann J., Sutcliffe A., & De Angeli, A. (2007*).* Assessing the Attractiveness of Interactive Systems. *CHI 2007 Conference Proceedings* (pp. 387-396), San Jose, CA, USA,.

Hasan, R. (1998). The Disempowerment Game: Bourdieu and language in literacy. *Linguistics and Education, 10*, 25-87.

Hassenzahl, M., & Tractinsky, N. (2006). *U*ser experience - a research agenda. *Behaviour & Information Technology, 25*, 91-97.

Hayward, C. R. (2000). *De-facing Power.* Cambridge: Cambridge University Press.

Hedberg, J. (2006). E-learning futures? Speculations for a time yet to come. *Studies in Continuing Education, 28*(2),171-183.

Heer, J., & boyd, D. (2008). *Visualizing online social networks.* Retrieved July 11, 2008 from http://jheer.org/vizster/

Heeter, C. (1989). Implications of new interactive technologies for conceptualizing communication. In J. L. Salvaggio & J. Bryant (Eds.), *Media use in the information age: Emerging patterns of adoption and computer use* (pp. 217-235). Hillsdale, NJ: Lawrence Erlbaum Associates.

Heider, F. (1958). *The psychology of interpersonal relations.* New York: Wiley.

Heinze, R. (2000) *The nature and function of rituals.* London: Bergin & Garvey.

Helland, C. (2000). Religion online / online religion and virtual communitas. In J. K. Hadden & D. E. Cowan (Eds.), *Religion on the Internet: Research prospects and promises.* JAI Press: New York.

Helms, D. (2007a). *Drug use and abuse.* Retrieved November 2, 2007, from http://druguseandabuse.ning.com/.

Helms, D. (2007b). *Group project.* Retrieved November 2, 2007, from http://www.msjc.edu/hs/hs123_group_project.html.

Hemetsberger, A., & Reinhardt, C. (2006). Learning and knowledge-building in open-source communities: A social-experiential approach. *Management Learning, 37*(2), 187-214.

Henderson, D.K. (1994). Accounting for macro-level causation. *Synthese, 101*(2), 129-156.

Henderson, J. V. (1998). Comprehensive, Technology-Based Clinical Education: The "Virtual Practicum". *International Journal of Psychiatry in Medicine, 28*(1), 41-79.

Herring, S., Scheidt, L., Bonus, S., & Wright, E. (2004). Bridging the Gap: A Genre Analysis of Weblogs. In *Proceedings of 37th Hawaii International Conference on System Sciences,* Hawaii. (*HICSS*-37). Los Alamitos: IEEE Computer Society Press. Retrieved 21st May 2008 from:http://csdl2.computer.org/comp/proceedings/hicss/2004/2056/04/205640101b.pdf

Herrington, A., & Herrington, J. (2006). What is an authentic learning environment? In A. Herrington & J. Herrington (Eds.), *Authentic learning environments in higher education* (pp. 1-13). Hershey, PA: Information Science Publishing.

Herrington, A., Herrington, J., Kervin, L. & Ferry, B. (2006). The design of an online community of practice for beginning teachers. *Contemporary Issues in Technology and Teacher Education, 6*(1), 120-132.

Herrington, J., & Oliver, R. (2000). An instructional design framework for authentic learning environments. *Educational Technology Research and Development, 48*(3), 23-48.

Heyse, V., Erpenbeck, J., & Michel, L. (2002). *Lernkulturen der zukunft. Kompetenzbedarf und kompetenzentwicklung in zukunftsbranchen* (No. 74). Berlin: Arbeitsgemeinschaft Betriebliche Weiterbildungsforschung, e.V.

Hillman, D. C., Willis, D., &, & Gunawardena, C. N. (1994). Learner-interface interaction in distance education: An extension of contemporary models and strategies for practitioners. *The American Journal of Distance Education, 8*(2), 30-42.

Hilton, J. (2006). The future for higher education: Sunrise or perfect storm. *EDUCAUSE Review, 41*(2), 58-71. Retrieved on 7th April 2008, from http://www.educause.edu/ir/library/pdf/erm0623.pdf

Hilton, J. (2006). The future for higher education: sunrise or perfect storm. *EDUCAUSE Review, 41*(2), 58-71.

Hines, A. (1993). Transferable skills will land you a job in the future. *HR Magazine, 38*(4), 55-56.

Hirschbuhl, J., Zachariah, S., & Bishop, D. (2002). Using knowledge management to deliver distance learning. *British Journal of Educational Technology, 33*(1), 89-93.

Hirschorn, M. (2007). The web 2.0 bubble. *The Atlantic*, http://www.theatlantic.com/doc/200704/social-networking

HitWise (2006). *Is Bebo next?* Retrieved June 29, 2007 from http://weblogs.hitwise.com/heather-hopkins/2006/11/bebo_and_myspace_network_maps.html.

Hogg, M. A. (2001). Social categorization, depersonalization, and group behavior. In M. A. Hogg & S. Tinsdale (Eds.), *Blackwell handbook of social psychology: Group processes* (pp. 57-85). Malden, MA: Blackwell.

Hogg, M. A., & Hains, S. C. (1996). Intergroup relations and group solidarity: Effects of group identification and social beliefs on depersonalized attraction. *Journal of Personality and Social Psychology, 70*(2), 295-309.

Hogg, M. A., & McGarty, C. (1990). Self-categorization and social identity. In D. Abrams & M. A. Hogg (Eds.), *Social identity theory: Constructive and critical advances* (pp. 10-27). New York, NY: Harvester Wheatsheath.

Hogg, M. A., Cooper-Shaw, L., & Holzworth, D. W. (1993). Group prototypicality and depersonalized attraction in small interactive groups. *Personality and Social Psychology Bulletin, 19*(4), 452-465.

Hogg, M. A., Terry, D., & White, K. M. (1995). A tale of two theories: A critical comparison of identity theory with social identity theory. *Social Psychology Quarterly, 58*(4), 255-269.

Hollenbeck, K. (1994). *The workplace know-how skills needed to be productive.* (Technical Report). Michigan: Upjohn Institute for Employment Research. (ERIC Document Reproduction Service No. ED 413 712)

Homik, M., & Melis, E. (2006). Using Blogs for Learning Logs. *In Proceedings of ePortfolio*, Oxford UK.

Höök, K. (2003). Social Navigation: from the web to the mobile. In G. Szwillus & J. Ziegler (Eds.), *Mensch & Computer 2003: Interaktion und Bewegung* (pp. 17-20). Stuttgart.

Höök, K., Benyon, D., & Munro, A. J. (2003). *Designing information spaces: The social navigation approach.* London New York: Springer.

Hope, J. E. (2004). *Open Source Biotechnology.* Unpublished doctoral dissertation, Australian National University.

Horne, R., & Weinman, J. (1999). Patients' beliefs about prescribed medicines and their role in adherence to treatment in chronic illness. *J Psychosom Res 1999, 47* 555-67.

Horowitz, B., (2006). Creators, Synthesizers, and Consumers. Retrieved June 2007 from http://www.elatable.com/blog/?p=5.

Horvitz, E., Apacible, J., & Subramani, M. (2005). Balancing Awareness and Interruption: Investigation of Notification Deferral Policies. In *User Modeling 2005*, (pp. 433-437). Heidelberg: Springer.

Horvitz, P. M. (1965). A note on textbook pricing. *The American Economic Review, 55* (4), 844-848.

Howard, J. (1995). The future of work in Australia. In Department of Employment, Education and Training (Ed.), *The future of work* (pp. 119-126). Sydney: Australian Council of Social Service.

Hudson, S., Fogarty, J., Atkeson, C., Avrahami, D., Forlizzi, S.K., Lee, J., & Yang, J. (2003) Predicting human interruptibility with sensors: a Wizard of Oz feasibility study. In *Proceedings of the SIGCHI conference on Human factors in computing systems,* April 05-10, 2003, Ft. Lauderdale, Florida, USA

Hug, T., Lindner, M., & Bruck, P. (Eds.). (2006). *Microlearning: emerging concepts, practices, and technologies after e-learning. Proceedings of Microlearning 2005: Learning & working in new media* (pp. 121-130). Innsbruck, Austria: Innsbruck University Press.

Hughes, G. (2004) *RSS/Blog Overload - How do you deal with the glut of information?* Retrieved 6th November 2007, from: http://www.greghughes.net/rant/Blogger-ConRSSBlogOverloadHowDoYouDealWithTheGlutOfInformation.aspx

Hughes, H. (2006). Responses and influences: A model of online information use for learning. *Information Research, 12*(1). Online: Accessed 14.06.07. http://eprints.qut.edu.au/view/person/Hughes,_Hilary.html

Hughes, J., & Lang, K. (2006). Transmutability: digital decontextualization, manipulation, and recontextualization as a new source of value in the production and consumption of culture products. In *Proceedings of the 39th Annual Hawaii International Conference on System Sciences (HICSS'06)* (p. 165a). Los Alamitos, CA: IEEE Computer Society.

Hugo, G. (2005). Academica's own demographic time bomb. *Australian Universities Review, 48*(1), 16-23.

Hummel, J., & Lechner, U. (2002). Social profiles of virtual communities, In *Proceedings of the 35th Hawaii International Conference on System Sciences..*

Hutchins, E. (1991). Organizing work by adaptation. *Organization Science, 2*(1), 14-39.

Hutchins, E. (1995). *Cognition in the wild.* Cambridge, MA: MIT Press.

Hylén, J. (2005). *Open Educational Resources: Opportunities and Challenges.* OECD-CERI.

IBM. *What is social computing?* Retrieved July 7, 2007, from http://www.research.ibm.com/SocialComputing/SCGFAQs.htm#WhatIsSocialComputing.

IDEF5 method report (1994). Retrieved oct 7th 2007 from http://www.idef.com/pdf/Idef5.pdf

Illich, I. (1971). *Deschooling Society.* New York: Harper & Row.

Industry Task Force on Leadership and Management Skills. (1995). *Enterprising nation: Renewing Australia's managers to meet the challenges of the Asia-Pacific century.* Canberra: Australian Government Publishing Office.

Ingwersen, P., & Jarvelin, K. (2005). *The turn: integration of information seeking and retrieval in context.* New York: Springer

Ip, R., & Wagner, C. (2008). Weblogging: A Study of Social Computing and Its Impact on Organizations, *Decision Support Systems, 45*(2), 242-250.

Ipsos MORI (2007). *Student expectations study.* Retrieved November 5, 2007 from http://www.jisc.ac.uk/media/documents/publications/studentexpectations.pdf.

Ipsos MORI (2007). *Student expectations study: key findings from on-line research and discussion evenings held in June 2007 for the Joint Information Systems Committee* JISC.

Irving, C., & Crawford, J. (2007). *A National Information Literacy Framework Scotland.* Glasgow Caledonian University, ILS Report Project. Retrieved on 7 April, 2008, from http://www.caledonian.ac.uk/ils/framework.html

Ittelson, J. (2001). Building an E-dentity for Each Student. In *Educause Quarterly, 4*, 43-45. Boulder: Educause. Retrieved April 12, 2007 from https://www.educause.edu/ir/library/pdf/EQM0147.pdf

Jäkälä, M., & Berki, E. (2004). Exploring the Principles of Individual and Group Identity in Virtual Communities. In the Proceedings of P. Commers, P. Isaias, & M. Baptista Nunes (Eds.), *1ˢᵗ IADIS Conference on Web-based Communities* (pp 19-26). Lisbon, Portugal, 24-26 Mar.

Jäkälä, M., & Mikkola, L. (2001). Technology Makes You Feel Better? Attempts to Mediate Social Support through Technology in Health Care. In M. J. Smith, & G. Salvendy (Eds.), *Systems, Social and Internationalization Design Aspects of Human-Computer Interaction* (pp. 137-141). Lawrence Erlbaum Associates, Mahwah, NJ.

James, W. (1891/1950). The consciousness of self. In *Principles of Psychology*. New York, NY: Dover Publications.

Jaokar, A., & Fish, T. (2006). *Mobile Web 2.0: The innovator's guide to developing and marketing next generation wireless mobile applications*. London: Futuretext.

Jarche, H. (2006). *My PKM System, blog post and comment*. 29th August 2006. Retrieved on 7 April, 2008, from http://www.jarche.com/?p=865

Jarman, S. (2005). *Open Content Initiative Application to The William and Flora Hewlett Foundation*. Retrieved on January, 17, 2007 from http://www.open.ac.uk/openlearn/__assets/06sngpqpwminsmwxov.pdf

Jenkins, H. (2001). Convergence? I diverge. *Technology Review*, (June), p. 93, and at http://www.technologyreview.com/Biztech/12434/, accessed 23 June 2007

Jenkins, H. (2006). *Fans, Bloggers, and Gamers: Exploring Participatory Culture*. New York: New York University Press.

Jenkins, H. (2007). *Confronting the challenges of participatory culture: media education for the 21st Century*. Chicago, IL: MacArthur Foundation. Retrieved January 4, 2007, from http://www.digitallearning.mac-found.org/atf/cf/%7BE45C7E0-A3E0-4B89-AC9C-E807E1B0AE4E%7D/JENKINS_WHITE_PAPER.PDF.

Jenkins, R. (2000). Categorization: Identity, social process and epistemology. *Current Sociology, 48*(3), 7-25.

Jenkins, R. (2004). *Social Identity*. New York, NY: Routledge.

Jepperson, R., Wendt, A. & Katzenstein. P. (1996). Norms, identity, and culture in national security. In Katzenstein, P. *Culture and Security*, (pp. 33–78). New York: Columbia University Press.

JISC. (2006). *Designing spaces for effective learning: a guide to 21ˢᵗ century learning space design*. London, England: Joint Information Systems Committee. Retrieved July 2, 2007, from http://www.jisc.ac.uk/media/documents/publications/learningspaces.pdf.

Johannessen, O. (2006). *Digital competencies in the national education policy*. Ministry of Education and Research, Norway. EU eLearning Conference 2006. 4ᵗʰ-5ᵗʰ July 2006. Espoo 04072006. Online. Accessed 09.09.07. http://www.google.com.au/search?hl=en&q=norwegian+ministry+digital+competencies&meta=

Johnson, C. M. (2001). A Survey of Current Research on Online Communities of Practice. *Internet and Higher Education, 4*, 45-60.

Johnson, J.C., Palinkas, L.A., & Boster, J.S. (2003). Informal social roles and the evolution and stability of social networks. In R. Breiger, K. Carley & P. Pattison (Eds.), *Dynamic social network modeling and analysis: Workshop summary and papers* (pp. 121-132). Washington, D.C.: National Research Council.

Johnson, M., & Liber, O. (2008). The personal learning environment and the human condition: From theory to teaching practice. *Interactive Learning Environments, 16*(1), 3-15.

Johnson, M., Beauvoir, P., MIlligan, C., Sharples, P., Wilson, S., & Liber, O. (2006a). Mapping the future: The personal learning environment reference model and emerging technology. In D. Whitelock & S. Wheeler

(Eds.), *Alt-c 2006: The next generation - research proceedings* (pp. 182-191). Totton: Association for Learning Technology.

Johnson, M., Hollins, P., Wilson, S., & Liber, O. (2006). *Towards a reference model for the personal learning environment. Proceedings of the 23rd annual ascilite conference: Who's learning? Whose technology?* Australia.

Johnson, M., Liber, O., Wilson, S., & MIlligan, C. (2006b). The personal learning environment: A report on the cetis ple project. Retrieved April 5, 2008, from http://wiki.cetis.ac.uk/image:plereport.doc

Johnson, N.F. (2007). *Two's Company, Three is complexity: A simple guide to the science of all sciences.* Oxford, UK: Oneworld.

Joinson, A. N. (2001). Self-disclosure in computer-mediated communication: The role of self-awareness and visual anonymity. *European Journal of Social Psychology, 31*, 177-192.

Jonassen, D. (1995). Supporting communities of learners with technology: A vision for integrating technology with learning in schools. *Educational Technology, 35*(4), 60-63.

Jonassen, D. (2003). Designing research-based instruction for story problems. *Educational Psychology Review, 15*(3), 267-297.

Jonassen, D. H., Peck, K. L., & Wilson, B. G. (1999). *Learning with Technology: A Constructivist Perspective.* Upper Saddle River, NJ: Merrill Prentice Hall.

Jonassen, D., Beissner, K., & Yacci, M. (1993). Structural Knowledge: Techniques for Representing, Conveying, and Acquiring Structural Knowledge. Lawrence Erlbaum Assoc Inc

Jones, C. (2008). Infrastructures, institutions and networked learning. *Sixth International Conference on Networked Learning,* Halkidiki, Greece.

Jones, P., Miller, C., Packman, G., & Thomas, B. (2004). *Student and tutor perspectives of online moderation.* Welsh Enterprise Institute, University of Glamorgan.

Jones, Q. (1997). Virtual –communities, virtual settlements & cyber-archaeology: A theoretical outline. *Journal of Computer-Mediated Communication,* 3(3). http://www.ascusc.org/jcmc/vol3/issue3/jones.html

Jones, R.H., & Norris, S. (2005). Introducing mediational means / cultural tools. In S. Norris & R. H. Jones (Eds.), *Discourse in Action* (pp. 49-51). New York, NY: Routledge.

Jones, S., & Madden, M. (2002). The Internet goes to college: How students are living in the future with today's technology [Electronic Version]. *Pew Internet & American Life Project.* Retrieved October 15, 2007, from http://www.pewinternet.org/pdfs/PIP_College_Report.pdf

Jones-Kavalier, B.R. & Flannigan, S.L. (2006). Connecting the digital dots: Literacy of the 21st Century. EDUCAUSE Quarterly, 29, 2, 8-10. Online. Accessed 11.11.07. http://www.educause.edu/ir/library/pdf/EQM0621.pdf.

Joseph, D. (2004). The Practice of Design-Based Research: Uncovering the Interplay Between Design, Research, and the Real-World Context. *Educational Psychologist, 39*(4), 235-242.

Jukes, I. A. (2007). *Born to be wired: NetSavvy and communication literacy for an information age.* web. mac.com/iajukes/thecommittedsardine/Presentations. html [Accessed 15 December 2007]

Jünger, S. (2004). *Selbstorganisation, lernkultur und kompetenzentwicklung.* Wiesbaden: Deutscher Universitätsverlag.

Kalz, M. (2005). Building Eclectic Personal Learning Landscapes with Open Source Tools. *Conference proceedings for the Open Source for Education in Europe, Research & Practise conference.* Heerlen: Open University of the Netherlands. Retrieved April 14, 2007 from http://www.openconference.net/viewpaper. php?id=16&cf=3

Kamel Boulos, M. N., & Wheeler, S. (2007). The emerging Web 2.0 social software: An enabling suite of sociable technologies in health and health care education. *Health Information and Libraries Journal, 24*(1), 2-23.

Kamel Boulos, M. N., Maramba, I., & Wheeler, S. (2006). Wikis, blogs and podcasts: a new generation of web-based tools for virtual collaborative clinical practice and education. *BMC Medical Education, 6*(41). [Online at: www.biomedcentral.com/1472-6920/6/41] Accessed 30 November, 2006.

Kanuka, H. (2008). Instructional Design and eLearning: A Discussion of Pedagogical Content Knowledge as a Missing Construct. *e-Journal of Instructional Science and Technology, 9*(2), http://www.usq.edu.au/electpub/e-jist/docs/vol9_no2/papers/full_papers/kanuka.htm [Accessed 20 of February, 2008].

Kanuka, H., & Anderson, T. (1998). Online social interchange, discord and knowledge construction. *Journal of Distance Education* [Online at: http://cade.icaap.org/vol13.1/kanuka.html] (Retrieved 13 November, 2007).

Kasperson, L. B. (2000). *Anthony Giddens: An Introduction to a Social Theorist.* Oxford: Blackwell Publishers Ltd.

Katz, I. R., & Macklin, A. S. (2007). Information and communication technology (ICT) literacy: Integration and assessment in higher education. *Systemics, Cybernetics and Informatics, 5*(4), *50-55*. Retrieved on 7 April, 2008, from http://www.iiisci.org/Journal/CV$/sci/pdfs/P890541.pdf

Katz, I. R., & Macklin, A. S. (2007). Information and communication technology (ICT) literacy: integration and assessment in higher education. *Systemics, Cybernetics and Informatics, 5*(4), 50-55. Retrieved November 17, 2007, from http://www.iiisci.org/Journal/CV$/sci/pdfs/P890541.pdf.

Katz, R. N. (2006). The ECAR study of Undergraduate Students and Information Technology 2006. Retrieved on 7 April, 2008, from http://www.educause.edu/ir/library/pdf/EKF/EKF0607.pdf

Keen, A. (2007). *The cult of the amateur: how today's Internet is killing our culture and assaulting our economy.* London: Nicholas Brealey.

Keen, A. (2007). *The Cult of the Amateur: How Today's Internet Is Killing Our Culture and Assaulting Our Economy.* Nicholas Brealey Publishing

Keen, A. (2007). *The Cult of the Amateur: How Today's Internet is Killing Our Culture and Assaulting Our Economy.* London: Nicholas Brealey.

Keller, K. L. (1993). Conceptualizing, measuring, and managing customer-based brand equity. *Journal of Marketing, 57*(1), 1-22.

Kember, D. (1989). A longitudinal process model of drop-out in distance education. *The Journal of Higher Education, 60*(3), 278-301.

Kember, D. (1997). A reconceptualisation of the research into university academics' conceptions of teaching. *Learning and Instruction, 7*(3), 255-275.

Kemp, J., & Livingstone, D. (2006). *Putting a second life "metaverse" skin on learning management systems.* http://www.sloodle.com/whitepaper.pdf

Kenagy, J. W., & Christensen, C. M. (2002). *Disruptive Innovation – New Diagnosis and Treatment for the Systemic Maladies of Healthcare, Business briefing: global healthcare*

Kenny, J., Quealy, J., & Young, J. (2002). *RMIT ICT DLS Competency Framework - A basis for effective staff development.* UltiBase Online Journal, November. Accessed 29.04.08. http://ultibase.rmit.edu.au/Articles/nov02/kenny1.pdf

Kerawalla L. J., Minocha S., Kirkup G., & Conole G. (2008). Characterising the different blogging behaviours of students on an online distance learning course. *Learning Media and Technology, 33*(1), 21-33.

Kerawalla L. J., Minocha S., Kirkup G., & Conole G. (in press). An empirically grounded framework to guide blogging in Higher Education. *Journal of Computer Assisted Learning.*

Kerawalla, L. J., Minocha, S., Conole, G., Kirkup, G., Schencks, M., & Sclater, N. (2007). Exploring students' understanding of how blogs and blogging can support distance learning in higher education. In S. Wheeler & N Whitton (Eds.), *Beyond control: learning technology for the social network generation.* Research Proceedings of the 14th Association for Learning Technology Conference (ALT-C 2007), Nottingham University, England UK; (pp. 169-178).

Kerka, S. (1993). *Career education for a global economy.* (Digest No. 135). Ohio: Clearinghouse on Adult, Career and Vocational Education. (ERIC Document Reproduction Service No. ED 355 457)

Kerres, M. (2007). Microlearning as a challenge to instructional design. Retrieved April 5, 2008, from http://mediendidaktik.uni-duisburg-essen.de/system/files/Microlearning-kerres.pdf

Kidwell, J. J., Vander Linde, K. M., & Johnson, S. L. (2000). *Educause Quarterly, 4*, 26-33.

Kiesler, S., Siegel, J., & McGuire, T. (1984). Social psychological aspects of computer-mediated communication. *The American psychologist, 39*(10), 1123-1134.

Kilby, T. (2001). The direction of web-based training: A practitioner's view. *The Learning Organization, 8*(5), 194-199.

Kimppa, K. (2007). *Problems with the Justification of Intellectual Property Rights in Relation to Software and Other Digitally Distributed Media.* Ph.D. Thesis. Turku Centre for Computer Science. University of Turku.

Kiousis, S. (2002). Interactivity: A Concept Explication. *New Media & Society, 4*(3), 355-383.

Kirschner, P. A. (2002). Can we support cscl? Educational, social and technological affordances for learning. Retrieved November 12, 2007, from http://www.ou.nl/Docs/Expertise/OTEC/Publicaties/paulkirschner/oratieboek_PKI_DEF_Klein_ZO.pdf

Kirsop, B., & Chan, L. (2005). Transforming Access to Research Literature for Developing Countries. In *Serials Review,*(31), 246-255. London: Elsevier. Retrieved February 01, 2007 from http://hdl.handle.net/1807/4416

Kisielnicki, J. (2002). *Modern Organisations in Virtual Communities.* IRM Press, Warsaw.

Kjeldskov, J., & Paay, J. (2005). Just-for-us: a context-aware mobile information system facilitating sociality. *ACM International Conference Proceeding Series; Proceeding of the 7th international conference on Human computer interaction with mobile devices & services table of contents, 111*, 23-30.

Klapp, O. (1982). Meaning lag in the Information society. *Journal of Communication, 32*(2), 56–66.

Kleck, C. A. (2007). *The company you keep and the image you project: putting your best face forward in on-line social networks.* Paper presented at 57th Annual Conference of the International Communication Association San Francisco, CA.

Klerkx, J., & Duval, E. (2007, September 17-20, 2007). *Visualizing social bookmarks.* Paper presented at the SIRTEL 2007 Workshop on Social Information Retrieval for Technology-Enhanced Learning, Crete, Greece.

KMI Knowledge Media Institute (2006). Open Sense Communities. Retrieved on January, 17, 2007 from http://kmi.open.ac.uk/projects/osc/index.html

Kolb, D. A., & Fry, R. (1975). Towards an applied theory of experiential learning. In C. Cooper (Ed.), *Theories of group processes.* London: John Wiley.

Kolbitsch, J., & Maurer, H. (2006). The Transformation of the Web: How Emerging Communities Shape the Information we Consume. *Journal of Universal Computer Science, 12*(2), 187-213.

Kollock, P. (1999). The Production of Trust in Online Markets. In E.J. Lawler et al. (Eds.), *Advances in Group Processes* Vol. 16. JAI Press, Greenwich, CT.

Korte, R. (2007). A review of social identity theory with implications for training and development. *Journal of European Industrial Training, 31*(3), 166-180.

Kosonen, M., & Kianto, A. (2008). Social Computing for Knowledge Creation? The Role of Tacit Knowledge. *In Proceedings of the 3rd Organization Learning,*

Knowledge and Capabilities Conference (OLKC 2008), Copenhagen, Denmark, 28-30 April 2008.

Kossinets, G., & Watts, D. (2006). Empirical analysis of an evolving social network. *Science, 311*, 88-90.

Kozma, R. B. (1994). Will media influence learning? Reframing the debate. *Education Technology Research and Development, 42*(1), 7-19.

Kraft, R., Chang, C. C., Maghoul, F., & Kumar, R. (2006). Searching with context. In *Proceedings of the 15th international Conference on World Wide Web* (pp. 477-486) (Edinburgh, Scotland, May 23 - 26, 2006). WWW '06. ACM, New York, NY.

Krause, K., Bochner, S., & Duchesne, S. (2003). *Educational psychology for learning and teaching*. Southbank, Australia: Thomson.

Krause, K-L. (2006). *Student voices in borderless higher education: The Australian experience*. June Report for The Observatory on borderless higher education. Retrieved July 25, 2007 from http://www.obhe.ac.uk. Subscription required.

Krause, S. D. (2004). When blogging goes bad: a cautionary tale about blogs, email lists, discussion, and interaction. *Kairos*, *9*(1). Retrieved 21st May 2008 from http://english.ttu.edu/kairos/9.1/binder.html?praxis/krause/index.html

Kreijns, K., Kirschner, P. A., & Jochems, W. (2002). The sociability of computer-supported collaborative learning environments. *Educational Technology & Society, 5*(1), 822.

Krikos, V., Stamou, S., Kokosis, P., Ntoulas, A., & Christodoulakis, D. (2005). DirectoryRank: ordering pages in web directories. In *Proceedings of the 7th Annual ACM international Workshop on Web information and Data Management* (pp. 17-22) (Bremen, Germany, November 04 - 04, 2005). WIDM '05. ACM, New York, NY.

Krüger, O. (2005). Discovering the invisible Internet: Methodological aspects of researching religion on the Internet. *Online-Heidelberg Journal of Religions on the Internet, 1*(1).

Kuhl, J. (1985). Volitional mediators of cognition-behavior consistency: Self-regulatory processes in action versus state orientation. In J. Kuhl & J. Beckmann (Eds.), *Action control: From cognition to behavior* (pp. 101-128). West-Berlin: Springer-Verlag.

Kuhlthau, C. C. (1988). Developing a model of the library search process: cognitive and affective aspects. *RQ* (Winter) (pp.232-242).

Kuhlthau, C. C. (1993). *Seeking meaning: a process approach to library and information services*. Norwood, NJ: Ablex; [Second edition published 2004].

Kuhlthau, C. C. (2007). From information to meaning: confronting the challenges of the 21st century. Keynote paper presented at *Information: interactions and impact conference*, Aberdeen June.

Kuhlthau, C. C., & Todd, R. J. (2007). Guided inquiry: a framework for learning through school libraries in 21st century schools. http://cissl.scils.rutgers.edu/guided_inquiry/characteristics.html [accessed 21 December 2007]

Kuhlthau, C. C., Caspari, A. K., & Maniotes, L. K. (2007). *Guided inquiry: learning in the 21st century*. New York: Libraries Unlimited Inc.

Kukulska-Hulme, A. (2005). *The mobile language learner – now and in the future*. Plenary session delivered at the Fran Vision till Praktik (From Vision to Practice) Language Learning Symposium, Umeå, Sweden, May 11-12. Retrieved February 3, 2006, from http://www2.humlab.umu.se/video/Praktikvision/agnes.ram.

Kvavik, R. B. (2005). Convenience, communications and control: How students use technology. In D. Oblinger & J. Oblinger (Eds), *Educating the Net Generation*, 7.1-7.20. Washington, DC: EDUCAUSE. Retrieved on 7 April, 2008, from http://www.educause.edu/educatingthenetgen

Kvavik, R., & Caruso, J. (2005). *ECAR study of students and information technology: Convenience, connection, control and learning*. Boulder: EDUCAUSE Center for Applied Research.

Lacey, C. (1985). Professional socialisation of teachers. In T. Husen and T. N. Postlethwaite (Eds.) *The International Encyclopedia of Education,* (pp. 4073-4084). Oxford: Pergamon.

Lacey, N. (1998). *Image and Representation: Key Concepts in Media Studies.* MacMillan Press Ltd, London.

Lakhani, K. R., & Eric von Hippel (2003). How open source software works: Free user to user assistance. Research Policy, 32(6), 923-943.

Lam, M. (1990). *Use your initiative. Enterprise skills for the future.* Canberra: Australian Government Printing Service.

Lamb, B. (2007). Dr Mashup; or, why educators should learn to stop worrying and love the remix. *EDUCAUSE Review, 42*(4), 12-25.

Lan, K. G., Xian, Y. Y., & Fu, Z. Y. (2000). Putting knowledge management technologies into distance education. *Proceedings of 2000 IRMA International Conference,* Anchorage, Alaska, USA, 1129-1130.

Lancaster University. The GUIDE Project. Retrieved 16.06.2007, from http://www.guide.lancs.ac.uk/overview.html

Land, R., & Bayne, S. (2001). 'Screen or monitor? Issues of surveillance and disciplinary power in online learning environments. In C. Rust (Ed.), *Proceedings of the "001 Ninth improving Student Learning Symposium* (pp. 125-138), Oxford: Oxford Centre for Staff and Learning Development.

Landow, G. P. (2005). *Hypertext 3.0: Critical Theory and New Media in an Era of Globalization.* Baltimore, MD: John Hopkins University Press.

Lange, P. (2007). *Commenting on Comments: Investigating Responses to Antagonism on YouTube.* Paper presented at Society for Applied Anthropology Conference Tampa, Florida,URL (consulted 17 September 2007). http://web3.cas.usf.edu/main/depts/ANT/cma/Lange-SfAA-Paper-2007.pdf

Lankshear, C., & Knobel, M. (2005). Digital literacies: Policy, pedagogy and research considerations for education In *Opening plenary address presented at the ITU Conference.* Oslo, Norway.

Lankshear, C., & Knobel, M. (2007). Researching new literacies: Web 2.0 practices and insider perspectives. *e-Learning, 4*(3), 224-240.

Lankshear, C., & Snyder, I. (2000). *Teachers and technoliteracy: Managing literacy, technology and learning in schools.* Crows Nest, Australia: Allen & Unwin.

Larner, A. J. (2006). Searching the internet for medical information: frequency over time and by age and gender in an outpatient population in the UK. *J Telemed Telecare 2006, 12* 186-8.

LaRose, R., & Eastin, M. S. (2004). A social cognitive theory of internet uses and gratifications: toward a new model of media attendance. *Journal of Broadcasting & Electronic Media, 48*(3), 358-377.

Laurillard, D. (2001). *Rethinking University Teaching: A Conversational Framework for the Effective Use of Learning Technologies.* Routledge.

Laurillard, D. (2002). *Rethinking university teaching in a digital age.* Retrieved November 1, 2007 from http://www2.open.ac.uk/ltto/lttoteam/Diana/Digital/rutdigitalage.doc.

Laurillard, D. (2002). *Rethinking University Teaching.* London: Routledge.

Laurillard, D. (2002). *Rethinking University Teaching: a conversational framework for the effective use of educational technology.* New York, USA: Routledge Falmer.

Lave, J., & Wenger, E. (1991). *Situated learning.* New York: Cambridge University Press.

Lave, J., & Wenger, E. (1991). *Situated Learning: legitimate peripheral participation.* Cambridge: Cambridge University Press.

Lave, J., & Wenger, E. (1991). *Situated learning: Legitimate peripheral participation.* New York: Cambridge University Press.

Lave, J., & Wenger, E. (1991). *Situated learning: legitimate peripheral participation.* Cambridge, England: Cambridge University Press.

Lawlor, R. (2007). Voices of the First Day: Awakening in the Aboriginal Dreamtime. at http://www.didgeridoos.net.au/dreamtime%20stories/Index%20dreamtime%20stories.html, accessed 20 June 2007.

Lea, M., & Spears, R. (1995). Love at first byte? Building personal relationships over computer networks. In J. T. Wood & S. Duck (Eds.), *Understudied relationships: Off the beaten track* (pp. 197-233). Thousand Oaks, CA: Sage.

Lea, M., Spears, R., & de Groot, D. (2001). Knowing Me, Knowing You: Anonymity Effects on Social Identity Processes Within Groups. *Personality and Social Psychology Bulletin, 27*(5), 526-537.

Leadbeater, C. (2006). *The ten habits of mass innovation.* London, England: NESTA. Retrieved November 3, 2007, from http://www.nesta.org.uk/assets/pdf/ten_habits_of_mass_innovation_provocation_NESTA.pdf.

Leadbeater, C. (2007). We-Think, URL (consulted 17 September 2007): http://www.wethinkthebook.net/home.aspx

Lee, M. J. W., Chan, A., & McLoughlin, C. (2006). Students as producers: second year students' experiences as podcasters of content for first year undergraduates. In *Proceedings of the 7th IEEE Conference on Information Technology Based Higher Education and Training (ITHET'06)* (pp. 832-848), Sydney, NSW: University of Technology, Sydney.

Lee, M. J. W., Eustace, K., Hay, L., & Fellows, G. (2005). Learning to collaborate, collaboratively: an online community building and knowledge construction approach to teaching computer supported collaborative work at an Australian university. In M. R. Simonson & M. Crawford (Eds.), *Proceedings of the 2005 AECT International Convention* (pp. 286-306). North Miami Beach, FL: Nova Southeastern University.

Lefcourt, H.M. (1966). Internal versus external control of reinforcement: A review. *Psychological Bulletin, 65*(4), 206-220.

Lemke, J. (2002). Becoming the village: Education across lives. In G. Wells & G. Claxton (Eds.), *Learning for life in the 21st Century: Sociocultural perspectives on the future of education.* London: Blackwell.

Lenhart, A., & Fox, S. (2006). *Bloggers. A portrait of the internet's new storytellers.* Report for Pew Internet and American Life Project. Washington DC.

Lenhart, A., & Fox, S. (2006). Bloggers: A portrait of the internet's new storytellers. Retrieved 12 November 2007 from: http://www.pewinternet.org/PPF/r/186/report_display.asp

Leslie, C. (2003). www.edtechpost.ca/gems/matrix2.gif, (01/24/2006).

Lessig, L. (2001). *The Future of Ideas: The Fate of the Commons in a Connected World.* Random House.

Leu, D., Mallette, M., Karcher, R., & Kara-Soteriou, J. (2005). Contextualising new literacies of information and communication technologies in theory, research and practice. In R. A. Karchmer, D. J. Leu, M. M. Mallette & J. Kara-Soteriou (Eds.), *Innovative approaches to literacy education: Using the Internet to support new literacies.* (pp. 1-12). Newark: International Reading Association.

Levin, H., & Rumberger, R. (1989). Education, work and employment in developed countries: Situation and future challenges. *Prospects, 19*(2), 205-224.

Levin, L. A., & Moore, J. A. (1977). Dialogue-Games: Metacommunication Structures for Natural Language Interaction. *Cognitive Science, 1*(4), 395-420.

Levine, F., Locke, C., Searls, D., & Weinberger, D. (1999). *The Cluetrain Manifesto.* New York: Cluetrain.

Levy, D. M. (2006). More, Faster, Better: Governance in an Age of Overload, Busyness, and Speed. *First Monday, special issue number 7* (September 2006).

Retrieved November 8th 2007, from: http://firstmonday.org/issues/special11_9/levy/index.html.

Levy, Y. (in press). Comparing dropouts and persistence in e-learning courses. *Computers & Education, 48*, 185-204.

Li, C. (2007) *Social technographics.* Available at: http://blogs.forrester.com/charleneli/2007/04/forresters_new_.html

Li, L., Helenius, M., & Berki, E. (2007). Phishing-Resistant Information Systems-Security Handling with Misuse-Cases. The Proceedings of E. Berki, J. Nummenmaa, I. Sunley, M. Ross, & G. Staples (Eds.), *Software Quality in the Knowledge Society* Software Quality Management XV, (pp. 389-404). BCS: GB, Swindon.

Liebowitz, J. (2001). Knowledge management and its link to artificial intelligence. *Expert Systems with Applications, 20*, 1-6.

Lim, C. P., & Chai, C. S. (in press). Teachers' pedagogical beliefs and their planning and conduct of computer-mediated classroom lessons. *British Journal of Educational Technology.*

Limberg, L. (2007). What matters: shaping meaningful learning through teaching information literacy Presentation at *Information: interactions and impact conference,* Aberdeen June.

Lin, C.-H., Li, L.-Y., Hu, W.-C., Chen, G.-D., & Liu, B.-J. (2007). Constructing an authentic learning community through Wiki for advanced group collaboration and knowledge sharing. In J. M. Spector, D. G. Sampson, T. Okamoto, Kinshuk, S. A. Cerri, M. Ueno, & A. Kashihara (Eds.), *Proceedings of the 7th International Conference on Advanced Learning Technologies (ICALT'07)* (pp. 342-344). Los Alamitos, CA: IEEE Computer Society.

Lindahl, C., & Blount, E. (2003). Weblogs: Simplifying Web Publishing. *Computer, 36*(11), 114-116.

Linden Research Inc. (2008). *About Second Life.* Retrieved April 21, 2008, from http://secondlife.com/

Linden Research Inc. (2008). About Second Life. Retrieved April 21, 2008, from http://secondlife.com/

Lindner, M. (2006). Use these tools, your mind will follow. Learning in immersive micromedia and microknowledge environments. In D. Whitelock & S. Wheeler (Eds.), *The next generation: Research proceedings of the 13th ALT-C conference* (pp. 41-49). Oxford, England: ALT.

Little, T.D., Hawley, P.H., Henrich, C.C., & Marsland, K.W. (2002). Three views of the agentic self: A developmental synthesis. In E. Deci & R. Ryan (Eds.), *Handbook of self-determination research* (pp. 390-404). Rochester, NY: University of Rochester Press.

Liu, W. (2006). Knowledge Exploitation, Knowledge Exploration, and Competency Trap. *Knowledge and Process Management, 13*(3), 144-161.

Liu, Y., & Shrum, L. J. (2002). What is interactivity and is it always such a good thing? Implications of definition, person, and situation for the influence of interactivity on advertising effectiveness. *Journal of advertising, 31*(4), 53-65.

Living Treasures of Los Alamos. Retrieved April 11, 2008, from http://livingtreasureslosalamos.org/default.asp

Livingstone, S., & Bober, M. (2005). *UK children go online: Final Report.* Swindon: ESRC.

Lockyer, L., Patterson, J. W., Rowland, G. S., & Hearne, D. B. (2007). ActiveHealth - Enhancing the Community of Physical and Health Educators through Online Technologies. In M. Keppell (Eds.), Instructional Design: Case Studies in Communities of Practice (pp. 331-348). Hershey, New York: Information Science Publishing.

Loedewyk, K., & Winne, P. (2005). Relations among the structure of learning tasks, achievement, and changes in self-efficacy in secondary students. *Journal of Educational Psychology, 97*(1), 3-12.

Loefler, I. J. (2000). Are generalists still needed in a specialized world? The renaissance of general surgery. *BMJ, 320*(7232), 436-40. Review.

Loertscher, D. V., & Woolls, B. (2002). *Information literacy: a review of the research. A guide for practitioners and researchers* 2ⁿᵈ Edition Salt Lake City: Hi Willow Publishing.

Lombard, M., & Ditton, T. (1997). At the heart of it all: The concept of presence. *Journal of Computer-Mediated Communication, 3*(2). Retrieved 12ᵗʰ November, 2007 from http://jcmc.indiana.edu/vol3/issue2/lombard.html

Lombardi, M. M. (2007). Authentic learning for the 21st century: An overview. In D. G. Oblinger (Ed.), *Educause Learning Initiative. Advancing learning through IT innovation* (pp. 1-12): EDUCAUSE.

Lorenz, K. (1977) *Behind the mirror: A search for the natural history of human knowledge.* New York: Harcourt Brace Jovanovich.

Lorenzo, G,. & Dziuban, C. (2006). *Ensuring the net generation is net savvy.* Washington, D.C.: EDUCAUSE. Retrieved July 10, 2007, from http://www.educause.edu/ir/library/pdf/ELI3006.pdf.

Lorenzo, G., & Dziuban, C. (2006). *Ensuring the Net-Generation is net savvy.* Washington, DC: EDUCAUSE. Retrieved on 7 April, 2008, from http://www.educause.edu/ir/library/pdf/ELI3006.pdf

Lorenzo, G., & Ittelson, J. (2005). *An Overview of E-Portfolios.* ELI Paper 1: 2005. Boulder: Educause Learning Initiative. Retrieved July 26, 2005 from http://www.educause.edu/ir/library/pdf/ELI3001.pdf

Love, D., McKean, G., & Gathercoal, P. (2002). Portfolios to Webfolios and beyond: levels of maturation. *EDUCAUSE Quarterly, 25*(2), 29-37.

Luke, A. (2006). On critical literacy: learning to question texts and discourses Keynote paper at *Bridging the Gap* Conference Yokohama November

Lynch, D. (2005). *Children's identity development in virtual spaces.* Unpublished Dissertation, McGill University, Montreal, QB.

Lytras, M. D., Naeve, A., & Pouloudi, A. (2005). A knowledge management roadmap for e-learning: The

way ahead. *International Journal of Distance Education Technologies, 3*(2), 68-75.

Ma, M., & Agarwal, R. (2007). Through a glass darkly: Information technology design, identity verification, and knowledge contribution in online communities. *Information Systems Research, 18*(1), 42-67.

Maarof, N. (2007). Telling his or her story through reflective journals *International Education Journal, 8*(1), 205-220.

Macgregor, G., & McCulloch, E. (2006). Collaborative Tagging as a Knowledge Organisation and Resource Discovery Tool. *Library Review, 55*(5).

Mackenzie, J. D. (1979). Question-begging in non-cummulative systems. *Journal of Philosophical Logic, 8*, 117-133.

Madden, M. (2007). On-line Video: PEW Internet and the American Life Project. Washington, DC.: PEW Research Center for People and the Press, URL (consulted 29 January 2008): http://www.pewinternet.org/PPF/r/219/report_display.asp

Mahoney, J. (1996). *Building the digital library. Networked information in an international context.* Paper presented at a Conference organized by Ukoln in conjunction with the British Library, CNI, CAUSE & JISC, Ramada Hotel, Heathrow, UK. 9ᵗʰ-10ᵗʰ February.

Male, S. A., Chapman, E. S, & Bush, M. B. (2007). Do female and male engineers rate different competencies as important? *Proceedings of the 2007 AaeE Conference*, Melbourne. The University of Melbourne, 2007. http://www.cs.mu.oz.au/aaee2007/papers/paper_61.pdf

Mangione, G. R., Cigognini, M. E., & Pettenati, M. C. (2007). Favouring a Critical, Creative and Ethical Use of the Network Resources Through Web 2.0 Applications. Proceedings from *Towards a Social Science of web 2.0 Conference*, 5 -6 September 2007, University of York, UK. Retrieved on 7 April, 2008, from http://www.york.ac.uk/res/siru/web2.0/cigognini.htm

March, J. (1991). Exploration and exploitation in organizational learning. *Organization Science*, 2, 71-87.

Marfleet, J. (2008). Enterprise 2.0 What's your game plan? What, if any, will be the role of the information. *Business Information Review, 25*(3), 152-157.

Margolis, E. (2001). *The hidden curriculum of higher education*. London: Routledge.

Markless, S., & Lincoln, P. (Eds.) (1986). *Tools for learning* British Library R and D Report 5892 London: British Library Board.

Markless, S., & Streatfield, D. R. (2000). *The really effective college library*. Library and Information Commission Research Report 51 Twickenham, Middx. IMA for the LIC.

Markless, S., & Streatfield, D. R. (2007). Three decades of information literacy: Redefining the parameters. In S. Andretta (Ed.), *Change and challenge: information literacy for the 21ˢᵗ century.* Adelaide: Auslib Press.

Markov, J. (2005). Web Content by and for the Masses. www.nytimes.com/2005/06/29/technology/29content.html (06/29/2005).

Markus, H.J., & Nurius, P.S. (1984). Self-understanding and self-regulation in middle childhood. In W. A. Collins (Ed.), *Development during middle childhood: The years from six to twelve.* Washington D.C: National Academy Press.

Marland, M. (Ed.) (1981). *Information skills in the secondary curriculum: the recommendations of a Working Group sponsored by the British Library and the Schools Council.* London: Methuen Educational

Maron, M. (2003). *the World as a Blog.* Retrieved on January, 17, 2007 from http://brainoff.com/geoblog/

Marques, J. M., Abrams, D., Paez, D., & Hogg, M. A. (2001). Social categorization, social identification, and rejection of deviant group members. In M. A. Hogg & S. Tinsdale (Eds.), *Blackwell handbook of social psychology: Group processes* (pp. 400-424). Malden, MA: Blackwell.

Martin, A. (2006). Literacies for the Digital Age. In A. Martin & D. Madigan (Eds.), *Digital literacies for learning.* London: Facet Publishing.

Martin, A. (2006a). The Landscape of Digital Literacy. *DigEuLit project.* Glasgow. Retrieved on 7 April, 2008, from http://www.digeulit.ec.

Martin, A. (2006b). Literacies for the digital age: preview of Part 1. In A. Martin & D. Madigan (Ed.), *Digital literacies for learning,* (pp. 3-25). London, Uk: Facet Publishing.

Martin, A., & Ashworth, S. (2004). Welcome to the Journal of eLiteracy!. *Journal of eLiteracy, 1*(1), 2 – 6. Retrieved on 7 April, 2008, from http://www.jelit.org/11/

Martin, C. (2003). Chronic illness care in General Practice – the practitioner-patient relationship. In C. Walker, C. Peterson, N. Milman, & C. Martin (Eds.), *Chronic Disease: New Perspectives and New Directions.* Melbourne: Tertiary Press.

Martin, J. (2003). Emergent persons. *New Ideas in Psychology, 21,* 85-99.

Martin, J. (2004). Self-regulated learning, social cognitive theory, and agency. *Educational Psychologist, 39*(2), 135-145.

Martin, J., Sugarman, J., & Thompson, J. (2003). *Psychology and the question of agency.* New York, NY: State University of New York Press.

Martindale, C. (1989). Personality, situation, and creativity. In J. A. Glover, R. R. Ronning, & C. R. Reynolds (Eds.), *Handbook of creutivdy* (pp. 211-232). New York, USA: Plenum.

Martinez-Miranda, J., & Arantza, A. (2005). Emotions in human and artificial intelligence. *In Journal Computers in Human Behaviour, 21,* 323–341.

Marton, F., & Saljo, R. (1976). On qualitative differences in learning-1: Outcome and process. *British Journal of Educational Psychology, 46,* 4-11.

Masie, E. (2005). *Nano-learning* [Podcast transcript]. Retrieved July 2, 2006, from http://www.masieweb.com/component/option,com_alphacontent/Itemid,122/section,9/cat,29/task,view/id,1321/.

Masie, E. (2006). Nano-learning: miniaturization of design. *Chief Learning Officer, 5*(1), 17.

Maslow, A. H. (1987). *Motivation and personality*. New York: HarperCollins.

Mason, B. L. (1998). E-Texts: The Orality and Literacy Issue Revisited. *Oral Tradition, 13*(2), 306-29.

Mason, R. (2002). Rethinking assessment for the online environment. In C. Vrasidas & G. Glass (Eds.), *Distance education and distributed learning.* (pp. 57-74). Greenwich, Co.: Information Age Publishing.

Mason, R., & Weller, M (2000). Factors affecting student satisfaction on a web course. Education at a distance. *Australian Journal of Educational Technology, 16*(2), 173-200.

Massachusetts Institute of Technology. (2008). *MIT OpenCourseWare*. Retrieved June 2, 2008, from http://ocw.mit.edu/.

Massey, B. L., & Levy, M. R. (1999). Interactive online journalism at English-language web newspapers in Asia. *Gazette, 61*(6), 523-538.

Mateer, G. D. (2007). *Teaching Economics with YouTube*. Retrieved March 3, 2008, from http://www.youtube.com/dmateer.

Mateer, G. D. (2008). *Teaching with YouTube: an economist's guide to free Web-based content.* Paper presented at the 2008 American Economic Association Conference, New Orleans, LA, January 4-6. Retrieved March 3, 2008, from http://www.aeaweb.org/annual_mtg_papers/2008/2008_669.pdf.

Materu, P. (2004). *Open source courseware: A baseline study.* The World Bank, Washington DC.

Mathes, A. (2004). *Folksonomies cooperative classification and communication through shared metadata.* Retrieved October 12, 2006, from http://www.adammathes.com/academic/computer-mediated communication/folksonomies.html.

Maturana, H. R., & Varela, F. J. (1980). *Autopoiesis and cognition. The realization of the living.* Dordrecht: Reidel.

Mayer Committee. (1992, September). *Key competencies.* (Report of the Committee to advise the Australian Education Council and Ministers of Vocational Education, Employment and Training on employment-related key competencies for postcompulsory education and training). Melbourne: Mayer Committee.

Mayes, T., & De Freitas, S. (2004). Review of E-Learning Theories, Frameworks and Models. *JISC E-Learning Models Desk Study.* JISC: 43.

Mayes, T., & Fowler, C (1999). Learning Technology and Usability. *Interacting with Computers, 11*, 485-497.

Mayes, T., & Fowler, C. (2006). Learners, learning literacy and pedagogy of e-learning. In A. Martin & D. Madigan (Ed.), *Digital literacies for learning*, (pp. 107-123). London, UK: Facet Publishing.

Mazer, J. P., Murphy, R. E., & Simonds, C. J. (2007). I'll see you on "Facebook": the effects of computer-mediated teacher self disclosure on student motivation, affective learning and classroom climate. *Communication Education, 56*(1), 1-17.

McAfee, A. P. (2006). Enterprise 2.0: The Dawn of Emergent Collaboration. *MIT Sloan Management Review, 47*(3), 21-28.

McAlister, S., Ravenscroft, A and Scanlon, E. (2004a). Combining interaction and context design to support collaborative argumentation using a tool for synchronous CMC, *Journal of Computer Assisted Learning: Special Issue: Developing dialogue for learning* 20/3, 194-204.

McAlister, S., Ravenscroft, A., & Scanlon, E. (2004b). Designing to promote improved online educational argumentation: an evaluation study, In *Networked Learning 2004.* Banks et al. Lancaster and Sheffield Universities, (pp. 541-548).

McCarthy, J., & Wright, P. (2005). *Technology as Experience*. Cambridge: MIT Press.

McCarty, S. (2005a). Similar proverbs in Chinese, Japanese, and English? *Japancasting* [weblog]. Retrieved March 10, 2007, from http://stevemc.blogmatrix.com/:entry:stevemc-2005-09-01-0000/.

McCarty, S. (2005b). Spoken Internet to go: popularization through podcasting. *The JALT CALL Journal, 1*(2), 67-74.

McCarty, S. (2006). *Japancasting* [weblog]. Retrieved December 3, 2006, from http://stevemc.blogmatrix.com.

McConnell, D. (2002). *Implementing computer supported cooperative learning*. London: Kogan-Page.

McCormack, A., Gore, J., & Thomas, K. (2004). *Learning to teach: Narratives from early career teachers*. Paper presented at the Australian Association for Research in Education, University of Melbourne, Melbourne.

McCrea, R. R., & Costa, P. T. Jr. (1987). Validation of the five-factor model of personality across instruments and observers. *Journal of Personality and Social Psychology, 66*, 574-83.

McDonald, J. (2003). Assessing online collaborative learning: process and product. *Computers & Education, 40*(4), 215-226.

McGill, L., Nicol, D., Littlejohn, A., Grierson, H., Juster, N., & Ion, W. (2005). Creating an information-rich learning environment to enhance design student learning: challenges and approaches. *British Journal of Educational Technology, 36*(4), 629-642.

McKelvie, G., Dotsika, F., & Patrick, K. (2007). Interactive business development, capturing business knowledge and practice: A case study. *The Learning Organization, 14*(5), 407-422.

McKenna, K. Y. A., Green, A. A., & Gleason, M. J. (2002). Relationship formation on the Internet: What's the big attraction? *Journal of Social Issues, 58*(1), 9-31.

McLagan, P. A. (1996). Great ideas revisited. *Training and Development, 50*(1), 60-65.

McLoughlin, C. & Lee, M. J. W. (2007). Social software and participatory learning: Pedagogical choices with technology affordances in the Web 2.0 era. *Proceedings Ascilite Conference, Singapore,* (pp. 664-675). www.ascilite.org.au/conferences/singapore07/procs/mcloughlin.pdf -

McLoughlin, C., & Luca, J (2001). Quality in Online Delivery: What does it Mean For Assessment in E-Learning Environments. Meeting at the Crossroads. *Proceedings of the Annual Conference of the Australasian Society for Computers in Learning in Tertiary Education (ASCILITE)*: http://www.ascilite.org.au/conferences/melbourne01/pdf/papers/mcloughlinc2.pdf [Accessed on February 14th 2008].

McLoughlin, C., & Oliver, R. (2000). Designing learning environments for cultural inclusivity: A case study of indigenous online learning at tertiary level. Electronic Version. *Australian Journal of Educational Technology, 16*, 58-72. Retrieved September 27, 2007, from http://www.ascilite.org.au/ajet/ajet16/mcloughlin.html

McLuhan, M. (1964). *Understanding Media*. London: Routledge.

McLuhan, M. (1989). *The Global Village: Transformations in World Life and Media in the 21st Century*. Oxford University Press, UK.

McMillan, D. W., & Chavis, D. M. (1986). Sense of community: A definition and theory. *Journal of Community Psychology, 14*(1), 6-23.

McMillan, S. J. (1999). Health communication and the internet: Relations between interactive characteristics of the medium and site creators, content, and purpose. *Health Communication, 11*(4), 375-390.

McMillan, S. J. (2002). A four-part model of cyber-interactivity: Some cyber-places are more interactive than others. *New Media and Society, 4*(2), 271-291.

Mcmillan, S. J., & Hwang, J. S. (2002). Measures of perceived interactivity: An exploration of the role of direction of communication, user control, and time in shaping perceptions of interactivity. *Journal of Advertising, 31*(3), 29-43.

McPherson, M., Smith-Lovin, L., & Cook, J. (2001). Birds of a feather: Homophily in social networks. *Annual Review of Sociology, 27*, 415-444.

McQuail, D. (2000). *McQuail's Mass Communication Theory.* London: Sage Publications.

McWhinney, I. R. (1996). The Importance of being Different. William Pickles Lecture 1996. *British Journal of General Practice, 46*(7), 433-436

Mead, G.H. (1932). *The philosophy of the present.* Chicago, IL: University of Chicago Press.

Mead, G.H. (1934). *Mind, self and society from the standpoint of a social behaviorist.* Chicago, Il: Chicago University Press.

Mejias, U. (2005). A nomad's guide to learning and social software. *The Knowledge Tree: An e-Journal of Learning Innovation, 7.* Retrieved November 10, 2006, from http://knowledgetree.flexiblelearning.net.au/edition07/html/la_mejias.html.

Mejias, U. (2005, November 23, 2005). A nomad's guide to learning and social software. *Knowledge Tree Journal, 7,* from http://flexiblelearning.net.au/knowledgetree/edition07/download/la_mejias.pdf

Melo, M. (2005). "Web Are You? Networked Emoticon Device". *Mauricio Melo Design.* Retrieved 12th November, 2007, from http://www.mauriciomelo.com/contents/interact05.htm

Menell, B. (2005). Atomization of learning (Beyond the learning object). *Learning 2.0,* [weblog], November. Retrieved January 8, 2006, from http://learning20.blogspot.com/2005/11/atomization-of-learning-beyond.html.

Mentor, K. (2007). Open access learning environments. *Online Journal of Distance Learning Administration.* Retrieved April 2007 from http://www.westga.edu/%7Edistance/ojdla/spring101/mentor101.htm

Mercer, N. (2000). *Words and Minds: how we use language to think together.* London: Routledge.

MERLOT. (2008). Retrieved February 19, 2008, from http://www.merlot.org/.

Merlyn, P. R., & Välikangas, L. (1998). From information technology to knowledge technology: Taking the user into consideration. *Journal of Knowledge Management, 2*(2), 28-35.

Merriam-Webster Online Dictionary (2007). Definition of " attitude". Retrieved on 7th April 2008, from http://www.merriam-webster.com/

Metaxiotis, K., Ergazakis, K. & Psarras, J. (2005). Exploring the world of knowledge management: agreements and disagreements in the academic/practitioner community. *Journal of knowledge management, 9*(2), 6-18.

Metid Center (2007). *Workshops on Web 2.0 in the classroom.* Politecnico of Milan, Retrieved on 7 April, 2008, from http://www.sidelab.com/workshops.htm

Mezirow, J. (1990). *Fostering critical reflections in adulthood: A guide to transformative and emancipatory learning.* San Francisco, CA: Jossey-Bass Publishers.

Midoro, V. (2007). Quale alfabetizzazione per la società della conoscenza? *TD - Tecnologie Didattiche, 41*(2), 47-54, Ortona, Svizzera: Menabò Edizioni.

Miettinen, M., Kurhila, J., Nokelainen, P., & Tirri, H. (2005). OurWeb - Transparent groupware for online communities. Paper presented at the Web Based Communities 2005, Algarve, Portugal.

Miles, M., & Huberman, A. (1984). *Qualitative Data Analysis.* London: Sage.

Miles, R. E., & Snow, C. C. (1995). The new network firm: A spherical structure built on a human investment philosophy. *Personnel Journal, 67,* 5-18.

Miller, D. B. (2006). Podcasting at the University of Connecticut: enhancing the educational experience. *Campus Technology,* October 18. Retrieved April 10, 2007, from http://campustechnology.com/news_article.asp?id=19424&typeid=156.

Miller, D. B. (2007). *iCube*. Retrieved April 10, 2007, from http://icube.uconn.edu/.

Milligan, C., Johnson, M., Sharples, P., Wilson, S., & Liber, O. (2006). Developing a reference model to describe the personal learning environment. In W. Nejdl & K. Tochtermann (Eds.), *Innovative approaches for learning and knowledge sharing - first european conference on technology enhanced learning, ec-tel 2006* (pp. 506-511). Berlin/Heidelberg: Springer.

Milne, A. J. (2007). Entering the interaction age: implementing a future vision for campus learning spaces. *EDUCAUSE Review, 42*(1), 12-31.

MIT (2006). *2005 Program Evaluation Findings Summary*. http://ocw.mit.edu/ans7870/global/05_Eval_Summary.pdf

Montgomery, J. D. (1992). Job search and network composition: Implications of the strength-of-weak ties hypothesis. *American Sociological Review, 57*(5), 586-596.

Moore, J. W. (2003). Are textbooks dispensable? *Journal of Chemical Education, 80*(4), 359.

Moore, M. (1989). Three types of interaction. *The American Journal of Distance Education, 3*(2), 1-6.

Moore, M. G., & Kearsley, G. (1996). *Distance Education: A Systems View.* Belmont, CA: Wadsworth.

Moore, M., & Kearsley, G. (2005). Distance education: A systems view. (2nd ed.). Belmont, CA: Thomson Wadsworth.

Moore, P. (1997). Teaching information problem solving in primary schools: an information literacy survey. *J of Contemporary Educational Psychology, 20*, 1-31.

Moore, P. (2005). An analysis of information literacy education worldwide in School. *Libraries Worldwide, 11*(2), 1-23.

Mortensen, T., & Walker, J. (2002). Blogging Thoughts: Personal Publication as an online Research Tool. In A. Morrison (Ed.), *Researching ICTs in Context.* Oslo. Intermedia, University of Oslo.

Muniz, A. M., & O'Guinn, T. C. (2001). Brand community. *Journal of Consumer Research, 27*(1), 412-432.

Munroe, R. L. (2000). Ethnography. In A. E. Kadzin (Ed.), *Encyclopedia of Psychology* (Vol. 3, pp. 267-269). Washington, DC: American Psychological Association.

Murray, E., Lo, B., Pollack, L., Donelan, K., Catania, J., White, M. et al. (2003). The impact of health information on the internet on the physician-patient relationship: patient perceptions. *Arch Intern Med., 163*, 1727-34.

MySpace, Inc. (2008). About MySpace. Retrieved April 21, 2008, from http://www.myspace.com/index.cfm?fuseaction=misc.aboutus

MySpace, Inc. (2008). About MySpace. Retrieved April 21, 2008, from http://www.myspace.com/index.cfm?fuseaction=misc.aboutus

Na Ubon, A., & Kimble, C. (2002). Knowledge management in online distance education. *Proceedings of the 3rd International Conference Networked Learning 2002,* University of Sheffield, UK, March 2002, 465-473.

Nardi, B. A., Schiano, D. J., & Gumbrecht, M. (2004). Blogging as social activity, or, would you let 900 million people read your diary? In *Proceedings of the 2004 ACM conference on Computer supported cooperative work,* New York, (pp. 222-228).

Nardi, B., Schiano, D., & Gumbrecht, M. (2004). Blogging as Social Activity, or, Would You Let 900 Million People Read Your Diary? *Proc. of CSCW'04, 3*(6), 222-231.

National Board of Employment, Education and Training. (1994). *Converging Communications and Computer Technologies: Implications for Australia's Future Employment and Skills.* Victoria: Australian Government Publishing Service.

Naumer, C., Fisher, K., & Dervin, B. (2008). *Sense-Making: A Methodological Perspective.* Paper presented at the CHI 2008, Florence, Italy. ACM.

NCREL. (2003). 21st Century Skills enGauge ® 21st Century Skills: Literacy in the Digital Age. Online. Accessed 11.11.07 (http://www.ncrel.org/engauge/skills/agelit.htm)

Neisser, U. (1994). Multiple systems: A new approach to cognitive theory. *The European Journal of Cognitive Psychology, 6*(3), 225-241.

Neji, M., & Ben Ammar, M. (2007). Agent-based Collaborative Affective e-Learning Framework. *The Electronic Journal of e Learning, 5*(2), 123-134.

Newcomb, T. M. (1961). *The acquaintance process.* Holt, Rinehart and Winston.

Newhagen, J. E., Cordes, J. W., & Levy, M. R. (1995). Nightly@ nbc. com: Audience scope and the perception of interactivity in viewer mail on the internet. *Journal of Communication, 45*(3), 164-75.

Newman, N. (2005). Power laws, pareto distributions and zipf's law. *Contemporary Physics, 46*, 323-351.

Nicolosi, J. (1991). **Constructing ethnicity: Creating and recreating ethnic identity and culture.** *Reparative therapy of male homosexuality.* Northvale: Jason Aronson.

Nielsen, A. P. (2006). Understanding dynamic capabilities through knowledge management. *Journal of Knowledge Management, 10*(4), 59-71.

Nkambou, R. (2006). Towards Affective Intelligent Tutoring System. Workshop on Motivational and Affective Issues in ITS. 8th International Conference on ITS 2006, (pp 5-12).

Noam, E. M. (1995). Electronics and the Dim Future of the University. *Science, 270*, 13 October 1995, 247-249

Nocera, Abdelnour J. L. (1998). Virtual Environments as Spaces of Sympolic Construction and Cultural Identity: Latin-American Virtual Communities. In C. Ess & F. Sudweeks (Eds.), *Proceedings of Cultural Attitudes Towards Communication and Technology '98*, Sydney, Australia, (pp. 193-195).

Nonaka, I., & Takeuchi, H. (1995). *The knowledge-creating company: how Japanese companies create the dynamics of innovation.* New York, NY: Oxford University Press.

Nonaka, I., & Takeuchi, H. (1995). *The Knowledge-Creating Company.* New York, NY: Oxford University Press.

Nonaka, I., & Toyama, R. (2003). The knowledge-creating theory revisited: knowledge creation as a synthesizing process. *Knowledge Management Research and Practice, 1*(1), 2-10.

Norman G. R., & Schmidt, H. G. (2000). Effectiveness of problem-based learning curricula: theory, practice and paper darts. *Medical Education, 34*(9), 721–728.

Norman, D. (1988). *The design of everyday things.* New York: Basic Books.

Norman, D. (2004). *Emotional Design: Why we love or hate everyday things.* New York: Basic Books.

Norman, D. A. (1988). *The psychology of everyday things.* New York: Basic Books.

Nov, O. (2007). What motivates Wikipedians? *Commun. ACM 50, 11* (Nov. 2007), 60-64.

Novak, T. P., Hoffman, D. L., & Yung, Y. F. (2000). Measuring the customer experience in online environments: A structural modeling approach. *Marketing Science, 19*(1), 22-42.

Nowak, A., Vallacher, R.R., Tesser, A., & Borkowski, W. (2000). Society of self: The emergence of collective properties in self-structure. *Psychological Review, 39*, 39-61.

Nunan, T. (1996) *Flexible Delivery - What is it and Why a part of current educational debate?* Paper presented at the Higher Education Research and Development Society of Australasia Annual Conference Different Approaches: Theory and Practice in Higher Education Perth, Western Australia, 8-12 July, 1996.

Nussbaum, E. (2007). Kids, the Internet and the end of privacy. *The Weekend Australian Magazine* March 23-24, (pp. 23-27).

O'Conner, M. (2002). *Personal Knowledge Management (PKM).* Millikin University Report. Retrieved on 7 April, 2008, from http://www.millikin.edu/webmaster/pkm/

O'Connor, T., & Wong, H.Y. (2002). Emergent properties. In E. N. Zalta (Ed.), *Stanford encyclopedia of philosophy*. Stanford, CA: The Metaphysics Research Lab, Stanford University.

O'mahony, S., & Ferraro, F. (2003). Managing the boundary of an 'Open' project. Retrieved on January, 17, 2007 from http://opensource.mit.edu/papers/omahonyferraro.pdf

O'Reilly, T. (2004). Open Source Paradigm Shift. [Online at: http://tim.oreilly.com/articles/paradigmshift_0504.html] (Retrieved 15 February, 2007).

O'Reilly, T. (2005) *What is Web 2.0: design patterns and business models for the next generation of software*. Retrieved December 15, 2006, from http://www.oreillynet.com/pub/a/oreilly/tim/news/2005/09/30/what-is-web-20.html.

O'Reilly, T. (2005). What Is Web 2.0 - Design Patterns and Business Models for the Next Generation of Software. Retrieved 20.04.2007, from http://www.oreillynet.com/pub/a/oreilly/tim/news/2005/09/30/what-is-web-20.html

O'Reilly, T. (2005). *What is Web 2.0? Design patterns and business models for the next generation of software*. Retrieved November 1, 2007 from http://www.oreilly.com/lpt/a/6228.

O'Reilly, T. (2005). *What is Web 2.0?* www.oreilly.de/artikel/web20.html (11/13/2007).

O'Reilly, T. (2005). *What is Web 2.0?: Design Patterns and Business Models for the Next Generation of Software* http://www.oreillynet.com/pub/a/oreilly/tim/news/2005/09/30/what-is-web-20.html

Oberholzer, F., & Koleman, S. (2004). *The Effect of File Sharing on Record Sales An Empirical Analysis*. http://www.unc.edu/~cigar/papers/FileSharing_March2004.pdf

Oblinger, D. (2004). Boomers, gen-exers and millenials: Understanding the new students. *EDUCAUSE Review, 38*(4), 37-47.

Oblinger, D. G. (2005). Learners, learning and technology. *EDUCAUSE review, September/October*, 66-75.

Oblinger, D., & Oblinger J. (2005). *Educating the Net Generation*. EDUCASE. Retrieved on 7 April, 2008, from http://www.educause.edu/content.asp?PAGE_ID=5989&bhcp=1

Oblinger, D., & Oblinger, J. (2005). Is It Age or IT: First Steps Toward Understanding the Net Generation. In D. G. Oblinger & J. L. Oblinger (Eds.), *Educating the Net Generation,*(p.21). EDUCAUSE, Washington, D.C.

Oblinger, D., & Oblinger, J. (Eds.) (2005). *Educating the net generation*. Educause. www.educause.edu/educatingthenetgen/

OECD (2005). *E-learning in tertiary education: Where do we stand?* Paris:OECD

OECD (2005). E-learning in Tertiary Education: Where Do We Stand? *Education & Skills 2005*, 2005(4), 1–293.

Ofcom (2003). Media Literacy Audit - Report on adult media literacy. at http://www.ofcom.org.uk/advice/media_literacy/medlitpub/medlitpubrss/medialit_audit/, accessed 20 June 2007.

Okada, A. (2005). The Collective Building of Knowledge in Collaborative Learning Environments. In T. Roberts (Org.), *Computer-Supported Collaborative Learning in Higher Education*. 1 ed. Idea Groups. London, v. 1, p. 70-99.

Okada, A., & Buckingham Shum, S. (2006). Knowledge Mapping With Compendium in Academic Research And Online Education. 22nd ICDE World Conference, 3-6 Sept. 2006, Rio de Janeiro [www.icde22.org.br]

Okada, A., Buckingham Shum, S., & Sherborne, T. (2008, forthcoming). *Knowledge Cartography: software tools and mapping techniques*. London: Springer.

OLPC (2007). *One Laptop Per Child*. wiki.laptop.org/go/Home. (11/13/2007).

Ong, W. J. (1982). *Orality and Literacy*. London: Routledge.

Online Encyclopedia of Criminal Justice. (2007). Retrieved November 15, 2007, from http://cjencyclopedia.com.

Ontology works, inc. What is Ontology? (2008). http://www.ontologyworks.com/what_is_ontology.php

Ontology-computer science. (2007, Aug 12) In Wikipedia. Retrieved oct 7th 2007 from http://en.wikipedia.org/wiki/Ontology_%28computer_science%29

Open Source Initiative (2007). Retrieved on January, 17, 2007 from http://www.opensource.org/

Openlearn (2006). Retrieved on January, 17, 2008 from http://www.open.ac.uk/openlearn/home.php

Oravec, J. A. (2003). Blending by blogging: weblogs in blended learning initiatives. *Journal of Educational Media, 28*(2-3), 225-233.

Organisation for Economic Co-operation and Development (2007). *Giving knowledge for free: The emergence of open educational resources.* Available online at: http://213.253.134.43/oecd/pdfs/browseit/9607041E.PDF

Osgood, H. M., William, C. E., & Murray, S. M. (1975). *Cross-cultural universals of affective meaning.* University of Illinois Press, Urbana.

Owen, M., Grant, L., Sayers, S., & Facer, K. (2006). *Opening Education: Social Software and Learning.* Bristol: Futurelab. [Online at: www.futurelab.org.uk/research] (Retrieved 20 November, 2006).

Owen, M., Grant, L., Sayers, S., & Facer, K. (2006). *Social software and learning.* Bristol, England: Futurelab. Retrieved April 11, 2007, from http://www.futurelab.org.uk/resources/documents/opening_education/Social_Software_report.pdf.

Owen, R., Grant, L., Sayers, S., & Facer, K. (2006). Social sofware and learning. *FutureLab.* Bristol, UK. Available at: http://www.futurelab.org.uk/research/opening_education/social_software_01.htm [Accessed 20 January, 2007].

Paavola, S., & Hakkarainen, K. (2005). The knowledge creation metaphor – An emergent epistemological approach to learning. *Science and Education, 14*(6), 535-557.

Palfrey, J. (2008). *Born Digital: Understanding the First Generation of Digital Natives (Hardcover).* New York, USA: Basic Books.

Palfrey, J., Gasser, U., & Weinberger, D. (2007). Digital Born. *John Palfrey. From the Bercam Center at haverval Law School.* Retrieved on 7 April, 2008, from http://blogs.law.harvard.edu/palfrey/2007/10/28/born-digital/

Palloff, R., & Pratt, K. (1999). *Building learning communities in Cyberspace.* San Francisco: Jossey-Bass.

Palloff, R., & Pratt, K. (2007). *Building Online Learning Communities.* San Franscisco, Jossey-Bass.

Palser, B. (2006). Artful disguises: sultans of spin masquerade as amateurs on citizen media Web sites. *American Journalism Review,* Issue October/November 2006, URL (consulted 31 July 2007): http://www.ajr.org/Article.asp?id=4215

Papadimitriou, C. (2003). *Turing (A novel about computation).* MIT Press, Cambridge, MA.

Papert, S. (1980). *Mindstorms: Children, computers and powerful ideas.* Brighton, Sussex: Harvester Press.

Papert, S. (2000). What's the big idea? Steps toward a pedagogy of idea power. *IBM Systems Journal, 39*(3-4), 720-729.

Papert, S., & Harel, I. (1991). *Constructionism.* New Jersey: Ablex Publishing Corp.

Paquet, S. (2003). *A socio-technological approach to sharing knowledge across disciplines.* Universite de Montreal.

Park, D., & Moro, Y. (2006). Dynamics of Situation Definition. *Mind, Culture, and Activity, 13*(2), 101-129.

Parsons, T. (1968). *The Structure of Social Action.* New York, NY: Free Press.

Passman, P. (2007). *Microsoft unlimited potential: Enabling sustained social and economic opportunity in the Unites States and around the world.* Online. Accessed 04.11.07. http://www.microsoft.com/about/adulteducation.mspx

Patel, N. (2003). Deferred System's Design: Countering the Primacy of Reflective IS Development With Action-Based Information Systems. In N. Patel (Ed.), Adaptive Evolutionary Information Systems (pp. 1-29). London: Idea Group Publishing.

Paton, S. (2005). *In Search of the Knowledge Worker. Labour Process Conference 2005.* Glasgow: University of Strathclyde. Retrieved April 29, 2008 from http://www.hrm.strath.ac.uk/ILPC/2005/conf-papers/Paton.pdf

Patrick, K., & Dotsika, F. (2007). Knowledge sharing: developing from within. *The Learning Organization, 14*(5), 395-406.

Paulsen, M. (1995). *The online report on pedagogical techniques for computer-mediated communication.* Available: http://www.emoderators.com/moderators/cmcped.html [Accessed on 10th November 2006].

Pauwels, L. (2002). Families on the Web. In D. Newman (Ed.), *Sociology: Exploring the Architecture of Everyday Life* (pp. 231-235). Fourth Edition, Thousand Oaks, CA: Pine Forge. P.

Pauwels, L. (2005). Websites as visual and multimodal cultural expressions: opportunities and issues of on line hybrid media research. Media, culture & society, 27(4), 604-613.

Pauwels, L. (2006). Ethical Issues of On-line (Visual) Research. *Visual Anthropology, 19*(3-4), 365-369. Taylor & Francis.

Pauwels, L. (2008). A Private Visual Practice Going Public? Social Functions and Sociological Research Opportunities of Web-based Family Photography. *Visual Studies, 23*(1). Routledge.

PBwiki. (2007). Retrieved September 7, 2007, from http://pbwiki.com/

PC Magazine (2006). July 2006.

Peal, D., & Wilson, B. (2001). Activity theory and web-based training. In B. H. Khan (Ed.), *Web-based Training.* New Jersey: Educational Technology Publications.

Peña-López, I. (2006). Position Paper for the Bazaar Seminar Hey Dude, Where's My Data? In *ICTlogy*, (37). Barcelona: ICTlogy. Retrieved October 24, 2006 from http://ictlogy.net/review/?p=471

Peña-López, I. (2007). Skills of an expert knower 2.0/leaner 2.0. *ICTlogy.* Retrieved on 7 April, 2008, from http://ictlogy.net/20071107-skills-of-an-expert-knower-20leaner-20/

Peña-López, I., Córcoles, C., & Casado, C. (2006). El Profesor 2.0: docencia e investigación desde la Red. In *UOC Papers*, (3). Barcelona: UOC. Retrieved October 10, 2006 from http://www.uoc.edu/uocpapers/3/dt/esp/pena_corcoles_casado.pdf

Penrod, D. (2007). *Using blogs to enhance literacy: The next powerful step in 21st century learning.* London: Rowman & Littlefield Education.

Perkins, D. N., & Salomon, G. (1992). Transfer of learning. In *International encyclopedia of education,* 2nd edition. Oxford, Pergamon Press.

Perlow, L. (1999). The time famine: Toward a sociology of work time. *Administrative Science Quarterly, 44*(1), \ 57–81, and at http://interruptions.net/literature/Perlow-ASQ99.pdf

Peters, J., & Cornu, R. L. (2006). *Successful early career teaching: More than engaging pedagogy.* Paper presented at the AARE 2006 International education research conference, Adelaide.

Petros, P. (2003). Non-linearity in clinical practice. *Journal of Evaluation in Clinical Practice, 9*(2),171-178.

Pettenati, M. C., & Cigognini, M. E. (2007). Social networking theories and tools to support connectivist learning activities. *International Journal of Web-Based Learning and Teaching Technologies (IJWLTT), 2*(3), 39-57, July-September 2007, Idea Group Inc.

Pettenati, M. C., Cigognini M. E., & Sorrentino, F. (2007a). Methods and tools for developing personal knowledge management skills in the connectivist era. Proceedings from *EDEN 2007 Conference NEW LEARNING 2.0? Emerging digital territories Developing continuities, New divides,* EDEN 2007 Annual Conference, 13-16 JUNE, 2007, Naples, Italy.

Pettenati, M. C., Cigognini, E., Mangione, J., Guerin, E. (2007). Using social software for personal knowledge management in formal online learning. *Turkish Online Journal of Distance Education, 8*(3). Retrieved April 23, 2008, from http://tojde.anadolu.edu.tr/tojde27/index.htm

Pettenati, M. C., Cigognini, M. E., Mangione, G. R., & Guerin, E. (2007b). Use of Social software for knowledge construction and management in formal online learning. *Turkish Online Journal of Distance Education (TOJDE), 8*(3). Retrieved on 7th April 2008, from http://tojde.anadolu.edu.tr/

Pew Internet and American Life Project (2004). *Faith online.* Available at http://www.pewinternet.org/pdfs/PIP_Faith_Online_2004.pdf , last accessed 4/29/2008.

Piaget, J. (1977). *The development of thought: Equilibrium of cognitive structures.* New York: Viking.

Piccoli, G., Ahmad, R., & Ives, B. (2000). Knowledge management in academia: A proposed framework. In *Information Technology and Management, 1*(4), 229-245. Hingham: Kluwer Academic Publishers. Retrieved May 09, 2006 from http://www.springerlink.com/index/M56672931049044P.pdf

Pierce, T. (2007). *Women, weblogs, and war: Digital culture and gender performativity. three case studies of online discourse by muslim cyberconduits of Afghanistan, Iran, and Iraq.* ProQuest Information & Learning, US.

Pintrich, P. (2000). The role of goal orientation in self-regulated learning. In M. Boekaerts, P. Pintrich & M. Zeidner (Eds.), *Handbook of Self-Regulations* (pp. 451-502). San Diego, CA: Academic Press.

Plato "The Phaedrus," trans. by Alexander Nehamas and Paul Woodruff. In John M. Cooper (editor), *Plato:*

Complete Works, Indianapolis, IN: Hacket Publishing, (1997).

Polanyi M. (1958). *Personal Knowledge. Towards a Post-Critical Philosophy.* London: Routledge.

Polanyi, M. (1966). *The Tacit Dimension.* Gloucester, MA: Peter Smith.

Polanyi, M. (1967). *The Tacit Dimension.* New York: Anchor Books.

Polhemus, L., Shih, L., Richardson, J., & Swan, K. (2000). *Building and Affective Learning Community: Social Presence and Learning Engagement.* Paper presented at the World Conference on the WWW and the Internet (WebNet) San Antonio.

Polsani, P. R. (2003). Network learning. In K. Nyíri (Ed.), *Mobile learning: essays on philosophy, psychology, and education.* Vienna, Austria: Pasagen Verlag.

Porter, C. E. (2004). A typology of virtual communities: A multi-disciplinary foundation for future research. *Journal of Computer-Mediated Communication, 10*(1).

Poster, M. (1995). *The Second Media Age.* Cambridge: Polity Press.

Poster, M. (1996). *The second media age.* Cambridge: Polity Press.

Postmas, T. (2007). The psychological dimensions of collective action, online. In A. Joinson, K. McKenna, T. Postmes, & U. Reips (Eds.), *Oxford Handbook of Internet Psychology.* (pp. 165-184). Oxford: Oxford University Press.

Postmes, T., Haslam, A., & Swaab, R. (2005). Social influence in small groups: An interactive model of social identity formation. *Europen Review of Social Psychology, 16,* 1-42. Retrieved June 2007 from http://psy.ex.ac.uk/~tpostmes/PDF/PostmesHaslamSwaabERSP05.pdf

Postmes, T., Spears, R., & Lea, M. (1998). Breaching or building social boundaries? SIDE-effects of computer-mediated communication. *Communication Research, 25*(6), 689-715.

Postmes, T., Spears, R., & Lea, M. (2002). Intergroup differentiation in computer-mediated communication: Effects of depersonalization. *Group dynamics: Theory, research, and practice, 6*(1), 3-16.

Preece, J. (2000). *Online Communities: Designing usability, supporting sociability.* John Wiley and Sons, Chichester.

Preece, J., Nonnecke, B., & Andrews, D. (2004). The top five reasons for lurking: improving community experiences for everyone. Computers in Human Behavior, 20(2), 210-223.

Prensky, (2001). *Digital Game-Based Learning.* McGraw-Hill Education.

Prensky, M. (2001). Digital natives, digital immigrants. *On the Horizon, 9*, 5.

Prensky, M. (2001). Digital Natives, Digital Immigrants. *On the Horizon, NCB University Press, 9*(5).

Prensky, M. (2001). Digital natives, digital immigrants. *On the Horizon, 9*(5) (October) www.markprensky. com/writing/Prensky%20-%20Digital%20Natives.%2 0Digital%20Immigrants%20-%20Part1.pdf [Accessed 21 December 2007]

Prensky, M. (2007). How to Teach With Technology -- keeping both teachers and students comfortable in an era of exponential change. *BECTA's Emerging Technologies for Learning, 2*, 4.

Prescott, L. (2007). *Hitwise US Consumer Generated Media Report, Feb 2007.*

Press, L. (2005). bpastudio.csudh.edu/fac/lpress/471/ blogfeedback.htm (04/30/2008)

Proboscis. (2003). *Urban Tapestries.* Retrieved 17.06.2007, from http://research.urbantapestries.net/

Prusak, L. (2000). Interviewed in "How Virtual Communities Enhance Knowledge", *Knowledge@Wharton*, March 21, 2000, available at http://knowledge.wharton. upenn.edu/article.cfm?articleid=152, last accessed 4/29/2008.

Puddifoot, J. (1995). Dimensions of Community Identity. Journal of Community & Applied Social Psychology, 5(5), 357-370.

Pullinger, K., & Joseph, C. (2007). "Inanimate Alice," at http://www.inanimatealice.com/, accessed 20 June 2007.

Pullinger, K., Schemat, S., & Joseph, C. (2004). The Breathing Wall. CD-ROM and at http://www.thebreathingwall.com, accessed 20 June 2007.

Putz, P., & Arnold, P. (2001). Communities of Practice: guidelines for the design of online seminars in higher education. *Education, Communication & Information*, 1(2), 181-195.

Rafael, M. L. G. (2001). *Sensing the presence of others in a work environment. Design and implementation of an awareness system: SIBO* (Sign-in Board Online). Masters thesis, Royal Institute of Technology, Stockholm. Retrieved 12th November, 2007, from ftp://ftp.nada.kth. se/IPLab/TechReports/IPLab-191.pdf

Rafaeli, S., Dan-Gur, Y., & Barak, M. (2005). Social recommender systems: Recommendations in support of e-learning. *Journal of Distance Education Technologies, 3*(2), 30-47.

Rainie, L., (2007). *28% of Online Americans Have Used the Internet to Tag Content.* Pew Internet & American Life Project. Retrieved June 2007 from http://www. pewinternet.org/pdfs/PIP_Tagging.pdf.

Ramsey, C. (2003). Using virtual learning environments to facilitate new learning relationships. *International Journal of Management Education, 3*(2), 31-41.

Ravenscroft, A. (2000). Designing Argumentation for Conceptual Development, *Computers and Education, 34*, 241-255. Elsevier Science Ltd.

Ravenscroft, A. (2001). Designing e-learning interactions in 21C: Revisiting and re-thinking the role of theory. *European Journal of Education: Special edition on On-line Learning, 36*(2), 133-156.

Ravenscroft, A. (2004). Towards highly communicative eLearning communities: Developing a socio-cultural framework for cognitive change. In Land, R and Bayne, S. (Eds.) *Cyberspace Education*, Routledge, Chapter 9, (pp. 130-145).

Ravenscroft, A. (2007). Promoting Thinking and Conceptual Change with Digital Dialogue Games, *Journal of Computer Assisted Learning (JCAL)*, *23*(6), 453-465.

Ravenscroft, A., & Cook, J. (2007). New Horizons in Learning Design. In H. Beetham & R. Sharpe (Eds.), *Rethinking pedagogy for the digital age: Designing and delivering e-learning* (pp. 207-218).Routledge.

Ravenscroft, A., & McAlister, S. (2006a). Digital Games and Learning in Cyberspace: A Dialogical Approach, *E-Learning* Journal, Special Issue of *Ideas in Cyberspace 2005 Symposium*, *3*(1), 38-51.

Ravenscroft, A., & McAlister, S. (2006b). Designing interaction as a dialogue game: Linking social and conceptual dimensions of the learning process. In C. Juwah, (Ed.), *Interactions in Online Education: implications for theory and practice* (pp 73-90). Routledge.

Ravenscroft, A., & Pilkington, R. M. (2000). Investigation by Design: Developing Dialogue Models to Support Reasoning and Conceptual Change. *International Journal of Artificial Intelligence in Education: Special Issue on Analysing Educational Dialogue Interaction: From Analysis to Models that Support Learning*, *11*(1), 273-298.

Ravenscroft, A., McAlister, S., & Baur, E. (2006). *Development, piloting and evaluation of InterLoc: An Open Source tool supporting dialogue games in education*. Final Project Report to UK JISC (Joint Information Systems Committee), Bristol, UK.

Ravenscroft, A., Sagar, M., & Baur, E. (2007). Cross-institutional implementation and evaluation of digital dialogue games for inclusive and personalised learning. *Annual Report to UK Joint Information Systems Committee (JISC)*, November 2007.

Ravenscroft, A., Wegerif, R. B., & Hartley, J.R. (2007). Reclaiming thinking: dialectic, dialogic and learning in the digital age, British *Journal of Educational Psychology*

Monograph Series, Learning through Digital Technologies, Underwood., J & Dockrell, J. (Guest Eds), Series II, Issue 5, (pp 39-57).

Ravitz, J., & Hoadley, C. (2005). Supporting change and scholarship through review of online resource in professional development settings. *British Journal of Educational Technology, 36*(6), 957-974.

Raymond, E. (2000). *The Cathedral and the Bazaar*. http://catb.org/~esr/writings/cathedral-bazaar/cathedral-bazaar/index.html

Raymond, E. S. (1999). *The Cathedral & the Bazaar*. (revised edition: original edition 1999). Sebastopol: O'Reilly.

Raymond, E. S. (2001). *The Cathedral and the Bazaar: Musings on Linux and the Open Source by an Accidental Revolutionary*. O'Reilly.

Read, B. (2005). Drexel U. will give free iPods to students in School of Education. *The Chronicle of Higher Education*, March 2. Retrieved May 8, 2005, from http://chronicle.com/free/2005/03/2005030203n.htm.

Reagle, J. (2004). Open content communities. M/C: A Journal of Media and Culture, 7. Retrieved on January, 17, 2008 from <http://journal.media-culture.org.au/0406/06_Reagle.rft.php>.

Reeves, T. C., Herrington, J., & Oliver, R. (2004). A development research agenda for online collaborative learning. *Educational Technology Research & Development, 52*(4), 53-65.

Remenyi, D., Williams, B., Money, A., & Swartz, E. (1998). *Doing research in Business and Management: an introduction to process and Method*. London: SAGE Publications.

Renner, W. (2006). Proceedings from EDU-COM 2006. Nong Khai:Thailand:Publisher?

Renninger, K. A., & Shumar, W. (2002). *Building Virtual Communities Learning and Change in Cyberspace. Learning in Doing: Social, Cognitive & Com-*

putational Perspectives. Cambridge University Press, Cambridge.

Rheingold, H. (1993). A Slice of Life in my Virtual Community. In L. Harasim (Ed.), *Global Networks: Computers and International Communication*. Cambridge, MA: MIT Press.

Rheingold, H. (1993). *The Virtual Community*. Harper-Collins, New York.

Rheingold, H. (1993). *The virtual community: home-steading on the electronic frontier*. Cambridge: Addison-Wesley.

Rheingold, H. (2002). *Smart mobs: The next social revolution*. Cambridge, MA: Perseus Publishing.

Rhie, K. (2000). From Desktop to Webtop: Achieving True Computing Freedom, Anytime, Anywhere. *Proceedings of the AACE WebNet conference*, Chesapeake, VA, URL (consulted 29 January 2008): http://www.editlib.org/index.cfm?fuseaction=Reader.ViewAbstract&paper_id=6328&from=NEWDL

Rice, R. E. (1993). Media appropriateness: Using social presence theory to compare traditional and new organisational media. Cited in Stacey, E. (2002) Social presence online: Networking learners at a distance. In D. Watson & J. Anderson (Eds.), *Networking the Learner: Computers in Education*. Boston, MA: Kluwer Academic Press.

Richardson, J. C., & Swan, K. (2003). Examining social presence in online courses in relation to students' perceived learning and satisfaction. *Journal of Asynchronous Learning Networks, 7*(1), 68-88.

Richardson, W. (2006). *Blogs, Wikis, Podcasts and other Powerful Web Tools for Classrooms*. Thousand Oaks, CA: Corwin Press.

Richardson, W. (2006a). *Blogs, wikis, podcasts, and other powerful tools for classrooms*. Thousand Oaks, CA: Sage.

Richardson, W. (2006b). The new face of learning: the Internet breaks schools walls down. *Edutopia*, October. Retrieved November 3, 2007, from http://www.edutopia.org/new-face-learning.

Richardson, W. (2007) *Random thoughts and admissions*. Retrieved 10th October 2007, from: http://weblogged.com/2007/random-thoughts-and-admissions/

Riegelsberger, J., Sasse, M., & McCarthy, J. (2007). Trust in mediated interactions. In A. Joinson, K. McKenna, T. Postmes, & U. Reips (Eds.), *Oxford Handbook of Internet Psychology*. (pp. 53-69). Oxford: Oxford University Press.

Roberts, G. (2006). "MyWORLD e-Portfolios: Activity and Identity". In *Brookes eJournal of Learning and Teaching, 1*(4). Oxford: Brookes University. Retrieved April 12, 2007 from http://www.brookes.ac.uk/publications/bejlt/volumeiissue4/perspective/roberts.pdf

Roberts, G., Aalderink, W., Cook, J., Feijen, M., Harvey, J., Lee, S., & Wade, V. P. (2005). *Reflective learning, future thinking: digital repositories, e-portfolios, informal learning and ubiquitous computing*. Briefings from the ALT/SURF/ILTA Spring Conference Research Seminar. Dublin: Trinity College. Retrieved April 12, 2007 from http://www.surf.nl/download/ALT_SURF_ILTA_white_paper_2005%20(2).pdf

Robichaud, A. L. (2003). Healing and Feeling: The Clinical Ontology of Emotion. *Bioethics, 17*(1), 59-68.

Rodgers, C. (2002). Defining reflection: Another look at John Dewey and reflective thinking. *Teachers College Record, 104*(4), 842-866.

Rogers, E. M. (1995). Diffusion of Innovations, 4th ed. New York, NY: The Free Press.

Rogers, E. M. (1995). *Diffusion of Innovations*. New York, NY: Free Press.

Rogers, P. C., Liddle, S. W., Chan, P., Doxey, A., & Isom, B. (2007). Web 2.0 learning platform: harnessing collective intelligence. *Turkish Online Journal of Distance Education, 8*(3), 16-33.

Rohde, M., Klamma, M. J., & Wulf, V. (2007). Reality is our laboratory: communities of practice in applied computer science. *Behaviour & Information Technology, 26*(1), 81-94.

Rohs, M. (2005). Real-World Interaction with Camera Phones. In *Ubiquitous Computing Systems* (pp. 74-89). Berlin/Heidelberg: Springer.

Rohs, M., & Gfeller, B. (2004). Using Camera-Equipped Mobile Phones for Interacting with Real-World Objects. In A. Ferscha, H. Hoertner & G. Kotsis (Eds.), *Advances in Pervasive Computing* (pp. 265-271). Vienna, Austria: Austrian Computer Society (OCG).

Rohse, S., & Anderson, T. (2006). Design patterns for complex learning. *Journal of Learning Design, 1*(3). Retrieved Nov. 2006 from https://olt.qut.edu.au/udf/jld/index.cfm?fa=getFile&rNum=3386817&pNum=3386813

Rosenblum, D. (2007). What anyone can know: the privacy risks of social networking sites. *IEEE Security and Privacy, 5*(3), 40-49.

Rossi, P. G., Pascucci, G., Giannandrea, L., & Paciaroni, M. (2006). L'e-Portfolio Come Strumento per la Costruzione dell'Identità. In *Informations, Savoirs, Décisions, Médiations*, (25), art.348. La Garde: Université du Sud Toulon-Var. Retrieved April 12, 2007 from http://isdm.univ-tln.fr/PDF/isdm25/RossiPascucciGiannandreaPaciaroni_TICE2006.pdf

Rotter, J.B. (1954). *Social learning and clinical psychology*. Englewood Cliffs, NJ: Prentice-Hall.

Rotter, J.B. (1966). Generalized expectancies for internal versus external control of reinforcement. *Psychological Monographs, 80*(1), 1-28.

Rowe, S. (2005). Using multiple situation definitions to create hybrid activity space. In S. Norris & R. H. Jones (Eds.), *Discourse in action: Introducing mediated discourse analysis* (pp. 123-134). New York, NY: Routledge`.

Rubin, A. (1975). Disclosing oneself to a stranger: Reciprocity and its limits. *Journal of Experimental Social Psychology, 11*, 233-260.

Ruggles, R. (1998). The state of the notion: knowledge management in practice. *California Management Review, 40*(3), 80-89.

Ruitenberg, C. W. (2003). From designer identities to identity by design: Education for identity de/construction [Electronic Version]. *Philosophy of Education 2003*. Retrieved October 12, 2007, from http://www.ed.uiuc.edu/EPS/PES-Yearbook/2003/ruitenberg.pdf

Russel, D., Jeffries, R., & Irani, L. (2008). *Sensemaking for the rest of us*. Paper presented at the CHI 2008, Florence, Italy. ACM.

Ryan, R. M., & Deci, E. L. (2000). The darker and brighter sides of human existence: Basic psychological needs as a unifying concept. *Psychological Inquiry, 11*(4), 319-338.

Ryan, R. M., & Deci, E. L. (2000a). Intrinsic and extrinsic motivations: Classic definitions and new directions. *Contemporary Educational Psychology, 25*(1), 54-67.

Ryan, R. M., & Deci, E. L. (2000b). Self-determination theory and the facilitation of intrinsic motivation, social development, and well-being. *American Psychologist, 55*(1), 68-78.

Ryan, R., & Deci, E. (2000). Intrinsic and extrinsic motivations: Classic definitions and new directions. *Contemporary Educational Psychology, 25*(1), 54-67.

Sachs, J. (1999). Teacher Professional Identity: Competing Discourses, and Competing Outcomes. Paper Presented at the AARE Annual Conference Melbourne November. Available [Online]: http://www.aare.edu.au/99pap/sac99611.htm. Retrieved on 11 September 06.

Safuto, R. (2007). *Why do we need OpenSocial?* Retrieved 12th November, 2007 from http://blog.awakenedvoice.com/2007/11/05/why-do-we-need-open-social/

Salam, P. (2003). *Salam Pax: The Baghdad Blog*. London: Guardian Books.

Salisbury, M. W. (2003). Putting theory into practice to build knowledge management systems. *Journal of Knowledge Management, 7*(2), 128-141.

Salmon, G. (2000). *E-moderating: The key to teaching and learning online*. London: Kogan Page.

Salvador Declaration on Open Access: the developing world perspective. (2005). *Declaration signed in the International Seminar Open Access for Developing Countries*. Salvador: BIREME/PAHO/WHO. Retrieved February 01, 2007 from http://www.eifl.net/docs/Dcl-Salvador-OpenAccess-en.pdf

Salwen, M. B., & Stacks., D. W. (Eds.) (1997). *An Integrated Approach to CommunicationTheory and Research*. Mahwah, JF, Erlbaum.

Sauer, I. M., Bialek, D., Efimova, E., Schwartlander, R., Pless, G., & Neuhaus, P. (2005). Blogs and Wikis are valuable software tools for communication within research groups. *Artificial Organs, 29*(1), 82-89.

Saunders, M. (2006). From 'organisms' to 'boundaries': the uneven development of theory narratives in education, learning and work connections. *Journal of Education and Work, 19*(1), 1-27.

Saveri, A., Rheingold, H., & Vian, K. (2005). *Technologies of Cooperation*. Palo Alto: Institute for the Future and at http://www.rheingold.com/cooperation/Technology_of_cooperation.pdf, accessed 20 June 2007.

Savolainen, R. (2007). Filtering and withdrawing: strategies for coping with information overload in everyday contexts. *Journal of Information Science, 33*(5) (Oct. 2007), 611-621.

Saxena, A. (2007). Knowledge management and its applications in distance education. *The Turkish Online Journal of Distance Education, 8*(4). Retrieved October 19, 2007, from http://tojde.anadolu.edu.tr/index.htm

Scardamalia, M. (2004). Knowledge building environments: Extending the limits of the possible in education and knowledge work. In A. Distefano, K. E. Rudestam & R. Silverman (Eds.), *Encyclopedia of distributed learning*. Thousand Oaks, CA: Sage Publications.

Scardamalia, M., & Bereiter, C. (2003). CSILE/knowledge forum. In A. Kovalchick, & K. Dawson (Eds.), *Educational and Technology: An Encyclopedia*. Santa Barbara, ABC-CLIO.

Schon, D. (1983). *The reflective practitioner*. New York: Basic Books.

Schuler, D. (1994). Social computing. *Communications of the ACM, 37* (1), 28-29.

Schuller, T. (2007). Reflections on the use of social capital. *Review of Social Economy, 65*(1), 11-28.

Schunk, D., & Ertmer, P. (2001). Self-regulation and academic learning: Self-efficacy enhancing interventions. In M. Boekaerts, P. Pintrich & M. Zeidner (Eds.), *Handbook of Self-Regulation* (pp. 630-649). New York: Academic Press.

Scoble, R., & Israel, S. (2006). *Naked Conversations: How blogs are changing the way businesses talk with customers*. New Jersey, US: John Wiley & Sons.

Scott, P. J., Tomadaki, E., & Quick, K. (2007). The Shape of Live Online Meetings. *International Journal of Technology, Knowledge and Society, 3*.

Scott, R. (2002). Matchmaker, matchmaker, find me a mate: Examination of a virtual community of single Mormons. *Journal of Media and Religion, 1*(4), 201-216.

Searle, J. R. (1969). *Speech Acts: An essay in the philosophy of language*. Cambridge University Press.

Semple, E. (2006). Rise of the wiki. EI Magazine, 3 (2), available at: http://www.eimagazine.com/xq/asp/sid.0/articleid.4E73DFF9-53B3-4FF1-BA27-E5127C5FD365/qx/display.htm, last accessed on 15/09/2008.

Sener, J. (2007a). *Podcasting student performances to develop EFL skills*. Retrieved March 10, 2007, from http://www.sloan-c-wiki.org/wiki/index.php?title=Podcasting_Student_Performances_to_Develop_EFL_Skills.

Sener, J. (2007b). *University of North Carolina at Pembroke – cjencyclopedia.com: Online Encyclopedia of Criminal Justice*. Retrieved March 10, 2007, from http://www.sloan-c-wiki.org/wiki/index.php?title=University_of_North_Carolina_at_Pembroke_--_cjencyclopedia.com:_Online_Encyclopedia_of_Criminal_Justice.

Senge, P. (1990). *The Fifth Discipline – The Art and Practice of The Learning Organization*, New York, NY: Doublebay.

Severance, C., Hardin, J., & Whyte, A. (2008). The coming functionality mash-up in personal learning environments. *Interactive Learning Environments, 16*(1), 47-62.

Sfard, A. (1998). On two metaphors for learning and the dangers of choosing just one. *Educational Researcher, 27*(2), 4-13.

Shaffer, C., & Anundsen, K. (1993). *Creating Community Anywhere.* Los Angeles, CA: Tarcher/Perigee Books.

Shaikh, A. N., & Macauley, L. (2001). Integrating groupware technology into a learning environment. *Association for Learning Technology Journal (ALT-J), 9*(2), 47–63.

Shankar, S., Kumar, M., Natarajan, U. & Hedberg, J.G. (2005). A profile of digital information literacy competencies of high school students. *Issues in Informing Science and Information Technology,* (pp. 355-368).

Sharma, P., & Fiedler, S. (2007). Supporting self-organized learning with personal web publishing technologies and practices. *Journal of Computing in Higher Education, 18*(2), 3-24.

Sharpe, R., Benfield, G., Lessner, E., & De Cicco, E. (2005). *Final Report: Scoping Study for the Pedagogy Strand of the JISC e-learning Programme.* www.jisc.ac.uk/uploaded_documents/scoping%20study%20final%20report%20v4.1.doc [Acessed on 2 June, 2006].

Shaw, J., & Baker, M. (2004). Expert patient"--dream or nightmare?' *BMJ, 328*(7442), 723-724.

Shirky, C. (2003). *Fame vs Fortune: Micropayments and Free Content.* http://www.shirky.com/writings/fame_vs_fortune.html

Shirky, C. (2004). Nomic World: by the players, for the players. Retrieved November 8th 2007, from http://www.shirky.com/writings/nomic.html

Short, J., Williams, E., & Christie, B. (1976). *The social psychology of telecommunications.* Toronto: John Wiley and Sons.

Short, J., Williams, E., & Christie, B. (1976). *The social psychology of telecommunications.* London: Wiley.

Short, J., Williams, E., & Christie, B. (1976). *The Social Psychology of Telecommunications.* London: John Wiley and Sons.

Shuen, A. (2008). *Web 2.0: A Strategy Guide.* Sebastopol, CA: O'Reilly Media.

Siemens, G. (2004). Connectivism: A Learning Theory for the Digital Age. *eLearnSpace.* Retrieved on 7th April 2008, from http://www.elearnspace.org/Articles/connectivism.htm

Siemens, G. (2005). Connectivism: a learning theory for the digital age. *International Journal of Instructional Technology and Distance Learning, 2*(1), 3-10.

Siemens, G. (2006). *Knowing knowledge.* Retrieved on 7 April, 2008, from http://www.knowingknowledge.com/

Siemens, G. (2007). PLEs – I acronym, therefore I exist. *elearnspace: learning, networks, knowledge, technology, community* [weblog], April 15. Retrieved November 1, 2007, from http://www.elearnspace.org/blog/archives/002884.html.

Siemens, G. (2007). *Relationships and content.* http://www.elearnspace.org/blog/archives/003078.html

Simonson, M. (1999) Equivalency theory and distance education. *Tech Trends, 43*(5), 5-8.

Sims, R. (Ed.). (2006). Online distance education: new ways of learning; new modes of teaching? [Special issue]. *Distance Education, 27*(2).

Sitkin, S. B., Sutcliffe, K. M., & Schroeder, R. G. (1994). Distinguishing control form learning in total quality management-A contingency perspective. *Academy of Management Review, 19*, 537–564.

Skoyles, J. R. (2007). Here's what I believe but cannot prove. "The Edge"Retrieved oct 7th 2007 from http://www.edge.org/q2005/q05_6.html#skoyles

Smith B, Kusnierczyk W, Schober D, Ceusters W. Towards a Reference Terminology for Ontology Research and Development in the Biomedical Domain, Proceedings of KR-MED 2006

Smith R (1996): What clinical information do doctors' need? BMJ 313:1062-1068

Smith, A.A. (2007). Mentoring for experienced school principals: Professional learning in a safe place. *Mentoring & Tutoring: Partnership in Learning, 15*(3), 277-291.

Smith. (2001). Group Development: A Review of the Literature and a Commentary on Future Research Directions. Group Facilitation, 31(3). Spears, R., Postmes, T., Lea, M., & Wolbert, A. (2002). When are net effects gross products? *Journal of Social Issues, 58*(1), 91-107.

Snoke, R., Underwood, A., & Bruce, C. (2002). *An Australian view of generic attributes coverage in undergraduate programs of study: An information systems case study.* Proceedings of HERDSA Conference, Perth: Edith Cowan University, (pp. 590-598). Online: accessed 29.04.08. http://www.ecu.edu.au/conferences/herdsa/main/papers/ref/pdf/Snoke.pdf

Socialtext, Dresdner Kleinwort Wasserstein Case Study, available at: http://socialtext.com/customers/case-studies/drkw/, last accessed on 15/09/2008.

Society of College, National and University Libraries (1999). *Seven pillars of information literacy.* http://www.sconul.ac.uk/activities/inf_lit/sp/model.html [Published 1999; re-published 2004 - viewed December 21 2007]

Sohn, D., & Lee, B. (2005). Dimensions of interactivity: Differential effects of social and psychological factors. *Journal of Computer-Mediated Communication, 10*(3).

Sonnesyn Brooks, S. (1995). Managing a horizontal. *HR Magazine, June,* (pp. 52-58).

Sorrentino, F., & Paganelli, F. (2006). *L'intelligenza distribuita. Ambient Intelligence: il futuro delle tecnologie invisibili.* Trento, Italy: Erickson.

Sparks, P., & Shepherd, R. (1992). Self-identity and the theory of planned behavior: Assesing the role of identification with "Green Consumerism" *Social Psychology Quarterly,* Vol. 55, (4) 388-399.

Spender, D. (1997). Online upskilling in the digital renaissance. *Australian Training Review, 21,* 4-5.

Spivack, N. (2006). The third generation web is coming. *KurzweilAI.net.*

St. Laurent, A. M. (2004). *Understanding open source and free software licensing.* Sebastopol, CA: O'Reilley Media.

Stefani, L., Mason, R., & Pegler, C. (2007). *The educational potential of e-Portfolios: supporting personal development and reflective learning.* Abingdon, England: Routledge.

Stein, D., & Wanstreet, C. (2003). Role of Social Presence, Choice of Online or Face-to-Face Group Format, and Satisfaction with Perceived Knowledge Gained in a Distance Learning Environment. *Midwest Research to Practice Conference in Adult, Continuing and Community Education*: http://alumni-osu.org/midwest/midwest%20papers/Stein%20&%20Wanstreet-Done.pdf [Accessed on 5th of May, 2006].

Stein, R. (2007). Amazon starts to close the loop. at http://www.futureofthebook.org/blog/archives/2007/03/amazon_starts_to_close_the_loo.html, accessed 21 June 2007

Stenmark, D. (2008). Web 2.0 in the business environment: The new intranet or a passing hype? *In Proceedings of the 16th European Conference on Information Systems (ECIS 2008)*, Galway, Ireland, June 9-11, 2008.

Stephenson, R. (2005). *How to Make Open Education Succeed Conference*, Utah State University, Logan, UT

Sternberg, R. J. (1999). *Cognitive psychology*. Fort Worth, TX: Harcourt Brace.

Stets, E., & Burke, J. (2000) **Identity theory and social identity theory.** *Social Psychology Quarterly*, 63(3), 224-237.

Stewart WF, Shah NR, Selna MJ, Paulus RA and Walker JM. Bridging the Inferential Gap: The Electronic Health Record and Clinical Evidence. Health Affairs 2007;26(2): w181-w191

Stewart, D. W., & Pavlou, P. A. (2002). From consumer response to active consumer: measuring the effectiveness of interactive media. *Journal of the Academy of Marketing Science*, 30(4), 376-396.

Stewart, M. 2001 'Towards a global definition of patient centred care', BMJ 322(7284): 444-5.

Streatfield, D. R., & Markless, S. (1994). *Invisible learning? The contribution of school libraries to teaching and learning. Report on ... a research project* Library and Information Research Report 98 London: British Library.

Streatfield, D. R., & Markless, S. (2007). Information literacy. In J. H. Bowman (Ed.), *British librarianship and information work 2001-2005*. Aldershot, Hampshire: Ashgate 2007 (pp. 413-430)

Streatfield, D. R., & Wilson, T. D. (1980). *The vital link: information in social services departments*. London: Community Care and the Joint Unit for Social Services Research.

Stromer-Galley, J. (2004). Interactivity-as-product and interactivity-as-process. *The Information Society*, 20(5), 391-394.

Sturmberg JP. The Foundations of Primary Care. Daring to be Different. Oxford San Francisco: Radcliffe Medical Press 2007

Suber, P. (2005). *Open Access Overview*. Retrieved April 28, 2005 from http://www.earlham.edu/~peters/fos/overview.htm

Suber, P., & Arunachalam, S. (2005). Open Access to Science in the Developing World. In *World-Information City*, October 17, 2005. Tunis: WSIS. Retrieved February 01, 2007 from http://www.earlham.edu/~peters/writing/wsis2.htm

Sumner, T., Domingue, J., & Zdrahal, Z. (1998). *Enriching representations of work to support organisational learning*. Milton Keynes: Open University, Knowledge Media Institute (Tech Rep No KMI-TR-60).

Sunal, D., Sunal C., Odell, M., & Sunberg, C. (2003). Research supported best practices for developing online education. *Journal of interactive Online Learning, 2*(1). Retrieved Oct. 5, 2003 from http://www.ncolr.org/jiol/archives/2003/summer/1/index.asp

Sunstein, C. (2001). *Republic.com*. Princeton NJ: Princeton University Press. Retrieved April 2007 from http://press.princeton.edu/chapters/s7014.html.

Suriowecki, J. (2004). *The Wisdom of Crowds: Why the Many Are Smarter Than the Few and How Collective Wisdom Shapes Business, Economies, Societies and Nations*. Little, Brown.

Surowiecki, J. (2004). *The Wisdom of Crowds*. New York: Random House.

Surowiecki, J. (2004). *The wisdom of crowds: Why the many are smarter than the few and how collective wisdom shapes business, economies, societies, and nations*. New York: Doubleday.

Surowiecki, K. (2004). *The wisdom of crowds*. New York, NY: Doubleday.

Svensson, M., Höök, K., & Cöster, R. (2005). Designing and Evaluating Kalas: A Social Navigation System for Food Recipes. *Computer-Human Interaction, 12*(3), 374-400.

Sweeney, J., O'Donoghue, T., & Whitehead, C. (2004). Traditional face-to-face and web-based tutorials: A study of university students' perspectives on the roles of tutorial participants. *Teaching in Higher Education, 9*(3), 311-323.

Szwed, J. (1981). The Ethnography of Literacy. In M. F. Whiteman (Ed.), *Writing: The Nature, Development and Teaching of Written Communication*. Baltimore, MD: Lawrence Erlbaum, pp.13-24.

Tabberer, R., & Altman, J. (1986). *Study and information skills in schools*. London: British Library.

Tajfel, H. (1974). Social identity and intergroup behavior. *Social Science Information, 13*, 65-93.

Tajfel, H. (1981). *Human groups and social categories: Studies in social psychology*. Cambridge, UK: Cambridge University Press.

Tajfel, H. (1982). *Social identity and intergroup relations*. Cambridge University Press, Cambridge.

Tan J, Ed. (2005). E-healthcare information systems, Jossey-Bass: Wiley Imprint

Tang H, Ng JHK. (2006) Googling for a diagnosis—use of Google as a diagnostic aid: internet based study *BMJ* 2006;333:1143-5.

Tapscott, D., & Williams, A. D. (2007). *Wikinomics: How mass collaboration changes everything*. New York: Portfolio.

Taylor, J., & MacDonald, J. (2002). The effects of asynchronous computer-mediated group interaction on group processes. *Social Science Computer Review, 20*(3), 260-274.

Teal, W., Leu, D. J., Labbo, L., & Kinzer, C. (2002). The CTELL project: New ways technology can help educate tomorrow's reading teachers. *Reading Online*. Retrieved March 12, 2007.

Teo, H., Oh, L., Liu, C., & Wei, K. (2003). An empirical study of the effects of interactivity on web user attitude. *International Journal of Human-Computer Studies, 58*(3), 281-305.

Tepper, M. (2003). *The Rise of Social Software. netWorker magazine*. September.

The Cape Town Open Education Declaration (2007). Available online at: http://www.capetowndeclaration.org/read-the-declaration

The Center for Remediation Design and Brandeis University. (ERIC Document Reproduction Service No. ED328786)

The Social Construction of Reality. (2007, July 26) In Wikipedia, Retrieved Oct 16th 2007, from http://en.wikipedia.org/wiki/The_Social_Construction_of_Reality

Thelwall, M. (2007). *Social networks, gender and friending: An analysis of MySpace member profiles.* Paper presented at the Towards a Social Science of Web 2.0 conference, York, UK, URL (consulted 29 January 2008): http://www.scit.wlv.ac.uk/~cm1993/papers/MySpace_d.doc

Thomas, B., Jones, P., Packman, G., Miller, C. (2004). *Student perceptions of effective e-moderation: a qualitative investigation of e-college*. Wales: Networked Learning Conference.

Thomas, L., & Harri-Augstein, S. (1985). *Self-organised learning. Foundations of a conversational science for psychology*. London: Routledge.

Thomas, S. et al. (2007). Transliteracy: Crossing divides. *First Monday, 12*(12). Available at: http://www.uic.edu/htbin/cgiwrap/bin/ojs/index.php/fm/article/view/2060/1908.

Thompson, L., & Fine, G.A. (1999). Socially shared cognition, affect and behavior: A review and integration. *Personality and Social Psychology Review, 3*(4), 278-302.

Time (2007). Person of the year. *You, 168*(26).

Time (Canadian Edition) December 25, 2006/January 1, 2007.

Tinto, V. (1987). *Leaving college: Rethinking the causes and cures of college attrition.* Chicago, IL: University of Chicago Press.

Tinto, V. (1998). Colleges as communities: Taking research on student persistence seriously," *The Review of Higher Education, 21*(2), 167-177.

Todd, R. (2001). Transitions for preferred futures of school libraries. Keynote paper to International Association of School Libraries (IASL) Conference, Auckland, Symposium. http://www.iasl-slo.org/virtualpaper2001.html [Accessed 15 December 2007]. [Since developed by Professor Todd in various conference papers and presentations].

Togsverd, T. (2002). Denmark at the Forefront of Information and Communications Technology (ICT) Competencies. *Global J. of Engng. Educ., 6*(2), 175-178.

Tornero P. (2003). *Understanding Digital Literacy Promoting Digital Literacy.* Final report EAC/76/03.

Torniai, C., Battle, S., & Cayzer, S. (2005). Sharing, Discovering and Browsing Geotagged Pictures on the Web.

Tosh, D., & Werdmuller, B. (2004). *Creation of a learning landscape: weblogging and social networking in the context of e-portfolios.* [online document]. Retrieved April 14, 2007 from http://eduspaces.net/dtosh/files/7371/16865/Learning_landscape.pdf

Townley, C. T., Geng, Q, & Zhang, J. (2002). Bilateral team learning: Using distance technologies to enhance global education. *International Education, 32*(2), 19-48.

Toye, E., Madhavapeddy, A., Sharp, R., Scott, D., Blackwell, A., & Upton, E. (2004). *Using Camera-phones to Interact with Context-aware Mobile Services*: University of Cambridge.

Transliteracies Project: Research in the Technological, Social, and Cultural Practices of Online Reading. (2007). Retrieved June 20, 2007 from http://transliteracies.english.ucsb.edu/category/research-project.

Treaty of Lisbon (2007). Taking Europe into the 21st century. Key document of Treaty of Lisbon, European web portal. Retrieved on 7 April, 2008, from http://www.consilium.europa.eu/cms3_fo/showPage.asp?id=1296&lang=en&mode=g

Tremayne, M. (2005). Lessons learned from experiments with interactivity on the web. *Journal of Interactive Advertising, 5*(2).

Trentin, G. (2008). Using a wiki to evaluate individual contribution to a collaborative learning project. *Journal of Computer Assisted Learning,* 10.1111/j.1365-2729.2008.00276.x

Tu, C-H and McIsaac, M. (2002). The Relationship of Social Presence and Interaction in Online Classes, *The American Journal of Distance Education, 16*(3), 131-150.

Tungare, M., Burbey, I., & Perez-Quinones. (2006). *Evaluation of a location-linked notes system.* Paper presented at the 44th ACM Southeast Regional Conference, Melbourne, Florida.

Turkle, S. (1997). *Life on the screen: identity in the age of the Internet.* Weidenfeld & Nicolson, London.

Turner, J. C. (1985). Social categorization and the self-concept: A social cognitive theory of group behavior. In E. J. Lawler (Ed.), *Advances in Group Processes (Vol. 2).* Greenwich, CN: JAI Press.

Turner, J. C. (1987). A self-categorization theory. In J. C. Turner, M. A. Hogg, S. D. Oakes, S. D. Reicher & M. S. Wetherell (Eds.), *Rediscovering the social group: A self-categorization theory* (pp. 42-67). Oxford, UK: Basil Blackwell.

Turner, J.C. (1975). Social comparison and social identity: Some prospects for intergroup behaviour. *European Journal of Social Psychology.* 5, 5-34.

Turner, V. (1969). *The Ritual process: Structure and anti-structure.* Chicago: Aldine.

Turney, P. (2002). *Mining the Web for Lexical Knoledge to Improve Keyphase extraction:Learning from Labeled and Unlabeled Data,* NRC/ERB-1096, July 19, NRC 44947.

Twigg, C. (1994). The Changing Definition of Learning. *Educom Review, 29*(4). http://educom.edu/web/pubs/reviewArticles/29422.html [Accessed on 15th of March 2005].

Tyler, T. R. (2002). Is the Internet changing social life? It seems the more things change, the more they stay the same. *Journal of Social Issues, 58*(1), 195-205.

Tyman, J., &Huang, E. M. (2003). Intuitive visualizations for presence and recency information for ambient displays. In *Proceedings of the SIGCHI conference on Human factors in computing systems*, Ft, Lauderdale.

Übernoggin (2007). Hypermediated Work Environments. *Übernoggin* at http://ubernoggin.com/?p=18, accessed 20 June 2007.

UNESCO (2002). Recommendations addressed to the United Nations Educational Scientific and Cultural Organization - UNESCO. Youth Media Education. Seville, 15-16 February 2002.

UNESCO (2003). *Conference report of the information literacy Meeting of Experts.* Prague, September.

UNESCO (2008). *ICT Competency Standards for teachers.* Paris: UNESCO. http://unesdoc.unesco.org/images/0015/001562/156207e.pdf

Universities Australia (2007). *Australian student finances survey 2006 final report.* Retrieved November 1, 2007 from http://www.universitiesaustralia.edu.au/documents/publications/policy/survey/AUSF-Final-Report-2006.pdf.

Uschold M,(2005)An ontology research pipeline. Applied Ontology 1 (2005) 13–16 13. IOS Press

Valkenburg, P. M., Schouten, A. P., & Peter, J. (2005). Adolescents' identity experiments on the Internet. *New Media & Society, 7*(3), 383-402.

Vallacher, R.R., Nowak, A., Froehlich, M., & Rockloff, M. (2002). The dynamics of self-evaluation. *Journal of Personality and Social Psychology Review, 6*, 370-379.

Vallacher, R.R., Nowak, A., Markus, J., & Strauss, J. (1998). Dynamics in the coordination of mind and action.

In M. Kofta, G. Weary & G. Seflek (Eds.), *Personal control in action: Cognitive and motivational mechanisms* (pp. 27-59). New York, NY: Plenum.

Vallerand, R. J. (1997). Toward a hierarchical model of intrinsic and extrinsic motivation. *Advances in experimental social psychology, 29*, 271-360.

Vallerand, R. J., Fortier, M. S., & Guay, F. (1997). Self-determination and persistence in a real-life setting: Toward a motivational model of high school dropout. *Journal of Personality and Social Psychology, 72*(5), 1161-1176.

Van de Poel, J. (2005), Intermediality Reinterpreted. at http://www.ethesis.net/worlds/worlds_contence.htm, accessed 20 June 2007.

Van der Wal, T. (2005). *Explaining and showing broad and narrow folksonomies*, Personal InfoCloud: February 2005 Archives. Retrieved November 22, 2007, from http://www.personalinfocloud.com/2005/02/.

Van Rossum, E. J., & Schenk, S. M. (1984). The Relationship between Learning Conception, Study Strategy and Learning Outcome. *British Journal of Educational Psychology, 54*(1) 73-83.

van Weert, T. J. (2006). Education of the twenty-first century: new professionalism in lifelong learning, knowledge development and, knowledge sharing. *Education and Information Technologies, 11*(3/4), 217-237.

Vander Wal, T. (2007). *Folksonomy Coinage and Definition.* Retrieved 10.08.2007, 2007, from http://vanderwal.net/folksonomy.html

Vannevar Bush, V. (1945). As We May Think. *Atlantic Monthly.*

Varis, T. (2005), New Literacies and e-Learning Competences. *elearningeuropa.info directory*. Retrieved on 7 April, 2008, from http://www.elearningeuropa.info/directory/index.php?page=doc&doc_id=595&doclng=6

Veen, W. (2007). Homo Zappiens and the need for new education systems. Paper presented at the 2nd international convention *New Millennium Learners: Schools, ICT and learning* Florence. March

Vinscak, T. (2000). The function of rituals among the Buddhists in Mustang District, Nepal. In R-I. Heinze (Ed.), *The Nature and Function of Rituals*. London: Bergin & Garvey.

Virilio, P. (1986). *Speed and Politics: An Essay on Dromology* (trans. M. Polizotti). New York: Semiotext(e).

Virilio, P. (1995). *Speed and information: Cyberspace alarm!* In A. Kroker & M. Kroker (Eds.), *CTHEORY, 18*(3), 1-5.

Vukovic, A. (1997). Information literacy. *Management,* April, 10-11.

Vyas, D. M., & van der Veer, G. C. (2005). Experience as meaning: Creating, communicating and maintaining in real-spaces. In M. F. Costabile & F. Paternò (Eds.), *Human-Computer Interaction – INTERACT 2005* (pp. 1-4). Berlin, Heidelberg: Springer

Vygotsky, L. (1978). *Mind and society: The development of higher psychological processes*. Cambridge, MA: Harvard University Press.

Vygotsky, L. S. (1978). *Mind in society: The development of higher psychological processes*. Harvard, Harvard university press.

Vygotsky, L.S. (1962). *Thought and language*. Cambridge, MA: MIT Press.

Vygotsky, L.S. (1978). *Mind in society: The development of higher psychological processes*. Cambridge, MA: Harvard University Press.

Vygotsky, L.S. (1981). The instrumental method in psychology. In J. V. Wertsch (Ed.), *The concept of activity in Soviet psychology* (pp. 134-143). New York, NY: M. E. Sharpe.

W3C Emotion Incubator Group, (2007) W3C Incubator Group Report 10 July 2007, Internet document retrieved on 7th November, 2007 from http://www.w3.org/2005/Incubator/emotion/XGR-emotion-20070710

Waddell, C. D., & Thomason, K. L. (2008). Is Your Site ADA-Compliant or a Lawsuit-in-Waiting? *International Center for Resources on the Internet.* Accessed 24.07.08. http://www.icdri.org/CynthiaW/is_%20your-site_ada_compliant.htm

Wagner, C. (2003). Put another (B)Log on the Wire: Publishing Learning Logs as Weblogs. *Journal of Informations Systems Education, 14*(2), 131-132.

Wakefield, J. (2007). Turn off e-mail and do some work. *BBC News Online 19 October 2007.* Retrieved 5th November 2007, from: http://news.bbc.co.uk/1/hi/technology/7049275.stm.

Wallace, P. (1999). *The Psychology of the Internet.* Cambridge University Press, Cambridge.

Wallace, P. (1999). *The psychology of the Internet.* Cambridge, UK: Cambridge University Press.

Wallace, P. (1999). *The Psychology of the Internet.* Cambridge: Cambridge University Press

Walther J. B., & Burgoon, J. K. (1992). Relational communication in computer-mediated interaction. *Human Communication Research, 19*(1), 50-88.

Walther, J. B. (1992). Interpersonal effects in computer-mediated interaction: a relational perspective. *Communication Research, 19*(1), 52-90.

Walther, J. B. (1994). Anticipated ongoing interaction versus channel effects on relational communication in computer-mediated interaction. *Human Communication Research, 20*(4), 473-501.

Walther, J. B. (1996). Computer-mediated communication: impersonal, interpersonal, and hyperpersonal interaction. *Communication Research, 23*(1), 3-43.

Walther, J. B. (2007). Selective self-presentation in computer-mediated communication: Hyperpersonal dimensions of technology, language, and cognition. *Computers in Human Behavior, 23*(5), 2538-2557.

Walther, J. B., & Burgoon, J. K. (1992). Relational communication in computer-mediated interaction. *Human Research Communication, 19*(1), 50-88.

Walther, J.B. (1996). Computer mediated communication: Impersonal, interpersonal, and hyperpersonal interaction. Communication Research, 23(1), 3-43.

Walton, D. (1984). *Logical Dialogue-Games and Fallacies*. Lanham: University Press America.

Warlick, D. (2007). *Life long learners 2.0. Who writes the blog 2 Cents Worth?* Blog post Retrieved on 7 April, 2008, from http://repairman.wordpress.com/2007/07/09/lifelong-learner-20/

Watts, D. J. (2003). *Six degrees: the science of a connected age*. New York: Norton.

Watts, D. J. (2004). *Six Degrees (The Science of a Connected Age)*. Vintage U.K.: Random House.

We Media. (2003). *We Media - How audiences are shaping the future of news and information.* Retrieved 24.10.2007, from http://www.hypergene.net/wemedia/weblog.php

Webb, M. (2007). Music analysis down the (You) tube? Exploring the potential of cross-media listening for the music classroom. *British Journal of Music Education, 24*(2), 147-164.

Webber, I. (1991). The changing nature of work and careers. *Business Council Bulletin, 75,* 24-26.

Weber, M. (1947). *Theory of social and economic organization*. New York: Oxford University Press.

Weblog search (2006). www.pewinternet.org/PPF/r/144/report_display.asp, www.technorati.com, blogs.feedster.com (04/29/2006).

Wegerif, R. B. (2007). *Dialogic, Education and Technology: Expanding the Space of Learning*. New York: Springer-Verlag. (In Press)

Wegerif, R. (2006). A dialogic understanding of the relationship between CSCL and teaching thinking skills. *International Journal of Computer Supported Collaborative Learning, 1*(1), 143-157.

Weick, K. (1979). *The Social Psychology of Organizing*. 2nd. ed. New York: Radom House.

Weick, K. (1995). *Sensemaking in Organizations*. Thousand Oaks, CA: Sage Publications.

Weinberg, H., & Toder, M. (2004). The Hall of Mirrors in Small, Large and Virtual Groups. *Group Analysis,* 492-507. Retrieved May 2007 from http://gaq.sagepub.com/cgi/content/abstract/37/4/492

Weinberger, D. (2005). The BBC's low-tech KM, KM-World, available at: http://www.kmworld.com/Articles/Column/David-Weinberger/The-BBC%E2%80%99s-low-tech-KM-14276.aspx, last accessed on 15/09/2008.

Weinberger, D. (2007). *Everything is miscellaneous: The power of the new digital disorder.* Times books.

Weller, M. J. (2007). *Virtual Learning Environments - using, choosing and developing your VLE*. Oxford: Routledge.

Weller, M. J. (2007). *Virtual Learning Environments: Using, choosing and developing your VLE*. Routledge.

Weller, M., Pegler, C., & Mason, R. (2005). Use of innovative technologies on an e-learning course. *Internet and Higher Education, 8,* 61-71.

Wellman, B. (2000). Social network analysis: Concepts, applications, and methods. In A. E. Kadzin (Ed.), *Encyclopedia of Psychology,7,* 351-352. Washington, DC: American Psychological Association.

Wellman, B. (2001). The rise (and possible fall) of networked individualism. *Connections, 24*(3), 30–32

Wellman, B., Salaff, J., Dimitrova, D., Garton, L., Gulia, M., & Haythornthwaite, C. (1996). Computer networks as social networks: Collaborative work, telework, and virtual community. *Annual Review of Sociology, 22,* 213-238.

Wenger, E. (1998). Communities of practice: Learning as a social system [Electronic Version]. *The Systems Thinker, 9.* Retrieved November 10, 2007, from http://www.ewenger.com/

Wenger, E. (1998). *Communities of Practice: Learning meaning and identity.* Cambridge: Harvard University Press.

Wenger, E. (1998). *Communities of Practice: learning, meaning and identity.* Cambridge: Cambridge University Press.

Wenger, E. (1998). Communities of Practice: Learning, Meaning, and Identity (pp. 318). Cambridge: Cambridge University Press.

Wenger, E. (2000). Communities of practice and social learning systems. *Organization, 7*(2) 225-246.

Wenger, E., McDermot, R.M., & Snyder, W.M. (2002). *Cultivating communities of practice: A guide to managing knowledge.* Boston, MA: Harvard Business School Press.

Wenger, E., McDermott, R., & Snyder, W. M. (2002). *Cultivating Communities of Practice.* Boston: Massachusetts Harvard Business School.

Wenger, E., McDermott, R., & Snyder, W. M. (2002). Cultivating communities of practice. Cambridge, MA: Harvard Business School Press.

Wenzloff, J. (2005). *Furl, furled, furling: social online bookmarking for the masses.* Retrieved July 10, 2007, from http://www.classroomhelp.com/workshop/Furl_Guide.pdf.

Werry, C., & Mowbray, M. (2001). *Online Communities: Commerce, Community Action, and the Virtual University.* Prentice Hall, Upper Saddle River, NJ.

Wertsch, J. V. (1991). Voices of the mind: A sociocultural approach to mediated action. London: Harvester Wheatsheaf.

Wertsch, J.V. (1985). *Culture, communication, and cognition: Vygotskian perspectives.* New York, NY: Cambridge University Press.

Wertsch, J.V., Tulviste, P., & Hagstrom, F. (1993). A sociocultural approach to agency. In E. A. Forman, N. Minick & C. A. Stone (Eds.), *Contexts for learning: Sociocultural dynamics in children's development* (pp. 336-356). New York, NY: Oxford University Press.

Wessner, M., & Pfister, H.I. *International ACM SIG-GROUP Conference on Supporting Group Work:* IEEE.

Westwell, M. (2007). Bending minds: how technology can change the way we think. Keynote paper presented at *Information: interactions and impact conference,* Aberdeen June.

Wexelblat, A., & Maes, P. (1999). *Footprints: History-Rich Tools for Information Foraging.* Paper presented at the SIGCHI conference on Human factors in computing systems: the CHI is the limit.

Wexelblat, A., & Maes, P. (1999). *Footprints: History-rich tools for information foraging.* Paper presented at the Conference on Human Factors in Computing Systems, Pittsburgh, PA.

Wheeler, D. (2007). *Why Open Source Software / Free Software (OSS/FS, FLOSS, or FOSS)? Look at the Numbers!* http://www.dwheeler.com/oss_fs_why.html

Wheeler, S. (2007a). Something wiki this way cometh: Evaluating open architecture software as support for nomadic learning. In I. Bo & A. Szucs (Eds.), *Proceedings of EDEN 2007 Annual Conference,* Naples, Italy. 13-16 June.

Wheeler, S. (2007b). The Influence of Communication Technologies and Approaches to Study on Transactional Distance in Blended Learning. *ALT-J: Research in Learning Technology, 15*(2), 103-117.

Wheeler, S., & Boulos, M. (2007). Mashing, Burning, Mixing and the Destructive Creativity of Web 2.0: Applications for Medical Education. *Electronic Journal of Communication, Information and Innovation in Health,* 1(1), 27-33.

Wheeler, S., Yeomans, P., & Wheeler, D. (in press). The good, the bad and the wiki: Evaluating Student Generated Content as a Collaborative Learning Tool. *British Journal of Educational Technology.* doi: 10.1111/j.1467-8535.2007.00799.x

White, D. (2007). *Results of the 'Online Tool Use Survey' undertaken by the JISC funded SPIRE project.* Oxford: David White. Retrieved March 19, 2007 from http://tallblog.conted.ox.ac.uk/index.php/2007/03/16/some-real-data-on-web-20-use

White, N. (2006). *Blogs and community: launcing a new paradigm for online community.* Available at: http://kt.flexiblelearning.net.au/wp-content/uploads/2006/12/white.pdf [Accessed 15 December 2006].

Wiggins, G., & Mctighe, J. (2005). *Understanding by design,* 2nd ed. Alexandria, VA: Association for Supervision and Curriculum Development.

Wiig, K. M. (1997). Knowledge management: Where did it come from and where will it go? *Expert Systems with Applications, 13*(1), 1-14.

Wikipedia (2008). en.wikipedia.org/wiki/Weblogs (04/26/2008).

Wilbur, S. P. (2001). An archaeology of cyberspaces: virtuality, community, identity. In D. Bell & B. M. Kennedy (Eds.), *Cybercultures Reader* (pp 45-53). Routledge, London.

Wilhelm, A. G. (2000). *Democracy in the digital age.* Routledge: New York.

Williams, D., & Wavell, C. (2006). *Untangling spaghetti? The complexity of developing information literacy in secondary schools,* Scottish Executive, Web publication of research report.

Williams, D., & Wavell, C. (2007). Making connections: the nature and impact of information mediation in the development of information literacy in schools. Paper presented at *Information: interactions and impact conference,* Aberdeen June.

Williams, F., Rice, R. E., & Rogers, E. M. (1988). *Research methods and the new media.* Collier Macmillan.

Williams, J. B., & Jacobs, J. (2004). Exploring the use of blogs as learning spaces in the higher education sector. *Australasian Journal of Educational Technology, 20*(2), 232-247.

Williams, J., & Jacobs, J. (2004). Exploring the use of blogs as learning spaces in the higher education sector. *Australasian Journal of Educational Technology, 20*(2), 232-247.

Willinsky J. (2006). The access principle: the case for open access to research and scholarship. Cambridge: MIT Press.

Willke, H. (2005). *Systemtheorie II: Interventionstheorie.* Stuttgart: Lucius & Lucius.

Wilson, S. (2007). *The personal learning environments blog.* Retrieved 30 June, 2008 from: http://zope.cetis.ac.uk/members/ple

Wilson, S. (2008). Patterns of personal learning environments. *Interactive Learning Environments, 16*(1), 17-34.

Wilson, S., Liber, O., Beauvoir, P., MIlligan, C., Johnson, M., & Sharples, P. (2006). Personal learning environments: Challenging the dominant design of educational systems. Retrieved November 20, 2007, from http://hdl.handle.net/1820/727

Wilson, S., Liber, O., Griffiths, D., & Johnson, M. (2007). *Proceedings from World Conference on Educational Multimedia, Hypermedia and Telecommunications 2007.* Chesapeake, VA: AACE.

Windham, C. (2005). The student's perspective. In D. G. Oblinger & J. L. Oblinger (Eds.), *Educating the Net Generation* (pp. 5.1-5.16). Washington, D.C.: EDUCAUSE.

Wiszniewski, D., & Coyne, R. (2002). Mask and Identity: The Hermeneutics of Self-Construction in the Information Age. In K. A. Renninger & W. Shumar (Eds.), *Building Virtual Communities Learning and Change in Cyberspace. Learning in Doing: Social, Cognitive & Computational Perspectives* (pp. 191-213). Cambridge University Press, Cambridge.

Wittgenstein, L. (1953). *Philosophical Investigations,* translated by G.E.M. Anscombe, Blackwell, Oxford, UK.

Wolters, C. (1999). The relation between high school students' motivational regulation and their use of learning strategies, effort, and classroom performance. *Learning and Individual Differences, 11*(3), 281-299.

Wolters, C. (2003). Regulation of motivation: Evaluating an underemphasized aspect of self-regulated learning. *Educational Psychologist, 38*(4), 189-205.

Wolters, C., Yu, S., & Pintrich, P. (1996). The relation between goal orientation and students' motivational beliefs and self-regulated learning. *Learning and Individual Differences, 8*(3).

Wood, A. F., & Smith, M. J. (2001). *Online Communication. Linking Technology, Identity & Culture.* Lawrence Erlbaum Associates, Maewah.

Wood, D., & Gow, K. (1996). Virtually a reality. *Australian Training Review, 20,* 26-27.

Wood, D., & Gow, K. (1997). Educating students for the virtual business era. *New Horizons in Education, 96,* 36-45.

Wray, D. (1985). *Teaching information skills through project work.* London: British Library.

Wrede, O. (2003). *Weblog and Discourse.* www.weblogs. design.fh-aachen.de/owrede (10/29/2005/cache).

Wright, K. (2005). Personal knowledge management: supporting individual knowledge worker performance. *Knowledge Management Research & Practice, 3,* 156-165.

WSJ (2007). The Good, the Bad, And the 'Web 2.0'. *The Wall Street Journal online.* Retrieved on 7 April, 2008, from http://online.wsj.com/article/SB118461274162567845.html?mod=Technology

Wu, G. (1999). Perceived interactivity and attitude toward website. *Proceedings of the 1999 Conference of the American Academy of Advertising,* (pp. 254-262).

Xu, Z., Fu, Y., Mao, J., & Su, D. (2006). Towards the semantic web: Collaborative tag suggestions. *In proceedings of the Collaborative Web Tagging Workshop at WWW2006,* Edinburgh, Scotland, May, 2006.

Yadav, M. S., & Varadarajan, R. (2005). Interactivity in the electronic marketplace: an exposition of the concept and implications for research. *Journal of the Academy of Marketing Science, 33*(4), 585.

Zarb, M. (2006). Modelling Participation in Virtual Communities of Practice. London School of Economics; London. Retrieved April 2007 from http://www.mzarb.com/Modelling_Participation_in_Virtual_Communities-of-Practice.pdf

Zeldes, N., Sward, D., & Louchheim, S. (2007). Infomania: Why we can't afford to ignore it any longer. *First Monday, 12*(8) (August 2007). Retrieved 5th November 2007, from: http://firstmonday.org/issues/issue12_8/zeldes/index.html

Zimbardo, P. G. (1969). The human choice: Individuation, reason and order vs. deindividuation, impulse and chaos. In W. J. Arnold & D. Levine (Eds.), *Nebraska Symposium on Motivation* (Vol. 17, pp. 237-307). Lincoln, NE: University of Nebraska Press.

Zimmerman, B. (1998). Academic studying and the development of personal skill: A self-regulatory perspective. *Educational Psychologist, 33*(2/3), 73-86.

Zimmerman, B. (2004). Sociocultural influence and students' development of academic self-regulation: A social-cognitive perspective. In D. M. McInerney & S. Van Etten (Eds.), *Big Theories Revisited* (Vol. 4 In: Research on Sociocultural Influences on Motivation and Learning, pp. 139-164). Greenwich, CT: Information Age Publishing.

Zimmerman, B., & Kitsantas, A. (1997). Developmental phases in self-regulation: Shifting from process goals to outcome goals. *Journal of Educational Psychology, 89*(1), 29-36.

Zimmerman, B., & Kitsantas, A. (1999). Acquiring writing revision skill: Shifting from process to outcome self-regulatory goals. *Journal of Educational Psychology, 91*(2), 241-250.

Zipf, G. K. (1949). *Human behaviour and the principle of least effort.* Cambridge MA: Addison-Wesley

About the Contributors

Chris Abbott is reader in e-Inclusion at King's College London. He taught in special schools before researching aspects of disability and technology. He is the author of many academic articles and publications including "*ICT Changing Education*" (Routledge 2000), "*SEN and the Internet. Issues for the Inclusive Classroom*" (RoutledgeFalmer 2002) and "*Symbols, Literacy and Social Justice*" (Widgit 2006). He is programme director for the MA in e-Inclusion at King's College London and is editor of the *Journal of Assistive Technologies*.

William Alder was a student at Trinity school in Croydon between 2001 and 2008. Next year he will return to the school as a theatre technician to further his interests in drama, music, and photography for part of his Gap year. He then intends to study all aspects of drama at university, before possibly returning to the education field for his future employment.

Terry Anderson is professor and Canada Research chair in distance education at Athabasca University - Canada's Open University. He has published widely in the area of distance education and educational technology and has co-authored or edited five books and numerous papers. Terry is also the director of CIDER - the Canadian Institute for Distance Education Research (cider.athabascau.ca) and the editor of the *International Review of Research on Distance and Open Learning* (IRRODL www.irrodl.org).

Antonella De Angeli is a senior lecturer in human-computer interaction at the Manchester Business School, the University of Manchester. Her research addresses cognitive, social and cultural consequences of information technologies and focuses on the application of this knowledge to the design of useful and usable interactive systems. Antonella was awarded a PhD in experimental psychology from the University of Trieste (Italy) where she also completed a 2 year post-doctorate research in applied cognitive psychology. Part of her research was conducted at the OGI (Portland, USA), Loria (Nancy, France) and IRST (Trento, Italy). From 2000 to 2004 she worked as a senior HCI researcher for NCR Ltd. She has published over 80 papers, served in the programme committee of leading conferences, and reviewed for international journals.

Michelle S. Bachler is project developer for the Compendium software project and the Knowledge Mapping component of the Open Content Initiative. She is responsible for Compendium code, Compendium Developer Web site and Compendium technical support.

Richard Baraniuk is the Victor E. Cameron professor of electrical and computer engineering at Rice University and founder of Connexions. Connexions is a non-profit start-up launched at Rice University in 1999 that offers a rapidly growing collection of free, open-access educational materials and an open-source software toolkit to help authors publish and collaborate, instructors rapidly build and share custom courses, and students explore the links among concepts, courses, and disciplines. Connexions is internationally focused, interdisciplinary, and grassroots organized. For his research in the area of digital signal processing, Dr. Baraniuk has received national young investigator awards from the National Science Foundation and the Office of Naval Research, the Rosenbaum Fellowship from the Isaac Newton Institute of Cambridge University, and the ECE Young Alumni Achievement Award from the University of Illinois. He was elected a Fellow of the IEEE in 2001 and a Plus Member of AAA in 2004. For his teaching, he has received the George R. Brown Award for Superior Teaching at Rice twice and the C. Holmes MacDonald National Outstanding Teaching Award from Eta Kappa Nu.

Enzian Baur is a research assistant for Learning Technology Research Institute (LTRI) at London Metropolitan University and has a Masters in IT usability. She is currently working on usability design and evaluation research on two separate learning technology projects, the Generative Learning Object Maker software, and, the JISC funded Digital Dialogue Game project.

Eleni Berki, BSc, MA, PhD is an assistant professor of information systems and software development in the Department of Computer Sciences at the University of Tampere, Finland. Her research interests include testing, security and trust, human factors in software development, total and software quality management. She has held lecturer and researcher positions in a number of European and international Universities and has been working as an IS quality consultant in industry and education.

Werner Beuschel is professor of information management/enterprise management at Brandenburg University of Applied Sciences, Germany. Dr. Beuschel received his PhD in computer science from the Technical University Berlin in 1987. He has been involved in CSCL (computer supported cooperative learning) research for many years. As a member of the board of directors, Dr. Beuschel completed the 5-year German government-supported project *"Virtual University of Applied Sciences"* in 2003. His current research interests include social software use in education and Web-based learning management systems. For publications and details on his current activities, visit www.vfh.fh-brandenburg.de or send mail to beuschel@fh-brandenburg.de.

Dimitris Bibikas is a research associate and PhD candidate at SEERC (South East European Research Centre), a Research Centre of The University of Sheffield and CITY College. He holds a BSc in mathematics from Aristotle University of Thessaloniki, a Masters in information systems and a Masters in business administration, both from the University of Macedonia, Greece. His research interests include the impact of information and communication technologies on knowledge and innovation management, social networks and organisational adaptive strategies. He has extensive experience in coordinating R&D projects awarded by the European Commission, the Greek General Secretariat for Research and Technology, and the Greek Information Society Programme.

Mark Bilandzic is a PhD student at the Technische Universität München, Germany. He finished his undergrad and grad in Media Informatics at the Ludwig-Maximilians-University in Munich, Germany and holds an honours degree in technology management. Working on applied projects as a visiting scholar at the University of California, Berkeley and the Queensland University of Technology in Brisbane, Australia, he has specialised in mobile technologies, web development and human computer interaction. His fields of interest are at the intersection of information technology and sociology. His research studies target the issue how emerging information technology can be leveraged to provide tools for a more efficient information and communication behaviour within communities. Mr. Bilandzic has gathered related work experience at the research labs of Infosys Technologies in Bangalore, India, BMW in Munich and Dalmatech, a Web development start-up company in Santa Clara, California. Mr. Bilandzic is a scholarship recipient of the German National Academic Foundation (Studienstiftung des deutschen Volkes).

Rakesh Biswas is a professor of medicine in People's College of Medical Sciences, Bhopal, India. He is actively involved in patient centred learning with an aim to create a learning network between patients, health professionals and other actors in a care giving collaborative process that has been termed 'user driven health care'.

Elisabetta Cigognini is currently a PhD student in telematics and information society (XXI cycle) at the Electronics and Telecommunications Department of the University of Florence. In 2003 she graduated in Communication Sciences at IULM University of Milan and in 2004 she completed her Masters degree in "e-Learning Project Management and Design" at the University of Florence. Since then she has been collaborating as eLearning contractor, instructional designer and eTutor both in corporate and in academic contexts. Her main research interests are personal knowledge management skills, personal learning environment, instructional design, collaborative working environment, learning and knowledge management, e-learning and e-knowledge. elisabetta.cigognini@unifi.it

Jillianne Code is a writer, researcher and lecturer the areas of self-regulated learning, agency, and online social dynamics. Her research includes the expression of agency in social networks, strategic membership and dynamics of massively multiplayer online role-playing games, and the role of self-regulation in video game environments. Jillianne also specializes in instructional design for 3D simulation and games. Jillianne is currently completing a PhD in educational psychology at Simon Fraser University.

Gráinne Conole is professor of e-Learning at the Open University, with research interests in the use, integration and evaluation of information and communication technologies and e-learning and impact on organisational change. She was previously chair of educational innovation at Southampton University and before that director of the Institute for Learning and Research Technology at the University of Bristol. She has extensive research, development and project management experience across the educational and technical domains. She has published and presented widely.

Ignacio Aedo Cuevas holds a degree in computer science and PhD in computer science from Universidad Politécnica de Madrid. He's currently a full professor at the Universidad Carlos III de Madrid and his interests mainly focus on topics such as hypermedia, interactive systems, Web systems, learning technologies, development methodologies and information systems for emergency situations. Since 2001, he has been the technical advisor of the Ministry of Internal Affairs for the application of ICT in the civil protection domain. He is actually in a sabbatical leave at the Computer Supported

Collaboration and Learning Laboratory of the College of Information Science and Technology of Penn State University, leaded by Prof. Carroll and Prof. Rosson. Moreover, he is co-organizing the "HCI for emergencies" workshop for CHI 2008 conference and a special session with the same name in the ISCRAM 2008 conference. He is also general co-chair of IEEE ICALT 2008.

James Dalziel is professor of learning technology and director of the Macquarie E-Learning Centre Of Excellence (MELCOE) at Macquarie University in Sydney, Australia. James leads a number of projects including: LAMS (Learning Activity Management System), including roles as a director of the LAMS Foundation and LAMS International Pty Ltd; MAMS (Meta Access Management System), a national identity and access infrastructure project for the Australian higher education sector; RAMP (Research Activityflow and Middleware Priorities), a project investigating open standards authorisation and e-Research workflows, and ASK-OSS (the Australian Service for Knowledge of Open Source Software), a national advisory service on open source issues for the Australia higher education and research sector. Prior to his current roles, James helped lead the COLIS (Collaborative Online Learning and Information Services) project, was a director of WebMCQ Pty Ltd, an e-learning and assessment company, and was a lecturer in psychology at the University of Sydney.

Utpal M. Dholakia is the William S. Mackey Jr. and Verne F. Simons distinguished associate professor of management at the Jesse Jones Graduate School of Management, Rice University, in Houston Texas. He has a master's degree in psychology (1997), and a PhD in marketing (1998) from the University of Michigan, a master's degree in operations research (1994) from the Ohio State University, and a bachelor's degree in industrial engineering (1993) from the University of Bombay. His research interests lie in studying motivational psychology of consumers and online marketing issues such as virtual communities and online auctions. He also studies relational aspects of consumer behavior. Among others, Dr. Dholakia's research has been published in *Marketing Science*, the *Journal of Marketing*, and the *Journal of Consumer Research*. He has worked extensively with large and small firms in financial services, high tech, packaged goods, and service industries. He is also a frequent speaker at marketing conferences.

Jon Dron is an associate professor in the School of Computing and Information Systems at Athabasca University, Canada and a senior lecturer at the Centre for Learning and Teaching, University of Brighton, UK. He has a first degree in philosophy, a masters degree in information systems and a PhD in e-learning. He has published widely in the area of e-learning and written a number of social applications for learning. He is the author of the IGI book *Control and Constraint in E-Learning: Choosing When to Choose*. He is a national teaching fellow of the English Higher Education Academy

Marc Eisenstadt is chief scientist at the Knowledge Media Institute, interested in fostering quality learning experiences with or without technology. His current work interests include very large scale presence via messaging and gaming; intelligent agents as mediating tools for human interaction; internet mapping and visualisation; ubiquitous bandwidth and the educational challenge summed up by the phrase "wired... now what?".

Sebastian Fiedler is a researcher at the Centre for Social Innovation, a non-for-profit research institute in Vienna, Austria. Sebastian's research and development work focuses on the conceptual and technological support of self-organisation and self-direction in formal and informal educational contexts. Since 2000 Sebastian explores the potential of tools and practices that have emerged in the context of personal and collaborative Web-publishing (Weblogs, Wikis, Webfeeds, ...) and social media. He has published and presented frequently at international conferences on related issues and topics. Sebastian holds degrees in psychology (Friedrich-Alexander-Universität Erlangen-Nürnberg, Germany) and instructional design and technology (University of Georgia, USA).

Robert Fitzgerald is the associate dean (Research) in the Faculty of Education at the University of Canberra. His research and teaching explores the role of information and communication technologies (ICT) in learning particularly as it relates to ICT integration, information literacy and building online communities. His work explores the application of social software and Web 2.0 technologies to the development of collaborative systems for research and learning. Robert is currently working on a development project in Cambodia working with maize and soy bean farmers and traders build an interactive information system using text messaging and mobile phones.

Marcus Foth is a senior research fellow at the Institute for Creative Industries and Innovation, Queensland University of Technology (QUT), Brisbane, Australia. He received a BCompSc(Hon) from Furtwangen University, Germany, a BMultimedia from Griffith University, Australia and an MA and PhD in digital media and urban sociology from QUT. Dr. Foth is the recipient of an Australian Postdoctoral fellowship supported under the Australian Research Council's Discovery funding scheme. He was a 2007 visiting fellow at the Oxford Internet Institute, University of Oxford, UK. Employing participatory design and action research, he is working on cross-disciplinary research and development at the intersection of people, place and technology with a focus on urban informatics, locative media and mobile applications. Dr. Foth has published over fifty articles in journals, edited books, and conference proceedings in the last four years. He is a member of the Australian Computer Society and the Executive Committee of the Association of Internet Researchers. More information at www.urbaninformatics.net

Kathryn Gow, at the Queensland University of Technology, has researched into transition from school to work, generic, specialist, entrepreneurial and virtual competencies, graduate capabilities, academic achievement, and apprentices' intention to quit. She has had a long term interest in coaching, mentoring and training. Dr. Gow has been a speaker at both national and international conferences and events. She believes that the secondary school system has to change dramatically to accommodate the needs of young people and to incorporate work and life skills in innovative ways, especially in the digital age.

Elizabeth Guerin is currently a PhD student in telematics and information society at the Telematics Laboratory of the Electronics and Telecommunications Department of the University of Florence. She also teaches English language and teaching methodology at the Faculty of Education, University of Florence. Language learning through ICT is one of her specific areas of interest together with cognitive learning processes and technology, teacher professional development and education, language testing, and research issues related to the Common European Framework of Reference for Language Learning, Teaching and Assessment (CEF). elizabeth.guerin@unifi.it

Patricia Hellriegel is a former member of the Visual Culture Research Group in the Communication Sciences department at the University of Antwerp. Currently she is working as a Web developer for Lessius University College in Antwerp, Belgium.

Anthony Herrington is associate professor in both adult education and IT in education in the Faculty of Education, University of Wollongong, Australia. He has a long history of teaching in schools and universities, nationally and overseas. His interests include adult and Information and Communications Technology education. Herrington has won national teacher development grants resulting in award winning publications that have focused on the professional development of teachers using technology. He is currently engaged in researching the benefits of online communities of practice for beginning teachers

Jerald Hughes holds a PhD in business with a specialization in computer information systems from the Graduate Center of the City University of New York. He currently teaches as an assistant professor at the University of Texas – Pan American. Among his research interests are digital information goods, emergent online user networks, information systems security, and information architectures.

Mikko Jäkälä, MA, MEd is a lecturer of computer-mediated communication in the Department of Computer Science and Information Systems at the University of Jyväskylä, Finland. He is interested in the human aspect in implementation, design and use of information technology. His research focuses on how technology is used to support and enhance human communication, and how technology influences communication practices and social behaviour.

Chris Joseph – digital writer and artist, currently IOCT Digital Writer-in-Residence and collaborator with Kate Pullinger on works including the award-winning Inanimate Alice. http://www.chrisjoseph. org

A.S. Kasthuri is a professor emeritus of medicine at the eminent Armed Forces Medical College in Pune, India. He continues to nurture a deep interest in patient centred learning along with regular involvement in health informatics.

Helen Keegan works as a research fellow and lecturer at the University of Salford, specialising in the use of ICT in teaching and learning (HE). She has a background in cognitive linguistics and multimedia production and has published and presented nationally and internationally on learning technology implementation and evaluation. Her research focuses on technology, society and education, specifically virtual communities, online social networking and digital identity; learning technologies and social software in education; and virtual mobility and online communities of practice, focusing on intercultural communication and collaboration.

Lucinda Kerawalla is a cultural psychologist and research fellow at the Institute of Educational Technology at the Open University. Her main research interests are in the technological mediation of collaboration and argumentation, and the use of technology to enhance links between school and home. She has worked as a research fellow and consultant on several research projects in primary schools, secondary schools and in higher education, and has published in the area of technology-enhanced learning.

Lisa Kervin is a senior lecturer in educational psychology and curriculum at the University of Wollongong. She has worked as a teacher, teaching from Kindergarten to Grade Six, and has been employed in consultancy roles. She has researched her own teaching and has collaborative research partnerships with teachers and students in both tertiary and primary classrooms. Her current research interests are related to the literacy development of children, the use of technology to support student learning and teacher professional development.

Gill Kirkup is a senior lecturer in educational technology at the Institute of Educational Technology at the Open University. Also, she is seconded presently for half her time to the UK Resources Centre for Women in Science Engineering and Technology as head of research and data. She has been engaged in research and teaching in aspects of educational technology for many years, as well as in gender and technology. She is at present trying to navigate the minefield of all these issues in her own blogging.

Jess Laccetti – IOCT doctoral student researching Web fictions within a narrative and feminist theoretical context. She is also an active researcher, teacher, and blogger. http://www.jesslaccetti.co.uk

Petros Lameras is a PhD candidate from the South East European Research Centre and he is interested in the facilitation of e-learning pedagogy in higher education –in particular, in academics' conceptions of and approaches to teaching and learning using information and communications technologies. He is also interested in qualitative research methodologies with a special focus on the phenomenographic research approach.

Deborah LaPointe is assistant professor and assistant director for the Education Development Health Sciences Library & Informatics Center at University of New Mexico's School of Medicine, as well as a professor for the Organizational Learning and Instructional Technology (OLIT) Program. Dr. LaPointe received her PhD degree from University of New Mexico in 2004. She is interested in communication in online learning, especially through the formats such as wikis, blogs and other social software including *Second Life*. She has worked with organizations and learners in Taiwan, Mainland China, Spain and Australia and continues to research peer interaction in online learning environments.

Mark J. W. Lee is an adjunct senior lecturer with the School of Education, Charles Sturt University, and an honorary research fellow with the School of Information Technology and Mathematical Sciences, University of Ballarat. Previously, he worked in a variety of teaching, instructional design and managerial roles within the private vocational education and higher education sectors. Mark has published widely in the areas of educational technology, e-learning and innovative pedagogy in higher education. He is presently chair of the New South Wales Chapter of the Institute of Electrical and Electronics Engineers (IEEE) Education Society, and serves on the editorial boards of a number of international journals in the area of educational technology and e-learning.

Edwin Wen Huo Lee had served as a manager for Intel Innovation center in Kuala Lumpur, Malaysia and is deeply interested in health informatics and learning promotion in health care. He has recently begun a company called *Health Connect* to further the goals of user driven health care.

Stefano Levialdi has worked for over twenty years in parallel image processing, moving to human-computer interaction in 1984 mainly interested in the visual channel: visual languages, visual interfaces and related usability issues. He has started the computer science curriculum at the University of Rome, Faculty of Sciences. He has published over 250 papers and started the *Journal of Visual Languages and Computing* (1990) and is IEEE Life Fellow. He has taught different subjects within computer science, his latest one is human-computer interaction. Levialdi has strong international ties and cooperates with a number of foreign universities; he is fluent in Spanish, English and Italian

Jennifer Linder-VanBerschot is a research associate at Mid-continent Research for Education and Learning (McREL) and a doctoral candidate at the University of New Mexico in the Organizational Learning and Instructional Technology (OLIT) Program. Her focus is on communication patterns of non-native English speakers on online courses. She is particularly interested in the use of social software to promote interaction across cultures and between international learning communities. She has also conducted educational research and evaluation on the topics of leadership, English language learners and classroom instruction.

Bernard Lisewski works as an educational developer in the Education Development Unit at the University of Salford. He is the programme leader for the MA in higher education practice and research. Previously published work has focused on critical examinations of the five stage e-moderating model and strategic learning technology implementation. His current research interests revolve around using self-ethnography to examine the role of discourse and the formation of power relations within university-based communities of practice.

Alex Little is a developer in social software. He is part of KMi's contribution to the OpenLearn team, mainly developing and integrating BuddySpace/MSG messaging systems into the Moodle VLE. His interest focuses on the software development of systems for social networking

Alessio Malizia is currently with the DEI group holding an associate professor position at the University Carlos III, at Madrid, Spain. He holds a degree in computer science and PhD in computer science from University "La Sapienza" of Rome, Italy (Thesis title: *A Cooperative-Relational Approach to Digital Library Environments*). From 1999 to 2002 he worked for the Rome IBM Tivoli Laboratory, and Silicon Graphics. From 2003 to 2004, he was visiting researcher at the XEROX PARC (Palo Alto Research Center, Palo Alto, CA, USA) in the ISTL (Information Science and Technology) Lab working on visualization and small display devices. He authored the book *"Mobile 3D Graphics"* published by Springer (September 2006). Until February 2007, he was a research fellow at the Computer Science Department of the University of Rome "La Sapienza", Italy. In the past his research activities focused on theory and algorithms for pattern recognition, machine learning and visualization. Today he is working on human computer interaction, visual languages and social networks.

G. Rita (Jose) Mangione obtained her PhD in telematics and information society from the Electronics and Telecommunications Department of the University of Florence. In 2003 she completed her Master degree in "e-Learning Project Management and Design" at the University of Florence. In 2004 she completed her Master degree in "Multimediality for E-learning" at the University of Rome; she collaborated as instructional designer and eTutor both in corporate and in academic contexts. Her main research interests concern trust in online collaboration, knowledge representation and management and instructional design. Since 2006 she is a scientific collaborator at CEMSAC, University of Salerno, where she works on the ELegi European IP project and Learning & Knowledge Project. mangione@ crmpa.unisa.it

Jessica Mantei teaches in the Faculty of Education at the University of Wollongong, Australia. As a primary school teacher, she taught Kindergarten to Year 6 and reading recovery, worked as a teacher mentor and professional development facilitator within and across schools. As a tertiary educator, Jessica teaches undergraduate and postgraduate education students in research methods, curriculum and pedagogy subjects. Her PhD project explores the ways that teachers plan, organise and facilitate authentic learning experiences in their primary school classrooms.

Sharon Markless is a lecturer in higher education in the King's Learning Institute at Kings' College, London. She also works part time as a freelance researcher and educator in the fields of information literacy and the contribution of libraries to teaching and learning. Her research career began over twenty years ago when she was a senior research officer at the National Foundation for Educational Research. Markless has been a guest speaker on the development of information literacy and the impact of libraries and information services at numerous national and international conferences, most recently in the USA, Japan and Denmark.

Carmel M Martin is an associate professor of Family Medicine at the Northern Ontario School of Medicine. She is a health services researcher with a special interest in primary health care systems in Canada, Australia, the UK and internationally. Her research themes include complex adaptive chronic care, equity and health disparities.

Bruce Mason specializes in ethnography, folklore, linguistics and artificial intelligence and is currently a postdoctoral research fellow at De Montfort University where he works on a project analyzing the impact of the Million Penguins wiki novel. http://www.hum.dmu.ac.uk/blogs/part/2006/05/bruce_mason.html

Catherine McLoughlin is an associate professor with the School of Education at the Australian Catholic University, Canberra. She also serves as the coordinator of the Australian Capital Territory branch of the Research Centre for Science, Information Technology and Mathematics Education for Rural and Regional Australia (SiMERR). With over 20 years experience in higher education in Europe, South East Asia, the Middle East and Australia, Catherine has experience and expertise in a variety of educational settings, with diverse students and across a wide range of cultural contexts. She is editor of the *Australasian Journal of Educational Technology* and an editorial board member of a several leading journals, including the *British Journal of Educational Technology*.

Shailey Minocha is senior lecturer of human-computer interaction (HCI) in the Department of Computing of the Open University (OU), UK. Shailey's research focuses on the effective design of electronic environments, with two related strands: (a) customer relationship management and service quality of e-business environments, and (b) information design and pedagogical effectiveness of e-learning environments. The core thrust of Minocha's research has been on investigating user behaviour with computer systems, users' requirements from technologies, and the nature of the user-system interactions, which influence the design and usability of electronic environments. Minocha has a PhD in digital signal processing from the Indian Institute of Technology, Delhi, India, post-doctorate in adaptive user interfaces from Technical University, Braunschweig, Germany, and an MBA from the OU.

Kamalika Mukherji is a consultant psychiatrist in learning disabilities. She works in hospital and community outreach settings. She has been involved in training patients and care givers to improve their understanding and management of disease models such as epilepsy and dementia. From 2002 she has worked in teaching projects exploring attitudes towards disability.

Sridhar Nerur is an assistant professor of information systems at the University of Texas at Arlington. He received his BE in electronics from Bangalore University; a PGDM from the Indian Institute of Management, Bangalore; and a PhD from the University of Texas at Arlington. His publications include articles in leading research journals such as *Strategic Management Journal (forthcoming)*, *MIS Quarterly, The Data Base for Advances in Information Systems, Communications of the ACM, and Information Systems Management*. He serves as an associate editor of the *European Journal of Information Systems*. His research and teaching interests are in the areas of object-oriented analysis and design, adoption of software development methodologies, social computing, cognitive aspects of programming, knowledge management, and agile software development.

Alexandra Okada is a researcher in Knowledge Mapping for Open Content Initiative at the Knowledge Media Institute, Open University. She is a visiting lecturer at the FGV University in Brazil and heads up the CoLearn Community in the OpenLearn Project. She is interested in how knowledge media tools can be used to facilitate research, teaching and learning.

Peter Oriogun is currently an associate professor of information technology and commujnications. Prior to this he was a senior lecturer in software engineering at London Metropolitan University. His current research interests are in semi-structured approaches to online learning, CMC transcript analysis, software life cycle process models, problem-based learning in computing and cognitive engagement in online learning. He is a chartered member of the British Computer Society. The title of his PhD thesis by prior output is *"Towards understanding and improving the process of small group collaborative learning in software engineering education"*.

Iraklis Paraskakis is a senior research officer, academic director of the doctoral programme at SEERC and senior lecturer at Computer Science Department of CITY College. His research interests are in the area of education and information technology, information systems, knowledge management and Semantic Web services. He is interesting in exploring the impact and overlap of these areas into learning and organisations. He has published in various journals and conferences (ITS, CAL, PEG, EARLI, ESWC, BIS) and is a member of the Artificial Intelligence and Education Society (AIED), European Association for Research on Learning and Instruction (EARLI) and IEEE. He has been the principal investigator in a number, of successfully completed, EU projects as well as current ones in the areas of eLearning, Knowledge Management and Semantic Web Services.

Kai Pata is the senior researcher in the Center of Educational Technology, Institute of Informatics, Tallinn University. Her main expertise is in learning management in distributed learning environments and social systems for inquiry learning, tutoring models and scaffolding elements in web-based synchronous collaborative learning environments, and cognitive aspects of learning with visual models in inquiry learning environments. She has the background of science education and ICT in learning. Her experience in the field started at 1994 as a designer and virtual teacher in an online elearning portal Miksike, from 2000-2007 she worked at research positions at the University of Tartu, Science Didactics Department in various science related ICT projects.

Luc Pauwels is professor of visual communication, vice-dean of the Faculty of Political and Social Sciences, University of Antwerp, and chair of the Visual Culture Research Group. He teaches and writes about visual research methodologies, visual ethics, family photography, Web site analysis, anthropological filmmaking, visual corporate culture, and scientific visualization.

Ismael Peña-López, Bachelor in economics, Master en ecoaudit and environmental planning. Specialist postdegre in knowledge management. MPhil in political science, lecturer of public policies for development and ICT4D at the Open University of Catalonia, his main research fields are twofold. On the one hand, the aspects related with information and communication technologies for development (ICT4D): e-Readiness, the digital divide, ICTs in cooperation for development, nonprofit technology, online volunteering, e-inclusion; on the other hand, aspects related with e-learning and empowerment: digital capacity building and literacy, e-portfolios, open access, open science, access to knowledge. He has been founder of the University's cooperation for development programme, mainly about e-learning for development. He is editor of *ICTlogy.*

Simon Perril – poet and senior lecturer in creative writing and English with an interest in experimental poetry. His current creative project is a book of poems concerning early and silent cinema. Samples of work and mp3 files of readings can be found in the 'authors' section of The Archive of the Now http://www.archiveofthenow.com

Maria Chiara Pettenati is senior researcher at the Telematics Laboratory of the Electronics and Telecommunications Department of the University of Florence since late 2004. In 2000 she received her PhD degree in telematics and information society from the University of Florence. Until 2004 she held a post-doctoral research position in the same laboratory. Her main research interests include collaborative working and learning environments, knowledge bases, e-knowledge and network mediated knowledge, trust intermediation architectures, and information interoperability architecture. mariachiara. pettenati@unifi.it

Alexandros G. Psychogios is a lecturer and academic research coordinator of the Business Administration and Economics Department of CITY College, Affiliated Institution of The University of Sheffield. His research interests include knowledge management, organisational learning, organisational change and its impact on human resources and total quality management. He has published in a variety of journals, such as the *International Journal of Human Resource Management, The TQM Magazine, The Qualitative Report,* etc

Kate Pullinger – author of *A Little Stranger* and *Weird Sister* among other works of print fiction; collaborates with Chris Joseph on the digital fiction, *Inanimate Alice*. She worked with Sue Thomas to develop and teach online MA in creative writing and new media at DMU where she is reader in creative writing and new media. http://www.katepullinger.com

Andrew Ravenscroft is professor of technology enhanced learning and deputy director at the Learning Technology Research Institute (LTRI) of London Metropolitan University. Previously he was director of the Dialogue and Design for New Media Research Group that he established at the UK Open University whilst working in the Institute of Educational Technology (IET). He gained his PhD in psychology and intelligent media design whilst working as a research fellow in the Computer Based Learning Unit (CBLU) at the University of Leeds and is a chartered psychologist. His current research focus is on 'advanced learning and interaction design'.

Scott Robinson's work in systems analysis spans several disciplines, including engineering, distributed systems and neuropsychology. He has supervised applied research for DARPA, the Department of Defense, and the Department of Energy, and did his graduate research in infant neurological development. He is a consultant in the information technology industry, and frequently gives seminars in systems interface technology, distributed systems architecture and computer security. His current research interests include new information storage/retrieval paradigms and social evolution in cyberspace.

Yoni Ryan is director of the Institute for the Advancement of Teaching and Learning, Australian Catholic University, following several years with the University of Canberra, where she was involved in a number of Carrick projects as team member or reference group member, including the project described in this chapter. She has extensive experience in staff development, and educational design and development with new technologies, at various universities in Australia and the Pacific. Her current research interests span the challenges of teaching new generation students, and using social technologies. Her publications span staff development via formal award programs, and new generation students.

Vishal Sachdev is an assistant professor at the Department of Computer Information Systems at Middle Tennessee State University, Murfreesboro, TN. He received his PhD from the University of Texas at Arlington, and his Masters in international business, from the Indian Institute of Foreign Trade in New Delhi, India. His publications include a refereed book chapter and several conference proceedings. His research interests are in social computing, outsourcing and multi-agent modeling. He has teaching interests in the use of technology to enable active learning, particularly the use of multi-user virtual environments in education.

Musbah Sagar is a research fellow at the Learning Technology Research Institute (LTRI), London Metropolitan University, working on the JISC funded Digital Dialogue Game project. He has a BSc in computer engineering and an MSc in Web technology from Oxford Brookes University. He worked as a Web programmer for Danfoss UK and as a research assistant for Oxford Brookes University on an e-science project called gViz. He also worked as a research fellow for Oxford Brookes University in a project called Open Overlays, funded by the EPSRC Fundamental Computer and e-Science Program.

Peter Scott is the director of KMi. He is also head up the KMi's Centre for New Media research, where he works on numerous prototype applications of networked learning media. His interests focus on stadium telepresence, professional learning, streaming media and peer-supported open learning through FM.

Simon Buckingham Shum is senior lecturer at the Knowledge Media Institute, Open University and coordinator of knowledge media technologies for the OpenLearn project. He is interested in technologies for sensemaking, specifically, which structure discourse to assist reflection and analysis.

David Streatfield is an information researcher and consultant specialising in the evaluation of information services and libraries. After an academic research career at the University of Sheffield and the National Foundation for Educational Research (where he was head of information research and development) he now trades as Information Management Associates, undertaking national UK research and consultancy projects. His clients have included the Department for Children, Schools and Families, the NHS Executive, the British Film Institute, the Museums, Libraries and Archives Council, the British Library and the Research Information Network.

Joachim P. Sturmberg is a/prof of general practice at Monash University Melbourne and The University of Newcastle, Australia. He has a longstanding involvement in under- and post-graduate teaching in general practice. His main research interest relates to the complex adaptive nature of health service structures and their impact on patient care.

James T. C. Teng is the Eunice and James L. West distinguished professor in the Department of Information Systems and Operations Management at the University of Texas at Arlington. He received a MS degree in mathematics from the University of Illinois at Urbana-Champagne prior to completing PhD study in information systems at the University of Minnesota. His publications include numerous book chapters and articles in leading information systems research journals such as *Information Systems Research, MIS Quarterly, Journal of AIS, Journal of MIS, IEEE Transactions on Engineering Management, Communications of ACM, and Decision Sciences.* His current research interests include knowledge management, implementation of enterprise systems, and the impact of information technology on organizations and the economy.

Sue Thomas – writer and professor of new media who founded the trAce Online Writing Centre in 1995 and, with Kate Pullinger, the online MA in Creative Writing and New Media in 2006. Her most recent book is *Hello World: Travels in virtuality* (2004). http://www.suethomas.net

Eleftheria Tomadaki is a research fellow in the Centre for New Media, working on cooperative learning systems. She is mainly concerned with the integration of the video conferencing tool FM with the OpenLearn platform and the study of large-scale synchronous collaborative media.

Shashikiran Umakanth is currently working as associate professor of medicine at Melaka-Manipal Medical College (Manipal University) in Malaysia. His areas of interest are diabetes, metabolic syndrome and medical education including health informatics.

Ana C. Vasconcelos is a lecturer at the Information Studies Department of the University of Sheffield. Her research interests include the interface between information systems development and the management of knowledge and information, with a focus on discourse and identity, the role of discursive practices in IS adaptation, organisational and political arenas, communities of practice and virtual communities, professional discourses and identity in information work.

Martin Weller is professor of Educational Technology at the Open University in the UK. He developed the Open University's first fully online course, which attracted 12,000 students annually. He was the VLE project director and is the author of two text books *Delivering Learning on the Net* and *Virtual Learning Environments*. His research interests are in social networking, elearning, learning design and the application of new technologies. He blogs at edtechie.net

Steve Wheeler is senior lecturer in education and ICT in the Faculty of Education at the University of Plymouth. His research interests include e-learning and distance education, and he has published more than 180 scholarly articles in this field. His most recent book is entitled '*The Digital Classroom*' (Co-authored with Peter John) which is published through Routledge. He serves on the boards of 7 international peer reviewed journals and is currently the chair of IFIP Working Group 3.6 on Distance Education. Steve lives in Plymouth, South West England, with his wife and three children.

Scott Wilson is a senior research officer in the Institute for Educational Cybernetics at the University of Bolton, and an assistant director of the JISC CETIS service. His current research interests include advanced Internet technologies for presence and identity, information systems design, and the use of cybernetics in the strategic development and adoption of new technologies. Wilson has also worked for a number of companies working in the areas of strategic technology and intelligence analysis.

Nicholas Zap is a writer, lecturer, researcher and consultant in the areas of educational engagement, communication, and virtual learning environments. His research includes such diverse areas as video games in education, cognitive development, problem solving, and educational neuroscience. A hardcore video game player his whole life, much of his research is focused on the psychology of games and play and the impact of these environments on cognitive development. Zap is currently completing a PhD in Educational Psychology at Simon Fraser University.

Index